COLLEGE OF ALAMEDA LIBRARY

WITH

D1135026

NA
7205
P68

Pratt, Dorothy
    A guide to early
American homes

DATE DUE

OCT 27'84			
OCT 8'85			
MAY 20'92			

WITHDRAWN

A Guide to

EARLY

AMERICAN

HOMES

North & South

COMBINED EDITION—TWO VOLUMES IN ONE

DOROTHY & RICHARD PRATT

Bonanza Books • New York

A Guide to

EARLY

AMERICAN

HOMES

North

A GUIDE TO EARLY AMERICAN HOMES—NORTH

Copyright © 1956 by Dorothy and Richard Pratt. All rights in this book are reserved. It may not be used for dramatic, motion-, or talking-picture purposes without written authorization from the holder of these rights. Nor may the book or parts thereof be reproduced in any manner whatsoever without permission in writing, except in the case of brief quotations embodied in critical articles and reviews.

Library of Congress Catalog Card Number: 56–10867

This edition published by Bonanza Books,
a division of Crown Publishers,
by arrangement with the copyright owners.
Printed in the United States of America

(EE)

PREFACE

It would be a slight exaggeration to say that nothing could be less alike than the early houses of the North and those of the South. Yet it is striking what differences do appear as from either direction you break through the boundaries marked out by Mason and Dixon and the Ohio River. Here in this book the early homes in the fourteen states that lie above those boundaries and between the Atlantic Seaboard and the valley of the Mississippi furnish the explanation of how and why they are different from the houses down south. Even more interesting will be their demonstration of how they happened to be different from one another. And it isn't merely that the various types of early houses in Massachusetts are different from those of Michigan. They are different even from those of the next-door states of New Hampshire, Vermont, New York, Connecticut, and Rhode Island. Pennsylvania houses are quite remarkably different from those of New Jersey. And the early houses of Ohio have a mood and manner very much their own. All this will appear as you pick your way through the pages of this book.

In the South the early houses are mainly to be found in the country; in the North they are mainly to be found in the cities, towns, and villages, thus explaining to some extent the essential nature of the two regions—the one a rural, the other a town economy. That may or may not be the reason why there are so many restoration communities in the North, such as Shelburne in Vermont; Sturbridge, Deerfield and Storrowton in Massachusetts; Mystic Seaport in Connecticut; the Farmer's Village in Cooperstown, among many others

in New York; Hopewell and Old Economy in Pennsylvania; Greenfield Village in Michigan, and a dozen or more others here and there. In the South, on the other hand, aside from Old Salem in North Carolina, there is only one other of any stature, namely Colonial Williamsburg, the most stunning of them all, of course, anywhere in the country.

And while, again, there are any number of organized house tours in the North, hardly any can even begin to compare in scope and attendance with a good half-dozen famous ones in the South.

As against the nearly seven hundred houses that can be visited in the South, there are well over nine hundred in the North, as described herein. Approximately two-thirds of these are houses that are open to the public and maintained for that purpose. The remaining one-third are private homes. We believe you will find in this book, for the first time anywhere, virtually every open early house of any merit in the North. We *know* that you will find here, for the first time anywhere, the hundreds of private homes whose owners, through the *Guide,* have generously agreed to let their homes be visited under conditions set down in each case. The authors are as pleased to have helped make possible this unprecedented privilege as they are grateful to all the various owners involved for granting it. Readers will readily appreciate that to abuse this privilege will be to run the risk of ending it for others.

The order in which the states are arranged gives the same precedence to Massachusetts here as is given to Virginia in the South. After Massachusetts it is merely a matter of working your way through the rest of New England and striking down through New York, New Jersey, and Pennsylvania. From the seaboard states you start westward as the pioneers did before you. When it seemed to us an advantage for the reader that the localities in any given state should be arranged regionally, this was done—just as an alphabetical order was followed when that seemed better.

¶ Things to remember

Automobile road maps are accurate, up to date, and free. We believe that with the *Guide* and a good road map you can find every house listed herein, except some of the *private houses*. For these, which are often isolated, get explicit directions from the owners when making appointments by letter or phone.

For further local guidance, we suggest that the town or county historical societies, the chambers of commerce, the public libraries, the post office, and even sometimes the gas station or the police, will prove helpful—more or less in the order given.

It goes without saying that days, hours, and entrance fees are subject to change. Advance inquiries sometimes save disappointments. When two fees are given, the first is for adults, the second for children. If no fee is mentioned, no fee is required. Voluntary contribu-tions are suggested in many cases but not obligatory.

¶ To those who helped

Mention of all the individuals who have given helpful information, and all the books which have been consulted, would fill a volume in themselves. We have tried the patience of countless home-owners, of house custodians and curators, of endless officers of state and local historical societies, of development commissions, of landmark and antiquarian societies, of pilgrimage and house-tour people, of chambers of commerce, women's clubs, librarians, town clerks, of the Colonial Dames and the D.A.R.—and we thank them all for the time they have taken in our behalf during the more than three years we have been working intensively on the books. For expert assistance on the manuscripts, we wish to give sincere thanks in particular to Miss Lorinda Ballard and Mrs. Anthony Salisbury—bless their hearts!

To the LADIES' HOME JOURNAL *and its editors, Bruce and Beatrice Blackmar Gould, and to the parent organization, the Curtis Publishing Company, a special note of appreciation for putting picture material at our disposal, along with indispensable facilities and advantages of many kinds, without which it would have been impossible to produce these* Guides.

CONTENTS

A GUIDE TO EARLY AMERICAN HOMES

North

Here at the fascinating Saugus Ironworks restoration, of which this is the Ironmaster's house, you are in one of the richest seventeenth-century regions of Massachusetts (see page 22), with both the Parson Capen and Scotch Boardman houses nearby. This many-gabled and weather-darkened house was restored some forty years ago by Wallace Nutting, a pioneer in promoting public appreciation of our heritage homes. Across the page is a typical interior of the Wayside Inn at South Sudbury, celebrated by Longfellow, and forming part of an extensive restoration by Henry Ford.

MASSACHUSETTS

*T*HERE is great equality in the people of this state. Few or no opulent men—and no poor—great similitude in their buildings, the general fashion of which is a chimney (always of stone or brick) and door in the middle, with a staircase fronting the latter . . . two flush doors with a very good show of sash and glass windows. The size generally is from 30 to 50 feet in length, and from 20 to 30 feet in width, exclusive of a back shed, which seems to be added as the family increases."

Thus did the man who slept in probably more early American homes than anyone else in our history put down in his Journal his impressions of Massachusetts houses as he passed among them in the peaceful golden autumn of 1790, on his first great Presidential tour. He had driven that particular morning through the village of Longmeadow with its lovely green, and he could have had the Storrs Parsonage in mind because of its "two flush doors with a very good show of sash and glass windows."

But he should have known better than to mention "similitude," for even at this early date the houses of Massachusetts were outstanding for their wide variety. With one house of a very elegant variety Washington had reason to be well familiar, for with his unerring eye for the best, the General had chosen it for his Cambridge headquarters back in 1775—a big Georgian beauty of a house that nearly everyone now knows as the "Longfellow Home."

The gap between Storrs Parsonage

and the Cambridge mansions was great enough, but there were many Massachusetts houses in 1790 that were much earlier than the parsonage—a good hundred and fifty years earlier, represented now by those dark, brooding Elizabethan dwellings, like the "Ward," the "Witch," and the "Seven Gables" group in Salem; the "Boardman" and the "Capen"; and a whole collection at Ipswich. And after Washington's time the variety was to be enriched by houses, still early in our terms, as different as Gore Place at Waltham, the fine foursquare Federal houses in Newburyport, the McIntire masterpieces in Salem, and the Bulfinch houses on Beacon Hill.

Nor is any other state a match for Massachusetts in the total number of houses that can be visited. And because a great majority of the early houses are located in the eastern portion of the state, a concentration of early houses here is something to consider.

The density is greatest in the crescent of land which lies back from the borders of Massachusetts Bay. On your road map you will see that Newburyport would be the tip of the crescent, Plymouth the toe, and the landward curve would cut right through Concord. Between that outward sweeping line and the waters of the Bay there are, of early American houses that matter, more to the square mile than in any other area of similar extent in the country.

Another situation exists, namely the peculiar perplexity that confronts the stranger endeavoring to find his way from one place to another. We suggest the planned approach. To that end, instead of attempting to relate the towns geographically to each other, which would have been pure madness, we have taken the more or less accepted geographical areas of the state, as indicated above, and in these areas have simply arranged the towns in alphabetical order. The reader now merely marks on his road map the towns he wishes to visit, and works out his own itinerary to fit. It couldn't be simpler!

IN & OUT OF BOSTON

On & off Beacon Hill; Arlington; Brookline; Cambridge; Chelsea;
Dorchester; Medford; Watertown & Waltham; Winthrop

¶ On & off Beacon Hill

Up on Beacon Hill there is a profusion of fine Federal architecture. Credit much of its beauty and abundance to Charles Bulfinch, who crowned the Hill in 1795 with his golden-domed State House. He was a darling of his day, famous for the purity of his façades. He made a fashion of shallow recessed arches in his walls, and his Adam details were always done with wit, taste, and delicacy.

Down the Hill, in the direction of Dock Square, Faneuil Hall brings you face to face with your Revolutionary past, as does the elegant old State House around on State Street, its Dutch gables adorned with the unicorn and lion of the Crown. Take in the spiral staircase of the State House and the grasshopper weathervane of Faneuil Hall.

PAUL REVERE HOUSE (*1680*)
19 North Square; daily 10 to 4 except Sundays and holidays; 25 cents; Paul Revere Memorial Association.
There couldn't be a better house to begin with here than Paul Revere's. Down below Beacon Hill on ground hallowed by history in what is now Boston's "Little Italy," this dark, medieval dwelling, close-clapboarded,

Hemmed in as it is, the Paul Revere house stands out from its surroundings with an aura of history and age.

with corbeled overhang, leaded diamond panes, and peek-hole shutters, has the Elizabethan look that early Boston builders brought here in memory from England. The house was already a hundred years old when Revere moved in before the Revolution, and it is furnished now as it must have been when Paul occupied it, and the house was bursting at the seams with sixteen little Reveres. Four rooms and attic are filled with mementos of the famous silversmith and midnight rider, who was descended from the French Huguenot family of Rivoire. He worked in copper as well as silver, and became one of the most successful craftsmen of his day. He was also accounted very skillful at fashioning false teeth from ivory.

MOSES PIERCE-HICHBORN HOUSE
(c. 1676)
29 North Square adjacent to Paul Revere House; weekdays 10 to 4 and Sundays 2 to 4 November 1 to April 30, (closed Tuesday and holidays), daily 10 to 6 except Mondays May 1 to October 31; 25 cents.

Hichborn was a prosperous cousin of Paul Revere's who occupied this nearby fine red-brick residence with big chimneys, fireplaces in every room, and one of the first cove ceilings in the Colonies. If the date is correct, it is one of the rare remaining pre-Georgian brick houses in New England. Unfortunately, the most remarkable one in the country (the Foster-Hutchinson House) was torn down here as long ago as 1833.

HARRISON GRAY OTIS HOUSE (1795)
141 Cambridge Street; daily, 9 to 4:45, except Saturdays and holidays; 25 cents; S.P.N.E.A.

Bulfinch undoubtedly did this one, the only "open" house on the Hill today. Don't dream of missing it. Otis was a wealthy politician with a passion for stylish houses. This was his first one, but there is a second and a third. The dining room here is a special delight. There are fine collections of silver, glass, pewter, ceramics, costumes, and Shaker pieces. The house is also the home today of an organization dear to the hearts of early-house devotees, the Society for the Preservation of New England Antiquities, whose good works are duly noted most happily on many occasions in this *Guide*. They administer more than half a hundred old New England houses; many, like this one, of great distinction.

The first Harrison Gray Otis house has one of the finest Adam dining rooms in America.

THE SECOND HARRISON GRAY OTIS HOUSE (*1800*)

85 Mt. Vernon Street; on request by letter, December through April; Miss Evelyn Sears.

Furnished and used as a lived-in home, with pieces of many periods and countries, this house offers a rare opportunity without and within to enjoy at first hand the Bulfinch flavor and distinction.

TOWNSEND HOUSE (*1820*)

48 Chestnut Street; by appointment; Mr. and Mrs. Charles Townsend.

Built on land that was once a terraced garden, this house has two flights of stairs below the first floor. A tall, handsome Federal-style dwelling, with stunning interiors, furnishings of museum quality, and one of the finest small city gardens in the country.

At Numbers 54 and 55 BEACON STREET you pass a pair of houses by Asher Benjamin, now occupied by the Colonial Dames; at 45 the THIRD HARRISON GRAY OTIS HOUSE, by Bulfinch; at Number 39 and Number 40 two beauties, most probably by Bulfinch, now the WOMEN'S CITY CLUB. The big gray wood-and-brick 1805 house, with its black shutters, at 14 Walnut Street, was the home of Ellery Sedgwick, famous editor. Two notable houses on Mt. Vernon Street, in addition to the "Otis Number Two," are Number 57 and Number 59, once the homes of Charles Francis Adams, Civil War Ambassador to England, and of Thomas Bailey Aldrich, respectively. As for privately maintained LOUISBURG SQUARE, with its cobbled paving, there is nothing quite like it this side of London.

There is a galaxy of early rooms to be seen at the MUSEUM OF FINE ARTS, among them two McIntire rooms from Peabody, with the master's exquisite carving; a wonderfully paneled fireplace wall from Fiskdale; and seventeenth-century rooms with massive medieval framing from Ipswich and West Box-

ford—a good introduction to the many wonders you will walk into throughout Massachusetts.

¶ *Arlington* (*out past Cambridge*)

JASON RUSSELL HOUSE (*1680*)

7 Jason Street; daily 2 to 5 except Mondays, April to November; contribution; Arlington Historical Society.

The bloodiest fighting on April 19, 1775, in what is now this Boston suburb between Cambridge and Lexington, took place in and about the Jason Russell House, when a group of Minute Men were caught off guard by the British. Jason Russell and eleven others were killed and lie together in a common grave in the Arlington burying ground. The house has been put into pre-Revolutionary shape, as a well-to-do farmer's home. Many relics, some Paul Revere silver, and plenty of bullet holes.

¶ *Brookline* (*out Beacon Street to Harrow*)

EDWARD DEVOTION HOUSE (*c. 1680*)

347 Harvard Street; Saturday afternoons 2 to 4, other times by appointment; 25 cents.

This is one of the few remaining houses that Paul Revere passed on his midnight ride, and on the annual reenactment of the ride a stop is made at the doorstep.

¶ *Cambridge*
(*out Memorial Drive*)

In addition to the houses listed below, after you leave the Longfellow House you will certainly want to stroll down Brattle Street, once known as "The King's Highway" and for a long time as "Tory Row." It is a street of ample lawns and ancient trees, and many of its houses still breathe the opulent yet conservative living habits of their early inhabitants. At 153 stands the handsome THOMAS LEE HOUSE (1685), at 159 the NICHOLAS LEE HOUSE, an interesting oblong mass painted brown, set off by ivory-colored corner quoins and broad doorway and a central chimney twelve feet in width. At 94 Brattle is the massive BELCHER HOUSE, an impressive yellow frame mansion with main entrances at either end; the east end, dated 1700, retains its fine features. The READ HOUSE (1725) is at Number 55, and at 76 is the SAMUEL LONGFELLOW HOUSE (1725), of the brother of the poet.

In addition to the houses listed below, you may want to stroll past the following. The large yellow mansion with the balustraded roof at the corner of Mt. Auburn Street and Elmwood Avenue (1767) was the HOME OF JAMES RUSSELL LOWELL, built for an Englishman named Oliver, the last of the King's deputies here.

BRATTLE HOUSE (c. 1735)

42 Brattle Street; Monday to Saturday, 9 to 5 (except when rooms are being used for courses); Cambridge Social Union.

The first of the stylish eighteenth-century houses still standing here has quite a lot of its style still remaining; a three-story clap-boarded gambrel with dormers, it has some fine paneling and a handsome staircase. Brattle was one of the prominent royalists who left Cambridge in a hurry when Boston was evacuated by the British. Then for a while in the Emersonian era, when it was occupied by Margaret Fuller, brilliant editor, teacher, and critic, the house was aglow with the literary lights who clustered where today the Cambridge Social Union holds its classes.

LONGFELLOW HOUSE (*1759*)

105 Brattle Street; daily 10 to 5, Saturdays 12 to 5, Sundays 1 to 5; 30 cents; Longfellow Memorial Trust.

The last and most elegant of this Cambridge triumvirate is the great square white and yellow mansion in which the poet Longfellow lived. A royalist, Maj. Henry Vassall, built it, but, like Mr. Brattle mentioned above, left it suddenly one night fifteen years later with all his Tory neighbors. The next occupant was Gen. George Washington, who managed to pick some very handsome headquarters here and there. The side piazzas and other additions were made right after the Revolution by Dr. Andrew Craigie, Apothecary General

Long before this famous old house became the home of Longfellow, it served as Washington's headquarters during the early days of the Revolution.

of the Army, whose widow, following the doctor's financial failure and death, rented out rooms to Harvard students and other eligibles—among the latter Longfellow, in 1837, when he was a young professor. When the poet married after a seven-year courtship, the bride's father gave the pair the house as a wedding present; and here Longfellow lived until he died in 1882. Still lived in by his grandson, the house has been kept exactly as it was during the poet's lifetime.

COOPER-FROST-AUSTIN HOUSE
(1657)

21 Linnaean Street 1 mile from Harvard Square, to left of Massachusetts Avenue; Mondays, Thursdays, and Fridays 2 to 5 June to October, Mondays and Thursdays 2 to 5 November to May; 25 cents; S.P.N.E.A.

This earliest house in Cambridge is a seventeenth-century beauty, of size and substance, with great modesty of manner, built by Deacon John Cooper. It is a two-story, foursquare white clapboard structure with monumental central chimney. Expertly maintained to set it all off to the best advantage both inside and out.

WADSWORTH HOUSE (1726)

Open during office hours, except during commencements; Harvard Alumni Association.

This big yellow house, full of Cambridge character (for yellow-painted clapboards, green shutters, and white trim combined to make a favorite Cambridge color scheme, as you can see), was built by Benjamin Wadsworth, the first of nine Harvard presi-

The Royall house in Medford is adorned with a great variety of architectural delights.

dents to live in it; Wadsworth's tenure was 1725–1737, while Edward Everett's (the last one to live here) was 1846–1849. A Stuart portrait of E. E. as a young man hangs in the Board Room to the right of the front door. The visiting preacher used to have his rooms here; students have lived here in the past, among them Emerson and "Light Horse Harry" Lee. The interior woodwork (and it is very handsome) has been well preserved, and there are eighteenth-century furnishings in most of the rooms and offices. The house is now used mainly as the alumni center.

¶ *Chelsea (out across the Mystic River Bridge past Bunker Hill and the Constitution)*

GOVERNOR BELLINGHAM-CARY HOUSE (1659)

34 Parker Street; by appointment; Mr. Charles W. Bennett, 20 Lawrence Street.

This is the house built here by a seventeenth-century colonial governor named Richard Bellingham, whose eccentricities you will hear about at the house. In the siege of Boston it was the last outpost of the Continental Army's left wing. Later the original frame structure was somewhat refashioned, but from the two periods there is some fine paneling, much original hardware, and a secret passage.

¶ *Dorchester (southeast section of city)*

CLAPP HOUSE (1806) or EMMA M. E. REED MEMORIAL

195 Boston Street; by appointment with caretaker; Dorchester Historical Society.

CLAPP HOUSE
(seventeenth century)

Adjoining on Willow Street; same as above; librarian in charge.

The two adjoining Clapp Houses—one early, one late—here in this southeast section of Boston, give a good opportunity to compare the building manners of the late seventeenth and early nineteenth centuries. The later one is being restored with furnishings of the Federal period; the earlier has an interesting contemporary in the James Blake House (1648) on Edward Everett Square, where the caretaker lives.

The country seat of Governor Gore out Waltham way is once again a wonder of the opulence and sophistication of the early 1800s hereabouts.

¶ *Medford (north on Route 1)*

This northerly suburb, where some of the first New England bricks were baked and the first rum was distilled, has two "open" houses of particular and contrasting interest: the seventeenth-century Tufts House, and the eighteenth-century Royall House, the former built as a garrison house, and the latter as a wealthy merchant's establishment.

PETER TUFTS HOUSE, *formerly*
CRADDOCK HOUSE (*1678*)
> *350 Riverside Avenue, near Spring Street; Mondays, Thursdays, and Fridays 2 to 5 June to October, Mondays and Thursdays 2 to 5 November to May; 25 cents; S.P.N.E.A.*

A big gambrel-roof house of early brick, with a pair of first- and second-story portholes at either end of the front face that are architecturally delightful. Beautiful oak beams and furnishings to fit.

ISAAC ROYALL HOUSE (*1732*)
> *15 George Street; daily 2 to 5 except Mondays and Fridays, May 1 to October 1; 50 cents and 25 cents; Royall House Association.*

Be prepared to see quite a house when you visit the mansion Col. Isaac Royall built for himself around a seventeenth-century farmhouse after he came here from the West Indies, with twenty-seven slaves, to live in style. The brick ends gable up into

great chimneys. The full three-story eastern façade is filled with richly framed windows, corniced and quoined; the western façade has one of the first rusticated wooden walls in the Colonies, with end pilasters to the eaves. From a lookout in the attic roof, Mollie Stark kept her eye on the British troops over on the Mystic shore, while Gens. Washington, Charles Lee, Sullivan, and Stark held councils of war in the richly paneled and furnished rooms below —rooms that are once more as they were. There are commodious slave quarters on the grounds. It was Gen. Charles Lee who left Washington at the Vassall House (some say in a huff) and made this mansion his headquarters.

¶ *Watertown & Waltham*
(*out Route 20*)

ABRAHAM BROWNE, JR., HOUSE
(*1698, addition 1720*)
> *562 Main Street; daily 2 to 5, except Saturdays; 25 cents; S.P.N.E.A.*

The first and by far the oldest of the three important houses in this area contains rooms and furnishings from both seventeenth- and eighteenth-century times, and a fireplace whose heroic dimensions make you wish we had the courage to do things this way today. The house is rightly proud of its three-part casements of rare early design. And while you are here, ask the custodians to show you the McIntire stable brought from the Derby farm at Peabody. It contains a nice collection of early carriages.

GORE PLACE (*1804*)

Main and Gore Streets; daily 10 to 5 except Mondays, Sundays 2 to 5; 50 cents; Gore Place Society, Inc.

Next, where Watertown and Waltham meet, you come to the showpiece of Massachusetts, a country mansion of princely appearance. And so it is, as you will see— in its scope and scale, its park, its style (very English in the Regency or Adam manner), its furnishings. It is filled with fascinating contrasts. Along with rooms for entertaining in the grand manner, there are family rooms of true intimacy, the Gores being people whose home provided as well for their private life as their public one. Christopher Gore was obviously a very wealthy personage—lawyer, diplomat, and a Governor of Massachusetts. Daniel Webster was a law clerk in Gore's office, and the elegant chandelier in the state dining room of Gore Place today is from the later law offices of the great orator. The whole effect is choice; the banquet hall impressive, and the staircase stunning.

LYMAN HOUSE *or* THE VALE (*1795*)

Lyman and Beaver Streets; Wednesday through Saturday 11 to 5, May 19 to September 11; 50 cents; S.P.N.E.A.

Farther along, and off to the right, the Lyman House is of equal eloquence in its own way, having been designed by the great Samuel McIntire of Salem. This was the farthest from Salem that the celebrated woodcarver ever worked. The master's carving is, as ever, a joy. The ballroom is one of his best, and the bow parlor has some rare McIntire furniture. The setting is delightful; the McIntire stable and the old greenhouses and gardens are reminders of the style in which the Lymans lived.

As an indication of Gore house glamour, the circular staircase leading up from the marble-floored entrance hall will do very nicely.

Out beyond Gore Place, the Lyman house by McIntire stands up imposingly from its lovely sylvan setting; fine interiors, fascinating dependencies.

¶ *Winthrop* (*out past airport; bear right on Bennington and Saratoga Streets*)

DEANE WINTHROP HOUSE (*1637*)
40 Shirley Street; Wednesday and Friday afternoons, 3 to 5; 10 cents; Winthrop Historical and Improvement Association.

This old peninsular community of the metropolitan area lies just across the harbor waters from the airport, and the little unassuming Deane Winthrop House here just happens to be one of the very first salt boxes in America. At 49 Siren Street you can see, in passing, the red-brick house that John Hancock built as his summer home in 1756. Frequent partakers of the famous fish-and-game dinners served at the old Tufts Inn were four old friends named Emerson, Lowell, Holmes, and Longfellow.

NORTH OF BOSTON

Amesbury; Andover; Beverly; Boxford; Danvers; Gloucester;

Groton; Haverhill & East Haverhill; Ipswich; Lowell; Lynn;

Marblehead; Melrose; Manchester; Newbury; Newburyport;

North Andover; Peabody; Reading; Rockport; Rowley;

Salem; Saugus; Topsfield; Wakefield; Wenham; Woburn

¶ *Amesbury* (*up near the New Hampshire corner on Route 110*)

MACY-COLBY HOUSE (*1654*)
259 Main Street; Wednesdays 2 to 5, June 1 to August 31; contributions; Bartlett Cemetery Association.

A fine little salt box, delightfully kept up. It has a fireplace ten feet wide. The house figures in Whittier's poem *The Exile*, describing how Thomas Macy was banished to Nantucket in 1655 for sheltering Quakers here in a storm.

In the 1860s Mary Baker Eddy lived and worked practically next door in the SQUIRE BAGLEY HOMESTEAD.

JOHN GREENLEAF WHITTIER HOUSE (*before 1836*)
86 Friend Street; daily 10 to 5, Sundays by appointment; Whittier Home Association.

The house where the poet lived for fifty-six years is special mostly for its Whittier associations—associations that permeate the town and the countryside all the way to Haverhill.

¶ *Andover* (*23 miles up from Boston on Route 28*)

DEACON AMOS BLANCHARD HOUSE (*1819*)

97 Main Street; daily; contribution; Miss Caroline Underhill.

A big foursquare house in the Federal style, attractively fenced, and fittingly furnished with local pieces from as far back as the late 1600s.

A mile away, on Argilla Road, is the 1680 BENJAMIN ABBOTT FARMSTEAD, weathered and worn, but soon to be restored. Don't miss it.

¶ *Beverly* (*turn south off 128 onto 97*)

BALCH HOUSE (*1638, later additions*)

448 Cabot Street; daily 10 to 4 and Sundays 2 to 4 June 15 to September 15, other times by appointment; 25 cents and 10 cents; Beverly Historical Society.

Said to be the oldest New England house with a recorded history, both the house and its history worth looking into. It is part of the record that John Balch built it for the bride he went all the way back to England to fetch.

HALE HOUSE (*1694*)

39 Hale Street; daily 10·30 to 4:30 except Sundays, Mondays, and holidays June 15 to September 15, other times by appointment; Beverly Historical Society.

This place clearly shows how radically styles had begun to change even before the seventeenth century was over. Under its gambrel roof the goodly wife of the Reverend John Hale, an early ancestor of the patriot Nathan and of Edward Everett, was accused of witchcraft—a canard so preposterous as finally to cause the persecutions, one and all, to collapse.

JOHN CABOT MANSION-HOUSE (*1781*)

117 Cabot Street; daily 10 to 4 July and August, Saturdays 10 to 4 rest of year; Beverly Historical Society.

A full-blown foursquare Georgian mansion of brick, with monumental chimneys, captain's walk, and the formality that went with a wealthy merchant's town house of the time. A very handsome sight, with some finely furnished rooms.

¶ *Boxford* (*left on Topsfield Road off Route 1*)

HOLYOKE-FRENCH HOUSE (*1760*)

Elm Street and Topsfield Road; Sundays 3 to 5 May 1 to November 1, or on request to custodian; 25 cents; Boxford Historical Society.

The proportions of this great gambrel-roof house are truly impressive. Mt. Holyoke College was named after the great-grandfather of its builder, and in it are many heirlooms of the French family who followed the Holyoke occupancy—some good primitives, dolls, and toys, and in the barn a fine collection of early farm tools.

¶ *Danvers*

(*turn north off 128 onto 97*)

There are many good early houses here which are private homes to be visited only on special occasions, but at the Historical Society in the Page House readers of the *Guide* will be furnished with directions for seeing them. It was from Danvers, by the way, that "The Lindens" was removed in 1927 to Washington, D.C.

PAGE HOUSE (*antique shop*) (*1754*)

11 Page Street; Saturday afternoons and by appointment; small charge.

This place shows comparatively recent modifications through which the good original gambrel-roof house emerges. Contains collections of antiques and historical relics.

JUDGE SAMUEL HOLTEN HOUSE (*1670*)

Holten and Center Streets; preferably by appointment; contribution; General Israel Putnam Chapter, D.A.R.

A seventeenth-century house now grown into a dwelling of considerable substance, containing many early furnishings and features of interest including the partitioned privy at the rear, with two doors and seven seats.

REBECCA NURSE HOUSE (*1678*)

149 Pine Street; daily 10 to 5 or by appointment, mid-June to mid-October; 25 cents; S.P.N.E.A.

The wife of Francis Nurse was taken from her house here and hanged in Salem as a witch. A fine old clapboard house, filled with much honest workmanship of a simple, primitive nature. The tragic circumstances of its early history are in striking contrast to its present serenity.

SAMUEL FOWLER HOUSE (*1810*)

166 High Street; Wednesdays 3 to 5 and Saturdays 10 to 5, other times by appointment; 25 cents; S.P.N.E.A.

This is a real beauty of a large brick house, designed with uncommon restraint and immensely rewarding within for such features as its notable woodwork and the Zuber wallpapers of 1829. It is furnished in excellent style and there are fine collections of good china and pewter. The Fowlers were an old family hereabouts, an ancestor, Philip Fowler, having settled at Ipswich in 1632.

¶ *Gloucester* (*out past the end of Route 128*)

BEAUPORT (*1907*)

Eastern Point Boulevard; weekday afternoons for guided tours only (2:30, 3:30, and 4:30), June through September (closed Sundays and holidays); $1.00 and 50 cents; S.P.N.E.A.

This is an extraordinary museum out here by the sea, containing a surprising assortment of period rooms assembled by a collector named Henry Sleeper, which are housed in this late château-like structure made up of many parts and pieces of architecture. It has been called the most fascinating house in America, and not without some justification. There is plenty of color and variety, and no matter what your taste, you are almost certain to find it entertaining.

SARGENT-MURRAY-GILMAN-HOUGH HOUSE (*1768, remodeled 1916*)

49 Middle Street; weekdays 11 to 5, July 1 to September 25; 30 cents; Sargent-Murray-Gilman-Hough House Association.

The handsome hip-on-gambrel house that Winthrop Sargent built as a pre-Revolutionary wedding present for his daughter Judith brings you back from the theatrical to the serene. It discloses with dignity and warmth, and with just a pleasant touch of ostentation in its heroic corner pilasters, how homelike a stylish early house could be.

CAPE ANN HISTORICAL HOUSE (*c. 1805*)

27 Pleasant Street; daily 11 to 4, June to September; 25 cents; Cape Ann Scientific, Literary and Historical Association.

This place reflects without and within the typical seaport town house of Federal times. It is simple, straightforward, and nautical in its neatness; even the quoins that decorate its corners do so with crisp and clean restraint. Inside, it is furnished in a way that old seafarers would admire.

RIGGS HOUSE (*1638–1700*)

By appointment; 50 cents.

The oldest dwelling in the vicinity, it was the first schoolhouse of the town, and there are collections of early household equipment.

¶ *Groton* (*turn right on Route 110, then 40 miles out on Route 2*)

GOVERNOR BOUTWELL HOUSE (*1851, remodeled 1938*)

Main Street; Saturday afternoons 3 to 5, June to November; Groton Historical Society.

An interesting frame house of a late but fascinating period, painted yellow with green trim. A nice piece of preservation, portraying the background of a notable of this community.

¶ *Haverhill & East Haverhill* (*up near the New Hampshire line*)

THE BUTTONWOODS (*1814*)

240 Water Street; Tuesdays, Thursdays, and Saturdays, 2 to 5; contribution; Haverhill Historical Society.

"The Buttonwoods" is one of those orderly, square two-story hip-roof houses that the builders who used the books of Asher Benjamin did so well in the early 1800s. The rooms are foursquare and capacious, well lighted by four large windows apiece. Some of them here are finely furnished and filled with items of local historical interest.

JOHN WARD HOUSE (*before 1645*)

240 Water Street; Tuesdays, Thursdays, and Saturdays, 2 to 5; voluntary contribution; Haverhill Historical Society.

The little white Ward House next door is twice as old as "The Buttonwoods."

The bedroom of the grand old Whipple house in Ipswich.

The SPILLER HOUSE, at Groveland and Water Streets, and the AYER HOMESTEAD, overlooking the green, are both seventeenth-century houses worthy of attention.

JOHN GREENLEAF WHITTIER HOMESTEAD (*1688*)

> Route 110 just off Amesbury Road; daily 10 to 6 except Mondays, Sundays 1 to 6; 25 cents and 15 cents; Trustees of the John Greenleaf Whittier Homestead.

Three miles out on Route 110, the Whittier birthplace is architecturally a much more enjoyable house than the one at Amesbury in which the poet spent so much of his later life. This is a typical New England farmhouse in the best tradition—a fitting birthplace for this particular poet. Also, as you might know, it is the scene of *Snowbound*. Filled with Whittier belongings.

¶ Ipswich

The assortment of seventeenth-century houses here is probably as large as any in the country. Eight houses in all can be visited. One is a sea captain's house from the mid-1800s and one a wealthy merchant's mansion from the century before that; but all the rest are of the 1600s. If you come here on Seventeenth Century Day in August (write the Waters Memorial for dates), you will hit the jackpot, for many more will be open.

LAKEMAN-JOHNSON HOUSE (*before 1850*)

> 16 East Street; Tuesdays, Thursdays, and Saturdays, 10 to 5, mid-June through September; contribution; S.P.N.E.A.

This is the sea captain's house, the first but by far the latest in our Ipswich listing. It is being kept up in character simply and attractively.

THOMAS FRANKLIN WATER MEMORIAL, *formerly* JOHN HEARD HOUSE (*1795*)

> Daily 10 to 5, except Mondays, Sundays 1 to 5, April to November; 75 cents; Ipswich Historical Society.

Likewise late for Ipswich, this foursquare three-story house also belonged to an old seafaring family. It has many attractive features like the Chinese Chippendale stair rail and the furnishings of its period.

JOHN WHIPPLE HOUSE (*1640, 1670, and 1700*)

> 53 South Main Street; daily 10 to 5, except Mondays, Sundays 1 to 5, April to November; 50 cents; Ipswich Historical Society.

This famous and venerable house is able to show off to wonderful advantage the character of our home-building pioneers. The way they worked those massive oaken beams and girders and posts into an everlasting frame makes it plain that these people felt they were here to stay. And, of course, what time has done to the color and feel of that oak is a treat to the senses of sight and touch. Fortunately, the house has not been made into a piece of period perfectionism. The furnishings are complete in all that matters—possessions that any ancient house would acquire, with discrimination, in the course of several centuries.

THE HOUSE OF THE ORANGE SHUTTERS (*1680 and 1715*)

106 High Street; by written or phone appointment; may be seen 11 to 12 and 1 to 4 (phone: 889M); 50 cents; Mr. and Mrs. Roy Lee Bulger.

This house offers a rare opportunity to see how well these ancient dwellings can be adapted to modern living.

EMERSON-HOWARD HOUSE (*c. 1648*)

Turkey Shore Road at eastern end of Green Street bridge; Monday through Thursday June 15 to October 15, other times by appointment; contribution; S.P.N.E.A.

The house that Thomas Emerson built here more than a hundred and fifty years before his famous philosopher descendant was born in Boston has the narrow,

weathered siding, hewn overhang, and vast framing members that become a familiar sight in Ipswich. Sparsely but expertly furnished.

PRESTON-FOSTER HOUSE (*c. 1640*)

6 Water Street; daily 10 to 5 except Mondays June 15 to October 15, rest of year by appointment; contribution; S.P.N.E.A.

The pitch of the roof of the Preston-Foster House has been left as it was when thatching was still the habit, showing how much steeper a roof had to be before shingles superseded straw. Very simply maintained at the moment, but many things about the house itself claim your attention.

HART HOUSE (*an inn*) (*1640*)

Line Brook Road, 0.7 mile off Route 1A; April to December; Mrs. Elizabeth L. Marr.

No doubt the oldest house in the country now used as an inn. A first-floor room is at the Metropolitan, and a second-floor room at Winterthur—a rather wry kind of recognition; but both rooms have been faithfully reconstructed here. It is all furnished with feeling. An excellent inn.

Ipswich itself and the Whipple house here make a real seventeenth-century combination.

STRAWBERRY HILL *or* PROCTOR HOUSE (*c. 1670*)

> *Jeffrey's Neck Road, 2 miles from center of town; by appointment only; Mr. and Mrs. Daniel S. Wendell.*

The Wendells rescued this from its town site and took it to its present hilltop location two miles out of town. There, as "Strawberry Hill," today very much a home, it stands as one of the most remarkable examples in America of the seventeenth-century style and structure which followed Elizabethan lines. It is a great privilege to see it and one of the choice pleasures of a *Guide*-d visit to Ipswich.

¶ *Lowell*

WHISTLER HOUSE (*an art gallery*) (*1823*)

> *243 Worthen Street; daily 1 to 5, except Mondays; Lowell Art Association.*

This simple and retiring birthplace of the painter—who was anything but—is primarily interesting for its Whistleriana and for its art exhibits.

¶ *Lynn*

HYDE-MILLS HOUSE (*c. 1838*)

> *125 Green Street; by appointment with custodian there part of every day except Sundays; Lynn Historical Society.*

Exhibits in this good-looking house include an early Lynn shoeshop, early household objects, a few period rooms, and a McIntire eagle. The lack of lengthy and elaborate descriptions, we might reiterate here, does not indicate lack of excellence or things of interest. To this general rule the Hyde-Mills House is no exception.

¶ *Marblehead*

Just to pick your way through the tangled streets and lanes of this famous and delightful old harbor town is a pleasure. And every now and then you will be stopped in your tracks by the style and polish of a fine old mansion from the days when commerce by sea was a paying proposition here.

This extraordinary example of a seventeenth-century house was moved from Ipswich to its present location outside the town, restored to perfection, and named Strawberry Hill.

COL. JEREMIAH LEE MANSION
(*1768*)
161 Washington Street; weekdays May 15 to October 15, Sundays 2 to 5 July and August; 50 cents; Marblehead Historical Society, Miss Gretchen Girdler.

This ranks among the finest old homes in America. The stateliness of its rusticated exterior is more than matched by its inside. One of the most monumental of domestic staircases mounts from the immense hall, the walls dramatically covered by paper painted in England. Although Lee lived in princely fashion here, his death was due to exposure: having been ambushed by the British while on a Revolutionary mission out beyond Boston, he was forced to flee his lodging in very little clothing.

KING HOOPER MANSION
(*1728–1745*)
Hooper Street; daily 2 to 5, except Mondays; 30 cents; Marblehead Arts Association.

This is another luxurious home, of nearly the same scale. Its formal front, beautifully quoined and corniced, almost conceals an earlier tall Hooper House that had to be turned endwise on its lot to make street room for this more imposing addition. The ballroom is used for art exhibitions.

HOOPER-PARKER HOUSE
(*before 1775*)
181 Washington Street; Mondays, Wednesdays, and Fridays 2 to 4, June 15 to September 15; 25 cents; S.P.N.E.A.

This other Hooper House has once again that stateliness and charm which mark these fine Marblehead mansions.

As you walk around, keep your eyes open for the PEDRICK MANSION, at 52 Washington Street; for the COL. WILLIAM R. LEE, at 185; and the MANSION HOUSE, at 187.

¶ Melrose

PHINEAS UPHAM HOUSE (*1703*)
225 Upham Street; by appointment with Mrs. W. C. Rogers (phone: Melrose 4–3335); contribution; The Upham Family Society, Inc.

The weather-darkened siding of the house that Phineas Upham built in what is now this Boston suburb has been saved by a society formed by his present-day descend-

The picturesque town of Marblehead has a wonderful collection of Early American homes, but none with quite the nobility of the Lee mansion, or one with such impressive interiors and handsome furnishings.

ants to restore and perpetuate their family heirloom.

¶ Manchester

TRASK HOUSE (*1830*)
12 Union Street; Wednesdays 2 to 5, July 1 to August 31; Manchester Historical Society.

A Late Federal house, prettily fenced and balustraded as becomes this attractive North Shore town, containing exhibits of a nautical nature, including a sailor-made model of the frigate *Constitution*.

¶ Newbury

TRISTRAM COFFIN HOUSE (*original ell c. 1651, later additions in the same century*)
14 High Road; Mondays, Wednesdays, and Fridays 2 to 5, other times by appointment; S.P.N.E.A.

Of the three listed here, the Coffin House probably depicts best the household life in those early days. It remained in the Coffin family almost three hundred years—possibly a record in this country.

SHORT HOUSE (*1733*)
33 High Road; daily 10 to 5, Tuesdays and
Thursdays 2 to 5, mid-June through
September, other times by appointment;
25 cents; S.P.N.E.A.

Recommended are the red door and window trim on the weathered face of the Short House. The ends are brick; inside there is a lot of excellent paneling.

SWETT-ILSLEY HOUSE (*1670*)
4 and 6 High Road; Tuesday through
Saturday, 12 to 7; S.P.N.E.A.

This place has at one time been a tavern, a chocolate works, and is now, at least in part, a tearoom—recommended along with the house.

¶ *Newburyport*

High Street here is a picture of the prosperity that came to the town in the days when this was a shipbuilder's paradise.

PETTINGILL-FOWLER HOUSE (*1793*)
High and Winter Streets; daily, except
Sundays and holidays, June through
September; 10 cents; Historical Society of
Old Newbury.

In outward appearance this is an exception to the general run of tall, square, three-story High Street houses—shallower, lower, with a hip-on-gambrel roof. Its date would account for the difference; most of the others came along twenty-five years later. There is nothing better in town than its drawing-room mantel.

TRACY HOUSE (*1771*)
94 State Street, 9 to 9, daily except Sunday;
city of Newburyport.

This is still earlier—Late Georgian in character. It is the public library, and the directors' room with its carving and its alcove windows is something to look at.

BRADBURY-SPALDING HOUSE
(*1788–1791*)
28 Green Street; Mondays, Wednesdays,
and Fridays 10 to 5, other times by
appointment; S.P.N.E.A.

Except for its roof, which is a regular and very good gambrel, the Bradbury-Spalding House has much in common with the Pettingill House, its contemporary. Compare, for instance, the drawing-room mantels.

The collections and the furnishings are of special interest.

¶ *North Andover (turn off Route 28 at Andover)*

THE COTTAGE *or* SAMUEL DALE STEVENS MEMORIAL (*1790*)
153 Academy Road; Mondays, Wednesdays,
and Saturdays, 2 to 5; North Andover
Historical Society.

They don't come any neater and trimmer than this, inside or out.

BRADSTREET HOUSE (*1666–1667*)
179 Osgood Street; Wednesdays and by
appointment; North Andover Historical
Society, Mrs. Woodbury K. Howe
(custodian and tenant).

This is an unusually interesting house, not only as a dwelling, but because of those whom it housed. Simon and Anne Bradstreet, ardent Puritans, came here in Governor Winthrop's party on the *Arabella* in 1630. Simon Bradstreet, as the first secretary of the colony and later its Governor, was a man of importance in his day, but it remains for time to tell that it was his fragile wife, Anne, who will best be remembered. Anne, the mother of eight children, lived to be only sixty. But she left a small body of poetry which has increasingly redounded to her fame. She is the first American poet. Her poetry was published in England in 1650, and there became so popular that the bookseller catalogued it as "the most vendible book." Conrad Aiken, in his *Comprehensive Anthology of American Poetry* (1944), devotes twelve pages to her poems, four to Lowell, six to Whittier, and eight to Longfellow.

¶ *Peabody (at intersection of Routes 1 and 128)*

GEN. GIDEON FOSTER HOUSE
(*between 1808 and 1815*)
35 Washington Street; Wednesdays 2 to 5,
July 1 to September 30; Peabody
Historical Society.

A pleasant example of the tall, three-story, hip-roof house so numerous hereabouts. They vary in distinction; this one being not quite the equal of the High Street houses in Newburyport, though they vary too.

¶ Reading (just north of Route 128 on
Route 28)

PARKER TAVERN (1694)

*103 Washington Street; Sundays 2 to 5
June 1 to October 1, and by appointment
with Mrs. Robert Barclay; contribution;
Reading Antiquarian Society.*

It is the unusual claim of this weather-
darkened salt box that "no famous people
have either lived or visited here." It is preserved simply as a typical early homestead,
and filled with fascinating collections of
woodenware, lighting devices, children's
toys, and early household paraphernalia.

¶ Rockport (out on the point of Cape Ann)

OLD GARRISON HOUSE or WITCH
HOUSE (possibly c. 1675)

*188 Granite Street; open to students of
architecture by written request, May to
November; Mrs. Oliver Williams and
daughter Mrs. McKinney.*

The Garrison House, built of logs hewn
square to resist attack, with a second-
story overhang, was used as a garrison during King Philip's War, but is now a summer home.

OLD CASTLE (1715–1792)

*Castle Lane; Saturdays and Sundays 2 to 5,
July and August; Pigeon Cove Village
Improvement Society.*

How the fine old shingled house with its
overhang and added lean-to came to be
called the "Old Castle" is worth a question
when you call to see its collections of early
household equipment.

¶ Rowley (between Ipswich and
Newburyport)

CHAPLIN-CLARK-WILLIAMS HOUSE
(1671)

*Route 133, Bradford Street between
Newburyport Turnpike and Old Bay Road;
by appointment with custodian;
contribution; S.P.N.E.A.*

PLATTS-BRADSTREET HOUSE

*(c. 1670; restored in eighteenth
century and again in 1919)
Main Street; on request, June 1 to
October 1; contribution; Rowley
Historical Society.*

The unpretentious Chaplin farmhouse has
features of historical and structural interest, and, together with the larger Platts-

Bradstreet House, which has a beautiful
setting, makes a pleasant pause on the way.

¶ Salem

Largely because of the work of the master craftsman, Samuel McIntire, connoisseurs consider this the treasure
town of the state. And when you have
taken in the Peirce and Pingree Houses,
walked back and forth a few times on
Chestnut Street, and made your way
around Washington Square, very likely
you will come to the same conclusion.

But there is still the fine Georgian
Derby House to visit down by the Derby
wharf. And to get way back to the
Salem version of the dark Elizabethan
look, there are still the ancient House
of Seven Gables group and other houses
like the Ward and the Witch to in-
vestigate.

After the austerity of pioneer days,
and the passion of witchcraft in the
seventeenth century, the eighteenth century brought something that was a welcome relief in a wonderful, swash-
buckling way: namely, trade with
Europe and the West Indies, in fleet
little ships that were Salem-built to fit
snug Salem harbor. And from the wealth
that began piling up on the Derby wharf
was built the lovely Georgian house right
across the way from the wharf; a house,
however, not to be compared in size
and glamour with the great Derby Mansion by McIntire that went up on Essex
Street forty years later, only to be torn
down fifteen years after it was finished.

Then, all of a sudden, a new kind of
Yankee ship was created that could out-
sail and outcarry the little Salem craft.
What was worse, these new, deep-draft
clippers needed deep-water harbors, and
Salem simply didn't have one that would
accommodate them. But Salem had her
houses. And in time she became a big

bustling modern industrial city. But by some miracle a lot of Old Salem still stands, and with it some of the finest old houses in America.

ROPES MANSION

(1719, additions 1804 and 1894)
318 Essex Street; afternoons except Sundays, Mondays, and holidays; 25 cents; Board of Trustees of Ropes Memorial.

This began as one of Salem's most important pre-Georgian houses, and in spite of alterations, its proud distinction is still strongly in evidence. In 1804 it acquired its extremely handsome fence in McIntire's best manner, even if not by the hand of the master. Filled with handsome mementos of many Salem generations.

HOUSE OF SEVEN GABLES *(1668)*

54 Turner Street; daily, 10 to 5, except Thanksgiving and Christmas; 75 cents and 30 cents to settlement work; House of Seven Gables Association.

It takes its name from Hawthorne's 1852 novel, having previously been the Turner House for almost two hundred years. It started off with four gables—two end ones and two cross ones in front. Then seafaring prosperity brought about additions that made the seven. For a while there were

eight. It was in the year of the witchcraft delusions that the secret staircase was installed within the original chimney, which is now a feature of interest. It is a fascinating old house, weather-darkened and rambling, and picturesque—one of the most extensive and important of the country's Early Gothic constructional types.

RETIRE BECKETT HOUSE *(1655)*

54 Turner Street near House of Seven Gables; weekdays, 10 to 6; House of Seven Gables Settlement Association.

HATHAWAY HOUSE *(1682)*

54 Turner Street; July 1 through Labor Day (two exhibition rooms open); 15 cents; House of Seven Gables Settlement Association.

The Retire Beckett and Hathaway Houses contribute their own ancient charms to the beautiful group they now form with the House of Seven Gables.

JOHN WARD HOUSE *(1684)*

132 Essex Street; weekdays 9 to 4:15, May 1 through October 31; 25 cents; Essex Institute.

One of the same vintage, featuring the same bold cross gables and overhangs, which added much light and space to the second-floor rooms. It was moved to the Essex Institute Garden in 1909.

The House of Seven Gables will deservedly always be one of the greatest of Salem's ancient attractions.

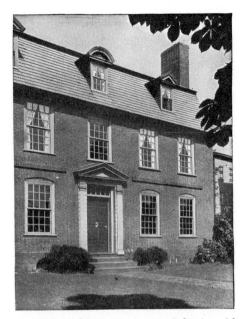

The Derby house represents Salem's middle period at its best, a choice piece of New England Georgian.

WITCH HOUSE (*a restoration*) (*1692*)
Daily 10 to 6, June 15 to October 12;
30 cents; city of Salem.

Another one of those seventeenth-century rarities that help to put Salem in a class by itself as a storehouse of treasures, early and late alike. This is the house in which Jonathan Corwin, a judge in the witchcraft court, lived and held preliminary examinations of the accused. Now restored and furnished as it was in that fateful year.

PEIRCE-NICHOLS HOUSE (*1782*)
80 Federal Street; daily, 2 to 5, except
Sundays and Mondays; 50 cents;
Essex Institute.

Samuel McIntire's first enduring triumph. Probably the greatest and most elegant of the country's early wooden houses; big, white, beautiful, and bold. An incomparable craftsman, McIntire brought to his architectural conceptions a quality of naïveté which accounts for their non-academic manner—wonderfully illustrated here in this house's exterior. The woodcarving within is among McIntire's most brilliant. The furnishings do full justice to the house—which couldn't be higher praise.

DERBY HOUSE (*1762*)
168 Derby Street; daily, 10 to 5; 25 cents;
National Park Service.

The Georgian gem that the great Salem maritime merchant built for his son Elias across from the long Derby wharf, was once the center of colonial seafaring trade. The oldest fine brick house in Salem, it has been faithfully restored and related to its surroundings—the RUM SHOP, the HAWKES HOUSE (a much-remodeled McIntire house that Derby didn't finish), and the CUSTOMS HOUSE, beautiful, stylish, and famous for the fact that Hawthorne worked in it for three years as surveyor of the port.

PINGREE HOUSE (*1804*)
128 Essex Street; daily; 50 cents and 25
cents; Essex Institute.

This great house came along in the latter part of McIntire's career, and here in the fine pale brick façade, set with a lovely semicircular entrance porch, the symmetry is expert in its rhythm and restraint. The carving inside is indescribably exquisite, and the rooms are among the most beautifully furnished in America, thanks to Mrs. Frances Crowninshield.

ANDREW SAFFORD HOUSE (*1818*)
13 Washington Square; to be open soon;
Essex Institute.

One of Salem's largest and costliest Late Federal brick mansions. High, wide, and handsome, it has a double balustrade whose decorative purpose was to minimize the roof—it being a foible of the Federal style

Considered by many to be McIntire's masterpiece, the Peirce-Nichols house is naturally one of the wonders of Salem.

that roofs, like petticoats, should not show. Now in process of restoration, its garden is connected with that of the Pingree House, around the corner.

THOMAS WOODBRIDGE HOUSE
(1810)
48 Bridge Street; not always open; occupied by a dealer in antiques.

The Woodbridge House has some McIntire paneling, as has the earlier DEAN HOUSE— now the EAST INDIA, operated as an inn. The very early and picturesque DANIELS HOUSE is also an inn, while the PIONEERS' VILLAGE represents Salem at its very earliest and bitterest—an expert piece of reconstruction demonstrating the indomitable fiber of the first settlers hereabouts.

¶ Saugus (between Boston and Lynn)

OLD IRON WORKS HOUSE
(1636–1642)
237 Central Street; daily, 10 to 5, except Thanksgiving, Christmas, and New Year's; 50 cents and 25 cents; First Iron Works Association, Inc.

An Elizabethan beauty, now restored with great skill and understanding as part of the restoration here of the first ironworks in America. It was really the ironmaster's house, furnished in true seventeenth-cen-

tury fashion—the whole instructive enterprise subsidized by the American Iron & Steel Institute, with no effort or expense spared to achieve authenticity, in a project of which the house itself is only a part.

SCOTCH BOARDMAN HOUSE *(1651)*
From Newburyport Turnpike at crossing of Saugus and Melrose Street railway, following tracks toward Melrose, Howard Street; June through September (apply to custodian); 15 cents; S.P.N.E.A.

A survival from the seventeenth century, more nearly intact than any other New England dwelling of its age. It has the overhang, the narrow, weather-darkened siding, the central immense medieval chimney, and carries lightly, movingly, its more than two and a half centuries. Someday to be fittingly restored and furnished.

¶ Topsfield (off Route 1 near intersection of 97)

PARSON CAPEN HOUSE *(1683)*
Just off village common on Howlett Street; weekdays 10 to 4:30, except Mondays, Sundays 12 to 5, May 15 to October 15, other times by appointment; 25 cents; Topsfield Historical Society.

One of the most famous, it answers closely the Scotch Boardman House description, though containing more sophisticated

touches on its exterior. It has the advantage of a more suitable setting, and is furnished in full conformity with what might be expected of a seventeenth-century parsonage. To have such a house the Capens could only have been people of dignity and distinction.

¶ *Wakefield (near Reading, just north of Boston)*

COL. JAMES HARTSHORNE HOUSE
(west end 1681, east end late 1700s)
Church Street, on Lake Quannapowitt; by appointment, at all times; voluntary contribution; Hartshorne House Association and town of Wakefield.

The Colonel Hartshorne House is a good example of a local preservation project. The home for many years of an officer in Washington's Rifle Greens, it has an unpretentious charm and a heart-warming neighborhood interest.

¶ *Wenham (off 128 above North Beverly)*

WHITEGATES (c. 1646)
162 Cherry Street; by written appointment only; Henry A. Erhard.

Clearly a seventeenth-century house built by a man of moderate means with neighborly assistance, all of it quite amateur and "without benefit of ruler," as its present owner testifies. Of special interest as a personal restoration.

CLAFLIN-RICHARDS HOUSE (1664)
Opposite the village green on Main Street; Monday to Friday, 1 to 4 (closed February and legal holidays); Wenham Historical Association and Museum, Inc.

An early cross-gabled house with later alterations, and with its weathered siding now painted. Good rooms with curved-brace framing and nice paneling, and a remarkable collection of dolls and figurines.

¶ *Woburn (just north of Boston on Route 38)*

RUMFORD HOUSE (early 1700s)
80 Elm Street, 2 miles east of town center; daily, 2 to 5, except in winter; Rumford Historical Association.

Count Rumford's birthplace happens to be an attractive early country house, made famous by the remarkable man born here as "Benjamin Thompson," knighted by George III and made a Count of the Holy Roman Empire. He was a scientist, philanthropist, and inventor of the Rumford Roasting Oven, the last word in cooking convenience for our grandmothers.

At the left the keeping room of the Ironmaster's house at Saugus contains a mouth-watering array of Early American articles and furnishings.

When you come upon the Parson Capen house you immediately feel yourself to be in the presence of a house with an almost human personality.

SOUTH OF BOSTON

Assinippi; Attleboro; Dedham; Duxbury; South Duxbury;
Hanover Center; Hingham; Kingston; Mansfield; Medfield;
Millis; Milton; Marshfield; North Swansea; Plymouth;
Quincy; Scituate

¶ *Assinippi (at intersection of Routes 3 and 123)*

JACOBS FARMHOUSE
(1726 and 1839)
Main Street and Jacobs Lane; Mondays, Tuesdays, and Fridays 2 to 5 June to October, and by appointment with caretakers; S.P.N.E.A.

This typical early farmstead is another good demonstration of well-organized domestic arrangements in the eighteenth century. In the barns is a collection of fire apparatus of 1760 to 1900.

¶ *Attleboro (on Route 123 almost to Providence)*

OLD PECK HOUSE (*early 1700*)
North Main and Elizabeth Streets; daily by arrangement with custodian, Mrs. Myra Hoxie; Attleboro Chapter, D.A.R.

A delightful and diminutive gambrel-roof cottage, important for the motive that inspired its preservation: "Acquired as an ancient landmark . . . for keeping ancient relics and curios."

¶ *Dedham (on outskirts of Boston)*

FAIRBANKS HOUSE (*1636*)
Eastern Avenue and East Street; daily 9 to 5, May 1 to November 1; 35 cents and 15 cents; Fairbanks Family in America, Inc.

This has been called the oldest frame dwelling still standing in this country, a title very difficult to establish. Its numerous very early additions make it not only picturesque but an extraordinary document. It was lived in by one family for nearly three centuries.

DEXTER HOUSE (*1761–1763*)
699 High Street; by appointment; George C. Seybolt.

A full, foursquare Newbury-type mansion, built by a distinguished colonial merchant, this house is rich in Revolutionary lore. It has paneled rooms and a carved staircase. Very worthwhile.

The ancient Fairbanks house at Dedham makes an interesting study of a domestic establishment that has been actively lived in for more than three centuries, and for the most part by one family.

Altogether appealing in many ways, the Jabez Wilder house at Hingham is famous for its bowed roof, obviously the work of ship carpenters turned housebuilders.

¶ *Duxbury & South Duxbury*
(*off Route 3 down by Plymouth Bay*)

JOHN ALDEN HOUSE (*1653*)
> *Alden Street, near the station; daily, April 15 to November 15; 35 cents; Alden Kindred in America, Inc.*

The Alden House has always been occupied by Aldens (including John and Priscilla) and still is today. Naturally, the ancient cottage and its colonial furnishings, which housed one of America's first families, have romantic as well as eye appeal.

ALEXANDER STANDISH HOUSE
(*1666, remodeled 1946*)
> *Standish Street, South Duxbury; will show when at home; David L. Patten.*

A remarkably well-preserved shingled house with gambrel roof and central chimney, built by the eldest son of Miles Standish, who married John Alden's daughter, you will recall. Captain Standish's own house once stood nearby, but was destroyed by fire.

KING CAESAR HOUSE (*c. 1798*)
> *King Caesar Road, Powder Point; by appointment, through the summer season; Miss Alice Moran and Mr. and Mrs. Weber-Fulop.*

This great imposing white house was built by Ezra Weston, Jr., known as "King Caesar II," his father being "King Caesar I." They were shipbuilders and bankers, and practically owned Powder Point. There is a slave house in the rear, and there goes with the house the story of a secret passage leading from the slave house to the bay.

There is also a monument to Honest Dick, the horse who died at thirty-nine after serving both Caesars. Scenic papers; fine furnishings.

FOUR CORNERS (*1780*)
> *Washington Street; by appointment; 50 cents for Winslow House Fund; Mr. and Mrs. Harold E. Fitzgibbons.*

A typical Duxbury Colonial, i.e., square, with a great central chimney, "Four Corners" is of the period just preceding the more ostentatious ship captains' houses of the turn of the century.

¶ *Hanover Center*

SAMUEL STETSON HOUSE
(*1694, enlarged 1716*)
> *Near Village Green, off Route 3; 10 to 5 daily except Mondays June through October, other times by appointment; 25 cents; S.P.N.E.A.*

Portions of the original chamfered frame are still visible, though the present trim is largely of the second, or "Drummer" Stetson, period. The house has been restored, with one room serving as a memorial to the Briggs family who gave the house to the Society. Another room contains local collections.

¶ *Hingham (beyond Quincy on Hingham Bay)*

JABEZ WILDER HOUSE (*1690–1790*)
> *557 Main Street (Route 128); by appointment; Lois Williams.*

Known locally as the "Rainbow Roof House," this is sparkling white and ship-shape. It is remarkable for its bowed, convex roof, the rafters for which were bent for strength by local shipbuilders, as were the ribs of ships. The corners of the clapboard walls are neatly trimmed with wooden quoins. The original pine floor contains boards as wide as twenty-seven inches; the steep divided staircase has a shiplike look, too, and three of the rooms retain their original paneling. Built by Jabez Wilder, the house remained in the family until 1950.

THE OLD ORDINARY (1650)

19 Lincoln Street; weekdays 2 to 5, April to November; 25 cents; Hingham Historical Society.

One of the old New England roadside inns. Well preserved, with most of the country-tavern features still intact, it is fitted out and furnished as it should be.

The OLD SHIP MEETINGHOUSE is another feature of the town.

SAMUEL LINCOLN HOUSE (1741)

182 North Street; Mondays, 2 to 5 (two rooms open); S.P.N.E.A.

The oldest house in town, with two rooms open as a Lincoln family memorial.

¶ Kingston

(on Routes 3 and 3A, 4 miles above Plymouth)

SQUIRE WILLIAM SEVER HOUSE (1760)

2 Lindent Street; by appointment several days in advance; $2.00 per person for Historic Winslow House Association; Mr. and Mrs. Arthur E. Beane, Jr.

This is a beautifully preserved house, simple, fine, and foursquare, with a handsome doorway, all lovingly restored and most appropriately furnished.

OLD BREWSTER HOUSE (1690)

Brewster Road (intersection of 3 and 3A, about 150 yards south of sign); weekdays 10 to 5, June to October; 30 cents and 15 cents; Edward L. Singsen.

Built by Joseph Holmes, stepson of Maj. William Bradford, who married Mary, daughter of Love and Wrestling Brewster. Now occupied by the sixth generation of Brewsters, it contains period furnishings and relics of the Brewsters from the time of the landing of the *Mayflower*.

MAJ. JOHN BRADFORD HOUSE (1674 and 1720)

Landing Road; daily 10 to 5:30 and Sunday afternoons, July 1 to Labor Day; 35 cents and 10 cents; Jones River Village Club.

Built when Kingston was part of Plymouth by a grandson of Governor Bradford, who chose a lovely knoll overlooking the landing on the Jones River. He moved into it as a honeymoon house with his bride Mercy Warren. Later additions were made as the family grew to nine, and the house shows the transition from leaded casements to sliding sash. There are furniture, household utensils, and tools of the period, and the looms are in operation daily.

¶ Mansfield (on Route 140 about 30 miles south of Boston)

FISHER-RICHARDSON HOUSE (built 1704, enlarged 1800)

Willow Street; Saturdays and Sundays 2 to 5 and by appointment, June 15 to October 1; town of Mansfield.

This is an interesting primitive, with a wide gambrel, and a well sweep in the yard. A good restoration, it is furnished in its period and contains exhibits of early industries.

¶ Medfield (on 109, 7 miles below Dedham)

PEAK HOUSE (rebuilt 1680)

Main Street; by appointment; town of Medfield.

So called because of the sharp pitch to its once thatched roof, this little house is unfurnished, but it is an interesting and nicely restored relic, with its leaded diamond-paned windows, said to be the originals. It is the immediate successor to the similar house destroyed when King Philip's Indians burned the town of Medford in 1676.

¶ Millis (3 miles beyond Medfield)

BASIL GAVIN HOUSE (c. 1740)

Millis State Road; by appointment; Basil Gavin.

A fine Colonial house built by a member of the Adams family on land deeded to him by the King, it is notable for its woodwork. The moldings and doors of the master bedroom are very good examples of early work, and a duplicate of the mantel here is in the Boston Art Museum. An annual tour has been started here which takes in seven or eight houses dating from 1691 to 1810, all of interest. Mr. Gavin will give you more information about it on request.

¶ Milton (southern environs of Boston via Route 28)

GOVERNOR BELCHER PLACE (*1777*)
401 Adams Street; on application to custodians, Mr. and Mrs. Nathaniel Lord; Milton Historical Society.

This is an interesting Revolutionary house, built by the widow of Governor Belcher after fire destroyed a previous house on the same spot. Not a manor house, but distinctly more than a farmhouse. Interior restoration in progress.

SUFFOLK RESOLVES HOUSE
(*1765 and 1780*)
1350 Canton Avenue; on request to owner; Mrs. James B. Ayer.

This is where the Suffolk Resolves of 1774, one of the major acts leading to the Revolution, were signed. Built by Capt. Daniel Vose, it was brought here from Milton Lower Mills Village and completely restored.

¶ Marshfield (on 3A above Duxbury)

WINSLOW HOUSE (*1699*)
Careswell and Webster Streets; July 1 to September 15; 30 cents; Historic Winslow House Association.

Built by Isaac Winslow, the son and grandson of two Massachusetts governors, it was later owned by Daniel Webster, a Duxbury man. Framed with "gunstock" timbers, it has a massive chimney, wide windows, and steep stairs adorned with acorn drops that give it a Jacobean look. Some Georgian remodeling was done in 1756 by the Gen. John Winslow who had just driven the Acadians from Grand Pré, but there is also evidence of Georgian detailing in the original structure, which would make this one of the earliest examples of Georgian work in New England, if not the first.

¶ North Swansea

MARTIN HOUSE (*1728*)
Fall River Avenue (highway between Providence and Fall River); daily 10 to 6, May 15 to November 1; 25 cents and 15 cents; National Society of Colonial Dames of Massachusetts.

A most attractive gambrel-roof farmhouse with silvery shingles and with one of those collections of local interest inside which always manage to strike a spark.

¶ Plymouth
(*36 miles south of Boston on Plymouth Bay*)

There is a good deal to see here which is of a historical nature not directly connected with the houses themselves, and individuals and groups who wish to arrange for a guided tour should write for detailed information to Arthur G. Pyle, Box 1620, Plymouth. Out of season individual houses may be visited by special arrangement with their custodians.

THE WINSLOW HOUSE (*1754*)
Winslow and North Streets; daily 10 to 5 except Mondays, June until it gets too cold in October; donation; General Society of Mayflower Descendants.

A large white frame Georgian house with balustraded roof, very handsome and distinguished, built by Edward Winslow, grandson of Governor Winslow of the *Mayflower*. It is furnished in Queen Anne and early Chippendale. It was in this house that Ralph Waldo Emerson was married.

ANTIQUARIAN HOUSE (*1809*)
126 Water Street; daily 10 to 5, June 14 to September 11; 50 cents and 15 cents.

This mansion of the Federal period is historically a far cry from the dwellings erected here by the early arrivals. It contains collections of dolls, costumes, toys, fans, lace, and books.

PILGRIM JOHN HOWLAND HOUSE
(*1666 and 1750*)
Sandwich Street; daily 9 to 5, May 15 to November 1; 25 cents and 15 cents.

The only house still standing in Plymouth

which was occupied by actual Pilgrims, it was the home of Jabez, son of John, who came over on the *Mayflower*. The original paint is still on the walls of the 1750 living room, and the furnishings are mostly family heirlooms. Howland descendants meet here every year to keep alive the family traditions.

OLD FORT HARLOW HOUSE (*1677*)

119 Sandwich Street; daily 10 to 5, May 30 to September 15; 30 cents and 15 cents.

A museum of life as it was lived in seventeenth-century Plymouth, and furnished in the period. There are collections of early utensils, and demonstrations are given of spinning, weaving, candlemaking, dyeing, and fireside cookery.

RICHARD SPARROW HOUSE (*1636–1640*)

42 Summer Street; daily, 10 to 5, except Sundays; 20 cents and 10 cents; Miss Katharine Alden (custodian) 42 Summer Street (phone: Plymouth 1024–M).

This restored red clapboard house is probably the oldest in Plymouth. It serves as a home and as the headquarters of a co-operative guild known as the "Plymouth Potters," and several rooms are furnished with early things.

HARLOW-HOLMES HOUSE (*1649*)

8 Winter Street; open all year; 30 cents; Harlow Family Association, Mr. and Mrs. Knowlton B. Holmes.

This ancient gambrel-roof house is now lived in by the ninth generation of the Holmes family. It is completely furnished with family pieces left by previous generations, including the captain's table from the *Mayflower* itself. Every effort has been made to preserve the house in its original form.

PLIMOUTH PLANTATION

(*a reproduction*)

On waterfront adjacent to Plymouth Rock; First House 9 to 7 May 30 to Labor Day and weekends through Thanksgiving, First Fort 9 to 7; May 30 to Labor Day and weekends through Thanksgiving; 10 cents; Mrs. Deane Eldridge (custodian).

This is an interesting reproduction project in the process of development, containing among other exhibits a typical permanent Pilgrim dwelling of the period of 1623, complete with appropriate furnishings. Plans are under way for a reconstruction of the first fort and meetinghouse of the Pilgrims; and a full-size replica of the *Mayflower* is, or will be, a feature of great interest.

This is the fascinating old home of the famous Adams family at Quincy.

Speaking of family houses, this one at Plymouth is presently sheltering its ninth generation of Holmeses.

¶ Quincy

(virtually now the southeastern section of city of Boston)

ADAMS MANSION *or* THE OLD HOUSE (*1731*)

> *135 Adams Street; daily 9:30 to 4:45, May 10 to November 10; 30 cents; National Park Service.*

This is one of the most remarkable American family mansions of one of America's most remarkable families, and constitutes, for all to see, a document of their lives through four generations of Presidents, great statesmen, and historians. In an intimate way, it tells the story of how the Adamses lived from 1787 to 1927—from the year John Adams bought it from a grandson of wealthy Maj. Leonard Vassall, who had built it fifty-six years before, to the year Brooks Adams, the last of the family to occupy it, died. The house contains the family furnishings as they came down from generation to generation, and with them it contains some of the character and culture that made the name of this family one of our greatest.

BIRTHPLACE OF PRESIDENT JOHN ADAMS (*1663*)

> *129 Franklin Street; daily 10 to 5 except Mondays, April 19 to November 1; 30 cents or 50 cents; city of Quincy and Quincy Historical Society.*

BIRTHPLACE OF JOHN QUINCY ADAMS (*1675*)

> *131 Franklin Street; same.*

These two old neighboring houses of the salt-box persuasion, clapboarded and each with its great central chimney, are as simple and unpretentious as most of their contemporaries. Neither President—father or son—was born in luxury, though the family had solid standing and belonged to the only aristocracy that existed then—that of brains. Both houses are attractive in their sturdy plainness. In the later house was also born the constitution of Massachusetts.

QUINCY HOMESTEAD *or* DOROTHY Q HOUSE (*1706*)

34 Butler Road, at Hancock Avenue; daily 10 to 5, April 19 to November 1; 25 cents and 15 cents; Commonwealth of Massachusetts; Massachusetts Society of Colonial Dames.

This Early Colonial mansion, with its inklings of the Queen Anne style—hip on gambrel, the hip hidden by balustrading—has great architectural charm. Within a very feminine feeling prevails. Fine paneling and the very French wedding wallpaper that was imported for the marriage of "Dorothy Q" and John Hancock.

COL. JOSIAH QUINCY HOUSE (*1770*)

20 Muirhead Street, Wollaston; Tuesday through Friday and Sunday 11 to 5 May to October 13, other times by appointment; S.P.N.E.A.

Imagine this fine foursquare white and yellow house as a gentleman's country seat, as it was before the encroachments of Quincy Town. This former home of a prominent patriot, wealthy merchant, and shipbuilder has a pleasant portico with columns, and the corners of the clapboard walls are trimmed with imitation stone-block quoins, typical of the times.

¶ *Scituate (on Route 3A halfway between Quincy and Plymouth)*

CUDWORTH HOUSE (*1723*)

Opposite schoolhouse; daily 1 to 6, July 1 to Labor Day; contribution; Scituate Historical Society.

This is the kind of house that twentieth-century Americans hanker for: shingled walls neatly trimmed in white, gambrel roof, king-size central chimney. No matter how many of these modest eighteenth-century dwellings Massachusetts may have to offer, each one has its unique character. The barn of this one contains interesting collections of carriages and farm implements.

WEST OF BOSTON

Concord; Harvard; Lexington; South Sudbury; Sturbridge;

Templeton; Newton Lower Falls; Shrewsbury

¶ *Concord*

The houses here make vivid the events and personalities for which the town is famous, from Revolutionary heroes and happenings to the literary circles, figures, and families that lived here through the later years.

ANTIQUARIAN HOUSE

(a museum)

Daily and holidays 10 to 5 and Sundays 2 to 5, April 19 to November 11; 50 cents and 20 cents (plus tax); Concord Antiquarian Society.

The building was carefully designed to reflect the fine middle ground of early domestic architecture in New England. Incorporated in the museum as a wing, is the seventeenth-century house that was rebuilt here to contain some of the early collections. This has the true medieval look, from diamond-paned casements and clamshell plastered walls down to the wooden latches and locks. The transitions of styles through which you pass—from the seventeenth-century-house wing to the Victorian room on the third floor of the museum proper—make an illuminating journey through time and taste. In addition, two "personality rooms" are placed as cul-de-sacs en route: a little Thoreau room, and an Emerson study.

EMERSON HOUSE (*1828*)

Cambridge Turnpike, opposite Antiquarian House; daily 10 to 11:30 and 1:30 to 5:30 except Mondays, Sundays 2:30 to 5:30, April 19 to November 15 (large groups by appointment); 35 cents and 15 cents; Emerson Memorial Association.

Having "dodged the doom of building," to quote the great man himself, Emerson purchased this house in 1835 and lived here the rest of his life. A large white house of quiet dignity and no stylistic pretentions, it reflects the cultivated American who was more interested in essence than appearance.

THE WAYSIDE (*1717*)

Lexington Road, near Hawthorne Road; weekends and most other days except Monday; daily except Monday, June 16 to September 30; 40 cents and 20 cents; Miss Margaret Lathrop.

Associated primarily with Nathaniel Hawthorne, the house was occupied first by the Alcotts as "Hillside." Later it was inhabited by Margaret Sidney, author of the popular series *The Five Little Peppers.* An early house to begin with, it shows plainly its later additions. The ungainly tower room was built by Hawthorne to avoid visitors while he was writing two of his masterpieces, *The Marble Faun* and *Tanglewood Tales.*

THE OLD MANSE (*1769*)

Weekends and by appointment 2 to 5 April 19 to June 1, daily 10:30 to 5 and Sundays 2 to 5 June to October, weekends October to November 11; 35 cents and 10 cents; Trustees of Public Reservations.

Built by Emerson's grandfather, the Reverend William Emerson, chaplain at Ticonderoga, it was here that Ralph Waldo began the writing of his famous essay *Nature.* Here, too, Hawthorne lived the first three idyllic years of his marriage and wrote many of the *Mosses from an Old Manse,* in the first of which there is a description of the house. A plain but well-built gambrel-roofed house, with an odd double dormer probably added by one of its later occupants, it had a front-row seat for the Battle of Concord. Right here, at the nearby river, was fired the shot that was to be "heard around the world."

ORCHARD HOUSE (*1650 and 1730*)

Lexington Road; daily 10 to 5 except Mondays, Sundays 2 to 6, April 19 to November 1; 35 cents and 20 cents; Louisa May Alcott Memorial Association.

Bronson Alcott brought two old houses together here and made them into one, in which his daughter Louisa May was to write *Little Women,* a classic book for girls as well as the tale of the delightful and improvident family who lived here. Bronson Alcott, a remarkable man and a domestic disaster, called by Emerson in his Journal "a tedious archangel," encouraged imagination and the creative urge in his daughters. But it is Louisa May's personality which predominates here, just as it must have during her lifetime. It is a house in which the emphasis on "simple living" is still evident, for little has been changed inside since the Alcotts' day.

There are three colonial inns on Lexington Road, all still operating: THE WRIGHT TAVERN (1747), HARTWELL FARM (pre-Revolutionary), and the REUBEN BROWN HOUSE (before 1775), which was the home of the colonial saddler who carried to Concord the news that hostilities had occurred, and is now a tearoom.

¶ *Harvard* (*12 miles beyond Concord via Route 111*)

FRUITLANDS (*early eighteenth century*) and the WAYSIDE MUSEUMS, INC.

On Prospect Hill; daily 1 to 5:30, May 30 to September 30; founded by Miss Clara Endicott Sears.

This is a fascinating cluster of various restorations, including an old Shaker house, an Indian mansion, a picture gallery, and a library, among which you will be amused to find to what lengths the Transcendentalists attempted to carry their experiments— this one a way of life which would not exploit man, beast, or even insect. It lasted only four months. There are fine collections of Shaker furniture and household ware and of Indian relics. House interest and human interest both.

¶ *Lexington* (*in northwest suburban area of Boston*)

HANCOCK-CLARK HOUSE (*1698, enlarged 1734*)

35 Hancock Street; weekdays 10 to 5 and Sundays 2 to 5, May 30 to October 12; 35 cents; Lexington Historical Society, 1774 Massachusetts Avenue.

The typical unpretentious house of a substantial eighteenth-century citizen. One occupant here (for seven years) was John Hancock. Samuel Adams was here with him the night Paul Revere came by.

MUNROE TAVERN (*1695*)

1332 Massachusetts Avenue; weekdays 9:30 to 5 and Sundays 2 to 5, April 19 to November 11; 35 cents.

This tavern was eighty years old and a going concern the day in April, 1775, when Earl Percy took it over as his headquarters and as a hospital for his wounded redcoats. A sturdy, attractive two-story frame house, with a very pleasantly pedimented doorway, it contains fine early furnishings and fascinating mementos.

BUCKMAN TAVERN (*1712*)

Facing Battle Green; weekdays 10 to 5 and Sundays 2 to 5, Memorial Day to Columbus Day; 35 cents; Lexington Historical Society.

The Minute Men assembled here in this good-looking inn on the morning of that famous April 19. Its fine façade looks out over the village green, where they subsequently fought. Its well-maintained interior contains an abundance of Revolutionary household and tavern paraphernalia.

¶ *South Sudbury (20 miles beyond Waltham on Route 20)*

LEONARD P. GOULDING HOUSE

(antique shop on premises) (*built 1700 in Wayland, Massachusetts, moved 1925*)

Daily; Mr. and Mrs. Leonard P. Goulding.

This old, deeply weathered dwelling, two stories and an attic, is a first-rate restoration with its diamond-paned casements and its almost Tudor chimney. The great living room in the lean-to is paneled even to the summer beams, and the whole house is furnished with the skill of veteran collectors. Don't miss it for anything.

¶ *Sturbridge (on Route 20 between Worcester and Springfield where Route 15 from Hartford intersects)*

OLD STURBRIDGE VILLAGE

(*re-creation of a New England village of 1790*)

At junction of Routes 15 and 20; April 1 to November 11; May 16 to November 11 $1.75, November 12 to May 15 $1.00 (groups of 20 or over $1.25 each).

This is a three-hundred-acre community created to represent, in effect, a far-flung New England village, with homes, church, store, farm, sawmill, gristmill, tavern, and all the various shops that supplied the household and business needs of an early Yankee rural community. There are thirty-five or more buildings, bridges, and other installations, dating from 1704 to 1840, which have been brought together here

from various parts of New England, properly placed, expertly restored, and appropriately furnished and equipped. Incidentally, it has been made into an entertaining place to visit. It is essentially a performance, painstakingly prepared and presented. You can learn a great deal about our past that you never knew before and have a lot of fun doing it. Complete information on travel and accommodations will be furnished by the director's office.

¶ *Templeton* (*on Route 2, 4 miles beyond Gardner*)

NARRAGANSETT HISTORICAL SOCIETY (*c. 1810*)

> *Saturday afternoons, June until October; Tuesdays and Saturdays 2 to 5, July 1 to September 15; Narragansett Historical Society.*

Built by a man of obvious taste and talent named John Stiles, this is a very stylish foursquare brick dwelling in the prim, Late Georgian, symmetrical manner. Stiles had the store and post office occupying a portion of the house, and these now form part of the present display. The residential rooms are furnished with appropriate early pieces, mostly from hereabouts, and there are exhibits and collections of early local objects.

¶ *Newton Lower Falls* (*the Newtons form the western part of metropolitan Boston*)

JOHN PARKER HOUSE (*1750*)

> *2349 Washington Street; first Thursday in month all year and second Monday in month October through May; Lucy Jackson Chapter, D.A.R.*

A foursquare Colonial with some Federal remodeling, this is a town house of considerable style, with a fine recessed doorway decorated with a fleur-de-lis and with many well-restored rooms of interesting furniture, china, glass, toys, and costumes. It was once the parsonage of the charming white church next door.

¶ *Shrewsbury* (*35 miles out on Route 9 and 1 mile off to the right on 140*)

ARTEMUS WARD HOUSE (*before 1775*)

> *May 15 to October 1; Harvard University, Mrs. Busbey (custodian).*

An unusually handsome pre-Revolutionary house in unusually good condition, certainly very much worthwhile turning off to see. The home of Gen. Artemus Ward of Revolutionary fame, it was always lived in by the family, many of whose things are still there.

Across the page in this winter glimpse of Old Sturbridge Village, the Fitch house lies off to the left of the country store, and above it rises the steeple of the Greek Revival meetinghouse.

This very trim, attractive house that was built by John Stiles in Templeton is now the interestingly furnished headquarters of the Narragansett Historical Society.

THE CONNECTICUT RIVER VALLEY

Amherst; Bernardston; Deerfield; Hadley; Holyoke;

Longmeadow; Northampton; Springfield; West Hatfield;

West Springfield

¶ *Amherst*

NEHEMIAH STRONG HOUSE (*1744*)

67 Amith Street; Tuesdays and Fridays 2 to 5, June 1 to October 1; 25 cents; Amherst Historical Society.

This is the oldest house in town. Three and a half stories, with a gambrel roof and the well-known weathered hue, it is fascinatingly constructed, of course, and contains fine collections of local early objects and furnishings.

¶ *Bernardston (a few miles below the Vermont line on Route 5)*

RYTHER HOUSE (*1745*)

Daily when convenient, on special request; Fred A. and Grace M. Donaldson.

An interesting house in which all of the old features have been preserved, including a painting of a British spy on the plaster wall over the mantel (c. 1812) and, next to it, a wall of early stenciling. There are fourteen rooms, all furnished with American antiques, and original Indian shutters, made in one piece to slide over the window in case of attack.

¶ *Deerfield*

The ancient elms of Old Deerfield Street arch over one of the most homogeneous avenues of eighteenth-century buildings in America. At least twenty of the houses here were built before the Revolution, and Mr. Henry N. Flynt, the good angel of these precincts, numbers more than thirty from that century alone. The fact that almost every house is being used and that even the museum houses are occupied by their devoted custodians brings a town of museum quality to life.

Deerfield was a byword for Indian savagery long before the Revolution. Actually there were three major massacres and countless minor raids, beginning with the attack in 1675 that wiped out the first little colony and continuing on, even after the friendship pledge had been signed in 1735. But in time safety was assured and Deerfield was free to develop its prosperous agricultural economy. Its citizens had the courage and finally the means to build themselves comfortably fine homes, so many of which, by great good fortune and great good construction as well, have survived—to embark on a new lease of life in the twentieth century.

Certainly no one should attempt to see Deerfield without securing a booklet at the information center in the Hall Tavern, with a map of streets and houses. Another word of advice: winter may be flattering to the houses, but few of the buildings can be seen during the school months, when the town is more or less concentrated on its academic life, centering on Deerfield Academy for Boys.

PARSON ASHLEY HOUSE
(*1726 to 1733*)

Weekdays 10 to 12 and 2 to 4:30 except Mondays, Sundays 2 to 5; 60 cents.

Perhaps you will begin at the north end of the wide avenue with the Parson Ashley House, one of the pick of the crop. The narrow weatherboarding, a feature of these houses, is dark with age and the tall narrow windows give the house an almost fortresslike appearance. Its walls were, in fact, bulletproof. Its magnificent broken-arch pediment over the doorway, and the door itself, tell that it was made in the Connecticut Valley. When you see the

The doorway of the Parson Ashley house is one of the finest in Deerfield, the house one of the most colorfully furnished and decorated.

beautiful interior, you will find it hard to believe that it was rescued, back in 1869, from service as a tobacco barn. Its present perfection is the work of the Flynts, as they conceive it was lived in by the prosperous parson. It can be seen that in Deerfield a parson was not lacking in the blessings of this world, as well as the next.

INDIAN HOUSE (*1698 reconstruction*) and BLOODY BROOK TAVERN (*c. 1785*)

> *Old Deerfield Street; weekdays 9 to 12 and 1 to 5 except Tuesdays, Sundays 1 to 5; both buildings 30 cents.*

You cannot mistake the Indian House, a darkly brooding reconstruction of a typical late seventeenth-century dwelling with second- and third-story overhangs, built on the site of a 1698 house built by Ens. John Sheldon within the stockade which was the scene of the 1704 Massacre—the one which resulted in the prisoners' being marched off in the dead of winter to Canada. Back of it stands old Bloody Brook Tavern (1675 to 1700), moved here from South Deerfield, where it had stood by the brook of evil memory.

As you pass, look at the JOSEPH STEBBINS HOUSE, a great gambrel-roof mansion of considerable style built for the hero of Bunker Hill in about 1772, his townsmen having helped him to become a tycoon by granting him perpetual tax freedom for his gristmill in appreciation of his war record. The rooftree easily accommodated his family of thirteen children. Corner quoins

and fine doorways distinguish it, the ornamentation hinting at the first advance of the Federal influences.

EPHRAIM WILLIAMS HOUSE (*1760*)

> *Upon application at Deerfield Academy office.*

Now the home of the headmaster of the academy, it was built in 1760 and enlarged in 1794. Its rear wing, Greek Revival in character, seems to have been added still later.

MEMORIAL HALL (*1797*)

> *Deerfield Academy; weekdays except Tuesday 9:30 to 12 and 2 to 5, Tuesdays 10 to 12 and 2 to 4, Sundays 2 to 5; 50 cents and 15 cents.*

This place has several rooms furnished in old Deerfield relics.

NIMMS HOUSE (*1710*)

The Nimms House can probably be visited upon request to the academy.

JONATHAN WILLIAMS HOUSE (*1707*)

> *Campus of Deerfield Academy; perhaps upon application at the Deerfield Academy office.*

Worth a good look is the Reverend Jonathan Williams House, whose owner was the first preacher to the people of Deerfield, for its doorway is admittedly the finest in a town which does not lack for them. From it, he and his five children were dragged captive to be marched in bondage three hundred miles to Canada, while his wife and two other children were murdered. Williams lived to return to Deerfield, when he was given this home by his thankful congregation, to write his account of those harrowing times in a locally famous source book, *The Redeemed Captive*.

FRARY HOUSE (*1683–1763*)

Weekdays 9 to 12 and 1:30 to 5 except Mondays, Sundays 2 to 5, April 1 to November; 50 cents and 15 cents.

The only house in Deerfield that escaped in large part the disaster of 1704. Not so its owner and his wife, however, who were massacred. Today the staunch, rambling house, deeply weathered, is an almost perfect example of its times, both inside and out. The doorway of its north and earliest end has the kind of rich austerity so typical of Deerfield craftsmanship. In 1763 Selah Bernard added the south part and made it a tavern. Twelve years later it was the place Benedict Arnold chose to stop in on his way to Ticonderoga, and to feed his army he ordered a collection of fifteen hundred pounds of beef from the local farmers. One of the features of this U-shaped structure is the yellow ballroom, a room almost as necessary as a taproom in those times.

THE OLD MANSE *or* WILLARD HOUSE (*1694–1768*)

Upon application at Deerfield Academy office.

This place has one of the prettiest façades in town. It is a charming square house painted yellow, an unusual note in Deerfield, and the detail of its corner quoins and delicate cornice, and its window lintels and doorway (another fine one) are brought out in white. The handsome hip roof, broken by close-set dormers, completes a picture which is unmistakably Salem in character. It is told that Joseph Barnard took thirteen years to collect the pine for it, so that no panel should show a knot.

HALL TAVERN AND STORE (*1765*)

Weekdays 9:30 to 12 and 1:30 to 5, Sundays 1 to 5; 50 cents.

The Hall Tavern and Deerfield Store, the former moved here from nearby Charlemont on the Old Post Road, was the focal point of entertainment for the whole neighborhood and typical of the best New England hostels of the day. Spacious and clean, such inns as this one were a boon to travelers who had been in the saddle or

Among the extraordinary collection of early houses which forms Old Deerfield Village, the Frary house is outstanding, its yellow ballroom a special feature.

The main body of the Old Manse is one of the more formal of Deerfield houses. Note the older gambrel-roof section at the right rear.

jolting over the rough roads from dawn to dark. Lucretia Hall, the hostess here during much of its history, was a notable cook and provider of cheer. Her Thanksgiving pies, whose upper crusts were enlivened by a flight of pastry doves, are legendary. The seven fireplaces in the inn kept out the long winter chill. The ballroom on the second floor, with its narrow benches built in all the way round the walls, has a vaulted ceiling, and the brilliant stencil pattern that covers the wall with a special overmantel picture is something not to be missed. Several of the best of the old papers and stencils in the various homes, as discovered by Mrs. Henry Flynt, have been well reproduced and are on sale here.

ASA STEBBINS HOUSE (*1799*)
Weekdays 10 to 12 and 2 to 4:30 except Wednesdays, Sundays 2 to 5; 50 cents.

The only two brick houses in town were both built by the wealthy Stebbins brothers. This one has the early rear wing attached, in which the father, Joseph, raised the family. The two sons, Asa and Joseph, were shrewd businessmen as well as patriots, and to this fact we owe the beauty of this little brick Federal mansion and the equally fine mansion which Joseph erected near the end of the avenue. Asher Benjamin, an unknown lad of twenty, was working on the academy at this time, and his influence is plain to be seen here. The Asa Stebbins House is as delicate as a shell inside and its lightness is in striking contrast to the houses already described. Its interior must have seemed a miracle of elegance when the Federal style was only just beginning to be seen. The pink walls of the drawing room (brick dust mixed with the plaster), its pargeted ceiling and elaborately decorated cornice, the brilliant freehand designs painted gaily on the dining-room walls (possibly by Jared Jessup), the graceful curved staircase—all these delicate innovations must have seemed almost frivolous to the townsfolk. If the house were half as finely furnished as it is today (thanks to the Flynts), they could not have failed to admire it.

Upstairs in the old Hall Tavern, which served as inn and village store, is one of the most interesting ballrooms in New England.

A glimpse of the restoration village of Storrowton with its interesting collection of early New England homes and other structures.

¶ Hadley (*on Route 9, 3 miles east of Northampton*)

PORTER-PHELPS-HUNTINGTON HOUSE (*1752 and 1799*)
> *Saturdays and Sundays 10 to 6, May to October; by appointment; 50 cents.*

This is a delightful old family establishment—a large, ingratiating three-story gambrel-roof house, with kitchen ell, woodshed, and carriage house in a long low line connecting it with a later and smaller house of simple Colonial design. Surrounded by a split-rail fence, it is set in a grove of elms, maples, and hemlocks. Household articles include pieces brought to Dorchester from England in 1631 and items from every generation who lived in the house for the next one hundred and seventy-five years.

¶ Holyoke (*on Route 5 between Springfield and Northampton*)

THE TAVERN (*1785*)
> *Halfway between Springfield and Northampton; Eunice Day Chapter, D.A.R.*

When this town was on the old coach line from Springfield to Boston, this old hostelry was known as "The Miller's Inn," and later became famous as "Craft's Tavern." Furnished in keeping.

¶ Longmeadow (*just above the Connecticut line on Route 5*)

COLTON HOUSE (*1734*)
> *Longmeadow Street; Mondays and Wednesdays 3 to 5 mid-June to mid-October, other times by appointment; 25 cents; S.P.N.E.A.*

STORRS PARSONAGE (*1786*)
> *697 Longmeadow Street; Thursdays 2 to 5, August and September; Longmeadow Historical Society.*

These two houses of considerable distinction grace an old street of noble beauty.

¶ Northampton

ISAAC DAMON HOUSE
(*1812, remodeled 1825*)
> *46 Bridge Street; summer, by appointment, (phone: 990); contribution; Northampton Historical Society.*

Damon was an early New England architect and bridge builder. Here are his drafting instruments, models of bridges, and other memorabilia; also a collection of Jenny Lind articles.

CORNET JOSEPH PARSONS HOUSE
(*1658, remodeled about 1806*)
> *58 Bridge Street; Wednesdays, Fridays, and Sundays, 2 to 5; contribution; Northampton Historical Society.*

This is the oldest house in the town; built by the first settler, it is furnished with a variety of pieces presented mostly by Northampton people. The list of its possessions is endless, and a matter of considerable local pride and general interest.

THE CAPEN HOUSE (*1825*), THE DEWEY HOUSE (*1827*), *and* THE SESSIONS HOUSE (*1700*) (*now dormitories*)

On request, at reasonable hours; Smith College.

The Capen and Dewey Houses are Greek Revival.

¶ *Springfield*

ALEXANDER HOUSE (*1811*)

284 State Street; weekdays by application to caretaker; S.P.N.E.A.

Designed by Asher Benjamin, which gives it special interest.

CONNECTICUT VALLEY HISTORICAL MUSEUM *or* WILLIAM PYNCHON MEMORIAL BUIDING

(*a reproduction of a Colonial mansion*)

Tuesday through Saturday 1 to 5, Sundays 2 to 5; City Library Association.

In the museum there are two interesting early rooms taken from the Chapin Tavern, which stood in Chicopee, Massachusetts, and some reproduction rooms furnished with excellent antiques.

¶ *West Hatfield (on Route 5, 4 miles north of Northampton)*

SOPHIA SMITH HOMESTEAD (*1796*)

By application to college.

This home of the founder of Smith College has been very well restored and becomingly furnished by the alumnae.

¶ *West Springfield (across river from Springfield)*

STORROWTON VILLAGE

Daily 9 to 5, May 1 to November 1; 75 cents; Rampagne Historical Society.

An assembled and re-created village consisting of early New England houses and miscellaneous buildings. Many of the installations are actively in use for the convenience and entertainment of visitors, including the tavern. Among the buildings brought here from various New England sites are the ATKINSON TAVERN (1789), the CHESTERFIELD BLACKSMITH SHOP (1850), the EDDY LAW OFFICE (1806), the GILBERT HOMESTEAD (1794), the LITTLE RED SCHOOLHOUSE (1810), the PHILLIPS HOUSE (1767), the POTTER HOUSE (1777), the SALISBURY MEETING HOUSE (1834), and the TOWN HOUSE (1822).

JOSIAH DAY HOUSE (*1754*)

Town green, corner of Hanover and Park Streets; Tuesdays, Thursdays, and Saturday 9 to 6, May 1 to November 1.

This is one of the extremely rare early salt boxes to be made of brick. It is very stylish with its broad chimney, and has never been lived in by any but the original Days and their descendants.

THE WESTERN HILLS

Great Barrington; Richmond; Sheffield; South Egremont;

Stockbridge; South Lee

¶ *Great Barrington (near junction of Routes 7 and 23)*

WILLIAM CULLEN BRYANT HOUSE (*1739*)

Berkshire Inn.

Now part of the inn. Bryant was married here when he was serving as town clerk in 1815. The handsomely paneled wedding room has been carefully preserved.

¶ *Richmond (on Route 41 halfway between Lenox and Pittsfield)*

SHAKER FARM

(*early nineteenth century*)

5 miles from Tanglewood; by written or phone appointment; August; Dr. and Mrs. Edward D. Andrews.

This is a rare opportunity to see some of the finest Shaker interiors in the country, in the house occupied by the two outstand-

The kitchen of the Shaker Farm at Richmond is filled with the kind of household wares and furnishings for which the sect was famous.

ing Shaker authorities. The utilitarian perfection which makes Shaker craftsmanship a uniquely American contribution to the art of cabinetry can be seen here in its purest form. To see the house and all that it contains is one of the rarest privileges offered to readers of this *Guide*.

¶ *Sheffield (on Route 7 in southwest corner of state near Connecticut line)*

COLONEL ASHLEY HOUSE (*c. 1735*)

Southern end of town off Cooper Road; open on request to interested visitors during 6 summer months; Mr. and Mrs. E. A. Brewer.

This is probably the oldest house in this part of the state, and a choice one beautifully restored and furnished by connoisseurs of the period. The high spot is the upstairs study, with impressive paneling and shell cupboard, and a raised hearth with fine original molding. Here Sheffield's

declaration of independence is supposed to have been written. The living hall in the southwest corner was willed by Col. John Ashley to his housekeeper for "her use and improvement during her natural life," having its own outside door.

¶ *South Egremont (on Route 23 in southwest corner of state near the New York line)*

EGREMONT TAVERN (*1730s*), MOUNT EVERETT INN (*1780*) and the OLD GRIST MILL (*1790*) (*still being operated as inns*)

All three together in center of town; daily; James Adie.

It was at the tavern here that Sir William Johnson stopped on his trips from New York to Connecticut on the King's business. Plans for Shays' Rebellion were laid here. Also used for barracks in the Civil War.

¶ *Stockbridge (on Route 7 between Great Barrington and Lenox)*

MISSION HOUSE (*1739*)

Main Street; weekdays 10 to 12:30 and 2 to 6 April 1 to November 1, Sundays 2:30 to 6 during summer months, during winter admittance by ringing bell of Cobbler's Shop; 35 cents; Trustees of Public Reservations.

The outstanding architectural feature of this fine old house is the often-photographed double-pediment doorway, beautifully carved and paneled. The house was built by John Sargeant, first missionary to the Housatonic Indians, and some of his furniture is still here, along with the Indian exhibits.

¶ *South Lee (just east of Stockbridge)*

MERRELL TAVERN (*1760*)

Main Street; Saturday and Sunday afternoons, July 14 to September 2; contribution.

When the ballroom was added to this atmospheric old brick inn, it was superimposed as a third story in frame, giving the building considerable distinction.

The stove, the cabinet, the chairs, are rare examples of Shaker craftsmanship in this rare example of a lived-in Shaker house.

CAPE COD & THE ISLANDS

Barnstable; Chatham; Edgartown; Falmouth; Nantucket;

Sandwich; North Falmouth; Woods Hole; Yarmouthport

¶ *Barnstable (on Route 6A, 15 miles past Cape Cod Canal)*

CROCKER TAVERN (*c. 1754*)

Main Street; Mondays, Thursdays, and Saturdays 10 to 5, June 1 to October 13; 25 cents; S.P.N.E.A.

This old inn is being carefully preserved as an example of the simplicity and honesty of our early building manners.

¶ *Chatham (on southeastern tip of Cape)*

OLD ATWOOD HOUSE (*1752*)

Stage Harbor Road, off Route 28; Wednesdays and Fridays 2 to 5 July and August, and by appointment; contribution; Chatham Historical Society.

Capt. Joseph Atwood, noted navigator, built it the year he stayed home because the pirates were so bad. The building tim-

The Thomas Cooke house points up the early attractiveness of charming Edgartown on Martha's Vineyard.

bers were cut and rough-hewn right here. It is the oldest and by far the loveliest house in town, now a veritable Cape Cod museum.

¶ *Edgartown (Martha's Vineyard)*

This is a charming old whaling village, now a most attractive resort in summer, with many a fine early house along its old streets. Over at Oak Bluffs is a picturesque cluster of tiny ornate Victorian cottages surrounding an old camp-meeting site.

THOMAS COOKE HOUSE (*special exhibits in summer*) (*1765*)

Cooke and School Streets; weekdays 10 to 12 and 2 to 4:30 and Sundays 2 to 4:30 June to October, winter hours on request; Dukes County Historical Society.

This trim, silvery-shingled salt-water house was built by ships' carpenters. Unaltered, its original fireplaces and paneling are still intact. Reflecting the life of the once great whaling port, the house contains furniture, china, and portraits by Vineyard primitives, ship models and gear, Indian relics, and special exhibits in summer.

¶ *Falmouth (in southwestern corner of Cape)*

WICKS HOUSE (*1790*)

Opposite green on Palmer Avenue; Tuesday, Wednesday, Thursday, and Friday afternoons 2 to 5, Saturday mornings 10 to 12; Falmouth Historical Society.

Recently restored, this old house has French eighteenth-century wallpaper, fine portraits, furniture of the period from Falmouth homes, and a fine whaling collection. The captain's walk, the two-story porch, and the restoration of the garden are special attractions.

JOHN JENKINS HOMESTEAD (*1820*)

20 Hewins Street on Green; on written request to Mr. and Mrs. Edward Richardson, 120 East 31st Street, New York City; 25 cents for Falmouth Historical Society.

A stately, small-scale house with some unusual features, including its lunette windows and staircase. It is furnished well with late-eighteenth- and early-nineteenth-century pieces and a number of good paintings. As the owner suggests, it has "a thin-lipped suggestion of Southern grace in a small Cape Cod seaport," inspired, she believes, by the old-time trade with Charleston, South Carolina. Other Falmouth houses around the green here seem to bear this out.

¶ *Nantucket*

There is nothing else like it in America. Twenty miles out in the sea from Cape Cod lies the "faraway" island whose town is a clustered harmony of old gray houses. The old section still contains four hundred houses antedating the great fire of 1846, which largely burned out the dwellings of the central district, most of which were immediately replaced by new ones that looked just like the old. That is the great thing about Nantucket —even the houses built today conform, and it is hard to tell them from the old gray-shingled or clapboarded dwellings. It is this homogeneous quality that makes the island unique, and the inhabitants intend to keep it that way. The good gray cottages, of which there is a preponderance, are the oldest type on the island, while the imposing Federal and Greek Revival façades lining both sides of Main Street are the results of the great whaling prosperity which hit its peak during the first decade of the nineteenth century. To see the interiors of some of these mansions you should be here in August when the annual tour takes place and several of them are on view. Contact The Hospital Thrift Shop for information on it.

JETHRO COFFIN HOUSE (*1686*)

Sunset Hill Road; weekdays, June 15 to October 1; 50 cents; Nantucket Historical Society.

The oldest house in Nantucket, of the medieval Ipswich type, its small, infrequent diamond-paned casements are among the many marks of its long-ago era. Inside it has been little changed, and much of the crude original construction remains to tell its story. It is furnished with fitting simplicity, mostly with island pieces.

MARIA MITCHELL MEMORIAL HOUSE (*1790*)

1 Vestal Street; daily 10 to 5 except Sundays, June 15 to September 15; Maria Mitchell Association.

The island woman of this name was born here in August, 1818, and here, when she had reached the age of twenty-nine, she awoke one morning to find herself famous —a fame which was to take her name not only to the mainland, but to many other lands as well. For she was the discoverer of a new comet. Descended from the same Folger ancestor as Benjamin Franklin, her father, called "William the Teacher," was among other things astronomical observer for the Coast Survey. When she was a small girl, she helped her father make observations from the captain's walk which perched steeply atop their house. In fact, the plain gray house is almost indistinguishable from many another plain gray house along these quiet streets, and is as simple within as without.

LYDIA S. HINCHMAN HOUSE

7 Milk Street; daily except Sundays, June 15 to September 15; Nantucket Historical Society.

This was one of the fine brick mansions whose exteriors remain much as they were; but inside the walls of most of the rooms have been removed to accommodate the exhibits. They are unusually interesting, devoted for the most part to whaling in all its aspects. One room contains some good portraits of a number of the first settlers. Observe family resemblances in the faces.

1800 HOUSE (*1800*)

Mill Street; daily 10 to 5, June 15 to September 15; 50 cents; Nantucket Historical Society.

Assembled in this house that once belonged to the high sheriff of the county are the

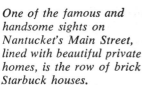

One of the famous and handsome sights on Nantucket's Main Street, lined with beautiful private homes, is the row of brick Starbuck houses.

furniture and possessions of former generations of islanders, covering a period of about seventy-five years, some of it made by local artisans. The interior has been restored with discretion.

DELL HOUSE (*c. 1800*)
Academy Hill; by written appointment, open afternoons August and September; Mr. and Mrs. Burnam Dell.

On a hilltop overlooking the sea, this captain's house, faced with narrow clapboards, is painted yellow with white trim. Its corner quoins and fine porticoed doorway are sparkling Federal details. The small captain's walk is perched as if on stilts over the roof ridge, as it is on so many of these houses, almost crowding the chimneys. They were meant for business, and not for decoration, so they aren't fancy. From this one the captain or his lady could have seen a sail for twenty miles.

BROOKS HOUSE *or* JOSIAH COFFIN HOUSE (*1723*)
60 Cliff Street; by written request well in advance, June 15 through Labor Day; Mr. and Mrs. Emerson Tuttle.

Mrs. Tuttle is the sister of Mrs. Frost of Sherburne (column 2), and her well-preserved house is one of the most unspoiled examples on the island. Tucked in behind tall hedges, its weather-frosted exterior, deceptively small in scale, hardly prepares you for the space you find within. Woodwork richly mellowed by time and attention has never been altered. In fact, the fine, heavy structural elements are everywhere in evidence. The house is furnished with simplicity and great taste.

SHERBURNE *or* ELIHU COLEMAN HOUSE (*1722*)
Hawthorne Lane, on the moors; upon request, Tuesday, Thursday, and Saturday mornings July and August; Mrs. Elizabeth Hollister Frost.

Perhaps no book could be a better introduction to the island and its people, or to Mrs. Frost's home, than her epic novel *This Side of Land*. This weathered gray-shingled house nestles into the moor, its long sweep of roof almost touching the earth on the far side. A garden of heather suits the landscape to perfection. Everything about the house has been done with thoughtful understanding of its quality and the kind of life that went on in it through the earliest years.

¶ Sandwich

OLD DANIEL WEBSTER INN (*1694*)
Open as an inn and not much altered downstairs. The food is good, and it is a pleasant

High on its hill overlooking the ocean, the Dell house is filled with true Nantucket character.

The Josiah Coffin house at the right is one of the more distinguished and venerable houses on the island.

place to stay. Daniel Webster often stayed here. It was originally the home of the Reverend Ferrenden, the greatest of all missionaries to the Indians.

HOXIE HOUSE (*1637*)
Grove and Canal Streets; apply for information to Sandwich Historical Society, Main Street.

¶ *North Falmouth*

MALONE HOUSE (*c. 1775*)
Old Main Road; on request, weekends in July, August, and April to December; Mrs. Joseph A. Malone.

A good early Cape Cod cottage, close to the ground and covered with hand-split shingles, it has a six-panel entrance door and a simplified Adam-style mantel typical of Falmouth. Nicely furnished with antiques of its period.

¶ *Woods Hole (on southwestern tip of Cape)*

TO WINDWARD (*1775*)
North Street; by appointment during summer months with owners; 75 cents for Falmouth Historical Society; Mr. and Mrs. Lawrence Saunders.

This large, handsome house, typical of its time, was built far away in East Bridgewater, thirty miles south of Boston, and a likely legend is that the day the roof was shingled the workmen felt the reverberations of the cannon at the Battle of Bunker Hill. Anyhow, it was moved here by the man responsible for Storrowtown, and has made itself very much at home.

¶ *Yarmouthport (on Route 28 past Hyannis)*

COL. JOHN THATCHER HOUSE (*1680*) *or* 1680 HOUSE
King's Highway and Thatcher Lane; daily 10 to 5, June to October 15; 25 cents; S.P.N.E.A.

This place has the atmosphere of a prosperous Cape Cod home of the early eighteenth century. In the later paneled rooms a fine collection of old silver is effectively displayed. The furnishings are charming throughout.

WINSLOW CROCKER HOUSE (*1780*)
Next to Thatcher House; by appointment; contribution; S.P.N.E.A.

A handsome house of sizable dimensions which was built two miles away at West Barnstable and moved here in 1934. Like the Thatcher House, it is appropriately furnished, and the two houses make an excellent pair to see.

Captain Moffatt had his ship room on the second floor of his stately Portsmouth mansion, where he could look down upon his wharves below the bluff in front of the house and watch his ships sail out the Piscataqua. The low building beyond the house was his office. There is an old-fashioned garden behind that goes with the house, and within the house there is great elegance of furnishing and décor, one of the most impressive interiors being the entrance hall opposite with its grand staircase all paneled and carved.

NEW HAMPSHIRE

PEOPLE have said that after the fine great Portsmouth houses, all other New Hampshire houses are an anticlimax. This canard, of course, is folderol, as town after town throughout the state will testify, and as house after house among the hills of this handsome countryside will bear witness. Still, we will say for Portsmouth that the stateliness of its outstanding old homes, along with their number and variety, leaves it few rivals among early American cities of its size. We would call it the New England counterpart of Charleston, South Carolina; and as for the rest of New Hampshire, we would say that only two other states could touch it for the number and attractiveness of its towns with unspoiled early architectural charm; those two states are Vermont and Connecticut.

As for the lover of early American homes, New Hampshire is particularly rich in two most ingratiating kinds—distinguished frame houses in the Federal style and white well-to-do frame farmhouses in the colonial tradition, both kinds dating from the early 1800s and indicating the prosperity of that period here.

A word as to the regional arrangement above. Portsmouth and vicinity seemed the obvious area in which to start our listings and descriptions. Geographically, historically, and architecturally important, it is, furthermore, practically the main entrance to the state. Since Concord is not only the capital of the state but the virtual center of a region that is rather rich in good early houses, at least of good old houses that can be visited, it is a convenient focal point for the section, even though it is not especially house-rich itself. And, of course, there is the Connecticut River Valley (right bank), a valley that is ever a rich region for the best in early domestic architecture, no matter whether the state is New Hampshire, Vermont, Massachusetts, or Connecticut.

By no means are all the good house towns listed, only those in which there are houses that can be visited, but you can be pretty sure that the best remaining possibilities will be found in the vicinity of the towns named. For example, anyone passing through Hanover, on the way to or from Orford, will want to pause for a look in the neighborhood of the Dartmouth College campus. And anyone who fails to look into little Bath Village, about eighteen miles above Haverhill, will have missed one of the most delectable early architectural treats in New Hampshire.

¶ Portsmouth

Above all, the thing that marks the houses of Portsmouth and gives them the unmistakable flavor of an English ancestry is style. They are not "great" houses, perhaps, in the sense of the mansions of Virginia or Maryland, but they are the *splendid* homes of wealthy merchants and sea captains who had pride in how they built and lived. Here balance and proportion are more important than ornament, though detail was by no means neglected either outside or within. With a history dating back over three hundred years, the town retains an eighteenth-century flavor, although you will find a range which extends from the earliest salt boxes, protected from the sea gales of winter by roofs that touch the ground, to houses of the Federal period. It was the eighteenth-century trade with the West Indies which brought the prosperity that built the houses. Mid-

The richly detailed façade of the Wentworth-Gardner house is a memorable sight down by the water.

dle Street, with its high, square, delicate white abodes is virtually unspoiled; flat hipped roofs and captain's walks, fine doorways, and beautiful fences are the rule rather than the exception.

The older stretches of Middle Street and vicinity will lead you directly into the most flavorsome period of the fine old Portsmouth houses; for while the highest architectural distinction of the town must be reserved for the best Georgian houses—the Moffatt-Ladd, the Warner, the Wentworth-Gardner, and the Governor Langdon—it is the big four-square Federal houses which play such a powerful part in the personality of the place. Ironically, none of these can, at this time, be listed for visiting, but you can enjoy to your heart's content their highly pleasing façades, which indeed constitute one of their chiefest charms.

The Warner is one of the great early brick houses of America, containing endless features of interest from top to bottom.

WARNER HOUSE (*1716*)

> *Daniels and Chapel Streets; daily 10 to 5, June 15 to September 15; 50 cents.*

This belongs to the nobility of early American brick homes. Built by Capt. Archibald Macpheadris, a Scotsman, whose daughter married Jonathan Warner, it housed their descendants until 1930, when the Warner House Association took over its care and security. It couldn't be in better hands. The astonishing staircase murals, accidentally discovered in the 1840s under many layers of wallpaper, the balustraded gambrel roof, which began as rare double gables with a valley between, and the lightning rod installed in 1762 under the personal supervision of Benjamin Franklin, are merely a few of its many arresting features. It is, of course, fitted out and furnished to perfection.

WENTWORTH-GARDNER HOUSE (*1760*)

> *Gardner and Mechanics Streets; daily 10 to 5 July 1 to September 15; 50 cents; Wentworth-Gardner and Tobias Lear Houses Association.*

Still another famous beauty. Down by the river, it has a waterside setting worthy of its white and yellow stateliness, with a wonderful doorway crowned with a broken scroll pediment, which in turn is placed against the wooden yellow-block front façade, framed in by white contrasting quoins and cornice. Within, the carved woodwork is superb, including the black-cherry staircase; brilliant scenic wallpapers and beautiful furnishings. The mansion has had many owners, among them the Metropolitan Museum, which at one time had in mind moving it to New York and putting it up in Central Park.

MOFFATT-LADD HOUSE (*1763*)

> *154 Market Street; daily 10 to 5, June 15 to September 15; 50 cents; Colonial Dames of America in New Hampshire.*

The fine great gray and white foursquare mansion from which Captain Moffatt could look down upon his ships sailing out the Piscataqua to all parts of the world makes a pretty exciting spectacle itself. Within, the paneled entrance hall and staircase bowl you over with the beauty of their design and workmanship. The Colonial Dames have made the appearance of the whole house one of their superlative performances. The terraced garden is a colonial delight, and the little counting house, all in keeping, in the side yard, is a

The carved woodwork of the north parlor in the Gov. John Langdon house called forth a pretty compliment from President Washington.

reminder of the money that must have gone, first and last, into the making of the proud Captain's establishment. One of the finest of the great New England four-squares; handsomely fenced, quoined, windowed, and balustraded.

GOV. JOHN LANGDON MANSION (*1784*)

143 Pleasant Street; daily 1 to 5, June 1 to September 15; 50 cents; S.P.N.E.A.

If you feel that "this is the handsomest house in Portsmouth," you will be glad to know that this was just what Washington said about it in 1789. It is without question one of the handsomest. Slightly more florid in effect than the three earlier homes mentioned above, it has a Chinese Chippendale balustrade crowning the roof, ornately pedimented dormers, Corinthian fluted pilasters up the corners, and a porch that is perhaps rather playful for the house. Within, the woodwork is richly and luxuriantly carved, and the furnishings are of a very high order indeed.

JOHN PAUL JONES HOUSE (*1758*)

Home of Portsmouth Historical Society, State Street; daily 10 to 5, June 15 to September 15; 50 cents; Portsmouth Historical Society.

This is the typically Portsmouth house with a fine big gambrel roof, that Capt. Gregory Purcell built when he was about to marry Governor Benning Wentworth's daughter Sarah—she who was destined to conduct here a genteel boarding house after her husband's death in 1776 and to attract

as a boarder a dashing young Captain Jones who had come to Portsmouth to get the U.S.S. *Ranger* outfitted for action, the same young man whose name the house bears today. Some of the rooms are furnished, and there are, of course, many fascinating collections of Portsmouthiana.

RICHARD JACKSON HOUSE (*1664*)

Jackson Hill Street; daily 11 to 5, June 1 to November 1; 25 cents; S.P.N.E.A.

The oldest house in Portsmouth; picturesque as only seventeenth-century houses can be, in a medieval way, with long sweeping rooflines and many details to delight the antiquarian, such as leaded glass, mammoth oversize framing, and furnishings to fit.

THOMAS BAILEY ALDRICH MEMORIAL (*1790*)

386 Court Street; daily 10 to 5, June 15 to October 15; 50 cents and 25 cents.

There is an intimate description of this house in *The Story of a Bad Boy,* whose author lived here in the Victorian period, in keeping with which the house is furnished today. However, the house itself, built by Aldrich's grandfather, is a good example of a simple white clapboard in the early Portsmouth tradition.

TOBIAS LEAR HOUSE (*before 1760*)

Hunking Street; not officially open or presently furnished; Charles M. Dale.

A Georgian dwelling with a steep hipped roof, nicely dormered, a real Portsmouth air, and considerable style. It stands near the Wentworth-Gardner House and was occupied by George Washington's secretary, Tobias Lear, who also tutored the general's two stepchildren.

GOV. BENNING WENTWORTH HOUSE (*1695 and later*)

On Little Harbor, out past the Hotel Wentworth-by-the-Sea, 2 miles south via Route 1A from the center of city; will be open daily; State Recreation Division.

This uncommonly impressive mansion of some thirty rooms, with a cellar in which a small troop of horses was kept stabled whenever there was need for cavalry protection, bids fair to be one of the more spectacular historical sights of Portsmouth when the restoration now under way is completed. It was the home of the Wentworth who became Royal Governor of the province at the time of New Hampshire's separation from Massachusetts—the same Wentworth who on the occasion of his sixtieth birthday banquet here, in the presence of many guests of high degree, called in his housekeeper, Martha Hilton, announced their intention to marry, and forthwith requested a clergyman present to perform the ceremony. Longfellow describes the house in his poem *Lady Wentworth*:

It was a pleasant mansion, an abode
Near and yet hidden from the great highroad,
Sequestered among trees, a noble pile,
Baronial and colonial in its style.

It was Benning who made it baronial, having inherited it as a much more modest house from his grandfather. In the dining room are three small ovens, which were used to heat the rum for toddies.

¶ Exeter

WELLS KERR HOUSE (*1783*)
Open on special request; house of the dean, Phillips Exeter Academy.

Built by John Phillips, founder of Phillips Exeter, as the first academy building, it served as the school for the original fifty-six students and *one* preceptor. It was moved in the early nineteenth century and then in 1917, relocated near its original site. It is a pretty, trim white house, now the dean's dwelling.

GARRISON HOUSE (*1650–1658*)
Water and Clifford Streets; by appointment; William Perry Dudley.

So fine is the woodwork in this house that one room went to the Metropolitan Museum. The oldest house in New Hampshire, the main part was built to meet Indian attacks. For this purpose, the upper story projected a foot or more over the lower and the windows were narrow. The door actually had a portcullis. The front wing was added in 1772 by Gen. Peter Gilman to provide a proper place to entertain Governor Wentworth, who was about to pay a visit. Later, while a student at Exeter, Daniel Webster boarded here with Mr. Clifford, a noted woodworker. The paneled rooms are very chaste and elegant, the furniture sparse but excellent. William Perry Dudley, the owner, has restored it with skill and devotion.

A dwelling of earlier distinction than the Georgian and Federal mansions of Portsmouth is the ancient Jackson house here.

CINCINNATI HALL, *formerly* **LADD-GILMAN HOUSE** (*1721*)
> *Governor's Lane; Thursdays 2 to 4, and by application to caretaker at any time.*

The lengthy façade, seven windows across, is not symmetrical, the windows in the later part being longer. There is some impressive paneling within, fluted pilasters, and a fluted summer beam. Purchased by the Society of Cincinnati in 1903, the house was the birthplace of Nicholas Gilman, delegate to the Constitutional Convention, and was used as the state treasury during the Revolution. It is furnished with some appropriate pieces and interesting portraits and engravings. A private meeting place of distinction, not a home.

GIDDINGS TAVERN (*1723 or 1728*)
> *Park and Summer Streets; on request; Mr. and Mrs. F. E. Kusiak.*

Built by Noah Webster for his daughter Debrah, who married Zebulon Giddings, it was in the family until 1884. Fortunately, the present owners have done little to modernize it; the old paneling is unchanged. They keep it painted and in repair, but it serves as a home for their seven children.

FULSOM TAVERN
> *1770 Spring Street.*

Washington had breakfast here.

Also worth noting are the GILMAN HOUSE (1736), at 46 Front Street, and the GILLEY HOUSE (1745), at 77 Park Street—the former used by Phillips Exeter Academy, the latter owned by the Colonial Dames.

❡ *Dover*

ANNIE E. WOODMAN INSTITUTE
> (*a museum*)
> *182 Central Avenue, owns the following group of houses at this address:* JOHN PARKER HALE HOUSE (*1813*), WOODMAN HOUSE (*1818*), *and* WILLIAM DAMM HOUSE (*1675*); *daily, 2 to 5, except Monday; Harry O. Berry (custodian).*

The Hale and the Woodman are large foursquare houses in the style of early nineteenth-century Portsmouth, and contain interesting collections of everything from china and furniture to birds and minerals. The William Damm House was built to withstand Indian attacks, of massive hewn timbers more than twenty feet long. It is one of the last of the old garrison houses.

❡ *Concord*

FRANKLIN PIERCE HOUSE
> *52 South Main Street; April 1 to December 25, by request; contribution.*

Although this later house is the last one Pierce lived in, and the one least associated with him, it is the only one which may be seen. It has furnishings of the 1850

What could be more attractively typical of New Hampshire village architecture than the foursquare Pierce homestead in Hillsboro?

period. At 18 Montgomery Street is the only house he owned here, and the one he lived in from 1842 to 1847, when he also served in the Mexican War. When he was elected President, the Pierces were living at 60 South Main Street. He boarded for two years at 52 South Main Street and died there in 1869.

¶ North of Concord

Boscawen

FORT ACRES (c. 1760)
On Daniel Webster Highway (King Street); daily, May through October; Mr. and Mrs. Omar T. Lassonde.

First came the fort and then the salt box house and barn a few rods away from it. The old house has outlasted the fort and commands a magnificent view of the Merrimack. Mrs. Lassonde is a direct descendant of the Reverend Robie Morril, who built it, which fact she discovered only by chance, after living in the house ten years. Mr. Lassonde, an artist, has converted the barn into a small art gallery. Both buildings are well preserved; on one of the beamed ceilings the date 1769 is clearly discernible.

¶ Franklin

THE PINE CUPBOARD (1790)
925 Central Street; by appointment; Mr. and Mrs. Raymond G. Clifton.

Once owned by Daniel Webster and moved to its present location in 1808. It is furnished with pine and maple antiques and collections of pewter and toleware.

DANIEL WEBSTER MEMORIAL
Off Route 127 between Franklin and Salisbury; daily May 15 to October 15; with guide 25 cents; State Parks and Historical Sites, Recreation Division; Mr. and Mrs. Orr (caretakers).

A miniscule house where Webster was born in 1782 on a hardscrabble farm, furnished sparsely with originals of the period and Webster belongings. The MANSION (1790) next door was occupied by Webster's father and family for many years; has authentic Webster relics. ABIGAIL WEBSTER HOUSE is also next door. Both private.

¶ Canterbury

SHAKER SETTLEMENT
(main dwellings 1793; white meeting-house 1792)
Off Boscawen Road. New Hampshire Historical Society.

It consisted originally of thirty buildings nestling among huge maples. Men and women lived apart. In 1949 there were still sixteen Shaker women living there; *no* men. In summer, now, they live scattered one or two in a house. The meeting-house (1792) dominates the compact group. The Community was formed in 1792 on the farm of Benjamin Whicher. He became Elder in 1794 and remained so until his death.

The parlor of the Hillsboro Pierce house in which the President lived for a while is papered in French scenics.

¶ *Bridgewater*

ELM LAWN INN, *formerly* HOYT'S TAVERN (*c. 1800*)
Newfound Lake; Robert E. Erickson.

A stagecoach stop, the original section was built by Hoyt, the first proprietor. Still used as an inn.

¶ *Wolfeboro*

CLARK HOUSE (*1778*)
South Main Street on Route 28; July and August, on varying days; headquarters of Wolfeboro Historical Society.

Fully furnished with early nineteenth-century pieces, including a display of rare pewter. Tea and punch served in old-fashioned garden without charge.

¶ *Laconia*

SHELTERFIELD
(*lunch or dinner by reservation*) (*1760*)
Off Parade Road; daily, May to November; Mr. and Mrs. William Allen Camp.

New Hampshire houses have their own distinction and character. This one, with its huge central chimney, double oak sills, wide floorboards, petticoat molding on staircase, original hardwood, and excellent paneling is in the tradition. It is furnished with some old pieces; the other furnishings are harmonious. A collection of blackberry milk glass.

¶ *Center Sandwich*

ELISHA MARSTON HOUSE (*c. 1847*)
Headquarters of Sandwich Historical Society.

The house is filled with the Society's collections of furniture, books, records, and mementos of early times. There is also a fine collection of early tools used in farming and industry on display, and the bar houses a replica of an old country store, cracker barrel and all. Elisha Marston was a shoemaker and tanner by trade who made copper-toed boots. The building is one and a half stories with barn attached, typical of Sandwich.

Other notable old houses in Sandwich are the SHERMAN HOIT HOUSE, built in 1810 by Gen. Daniel Hoit; the JERE-

Many of the early houses all through New England were specially built to serve as places of refuge in emergencies: log-built, heavily boarded, and so on. It was from such a house that Fort Acres at Boscawen got its start.

Ocean-born-Mary house does not need a colorful legend to give it real distinction, but a colorful legend it has, as you will see, along with its real distinction of design.

MIAH SMITH HOUSE, next to the above and built before 1810; the old BLANCHARD HOMESTEAD, built in 1822 by Augustus Blanchard and maintained in its original state by its owner, Miss Jessy Flanigen; the STEPHEN FELLOWS place, built in 1806 and now the summer home of Professor Cornelius Weygandt of the University of Pennsylvania, who takes such delight in the "survivals of yesterday"; and the THOMAS BURLEIGH PLACE, used as an inn in its early days (1806), recently restored and now called the VILLAGE INN.

¶ West of Concord

¶ Hopkinton (the first town below Concord)

THE TOWNE HOUSE (c. 1790)
June and October, Mondays, Wednesdays, and Fridays 10 to 4; $1.00;
Mabel K. Lomas.

An unusually imposing square white house with large fanlights in the gable ends. The hall, forty by twenty, gives an idea of its spaciousness; the hall, incidentally, is hung with its original French wallpaper. It was built by Joseph Towne, leading merchant banker, on what was then the Boston-Montreal Highway. Furnished with fine eighteenth-century American pieces.

¶ Henniker

OCEAN-BORN-MARY HOUSE (1760)
About 3 miles from town, well marked;
May to December, afternoons only; 25 cents; L. M. A. Roy.

This isolated house on a hill has a romantic history without parallel in New England. Why such a fine house with so many unusual features was built in this out-of-the-way spot is a part of the story. In 1720 a party of Scotch-Irish immigrants were on their way from Londonderry to New Hampshire when pirates boarded the ship. At this inauspicious moment, Mrs. James Wilson, recently widowed, gave birth to a girl. The pirate captain was moved to spare the ship provided the baby was named for his mother Mary. Boarding the ship again, he brought gifts to the infant, among them a fine piece of blue silk for her future wedding gown. His command was carried out. After doing service for the weddings of Mary and many of her descendants, a piece of the silk still survives, now in a frame in the house. There is some difference of opinion as to the builder of the house. But the present owner states that it was the pirate himself, who retired with his crew, which included ship's carpenters and Negro slaves, and built it so that in time Mary might live here with her sons. The pirate met with a violent death near the house, but Ocean-born Mary lived to be ninety-four years old and died in what is now called the eagle room, in 1814. The room was hers and the blue eagle with its *sixteen* stars painted over the mantel was her work, the stars representing the number of states then in the Union. The beautiful paneling in this room is unsurpassed in this section of the country. Deep cornices, large twenty-four-pane windows, wainscoting two feet wide, and six-panel doors fitted with box locks and H and L hinges; many of the doors have the Crusader cross. The front door has crane hinges. A door on the stair landing leads into the massive chimney, which was used to smoke hams. The house contains six fireplaces, two of which contain brick cooking ovens. The weather-beaten exterior, with its hip roof and two dormers, has unusually fine fenestration. Mr. Roy and his mother took the beautiful old house some years ago, after it had stood empty a long time, and rehabilitated it—for the most part with their own hands. Both of them are skilled in crafts, and they have treated it with an inspired affection and understanding. Mrs. Roy revived the old arts of spinning and baking here, and her spirit lives on in the house with that of its first occupant, Ocean-born Mary.

¶ *Hillsboro*

PIERCE HOMESTEAD (*1804*)

> *Near junction of Routes 9 and 31; daily 1 to 5, May 15 to October 15; State Recreation Division.*

Square and simple, with a fine doorway, this handsome house was the home of Franklin Pierce's father, who was twice Governor of the state. The parlor contains noteworthy French wallpaper, still in fine condition. Another room has a fine stencil by an early itinerant painter, well preserved. The grandnieces Misses Mary and Susan Pierce act as hostesses here, and are as interesting as the house.

¶ *Hancock*

HANCOCK HISTORICAL SOCIETY HOUSE (*c. 1809*)

> *Wednesdays, Saturdays, and holidays 3 to 5, May 30 to October 12; Hancock Historical Society.*

On one of the finest typically New England main streets in the state stands this simple, handsome brick building with flat hipped roof, tall end chimneys, and twenty-four-pane windows, widely spaced. Within, there are simple mantels, lovely dado paneling, and appropriately simple furnishing; also exhibits of all types of utensils, clocks, tools, and band instruments.

JOHN HANCOCK HOUSE (*an inn*) (*c. 1793*)

> *In town on Route 123 just off Route 202; Mr. and Mrs. William D. Roche.*

A drovers' inn at the turn of the nineteenth century, it is one of the prettiest places to stop in New England. Both spacious and gracious, the interior preserves the best of the old-time atmosphere, with modern conveniences added. The frescoed walls of one bedroom were painted by an itinerant at that time, and there is evidence that he may have done other rooms during his stay. Pay for these beautiful murals was often taken in board and lodging.

HISTORICAL HOUSE (*1809*)

> *Main Street; Memorial Day to October 12, Wednesday, Saturday, and holidays 2 to 5; donation; Hancock Historical Society.*

Built as a tavern by Charles Symonds on a farm that adjoined the property of Governor Hancock, this strikingly fine brick building, with its twenty-four-pane windows spaciously separated and its tall chimneys soaring above the hipped roof, is another demonstration of the pride and skill of the country craftsmen in the days when these far Northern states were almost wilderness. Tavernkeeper Symonds introduced an innovation in 1835—the first cookstove. Before that there was only the fireplace, of course. Later the building became the home of Albert Anthony, the town harness-maker. Today it is cherished by the residents of Hancock, who have donated many of the furnishings, most of which are of local interest and origin.

¶ *Sharon*

LAWS HOUSE (*c. 1800*)
New Ipswich Road (Route 123); by appointment; S.P.N.E.A.

This interesting old house is part of the Sharon Art Center.

¶ *New Ipswich*

BARRETT HOUSE (*1800*) *or*
FOREST HALL
Main Street (Route 123); daily 11 to 5 except Wednesdays and Saturdays 11 to 1, mid-June to mid-October; 25 cents; S.P.N.E.A.

An impressive three-story white clapboard mansion of the Federal period, it is surrounded by a beautiful iron fence. The grounds were landscaped in the early 1800s; ancient maples, fourteen all told, line the ascending terraces leading up to an old summer house. Within there are portraits, early wallpaper, delft tiles on eight of the fireplaces, Waterford and lusterware—a housefull of treasures. Across the front of the third floor is the "grand" ballroom, unspoiled. The musical glasses are still here.

South of Concord
Manchester

CURRIER GALLERY OF ART
129 Orange Street; daily 10 to 5 except holidays, Sundays 2 to 5.

Large collections of American furniture, silver, pewter, and textiles, of the seventeenth and eighteenth centuries; some rooms completely furnished.

STARK HOMESTEAD (*1736*)
1070 Canal Street; shown any time by occupant or member of Molly Stark Chapter, D.A.R.

Built by the father of General Stark, it remained in the family until 1821. Given to the D.A.R. by the Amoskeag Industries, it was restored as nearly as possible to its original state. A typical New England farmhouse, painted red with white trim, it has some fine paneled walls and high oak mantels, but only a few rooms are furnished in period. Three rooms are used for museum exhibits.

¶ *Derry*

PINKERTON HOUSE (*1735–1816*)
On request; Mr. and Mrs. Ralph A. Smith.

Fortunately, the fine paneling, said to have been brought from England, and the beautiful stairway, were not too badly damaged by a fire here in 1952. The house was built by Maj. John Pinkerton, one of the founders of the Pinkerton Academy, who operated a store in it. The scale of the woodwork is manorial, but why and how such a house happens to be here is not known.

¶ Up the Connecticut River Valley

¶ *Walpole*

HARMONY HILL (*1818*)
On written request, June 15 to October 15; 50 cents for Walpole Historical Society; Mrs. Robert A. Hubbard.

Built by Ephraim Holland, whose descendants still occupy it, it is in the clear-cut, appealing Colonial tradition of these parts, but with ornaments here and there on doorways and mantels which betoken the advent of the Classical Revival. Family furnishings of many generations back are here, along with old pewter and silver. In the kitchen many fascinating old household things are now on display.

¶ *Charlestown*

SAWYER HOUSE (*c. 1804*)
By appointment; Mrs. Eleanor Sawyer; antiques.

A very fine Federal house with unusual details. The furniture and furnishings couldn't be better for the house.

¶ *Claremont* (*12 miles below Hanover*)

RIVERFIELDS (*early 1800s*)
Route 12A, 20 miles south of Hanover, at D.A.R. marker; on written request, June 1 to September 15; Mr. and Mrs. Charles B. Officer (address other times: 810 2d Place, Plainfield, N.J.).

In 1825, when Lafayette visited Dartmouth College, some of the students pulled him to "Riverfields" in a wicker carriage. If he expected to see a farmhouse, he must have

This is one of a notable "row" of Federal houses set far back from the highway at Orford, of which the Capt. Samuel Morey house is another. The arched recesses that occur in some of them, as here, have given rise to the supposition that Bulfinch may have worked on them, this being a familiar device of his.

been quite astonished; for here is a façade full of hand-carved detail of a most unusual nature. The fluted pilasters, ornate Palladian window over a still more ornate entrance, and carved and dentiled cornice all go to make up one of the most charming exteriors in the state. It was built by Godfrey Cooke, whose father was said to have paid for the land with a bushel basket full of Continental money. A few pieces of his furniture have been purchased by the present owners and have been supplemented with Chippendale, Sheraton, and Hepplewhite. Two rooms have their original hand-blocked paper.

¶ *Cornish*

AUGUSTUS ST. GAUDENS MEMORIAL, formerly HUGGINS TAVERN (*1800*)
Route 12A, 2 miles north of covered bridge on Connecticut River at Windsor; daily

10 to 6, May 30 to October 15; 25 cents; Augustus St. Gaudens Board of Trustees.

The well-known sculptor lived in this large two-story brick house with its two fine chimneys and stepped gable ends, and it was remodeled for his greater convenience in the 1880s. The studio, reached through a lovely garden, was once the stable for the inn. Later a larger studio had to be built for his monument of General Sherman, which now stands at Fifth Avenue and 59th Street in New York City. The marble Ionic temple in the meadow is the tomb of the sculptor and his wife.

¶ *Orford*

CAPT. SAMUEL MOREY HOUSE (*1793-1798*)
May to October, written request; Mrs. Lyman Tiffany Dyer.

This is one of a remarkable row of seven

elegant houses of the Federal period, set well back from the road and all different— one of the rare collections of the state. The Captain Morey who built this house built a little steamboat at about the same time and ran it on the Connecticut River here some years before Fulton's more famous trip on the Hudson. The houses are all Federal in feeling. One *may* have been designed by Bulfinch.

¶ *Haverhill*

THE 1812 HOUSE (*an inn*)
(*1808 or 1809*)
Dartmouth College Highway; daily, June 15 to Labor Day; Miss Sue Ralston.

Charmingly small and personal. Miss Ralston, who is glad to show anyone around, has furnished it with assorted antiques and chosen appropriate wallpapers and wall colors. A good place to stop over, for Miss Ralston will arrange to show, or direct you to, other houses that may perhaps be visited.

THE MAINSTAY, *formerly* BLISS TAVERN
By appointment, July, August, and September; 50 cents; Mrs. Howard W. Sullivan.

This is a stately square white frame structure with identical doorway front and side and eight-paneled doors capped by fanlights and a broken pediment. Bliss was the first postmaster, commissioned by George Washington in 1790; he was probably also the innkeeper, and obviously a man of substance to be able to build such a fine house. It was later a station on the Underground Railway.

GEN. JOHN MONTGOMERY HOUSE
(*1785*)
June to October; Cecil and Grace Wilson-Lavery.

Now an antique shop, it is another charming house whose beautiful proportions and fine simple lines are typical of the abundant good architecture in this town, which represents New Hampshire unspoiled.

This little gem stands at the northerly end of the famous Orford "row."

The delicacy, fantasy, and naïveté which went into the design and execution of this mantel and chimney piece in the Ruggles house at Columbia Falls are rare qualities to encounter in such a faraway spot. This parlor is the prize room of the house, but on page 71 you will see the staircase which is equally fine. Across the page is the Hamilton house, standing in great style near South Berwick.

MAINE

*I*N THE *WPA American Guide Series,* Maine architecture is characterized as "eminently suited to its time and place" and as belonging "to its particular background and landscape." This pretty well describes the early houses in all the states, but especially so the early houses of Maine. The long cold winters of this coastal country were responsible for the evolution of the typical long, rambling farmhouse in which every outbuilding is connected to the main one, so that in bad weather one could keep under cover. Rooflines step pleasantly up and down, and woodshed openings often form a flat arch. The effect is not only trim and attractive, but gives the farmsteads a homey look of self-sufficiency much like the character of the people who live in them. The houses, like the famous Maine fishing boats, are built for practicability first of all rather than for mere attractiveness, but like the boats they manage beautifully to achieve both. This is a common characteristic throughout northern New England, but it seems to be most in evidence in Maine. Right here let it be said, however, that when Maine houses decided to be elegant, they did so with the best of them—as will be noted.

In such towns as York, Kittery, Saco, and Kennebunk you will see a number of eighteenth-century homes, and even a few dating back to the late seventeenth. But of the first French and British settlements along the coast few if any traces remain, except blockhouses or forts. Life in the territories granted by the Crown to the proprietors was unstable in the extreme. The bitter fighting, between the French and English, both sides enlisting the Indians when they could, or between red men and white, lasted a long time. It wiped out the early settlements on Monhegan Island, where Capt. John Smith made a landing in 1614; on Mt. Desert Island, where Champlain landed in 1604; and on the mainland as well, populated sparsely with adventurers and fur traders who were tough enough to brave the hard life.

With its long, deeply indented coastline strewn with islands, Maine has always been married to the sea, and whatever wealth it has accrued has come from the sea. This is why so many of the choice early houses here are to be found in the towns and villages that lie in close communication with the coast, all the way from Kittery to Canada. Some of the houses, especially near Kittery, reflect the tastes of the British aristocrats who built them in the early days, but they are the exception in Maine and not the rule. Their elegance may be found in similar modes of building in other parts of New England. But as time went on, the lords and ladies disappeared, and sea captains and merchants took their places. This later breed built houses with an eye toward comfort and durability—which is still the way many Maine houses are being built, so that sometimes you can hardly tell the new from the old.

From the latter part of June to the end of August there are ample opportunities

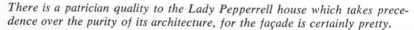

There is a patrician quality to the Lady Pepperrell house which takes precedence over the purity of its architecture, for the façade is certainly pretty.

for visiting some of Maine's more distinguished early houses which happen to be private homes. At least a dozen towns hold house-and-garden tours, but not all make yearly events of them. Some celebrate bi- and tricentennials; that's how old many Maine towns are getting to be.

To be absolutely sure when and where house-and-garden tours and open-house days are going to be held, write to the Maine Publicity Bureau, Gateway Circle, Portland, for its calendar of events for the summer, and also for a list of its information centers, which you will find to be extraordinarily helpful institutions.

The towns which follow are arranged as you would come upon them entering the state at Portsmouth, New Hampshire, and working your way "down East," with occasional forays inland as indicated.

¶ *Kittery Point*
    (*on Route 103, 4 miles from Portsmouth*)

On November 4, 1789, Washington landed here briefly from a barge while exploring Portsmouth Harbor—the farthest north he ever went.

LADY PEPPERRELL MANSION (*1760*)
    Daily 10 to 12 and 2 to 4, mid-June to mid-September; 50 cents; maintained by S.P.N.E.A.
This house, built for Lord Pepperrell's widow by British workmen brought over by her ladyship, is one of the great ones of New England. It is striking in appearance, with its Georgian façade of snow-white shiplap styled with unusual sophistication and strength of character. It is as elegant within as without, and beautifully finished. Even after the Revolution had rendered its owner's title null and void by transforming her into an American citizen, Lady Pepperrell still insisted that she be addressed with the deference she fancied to be her due. There was never any question about the nobility of the house itself.

SIR WILLIAM PEPPERRELL MANSION (*1682*)
    On request in advance; Mr. Joseph W. P. Frost.
Still occupied by a direct descendant of Sir William's, this two-and-a-half-story gambrel built of wood stands firm and unaltered, much of its interior paneled from floor to ceiling. The furniture is Queen Anne and Chippendale; the rugs, silver, and pewter are all handed down from the Pepperrells, the Brays, the Frosts, and the Goodwins. A complete eighteenth-century library contains, among other choice items, the diary of Chief Justice Samuel Sewall, who was the judge at the Salem witchcraft trials and a grandfather of Lady Pepperrell.

BRAY HOUSE (*1662*)
    By appointment in advance; Mrs. David A. Wasson and Mrs. N. C. Ayer.
Even older than Sir William's, the Bray House retains many of its medieval features, but the owners have made certain concessions to comfortable living which add greatly to its charm and interest—for there are plenty of early museum houses in which no such concessions are made. Maintained and furnished with feeling, its sunny windows open on a beautiful, boat-filled bay.

SPARHAWK HALL (*c. 1740*)
    Not open, but can be seen from the road.

CHAMPERNOWNE FARM (*1680–1880*)
    By appointment only; Miss Rosamond Thaxter.
This was the home of the Maine poet Celia Thaxter, grandmother of the present owner. It is the third of three houses built on the foundations laid by Capt. Francis Champernowne, who back in the seventeenth century planted the English elm that still stands on the lawn, a flourishing giant that people come from far to enjoy.

¶ *York Village*

Take your time here—lots to see. York celebrated its three hundredth anniversary in 1952, and though several other Maine towns have done the same, York can claim to be the oldest permanent settlement in the state.

Whoever has been enchanted by the writings of Sarah Orne Jewett will appreciate the personality that shines forth from her house, and nowhere so much as from her bedroom.

COVENTRY HALL (*c. 1790*)
By appointment, first and third Fridays of July and August; Mr. and Mrs. John Jacob Gunther (other address: Twilight Point, South Norwalk, Connecticut).

The mansion that Judge Sewall erected for himself here, and in which he entertained President Monroe, is still one of the finest in Maine. The wonderfully carved woodwork is much in the style of McIntire. It is fortunate for readers of the *Guide* that a connoisseur of Americana now owns the house and has agreed to let it be seen, even if only at limited times.

MOODY HOMESTEAD (*c. 1800*)
Moody Lane; by appointment, May 15 to early October (if owner there, may be seen also in winter); Mrs. William J. Neal.

The beauty of this house lies in its simplicity and directness. Its functional qualities mark it as the true Maine farmstead in which house, barn, and outbuildings join to form a harmonious whole. The owner is a descendant of the builder, which is part of the harmony.

ELIZABETH PERKINS HOUSE (*1686–1730*)
At Seawall's Bridge; daily, 11 to 4; 30 cents; York Society for Preservation of Historic Landmarks.

This was also a Sewall house and was the gift to the society of Miss Perkins, its recent owner. She left it furnished as she had lived in it, partly in antiques, both Victorian and earlier.

WILCOX HOUSE (*1740*)
In center of village; daily 10:30 to 5:30, Sundays 1:30 to 5:30; 50 cents; owned by Old Gaol Committee.

This had been a post office and tavern before it became first a private residence and then a museum house; its interior is now thoughtfully restored and furnished.

There are many other old houses of great interest in York: the SAYWARD MANSION, the JEREMIAH MOULTON HOUSE, the PATCH, the THOMAS CROCKETT, and WOODBRIDGE TAVERN. Mrs. Lucien Horton, an officer of The Antiquarian Society, will be glad to answer your questions about them. If you have a particular house you want to see that is not on our list, she may be able to arrange it for you. While you are there, don't miss the OLD GAOL, one of the town's most attractive possessions, with its bedroom for the gaoler, whose bed has the finest of crewelwork furnishings; JEFFERD'S TAVERN, brought here from Wells with some remarkable wall paintings intact (tea served from four to six); and the SCHOOLHOUSE, with its old school furniture (key at the Gaol).

¶ *In & out of South Berwick*

SARAH ORNE JEWETT HOUSE
(1774)
101 Portland Street; Wednesday through Saturday 12 to 5, late June to mid-September; 25 cents; S.P.N.E.A.

From the street this is a good example of a Maine town house of more than ordinary importance. Within it reflects the very special personality of a delightful and cultivated woman. The author was born here, and the fine furnishings are all hers. One of the lovely wallpapers was intended for a French colonial governor down Portsmouth way, but somehow the paper got here instead. The hall, with its charming wide arch and paneled dado, prepares you for the elegance of the little drawing room, with its delicate carved cornice and fluted corner posts. Built by Miss Jewett's grandfather, a wealthy shipowner, it was passed on to her father, a cultivated country doctor; but it is Sarah's own personality which is most clearly stamped on these rooms. Although some of the family furniture is here, much of it was of Sarah's own choosing and communicates an unmistakable fineness of feeling. The unassuming person who wrote that minor masterpiece *The Country of the Pointed Firs* and most of whose quiet life was spent here has left the imprint of a rare personality on the whole house.

HAMILTON HOUSE (*c. 1770*)
Ask at Jewett House for directions; Wednesday through Saturday 12 to 5 and Sunday 2 to 5, late June to mid-September; 50 cents; S.P.N.E.A.

This stately Georgian country seat reminiscent of Portsmouth grandeur has a beautiful riverbank setting above the Piscataqua, lovely to enjoy while relaxing on the terraced lawns. John Paul Jones was a frequent visitor. The accent inside is on color, and again feminine charm is in evidence, but of a less sensitive variety.

GEN. ICHABOD GOODWIN HOUSE
(1797)
Route 103, ½ mile from village square; on request to Miss Elizabeth Goodwin (phone: South Berwick 4362).

Across the field from the Hamilton House and in sharp contrast to it is this very attractive early country dwelling, now sheltering its fifth generation of Goodwins—namely, Miss Elizabeth, who is the hostess at the Hamilton House. Her own home is pleasantly furnished, and has a stenciled room of particular interest.

¶ *Alfred*

You can reach this nice little inland col-

The Jewett house is a simpler version of the Hamilton house just out of town and a relative of the Georgian mansions of Portsmouth not far away.

lege town from South Berwick via Route 4; then return to the coast at Kennebunk.

HOLMES HOUSE (*1802*)

Opposite village green; open upon request when owner is at home; Mrs. Elizabeth Marshall.

A remarkable house, with tall, slender two-story columns which support a roof whose balustrade is broken by square panels containing a delicate pattern of bows and arrows. Among other odd and charming features of this house is the vestibule room behind the porch columns, with its solid fan and shutters, whose roof forms a small square second balcony with colonnettes at its corners and a French window repeating the fanlight. John Holmes was one of the first two United States senators from Maine and chairman of the committee that drafted the state constitution. He employed a master builder with a mind of his own, for the house takes a lot of liberties with local traditions—with delightful results. There are many stories about the bow-and-arrow pattern of the roof balustrade, among them one that it was meant as a reply to those who said that Holmes was part Indian.

¶ *The Kennebunks*

THE BRICK STORE (*1825*)

117 Main Street.

A museum at which it is possible to obtain a map that points out the best early houses in town, dating from 1752 to 1826. None of these are open to the public except on special occasions, but they can be enjoyed from the street. Notable are the LORD MANSION, the BOURNE HOUSE, and the WEDDING CAKE HOUSE, the last a delightful fantasia of superimposed romanticism.

¶ *In & out of Portland*

The four houses below are the most entertaining in town, but three blocks of State Street from York to Congress Streets and a quick turn through High and Danforth Streets will give you, a bittersweet glimpse of what it must have been like around here in the early 1800s. Keep imagining, and note especially 116 High and Number 51, Number 106, and Number 162 State.

TATE HOUSE (*1755*)

Just off highway leading from turnpike entrance to Portland, in Stroudwater; daily 2 to 5 except Mondays, July to mid-September; 35 cents; Maine Society of Colonial Dames.

The Colonial Dames have restored this remarkable old house with sparkle, taste, and skill, with the old exterior siding left to weather as they believe it has been doing

In noting the slender colonnade that so effectively surrounds the Holmes house, do not fail to take in the bow-and-arrow panels of the roof railing.

since the day the house was built. Note especially the recessed continuous dormer that lights the attic rooms where the house slaves were quartered; and for a neat decorating idea note the black strip painted above the bolection molding of the dining room. This was the strategically located home of the King's agent, whose responsibility it was to provide masts for the British Navy from Maine forests.

WADSWORTH-LONGFELLOW HOUSE (1785–1786)

485 Congress Street; daily 9:30 to 4:30 except Sundays, June 19 to September 18; 40 cents and 30 cents.

This is very pleasant Late Georgian. Filled with Longfellow memories and much personalia, it was built by the poet's grandfather Peleg Wadsworth, who later moved to the home in Hiram.

SWEAT MANSION (1800)

Spring and High Streets; daily 10 to 4:30 and Sundays 2 to 4:30, except July and August; Portland Society of Art.

Reached through the Sweat Museum, this is one of several fine Federal houses here in Portland by Alexander Parris, an architect from Boston at a time when professional architects were still few and far between. The detailing inside is just as delicately academic as the outside, and the furnishings exactly as the last owner willed them to remain forever.

VICTORIA MANSION (1859)

Park and Danforth Streets; daily 11 to 4:30 except Mondays, June 13 to October 1; 60 cents; city of Portland.

Perhaps the most remarkable Victorian mansion in America, it is the work of Henry Austin, an outstanding eclectic architect of the period. The general stylistic scheme is Louis XV, and splendor is really laid on with a lavish hand. No expense was spared to put into play the finest of rare woods and imported marble. Anyone with a weakness for Victorian in its more monumental mood will find this rewarding.

WADSWORTH HALL (1787)

40 miles out on Route 25, 1 mile from Hiram; daily; 25 cents.

The Hiram house that Longfellow's grandfather came here from Portland to build after the Revolution. During the war he was captured by the British at Thomaston and imprisoned at Castine, but promptly escaped. The place has furnishings of both personal and historical interest.

BAXTER HOUSE (a museum) (1808)

15 miles out on Route 25, on South Street in Gorham; Wednesday and Saturday afternoons 2:30 to 5, July and August.

Now a local museum with collections of early and late military relics, Indian artifacts, and rare coins.

The Tate house has one of the most aristocratically turned-out interiors of any small house in the country. Take, for example, the dining room here.

¶ In & out of Brunswick

In addition to the houses below, Nathaniel Hawthorne roomed at 76 Federal. The CHANDLER HOUSE at 75, and the DUNLAP HOUSE at 27, are the work of Samuel Melchers III, a master builder of Brunswick, who also did the GILMAN HOUSE at Oak and Union Streets; all of these were built around 1800. Melchers also erected the ALDRICH and other interesting houses just across the river at Topsham. After seeing them, you may agree that his was an unusually attractive talent.

HARRIET BEECHER STOWE HOUSE
(an inn) (1804)
> 63 Federal Street; open all year; Mary Baxter White.

Uncle Tom's Cabin was written here, and Longfellow lived here while a student at Bowdoin. It retains much of the original interior and considerable Stowe-period charm. A very good inn as well.

GILMAN MANSION (1799)
> Union and Oak Streets; open by special permission; small fee; Mr. George Foster.

The great white Colonial Gilman House sits in its own small park with a long view down the Androscoggin River, protected by its fountainlike elms. Melchers designed the twenty-four-room mansion, with its balustraded roof and arched dormers, for a sea captain, John Dunlap, whose great-grandchildren are living in it today. The principal rooms are paneled in Brunswick white pine. The drawing rooms run the fifty-foot length of the house, and are papered with gilded wallpaper and lit by crystal chandeliers, all from France. The heirlooms and mementos are in themselves a history of Maine notables. The century-old garden should not be overlooked.

PENNELL MANSION (1837)
> Out of Brunswick between Harpswell and Merepoint on Pennellville Road midway down peninsula; by appointment in advance; Mr. and Mrs. Andrew Pennell.

Master builder James Pennell's house looks out upon the Atlantic. He was one of seven Pennells who came here, built their homes, and set up their shipyards nearby. His great map of the coast of China is unfurled on a wall with his sea chest beneath, and his spyglass is right where he left it. From the octagonal cupola there are sweeping views of the sea. The great white house has never been altered, and little has been added to the original old family furnishings. There are six or more Pennell houses here —all fascinating.

¶ The back country from Brunswick

¶ Winthrop (15 miles west of Augusta on Route 202)

METCALF HOUSE (1790)
> Occupied summers only, visitors welcome any time on request; Mrs. Guy E. Healey.

Deacon Metcalf, a cabinet and furniture maker who came to this section from Franklin, Massachusetts, in 1789, built his house of hewn native-oak timbers fastened with wooden pins, and two-inch elm planks. The interior, with its six brick fireplaces, has extensive native-pine paneling. There is a FAIRBANKS HOUSE here where Deacon Metcalf stayed when he arrived (see Dedham, Massachusetts), and there are the WILLIAMS and LONGFELLOW HOUSES nearby, both built in 1766, as well as the BISHOP TAVERN (1790). All are sturdy and simple dwellings, well worth a look. Mrs. Healey, a hospitable person, will help you to identify them, and you can probably get in to see the others if you ask.

¶ Hallowell (just south of Augusta)

PRECEPTOR MOODY HOUSE
(eighteenth century)
> Recently remodeled but not now occupied; Mr. and Mrs. Gilbert W. Maxwell, 14 Middle Street, will show it as long as it belongs to them.

THE BIRD CAGE
(nineteenth century)
> 159 2d Street; by appointment at owners' convenience; Mr. and Mrs. Charles Gatchell.

Known to local people as the "Bird Cage" partly because of its small size and partly because of its extraordinary iron balconies. Architecturally speaking, it is unique for the downstairs is made up of two twelve-sided rooms. The façade of this amazing villa, whose inspiration is Italian, has two windows and a door whose immense openings cover virtually the entire front wall. Tall chimneys, rising at the one-story level of these two rooms, bracket a pediment supported by Ionic columns. The proportions are odd but pleasing.

VAUGHAN HOMESTEAD (*1794*)
June to October, by written appointment with Mrs. Langdon Marvin; the Vaughan family.

Benjamin Vaughan came to the new country a man of parts, for he had been secretary to the English Prime Minister and a member of Parliament. Naturally he came to know all the important Americans of his time, and letters from Jefferson, Adams, Bowditch, Rush, and many others are part of the family possessions here. For his spacious home he could not have chosen a lovelier location: on a curve of the Kennebec River, with a section of virgin pine and spruce still covering the steep banks of a nearby ravine whose waterfalls cascade down to a swift stream. The house itself is in the foursquare Maine tradition, with hip roof, tall chimneys, and considerable elegance of country-seat quality. Ample to begin with, it has been augmented in the spirit of the original by the family who have always lived in it and still do. The original furniture, brought from England by Benjamin Vaughan, is for the most part still here.

¶ Augusta

BLAINE HOUSE (*1830s*)
Daily, 2 to 4, except Saturdays and Sundays; state of Maine.

The Blaine House, on the capitol grounds, built in the Classical Revival vein, is pleasantly impressive rather than picturesque or stylistic. It is now the residence of Maine governors. There are things to see inside if you have the time. It was once the home of James G. Blaine.

STATE HOUSE (*1829*)
Any time.

This place still has most of its Bulfinch exterior.

FORT WESTERN (*1754*)
Daily, May to October; 25 cents.

A very interesting example of the fortified communities in which Maine settlers sought refuge in wilderness days. As close as anything you will see to early provincial architecture here.

¶ Back to the coast and continuing down east

¶ *Pittston* (*10 miles from Fort Western toward Wiscasset*)

MAJ. REUBEN COLBURN HOUSE (*1765*)
Less than 1 mile from village; open by appointment in advance (phone: Gardiner 248); Mr. and Mrs. Paul S. Plumer, Sr.

Like the old houses in the little roadside town nearby, the Major Colburn House is a plain white frame country house with green shutters. It has twelve rooms, and was built by the four Colburn brothers, who came here with their four sisters from Dunstable, Massachusetts, in 1761. The Colburns built the two hundred and twenty boats that carried Col. Benedict Arnold's little army of eleven hundred soldiers on the Quebec expedition. Arnold and his officers lodged here; their men lived in crude shelters on the grounds.

¶ *Wiscasset*

Note the LEE-PAYSON-SMITH HOUSE on High Street opposite the library, and the ABIEL WOOD HOUSE on the corner of High and Lee Streets—both lovely. For that matter, there is a lot more that is lovely along the unspoiled streets of this notable old town.

TUCKER CASTLE (*1807*)
East End of High Street; by advance appointment; Miss Jane Tucker.

A sea captain's copy of a castle in Dunbar, Scotland, it is an unusual and fascinating house, full of the character of the family that lived in it for more than a hundred and fifty years. Miss Jane Tucker will show the house when she is able. She evokes the memories of this house so vividly that everything in it comes to life again.

NICKELS-SORTWELL HOUSE
(*1807–1808*)
*Main and Fort Streets; by written or
phoned appointment; $1.00; Miss Frances
A. Sortwell.*

A tall and most attractive town house with
a fine entrance portico, Corinthian pilasters,
and a central Palladian window. You enter
through one of the loveliest doorways in
Maine. The interior is correspondingly interesting and fine in detail, furnished with
many old family pieces.

¶ *Thomaston*

MONTPELIER (*reconstruction of Henry Knox House of 1795*)
*Route 1 1 mile north of town; daily 10 to
6, May 30 to October 31; 50 cents.*

This gleaming mansion which dominates
the landscape celebrates the hero of the
Battle of Bunker Hill and the Secretary of

*Still pretty fine in spite of the traffic, Wis-
casset has been one of the wonder towns of
Maine, and the Nickels-Sortwell house is a
prize possession.*

War in Washington's first Cabinet. The
façade is elaborate, the central section
elliptical and ornamented by four engaged
columns. The low roof is surrounded by a
balustrade. Its eighteen rooms are furnished
with antiques, many of them saved when
the original house burned down.

¶ *Belfast*

FIELD HOUSE (*1807*)
*139 High Street; on written or phone
request; Mrs. John R. Dunton.*

An imposing square hip-roofed house,
typically Maine, with the barn snugged in
close. It overlooks the whole city and the
Penobscot, and what a sight that is! Built
by the present owner's grandfather for his
bride, it has been occupied continuously
and lovingly by members of the family.
Well kept up and full of gracious family
atmosphere. Fine cornice carving both inside and out.

¶ *Castine*

As you approach Castine on either 166
or 166A, there are many fine Maine
houses to be seen, and plenty of them in
Castine itself, hanging over its harbor.
On Perkins Street the BARTLETT HOUSE
is known for its interesting fireplaces and
staircase. Opposite is the WHEELER
HOUSE (1810), of brick covered with
clapboard. FORT MADISON, on the same
street, was built before the War of 1812.
The ABBOT, DYER, WHITNEY, and
PARSON-MASON HOUSES all date from
1765 to 1805. Most of these are shown
in the annual tour, which usually takes
place the last week in July and includes
twelve houses. It is sponsored by the
Castine Women's Club.

JOHNSTON HOUSE (*1805*)
*Main Street; by appointment; reasonable
fee; Col. and Mrs. E. C. Gillette, Jr.*

The Johnston House has a lovely doorway
and a Palladian window. It is a sophisticated town house, with fine Adam detailing
inside and a flying staircase. Good furniture.

The flying divided staircase of the Ruggles house shares the honors there with the mantelpiece in the parlor shown on page 60.

¶ *Ellsworth*

COLONEL BLACK MANSION (*1802*)

Main Street on Route 1; daily 10 to 5, July to November; small charge for guide service; Hancock County.

This handsome house was designed by Asher Benjamin for the Blacks, who filled their big home with the fascinating things that go with affluence and fashionable taste; fortunately it is all still here. Little was added after the 1860s. It is a great period piece, a little on the cluttered side within, which we happen to like once in a while—especially when the house is an Asher Benjamin.

¶ *Columbia Falls*

RUGGLES HOUSE (*1818*)

Daily; contribution; Ruggles House Society; Mary Ruggles Chandler (custodian).

You are really "down East" now and will be delighted to find this exquisite and unexpected piece of country Adam, with a divided flying staircase, a drawing-room chimney piece of superb cabinetry, and remarkable carving. This is one worth com-

ing many miles to see, which is what you'll have to do. Its custodian, Mary Ruggles Chandler, is the granddaughter of the builder. A house close to our hearts.

¶ *Machias*

BURNHAM TAVERN (*1770*)

Saturday afternoons June to October, or inquire.

This old tavern, with its continuous dormer on the order of the Tate House, is full of relics. The first owner placed slips of paper beneath each of the four cornerstones reading "Hospitality," "Cheer," "Hope" and "Courage." They are still here.

¶ *Dennysville*

LINCOLN HOME

(guest house) (*c. 1787*)
Mrs. Lois M. Styles.

This is a sturdy, eye-catching country homestead on a green slope overlooking the Dennys River docks and sailing vessels, and the bay. It is now a guest house, and there couldn't be a better place to break your trip. Breakfast is served. It passed from the Lincoln family only recently. General Lincoln, who was Secretary of War and Lieutenant Governor of Massachusetts, came here with Gen. Henry Knox right after the Revolution on a scouting trip through the wilderness. Later on Audubon spent some time here while Tom Lincoln, who accompanied the famous naturalist on his Labrador expedition in 1833, fitted out the schooner in which the trip was made.

The Field house in Belfast is a picture of prim Maine proportions—simple, foursquare, and forthright.

Vermont is by no means a state of white clapboard cottages alone, as evocative as they are. The early houses here have great variety and a lot of individualism, the Langdon-Cole house in Castleton being an outstanding example of the latter, with its two-story bays and the attenuated columns of its entrance porch, the work of one of the rare early local architects. On the opposite page is the Dutton house at Shelburne Village, more typical of the early farmhouses, yet full of its own very personal character.

VERMONT

*S*ETTLERS were getting established in the rigorous Vermont wilderness at about the same time that pioneers were striking out into the Middle West. The earliest frame dwelling still standing in the state, said to be the Parson Dewey House in Bennington, was built well after 1750, when the earliest houses you can see today in Salem, Ipswich, and elsewhere were already a hundred years old.

Vermont has always been famous for frugality, so it may come as a surprise to find here so many stylish and handsome houses. It is surprising too that the granite and marble so plentiful here rarely found their way above the foundations and doorsteps. Wood and, later, brick were far and away the favorite materials, as they were elsewhere throughout New England. And Vermont styles are pretty much an extension of New England styles that prevailed from 1750 on. Still, as in every other state, you feel a special regional quality which you soon begin to recognize.

Every year the Federated Garden Clubs of Vermont hold a State Garden Tour in early August (exact dates can

73

be obtained from Walter R. Hard, JR., Vermont Development Commission, or from Miss Shoemaker, Greater Vermont Association—both in Montpelier). These tours cover the towns of Bennington, Newfane, Manchester, Brownsville, Rutland, Middlebury, Barre, and Burlington, and while they are more concerned with gardens, they "try to have one or two old houses on display in each community as they are popular always."

The following arrangement of towns in Vermont is a regional one, and should work very well hand in hand with a good road map.

¶ Up the western border

¶ Bennington

There is nothing "open" here except the OLD FIRST CHURCH and the BENNINGTON HISTORICAL SOCIETY BUILDING down the hill on the way to Bennington, but both of these are beauties, and the village itself is very well worth a long, lingering look.

¶ Shaftsbury Center

GOVERNOR GALUSHA HOUSE
(*1804*)
> *On request; Mr. and Mrs. D. Henry Werblow.*

A white Colonial frame house with a Palladian window over the front porch, whose fine qualities have caused authorities to attribute it to Lavius Fillmore, noted architect of the Middlebury and Bennington churches. Built for a Revolutionary hero who was nine times Governor, the house has always been so well cared for that everything is still intact, even the windowpanes and hardware. The present owners say that some of the Governor's own shirts, woven from flax grown on the farm, with even their buttons made of linen thread, are still preserved by his descendants. The house is furnished mostly with antiques. The southeast "best" bedroom has wall paintings done in 1810 by an itinerant French artisan.

MUNRO-HAWKINS HOUSE (*1820*)
> *Vacant at time of publication; apply for information to Herbert H. Leonard, Marhawlen Farm.*

This is one of the gems of Vermont, and it is hoped that a local group led by Mr. Leonard will succeed in their desire to preserve it and allow it to be seen. The house was probably designed by Lavius Fillmore

The house that Joshua Munro built for himself at Shaftsbury Center when the price of wheat went sky-high during the Napoleonic Wars has been rightly called "an aristocrat among farmhouses."

Also in Shaftsbury Center is the Governor Galusha house with its remarkably sophisticated detailing; a house that is even more fascinating within.

of Bennington fame, but Joshua Munro, who built it, probably did a great deal of the work himself and with the help available in the neighborhood. Munro's story is of the rags-to-riches variety. Having been left an orphan in Bennington when he was a child, bound out to a shoemaker, he became wealthy by trading wheat when the Napoleonic Wars inflated the price. He built himself an "aristocrat among farmhouses," as Herbert Congdon has remarked. There is no doubt of it, for the restrained but elegant detail of the façade, with its Palladian window and perfect proportions, can hold its own in the society of more sophisticated mansions. As you might expect, the woodwork of the mantels, cornices, and doorways within is carefully contrived to please without ostentation. However, there is a surprise in store on the second floor, for here the broad hallway, beautifully lit by a Palladian window,

has a vaulted ceiling; and naturally the hall is flanked on either side by quite impressive bedrooms. For Mr. Munro's guests—only the best!

¶ Manchester

THE OLD TAVERN (*an antique shop*) (*1790*)

There are two rooms here well worth seeing, with finely carved woodwork in both mantels and chair rails.

¶ East Poultney

"When I entered Poultney, an aspirant to apprenticeship in her printing office, I knew no one of her citizens . . . I have never since known a community so generally moral, intelligent, industrious and friendly—never one where so much good was known and so little evil said, of neighbor by neighbor." When Horace Greeley wrote that over a hundred years ago, the harmonious atmosphere that pervades the town must already have been in evidence. The meetinghouse and the Eagle Inn, on the green, will make you stop your car even if you had not intended to, and there are many others that are worth your attention as well. The RISING SUN TAVERN, built in 1790, would have been one of these; owned by Mr. and Mrs. Richard Davis, it burned to the ground soon after they had given the *Guide* their consent to allow visitors. As you can see, compiling a book like this is not without its sad occurrences. However, look at the RANSOM-LOVE-RIDGE HOUSE next to St. John's Church, with its beautiful fanlight and lunettes, built in 1800 and unchanged throughout. Mr. and Mrs. Gilbert Loveridge are

the owners. There is another equally fine doorway at the HOWE-DEWEY HOUSE (1813) with a triplicate window above and pilasters framing both door and windows, which are repeated full length on the façade. It is owned by Miss Lottie Dewey.

On the annual tour in the middle of August these homes and several more are thrown open to the public under the auspices of The East Poultney Historical Society, whose president, Miss Agnes Haynes, may be able to help you see some of the houses if you write or phone her in advance.

EAGLE TAVERN (*c. 1785*)
Route 30A and Horace Greeley Memorial Highway; always open; 50 cents; Walter E. Johnson.
Surely one of the loveliest and least typical buildings in Vermont, its parlor window looks out across the triangular green at the meetinghouse. Now a private home whose

The columns of the old Eagle Tavern at East Poultney, now a private home, were originally cut as masts for the British navy, but never managed to fulfill that purpose, creating instead the only colonnade of its kind hereabouts in its day.

hospitality is still in the tavern tradition, it is painted yellow, with twelve slender Doric columns supporting its hip roof on two sides. The columns were originally cut as masts for the British Navy, and for some reason are rather irregularly spaced. The interior, now furnished with antiques, has many fine features, but most interesting is the great vaulted room on the second floor, which served as a Masonic meeting place as early as 1791 and later was, of course, the scene of balls and entertainments for the whole countryside. Horace Greeley boarded here for two years, and much earlier Ethan Allen was a frequent guest. The rooms must have echoed to many a Revolutionary toast when the Green Mountain Boys passed this way.

GRANT-PEVERELLY HOUSE
(*c. 1780*)
April to January, by written appointment; Mr. and Mrs. A. O. Peverelly.

Built by John Grant, who was a cousin of Ethan Allen and father of Gen. U. S. Grant, this is one of the most interesting and oldest homes in town. The living-room woodwork is curious and beautiful, with wrought-iron medallions set into the window frames. Very little altered and furnished with heirlooms, it also contains a good collection of Currier and Ives. The key to the melodeon factory next door may be obtained here. The Historical Society is restoring the factory now.

THE OLD MELODEON FACTORY
(*1808*)
Key at Grant-Peverelly House; Poultney Historical Society.

THE OLD CHEESE FACTORY
(*an antique shop*)
Mrs. Arthur Williams.

THE BLACKSMITH SHOP
(*an antique shop*)
Mrs. Florence D. Clark.

¶ Castleton

Strung out along its wide country street, Castleton presents a rare opportunity to examine the work of a remarkable architectural craftsman who made this village his career. He was Thomas R. Dake

(1785–1852), and while there is no evidence that he was ever a pupil of Asher Benjamin's, his houses here show that he was familiar with Benjamin's books, though too much of an individualist to be a mere imitator. His Castleton houses have features you don't encounter anywhere else.

The first Wednesday in every August Castleton holds its Colonial Day, sponsored by the Castleton Women's Club. You can spend the night comfortably at CASTLETON INN (the ARMSTRONG HOUSE), which is really three houses joined together, the oldest dating from 1835. However, it is not essential to be there on that particular day to see most of the homes on the tour, for Castleton people are usually pleased to show their homes to visitors who are genuinely interested. A walk through Castleton, with pauses to see some of the unusual exteriors, will hardly consume a half hour. Be sure to see the MEACHAM-AINSWORTH HOUSE, with Dake's exquisite little portico carved, as is the frieze above it, in delicate, garlandlike traceries. The MALLORY JONES HOUSE has Dake's fine exterior detail—a paneled frieze with dentiled cornice. The RANSOM HOUSE is ambitiously Greek Revival (possibly not by Dake). Do not fail to see the staircase and paneling in the OLD DAKE HOMESTEAD; the fluted carving of the stringer is a delight. Another stairway which demonstrates Dake's great ability is that in the GRANGER-RANSOM HOUSE. The MALLORY-JONES HOUSE has a beautifully proportioned triple arch in the hallway, although the scale of the house is modest —as are, in fact, all the Dake houses (even the Langdon-Cole, in which he outdid himself.)

ST. JOHN-COLE HOUSE (*1806*)
On request.

Family heirlooms, Chippendale, and Hepplewhite.

LANGDON-COLE HOUSE (1823)
Summer and fall; owner's convenience; Mr. and Mrs. French Campbell.

This is Dake's masterpiece. No other house in the state has this scheme of two-story bays flanking recessed porticoes. Built for a popular gentleman named "B. F." Langdon, it was designed to suit his personality, it is claimed. From the free-wheeling style of the house, both odd and harmonious, we may gather that "B. F." went all the way with the gifted and original builder. The house is fittingly furnished with antiques.

HENSE HOUSE (early 1800s)
On request.

This place has hand-hewn beams and floors made of boards which are tapered like the trunks of the trees they were made from.

DEACON MERRILL'S COBBLER SHOP (c. 1785)
On request; Historical Society.

Being restored by the Historical Society, this is the oldest brick house in the state.

THE MAPLES (1811)
On request; Mr. and Mrs. Harold Brown.

Higley pewter and six ample fireplaces.

WOOLDRIDGE HOUSE (1850)
On request; Mr. and Mrs. Reginald Wooldridge.

Built for the owner's grandfather and left unchanged in memory of his good taste, this house has a Victorian parlor.

¶ Brandon

STEPHEN A. DOUGLAS BIRTHPLACE (before 1813)
4 Grove Street facing Conant Square; by appointment; Lake Dunmore Chapter, D.A.R.

In the room where the "Little Giant of Illinois" was born are his cradle and a table he made, for he was a cabinetmaker by trade before he became a debater. The simplicity of the house is its primary distinction.

¶ Middlebury

The Congregational church in this lovely old college town is one of the prettiest in New England. There are several houses of real distinction, and many of great charm. On the first Wednesday in August about ten of them are opened for the tour day; for further information write to Mrs. Chester M. Way, 1 Court Street.

MIDDLEBURY INN, THE ANNEX (1801)
Remainder modern.

SHELDON MUSEUM (1829)
May 31 to September 15 Monday through Saturday 10 to 5, September 16 to May 30 Tuesday through Friday 1 to 5; 50 cents and 25 cents; Board of Trustees.

In this three-story brick mansion each one of the dozen or more rooms represents a different phase of the early life of the community here and, in fact, of all Vermont. There is the comfortable, family-size kitchen with its huge fireplace; the schoolroom of 1810, complete with rum bottle; the country store, properly stocked; and the Victorian parlor, properly horsehaired. And in a building nearby there is a fine collection of early Vermont tools and vehicles.

COURT SQUARE (1802)
1 Court Street; first week in August; $1.00 for Veterans' Hospital; Mr. and Mrs. Chester M. Way.

Mrs. Way's own home is also permanently a part of the tour. This splendid Federal mansion with its double crown of balustrades on the hipped roof, looks as though it might have been brought here from Portsmouth, New Hampshire. If you are here when the house is open, there is much within to make a visit well worthwhile.

BATTELL HOUSE or COMMUNITY HOUSE (1814)
Main Street next to post office; daily September 25 to June 25 except Mondays; Middlebury.

This rates as one of Vermont's best "big" houses. Of yellow-painted brick, it is beautifully fenced along its sidewalk wall, and above a balustrade connects the two great gable ends. At the main entrance is a hood, oddly graceful, with its elaborate carved brackets resting on curved pilasters. The main entrance hall has a charming spiral staircase, overarched at its base. There are twelve mantels in the house, all well designed. The house is furnished with some antiques and some reproductions.

THE PRESIDENT'S HOUSE (*1840*)
3 South Street; any time on request by appointment; Mrs. Samuel S. Stratton.

This spacious residence has been very becomingly enlarged from what was originally a farmhouse. Now the home of Middlebury College presidents, it is furnished with some fine antiques and interesting pictures.

¶ *West Addison*

GEN. JOHN STRONG MANSION (*1796*)
Inquire at Vermont end of Lake Champlain Bridge; July and August, 10 to 5; 30 cents; Miss Erminie Pollard in charge; Vermont D.A.R.

Strong brought his family here in 1768 from Salisbury, Connecticut, traveling in winter because it was easier to make the trip by sleigh. Their first house was burned down in the border fighting, and Strong, who was away from home, lost track of his family. Finally one night at an inn one of his children heard his voice; his wife had taken a job in the kitchen there. Reunited, they returned to their land, and in the course of time were able to build this little mansion—an aristocrat among Vermont homes. The brick is laid in Flemish bond, and its Georgian elegance must have been something of an anomaly in its wilderness surroundings. Its perfect little portico, with delicate fluted colonnettes, is surmounted by a Palladian window, and that in turn by a fanlight in the low gable, giving it quite an air of sophistication. The lives of this courageous pioneer family, strong and simple, are reflected in the interior, with whose plainness the exterior seems to be delightfully at variance. The house was a station on the Underground Railway in slavery days, when the design of the brickwork provided a handy identification for the

A glimpse into the colorful old kitchen of the Langdon-Cole house at Castleton.

refugees. The false ceilings in the closets were installed as places of concealment, with secret access from the attic. The house, well cared for by the D.A.R., is furnished with Vermont antiques.

¶ *North Ferrisburg*

ROKEBY (*before 1792*)
> One mile north of Ferrisburg Center; daily, May to October; 25 cents; Mrs. Rowland T. Robinson.

Set high on a hill, this typical Vermont farmhouse was the home of Rowland Evans Robinson, famous and most loved Vermont author of nature and dialect stories. It was also a station on the Underground Railway. It has antique furniture and many of the author's possessions.

¶ *Vergennes*

GEN. SAMUEL STRONG HOUSE
(*an antique shop*) (*1793*)
> Southwest of Vergennes on Route 17, 1½ miles northeast of Lake Champlain Bridge; Mr. and Mrs. Samuel Wagstaff.

This house would be notable anywhere for its fine proportions and its masterly use of ornament on the façade. The handsome, unprotected doorway has successfully withstood the weather all this time, and its dignified and nicely executed entablature is repeated in small scale over the lower windows. The roof pitch is beautifully broken by a broad pediment with an oval window. The leaded glass in this window and in the fanlight over the doorway is particularly graceful in design, the latter centering on a gilt eagle.

¶ *Shelburne*

VERMONT VILLAGE
> 6 miles south of Burlington on Route 7; daily 9 to 3, May 15 to October 15; $1.75 and 50 cents (also group rates); Mr. and Mrs. J. Watson Webb (owner), Mr. Sterling D. Emerson (director).

A remarkable gathering of old buildings and one of the best collections of American folk art and early furniture and implements in the whole country. The project reflects the enterprise and taste of the owner, Mrs. J. Watson Webb, a collector of rare ability and discrimination, whose life has been devoted to bringing these things together. The Village and its collec-

The interiors of the Dutton house at Shelburne Village, whose exterior was shown on page 73, are masterly restorations, along with all the fascinating preservations of this museum village.

tions, which include the great old lake side-wheeler *Ticonderoga,* are constantly increasing. The VERMONT HOUSE, of gray stone, an austere building outside, has an extremely elegant interior both as to furnishing and woodwork, while the DUTTON HOUSE, an early red salt box from Cavendish, home of Gov. Redfield Proctor's mother, has a typical country-farmhouse interior of the early period, furnished to perfection. The STAGE COACH INN, a spacious building which dates from the wilderness period when Vermont was a republic, contains a ballroom extending across the whole east side. It houses what is probably one of the finest collections of folk art in the country. The QUILT ROOM contains over one hundred quilts and woven coverlets. The HAT SHOP contains half a hundred hat boxes covered with early decorative papers. The collections, including the early tools and the country-store items, constitute a complete education in each field. The STORE, by the way, with its cracker barrel and jiggle chair, dispensed men's corsets, shoes with copper toes, painkillers, and blood purifiers. Every detail is carried out by Mrs. Webb and her advisers with a human as well as a scholarly approach. Few restored villages in the country can compare with this one when it comes to making history colorful, entertaining, and human.

¶ *Burlington*

GRASSEMOUNT (*1804*)
> Public rooms may be seen on request to University of Vermont.

Regarded as the best example of Georgian in the state, this is now being used as a dormitory by the University of Vermont.

¶ *St. Albans*

HOUGHTON HOUSE (*1800*)
> 86 South Main Street; any time; Theodore S. Houghton.

The exterior of this frame house, in spite of its fine doorway beneath a Palladian window, hardly prepares you for the beauty of the woodwork and wall painting within, most of which was done in 1828 by the first Houghtons to occupy the house when they decided to remodel the interior. The

Houghton daughter's diary, which has been preserved, tells of living at the hotel while the work was being done; it also describes the wall painting of birds and flowers in one of the bedrooms which had to be papered over on account of plaster damage. The decoration on the raised center panel of the parlor mantel may be the work of the same hand. This mantel, flanked by richly carved recessed arches which in turn frame a recessed doorway, is a beauty. The south parlor is equally ornate though less formal, with rope moldings on chair rails and baseboards, and a cornice to match the one in the hall. The dainty colonnettes which support the mantel taper to the bottom in true country Adam style. The present owners of the house, direct descendants, are happy to show it to those who will appreciate its unusual features.

¶ *More or less down the center*

¶ *Brownington* (*near Orleans in the extreme north center on Route 5*)

OLD STONE HOUSE (*1836*)
> Orleans; daily, May 1 to October 31; 50 cents; Orleans County Historical Society.

It was Rev. Alexander Twilight's idea to build this four-story granite dormitory for the academy which he founded. It took six years to complete. The exterior is plain, the low fourth story being a continuous six-window dormer. Twenty-six rooms are filled with antiques, furniture, clothing, home appliances, farm implements, and a library of historical documents.

¶ *Calais* (*10 miles north of Montpelier on Route 12*)

KENT TAVERN *or* **FARMERS MUSEUM AND COUNTRY STORE** (*1835*)
> 10 miles north of Montpelier; daily by appointment, admission by card from Vermont Historical Society, Montpelier, or from Mrs. Louise R. Kent, next door; Museum of Vermont Historical Society.

Now used as a historical museum, this foursquare substantial brick-and-granite building has been preserved through the generosity of Atwater Kent, a Vermonter, who as a boy visited his grandfather Remember Kent here.

¶ *Morrisville* (*intersection of Routes 15 and 100, a little north of Stowe*)

NOYES HOUSE (*c. 1820*)

1 West High Street; daily in summer and any time by appointment; contribution; village of Morrisville, leased to Morrisville Historical Society.

This is set up as a local historical museum, one exhibit being a collection of 2,000 pitchers and Toby jugs and another a collection of clothing and household articles used by the first family of white settlers in the vicinity.

¶ *Brookfield* (*south from Barre on Route 14*)

MARVIN NEWTON HOUSE (*c. 1831*)

On request to custodian, Mrs. Ellen Bigelow; Brookfield Historical Society.

Partially furnished with belongings of its early residents, this house of primarily local interest was presented to the society by a descendant of the first owner. It has never been altered.

¶ *South Randolph* (*south of Brookfield on Route 14*)

THE ANTIQUE SHOP (*1781*)

Built by Experience Davis, this old house is said to contain one of the best collections of historic china in New England.

¶ *South Royalton* (*still farther down Route 15*)

FOX STAND (*1818*)

On written request; Mrs. Natalie Mickelson (usual address: 32 Adams Street, Oyster Bay, Long Island, New York).

Another impressive square red-brick house, with immense gabled ends, it was originally built as a hostelry, or "stand." Its doorways, both front and end, are amusingly off center. Neglected for some time, its present owner recognized its unusual distinction and is restoring it slowly. The simply paneled doors and wide fireplaces are in keeping with its impression as an inn of some substance, as is its grand ballroom on the second floor extending the whole length of the place. The owner plans to furnish it appropriately and to create an old-fashioned garden around it.

¶ *Woodstock* (*14 miles west of White River Junction on Route 4*)

This is one of the prettiest and most unspoiled towns in New England. It has become famous as both a summer and winter resort, partly because of its lovely situation on the Ottaquechee River, surrounded by mountains, and partly because so many of its old streets preserve the flavor of an early, prosperous rural village. The Woodstock Tour takes you into most of the fine old houses here. It takes place annually during the first week in August as a rule and lasts two days; The Historical Society, whose secretary is Mrs. A. W. Fowler, can furnish full information.

The only house which is regularly open to visitors (June through October) is the society's headquarters, the DANA HOUSE (1807), a pleasant village home on Elm Street furnished with antiques; various exhibits are displayed there during the summer. The WHITE CUPBOARD INN dates back to 1794, the RICHARDSON HOUSE to 1787, and the BENJAMIN SWAN HOUSE to 1801. The imposing LYMAN MOWER HOUSE (1823), built of brick with massive, broad chimney ends, is pictured in the *First Treasury,* as are the attractive JOHNSON HOUSE façade (1809), the early CONVERSE HOUSE, and the WARREN-KIDDER HOUSE (1807). The dates are all a good indication that the town is a delight to the eye, and the Woodstock Inn is excellent.

¶ *South Reading* (*south on Route 106 from Woodstock*)

EBENEZER ROBINSON HOUSE (*rear 1792, front 1824*)

Thursday through Sunday 2 to 5, June through October, by written or phone request only (Reading 4332); $1.00; Albert L. Brooks.

The new owners of the house have said, "Come for sunset"; for it is situated over one of the most exciting views of mountains and valleys in the state. The house, however, deserves daylight. The fanlight which crowns the triplicate window duplicates exactly the one over the doorway. The windowpanes are twelve over twelve below and twelve over eight above. There is a ceiling-to-floor stencil in the hallway, and another was discovered in the parlor behind the wallpaper. The present kitchen has the original maple paneling around the fireplace, including a little rum-cup cupboard paneled in the same. The early part of the house, in the back, was little more than a cabin.

¶ *Weston (west to Route 8)*

ORTON-ROSS HOUSE (*1828*)

On the green; by written request in summer; Mr. Vrest Orton.

Mr. Orton is the moving spirit of this out-of-the-way restored village. It is fitting therefore, that his fine tapestried brick house, presenting its façade to the green, should be the one that catches your eye first when you drive in here—and drive you must if you wish to visit this town. The walls are four bricks thick; the color is warm, but the arched doorway and the detail are chaste. In fact, it might easily have

One of the best off-beat early brick houses in Vermont, this is the home of Vrest Orton, who operates his early American country store nearby.

stood in any New England seaport fifty years before it was built here. The elegance of brick came late to Vermont as a rule, which makes these Weston houses all the more interesting. The Orton family, which settled in Vermont in 1763, left their descendant many fine pieces of local fabrication, late-eighteenth-century pine for the most part. Mr. Orton operates an early American country store nearby which stocks many of the items that were sold long ago. He tells us that he has upwards of fifteen hundred visitors a day here during the summer season.

FARRAR MANSUR HOUSE, MUSEUM, AND COMMUNITY HOUSE (*1797*)

Weston-on-the-Common; Tuesday to Sunday 1 to 5, June 27 to September 1; Weston Community Club.

Although this is a community house and is used as such, it is also a museum. It has retained much of its original flavor of a country tavern in an out-of-the-way village, which in early days was also the main center of communal activities and pleasures.

The Captain Farrar who built it came from a family of innkeepers in New Hampshire, but he made his public rooms so big that there was hardly room for extra bedrooms beside those needed for the family. Thus the tavern was well suited to becoming a private home, which happened in 1857 when it passed to the wealthy Mansur family whose mills and shops still stand behind it. They must have enjoyed the huge fireplace in the old barroom, whose heavy beams are smoked from countless fires and the rich fumes emanating from many a spitted roast turning there while it browned. The so-called "council chamber" was probably the best parlor, and well suited for that function by its odd and yet dignified mantel and the sliding inside shutters that afforded warmth and protection on cold winter nights. On the second floor, running across the whole front, is the ballroom, which was and still is the place for big gatherings, either festive or solemn. Most of the furniture here today was donated by people of the town, and so has a distinctively local quality, pleasantly informal, as

As typical an early Vermont village inn as there is to be found in the state is this large and famous one at Newfane.

you would expect. Some good primitive paintings on the walls.

¶ *Newfane (south from Weston via Routes 8 and 30)*

NEWFANE INN (*1787*)

> *On the green; open June 10 to October 25; Mrs. Gus Pucillo (proprietor).*

A large, rambling white building with long porches situated on an historic green, and facing other buildings of antiquity, such as the renowned OLD WINDHAM COURT HOUSE. The inn preserves much of its atmosphere, with no sacrifice of the comfort of the guests. Antiques are featured throughout. The food is said to be the best.

¶ *Up the Connecticut River Valley*

¶ *Vernon (a few miles south of Brattleboro on Route 30)*

JONATHAN HUNT HOUSE *or* **MANOR HOUSE** (*1770–1779*)

> *Power Plant Road; by appointment with owner by letter or phone (Alpine 4–2808); $1.00 for Vernon Children's Special Service Center of Brattleboro; Miss Florence Stol.*

You will see how it came by its second name when you go inside, for, while this oversize farmhouse with its big central chimney may seem a little austere, many people consider the interior, with its four paneled rooms, the very finest in Vermont. The elegance of the workmanship at the chimney end of the drawing room is as astonishing as the pine used for its creation; hewn from the giant first growth that Hunt found here, it is completely clear, without a knot. It is used in the wainscoting on three sides of these rooms as well. The rest of the house is unadorned like the exterior. Hunt started building his home on his land grant of ten thousand acres while he was still fighting in the French and Indian Wars. It was finished in time for him to bring his Boston bride here, and since it constituted a midway stop between Boston and Albany, it soon became a social and cultural center. After Vermont entered the Union, Hunt became the first Lieutenant Governor. His daughter founded one of the earliest hospitals for the treatment of mental illness, and his grandson was William Morris Hunt, the well-known nineteenth-century painter. The house has had its vicissitudes. It was famous as a station on the Underground Railway, and it is now being beautifully restored by an owner who appreciates it fully.

¶ *Brattleboro*

CARUSO HOME (*1768*)

> *140 Western Avenue, West Brattleboro; by written or phone appointment; 50 cents and 35 cents for local music center; Mr. and Mrs. Joseph Caruso.*

A typical Vermont house, the oldest in the township. The central chimney is intact, with a smoke chimney on the reverse side. All the floors are of unusual hardwoods, hand-planed. The house is pleasantly furnished in Early American, with some Victorian.

¶ *Putney*

DUMMERSTON (*mid-1700s*)

> *By appointment; Mr. and Mrs. John Locke, R.F.D. 2.*

An unusual example of a weathered Vermont farmhouse with "broken" clearstory gable. Built by Samuel Loughton, Jr., it was sold way back in 1790 to ancestors of the present owner. There is some interesting paneling, and the house, now remodeled for comfortable living, is suitably furnished for its display.

¶ *Weathersfield Center*

REVEREND DAN FOSTER HOUSE
> *(summer home of minister)*
> *(rear 1785, front 1825)*
> *On Meeting House Green; open summer months most of the time; voluntary contribution; First Congregational Church of Weathersfield (owners), headquarters of Weathersfield Historical Society, Box 275, R.F.D. 2, Springfield.*

A plain, typical Vermont farmhouse, it is furnished with examples of Weathersfield furniture, crafts, and pictures. There are many interesting old implements in the workshop and the kitchen. It was the home of the first minister, and later Cook's Tavern.

¶ *Windsor*

OLD CONSTITUTION HOUSE
(*c. 1768*)
> *15 North Street; daily, April 15 to December 1.*

A long, narrow frame building with a steeply pitched roof, built as a tavern, it is one of the earliest in Vermont. The Vermont constitution was drawn up and signed here in 1777, and the first session of the legislature took place here as well. It is furnished with antiques, and has many interesting documents and portraits.

¶ *Hartland*

SUMNER-STEELE HOME or HATCH'S ANTIQUE SHOP (*1804*)

This is an extraordinarily fine Adamesque house with an Asher Benjamin look. The white balustrade which surrounds the lawn is a fitting ornament to a most ornamental country residence. The interior may be viewed only at the owner's convenience. Antiques are in the barn.

¶ *Norwich*

HATCH-PEISCH HOUSE (*1771*)
> *By written appointment, June, July, and August; Mr. and Mrs. Archibald M. Peisch.*

Outwardly another austere New England farmhouse with a big central chimney, it has a living room considered one of the finest in the state. Built by Capt. Joseph Hatch, it was the first two-story structure in the area; the beams were cut from first-growth pine, as was undoubtedly the sheathing. The paneling in the living room is of first-rate workmanship; but of even greater interest are the walls of the hall and a bedroom of beautifully smooth pine planks with wide V joints. The staircase is a masterpiece of the joiner's art in its delicate simplicity. The owners had the delight of uncovering all this excellence, which was buried under plaster and wallpaper when they bought the house.

Mrs. Peisch will be able to tell you whether it is possible to see the OLCOTT-JOHNSON HOUSE nearby. The chimney wall in its dining room is pronounced the finest in Vermont, and there is little doubt that any better paneling will be found in the state.

¶ *Newbury-on-the-Bow*

This is one of the earliest settlements in the state, set in lush green pastures formed by the double bends of the Connecticut River. It has a long rectangular Common, and many of its dignified old homes are still standing in the northern and oldest section of the village, known as the "Oxbow." Here some of the descendants of the Johnson family are still living in the homes that were built by Col. Thomas Johnson, of Revolutionary fame, who came here as a young man in 1760 and helped to establish the settlement along with Isaac Bayley. One of these descendants is the well-known best-selling author, Frances Parkinson Keyes. Mrs. Keyes and her cousins, who live across the road, are the fifth generation of the Johnson family to live in both homes. These houses and the Isaac Bayley House, along with a few others, are also open during the Annual Cracker Barrel Bazaar (week of August 1), sponsored by the D.A.R.

DAVID JOHNSON HOUSE (*1806*)
> *Open on request when owner is in residence, with reasonable advance notice (when not there, her cousins at guest house across street have key and are authorized to take people through at their discretion. House dismantled and unheated in winter); Mrs. Frances Parkinson Keyes.*

As Mrs. Keyes wrote us, "The front part is an extremely interesting example of early American architecture . . . the ell is wholly Victorian in style. When my mother inherited the house, the ell was in a bad state of disrepair and, though she employed one of the leading architects of the day—Bowditch of Boston—to advise her in its reconstruction, he did so in accordance with the then prevailing taste. The result is extremely commodious and comfortable to this day, and, as a matter of fact, the ell, in its own way, is as much a period piece as the six rooms comprising the main part of the house and their exterior. It is furnished throughout with Victorian family pieces." The front hall and the brown sitting room in the 1806 part of the house still have the original wallpaper. In this older section are many early heirlooms of unusual interest.

OXBOW FARM (*c. 1820*)

By appointment in advance; Mr. and Mrs. William J. Taisey.

A handsome foursquare brick house with a long one-and-a-half-story wing. The fine fenestration, arched doorways, and four good chimneys give the house its forthright character. The interior of Oxbow Farm has lovely woodwork throughout, each room but one having its own fireplace. It is furnished with antiques—English, American, and French.

In back is the original JACOB BAYLEY HOUSE, a white frame structure of the late eighteenth century which has not been restored but will be shown on request.

ISAAC BAYLEY HOUSE (*c. 1786*)

Oxbow Road, left off Route 5; by written request; Mr. and Mrs. Frederick B. Cobb, Wells River.

A white frame house of ample proportions, with a balustraded hip roof. The present owner is the seventh generation to live in it, a descendant of Gen. Jacob Bayley, who founded the town, and of Isaac, who built this house. Originally six rooms, it has been augmented by successive generations five times, so that there are today seventeen rooms. The interior presents a picture of the changing tastes of a family, as some of the earliest pieces, along with examples of all the subsequent ones, are still here. The parlor is the outstanding room, having alcoves on either side of the fireplace—the so-called "courting" and "marriage" alcoves. In this room the sliding interior shutters may still be seen.

JOHNSON'S-ON-THE-OXBOW *or* HAINES JOHNSON HOUSE (*1800*)

Guest house mid-May to mid-November, at other times by special arrangement; Mr. and Mrs. Haines Johnson.

Your host and hostess here in this ample square New England farmhouse are the Haines Johnsons, for one of whose forebears the house was built—one of the four homes that Colonel Johnson erected for his sons after the Revolution. To savor the early atmosphere in this village, you could not do better than spend the night here. Little has been changed, except for the comfort of guests. The house has dispensed hospitality to the public before during its long history; the arched ballroom, running right across the front of the second story (now divided), tells a tale of the festivities and dances that made many of the early inns the social gathering places for the whole countryside.

For many years after it was erected in 1687, this was known as the "splendid mansion of Eleazar Arnold," and is a rare example of early Rhode Island dwelling, with many curious characteristics of construction inside and out. The masonry ends and the pilastered chimney are distinctive of the state. On the opposite page is the very stylish dining room of the fine Georgian Hunter house in Newport.

RHODE ISLAND

As far as heritage homes are concerned, the two particular high spots of this tiny but historic state are, first, the early part of Newport, with its rare assortment of colonial buildings, and, second, the College Hill section of Providence, with its remarkable array of post-Revolutionary mansions and other fine older houses. There might even be a man who would put Providence first and Newport second. If so, it would not be the first time that Rhode Island, small as it is, made room for another way of thinking. For remember, the Colony of Rhode Island, as founded by Roger Williams, embraced all beliefs, quite in con-trast to the one-way conservatism of neighboring Connecticut and Massa-chusetts; and there are architectural his-torians who suggest that the varieties of thought and opinion that found a haven here might have been reflected in the early building manners of the colony—in such a house, for instance, as the little Clemence-Irons House at Thornton (a very early survival if the date of 1680 is correct). It is a highly individual type, found only in the region fanning out north and west from Providence. Stone-ended, with the masonry gable end rising into a pilastered chimney, and heavily framed in medieval fashion, it has the air of a house built with the strength of its own convictions.

And look how different the Wanton-Lyman-Hazard House of an even slightly earlier date is in Newport. The latter's trimness, its stylishness for the time, are surely a reflection of the fact that Newport was being settled by people of wealth and social position (though they too came to Rhode Island as religious dissenters), who established in the town a tradition of aristocracy that is still very much in evidence.

It is then "out of Providence," as indicated in the headings above, that you will be most apt to find the early and more ruggedly individualistic houses of Rhode Island. It is in Newport that you will see the fine Georgian town houses of fashion and beauty, dating back to the period of the town's prosperity before the Revolution, when it was one of our five most important and populous colonial cities. And it is on College Hill that you will come face to face with the elegance that the merchant princes of Providence gave to their great houses on this eminence. These potentate owners of the time looked down from their doorways and windows onto a forest of masts in Providence River, where dockworkers in the early 1800s unloaded cargo after cargo of rum, tea, spices, and goodness knows what else from the Gold Coast, the Orient, the South Seas, the Indies. Unloaded too was a lot of lovely foreign miscellany for the adornment of these palatial establishments, adding to our delight as we look at them now.

Then you have still to take in the Rhode Island towns from Charlestown to East Greenwich that were served by the Old Post Road for two centuries before that ancient highway became known as "Route 1"—towns that are still made charming by choice examples of houses from both the earlier and later periods.

Warren and especially Bristol are both worthwhile for the fascinating Federal houses you can see there from the streets, on your way between the two high spots of Providence and Newport. And for another aspect of Newport we call your attention to the most spectacular sideshow of late-nineteenth-century houses in America—as instructive as it is entertaining. For here by the sea are the summer estates, staggering in size, conception, and maintenance, that provided a perfect setting for the fabulous fortunes of this country at a time, between the 1880s and the Crash, when no expense had to be spared for taxes. Not early houses, to be sure; yet they couldn't be a more irretrievable part of our past. A stroll along the Cliff Walk here and a visit to the vast Vanderbilt château, "The Breakers," make a fitting climax to your fling among the houses of old Rhode Island. They show that here a man was permitted to *build,* as well as believe, any way he wanted—just so he had enough money.

¶ *In & out of Providence*

The four "greats" of the College Hill houses are the JOHN BROWN and CARRINGTON HOUSES (both open and described below), THE NIGHTINGALE, and the IVES HOUSE (both private but viewable from the street). These comprise as splendid a quartet of post-Revolutionary town houses as you will find anywhere, all of them mansions in the true sense of the word. Between the owners and the builders there were wealth, taste, and skill to spare, all of which are good ingredients.

THE NIGHTINGALE (1792), at 357 Benefit Street, now occupied by John Nicholas Brown of the famous old Providence family, is probably the largest early frame house of distinction in the land, strikingly detailed in the good forth-right Georgian tradition, balustraded around the roof like its fellows, and the only frame house of the four—fine, white, and palatial. The big brick façade of the beautiful IVES HOUSE (1811), at 66 Power Street is decorated with a rounded and balustraded portico under a large, flat-arched window. Though it has a strong family resemblance to the John Brown House, Thomas Poynton Ives, who built it after marrying into the Brown family, is said to have sent to England for the plans which came labeled "for a Georgian Manor House." The JOHN BROWN HOUSE, on the other hand, was designed right here by Joseph Brown, the talented brother of the owner, who also designed his own house (1774) at 50 South Main Street—much altered now, but still outstanding for its bold, broad ogee-pedimented roof. What dominates the slope of College Hill, mansions and all, is not a house, but Joseph Brown's masterpiece, the stunning FIRST BAPTIST MEETING HOUSE (1775).

A few more unlisted houses to look at are the EDWARD DEXTER (1799), at 72 Waterman Street, very gaily adorned for its date; the TRUMAN BECKWITH (1826) (now the HANDICRAFTS CLUB), at Benefit and College Streets, Late Federal, trim and stylish, and the SULLIVAN DORR (1810), at 109 Benefit, modeled after Alexander Pope's house at Twickenham, with Roger Williams's grave behind it. At 159 Benefit the famous, bold GOLDEN BALL INN, now a rooming house, was once the social center of the town. The SARAH HELEN WHITMAN HOUSE (c. 1790), at 88 Benefit, was the home of the young widow to whom Edgar Allan Poe indited his poem *Annabel Lee*. Note finally at 9 Thomas Street the DEACON EDWARD TAYLOR HOUSE (1790), now occupied by a community

school of music and also by some particularly fine colonial carpentry.

PROVIDENCE ART CLUB (*brick portion 1793, wooden portion 1789*)
11 Thomas Street; 10 to 5 weekdays, 2 to 4 Sundays.

This is really two houses joined by an archway; the earlier one in particular, built by a silversmith named Cyril Dodge, has noteworthy woodwork.

STEPHEN HOPKINS HOUSE (*1743*)
Hopkins and Benefit Streets opposite courthouse; Wednesday and Saturday afternoons, year round; Colonial Dames.

The home of the man who was ten times Governor of Rhode Island, a member of the Continental Congress, a signer of the Declaration, and the first Chancellor of Brown University. When he signed the Declaration of Independence, he made the moving statement, "My hand trembles but my heart does not." A fine restoration of a choice small house, with many interesting details of woodwork, it is skillfully and suitably furnished. Like the Bishop Berkeley House it shows how unpretentiously some of the "great" men lived before the sea brought so much wealth to Rhode Island.

BETSEY WILLIAMS COTTAGE (*1773*)
Roger Williams Park; year round, from 9 to 5 daily, except Thursdays; city of Providence.

Once owned by a descendant of Roger Williams, who gave the land to the city to establish a museum of colonial furniture. An attractive gambrel-roofed cottage.

PENDLETON HOUSE (*a replica*)
224 Benefit Street; Monday through Saturday 10:30 to 5, Sundays and holidays 2 to 5, Wednesday nights until 10 (closed in August, except by appointment); Rhode Island School of Design.

A replica of a Georgian mansion of the Providence type, it was built to house the famous Leonard Pendleton Collection of English and American furniture and *objets d'art*.

SHAKESPEARE'S HEAD (*1763*)
21 Meeting Street; 9 to 5, Monday through Friday.

Once one of the most important buildings in the town, it is square, with a low hipped roof and central chimney. The home of John Carter, an apprentice of Benjamin Franklin's, it was used as a print shop for the first Providence newspaper. A colonial-style garden has been planted here.

JOHN BROWN HOUSE (*1786*)

52 Power Street; year round except holidays, 9 to 5 Monday through Friday (not open Sundays during June, July, and August, 3 to 5 other Sundays); headquarters of Rhode Island Historical Society.

John Quincy Adams wrote of it after visiting here, "The most magnificent and elegant private mansion that I have seen on the continent." And so it must have seemed, for the merchant princes of Providence were emerging from their period of Quaker sobriety and were having their fling. John Brown's brother Joseph was its enormously able designer. Its carved woodwork, ornate and forceful in character, its fine furniture of the same style, evoke, along with its distinguished neighbors, the heyday of Providence prosperity. The exterior is particularly striking and harmonious—built of red brick, trimmed with white wood and sandstone lintels and columns; the doorway is one of the best in town, and the balustraded parapet outstanding.

EDWARD CARRINGTON HOUSE (*1810–1811*)

66 William Street; daily, 1 to 5, except Mondays; Rhode Island School of Design.

When Capt. Edward Carrington bought this big brick house from John Corliss in 1812, it was only two years old. As new as it was, and already large, he set to work at once to add a third floor and to decorate it with a two-story porch and an all-round roof balustrade, both of brownstone. The house has the distinctive style of a period when money was pouring in faster than it could be spent. It has dignity of form, and the austerity of color you notice from the street does not continue indoors. Carrington, who was our consul in Canton as well as a shipowner and builder of means, filled his home with rare chinoiserie, furniture, and handmade scenic wallpapers from China, which are still wonderful today. The imposing mansion, presented to the city by the last member of the family, is preserved exactly as it was when the family lived in it, and looks as though they were still here. The first floor is the most resplendent in Providence; but don't by any means miss the rest—sitting rooms, sewing rooms, bedrooms, and baths.

¶ Pawtucket (*the adjoining city on the eastern side of Providence*)

DAGGETT HOUSE (*1685*)

> Slater Park; by appointment with Mrs. Irving K. White (phone: Pawtucket 2–4917); Pawtucket Chapter, D.A.R.

Containing period furnishings and personalia of Samuel Slater and Nathaniel Greene, it was built to replace an earlier house erected in 1644 by John Daggett which had been burned during King Philip's War. This house, built in 1685, was remodeled in 1790. The Daggetts were slaveholders, and the rings from which Prince, one of the slaves, swung his hammock can still be seen in one of the center beams. In the attic is a secret closet where the family could hide from the Indians. On display in the house are many historical items, including a blanket woven by Samuel Slater, builder of the first cotton mill. Interesting antiques here.

¶ Foster Center (*near the Connecticut line on 101*)

PARDON WILLIAMS HOMESTEAD

(*antique shop and tearoom, 1796*)

> On Dolly Cole Hill (Route 6).

¶ Cumberland Hill (*north of Pawtucket*)

ELDER BALLOU MEETING HOUSE

(*before 1749*)

> Elder Ballou Meeting House Road; year round, by obtaining key from Adelbert H. Whipple, R.F.D. 1, Woonsocket.

Not a house, but extremely interesting to house lovers for its very early and fascinating structural features.

¶Lincoln Woods (*Saylesville Village*)

(*5 miles north of Providence on 146*)

ELEAZAR ARNOLD HOUSE (*c. 1687*)

> 449 Great Road (leave Route 1 at Highland Avenue and follow "Lincoln Downs" signs); weekdays except Mondays 12 to 5, June 15 to October 15, other times upon application to custodian in adjacent house; 25 cents; S.P.N.E.A.

A remarkable example of an early Rhode Island stone-end dwelling, with a pilastered chimney. It was well restored in 1952 and fittingly furnished.

FIREPLACE HOUSE (*a restoration*)

(*1675–1710*)

> Lincoln Woods; a state restoration; Division Parks and Recreation of Rhode Island; open when restored fully.

A small stone house with a supersize chim-

Left: From its balustraded terrace to its balustraded roof, the John Brown symbolizes the residential splendor of Providence in its prime. Beyond it can be seen part of its famous neighbor, the Nightingale house.

Rarely if ever in this country will you find a more richly decorated pair of rooms than the double drawing rooms of the Carrington house on the hill in Providence, done chiefly in Chinese.

ney and fireplace, as the name implies; restored by the state as representing an outstanding example of its early type.

¶ *Anthony Village (a few miles west of 3 on 117)*

GEN. NATHANIEL GREENE HOUSE
(*1770*)
> 20 Taft Street; Wednesdays, Saturdays, and Sundays, 2 to 5; Valley 1–8630; The General Nathaniel Greene Homestead Association, L. E. Wagner (caretaker) (phone: Valley 1–8360).

Designed and built by Nathaniel Greene in 1770, when he was manager of the Coventry Ironworks, and before he was second in command to Washington. He made the hand-wrought hardware himself. In 1774 he brought his bride to the house, and a year later a son was born here and christened George Washington. The house is simple in form and substantial in size, with six rooms in the attic for the slaves. The entrance doorway is the ornamental exterior touch—a beautifully chaste composition of pediment and pilasters, put on like appliqué. Nice interiors too.

¶ *Coventry (5 miles west of Anthony Village on 117)*

THE TREASURE CHEST
(*early eighteenth century*)
> On Route 1; June 1 to October 1, daily 9 to 9; Virginia G. Salisbury (owner).

An early salt box, it has the original stairs, with a double Rhode Island rail. Almost everything is intact, including a very early mouse hole in a kitchen cupboard. If you stop by, ask to hear the fascinating history of the house. Filled with antiques for sale.

¶ *Thornton (just west of Providence on 14)*

CLEMENCE-IRONS HOUSE
(*c. 1680*)
> 38 George Waterman Road, Manton; open reasonable hours upon application; 25 cents; S.P.N.E.A.

Very small and very early, with diamond-paned windows and a primitive pilastered stone chimney; your attention was directed to it in the introduction to the state. It is another fine restoration of the S.P.N.E.A., whose houses are all worth seeing. It contains some interesting pieces of its period.

¶ *On & off the Old Post Road*

Now Route 1, this old highway has been in active service between New York and Boston since early colonial days. Every traveler of the time knew well its towns, taverns, and hospitable homes.

¶ *Wakefield*

COMMODORE PERRY FARM (*1750*)
> Post Road; by appointment; $1.00 to charity; Wisner H. Townsend, care of John H. Lewis & Co., 63 Wall Street, New York City, N.Y.

A small, pleasing gambrel-roofed cottage, with only two windows in front and a small wing. It has the typical big central chim-

The Nathaniel Greene house at Anthony Village has been restored and furnished as becomes a home of its time, place, and importance.

ney but no dormers. In addition to its unusual charm, it was the birthplace of
Oliver Hazard and Matthew C. Perry, and
there is a Perry family burying ground on
the place. The Japanese government
planted a cherry tree here in 1937 in honor
of the famous commodore.

¶ *Charlestown (halfway between
Westerley and Wakefield)*

GENERAL STANTON INN
(*before 1775*)
*May 30 through October; Mr. and Mrs.
Grafton M. Wilson.*

OLD WILCOX TAVERN, *formerly*
MONUMENT HOUSE (*dining and
overnight guests*) (*c. 1730*)
*Route 1, Bradford; April 1 to November
30; Joseph Szydlowski, Bradford.*

Gen. Joseph Stanton, a hero of the Revolutionary and French and Indian Wars,
was born in the Wilcox Tavern. He later
made the Stanton Inn his home, as did his
descendants until recently. The former is
now a private home, furnished throughout
with antiques; the latter is still an inn. Both
these eighteenth-century houses have been
moderately modernized.

¶ *Kingston (few miles north of Wakefield
on 138)*

HELME HOUSE
(*pre-Revolutionary*)
*Main Street; summer 3 to 5:30, Thursday
through Sunday; headquarters of South
County Art Association.*

Benjamin Franklin was frequently entertained here as he traveled the Post Road
between Boston and Philadelphia. From
the roof during the Revolution it was
possible to watch the British fleet blockad-
ing Newport. The house got its good name
from its longest occupant, Chief Justice
Helme. Previously it had been occupied
for a short time by Samuel Casey, a coun-
terfeiter.

KINGSTON INN (*1757*) *and* ELISHA
POTTER HOUSE (*now part of inn*)
(*1809*)
Main Street; Dr. Frederic Benschoten.

The inn has retained some of its eighteenth-
century charm, and the house makes an
interesting nineteenth-century addition.

¶ *Jamestown (138 halfway between
Saunderstown and Wickford
5 miles from toll bridge)*

CARR HOMESTEAD (*late 1600s*)
*On Carr's Lane; open during August (and
in July during tour) by written or phone
appointment with Mrs. A. W. Bowser
(Jamestown 191R); 25 cents toward upkeep
of house; Carr family (owners).*

The house and farm still form an un-
divided estate, with twenty-six heirs scattered all over the world. Built by Nicholas
Carr, oldest son of Gov. Caleb Carr, it
passed from father to son for seven generations. Except for a small addition, it is
as originally built—a simple, sturdy home,
with a central chimney. Much of the early
furniture and portraits are still here. This
is a home that has been well lived in and
cherished by its generations of owners.

MEADOWSWEET (*c. 1830*)
*131 Narragansett Avenue; on written
request; Mr. and Mrs. J. N. Porter.*

An excellent example of a post-Revolutionary "town house," finely furnished and
with several portraits by Sully.

¶ *Wickford (3 miles north of toll bridge)*

SMITH'S CASTLE (*1678*)
*2 miles north of Wickford on Route 1;
open daily 11 to 5 except Mondays,
Sundays 2 to 5, all year round; 25 cents;
Cocumscussoc Association, Mrs. Elizabeth
Warren Green (President), 126 West Main
Street, Wickford (phone: 2-0232).*

A "castle" in the sense that Richard Smith
built it in "the thickest of the barbarians"
as a substantial fortified dwelling in the
1637 wilderness. When it burned in 1676,
he rebuilt it in its own image within two
years. In 1740 the interior was modishly
remodeled. It is the only Rhode Island
house left in which Roger Williams lived
and wrote.

¶ *Saunderstown (between 1A and 138 just
north of Kingston)*

BIRTHPLACE OF GILBERT STUART
and EIGHTEENTH-CENTURY SNUFF
MILL (*1751–1752*)
*Hammond Hill Road; year round; 25
cents and 10 cents; maintained by Gilbert
Stuart Association.*

The birthplace and boyhood home of our
best-known colonial artist and foremost

This attractive town house in East Greenwich was the home of General Varnum, the Revolutionary hero.

painter of George Washington portraits is a large gambrel-roofed dwelling, rather austere but full of character, with a grist-mill adjoining that was operated for almost a hundred years after Stuart's day. Stuart's father operated a snuff mill in the present immense kitchen. Now that the house has been restored, the primitive manufacture of snuff is being demonstrated here today with an old water-driven snuff mill brought from England.

¶ East Greenwich

GEN. JAMES MITCHELL VARNUM HOUSE AND MUSEUM (*1773*)

57 Pierce Street; Wednesdays and Sundays 3 to 5, June 1 through November 1, also by appointment (phone: Turner 4–9260); maintained by General Varnum Association, Lt. Col. Howard V. Allen (Chairman).

A stately white town house of noble proportions. Foursquare, clapboarded, and done with restrained Georgian elegance, it has thirteen rooms, eight fireplaces, and two central chimneys. Among its many fine features are a broken pediment mantelpiece, original paneling, and old tiles. It is furnished with real distinction. In the rear is a historical museum; also a coach-

house museum covering early transportation.

THE WHITE SWAN (*1810–1820*)

4365 Post Road; appointment by letter or phone; Mrs. Arthur B. Lisle.

Owned by the late Arthur B. Lisle, President of the Society for the Preservation of New England Antiquities for twelve years, it is another very fine house of the Federal period, full of rare and interesting Oriental things as well as American antiques.

This is one of the most attractive early towns in the state, with a half dozen private homes to look at as you stroll around such as the CAPTAIN JOHN CONGDON HOUSE (1711), Division and Pierce Streets; the ELDREDGE HOUSE (1757), Division and Pierce Streets; the WINDMILL COTTAGE (1818), Division and West Streets; the GOV. WILLIAM GREEN HOMESTEAD (1680), Division and West Streets (opposite Windmill Cottage); the DANIEL HOWLAND (1677), Howland Road; the CAPT. THOMAS ARNOLD (1735), 28 King Street; and the old picturesque ALBERT C. GREENE HOUSE (1724), at 86 Main Street.

¶In & out of Newport

There are certain early American communities of less than metropolitan vastness in which anyone with a passion for searching out vintage houses will find his heart's desire. Outstanding in this respect are Portsmouth, Salem, Annapolis, Charleston, and Newport. These aren't museum towns in any sense of the word; they're just fine old colonial cities, somewhat smitten in spots by modernity, but holding on to certain ancient streets, certain old sections, and single houses here and there hemmed in by nondescript modern surroundings.

It is possible that in the popular mind today Newport is chiefly notable as the summer resort of legendary nabobs—a place, now somewhat dated and on the decline, of shingled châteaux, palatial cottages, and monumental seaside mansions on esplanades of lawn heaped with hummocks of huge blue hydrangeas. Yet, of the five cities mentioned above, it is perhaps Newport which offers the greatest historic variety of treasures, both early and late, to people on a house-hunting spree.

By all means get in touch on arrival with the Preservation Society of Newport County, at 5 Charles Street, for maps, further information, and good local guidance. The Hunter house and "The Breakers" are at present their two particular showpieces (and what an odd pair of showpieces!); but everything architecturally worthwhile in town is under the wing of the Society. Don't miss any of it!

HUNTER HOUSE (*1740*)
.   *Daily 10 to 5, July 1 to September;*
        admission (see "The Breakers").

It is an early eighteenth-century manor house which became the headquarters of Admiral de Terney during the Revolution. There is fine furniture made by Goddard and Townsend, the great eighteenth-century Newport craftsmen; Newport portraits; and silver. Restored with skill, expert knowledge, and taste, it is today the most important and beautiful eighteenth-century house in town, and has been called one of the best Georgian houses in the country. The interior colors are stunning.

One of the most distinguished houses of its day, the Hunter is now one of the showpieces of Newport not to miss by any means.

Second only to the Hunter house in Georgian distinction in Newport, the Vernon house has no rival here as far as historical fame is concerned. And while The Breakers is a very recent newcomer indeed by comparison, its palatial proportions and fabulous splendors make it a sightseers' paradise.

WANTON-LYMAN-HAZARD HOUSE AND GARDEN (*1675*)

82 Touro Street; daily 10 to 5, July 1 to September; admission (see "The Breakers").

This is the oldest house in town and one of the finest Jacobean houses in New England. It is furnished as an inn or tavern, and after the color and excitement of the Hunter house it may seem at first sight somewhat austere. However, it was built with a strength and solidity, and in a style which reflects the courage and culture of the early settlers here. Take note in the second-floor bedroom of the chimney end with its original and once colorful free-hand painting; but look too at the revealed structural features of this room, which gives it such a noble character.

VERNON HOUSE (*1708–1760*)

Clark and Mary Streets; Monday through Friday 9 to 5, by appointment, year round.

It was Rochambeau's headquarters, and here Washington planned his future campaign on March 6, 1781. It is not furnished. The mural paintings discovered behind the wall paneling, believed to be of eighteenth-century Chinese origin, are of considerable interest here.

THE BREAKERS (*1894*)

Ochre Point; daily 10 to 5, June 1 to September; adults $1.50 and children 60 cents, combination ticket (adults $2.00 and children $1.00) admits visitors to Wanton-Lyman-Hazard House, Hunter House, "Whitehall," and "The Breakers" stables (single admissions to each house may also be purchased).

Built for Cornelius Vanderbilt, modeled after north Italian palaces of the sixteenth century, furnished with the utmost luxury, and immensely ornate in every decorative detail, this is among the masterpieces of Richard M. Hunt, the great Beaux Arts architect of the 1890s. It was the pride of the Newport summer colony. To see it is an experience not to be missed.

MAWDSLEY-GARDNER-WATSON-PITMAN HOUSE (*center 1700, front 1747*)

228 Spring Street, corner John Street; at reasonable hours, by application to Mr. and Mrs. L. Feller, 18 John Street; S.P.N.E.A.

This is an interesting house with a paneled parlor and good staircase; but only the hall and parlor are shown.

¶ *Middletown (few miles north of Newport on 114)*

WHITEHALL (*1729*)

July 1 through Labor Day; 25 cents; Newport Society of Colonial Dames of Rhode Island (on 99-year lease from Yale University).

A beautiful restoration of the red frame house occupied by Bishop Berkeley during his three years' residence in the Colonies, during which time the famous British philosopher wrote the poem which contains the prophetic words "Westward the course of empire takes its way." It is sparsely furnished, as it would have been at the period, but with fine Jacobean pieces. The structural details are of great excellence. Original delft tiles in the study and some exceptional paneling in the northeast parlor.

The house called Bonnet Hill near Darien is a true collector's item, and fascinating for the reason that while the main body of the structure was brought from Stamford, various other parts were gathered from here and there in Connecticut, among them rare paneling of museum quality and this very appropriate mid-seventeenth-century doorway done in what might be called Connecticut Jacobean. On the opposite page is the ancient Glebe house on Hollow Road at Woodbury, one of the choice Connecticut towns.

CONNECTICUT

*I*T IS hard at times to tell which plays a more important part in the landscape of Connecticut—her boulder-strewn fields or her lean-to houses, also called "salt boxes," but known locally as "leanters." One thing is certain, however: no other type of house today harmonizes so attractively with the historic countryside.

A thing to keep in mind is that, of the two thousand or more carpentered houses built in Connecticut before 1700, less than twenty remain, and of these, only a very few, such as the Whitman House in Farmington and the Buttolph-

Williams House in Wethersfield, still stand in their original form. But you will see hundreds of simple Connecticut houses, at crossroads and in country towns, of vintages up to 1820 or so which emulate the earlier ones in both form and substance.

While the simple, utilitarian Connecticut salt box, of which many examples are actually quite large, with two full stories and an attic, and even often with wings, was always the basic house, you will discover from the dates that around the 1750s many houses began to be embellished with fashionable Georgian doorways, porches, cornices, pediments, and Palladian windows—for instance some of the more elegant houses in Litchfield. Yet underneath and through it all the conservative Connecticut character prevails, and along with it the scrupulous workmanship of the Connecticut carpenter. No builders in America had better woods to work with or were better able to work them; no builders in America left more enduring and delightful examples of colonial skill.

Connecticut house tours vary so much from year to year—listings would only mislead. For timely information write to Mr. Don Parry of the Development Commission, State Office Building, Hartford. The Connecticut Antiquarian and Landmarks Society (Mrs. Frank Cogan, Farmington) runs two tours each summer beautifully organized for members. Since membership includes free access to their several houses and covers a subscription to their excellent magazine, it is an antiquarian bargain at $3.50 a year.

O N & O F F T H E S H O R E R O A D

Greenwich; Darien; Fairfield; Stratford; Bridgeport;

Milford; New Haven; Guilford; Madison; Clinton; Old

Lyme; East Lyme; New London; Mystic; Stonington

¶ *Greenwich*

KNAPP TAVERN *or* PUTNAM COTTAGE (*1692–1729*)

243 East Putnam Avenue; Mondays, Thursdays, Fridays, and Saturdays, 10 to 5; Putnam Hill Chapter, D.A.R.

It was from this inviting early-eighteenth-century roadside inn, still faced today with round-ended shingles, that General Israel Putnam, surprised at his toilet, eluded the British by running from the house and plunging on horseback down a declivity which was steeper than his pursuers cared to tackle. It is part of the legend that he had seen the redcoats' arrival reflected in his mirror while shaving. The four rooms

Note as Connecticut characteristics the boldness of the window framing at Bonnet Hill, the great substantial central chimney around which the house was erected. On the opposite page, Churchside at Fairfield is charmingly restored.

open to view are fittingly furnished with antiques.

¶ *Darien*

BONNET HILL FARM *or* RICHARD WEBB HOUSE (*c. 1670*)

By written request; Monroe Dreher.

This delightfully restored Connecticut salt box was moved here in 1945 from Stamford, where Richard Webb had built it well over two centuries before, and where it had degenerated from being the nucleus of a prosperous colonial farmstead to being used as a glue factory. Its preserver has made it his home and an antiquarians' delight, furnished and finished to perfection. The exterior is pumpkin yellow trimmed with oyster white; the living room is one of the rare fully paneled rooms in Connecticut, and many of the furnishings are of museum rank.

¶ *Fairfield*

CHURCHSIDE (*1823*)

39 Meeting House Lane, Greenfield Hill, Fairfield; by appointment; Henry B. Spelman.

This is one of a cluster of charming old houses handsomely maintained for convenience and attractiveness. It was first occupied by the Reverend Richard Varick Day when he was called to the lovely old church here.

¶ *Stratford*

DAVID JUDSON HOUSE (*1723*)

967 Academy Hill; Fridays and Saturdays 2 to 5, May to October, and by appointment (Edison 7–0395); 25 cents and 10 cents; home of the Stratford Historical Society.

Overhanging gable ends, a monumental chimney, and a stunning entrance doorway with inch-thick panes of glass set in its paneling would make this an arresting house even apart from its fine interiors.

¶ *Bridgeport*

HARRAL HOUSE *or* WALNUT WOOD (*1846*)

350 Golden Hill Street; by written request to C. N. Gardner, c/o Archer C. Wheeler (owner).

This extraordinary Gothic mansion fills with joy all devotees of Alexander Jackson Davis, that most ardent of nineteenth-century American architects, who has been described with such enthusiasm by Wayne

Andrews in *Architecture, Ambition and Americans,* a book warmly recommended to readers of the *Guide.* "Preserved in all its original splendor by the present owner," Mr. Andrews writes, "Walnut Wood is one of our as yet unrecognized national monuments and it is difficult to know which to admire the more, the mirrored parlors or the intensely Gothic grand staircase, dining room and bedrooms. The complete convenience of the place is reflected in the brilliant asymmetry of the exterior."

¶ Milford

EELS-STOW HOUSE (*c. 1669*)

34 High Street; daily May to October, and by appointment; Milford Historical Society.

It is full of odd structural and historical items. For one thing, Capt. Stephen Stow's wife was named Freelove Baldwin. Also, there is a rare 1687 portrait of the Samuel Eels who built the house and willed one half of it to his daughter if his son should die—"Which halfe she pleaseth." For this eventuality two separate kitchens were provided. The gable overhangs, the coved cornice, and the dog-legged stairs are items to see. The furnishings and exhibits in this fine old salt box are mementos of all periods from Colonial to Victorian.

¶ New Haven

PARDEE-MORRIS HOUSE
(*1680–1685, 1780–1800*)

325 Lighthouse Road, 8 miles east of New Haven; weekdays 10 to 5 except Mondays, Sundays 2 to 5, May 1 to November 1; New Haven Colony Historical Society.

A great handsome ell of a house, with stone ends (unusual around here) laid up in mortar of oyster shells and lime. Its various roof levels are all composed with fine informality. The massive masonry end walls provide flues for eight fireplaces. There is a vaulted ballroom and a vast beamed basement kitchen. Not only is it finely furnished in character but attractively gardened in true colonial fashion. The original house was burned by the British in 1779, so that the rebuilding of 1780 had only a portion of the early house to start with; the ballroom part was added a little later. A house of great character has emerged as a result of the work done at

different dates. This fact together with its fine furnishings make it an instructive house to visit.

¶ Guilford

There may well be in the vicinity here more than a hundred houses from before the Revolution, putting Guilford almost on a par with Ipswich; and there is a Guilford style as clearly as there is an Ipswich style, with many characteristics in common. The great size of the village green gives a clue to the past importance of the place, and many of the best of the old houses can be covered in a brief stroll around it. Note in particular the tiny entrance-staircase hallways with their courting benches, the solid-paneled wall cupboards, and the general medieval manner of the houses as a whole.

PELATIAH LEETE HOUSE (*1730*)

Leete's Island, Guilford; by written request during summer months to resident, Mrs. Oliver Bowen; 75 cents for Dorothy Whitfield Society; Mrs. Harry E. Glen (owner).

The rosettes that decorate the doorway of this house were meant to ensure that no harm should come to the dwelling—and no harm ever has. It is one of the finest here of its time, with massive beams, lamb's-tongue-chamfered corner posts, a studded door with a wooden latch, and old cupboards and chests of Guilford cabinetry. Primitive interior woodwork was never in Connecticut finished with greater care and taste.

HYLAND HOUSE (*1660–1720*)

Boston Post Road; daily 11 to 5 except Mondays, June 15 to October 1; 25 cents; Dorothy Whitfield Society; Mrs. Woolsey Conover (President).

Expertly restored to its diamond-paned original appearance, the house has narrow clapboards and carved overhang, with supporting corner posts cut as corbels. Outwardly it corroborates the date given to it, but the high ceilings within have caused dispute among the experts. Its furnishing fits the early date. Very choice indeed.

DARIUS COLLINS HOUSE
(c. 1769)

56 Union Street; by written request (allow time for verification); Mr. and Mrs. Richard W. Beebe (Antiques).

A delightfully unspoiled salt box filled with many treasures collected by a connoisseur, and with a rare original Guilford cupboard built in. The woodwork and dado of the southwest parlor are painted with red buttermilk paint, much used in early days hereabouts. The entrance door is Cross-and-Bible, and other finely paneled doors open into the "borning room" and "keeping room."

HENRY WHITFIELD HOUSE *or* OLD STONE HOUSE (*1639*)

Whitfield Street; daily 10 to 5 except Mondays April to October, daily 10 to 4 except Mondays December to March; state of Connecticut, Miss Lois North (curator).

This is said to be the oldest stone house in Connecticut and is largely a reconstruction. The steep pitch of the roof reminds us that it was originally covered with thatching of rye straw. The main fireplace is immense —ten feet wide, with a lintel of oak that is monumental and a flue at either end for one or two fires, as required. The furnishing is sternly medieval. Perfectionist antiquarians may question the correctness of the 1903 interior restoration, pointing out that two rooms above and two below would have been right; however, this is a point for purists to ponder.

LYMAN BEECHER HOUSE (*1770*)

475 Whitfield Street; on written or phone request, at owners' convenience; Mr. and Mrs. Walter B. Dodge.

This house, built on the green, was moved in 1829 to its present site here near the water. The feat was accomplished by seventy yoke of oxen. The owner, himself famous, was the father of two more famous Americans: Harriet Beecher Stowe and Henry Ward Beecher, preacher and abolitionist. It is a plain white clapboard village house, typical of this section of the state, spacious and accommodating. A modern glass window at the rear of the large living room looks out on a lovely water view. Otherwise very little modernization is evident, and what there is only adds to the livability. The same may be said of the furnishings.

ISAAC STOWE HOUSE (*1743*)

77 Broad Street; on written request; Dr. and Mrs. Levin Lyttleton Waters.

An unspoiled example of the third period of Guilford architecture (1700–1750). The things to note are its massive framing, generous fireplaces, fine moldings, attic smokehouse, gun closet, and hardware made by the builder. The present owners are living in it while they restore it and taking their time so that they will make no mistakes. They already have collected some excellent pieces. (Mrs. Waters is a daughter of Mrs. Warnecke of "The Mowings," described under Moodus.)

JOSEPH CHITTENDEN HOUSE
(*1766*)

78 Petticoat Lane (Fair Street); by appointment only (phone: Glendale 3-2112); 50 cents for Dorothy Whitfield Historic Society; Mr. and Mrs. Russell M. Nichols.

This is a fine example of an integral salt-box house, in which many of the original features remain intact. These include a massive stone chimney serving three fireplaces, small panes in the windows throughout, and a "sparking bench" in the hall. It is a home which combines eighteenth-century charm and comfortable living. There are many ancestral portraits, all of descendants of Guilford settlers, as is Mrs. Nichols herself.

¶ Madison

NATHANIEL ALLIS HOUSE (*1739*)

Boston Post Road near library, east of town center; daily; 25 cents; Madison Historical Society.

The Allis House is one of a nice collection of seventeenth- and eighteenth-century houses in this town next door to Guilford. It has been furnished to retain the atmosphere and charm of the town from the 1740s on—which it does.

LEE ACADEMY (*1821*)

Next to town hall; Madison Historical Society.

In addition to Lee Academy take time to look from the street at the GRAVES HOUSE (1675), the MEYS HOUSE (a red salt box of 1690), and others that you can hardly miss.

¶ *Clinton*

STANTON HOUSE (*1789*)

Main Street near Congregational church green; daily 2 to 5, summer; Hartford National Bank and Trust Company.

The striking white clapboard house which claims your attention in this old town, where the brewing of witch hazel was a major industry, is like a large-scale cottage, extraordinarily capacious, with one of those hinged-panel partitions that can be swung up and hooked to the ceiling. It contains for your delectation everything from fine old furniture, china, and early costumes to a complete post-Revolutionary country store, attached.

¶ *Old Lyme*

This picturesque old parlor town, which has for many years attracted, along with well-to-do residents, a steady stream of painters, photographers, and summer visitors, was once a busy and wealthy world port, and many of its fine early houses were the homes of distinguished seafarers and sea traders. There are lots of attractive old houses to look at from the outside, apart from the two that can be visited.

FLORENCE GRISWOLD HOUSE (*1817*)

Post Road; daily 2 to 5 except Mondays, June 15 to September 15; 25 cents; Florence Griswold Association, Inc.

Attribute the likeness between the chaste Ionic portico here and that of the Congregational church nearby to the early Connecticut architect Samuel Belcher, who designed them both. The present church is a replica of the original, which was burned and rebuilt in 1906–1907. When, about that time, Old Lyme became an art colony, it was in this house that many of the artists boarded, and their work is now here to be seen in the charming antique setting provided by the old house.

WILLIAM SMITH HOUSE (*before 1778*)

Meeting House Hill, Johnnycake Hill Road; by appointment in advance; Mr. and Mrs. James Madison MacDonald.

It was from this house in 1815, when the Third Meeting House was struck by light-

The grand old Denison house at Mystic grows out of its boulder-set hillside in typical Connecticut fashion.

ning, that a daughter of Mr. Smith's with the surprising name of Union Sparrow ran to rescue the hymnbooks by carrying them out in her petticoat at the risk of her life. It is a fine, large example of Connecticut Late Colonial. It is a privilege to see the owners' collections of eighteenth- and early-nineteenth-century American, English, and Oriental furnishings—the last an indication of a seafaring community.

¶ East Lyme

THOMAS LEE HOUSE (*1664*)

> *Boston Shore Road, Route 56; daily 12 to 5 except Mondays, May 31 to September 15; donation; East Lyme Historical Society.*

To the student of seventeenth-century American dwellings the Lee House here is of rare interest, for it shows, in unusual fashion, the full development of the salt-box type from one room to many. Much of this growth and rearrangement was due to the fact that Mr. and Mrs. Lee produced, first and last, fifteen children, proof positive of the adaptability of the salt-box type.

¶ New London

JOSHUA HEMPSTEAD HOUSE (*1643*)

> *11 Hempstead Street; daily 1 to 4 except Mondays, May 15 to October 15; 25 cents, no charge to members; Connecticut Antiquarian and Landmarks Society.*

This may very well be the oldest frame house in Connecticut and one of the best documented, for the builder's son Joshua entered the whole operation in his diary. The walls are shingled on vertical boarding and filled with seaweed for insulation. It shows again, in a very different way, the evolution of a salt box.

SHAW MANSION (*1756–1840*)

> *11 Blinman Street; daily 1 to 4 except Sundays; donation; New London County Historical Society.*

It is plain to see from the size and style of the house that Capt. Nathaniel Shaw was a wealthy shipowner, and heartening to hear that he built it partly to give employment to a band of Acadian refugees. The eaves of both the gabled main house and its big foursquare wing are elegantly balustraded. There is much to see inside, including the carefully preserved room in

which Washington once stayed. Set on fire in the Revolution, the house was saved by the bursting of barrels of vinegar stored in the attic, which came flooding down on the flames.

¶ Mystic

The waterfront village of this historic maritime community wanders off into the rocky pastureland hills; but in the village itself there is the Living Museum of the Marine Historical Association, known as "Mystic Seaport." For lovers of the sea, ships, and boating lore this is a must. For lovers of houses there are several old ones in the Seaport, of varying interest. The SAMUEL BUCKINGHAM HOUSE (1768) was brought here by barge from Saybrook to help form an attractive part of this historical establishment—a simple, clean-cut Connecticut Colonial. Then there are the houses the three shipbuilding Greenman brothers built side by side on Greenmanville Avenue—evocative of the romantically classical 1840s.

DENISON HOUSE *or* PEQUOTSEPOS MANOR (*1717*)

> *Daily 1 to 5 except Mondays May 1 to November 1, by appointment November 1 to May 1 (phone: Jefferson 6–9248); Denison Society, Inc.*

This fine old house clad in wonderfully weathered shingles has been most delightfully restored. Each of its various rooms has been made to represent, in its own period attire, one of the eleven generations of the Denison family whose home it was, producing a panorama of furnishings from early colonial times to the Gay Nineties. We consider this one of the most interesting "family" houses in the country.

CAPT. PEREZ WOODWARD HOUSE (*1815*)

> *Pistol Point Road; summer months, by appointment in advance; Mr. and Mrs. Paul J. Kingsley.*

When Charles Mallory, the great Mystic shipbuilder who constructed the famous clipper *Twilight,* bought this then-unadorned house from Captain Woodward in 1828, he put on the Ionic portico to be in fashion, caused the egg-and-dart motif of the columns to be repeated on the front-door panel, and placed a cupola on the roof. Thus do architectural fashions work, their wonders to perform.

PACKER HOMESTEAD (*1720*)

Irving Street; by written or phone appointment only; Mrs. Carl C. Cutler.

This pleasant colonial family home, given truly ample proportions by enlargements made before the Revolution, has been lived in ever since it was built by lineal descendants of the original Packers. It is furnished to be comfortable with many personal pieces of no particular antiquity.

OLD WOODBRIDGE TAVERN (*1745*)

On the green; daily 1 to 5, by appointment; Mr. and Mrs. E. Fletcher Ingalls II.

Dr. Dudley Woodbridge was at one time the tavernkeeper, doctor, and preacher here. There are still two tiny rooms over the taproom in which the stagecoach drivers slept. There is a most interesting gun closet on the staircase, a secret passage, and fine old paneling everywhere. The curator of the New London Museum owned this choice house until recently.

¶ Stonington

Here, next door to Mystic, is another seaport village—an especially trim and attractive one. It also rambles far off into the rocky hills, its houses closely related to those in and out of Mystic. These all happen to be private homes that may be seen by appointment. There are eight altogether, next in number to Litchfield, and likewise in a community very con-

The brick trimmer arch above the vast cavern of the fireplace in Stonecrop Farm is one of the structural details common almost exclusively to the Stonington area.

scious of the priceless nature of its heritage houses. Be sure to walk around the village proper—one of the loveliest in New England. Local historians from all localities will do well to acquaint themselves with the chronology of Stonington prepared by Mr. Williams Haynes of Stonecrop Farm, who has also played an important part in the restoration of the Denison Homestead in Mystic, adjoining.

HEWITT HOUSE (c. 1699)

Off Route 2 near town; by phone appointment, July to Labor Day; Mr. and Mrs. Amos G. Hewitt (phone: Jefferson 6-2154).

The owners say that the simple finish of this earliest type of salt box indicates it was built by farmers; but don't forget that farmers were the great builders of early America. The massive oak beams, girts, sills, and corner posts have improved with age. The original floors are still intact—oak downstairs, sycamore upstairs. A house of great interest to all would-be restorers.

STONECROP FARM (1750)

Taugwonk Road, off Route 84; by appointment only, 24 hours in advance; 50 cents for Stonington Tricentennial Scholarship Fund; Mr. and Mrs. Williams Haynes.

The builder, the Hon. Paul Wheeler, was chairman of the local Committee of Safety in the Revolution and a veteran of the Indian wars. One outstanding feature of this in-every-way-delightful house is the huge old kitchen fireplace, with its trimmer arch, seen only hereabouts. The rock-ledge site is superb, and inside are unique collections —old pigeon prints and unusual spoons, among the family heirlooms. In the great fireplace room, with its immense dining table, are beautiful silver and pewter pieces. Here is a chance to catch up on local history, for the owners are the experts of the neighborhood, and are deep in Stonington lore.

PELEG DENISON HOUSE (1775)

Harvey Road; upon request, when owner is there; Mrs. Helen Joy Lee.

The attic here has pegged and numbered rafters, and a door into the chimney for smoking meat. Most of the original woodwork is still here. Across the road is the Deacon Joseph Denison Burying Ground. This, you will begin to comprehend, is Denison country.

EDWARD DENISON HOUSE (c. 1710)

Pequot Trail, west of North Road; upon request when owner is there; Mr. and Mrs. Minot Pittman.

The wife of Edward's son John was drowned in the well. The house later became a tavern. The bar cupboard is still here, and upstairs a ballroom with a floating partition, better to accommodate an overflow of guests. The house has corner fireplaces, unusual in this section.

JOSEPH DENISON HOUSE or GREAT HEARTH (1730)

Harvey Road; by appointment, with 24 hours' notice; 50 cents for Stonington Historical Society; Mr. and Mrs. James Reid Johnson.

With some of the finest eighteenth-century interior woodwork around Stonington and furnished in English and American pieces of the same period, this house is something to see.

CAPTAIN AMOS PALMER HOUSE (c. 1780)

24 Main Street; by written appointment at convenience of family, June through September; Mrs. Stephen Vincent Benét.

This house in the village has many distinctions, not the least of which is the fact that it is still occupied by the family of the poet, the late Stephen Vincent Benét. Earlier it was inhabited by another celebrated American, James McNeill Whistler. It is considered to be one of the best houses in this part of the state, with fine paneling, mantels, and a rather special double stairway to the front door.

PALMER MINER HOUSE (c. 1790)

Hangman's Hill Road; by appointment; Mr. and Mrs. Palmer Miner.

Owned in a straight line of descent since the 1830s, when the first Palmer Miner purchased it from Samuel Peabody, it is a Connecticut farmhouse of substance and distinction, with two upstairs rooms hung in French wallpapers brought over around 1800.

UP THE CONNECTICUT RIVER VALLEY

Essex; Moodus; Middletown; Wethersfield; Hartford;
Windsor; Suffield

¶ *Essex*

This town, on the west bank of the Connecticut River, is one of the loveliest and most colorful of the towns of this region.

LORD HOUSE (*c. 1800*)
> *28 Main Street; on request; Mr. and Mrs. Robert I. Carter.*

On a street of old captains' houses leading down to the water, this is an old captain's house itself—a charmer from the street and a beauty within.

GRISWOLD INN
> (*mid-eighteenth century*)
> *Main Street; always open; the Lovell Family (custodians).*

A grand old inn, very little changed except for the renovation of an old schoolhouse into a taproom. You can eat and sleep here.

PRATT HOUSE (*c. 1720*)
> *20 West Avenue; daily 1 to 4, Saturdays and Sundays by appointment; closed holidays June 15 to September 15; 25 cents; S.P.N.E.A.*

Among other attractions, this house contains the very fine Griswold collection of American furniture and furnishings.

¶ *Moodus*

There are many good houses to be seen from the road in this neck of the woods, even though they cannot be visited. One of the best exteriors in Connecticut is that of the GENERAL CHAMPION HOUSE in East Haddam.

THE MOWINGS (*seventeenth century*)
> *Afternoons summer months only, upon request by letter or phone (Moodus 202W2); Mr. and Mrs. Heinz Warneke.*

This mellow old farmhouse in the woods has been restored with rare feeling and

The woodwork in the dining room at The Mowings, like the woodwork all through this old house, is a glowing example of the color and finish inherent in ancient planks, paneling, and beams.

The kitchen chamber of the famous old Buttolph-Williams house in Wethersfield is furnished with great understanding in pieces that belong perfectly to its time and place.

skill by its owners, a well-known sculptor and his painter wife, who have furnished it with family heirlooms, portraits, and many unusual country pieces. Few houses anywhere have been treated with such tangible understanding, even more apparent on closer acquaintance. But get your directions straight and look out for deer.

¶ Middletown

ALSOP HOUSE, *now* DAVIDSON ART CENTER OF WESLEYAN UNIVERSITY (*1840*)

High Street; Monday to Friday 8 to 5, Saturdays 8 to 12 and 1 to 4, Sundays 2 to 4 (only when college is open, not during vacations or summer); Wesleyan University.

In a town containing some of the most interesting Greek Revival and Gothic houses in Connecticut, this is one of the most famous examples of the former fashion, now restored and furnished to show the graceful manner of living when Middletown was a flourishing center of commerce and culture, before the Civil War. On the outside walls are lifesize paintings of mythical figures, which appear from the street to be statues set in niches. The house is an experience not to be missed.

RUSSELL HOUSE, *now* HONORS COLLEGE OF WESLEYAN UNIVERSITY (*1828*)

High Street; daily, when school is in session; Wesleyan University.

One of the country's great Greek Revival mansions, designed by Ithiel Town of nearby New Haven, with an assist from Alexander Jackson Davis. The interiors are beautifully preserved, with decorated wall painting intact. The woodwork is becomingly ornate, and the great glass gaslight chandeliers are the very essence of their period. Count it a major opus of an eminent early team of architects.

¶ Wethersfield

BUTTOLPH-WILLIAMS HOUSE (*1692*)

Broad and Marsh Streets; daily 12:30 to 4 except Mondays, May 15 to October 15; 50 cents, members free; Antiquarian and Landmarks Society.

One of the finest examples of seventeenth-century architecture in Connecticut (which means in the country). Dark, stark, but filled with vitality, its medieval character is revealed in the narrow clapboards, overhangs, big chimney, small windows, and furnishing of period perfection. One of the most important preservations in the state.

WEBB HOUSE (*1752*)

> *211 Main Street; daily 10 to 5, Sundays ◀ to 5, during winter closes at 4; 50 cents and 10 cents; Connecticut Society of Colonial Dames.*

As beautifully urbane as the nearby Buttolph-Williams House is fascinatingly primitive, this is the house that Washington headed for in the spring of 1781 to effect a meeting with the Count de Rochambeau. Its paneling is one of the prides of Connecticut, and it is furnished with all the fitness and finish for which the Colonial Dames are famous. The red flock paper Mrs. Webb put up in honor of the general's coming is still on the walls of the room wherein he slept.

¶ *Hartford*

Three houses on the corner of the block at Farmington Avenue and Forest Street are as far from Early American as the 1870s could make them. They have a romantic-period interest, but it was mostly from the people who have lived there that they derived their distinction.

HARRIET BEECHER STOWE HOUSE (*c. 1870*)

> *73 Forest Street; by appointment; 50 cents; Miss Katharine S. Day (phone: Jackson 2–8635).*

You enter this mid-Victorian gray-brick house through a gabled porch. Mrs. Stowe always referred to it as a "cottage." It is furnished pretty much as it was when the author of *Uncle Tom's Cabin* lived there.

The many-gabled and -chimneyed CHARLES DUDLEY WARNER HOUSE (1872), the home of Mark Twain's great literary friend, can be seen from the street. In the AVERY MUSEUM you will find the famous Wallace Nutting Collection of Early American furniture, many notable Early American paintings, and collections of pottery and glass.

The Webb house in Wethersfield is among the greats of Connecticut, both for its intrinsic beauty inside and out and for its distinguished historical associations.

MARK TWAIN HOUSE (*1873*)

351 Farmington Avenue; daily 9 to 12 and 1 to 6, except Sundays and holidays; no charge, except for one room; Mark Twain Library and Memorial Committee.

Now the Mark Twain Library downstairs and apartments upstairs, only one room at present is furnished as it was when the great writer lived here—his bedroom, with the fantastically carved Venetian bedstead he bought in Italy. But there are hopes for the future of this, the only home he ever built for himself and his wife. He had what appears to be a pilothouse fitted to the rear to remind him of his life on the Mississippi.

¶ *Windsor*

This inland town way up the Connecticut River, you may be surprised to hear, carried on quite an extensive seagoing trade with the West Indies during the latter part of the eighteenth century. Carpenters from around here helped build some of the best houses in New Bern, North Carolina, for a little winter work.

LOOMIS HOMESTEAD AND SCHOOL

(*main house 1690, wing 1640*)

By appointment (phone: 8–8191); Loomis Institute.

It is a well-preserved rural house from the latter part of the seventeenth century, but with chimneys, trim, and rooflines which have eighteenth-century characteristics. The house, furnished with family heirlooms, is in good hands, being used for faculty housing by the school.

ELLSWORTH HOMESTEAD *or* ELMWOOD (*1740*)

778 Palisade Avenue, between Windsor Locks and Windsor; daily 9 to 5 except Mondays and Wednesdays, Sunday 1 to 6, May 1 to December 1; 25 cents; Connecticut D.A.R.

This fine big central-chimney mansion in its own three-acre park was the home of Oliver Ellsworth, one of the five senators in the First Congress who made the first draft of our Constitution. He didn't even wait to sign but galloped home to see that Connecticut did its part toward ratification.

Both Washington and John Adams were visitors here when the antiques were brand-new.

HEZEKIAH CHAFFEE HOUSE *or* THE CHAFFEE SCHOOL (*used for faculty housing*) (*soon after 1755*)

By appointment only; The Loomis Institute.

This elegant eighteenth-century brick house, with its central chimney and its wing, where Doctor Hezekiah had his office before the Revolution, faces the old Windsor green. The little brick building in back was either a countinghouse or slave quarters; beyond were the warehouses and the landing where seagoing vessels tied up, many miles from the sea.

LIEUT. WALTER FYLER HOUSE

(*one room 1640, later additions 1773*)

96 Palisade Avenue; Thursdays 10 to 5, or by appointment (phone: Windsor 8–3813); Windsor Historical Society.

This began as a one-room house, but when Capt. Nathaniel Howard bought it from Lieutenant Fyler in 1772 for one hundred and seventy pounds sterling, it began to get bigger, for every time the captain returned from a voyage he added a room. From the house his wife would sell the fine silks and other foreign goods her husband brought back. Later the three Styles sisters bought it for six hundred and seventy dollars. The side walls are filled with corncobs for insulation. The interior walls are wainscoted paneling, with cupboards built in.

¶ *Suffield*

HASTINGS HILL (*1737*)

Upon request by letter or phone, if convenient to owner; Mr. and Mrs. Henry M. Clark.

On the outskirts of another lovely old town is this red salt box, furnished and finished with such fine understanding and taste that few similar houses in the state can hold a candle to it. Mrs. Clark, a restoration expert, has collected pieces that museums might envy. If it happens that the owner can let you see it, ask her about the other houses in the neighborhood, which may at least be looked at from outside; she is an authority.

WEST OF THE CONNECTICUT RIVER

Ansonia; Hamden; Northford; Wallingford; Meriden;

Farmington; Weatogue; West Simsbury

¶ *Ansonia*

RICHARD MANSFIELD HOUSE
(1754)
35 Jewett Street; daily 2 to 5, May 15 to October 15; 25 cents; Antiquarian and Landmarks Society.

The builder of this fine old salt box was the first minister of the Episcopal church and made this his parsonage for seventy-two years. It has twenty-four-pane windows, a central chimney, and overhangs.

EZRA DICKERMAN HOUSE
(early eighteenth century)
3217 Whitney Avenue; upon request; Mr. and Mrs. Christopher P. Fredericks and Mr. and Mrs. Edward John Albert, Sr.

Some of the finest paneling and woodwork hereabouts. This excellent example of an early-eighteenth-century Connecticut dwelling is being occupied and preserved with keen appreciation.

¶ *Hamden*

JONATHAN DICKERMAN HOUSE *or* OLD RED HOUSE (1770)
Mt. Carmel Avenue, near park headquarters; Saturday afternoons during summer; Hamden Historical Society; William A. Reynolds (President).

This is something quite special: a one-and-a-half-story central-chimney house with a wide roof overhang which forms an effective and attractive sunshade. It has never been marred by modern improvements. Everything is original, including paint colors and wonderful woodwork.

¶ *Northford*

JONES HOUSE (1700)
Village Street; by appointment, May 1 to December 1; contribution for Wayside Museum, Inc., Clintonville; Mr. and Mrs. W. Spencer Smith.

A fine salt box inside and out, with much heirloom furniture, original paneling of pine, oak, and cherry, original floors and hardware throughout, a Y stairway to the attic, and a fireplace of *black* brick.

WARHAM WILLIAMS HOUSE
(1745–1750)
Middletown Avenue; upon request, May 1 to November 1; Mrs. Victor Schaeffer.

Two stories with a central chimney and an attic overhang, this is said to be an exact copy of Warham Williams's grandfather's house at Deerfield (listed in Massachusetts). It has a cherry-paneled buttery, one of the best entrance doorways hereabouts, and an enchanting stenciled room upstairs. Inside a closet door every painter who has worked on the house has left his

The venerable Nehemiah Royce house at Wallingford has the great stone central chimney and the gable-end overhang so characteristic of Connecticut, also its proper share of history and of interior period attractiveness.

name and date, from before 1792 up to the present.

THE RED HOUSE ON SOL'S PATH
Farm River Valley; by written appointment, July and August; Mrs. Morris E. Alling.

According to the *Connecticut Guide,* "In the early days, when this section was used as a pasture by settlers at the shore, Solomon, a colored man with an Indian wife, made a path of convenience across Totoket Mountain." A handsome old house, with a Dutch-type cantilevered hood above the entrance.

¶ Wallingford

SAMUEL PARSONS HOUSE (*1759*)
180 South Main Street; Sundays 3 to 5 July 1 to September 30, or by appointment (phone: Wallingford 9–5216); Wallingford Historical Society.

Restoration probably completed by now; if so, well worth a visit.

NEHEMIAH ROYCE HOUSE *or* WASHINGTON ELM HOUSE (*1672*)
538 North Main Street; daily 3 to 5, July 1 to September 1; donation; S.P.N.E.A., Helen E. Royce (custodian).

A fine example of a typical Connecticut Valley "leanter," with all furniture from local sources, it has a double-paneled doorway of distinction. It was under the great elm here that Washington paused to bid good-by to the people of Wallingford. He mentioned in his diary the mulberry trees, some of which are still here.

¶ Meriden

MOSES ANDREWS HOMESTEAD (*1760*)
242 West Main Street, west of center on Route 14; Sunday afternoons, 2 to 4; 25 cents; Meriden Historical Society.

Another nice central-chimney salt box, with double overhangs and good interior paneling; but still more noteworthy as a heartening example of a local restoration project, making it a house that will improve as time goes on.

¶ Farmington

Along with Litchfield and Old Lyme, this is one of the three principal parlor towns of Connecticut. Unfortunately only one early house is open to the public, but that is a very early one indeed. Main Street, High Street, and Farmington Avenue are by far the best for old houses.

HILL-STEAD MUSEUM (*1901*)
Farmington Avenue; Wednesday, Thursday, Saturday, and Sunday afternoons 2 to 5, or by appointment (phone: 7–9064); 50 cents; trustees of museum.

This great country mansion of twenty-nine rooms, twelve baths, two pantries, and a "Mount Vernon front," designed by the late Theodate Pope for her parents, is shown as it was when occupied by those wealthy collectors. The house is filled with fine (mostly English) furniture and furnishings—clocks, lusterware, and paintings galore by Monet, Manet, Degas, Whistler, and Cassatt. It attracts about four thousand visitors a year.

STANLEY-WHITMAN HOUSE *or* FARMINGTON MUSEUM (*c. 1660*)
37 High Street; daily 10 to 12 and 2 to 5 except Mondays April 1 to December 1, Fridays and Saturdays 10 to 12 and 2 to 5 and Sundays 2 to 5 December to April; 30 cents and 10 cents; Village Green and Library Association.

You will agree with the Landmarks Society's description of this house as "one of the best preserved 'framed overhangs with drops' in Connecticut." Its medieval character is evident even in its original corpus of hand-worked oak and hardware. The casements are authentic if not original, though the glass panes are old. The restoration was done by the famous architectural authority on old Connecticut houses, the late J. Frederick Kelly, held in high esteem by every serious antiquarian in the country.

THE ELM TREE INN
(built about 1755 around a mid-seventeenth-century house)
Open for guests.

This inn may be the oldest in the country, for it has been doing business here since 1665, when Philip Lewis was the host. The rear ell of the building encloses the ancient part of it. Today it is still a picturesque inn of brick and frame, with the west-end clapboard beaded.

¶ *Weatogue*

This is the Simsbury area, worth investigating.

JONATHAN HUMPHREY HOUSE
(*1720–1723*)
> *Route 10 (College Highway); by request at least 24 hours in advance; Mr. and Mrs. Julian I. Milliman.*

A very good salt box in fine condition and beautifully furnished with early eighteenth-century pieces. The entrance is decorated with pilasters surmounted by rosettes, and the door itself has the Cross paneling characteristic of Connecticut.

¶ *West Simsbury*

ORKIL FARMS (*c. 1781*)
> *Old Farcus Road; by appointment, May 15 to October 1; $1.00 to Antiquarian and Landmarks Society of Connecticut, Mr. Orrin P. Kilbourn.*

The basic structure of the house remains, but many characteristic features have long since been removed, its owner says. It is beautifully furnished, and the total effect is one of great charm, both inside and out. You can't entirely erase the essential personality of such a fine early house. This one is now being treated with the consideration that it deserves.

LEADING UP TO LITCHFIELD

¶ *Danbury*

ST. JOHN HOUSE *or* **SCOTT FANTON MUSEUM** (*pre-Revolutionary*)
> *43 Main Street; Wednesdays and Thursdays 2 to 5, or on request; Danbury Historical Society, Albert Meserve (President).*

This old village mansion is filled with many valuable American antiques of all periods and displays periodical exhibitions of contemporary painting and sculpture.

¶ *Woodbury*

Just before you get to Woodbury, there is Southbury to look at. The two villages are rare antiques in themselves, and there are a dozen early private homes of great worth in the vicinity.

GLEBE HOUSE
(*c. 1690, enlarged 1740*)
> *Hollow Road; daily 10 to 5, Sundays 1 to 5; donation; Seabury Society for Preservation of Glebe House.*

The Glebe House is known as the "birthplace of American Episcopacy" because it was the scene of the election of the first Episcopal bishop in America, Samuel Seabury. It is an engagingly simple house, with gambrel roof, center chimney, and all the original paneling. Many of the furnishings have also always been here, and there are besides many historical pictures and documents. A good place to get local old-house information.

¶ *Litchfield*

Let it be said at once that Litchfield is one of the few truly unspoiled *old* towns in America. Authorities have called it our finest example of a "live" colonial town, which simply means that people are living in and enjoying these houses as much as they did two centuries ago. Through their generosity you are now able to visit some of the finest of these houses—otherwise to be seen only once a year on the October tour sponsored by the Litchfield Junior Republic.

TAPPING REEVE HOUSE AND LAW OFFICE (*1773*)
> *South Street; daily 2 to 5 except Wednesdays June to November, by appointment in winter; 30 cents; Litchfield Historical Society.*

Of Tapping Reeve, Lyman Beecher said after his death, "Oh, Judge Reeve, what a man he was! When I go to heaven and meet him there, what a shaking of hands there will be." Reeve, the son of a Long Island minister and a graduate of Princeton (1763), founded here the first law school in America. The little building that housed the classes now adjoins the house. The beautiful old white house has been restored and furnished with taste and scholarship by the Historical Society.

OLIVER WOLCOTT, SR., HOUSE
(*1753*)

South Street; by appointment, at owner's convenience; Mrs. Frederick W. Sherman.

There are many reasons why this might be called the most interesting house in Litchfield. In addition to its architectural distinction, it happens to be the earliest house in town. Its illustrious first owner was a member of the Continental Congress, a signer of the Declaration, a governor of the state, and many other things; he entertained all the notables of the day, among them Washington. His descendants are still living right here. There are so many things to observe about this house that we will note here only a few: the porch with its Ionic columns supporting a fanlighted pediment; a room in which three walls are sheathed in wide feather-edged boards, one wall horizontal, the other two vertical; and a fine bolection molding over a bedroom fireplace. Since the house has always been occupied by the family, the furniture, as you would ex-

The Tallmadge house in Litchfield, showing the wings with their two-story columns added, it is said, after its first owner's visit with Washington at Mt. Vernon.

pect, is mostly eighteenth-century, handed down. This is not a house to miss.

TALLMADGE HOUSE (*1775*)

North Street; by appointment, at owners' convenience; Mr. and Mrs. C. Van Courtland Moon.

In the early golden era of Litchfield Colonel Tallmadge, late of General Washington's staff, entertained at one time his commander in chief, thereby acquiring for the house one of its more priceless souvenirs—George Washington's signature on a windowpane of what used to be the ballroom. The central part of the gambrel-roofed mansion, with its three dormers, was built of frame in the traditional Connecticut manner by Thomas Sheldon, but Tallmadge (after a visit to Mt. Vernon, it is said) added abbreviated wings at the ends with two-story porticoes, each supported by two slender columns. The unique style has been repeated elsewhere in town, and has come to be known as distinctive of Litchfield.

SEYMOUR HOMESTEAD (*1807*)

South Street; by appointment; Mr. and Mrs. Warren P. Smith.

One of those narrow-clapboarded, simple, but spacious houses for which the town is famous, this was built by Maj. Moses Seymour for his son Ozias, and never left the possession of the family until 1950. The major, a Revolutionary War hero, held the British mayor of New York City as hostage for a time, presumably in his own family house, built in 1735. The mayor aroused a good deal of bad feeling in town, and at one time had to be spirited away to save his life. In thanks for the good treatment he gave the Seymours the first "pleasure carriage" to appear hereabouts. But having gained the family's confidence, he strolled down the street one day and neglected to return.

JULIUS DEMING HOUSE (*1790–1793*)

North Street; on request by letter or phone, May to November, at least a day's advance notice; Mrs. Ludlow Bull.

First called "The Lindens," this house was built by a wealthy merchant who helped finance the Revolution, lost money on his loans, and recouped his losses with his general store and the China Trading Company, in which he was a partner along with

Oliver Wolcott and his friend and neighbor Colonel Tallmadge, aide-de-camp to Washington. In this big white house the handiwork of William Spratt is evident. Originally the house much resembled the more elegant of the foursquare captains' houses seen in many seacoast towns in New England. Square and white, with tall chimneys, quoined corners, and a hip roof balustraded all around, it nevertheless has its unusual Spratt features, such as the pillared entrance, and the heavy eyebrows over the lower windows.

ALEXANDER CATLIN HOUSE (*1778*)

By appointment, at owner's convenience; Mr. and Mrs. Eugene H. Dooman.

The unexpected thing about this house is the widow's walk so far from the sea (though at one time there was here in town the Litchfield China Trading Company, and merchants waxed wealthy from the trade).

CHARLES G. BENNETT HOUSE (*1814*)

East Street; by written appointment, May to November; Mrs. Arthur Goodwin Camp.

This fine brick Federal house stands imposingly on East Hill as you enter town, with its gable end facing the street and an unexpected Palladian window in the gable. The plan here is still essentially Colonial, but the graceful staircase and the mantels show the attenuated detail of the new era.

What makes this house a "must" in a town of such great attractions is the remarkable collection of museum-quality furniture you will find here—most of it seventeenth- and eighteenth-century Connecticut.

CATLIN HOUSE (*c. 1770*)

3 miles east of green on East Chestnut Hill; by appointment (phone: Jordan 7–5310); Mr. William L. Warren.

The owner of this house describes it as "a good farmer's mansion unspoilt . . ." This it is, and though probably built before the Revolution, "like many Connecticut houses it was not finished at once, and the finishing of certain rooms reflects the taste of a later date." The living room and kitchen have fine pre-Revolutionary paneling. One of the rooms has molding and fireplace trim typical of William Spratt, as well as some freehand wall painting which may have been done in the 1780s by a British prisoner quartered here. Its wide doorways, paired window placements, and double overhangs on the gable ends help to make it one of the choicest places to visit in the vicinity.

DAVID WELCH HOUSE (*c. 1754*)

Milton Steading; mid-May to mid-October, by written or phone appointment; Dr. Edward Holman Raymond.

The first owner of this fine salt box was later a major in the Revolution and a close friend of Ethan Allen. They were partners in the iron-ingot business and sold the metal from this house.

You can tell from this picture of the Nathan Hale homestead in winter what a distinct advantage it was to have the whole range of sheds and barn connected to the house under a single roof.

WILLIAM HALL HOUSE
(1758–1760)
Saw Mill Road, Milton Steading; all year round, on written request; Mr. and Mrs. J. R. Busk.

The village of Milton Steading was settled by Litchfield folk about 1740, but some settlers came from towns along the shore, notably William Hall, who came here from Guilford and brought with him certain Guilford building mannerisms—thus linking the two chief architectural localities of Connecticut.

EAST OF THE CONNECTICUT RIVER

¶ Norwich (*on the Thames 15 miles above New London*)

ROCKWELL HOUSE (1818)
42 Rockwell Street; Wednesday afternoons July and August, or by appointment; Faith Trumbull Chapter, D.A.R.

The house, of native-stone blocks quarried on the place, was the home of Maj. Joseph Perkins, a member of the local Committee of Safety. It contains twelve rooms, a separate building for the kitchen, and a large garden. Furnished with early American and Victorian pieces, it features an outstanding collection of china.

NATHANIEL BACKUS HOUSE (1750)
Near Rockwell House; Wednesday afternoons July and August, or by appointment; D.A.R.

The oldest house in the city, it was moved next to the Rockwell House in 1950, with which it is shown in conjunction. It is also furnished as a home of the period.

¶ Colchester (*20 miles up from New London on 85*)

NATHANIEL FOOTE HOUSE (1702)
South side of Norwich Avenue opposite Hayward Street; open by request; Col. Henry Champion Chapter, D.A.R.

A historical museum and chapter house.

¶ Marlborough (*10 miles northwest of Colchester on Route 2*)

MARLBOROUGH TAVERN (1740)
Always open.

¶ Lebanon

GOV. JONATHAN TRUMBULL HOUSE
(1740)
West side of town green; Mondays and Wednesdays 10 to 5, Saturdays 2 to 5, May to November; 25 cents; Connecticut D.A.R.

Built by Joseph Trumbull, father of Jonathan and successful farmer and storekeeper, it was a pretentious mansion for those days. Jonathan Trumbull was the last Governor of the colony and the first of the new state. He was a remarkable man —so resourceful in furnishing supplies to the Revolutionary Army that Washington made him his confidential adviser. Washington's oft-repeated remark in a crisis "We must ask Brother Jonathan" gave rise to the fact that our nation was often personified in those days as "Brother Jonathan" rather than "Uncle Sam." The house in which he was born has been moved a little and, in the process, slightly remodeled. It has nine rooms and an attic. At the head of the stairs is a tiny sentry room. The furnishings, consistent with the period, include a number of Trumbull pieces.

¶ Coventry

NATHAN HALE HOMESTEAD (1776)
South Street; daily 1 to 5, except Sundays, May 15 to October 15; 50 cents; Connecticut Antiquarian and Landmarks Society.

In September of the year in which this fine old fullsized farmhouse was being built by Nathan Hale's father, the unfortunate son was caught in school-teacher's clothes behind the British lines, and suffered the fate of a patriot spy. The house that he did not live to inherit has now become his memorial. It has also been made into one of the most charming house museums in Connecticut. The paneling, the mantels, and the woodwork all through the house show the remarkable refinement and finish for which the early carpenters hereabouts were famous; and the way in which the house is furnished and fitted out by the experts of the Landmarks Society is a tribute to their skill and taste, and a joy to behold. Mary Hale heirlooms here.

One of the finest and most beautifully preserved Greek Revival interiors in America, the double parlor of the Campbell-Whittlesey house in Rochester, is shown at the top of the page; under it is the music room of Rock Hall at Lawrence and, on the opposite page, Schuyler mansion at Albany.

NEW YORK

EVEN before the Revolution, the population of New York was polyglot in character. The colony, while it was still the "New Netherlands" of the Dutch, already contained settlers of a dozen other nationalities. These included, in addition to the Dutch, their neighbors the Walloons, a French-speaking people; the French Huguenots, refugees from religious persecution, who settled on the Hudson at New Paltz as early as 1677; Germans, Swedes, Welsh, Norwegians, and Danes from Northern Europe; and English from England, as well as those from New England, coming by sea to Long Island. It is on record that in 1644 as many as eighteen lan-guages were being spoken in the state!

All these people brought with them memories of the houses they'd come from, and all, naturally, had to adapt their building ideas to the materials and means at hand. So, while the old houses that survive have among them various national accents, the prevailing architec-tural language soon became as English as the common speech, and, like it, the idiom became more and more American. When finally in the nineteenth century an American Romantic Movement got under way, New York provided its two outstanding exponents, A. J. Downing and A. J. Davis, some of whose work is represented here.

121

It is a far cry from the surviving tall Dutch town houses with stepped gables, steep-roofed French farm dwellings, and salt boxes with mossy roofs sweeping to the ground, to the manor houses in the Hudson and Mohawk Valleys—Queen Anne, Georgian, Federal, and Regency. And even further removed in spirit from the early utilitarian dwellings are the multitudinous examples of the Greek Revival fashion, which from 1820 on put record numbers of columns not only on mansions but on farmhouses as well throughout the state. A little later, when romantic aspiration took another and even giddier flight into the Gothic, this state took the lead in the rage for the picturesque, just as it did finally in the Beaux Arts mansions for its millionaires (as will be noted).

IN & OUT OF NEW YORK CITY

Manhattan; The Bronx; Staten Island; Brooklyn; Queens;

Long Island: Lawrence, Oyster Bay, Huntington, South

Huntington, Mastic, St. James, The Setaukets, Cutchogue,

Sag Harbor, East Hampton; Westchester County: New

Rochelle, Eastview, Port Chester, North White Plains,

Scarsdale

¶ Manhattan

FRAUNCES TAVERN (*a restaurant*) (*1719*)

> *Broadway and Earl Streets; daily 10 to 4 except Sundays, Saturdays 10 to 3; Sons of the Revolution in the State of New York.*

Four stories of Georgian Colonial brick nobility denoting the erstwhile nature of the neighborhood, this is the oldest house of distinction still standing on Manhattan. A Dutch note are the dormers sloping from the balustraded roof. Built as the residence of a wealthy Frenchman, Etienne de Lancey, it was purchased and turned into a tavern more than two hundred years ago by Samuel Fraunces, a French West Indian who subsequently became a steward for George Washington. Still an eating place downstairs, it serves upstairs as state headquarters for the Sons of the Revolution, with many Revolutionary exhibits to be seen. It was here that Washington said farewell to his officers in December, 1783.

OLD MERCHANTS HOUSE (*1830*)

> *29 East 4th Street; daily 11 to 5, Sundays and holidays 1 to 5; 50 cents; Historical Landmark Society.*

The "old merchant" who built it was Seabury Tredwell, who lived here until 1865 at a time when this whole part of town was very chic, and when Colonnade Row—around the corner on Lafayette Street—was the most talked-about residential row in the city (half of it still there, at "428"). The entrance doorway of this house in the Late Federal style is something to talk about now, with a richly detailed fanlight and ornamental ironwork newels on the steps. Greek Revival indoors, with plenty of Duncan Phyfe furniture, splendid drapes and carpets, silver hardware, and all kinds of personal belongings from the past.

THEODORE ROOSEVELT HOUSE (*before 1858*)

> *28 East 20th Street; daily 10 to 5 except Mondays, Sundays and holidays 1 to 5; Theodore Roosevelt Association.*

This typical brownstone in which the twenty-sixth President was born represents the next architectural phase of domestic building in the city's march uptown. It is a narrow four-story house with a high stoop and "English basement," with five of its rooms fashionably furnished with Roosevelt family possessions of the Victorian era, when "Teddy" was a boy here. The room in which he was born and the

Jumel Mansion, one of the most distinguished country houses of colonial times, stands handsomely still today in the heart of upper Manhattan.

drawing rooms are much as they were when occupied; others are devoted to museum collections covering his lifelong activities.

JUMEL MANSION (c. 1765)
Edgecomb Avenue and West 160th Street; daily 11 to 5, except Mondays; City of New York.

This was one of the stylish Georgian country "great houses" of its day, and today it still holds its own both inside and out, standing in its small park uptown. Noteworthy features are rusticated board siding with quoins, a beautifully balustraded rooftop, and the first tall, slender classical portico on record in the Colonies. It is really the Col. Roger Morris House; Morris was

a Royalist who fled the country at the outbreak of the Revolution. Washington made it his headquarters during the fall of 1776. For a while it was a fashionable hostelry, until it was bought in 1810 by the wealthy Frenchman, Stephen Jumel, whose widow lived on in it until she died in 1865. She had a brief marriage in the 1830s with Aaron Burr, whose desk is now among the many choice furnishings here.

DYCKMAN HOUSE (1783)
204th Street and Broadway; daily except Mondays; City of New York.

This charming old Dutch farmhouse in its present unfarmlike situation has the easy sweeping rooflines of its Flemish Colonial

Also in Manhattan, finely maintained, is the Dyckman house, a delightful Dutch Colonial farmhouse.

style, creating a long covered front porch, with posts and railings. White clapboards above, white-painted fieldstone walls below, and a little wing at a lower level add up to a pretty and picturesque effect. Filled with furnishings of the time provided by the Dyckman family, which give the house additional interest today.

METROPOLITAN MUSEUM OF ART

Fifth Avenue and 82d Street; daily 10 to 5, Sundays 1 to 5.

The American Wing here contains one of the two largest and finest collections of early American rooms in the country, reassembled here, superbly furnished and displayed.

MUSEUM OF THE CITY OF NEW YORK

Fifth Avenue and 104th Street; daily 10 to 5 except Mondays, Sundays and holidays 1 to 5.

Several rooms of various periods from the city itself.

NEW YORK HISTORICAL SOCIETY

170 Central Park W.; daily 1 to 5 except Sundays, Saturdays 10 to 5.

Three outstanding rooms and their furnishings, of seventeenth- and eighteenth-century New England origin, given by Mrs. Katharine Prentis Murphy and her brother, Edmund Astley Prentis.

¶ The Bronx

VAN CORTLANDT MANOR (*1748*)

Van Cortlandt Park at 242d Street, east of Broadway; daily 10 to 5, Sundays 2 to 5; 25 cents Thursdays, other days free; leased and maintained by National Society of Colonial Dames.

Built to be the country seat of the famous old Flemish family whose name it bears, this great early stone house has for many years now created for countless visitors a vivid impression of well-to-do home life in those distant days. This house has a rugged dignity in comparison with the graceful manners of the Morris-Jumel mansion. It is furnished with appropriate ostentation— English in the formal rooms, Dutch in certain bedrooms, and very delightful Dutch indeed in the cavernous downstairs kitchen.

POE COTTAGE (*1812*)

Grand Concourse and Kingsbridge Road; daily 10 to 5 except Mondays, 10 to 4:30 Sunday afternoons in winter; City of New York, Bronx Society of Arts and Sciences.

The poet came here to what was then the country (!) for his wife's health for a few tragic years in the 1840s; his wife died here, and he left to die in Baltimore. In this simple clapboard cottage, with its long lean-to wing, Poe wrote *The Bells, Annabel Lee,* and some of his best-remembered stories.

BARTOW MANSION (*1820*)

Pelham Bay Park, entrance at East Boulevard and Westchester Avenue; Sundays, 10 to 5; 25 cents; City of New York, headquarters of International Garden Club.

Built by descendants of lords of the Manor of Pelham, this two-story gray-stone mansion is now used as headquarters of the International Garden Club. There are excellent Greek Revival details inside and a lot of fine furniture of the 1830s.

¶ Staten Island

Richmondtown, when it was founded in 1665, was known as "Cocclestown" for the mounds of shells left by the departing Indians. Debased to "Cuckoldtown," it was obliged to change its name for the honor of its menfolk. The forthcoming Richmondtown restoration promises to be one of the outstanding evocations of our earliest history. It will show the evolution of an American village during the seventeenth, eighteenth, and nineteenth centuries—buildings, furnishings, orchards, lanes, and gardens. Most of the houses are to be existing originals, with some reconstructions. The plan includes thirty buildings in all—eight to be left standing where they are and restored, eleven to be moved in from other sections of the island, and twelve replicas. This immense project is scheduled to be completed in 1960, but already a number of houses are open to the public. The Staten Island Historical Society, ensconced in the restored COUNTY CLERK'S OFFICE (1848), at Court and Center Streets, where it is to remain, will be the information center for the restoration; the office will remain a museum for study and display.

STILLWELL-PERINE HOUSE (*1679*)

1476 Richmond Road, Dongan Hills; Sundays 2 to 5 April to November, other times by special appointment with caretaker on premises; 15 cents; Staten Island Historical Society.

This is an interesting and picturesque example of a house put together in progressive stages. The original stone section, built by Thomas Stillwell, Staten Island's first important personage, was augmented about 1710 by Stillwell's son-in-law Col. Nicholas Britton—with a still older stone house brought here from another location. Further additions in 1750, 1790, and 1830 merely add to the total picturesque effect.

VOORLEZER'S HOUSE (*1695*)

Arthur Kill Road opposite Center Street, Richmondtown, daily 10 to 5 except Mondays April through November, open by arrangement with caretaker other times; 10 cents and no charge; Staten Island Historical Society.

"Voorlezer" was the name given by the Dutch congregation to the layman chosen to teach school and conduct church services, and his house was built to be a church, school, and dwelling. This was the first building in the whole country to house an elementary school, and today three rooms are furnished as schoolrooms—one of that earliest period, one of the eighteenth century, and one of the 1840s. There are also a living room and an old Dutch kitchen with early furnishings.

BILLOP CONFERENCE HOUSE (*c. 1680*)

Foot of Hyland Boulevard, Tottenville; daily 10 to 5, except Mondays; Conference House Association.

For more than two and a half centuries the most imposing house on Staten Island, it has beautiful walls of stone masonry two feet thick and a fine rather Dutch pre-Georgian appearance. It was built by a British naval captain named Billop, and during the Revolution, when Staten Island

was in the enemy's hands, Benjamin Franklin, John Adams, and Edward Rutledge came here to discuss terms with the English admiral Lord Howe. As the British terms did not include colonial independence, the conference failed; but it is memorialized in the name of the handsome and historical old house.

¶ Brooklyn

LEFFERTS HOMESTEAD (*1804*)

Near entrance to Prospect Park; Monday, Wednesday, and Friday afternoons; City of New York, Brooklyn Institute of Arts and Sciences.

Peter Lefferts built this ample but simple farmhouse after the British had burned him out during the Battle of Long Island. It was moved here to the entrance of Prospect Park from Flatbush when Peter's descendants gave the old house to the city in 1918. Its roof has the downswept slope of Dutch Colonial. Fittingly furnished.

THE BROOKLYN MUSEUM

Eastern Parkway; daily 10 to 5, Sundays and holidays 1 to 5.

The museum contains sixteen representative rooms, whose dates range from the 1720 paneling in a 1665 Maryland house to the smoking room of the old John D. Rockefeller House in New York City (1884). Between these extremes of taste you will soon find the Schenk-Crook House in its entirety, among the finest surviving homes of the seventeenth century in this country. All five rooms have been transported to the museum from Canarsie Park in Brooklyn, where the house had been standing since 1656.

¶ Queens

BOWNE HOUSE (*1661*)

Bowne Street and Fox Lane; daily, 3 to 5; Bowne House Historical Society.

Farmer John Bowne built this frame house, with its long Dutch dormers, when the settlement was under Dutch rule. He won everlasting fame by defying Governor Stuyvesant's ban against harboring Quakers, for which he was imprisoned and deported. By bringing the unfair edict to the attention of the Dutch governing body he gained religious freedom for the whole

Only a matter of minutes away from Manhattan is Long Island's finest colonial mansion, Rock Hall, at Lawrence.

colony. Quakers continue to worship in the house, and their meeting room, with its huge fireplace, may still be seen here. A couch on which George Fox, founder of the sect, rested while he was here, many of Bowne's possessions, and later acquisitions of the family furnish the house.

KING MANSION (*before 1750*)

> *King Park, Jamaica Avenue, between 150th and 153d Streets; Monday, Wednesday, and Saturday afternoons; village of Jamaica, Rufus King Chapter, D.A.R.*

This country seat of Rufus King, our first Minister to Great Britain, one of the first New York senators, and a member of the Continental Congress, was already an old place when King bought and enlarged it shortly after 1800. The white-shingled house has three stories and an attic. Its chaste portico is Georgian, while its gambrel, like those on some of the early upstate buildings, is Dutch. The house remained in the King family until 1896, when it was acquired, along with its sur-

rounding acres of park, by the village of Jamaica. The D.A.R. has supplied it with furniture, a toy collection, books, and other exhibits.

¶ Long Island

¶ Lawrence

ROCK HALL (*1767*)

> *Daily 9 to 5 except Tuesdays, May 9 to November 1; 50 cents and 25 cents, student groups free by appointment; town of Hempstead.*

This is one of the finest Georgian Colonial houses in the state. Now on the very verge of the metropolis, the imposing three-story white-shingled mansion still sits gracefully in its little park, its gambrel roof crowned by a Chinese Chippendale balustrade. The interior is truly notable, with its eight rooms paneled from floor to ceiling and most of the fireplaces faced with delft tiles. Recently and carefully restored and furnished, the rooms achieve the rare combination of museum perfection and the "lived-in" look. The color here is lovely; particularly fine, too, are the accessories, rugs, drapes, and portraits. Most of the rooms are eighteenth-century; the double drawing room, however, is as of 1810 to go with the woodwork there, whose style was brought up to date for a great wedding celebration in that early Federal year.

¶ *Oyster Bay*

RAYNHAM HALL (*1740s*)
West Main Street; turn north from 25A onto Route 106, to Main Street; Wednesdays, Fridays, and Sundays, 2 to 5; 25 cents; village of Oyster Bay.

Recently restored to its original colonial core, this old farmhouse is famous because of the part played by its first owner, Robert Townsend, called "Culpepper Junior," who was Washington's principal New York spy, in the capture of Major André and the exposure of Benedict Arnold's treachery.

SAGAMORE HILL (*1886*)
Cove Neck Road, off Cove Road from Route 25A; daily 10 to 5, except Tuesdays; 50 cents; Roosevelt Memorial Association.

Built by Theodore Roosevelt, this Edwardian country home, typical of the era, served as a summer White House from 1901 to 1908. It contains countless mementos of one of our most colorful Presidents. A "personality" house.

¶ *Huntington*

CONKLIN HOMESTEAD (*before 1760*)
New York Avenue and High Street; Wednesdays, Thursdays, and Fridays, 2 to 5, by appointment; Huntington Historical Society.

This mid-eighteenth-century house is furnished in that period and in early-nineteenth. It houses the Huntington Historical Society and its reference library on local history.

¶ *South Huntington*

BIRTHPLACE OF WALT WHITMAN (*1810*)
East Side of Route 110 about 1 mile north of Northern State Parkway; Saturdays and Sundays 2 to 5, May 31 to October.

Whitman's father built this two-story shingled farmhouse with his own hands. When Walt was four, the family moved to Brooklyn, where the father became a house builder. Whitman always considered himself an Islander. Eventually, after some wandering, he came back to teach school nearby and founded *The Long Islander,* a famous weekly in its day.

¶ *Mastic*

MANOR OF ST. GEORGE (*1700*)
In park; June 1 to November 30th; estate of Eugenie G. T. Smith.

Sitting in its own park, an original English land grant of 1693 by William and Mary, the manor was the site of Fort St. George and was occupied by the British in the Revolution. Left to the town by the last descendant of the original owners, it will remain intact, with all its heirloom furnishings of two and a half centuries.

¶ *St. James*

THE OLD WOODHULL HOUSE (*before 1719*)
Moriches Road near Setauket; on appointment by letter; Mr. and Mrs. Robert James Malone.

This long, low, shingled, vine-clad dwelling combines all the time-mellowed qualities of these early Island homes. Job Smith, who built it, was the son of Richard Smith (the "Bull-Rider") and patentee of nearby Smithtown.

¶ *The Setaukets*

Inquire about the Open House Day, usually in early September, at the Society for the Preservation of Long Island Antiquities, with headquarters at the Thompson House.

THOMPSON HOUSE (*early eighteenth century*)
In Setauket on North County Road, about 1 mile north of Stony Brook station; Saturdays 1 to 5 and Sundays 2 to 6, May 30 to October 11; 25 cents; S.P.L.I.A.

A very choice Long Island salt box which has been faithfully restored by Mr. and Mrs. Ward Melville. It is furnished with beautiful austerity, for the most part with Long Island furniture of the earliest period.

HAWKINS-MOUNT HOUSE (*c. 1750*)

Gould Road, Stony Brook; by appointment only through Suffolk Museum, Stony Brook.

This simple white frame house was the home of William Sidney Mount, one of our foremost genre artists. He and his brothers Henry and Shepherd, both also talented painters, spent their childhood here and used the familiar and charming scenes of this peaceful countryside by the Sound for their subject matter. The nearby museum contains some of William's and Henry's choice works.

JAYNE HOUSE (*1725*)

Old Post Road, which crosses Route 25A at Bailey Hollow Road, East Setauket; home of Mr. Howard G. Sherwood, not open at present; willed to S.P.L.I.A.

An early shingled house of rare quality, it was built by William Jayne, a chaplain in Cromwell's army and an Oxford graduate. Upon the accession of Charles II to the throne Jayne fled to this country and promptly acquired this property in what is now one of the most serene old sections of Long Island. Mr. Sherwood, a connoisseur, has cherished its early wall painting

in two rooms, possibly the best example of unspoiled freehand wall decoration in America. The woodwork is of museum quality, and so is the furniture.

¶ *Cutchogue*

THE OLD HOUSE (*1649*)

One block west from traffic light on south side of Route 25; weekends 2 to 5 May 30 to July, daily 2 to 5 July and August; 25 cents and 10 cents; Congregational Society of Cutchogue.

As a wedding present to his daughter Anna and her husband, Benjamin Horton moved this house here in 1660 from Southold, ten miles away, where he had built it ten years before. It is one of the best of its early vintage, with four immense fireplaces, and is furnished as befits its medieval style. It should be mentioned here that the moving of early houses, which was a fairly common practice out here on Long Island, as it is in Connecticut and Massachusetts, is made relatively simple when the houses are framed, as these are for the most part, with posts and beams mortised and pegged. The houses are stiff enough to

move all in one piece, and easy to dismantle and reassemble as well.

¶ *Sag Harbor*

OLD CUSTOMS HOUSE (*1789*)

East side of Garden Street; July 4 to October 12, daily 10 to 5, Sundays and holidays 2 to 5; Old Sag Harbor Committee.

Now between the Whaling Museum and the Hannibal French House, this old post-Colonial dwelling originally stood opposite the Whaler's Church. In those days a flag flew over the lean-to, indicating that Mr. Dering's house was not only the customs house for the first port of entry in the State of New York but also the post office. The Derings, father and son, were deep in shipping enterprises, and the latter was at one time a shipping partner of James Fenimore Cooper. The gray-shingled house, weathered and solid, with its two broad chimneys, is just about typical of the way Sag Harbor homes were built in the early days of whaling. Simple and functional, the doorway shows the skill of the ship's carpenters who built it, as do the

various mantels inside; for the original fireplaces are all here, and in the kitchen the old warming ovens and built-in cupboards can be seen. The early-home atmosphere has received real consideration here.

THE HANNIBAL FRENCH HOUSE (*1799 and 1825*)

Main Street; possibly shown on request; vacation home for The Servants of Relief for Incurable Cancer.

Perhaps the loveliest house in Sag Harbor, it was erected by Augustus Howell but later redesigned by Minard Lafever, who is said to have lived here himself for a period. It did not come into the French family until the 1860s. French & Hannibal was the last of the great whaling firms in the town, and its wealth brought gala days to the house. Lafever, according to Talbot Hamlin, "was perhaps the greatest designer of architectural decoration of his time in America." In the ornate exterior of this house and in its exquisite drawing room carving he left the town a legacy to be cherished. Fortunately Charles Edison, former Governor of New Jersey, pur-

In the atmospheric antique seaport of Sag Harbor, the old Customs House at the right is one of the choice early dwellings.

Opposite is the Thompson house at East Setauket, expertly restored and maintained in museum perfection.

chased the house in 1948 and undertook its restoration. His objective is to place the houses he can buy in the hands of those who will collaborate in keeping them unspoiled.

THE WHALING MUSEUM (*1846*)
Main and Garden Streets; daily, June to September.

The Whaling Museum was built as a home for the second of three Benjamin Hunttings and is said to be the work of Minard Lafever also. Lafever had the most able of collaborators in the shipwrights and master builders who executed his designs, and the beauty and elaboration of the Greek ornamentation on this building were brought to flower by skillful craftsmen here as elsewhere in the country. The house, with its great two-story Corinthian columns, was later a Masonic temple. It is fitting that the mansion should be devoted to the display of a fine whaling collection, for it was from that enterprise that the Hunttings derived their fortune.

Beside these places which are regularly open you may see four private homes—not always the same four. Mrs. Lloyd Bassett, Jr., will conduct this little tour for *Guide* readers for a fee of one dollar, provided that she is notified well in advance so that she may be able to make the arrangements with the owners. She recommends an excellent local guidebook, "A Tour of Historic Sag Harbor" (send fifty cents to the Old Sag Harbor Committee to get it), in which some eighty places of historic interest are noted and mapped.

¶ *East Hampton*

HOME, SWEET HOME (*c. 1764*)
Main Street; daily 10 to 12:30 and 1:30 to 5 and Sundays 2 to 5 June through August, daily except Tuesdays September through May; 50 cents; village of East Hampton.

This weathered old shingle salt box, under its high canopy of ancient elms, overlooks one of the prettiest village greens in the country. The chimney wall of a rather sophisticated living room is covered with ecclesiastical paneling. Moldings are emphatic in the parlor and bedrooms, and the construction of the house throughout is "for the ages." Beside the furniture, which is appropriate, the colonial kitchen and the buttery are completely equipped. A very

A portrait of John Howard Payne hangs above the mantel in the paneled parlor of his boyhood home in East Hampton— Home, Sweet Home.

fine collection of lusterware is scattered throughout the house. The old windmill behind the house also contains collections.

MULFORD HOUSE (*late 1600s*)

Next to "Home, Sweet Home" on green; Friday, Saturday, and Sunday afternoons in summer; East Hampton Historical Society, Edward Mulford Baker Strong (Curator).

This remarkable old farmhouse much resembles its next-door neighbor. It was built by an ancestor of Mr. Strong, a gentleman still known hereabouts as "Old Fish Hook" Mulford in reference to his trip to England in 1704 to protest the tax on whale oil: warned to expect pickpockets in London, he providently lined his pockets with fishhooks. His eleven-room, five-fireplace house, very spacious for its time and place, was framed with the timbers of the village church when the church, which had been built in 1650, became too small for its congregation.

¶ *Westchester County*

The Westchester County Historical Society, with headquarters at 626 County Building, White Plains, holds a yearly Open House Day the first week in October. Eight or ten houses are displayed each year in different parts of the county.

¶ *New Rochelle*

PAINE COTTAGE (*c. 1800*)

North and Paine Avenues; daily 2 to 5, except Mondays; Huguenot and Historical Association of New Rochelle.

Thomas Paine, the great pamphleteer of the Revolution, lived in this shingled cottage for a period of three years, off and on.

¶ *Eastview (near Scarsdale)*

HAMMOND HOUSE (*1719*)

Route 100C, near Grasslands Hospital; daily 1 to 5 except Mondays, April 1 to November 1; Westchester County Historical Society, White Plains.

This very early house has the steep roof with overhang, unbroken by dormers, which characterizes the early farmhouses

The Hammond house at Eastview is one of Westchester County's most inviting colonial cottages, a pleasure to visit.

of the neighborhood. Three successive generations of Hammonds, each one a distinguished officer of the militia, were the first three owners here. The family was well known and lived with some style, for the living room is paneled from floor to ceiling on two walls and enriched by pilasters and fine cornices and moldings, probably made in New England. Three of the rooms have been furnished with early Westchester items, and the remainder contain exhibits of interesting miscellany.

¶ *Port Chester*

BUSH HOMESTEAD (*c. 1700*)

479 King Street; Tuesdays, Thursdays, and Saturdays, 1:30 to 4:30; village of Port Chester.

Built by Abraham Bush, a sea captain, this is an interesting Georgian house which became the headquarters of Gen. Israel Putnam in 1777–1778. The bed and desk of "Old Put" are here.

¶ *North White Plains*

WASHINGTON'S HEADQUARTERS
(1738–1770)
Virginia Road; daily 10 to 4, except Mondays (closed in winter); county of Westchester, D.A.R. (custodians).

An unpretentious story-and-a-half farmhouse with a characteristic roofline, this comfortable home that Elijah Miller built was not only Washington's headquarters in the successful Battle of White Plains but subsequently, in 1778 and 1781, that of Generals Lee, Clinton, and Gates. Its secluded position—high yet out of sight of the British—made it serviceable. The floor of the room where Washington slept is now raised several inches by the roots of an ancient sycamore tree which even then gave it shade. The D.A.R. have furnished it as an eighteenth-century farmhouse with some Washington belongings of special interest.

¶ *Scarsdale*

WAYSIDE COTTAGE *(1729)*
1039 Post Road; being restored, open on request; Junior League of Scarsdale (custodians).

One of the eighteenth-century landmarks of Westchester County, this attractive old shingle-and-clapboard cottage, restored by the Junior League of Scarsdale and the D.A.R., was the home of the Varian family, who were driven from it, after serving in the Revolution, by the "skinners and cowboys" (equivalent of gangsters) who infested the area.

UP & DOWN THE HUDSON RIVER VALLEY

Yonkers; Tarrytown; Croton-on-Hudson; Garrison-on-Hudson; Beacon; Fishkill; Poughkeepsie; Pleasant Valley; Hyde Park; Rhinebeck; Staatsburg; Tivoli; Barrytown; Hudson; Kinderhook; Old Chatham; Rensselaer; Troy; Albany; Athens; West Coxsackie; Kingston; Old Hurley; New Paltz; Newburgh; Tappan; Monroe

¶ *Yonkers (15 miles north of Times Square)*

PHILIPSE MANOR HALL
(early and mid-eighteenth century)
Warburton Avenue and Dock Street; Monday to Saturday 9 to 5, Sundays 1 to 5; State of New York; American Scenic and Historic Preservation Society (custodians).

Frederick Philipse was lord of the Manor of Philipseborough, comprising a large part of what is now Westchester County; so, while this manor house is immense, its palatial scale was quite in keeping with the prosperity and importance of the Philipse family. The stone south wing is the earlier, though it must be somewhat later than its given date of 1682 on the evidence of its architectural details, and the brick side wing later still. There may have been an earlier manor house on this spot in which lived the first lord, who died in 1703; for the chances are that the present manor was both built and enlarged by his grandson, the second lord, also Frederick Philipse. In any event, it is one of the truly notable early American houses done in the Georgian manner (or manners). It is certainly the sight to see in Yonkers.

¶ *Tarrytown*

PHILIPSE CASTLE *(a Rockefeller restoration) (1683–1785)*
On Route 9 in North Tarrytown; daily 10 to 5, Sundays 12 to 5; $1.00 and 60 cents, combination ticket with "Sunnyside" $1.60 and $1.00.

The first lord of Philipseborough is said to have started the stone section of this "castle," in the northern part of his vast manorial grant, in the 1680s. The frame

The two main sections of Philipse Castle at Tarrytown—the stone and the frame—were built a hundred years apart.

addition was made in the 1780s, when the building was owned by the wealthy Beekmans. Now the "castle," along with its various dependencies, has been expertly restored in the Rockefeller manner—neither money nor experts spared. It is fitted with rare Dutch and English furniture appropriate to its two widely separated periods. This place and "Sunnyside" together provide a view of three contrasting periods and the ways of life of three prominent American families. Much to be learned here in an easy, entertaining way.

SUNNYSIDE *or* THE WASHINGTON IRVING HOUSE (*a Rockefeller restoration*) (*1835–1859*)

> *Off Route 9 between Irvington and Tarrytown; daily, 10 to 5; $1.00 and 60 cents.*

Three miles from Philipse Castle a much later "castle" has been preserved—the former home of Washington Irving. The Gothic and ultraromantic residence nearly hides what remains of the original old Dutch farmhouse that Irving bought in 1835 as the nucleus for the remarkable remodeling job that he commissioned. The Victorian interior is enchantingly un-

touched and is just as Irving and his sisters occupied it during the nineteenth century, with every evidence of the taste of a cultivated family who could afford to live with a window view of the Hudson.

¶ *Croton-on-Hudson*

VAN CORTLANDT MANOR HOUSE (*a restoration*) (*1665*)

> *John D. Rockefeller, Jr.*

This is a major restoration of one of the most important of the early Hudson River houses, built by Van Cortlandts and occupied by them until 1940—or more than two and a half centuries. Commanding a broad expanse of the lordly river, it was originally of fortress construction and was used as a refuge from the Indians. When ready, this will be one of the most important house museums on the Hudson.

¶ *Garrison-on-Hudson*

MANDEVILLE HOUSE (*1737*)

> *Four Corners; open on written request in late summer and fall; Miss Nancy Allan.*

One of the most ingratiating houses on the Hudson, it was begun by Jacob Mandeville, grandson of a Dutch immigrant who arrived here from Holland in 1659. The original house was two rooms with an attic; next came the kitchen wing; then, still before the Revolution, a parlor was added, with a bedroom above to accommodate the family. The library was added in 1850. The ecclesiastical paneling of the chimney wall in the oldest part, now the dining room, is of a rare quality and is repeated in the doorway, reminding us that the first church services in the vicinity were held here in the fall of 1770 and were continued regularly until a church was built. Other rooms are paneled as well, and there are built-in cupboards throughout the house. Since it was on an important highway between the southern part of Connecticut and West Point, Mandeville House was an overnight stop for many of the Revolutionary generals, among them Washington himself, and it was General Putnam's headquarters from May until October (his wife died here).

¶ Beacon

Edwin R. Corwin, Beacon historian, will be glad to give assistance in the vicinity. He is familiar with all the houses and with many of the owners.

BRET-TELLER HOUSE (1709)
Van Nydeck Avenue; vacant now but restoration in progress; D.A.R.

Dutch Colonial in feeling, with some of the walls covered with the original round-headed cedar shingles, this house is a good example of an early gambrel. Catharyne and Roger Brett built it, and their descendants lived in it until after 1940.

DE WINDT-BOGARDUS HOUSE (c. 1790)
16 Tompkins Avenue; open by request; Mr. and Mrs. Carl E. Cummings.

This attractive early Dutch cottage was built on Peter de Windt's estate for a relative. The de Windt House itself is long since gone, destroyed by fire, as was the famous Verplanck House. This is the third oldest house in town, and has been continuously occupied. The present owner has done a faithful job of restoration even while incorporating modern requirements and can furnish voluminous lore that does much to bring the old house back to life.

¶ Fishkill
(*just above Beacon*)

HENDRICK KIP HOUSE (1753)
On north side of road from Beacon, near Fishkill; preferably by written appointment, May 1 to November 1; Mr. Wilbur John Hammond.

This much-written-about house is a fine example of the early Dutch stone dwellings of the Hudson Valley. Except for an extension on the rear, its one and one half stories stand much as they looked when the place was built. It is thought by some that its builder James Hussey may have erected the east section as early as 1720. Baron von Steuben made his headquarters here while he was training the raw recruits in the area for Washington's army.

COL. JOHN BRINKERHOFF HOUSE (1738)
East of Fishkill and south of road to Hopewell; by written appointment; Mrs. Eleanora M. Lagerholm.

With one of the purest examples of a Dutch exterior of the early period in the Hudson Valley, it has only recently been restored. Its new owner assures us that it is unchanged, except for a modern kitchen. It is another of the houses that Washington slept in. The motherly colonel's lady is said to have tucked him in snugly on cold nights. Mrs. Lagerholm plans to furnish the house in period.

VERPLANCK-VAN WYCK HOUSE or CRYSTAL SPRING MANOR (1768)
Fishkill Plains; on request; Mrs. E. B. Stringham, Sr., R.F.D. Wappingers Falls (phone: Hopewell Junction 6-2542).

This great brick house, high, wide, and handsome, was built by wealthy Philip Verplanck, Jr., owner of a prosperous nearby gristmill and landing on Wappingers Creek. Philip improved his fortunes further by marrying the daughter of Burgher Gerard Beekman. The gambrel roof was a not uncommon feature of the brick manors in this section, but the balustrade and circular window in the gable are decorative notes not seen as frequently.

¶ *Poughkeepsie* (*on Route 9, 17 miles above Beacon*)

CLINTON HOUSE (*1765, rebuilt 1783*)
    549 Main Street; daily 9 to 5, Sundays 1 to 5; State of New York.

The original house, reputedly the headquarters of Gov. George Clinton during the Revolution, was burned in 1782. But the very next year Washington, out of respect for Clinton, ordered artisans from the Temple Hill camp to rebuild the house, at which time it was enlarged. A fieldstone home typical of the Hudson Valley, simple and solid, it is furnished with museum objects today as a memorial to the state's first governor.

LOCUST GROVE (*1827, augmented 1850 and again in 1901*)
    370 South Road; by appointment; Miss Annette I. Young.

This is one of the countless houses designed by Alexander Jackson Davis, whose notable career in architecture occupied more than half of the nineteenth century. It is also one of his best-known works, partly because it was bought by Samuel F. B. Morse with the first money he received from his invention of the telegraph. Morse remodeled it in 1850, and Miss Young's father made the final addition in the same style. It contains many fine Early American antiques.

GLEBE HOUSE (*1767*)
    635 Main Street; being restored by Dutchess County Historical Society and Junior League, open by written request and several afternoons weekly; city of Poughkeepsie.

A small brick building with one dormer whose first occupant was the Rev. John Beardsley, exiled in 1777 because of Loyalist sympathies. The house was built in three stages, and each of the rooms downstairs is being furnished as nearly as possible in the period in which it was built.

¶ *Pleasant Valley*

BRICK HOUSE FARM (*1777*)
    On written request only; Mr. and Mrs. Edwin H. Keith.

As an example of how a woman can pass the time when her husband is "off to the wars," Brick House Farm was built by Sophia Newcomb while husband Zaccheus was serving in the Revolution. Sophia's slaves made the brick for her house, which she constructed handsomely with a sweeping gambrel, ample windows, and charming details of cornice and entrance. Near the house, where the slaves dug out the clay, she made a duck pond. When Zaccheus returned, it is said he was astonished to find this delightful Georgian mansion, with his initials formed in the west wall by the ends of the beam anchors. Four spacious rooms downstairs are built around a wide hallway with Dutch doors at either end. Each of the rooms has its corner fireplace, and the woodwork throughout is of the first quality.

¶ *Hyde Park* (*on Route 9, 4 miles above Poughkeepsie*)

ROOSEVELT HOME (*1826*)
    Daily 10 to 5, except Mondays; 25 cents; National Historical Site.

This famous country seat, built in the year of Jefferson's death, has undergone many changes, adapting itself to the needs and tastes of the important family that grew up here. Basically it is a big Federal mansion, now just as it was while a Presidential home. F. D. R. was born here January 30, 1882, and buried here April 15, 1945. His parents bought it in 1867, and the house reflects their tenure—but with all the added memorabilia of a great man whose aura will always pervade it.

VANDERBILT MANSION (*1895–1898*)
    West side of Route 9; daily 9 to 5, except Mondays; small fee; National Park Service.

Not an Early American house by any means, but, like "The Breakers" at Newport and "Biltmore" at Asheville, affording not-to-be-missed opportunity to see the heights of a sumptuous magnificence which unlimited wealth can achieve. Although pleasing and enlightening, it is far from equalling McKim, Mead and White's best houses, though it may be their biggest. The Vanderbilt who built this was Frederick, brother of Cornelius, of "The Breakers," and George, of "Biltmore."

¶ *Rhinebeck (on Route 9, 5 miles above Staatsburg)*

GENERAL MONTGOMERY HOUSE
(before 1773)
East Livingston Street; daily, courtesy of caretaker; Chancellor Livingston Chapter, D.A.R.

This is the cottage in which the general and his wife lived while they were building "Grasmere," two miles to the south, which burned before it was finished. Montgomery captured Montreal in 1777 only to lose his life in the assault on Quebec. The cottage contains some good pieces of furniture donated by chapter members through the years.

THE BEEKMAN ARMS *(an inn)* *(1700)*
Route 9.

Open all the time as a comfortable, commodious hostelry, it began as a one-story, two-room stone house. Its enlargement began in 1769. There were later additions as trade became more brisk, but the old part still preserves its original character.

¶ *Staatsburg (on east bank above Hyde Park)*

THE MANSION *(1830 and 1895)*
Ogden and Ruth Mills Memorial Park, near Staatsburg; daily, 11 to 4:30; 30 cents and 10 cents.

A sixty-five-room palace built by the late Ogden Mills in what is now a two-hundred-acre memorial park near the town. The setting is fabulous, and the mansion is completely furnished as it was during the Mills' occupancy, with antiques, paintings, sculpture, Gobelin tapestries, and many other works of art. The furniture is chiefly Louis XV and XVI. Some of the furnishings belonged to the owner of the original house and great-grandfather of Ruth L. Mills, Morgan Lewis, who served in the Revolution and was the third Governor of New York State. The first house (1795) burned in 1832. The new one built here forms the central section of the present mansion, the wings having been added and the whole remodeled for the Mills family by Stanford White in 1895.

¶ *Tivoli (10 miles above Rhinebeck on the river)*

CALLENDAR HOUSE *(1794)*
On written request; Mrs. William H. Osborn.

This impressive old country seat has one of those breath-taking views of the valley for which the Livingston houses are fam-

Montgomery Place, near Barrytown on the Hudson, set in its velvety green park, has much of the charm of a minor French chateau.

Callendar House, near Tivoli on the Hudson, like a great Regency villa, looks out across the lordly river.

ous. Choosing this choice spot for his house, Henry G. Livingston built it and sold it at once to his cousin Philip, who named it "Sunning Hill." In 1860 it was repossessed by John Livingston, who gave it the present name. When first built, it was a manor house of stately proportions, with a hipped roof crowned by a broad, flat cupola. It had one-story wings originally, but they were apparently raised about 1830, when the portico was added to the west front, to create a classical colonnade of twelve Doric columns, giving the place the look of a great Regency villa. Other features are virtually unchanged, and it is furnished with many Livingston heirlooms.

¶ *Barrytown*

MONTGOMERY PLACE

(between 1802 and 1805)
On written request when owner can arrange to show; Gen. and Mrs. John Ross Delafield.

In the history of the Hudson Valley the name of Livingston bulks larger than any other, and so too did their lands. Montgomery Place is one of many mansions built by this family that literally dominated the valley for a century or more,

and some of whose descendants are still living today in the homes. In this case it was Janet Livingston, the daughter of the great Chancellor and the widow of General Montgomery, the hero of Quebec, who built the house. She and her husband had begun to build their home near Rhinebeck when the news of his death caused her to abandon the house, which burned. Later she built Montgomery Place, overlooking one of the finest views the majestic river affords. In 1844 the north pavilion, west veranda, and south wing were built; further ornamentation was added in 1860, and today it resembles nothing so much as a charming French château, set in its spacious green park. However, the interior is virtually unchanged, and the stately rooms contain nothing but the heirlooms of an illustrious family, many of the pieces purchased by the widow Janet when it was built. Not the least interesting things to see in this mellow house are the fine family portraits.

Nearby is EDGEWATER (1820), still another Livingston house, with a library by A. J. Davis, now owned by Gore Vidal, the novelist. It is one of the outstanding Federal-style houses of the valley, with a most impressive two-story Doric portico.

¶ *Hudson (on Route 9, 25 miles above Rhinebeck)*

OAK HILL

(*between 1790 and 1800*)
On written request at owner's convenience, summer months only; Mrs. Herman Livingston, R.D. 2.

The first manor house of the Livingstons stood scarcely more than a mile from here; built in 1699, it burned in 1800. "Oak Hill" was built by John, one of the sons of the last lord of the manor, who selected for himself one of the choicest bluffs along the length of the Hudson, with a view of the blue Catskills, rising beyond the opposite bank. The character of the Late Federal brick house has been somewhat altered by the later addition of a mansard roof and a veranda. However, within the high-ceilinged rooms all is much as it has been since John Livingston built it, for his great-grandson's wife is still residing here. The furniture which Duncan Phyfe made in his shop in New York especially for the drawing room, richly ornate in design, is placed where it has always been. Magnificent mementos of the China trade, fine carpets, family silver, and portraits of the first lord and his lady make this a Livingston house which breathes the history of the English family whose fortunes were identified with their great landholdings on the Hudson.

¶ *Kinderhook (on Route 9J, 12 miles above Hudson)*

HOUSE OF HISTORY (*1810*)

Route 9 (Main Street); daily 10 to 5 except Sundays June to November, other months by request to James E. Leath (residence across street); Columbia County Historical Society.

Built for James Vanderpoel by Barnabas Waterman, its most talented architect, this is one of the Hudson Valley's loveliest brick Federal houses. Not the least of its many charms are its livable scale and its elegance of detail. The color of the brick is a mellow russet. Marble arches frame the fanlight of the entrance door, a delicate white railing ornaments the roof, and four well-proportioned chimneys top off an exterior of real distinction. The interior is also consistently fine. The hallway is one of the best in the state. The arch at the foot of the exceptionally graceful staircase is flanked by delicate fluted pilasters of the Corinthian order. The beauty of these flat arches, which Waterman designed so successfully, can best be appreciated here in the hall. The house is furnished as exquisitely as it is designed, fortunately having been restored by Mr. Leath, a perfectionist who understood its rare quality. The furniture, portraits, and accessories make it one of the most satisfying small house museums in the country.

¶ *Old Chatham (a few miles east of Kinderhook)*

SHAKER MUSEUM

(*eighteenth century*)
May to November; Shaker Museum Foundation, Mr. H. Phelps Clawson (phone: Old Chatham 5271).

Here in the eighteenth century the Shakers set up their largest and most significant colony. A carpentry shop, a forge, the medicine-making room, and the weaving room are now on view, as well as typical rooms occupied by the brothers and sisters. A very fine collection of their furniture, notable for its beauty and simplicity of design, can be admired here. Considered by connoisseurs to be American craftsmanship at its most clean-cut and functional, this furniture and the other articles of household furnishings and equipment here have a beauty all their own.

¶ *Rensselaer (across from Albany)*

FORT CRAILO (*1704*)

Riverside Avenue; daily 9 to 5, Sundays 1 to 5; State of New York.

This rare old residence of the Rensselaers was built in two sections fifty years apart, the earlier serving double duty as a fort, as shown by its gun ports. It has been carefully restored by the state, and illustrates inside and out how the great Dutch landowners lived here in the eighteenth century. The old brick walls are laid in English bond, with headers of brick laid obliquely over the narrow windows and doors. The windows have leaded diamond panes, and the roof is tile. The furniture is for the most part regional and includes

The dining room of the House of History at Kinderhook is notable for the finish and perfection of its furnishings.

One of the great early brick houses of the state, Fort Crailo was built to serve both as a home and as a place of refuge.

many fascinating Dutch pieces. The house has been popularly linked to "Yankee Doodle" by a story which has it that a British Army surgeon staying here invented the words of that immortal ditty as he watched the raw colonial recruits tramp by. It was, of course, derisive, but the "Yankee Doodles" picked it up and made it the most popular marching song of the Revolution. Ask the way here to the nearby JAN BRIES HOUSE (1723), which is not open but still of interest from the outside.

¶ Troy (on east bank 5 miles above Albany)

CLUETT HOME (1827)
> 59 2d Street; daily 11 to 5, probably not on Sundays; 35 cents; Rensselaer County Historical Society.

The arched doorway and lintels of this delightful brick Federal town house are trimmed with contrasting sandstone, which along with the balustrade which edges the eaves and the round-headed dormers, all adds up to a sprightly appearance. The interior is even more debonair. A stairway of remarkable grace rises from a broad hall whose scenic paper has fortunately been preserved. One of the many fanciful features of the house is the repetition of the overdoor fanlight at every possible opportunity.

¶ Albany

SCHUYLER MANSION or
THE PASTURES (1762)
> Southwest corner Clinton and Schuyler Streets; daily 10 to 5, Sundays 1 to 5; State of New York, maintained by State Education Department.

This is one of the great Georgian houses of this country, with walls of beautifully patterned brick topped with a delicate balustrade of the Chinese Chippendale pattern. Built by young Philip Schuyler, later to become an outstanding Revolutionary general, a member of the Continental Congress, and an adviser and friend of Washington's, the house sits on its high knoll as handsome as ever, with its interior strikingly and elegantly restored—carved mantels, dignified paneling, and all the panoply of colonial wealth and position. In its south-

east drawing room Elizabeth Schuyler was married to Alexander Hamilton, only one of the countless colorful occasions which brought here at one time or another practically every notable of the day.

TEN BROECK MANSION (1798)
> 9 Ten Broeck Place; daily 3 to 4, other times by appointment; 35 cents, no charge Mondays; Albany County Historical Association.

It had to be an imposing house, for its owner, Gen. Abraham Ten Broeck, was a hero of the Battle of Saratoga and thrice Mayor of Albany. A big brick mansion with fine Georgian features, four great chimneys, and a balustraded roof, it breathes the solidity, the concern with good living that the wealthy Dutch descendants imparted to their surroundings. A certain sober splendor marked their homes, and this effect has been preserved here both without and within.

¶ Athens (just above Catskill on the Hudson)

VAN LOON HOUSE (c. 1812)
> 385 Franklin; on written or phone request (Hudson 8–6932); preferably warm-weather months; Mr. and Mrs. Eugene M. Van Loon.

This beautiful Federal mansion was designed by the talented Barnabas Waterman who built the House of History at Kinderhook. This one has, among other interesting features, a large oval ballroom with brick-red walls and white trim. The village was settled in 1686 by Jan Van Loon, and two other Van Loon houses still stand: a one-story house of 1724 at the north limits of the town, and a solid field-stone house with a gabled Dutch roof (1706) at the foot of Washington Street.

¶ West Coxsackie (on Route 385, 18 miles below Albany)

PIETER BRONCK HOUSE (1663, brick addition 1738)
> On west side of Route 9W; daily 9 to 5:30, June to October 15; donation; Greene County Historical Society.

Of stone and brick, with casements and early-Dutch-style gable ends, the house was built by the only son of Jonas Bronck, who settled in Westchester County in 1639, and

Chaste as only a fine Federal dwelling can be, the Van Loon house is one of the loveliest landmarks on the west bank of the Hudson River.

after whom the Bronx was named. It is actually three connecting houses, one of which was built in 1800 when a daughter refused to live under the original roof with her stepmother. In the oldest part are two large rooms with heavy-beamed ceilings, great fireplaces, and wide floorboards. The doors have all their handmade hardware, including the knockers. The fortresslike loopholes upstairs were to be used in case of Indian attack. Bronck furniture from the seventeenth down to the nineteenth century includes Revolutionary silver, fine paintings, and a rare early Bible.

¶ *Kingston (on Route 9W, 23 miles below Catskill)*

VAN LEUVEN MANSION (*1784, addition 1795*)

Main and Wall Streets; Thursdays and Saturdays, 10 to 5 (closed February and March); Fred J. Johnston.

One of the choice Federal houses of the Hudson Valley, this was built by John Suydam, an early Senator, whose portrait, by John Vanderlyn, hangs over the living-room mantel. Among the many treasures in this house, the Waterford chandelier in this room and the carpet which once graced the home of Duncan Phyfe are outstanding. The mahogany dining room is furnished in American Hepplewhite, with a sideboard that belonged to the first governor of Vermont; the library is Philadelphia Chippendale, with a serpentine

secretary made by John Goddard, of Newport, about 1760. Mr. Johnston sells antiques in his shop nearby; his knowledge of the neighborhood is extensive.

OSTERHOUDT HOUSE
(*1688 and 1740*)

Neighborhood Road off Route 9W, 3 miles from Kingston; by arrangement with Mrs. Charles S. Dana (phone: Kingston 7349W); Rev. Anita Trueman Pickett (owner).

A long, low stone dwelling with five dormers, painted white, it was built by three successive generations of the Dutch family of this name. The beams, among the largest known to experts in these parts, measure eighteen by ten and a half inches, and are set in the stone wall. A grandson of the first builder placed a 1740 date stone in the east end. It is furnished simply, in keeping.

SENATE HOUSE (*1666 or 1676*)

Clinton Avenue and Front Street; daily 9 to 5, Sundays 1 to 5; State of New York.

Very snug and full of character, it had its moment of history too. In September 1777 Kingston was temporarily the state capital by the fortunes of war, and the Senate convened in this house, then owned by Abraham Van Gaasbeek. A few days later the British burned the town, but the old stone dwelling was hardly scorched.

¶ *Old Hurley*

Old Hurley is unique in its aggregation

of unspoiled old Dutch houses built of the native stone. The owners of ten of them open them yearly under the auspices of the Old Hurley Dutch Reformed Church (itself built in 1790), usually the last week in July on a Saturday, for a modest fee. The essential character of these houses has been carefully preserved by their owners, and you will find them full of unexpected treasures. Probably nowhere else will you get a better idea of what a Dutch village in America actually looked like at that time.

JAN VAN DUESEN HOUSE (*1723*)
By written request; Mrs. Ruth C. Waterbury, Hurley.

The governing body of New York State met and hid their records in a secret room here after the British burned Kingston in 1777. Built flush with the street, like so many others in the Dutch towns hereabouts, it has the usual roofline meeting the wall not far above the twenty-four-pane first-story windows. Four dormers swoop down from the peak of the gable almost to the edge of the roof. The stone is light in color and uneven in texture; it typifies the best in this sturdy style of building.

Others to note here are the OLD GUARD HOUSE (1745), where David Taylor, a British spy, was imprisoned, a tiny stone house with one dormer and a scalloped bargeboard trimming the steep gable ends of the roof; THE SOJOURNER TRUTH HOUSE (1750), with its five dormers, the birthplace of the Negro evangelist whose name the house bears and whose religious influence was so marked hereabouts; and THE PARSONAGE (1790), with its clapboarded gable over the front porch.

¶ *New Paltz (on Route 32 16 miles below Kingston)*

New Paltz, on the banks of the Wallkill River, is one of the most picturesque towns in the country. Its Huguenot Street looks almost exactly as it did in the early part of the eighteenth century, and the low fieldstone houses with their steep-pitched roofs are much like the medieval farmhouses the Walloons left behind them in Pfalz, on the banks of the Rhine. They came to escape the religious persecution of Louis XIV, some

Washington lived longer here in the Hasbrouck house at Newburgh than in any other of his many Revolutionary headquarters; a house with much architectural interest as well.

The old stone Huguenot houses of New Paltz make this one of the most enjoyable villages in the state to visit.

of them establishing themselves at Hurley and others settling here. Four of these houses stand in their original state, and there are two others of equal interest and antiquity. A tour, called "Stone House Day" and sponsored by the Dutch Reformed Church, is held from time to time, on which occasion some of the homes described below may be visited. Mr. Kenneth E. Hasbrouck, the guiding spirit here, will arrange for special visits to private homes in the vicinity if notified in advance.

JEAN HASBROUCK HOUSE, *now* MEMORIAL HOUSE (*1712*)
> *Daily, 9 to 12 and 1 to 4; Huguenot Patriotic Historical Society.*

This is one of the bright gems of this old Huguenot settlement; of stone, of course, sharply gabled and low-eaved.

COL. JOSIAH HASBROUCK HOUSE (*1814*)
> *Gardiner, south of New Paltz on Route 32; Open afternoons 1 to 5, June until Labor Day; donation for Huguenot Historical Society of New Paltz; Miss Annette I. Young (owner), Mr. Kenneth E. Hasbrouck (custodian).*

Formerly known as "Locust Lawn," it was built by Josiah Hasbrouck, a colonel in the Revolution who served in the House of Representatives before 1800. It is said that the reason he moved from the Jean Hasbrouck House (Memorial House) in New Paltz is because he feared the village might

prove too gay for his only son Levi. His daughter, however, continued to live in that house after her marriage to Josiah Du Bois. Miss Young, the present owner, is a direct descendant of Josiah.

¶ *Newburgh (on Route 9W, 16 miles below New Paltz)*

HASBROUCK HOUSE *or* WASHINGTON'S HEADQUARTERS (*1750–1770*)
> *Liberty and Washington Streets, in a park; Monday through Saturday 9 to 5, Sundays 1 to 5; State of New York.*

Famous as the headquarters in which Washington remained for sixteen months, his longest continuous residence during the war. Here he established the Order of the Purple Heart and wrote his letter of advice to the governors of the states that were forming, and from here he finally announced the end of hostilities. A steep-roofed stone house with tall chimneys, it was built in three stages, which contributes to its present attractiveness. Washington's staff was quartered on the second floor. The house was returned to the widow Hasbrouck after Washington's departure. Nearby is a museum containing many Washington items.

GENERAL KNOX HEADQUARTERS *or* JOHN ELLISON HOUSE (*1734–1754*)
> *4 miles south on 94; weekdays 9 to 5, Sundays 1 to 5; State of New York.*

Five miles from Washington's Headquarters at Vail's Gate on a fifty-acre tract of land, is a comely colonial fieldstone house with a low wooden wing, whose rusticity is unusually pleasing. Its two small dormers, fine roofline, and twenty-four-pane windows give its plainness plenty of style. The fireplace mantels and woodwork are of unusually excellent quality, and the house is now being furnished with good period pieces. Mrs. Knox, who was noted for her hospitality, kept "open house" here for the officers encamped at Temple Hill.

¶ *Tappan (on Route 303 at New Jersey line)*

DE WINDT HOUSE, now GEORGE WASHINGTON MASONIC SHRINE (*1700*)
1 mile west of Route 9W; daily, 10 to 4; Grand Lodge, Free and Accepted Masons of New York.

This early brick and stone house was restored after many vicissitudes as nearly as possible to its original state when Washington occupied it as headquarters during the darkest days of the Revolution. Here the general signed the death warrant for Major André, who was hanged nearby.

THE 1776 HOUSE (*an inn*) (*1776*)
Tuesday through Sunday, 9 to 11; Russell and Robert Killoran.

This tailored stone house, with four chimneys, was Major André's place of confinement during his trial for treason, and from it he went to be hanged on October 2, 1780. It was an inn even then. Interesting eight-paneled shutters on the lower windows.

¶ *Monroe (on Route 17, 10 miles west of Bear Mountain)*

OLD MUSEUM VILLAGE OF SMITH'S CLOVE
1 mile west on Route 17; daily 10 to 5, May to November; $1.00 and 50 cents (groups less); Roscoe W. Smith.

This remarkable collection of old country buildings has been the hobby of Mr. Smith for many years. It now contains more than twenty structures, including many varieties of shops and country stores, log cabins, and farm structures, each housing collections of equipment, utensils, tools, and early machinery—a complete education in the early American rural utilities of a century or more ago.

THE MOHAWK VALLEY & VICINITY

Amsterdam; Constableville; Cooperstown; Johnstown; Little Falls

¶ *Amsterdam*

FORT JOHNSON (*1749*)
Fort Johnson Village, 3 miles west of Amsterdam on Route 5; daily 1 to 5 April to November, weekdays 10 to 5 July and August; Montgomery Historical Society.

Superintendent of Indian Affairs for the Crown Sir William Johnson lived in baronial state with his Indian wife, Molly Brant, in this great foursquare stone mansion with its tall chimney, hipped roof, and staggered dormers. Now a vine-covered house looking nothing like a fortress, it was surrounded by a high stockade during the French and Indian War. The Indians, however, trusted Sir William, and his power over them was said to be greater than that of any other white man. Here were held Mohawk and Iroquois powwows, at which the red men were liberally entertained. The

paneling and all the mantels except one are the originals. An invoice shows that woodwork, as well as glass and hardware, were imported from London. The two great halls, living room, dining room, and two bedrooms are furnished; some of the pieces belonged to Sir William, and the rest are of the same early period, except for the Sheraton dining room. The third floor and four small rooms are devoted to Indian displays—a large and significant collection.

GUY PARK MANOR (*1773*)
336 West Main Street; daily and Sunday afternoons; Amsterdam Chapter, D.A.R.

Built by Sir William for his daughter Mary and her husband and cousin Col. Guy Johnson, who not only inherited his uncle's great fortune but also his widespread influence with Indians; he was appointed superintendent of them in Sir William's place. The house has lost much of its character, both inside and out, by the reconstruction of the roof and cornice in 1848 and of the wings in 1858. The interior trim is typical Greek Revival now.

¶ *Constableville (on Route 26, 24 miles north of Rome)*

CONSTABLE HALL (*1810–1819*)

Route 26; daily 10 to 5 except Monday, Sundays 1 to 6, June to November; 50 cents and 25 cents; Constable Hall Association.

Remote and unspoiled in its beautiful country setting, the house itself is virtually as it was when occupied by William Constable. Of gray cut stone, its two bays bracket a pedimented portico with tall columns, and a similarly generous scale and simplicity of detail mark the interior. Much of the original Constable furniture is still here. The library and family papers are of great interest, since they concern the development of a tract of four million acres purchased in part by Constable's Dublin grandfather, Dr. John, who came here in 1754—the largest land transaction ever to be made in the state.

¶ *Cooperstown (60 miles west of Albany on Otsego Lake)*

FARMER'S MUSEUM AND FENIMORE HOUSE

1 mile north of town on 80 between lake road and lake; daily 9 to 6 May through October, winter Mondays and Fridays 9 to 5; 80 cents and 12 cents; New York Historical Association.

In the words of its administrator and one of its chief architects, Louis C. Jones, "Fenimore House and the Farmer's Museum tell the story of life as it was lived by the average citizen in the years between the close of the Revolution and the Civil War." In Fenimore House, a stately replica of a Georgian mansion, the story is told by "the artists who reported the world around them," and the place also contains an outstanding collection of folk art. In the numerous buildings of the Farmer's Museum "the rural life of the earlier period is re-created in as many ways as possible." In this group stands an immense stone barn which contains a number of living exhibits; for instance, you can see the whole process of weaving, from the braking of the flax to the spinning of the cloth. The other buildings comprise a small cross-

The way the two front bays of Constable Hall advance to embrace the entrance portico recalls a similar feature of the Langdon-Cole house in Castleton, Vermont.

roads village: the country store, the doctor's office, the school, the print shop, the tavern, and the homestead. And as an indication of how credulous these folk were, there is the Giant of Cardiff, the great hoax that fooled some of the wisest minds of the 1860s. It was carved by a Chicago stonecutter, buried in the ground, and unearthed by well diggers. Some thought there had been giants in our land!

THE LIPPIT HOMESTEAD is of particular interest; for not only has painstaking research made this as nearly as possible like a comfortable upstate farmhouse of the period, but the actual uses of the household equipment are shown here. A young woman comes daily to occupy herself with a typical farm routine. She bakes bread or beans in the beehive oven in the back of the huge fireplace, in which a roast may be turning on the spit. She collects fat for burning in the Betty lamps, churns, makes cheese, or dyes yarn in the back yard. Flax, broom, and Indian corn are grown in the nearby fields, as they must have been, and you may hear the lowing of oxen or the cry of the guinea hens and peacocks nearby. All is as it was, as if time had really stood still here since 1800.

BUMP TAVERN was built at the end of the eighteenth century. In 1844 the front was remodeled, the roof raised, and the four Ionic columns added, as well as the second-story gallery with its fine railing. It was a drover's tavern originally, standing on the old Catskill Turnpike at Windham,

seventy-five miles away from its present site. It was moved here in six huge pieces.

At Fenimore House you can obtain a "talk sheet" and map which will guide you through the town itself, which is full of fascinating architecture and associations. For special houses, see Mrs. Jones.

¶ *Johnstown (on Route 67, 11 miles west of Amsterdam)*

JOHNSON HALL (*1761–1762*)
Hall Avenue; daily 9 to 5, Sundays 1 to 5; State of New York.

In 1760 Sir William built himself another mansion, leaving the fort, nine miles distant, for his son Sir John, whose lands were later confiscated because of his Tory sympathies. Johnson Hall, whose much greater pretentions better fitted Sir William's growing importance, is a large two-story white frame dwelling whose rusticated siding and heavily dentiled cornices over windows and under eaves give it the elegant severity Sir William wanted. Lemuel Baker, the housewright, was brought from Schenectady to build it, and may also have built the house at Guy Park, which Sir William gave to his daughter. There were two stone blockhouses flanking Johnson Hall (of which one is still standing), testimony to the unsettled times. On the lawn there is a lilac circle where Sir William held conferences with the chiefs of the Six Nations. Among the other outbuildings are the carpenter shop, gristmill, slave quar-

Fenimore House at Cooperstown contains a great variety of entertaining collections relating to the history of upstate New York.

ters, and houses for personal musician, surveyor, and head butler. This was indeed a feudal barony. The mahogany chair rail in the wide hall is chipped the length of the banister; the scars are supposed to have been made by the tomahawk of Joseph Brant, brother of Sir William's wife and famous Mohawk war chief. Johnson lived here a little over a decade and died after holding a council with the Iroquois under the hot July sun, in the arms of Joseph Brant, it is told. The house, restored as it was then, contains much of the original furniture and many of Johnson's personal belongings.

¶ *Little Falls* (*on Route 5, 22 miles east of Utica*)

Offices and shops on the village street of the Farmer's Museum at Cooperstown.

HERKIMER HOME (*1764*)
3 miles east on south bank of Mohawk; daily 9 to 5, Sundays 1 to 5; State of New York.

The largest home west of Sir William Johnson's mansions, it is a two-story brick house of Dutch Colonial design, built by the hero of the Oriskany battle, the son of

Johan Joost. Gen. Nicholas Herkimer had little more than ten years to enjoy his new mansion. Ambushed with his men by Joseph Brant, the Mohawk chieftain, he died of his wounds here ten days after the battle. Some of his personal effects are still here—his chair, pistols, and bed.

WESTERN NEW YORK

Auburn; Canandaigua; Le Roy; Penn Yan; Rochester; Youngstown; Westfield

¶ *Auburn*

SEWARD HOUSE (*1816–1817, additions in 1840, 1847, and 1870*)
33 South Street; November 1 to April 30 Monday through Saturday 1 to 5; May 1 to September 30 Tuesday through Saturday 11 to 5 and Sundays 2 to 5; adults 25 cents, children free; The Foundation Historical Association, Inc.

William Henry Seward was Secretary of State in Lincoln's war Cabinet and his principal adviser, founder of the Republican party, twice Governor of New York State, and Senator. The great house presents the appearance of a handsome Regency villa, while a Victorian wing and porte-cochere add to its charm. The interior is a living picture of the life of the great statesman, about whose dramatic and sometimes tragic career very little has been written. The mantel in one of the parlors was carved by

Brigham Young, the Mormon leader, who as a lad was engaged as a journeyman carpenter by Judge Miller when he built the house. The spiral staircase in the hall was a gift of the forty-niners after Seward had won the admission of California as a "free" state.

¶ *Canandaigua* (*23 miles southeast of Rochester*)

The town is decidedly worth a leisurely walk-around in the general neighborhood of the Granger Homestead. At least a dozen private early homes of character and charm.

GRANGER HOMESTEAD (*1814*)
295 North Main Street; daily, 10 to 5; Mrs. Percy Pettit (hostess).

Built by Gideon Granger, Postmaster Gen-

The library of the Seward house in Auburn.

eral under Jefferson and Madison, this lovely Palladian country seat is one of the great beauties of this attractive old town. It has notable mantels and woodwork. The furniture has all come down from the Granger family and includes the dining-room set which Dolly Madison gave to Gideon when he was a member of her husband's Cabinet.

¶ Le Roy

LE ROY HOUSE *(1815)*
> *23 East Main Street; June 1 to October 1, Wednesdays, Fridays, and Sundays 2 to 5; Le Roy Historical Society.*

Built to serve both as land office and residence, this two-story house of plastered masonry played an important part in the development of western New York. Jacob Le Roy, its second owner, and owner of half of this portion of the state as well, became Daniel Webster's brother-in-law.

¶ Penn Yan (on Keuka Lake 16 miles south of Geneva)

POTTER HOUSE *(1790)*
> *Gorham Road, 1 mile from Keuka Lake; groups, by appointment; fee according to time consumed; Mr. and Mrs. Fenton H. Wager.*

A Georgian frame house built for Judge Arnold Potter by a Rhode Island house-wright, this was the refuge of Louis Philippe during his stay in this section.

¶ Rochester

By the 1830s Rochester was already being spoken of as "the young lion of the West." Mayor Jonathan Child explained its prosperity in a speech made at the city's incorporation ceremony. "It has been settled for the most part by mechanics and merchants whose capital was economy, industry and perseverance," he said. "It is their labor and skill that converted a wilderness into a City." Thus it came about that through industry the sons of mechanics and merchants were able to build themselves fine Federal mansions, romantic Gothic and Italianate villas, and impressive neoclassic temples in this bustling town, so lately wilderness. Mayor Child's own house, built in 1837 and still standing at 37 Washington Street, was not the least of these. On the monumental scale, strikingly adorned in the Corinthian order both inside and out, its gold-and-black-marble mantels and its crystal chandeliers are an indication of amazing wealth for a pioneer city. Its condition is not good at present but it is due for restoration. At the corner of Spring and Washington Streets, now used by Mechanics Institute, is the BURKE HOUSE (1840), whose portico was inspired by a sketch of the Taj Mahal from the popular book *Views of India*. On East Avenue, wide and elm-arched—whose bosomy houses, set back on deep lawns, are little enough changed to afford a complete picture of the whole gamut of taste of the latter part of the century— stand Gothic, Greek Revival, Edwardian, and rococo rubbing elbows. The HOME OF SUSAN B. ANTHONY, at 17 Madison Street, is now open for all to see how this great woman lived.

There are few cities in which the progression of styles from the 1830s on can be seen to better advantage. Nowhere were Americans more affected by the impact of the Greek Revival than in this western region of New York State, and nowhere are there more noble temple façades. The Society for the Preservation of Landmarks in Western New York, listed below, is doing a magnificent job of focusing interest on this heritage. It has recently issued a booklet and map of the houses in the city, and further plans a brochure devoted to that unique architectural expression of this area between the 1830s and 1850s, the cobblestone house, of which there are literally hundreds still being comfortably occupied. One of the most imposing of these can be seen at the intersection of Routes 20 and 5 between Canandaigua and Geneva. Built of red lake-washed cobbles carefully graded for color and size, its applied face reminds one of the jeweler's art. This particular house is in-

teresting too because of its size, its flanking wings, and the high Ionic façade that it presents to the road. It is now a tourist home.

CAMPBELL-WHITTLESEY HOUSE (1835)

South Fitzhugh and Troup Streets; daily 1 to 5, except Mondays; 50 cents; Society for the Preservation of Landmarks in Western New York, Miss Elizabeth Holahan, President.

This Greek Revival mansion is a beautiful example of an imposing town house in which no expense was spared. It takes its place with the finest museum houses in the country. The ornament of the window and door frames and ceiling cornices is of unusual splendor, the lavish use of color bringing out the beauty of the decoration. The restoration has been accomplished with artistry and imagination by painstaking experts. As for the furniture, it has been assembled and arranged with the greatest skill and fidelity to the period of the place and its Empire elegance.

The dining room of the Campbell-Whittlesey house in Rochester, the double parlor of which appears on page 120.

The front parlor of the Eastman Birthplace in Rochester.

THE OLIVER CULVER HOUSE (1815)

70 East Boulevard (first house north of East Avenue); by request (phone: Browning 6675); Miss Elizabeth G. Holahan.

Oliver Culver first viewed the region when he came here in 1798. Like Washington, he was only seventeen and a surveyor of the wilderness when he came upon the land of his choice. So in 1805 he returned to it and built a story-and-a-half frame house. This in only ten years became the ell for this infinitely more impressive abode, which has been restored with great skill and elegance and furnished for the most part with early Rochester pieces. As you enter the broad hallway, the lovely stairway is seen through an elliptical arch with a remarkable sunburst boldly carved above it. Oliver Culver's portrait hangs here, returned to the house by his family, who lived here until 1945. Upstairs the great hall becomes the ballroom, with twin mantels of freestanding triple columns, a vaulted Gothic ceiling, and a "springboard" floor built especially for dancing.

WOODSIDE (1838)

485 East Avenue; weekdays, 9:30 to 5; headquarters Rochester Historical Society.

A three-story mansion of unusually fine proportions and workmanship, it was designed by Alfred Badger for Silas O. Smith, a citizen of obvious means. The Federal style combines with the Greek Revival in a most satisfactory fashion. Some of the rooms are furnished with upstate New York pieces of the period.

Nearby, at 421 East Avenue, set in spacious grounds given a mellow appearance by the great Greek Revival structure they surround, is the old ERICKSON-PERKINS HOUSE (1842), now the GENESEE VALLEY COUNTRY CLUB.

THE HERVEY ELY HOUSE (*c. 1835*)
Livingston Park; by appointment with the Society for the Preservation of Landmarks; Irondequoit Chapter, D.A.R.

Here is another beauty of the same period, designed by Hugh Hastings, with a monumental Doric portico and flanking one-story wings with railed balconies. There is beautiful plaster ceiling ornament within, and the furniture is also of the period of the early republic. The original paint colors have been recently restored.

GEORGE EASTMAN BIRTHPLACE
(*early 1830s*)
900 East Avenue; daily 10 to 5, except Mondays; 25 cents; Eastman House Museum.

A story-and-a-half Greek Revival house, small-scale and charming, it was moved from Waterville, where George Eastman, of Kodak fame, was born in 1854. Brought to Rochester in 1954 in eight separate parts, reassembled in thirty-nine days by a crew of over fifty skilled workmen, it is now furnished with the type of things that the family must have owned at the period. The original wallpapers are also being reproduced, and the parlor stoves are especially appealing.

PATRICK BARRY HOUSE (*1855*)
692 Mt. Hope Avenue; by written request through the Landmarks Society (house to qualified students only); Mr. Frederick Barry.

This engaging example of the Italianate villa, a style which was spreading rapidly westward a century ago, is built of pink brick, with stone lintels. It was designed by Gervase Wheeler, whose plans may be seen in the library. Its carriage house and stables are still standing, and so is a delightful office building of the period (of the famous firm of nurserymen, Ellwanger & Barry), designed by Davis in the Gothic style, with narrow lancet windows. Incidentally, the buildings sit in a parklike arboretum in which many of the rare plants and trees have been growing for a hundred years. The house, with its original décor and all its original furnishings, is practically pristine.

At the left, the Eastman Birthplace is seen as it appears today on the grounds of the Eastman Museum in Rochester, a real gem of the Greek Revival.

One of the more memorable of the many fine sights of Rochester's East Avenue is the mansion called Woodside, with some most impressive Greek Revival interiors.

¶ *Youngstown (on Niagara River near Lake Ontario)*

OLD FRENCH CASTLE or FORT NIAGARA *(1679)*
> *6 miles north on Route 18; open summer 9 to 9, other times 9 to 5 (guide available); 35 cents; State Conservation Commission.*

René Robert de Salle put up this extraordinary structure, with walls *four* feet thick, for use as a home, a warehouse, and a refuge. Later occupied by the French in 1725, it was rebuilt at that time to look even more formidable to the Indians. However, it fell to Sir William Johnson in 1759, and during the Revolution it was a base for British supplies. A vast and successful restoration undertaken by the state has made it one of the best preserved of all of the great historic fortifications in the United States. The "castle" is furnished with both original and period pieces, in which many patriotic societies have assisted.

¶ *Westfield (on Routes 20 and 17 near Lake Erie)*

MC CLURG HOUSE *(1818–1819)*
> *Junction Routes 20 and 17; daily 9 to 12 and 1 to 5, June to November; Chautauqua Historical Society.*

This sixteen-room brick manor, with a style faintly reminiscent of a Scottish castle, must have been cause for amazement in the countryside even while still in the log-cabin stage. At any rate, it became known as "McClurg's Folly." Fortunately little changed through the years, the plan is to furnish it in the period of the 1820s, as it was when Mr. McClurg, a wealthy merchant with grandiose ideas, made it his home.

NORTHERN NEW YORK

Brownville; Essex; Schuylerville; Ft. Edward;

Plattsburg; Oswego; Peru

¶ *Brownville (5 miles west of Watertown on Route 12E)*

BROWN MANSION *(1814–1815)*
> *Main Street; Tuesday and Friday evenings 7 to 5, Saturdays 1 to 5; Brownville Civic Association.*

An imposing two-story house with a high attic and four tall chimneys, beautifully proportioned and built of native limestone, it was Jacob Brown's stately Georgian home until he moved to Washington as Commander of the Army in 1812. About to become a museum.

¶ *Essex (on Lake Champlain 30 miles north of Ticonderoga)*

HICKORY HILL *(1820)*
> *By appointment only; $1.00; Mrs. Winfield A. Townsend.*

The builder, William Gilliland, took his own and about twenty other families to Lake Champlain in 1765 to establish a manor such as he had seen in the Hudson Valley. His grandson, the great-great-grandfather of the present owner, built this brick house with marble exterior trim. The twenty-room mansion has fine woodwork, the drawing room is Adamesque in character. The furniture was bought the year the house was built.

¶ *Schuylerville*

SCHUYLER MANOR HOUSE *(1777)*
> *Saratoga National Historical Park; Monday to Saturday, 9 to 5; 25 cents and 15 cents; National Park Service.*

The Saratoga Battleground nearby saw the defeat of General Burgoyne, in which Gen. Philip Schuyler, the builder of this manor, took a decisive part. It became his summer residence, an earlier one having been burned in the battle. The house, little changed since it was built, is a substantial but unpretentious country dwelling of frame and brick. There are seven large rooms and a kitchen on the first floor and eleven bedrooms above—ample space for the many notable visitors, among whom were Washington, Lafayette, Hamilton, Governor Clinton, and goodness knows who besides.

¶ *Ft. Edward (on Route 4 and the Hudson 40 miles north of Troy)*

OLD FORT HOUSE *or* PATT SMYTH HOUSE (*1772–1773*)

29 Lower Broadway; daily 1 to 5 and Sundays 1 to 8 May 30 to October 3, or on request; Fort Edward Historical Association.

Given this name because of its proximity to the fort, which was razed in 1775, the house was built of material from a hospital used in the French and Indian War. The labor of restoration was a community project, and the town is proud of it. The place contains period furniture, pictures, and other exhibits.

¶ *Plattsburg (on Lake Champlain)*

KENT-DE LORD HOUSE (*1797*)

17 Cumberland Avenue; daily 9 to 6, Sundays 1:30 to 6; 50 cents; Kent-De Lord Corporation, Saranac Chapter D.A.R. (custodians).

The original section of this long two-story frame house was built soon after the Revolution by James Kent, State Chancellor and Justice of the state supreme court, who was known as the "American Blackstone." Purchased by De Lord, a French refugee, in 1812, it was enlarged and inhabited by his hospitable descendants for more than a century. It was occupied by the British briefly during the Battle of Plattsburg; they left in such a hurry that they forgot a chest of table silver, which is on display here today, along with fine furniture and various family treasures, both French and American.

¶ *Oswego (southeast corner of Lake Ontario)*

BATES RICHARDSON HEADQUARTERS HOUSE (*1850, remodeled 1880*)

135 East 3d Street; Sunday afternoons 3 to 6 April to November, other times by appointment; Oswego County Historical Society, Charles M. Snyder (President).

Given to the Historical Society completely furnished in Victorian by the Bates heirs, this massive, ornate house is a good example of a Late Victorian mansion. The dining room is paneled in oak and the library in cherry, and the ceilings of the parlor and drawing room are molded. The society has added an "Indian Room" and an early kitchen.

¶ *Peru (on Route 22, 10 miles south of Plattsburg)*

KEESE HOMESTEAD (*1834*)

Rogers Old Road, 4 miles off Route 22 between Harkness and Peru; daily, 10 to 7; 25 cents; the Keese family.

Built by Pieter Keese, a Quaker, of native sandstone, this house is now occupied by the seventh generation of the family.

Typical of South Jersey are the quite English-appearing tall brick houses which rise from the fields that roll like the swell of the ocean. The pent roofs that break across the fronts are part of the pattern, and the first floors are generally well off the ground, contributing to their tallness. This is Homeland, down near Salem, now restored with understanding and affection by its owners. On the opposite page, and at nearly the opposite end of the state, is the Zabriskie–von Steuben house, one of the rare remaining examples of the Dutch Colonial houses still in practically pristine condition.

NEW JERSEY

HE TWO most interesting architectural forms indigenous to New Jersey are exemplified, one in the upper, and one in the lower part of the state. Near the northeastern corner we have the well-known and well-loved Dutch Colonial types, an outstanding example of which is the Zabriskie-von Steuben House at North Hackensack; and down in South Jersey, around Salem, we have the distinctive tall brick houses built there by English settlers. These latter deserve to be better known than they are, just as the Dutch Colonial houses of Bergen County and vicinity deserve better fates than have befallen most of these unique dwellings. It would seem almost better to have them disappear altogether than for them to stand in a state of mutilation and disrepair, if it weren't that, while they at least exist, there is hope that some means will be found to preserve and restore them before it is too late.

The best of the big early mansions are the Trent in Trenton, the Ford in Morristown, and the Dey in Preakness Valley Park—all beauties, but comprising not too numerous a collection of well-preserved "great houses," open to the public for a state with so much historical importance.

FROM TRENTON NORTH

¶ Trenton

WILLIAM TRENT HOUSE (1719)

539 South Warren Street; daily 10 to 5 and Sundays 2 to 5 May through September, daily 10 to 4 and Sundays 2 to 4 October through April; 25 cents and 10 cents; city of Trenton.

An eighteenth-century sales bill describes this stately Queen Anne residence as "a genteel brick dwelling house, 40 x 48 feet, two stories high, four rooms on a floor, with a large handsome staircase and entry, with a cellar under the whole building, and a court yard on each front of the house, one fronting down the River Delaware to the ferry, through a large handsome avenue of English cherry trees, the other fronting up the river to Trenton." The description hardly does justice to this beautiful mansion, with its elegantly gardened grounds, much as they were two hundred years ago. In 1682 William Trent came from Scotland to Philadelphia, where he made his residence in the famous Slate Roof House, which had been William Penn's mansion—long since gone—on 2d Street. When he built his own mansion, up the Delaware on the Jersey side, he had Trent Town laid out around it. The genteel dwelling is stunningly restored, both inside and out. Most of the rooms have paneled dados and paneling over the corner fireplaces, as well as in the window reveals. Museum furniture of the early eighteenth century—William and Mary,

and Queen Anne—throughout; rugs in keeping; and distinctive curtains by the bountiful and ubiquitous Scalamandre.

OLD BARRACKS (*1758–1759*)
Willow Street opposite West Front Street; Wednesdays 10 to 5, May through August, Wednesdays 10 to 4 September through April; 25 cents and 10 cents; Old Barracks Association.

This is the only surviving one of five barracks erected during the French and Indian War to protect the colonial troops. In 1776 it quartered the Hessians. The building itself is like a long, oversize house, gaining its beauty from good construction and an aura of age. Simply furnished with antiques of the Revolutionary period, with some formal exhibits of china, silver, and costumes.

OLD MASONIC LODGE HOUSE (*1793*)
Northeast corner South Willow and Lafayette Streets; Monday to Friday, 10 to 12 and 1:30 to 4.

The first Grand Master of American Masonry was Col. Daniel Coxe, from Trenton. The lodge here was organized in 1787, and the Georgian fieldstone building with white trim is one of the oldest Masonic houses standing. The building is distinguished, and contains many relics of the day.

¶ Titusville (Washington Crossing State Park, a few miles up the Delaware from Trenton)

MC KONKEY FERRY HOUSE *or* JOHNSON HOUSE (*before 1776*)
Route 202; Tuesday to Saturday 10 to 5, Sundays 2 to 5; adults 25 cents, children 10 cents; state of New Jersey.

This is the house in which Washington and his staff spent the night before the Battle of Trenton after crossing the ice-packed Delaware. It served as a tavern then as well as a ferryhouse, and has been furnished as it was on that historic night. Across the Delaware at the other end of the bridge on the Pennsylvania side is a group of stone buildings which are a living souvenir of that historic occasion.

¶ Princeton

Princeton is a parlor town in the true sense of the word. Not only does it go far back into colonial times, with many landmarks and many pages of history to show for it (not quite so many lovely landmarks as in Litchfield or New Castle, say, but perhaps more pages of history), but, as with other parlor towns, it has had the good fortune of lying somewhat off the beaten path that inevitably demolishes any pristine beauty in its way.

The McKonkey Ferry House, on the left, has great appeal with its round-headed shingles.

The William Trent house in Trenton is an elegant Queen Anne mansion elegantly furnished and maintained.

Furthermore, well-directed civic pride has here, as in a few other communities, made a point of preserving as much as possible of the past and placed controls upon the worst excesses of the present. In other words, it remains a most appetizing old town and has not tried to be too pointedly picturesque. The time to see it is on the annual visiting day in spring, when many of the fine old private homes are opened. But, as dates differ from year to year, find out ahead of time from the Garden Club of Princeton or from the Princeton Book Shop.

MORVEN (1701)

Stockton Street and Library Place; will be open at specified times as Governor's Mansion (planned for 1957); state of New Jersey.

This great house of yellow-painted brick trimmed with white occupies its little park in Princeton with an air of pleasant importance. A wide porch now adds a picturesque note to the Early Georgian appearance of the fine old mansion, which has lived through a lot of history. The British ransacked and partially burned it when they retreated from Princeton in 1776. Washington and Cornwallis have both slept here (at different times) in the carved and canopied four-poster. A carved mantel in the dining room was brought to this country before 1700. Single-arm wrought-iron latches were installed before the birth of Thomas Jefferson, who visited here, along with most of the other Revolutionary notables. A colonial bath tub is still in use. Turned over to the state in 1953 by former Governor Edge for use as a permanent executive mansion, it is being restored and modern comforts added.

PROSPECT *or* THE PRESIDENT'S HOUSE (1849)

On campus; grounds during daylight hours, house on special occasions only; Princeton University.

Designed by John Notman of Philadelphia, this great brownstone mansion is romantically austere in the Florentine style that was chosen for so many of our grander Victorian homes. It has a side porch whose decorative ironwork (clusters of grapes painted blue) is in the large scale of the house. The house itself has much interest, especially as seen from the lower terraces of the extensive garden to the rear. The trees alone are worth a visit.

DEAN'S HOUSE (1756)

On campus; open only on special occasions; Princeton University.

Occupied during two centuries by ten college presidents, it was first inhabited by Aaron Burr, Sr. During the Battle of Trenton it was General Leslie's headquarters, and John Adams visited here while en route to the Continental Congress. The two giant sycamores at the gate were planted in 1765. The house was designed by Robert Smith, of the Carpenters Company of Philadelphia.

ELMWOOD (c. 1732)

Princeton Pike; on request by letter or phone (1–2879); Mr. and Mrs. William H. Jackson.

One of the loveliest early houses in the Princeton area, built of the pale ledge stone of the locality, the house has great style and has been understandingly restored. It is charmingly furnished, the owners having made it livable without changing its essential character.

YEATMAN HOUSE (1836)

72 Library Place; by advance appointment when convenient to owners; Mr. and Mrs. Phillip W. Yeatman.

Designed and built by an architect named Steadman along with four other houses in the Federal style, all of which are standing nearby. Beside being a typical urban dwelling of the period in this university town, it has other claims to distinction. Woodrow Wilson lived in it for many years while a professor at Princeton, but it came into the news in a controversial manner some time before his occupancy; for in it was installed the first indoor toilet in the vicinity, which immediately became a *cause célèbre.* The present owners have restored the house very well and have furnished it harmoniously with a number of fine late-eighteenth-century pieces.

TUSCULUM (1773)

Bayard Lane, less than a mile from town; open on written request; Mrs. Ario Pardee.

A Late Georgian house of local brownstone and singular charm, cushioned in boxwood. The great stone barn was built in 1792, and "Tusculum" has been a going farm ever since. It was the home of John Witherspoon, an outspoken patriot, a signer of the Declaration, and President of Princeton (1768–1794). Washington was a frequent visitor here.

¶ Rocky Hill (5 miles north of Princeton on the Kingston road)

BERRIEN MANSION *or* ROCKINGHAM (*1730*)
Daily 10 to 5 except Monday, Sundays 2 to 5; 10 cents and 35 cents; state of New Jersey, Department of Conservation and Economic Development.

A white clapboard farmhouse which served as headquarters for Washington from August to November, 1783, while the Continental Congress was in session at Princeton. In the upstairs blue room he wrote his Farewell Address to his army, and from its balcony he later delivered it to some three hundred of his men, who sat on the lawn or leaned against the trees. Here, in the midst of these serious matters, he also had time to entertain and attend banquets in his honor, as was his wont. Furniture and other articles used by George and Martha are here.

¶Freehold (23 miles east of Princeton via Hightstown)

COVENHOVEN-HANKINSON MANSION (*1775*)
150 West Main Street; by written or phone appointment, May 15 to October 15; Mr. and Mrs. Rhea Moreau.

The Covenhoven-Hankinson Mansion, the oldest residence in town, is a white-shingled, green-shuttered "farmstead," sitting on a broad lawn with old shade trees. It faces away from the street, run through long after the main section of the house was built by master builder John Middleton who constructed the nearby Tennant Church. The lovely proportions of the church and its many other fine details are repeated in the mansion. An unfinished overmantel painting has been attributed to the Hessians. Clinton stayed here the night before the Battle of Monmouth, forcing the widow Connover, then owner, to betake herself to the milk room with her

household to spend the night there on the brick floor. The Moreau family has occupied the house for a long time, and it is furnished with family heirlooms, many as old as the house itself.

¶ Red Bank (15 miles east of Freehold)

WHITEHALL HOUSE (*before 1776*)
Battlefield National Park near Woodbury, Route 130; daily, 10 to 12 and 2 to 4; 35 cents; National Park Service.

While the Battle of Red Bank raged around her, Mrs. Whitehall, a Quaker, kept on spinning. The famous spinning wheel is here, along with the other colonial furnishings.

¶ Middletown (5 miles north of Red Bank)

MARLPIT HALL (*1684*)
Route 35 between Keyport and Red Bank; Tuesdays, Thursdays, and Saturdays 11 to 5, Sundays 2 to 5; Monmouth County Historical Association.

In a village dating back to the seventeenth century, it is one of the rare houses of this type and age in the state, showing the strong Dutch influence. It is a long wide-shingled one-and-a-half-story house with small dormers. The interior has many interesting early features, among them a pilastered fireplace and a carved shell cupboard. Furnished with very early Jersey pieces.

¶ New Brunswick

BUCCLEUCH MANSION *or* THE WHITE HOUSE (*c. 1729*)
Buccleuch Park, near intersection of College Avenue and George Street; Sundays and holidays 3 to 5 Memorial Day to Labor Day, or by appointment for fee; city of New Brunswick.

Built by Col. Anthony White of the British Army, this is a fine Early Georgian house through which have passed many important figures in the history of the state. Elizabeth Morris, daughter of the colonial governor, was its mistress. It was renamed "Buccleuch" for his royal Scotch kin by Col. Joseph W. Scott, who bought it in 1821. He was the son of Moses Scott, Surgeon General of the Revolutionary Army. There are furniture and portraits of considerable interest here, and the Dufour wallpaper of 1807 and 1815 is outstanding; on the lower-hall wall is "The Banks of the Seine"; and on the upper-hall wall "Hindustani Scenery," consisting of twenty strips. Both are the first and only paper on these walls.

WOODLAWN ALUMNAE HOUSE (c. 1835)
Open on request to college; New Jersey College for Women.

This is a handsome building, but used as a place to entertain faculty and guests, with mostly modern equipment.

HENRY GUEST HOUSE (1760)
60 Livingston Avenue; daily, 9 to 5; apply at adjoining public library.

This house sheltered Tom Paine, who was forced to hide from the British here. It was owned by a successful tanner and whaler, Henry Guest. It is not furnished, but has an exhibit of laces and shawls.

IVY HALL *or* CORNELIUS LOWE HOUSE (1729–1740)
River Road; by written request well in advance; Theodore Voorhees.

Once the largest and most costly house in the busy shipping center known as "The Landing," this is one of the outstanding examples in the state of a Georgian mansion. It is fortunate that it has an owner who appreciates its rare qualities. Built of local sandstone, it has a splendid entrance, and the hall is beautifully paneled. In addition to fine paneling in many of them, each of the other rooms has a fireplace with a carved mantel, and the old tiles have been preserved in a number of them; so has much of the original hardware. Among other features are the shell cupboards. The house is furnished, says the owner, largely in period but "as a home, not a museum."

¶ *South Bound Brook (7 miles northeast of New Brunswick on Route 44)*

STAATS–VON STEUBEN HOUSE (1690)
165 Main Street; by written request; Mr. and Mrs. Charles Gurney Hollister.

Built by a Dutch landowner as a manor house for his farmlands, it remained in his family until 1935—almost a record tenure. During the Revolution it was von Steuben's headquarters and is usually known by this name. Washington and Lafayette were frequent visitors. The house has most of its original features—the hardware, the "Holy Lord" hinges, the hand-hewn oak beams in the ceilings, the hand-carved mantels, and the bull's-eye windows. It has recently been restored and made comfortable for modern living without destroying its character.

¶ *Somerville*

WALLACE HOUSE (1778)
38 Washington Place; daily 10 to 12 and 1 to 5 except Mondays, Sundays 2 to 5; 35 cents and 10 cents; state of New Jersey, Department of Conservation and Economic Development.

Occupied by George and Martha Washington from the fall of 1778 to June, 1779, while the Army was stationed at Camp Middlebrook, now Somerville. While here, Washington planned the Indian Campaign of 1779 which broke the power of the Six Nations. It is an unpretentious white-clapboard house, the rooms not large and the woodwork simple. There is some interesting old furniture and glass. Washington's ten-foot iron army trunk, lined with oak, which stands in the hall, is memorable when you learn the reason for its dimensions: in case of Washington's death, it was designed also to serve as his coffin. The rigors of the campaigns come intensely and intimately to life when you look at its grim length. Mrs. Washington told friends later that her most vivid memories of the house were the piercingly cold nights when she huddled under the quilts while guards knelt at her windows with guns pointed out into the night, ready for the ever-present danger of attack.

OLD DUTCH PARSONAGE (1751)
65 Washington Place; daily 10 to 12 and 1 to 5 except Mondays, Sundays 2 to 5; 35 cents and 10 cents; state of New Jersey, Department of Conservation and Economic Development.

Built of brick brought from Holland, so it is said, this place stands only a short distance down the street from the Wallace House, and was frequently visited by Washington. It was built by the congregation of the Reformed Dutch Church for the Rev. John Frelinghuysen and his Dutch bride, Dinah van Bergh, who came here with him because she believed the Lord wanted her

In the Dayton Room of Boxwood Hall the portrait over the Adamesque mantel is of Jonathan Dayton, youngest signer of the Constitution, who lived here in the early 1800s.

to help in the work of the churches of New Jersey. Here young men came to study for the ministry, and the building later became the seminary that was to be the nucleus of Rutgers University.

¶ *Plainfield*

NATHANIEL DRAKE HOUSE (*1746*)

> *602 West Front Street facing Plainfield Avenue; Tuesdays, Thursdays, and Saturdays, 2 to 5; 35 cents and 10 cents; Plainfield and North Plainfield Historical Society.*

A Dutch Colonial white-clapboard house of two and a half stories which was a stopping place for Washington while he was reconnoitering during the spring of 1777. Exhibits only.

¶ *Elizabeth*

BOUDINOT MANSION *or* BOXWOOD HALL (*1750*)

> *1073 East Jersey Street; daily 10 to 12 and 1 to 5 except Mondays, Sundays 2 to 5; state of New Jersey, Department of Conservation and Economic Development.*

A well-restored shingle house with a plain exterior and twenty-four-paned windows, some of them with the original glass. This deceptive façade leaves you unprepared for the amazing interior. The entrance hall is broad enough for a ball. There are richly carved mantels, unusual cornices, blue and white delft tiles in two fireplaces, and period wallpaper copied from the original. It

was the home of the first president of the Continental Congress, the son of Elias Boudinot, a Princeton silversmith.

¶ *Madison* (*on the way to Morristown*)

MEAD HALL *or* THE OLD GIBBONS MANSION (*1833–1836*)

> *On campus of Drew University; open daily, including Sunday; Drew University.*

An impressive and quite beautiful brick structure, painted white, with six stately Corinthian columns thirty-six feet in height supporting a flat roof with a fine balustrade and tall chimneys. The porch, which is ninety feet long, is paved in marble and is reached by flights of stone

Mead Hall began as the monumental mansion of William Gibbons, from Savannah.

steps. The place has for the most part been made into offices, but the former ballroom and dining room serve for social purposes, and may be seen at all times. The former is the only furnished room, containing Victorian pieces. A mansion whose original builder, William Gibbons, of Savannah, Georgia, was obviously a gentleman of wealth and taste.

¶ Morristown

FORD MANSION (1774)

230 Morris Avenue, Morristown National Historic Park; daily 10 to 5, except Mondays; 10 cents; National Park Service.

It is one of our great white flush-boarded Georgian houses, of robust proportions and with a delightful doorway, full of sturdiness and grace. It was built by Col. Jacob Ford, Jr., with wealth acquired from the neighboring iron mines. Morristown was, in effect, the military capital during the winter of 1779–1780, and, thanks to the widow Theodosia Ford, the house was a comfortable home for the Washingtons, serving as host during those months to most of the important men of the time.

It has been beautifully restored, and its fine interior can now be seen much as it looked during the Washington occupancy. In the living room is the desk on which many of his letters were written; the looking glass, table, and Queen Anne chair were also here during his stay. The kitchen, which in very cold weather served as dining room too, has a huge and fully equipped fireplace. On January 18 Washington wrote, "Eighteen belonging to my family and all Mrs. Ford's are all crowded together in her kitchen and scarce one of them able to speak for the colds they have caught." Mrs. Ford had kept only two rooms for her own living quarters. In May, 1780, Lafayette brought the good news to the general that France was sending a second expeditionary force.

SCHUYLER-HAMILTON HOUSE (before 1765)

5 Olyphant Place; Tuesday and Friday 10 to 12 and 2 to 5, ring bell and ask caretaker other times; Morristown Chapter, D.A.R.

The scene of Alexander Hamilton's courtship of Elizabeth Schuyler in 1779, the building is a simple one, with flush eaves at

The Ford house in Morristown, probably the finest Georgian house in Jersey, served Washington as his headquarters during the winter of 1779–1780.

There aren't many of the old Dutch Colonial houses left in presentable condition, a fact which makes the little Van Horn–Branford house at Wyckoff a rare exception.

the gable ends and bracketed cornices. The porch is a later addition. Dr. Jabez Campfield, Senior Surgeon of the Continental Army and Washington's personal physician, was quartered here in 1780. Beautifully furnished as a home of the period.

WICK HOUSE (*1750*)

> *Northeast corner Mendham-New Vernon road and Jockey Hollow Road; daily 1 to 5 except Mondays, Sundays 10 to 5; National Park Service.*

An appealing old farmhouse with sweeping rooflines, low eaves, and a single chimney in which Temperance Wick, daughter of a cavalry officer, made history by hiding her horse in her bedroom to save it from the British. The house is furnished with simplicity, as it must have been.

¶ Hanover (7 miles east of Morristown on Route 10)

THE OLD PARSONAGE *or* ASHBEL GREEN HOMESTEAD (*1757*)

> *On left of highway; open by appointment with Mr. and Mrs. Richard P. Heppner; Stockton Green (owner).*

Built as a parsonage for Jacob Green, the great-great-great-grandfather of the present owner—a teacher, pastor, doctor, and distiller. The house is a low, rambling, shingle structure. It housed Washington's staff during the winter at Morristown. Voluminous diaries of Ashbel Green, son of Jacob, second President of Princeton, and Chaplain of the Continental Congress, may be examined here. They contain a wealth of incidents and intimate comments

on personages of the Revolutionary period never yet published.

¶ Caldwell (around the mountain on Route 46)

GROVER CLEVELAND BIRTHPLACE (*1832*)

> *207 Bloomfield Avenue; daily 10 to 12 and 1 to 5 except Mondays, Sundays 2 to 5; 35 cents and 10 cents; state of New Jersey.*

This was a church manse when the future President was born here in 1832. There are memorabilia of Cleveland and his period—his cradle, which was an old one given to his mother by a neighbor; a chair he used in the White House; his desk when he was the Mayor of Buffalo; and similar items.

¶ North Hackensack

ZABRISKIE–VON STEUBEN HOUSE (*1739–1752*)

> *New Bridge Road, ½ mile off Route 4; daily 10 to 12 and 1 to 5 except Mondays, Sundays 2 to 5; 25 cents; state of New Jersey, Department of Conservation and Economic Development, and headquarters of Bergen County Historical Society.*

One of the finest examples of an Early Dutch Colonial house to be seen anywhere. Built of tailored native stone, its rooflines, sweeping in a long, flattening curve to create the porch roofs, have an almost pagodalike effect at the gable ends. The house is of great length, with nine delicate columns supporting the roof and forming the porch. It was Washington's headquarters during the retreat from Fort Lee in

A house of unusual dignity, substance, and true architectural merit is the famous old Dey mansion in what is now Preakness Valley Park not far from Paterson.

November, 1776. Two years later it was the headquarters of General Cornwallis. And again, in September, 1780, after the war, Washington used the house on his way to Hartford, Connecticut. It gets its name from Baron von Steuben, who was given the house and surrounding land in appreciation of his services with the ragtag army into which he had drilled military precision. However, he never occupied it, and it reverted to the Zabriskie family, from whom it had been taken because of their Tory sympathies. It has Dutch and Colonial furniture, and many curios of the late eighteenth century; and the house itself remains very much as it was in 1752.

¶ *Preakness Valley Park (Wayne Township)*

DEY MANSION *(1740)*
> *Route 6, 4½ miles west of Paterson, on Totowa Road near Mountain View Avenue; Tuesdays, Wednesdays and Fridays 1 to 5, Saturdays after 1; 35 cents; Passaic County Park Commission; Mrs. R. Rauchfuss (custodian).*

Washington knew how to pick the best! This remarkable brick house, set in its small, attractive park, is another of his headquarters in New Jersey—this time during July, October, and November, 1780. A Dutchman named Dirck Dey (pronounced *Dye*), who bought 611 acres of wilderness here and who was unquestionably a man of great skills, erected this distinguished eight-room manor house with the help of his slaves

and artisans. It was inherited by his son Theunis; he brought to the place his bride Hester Schuyler, to whom were born ten children, five of whom fought in the Revolution. The beautiful exterior is unusual, with the old red brick set off by the window and door openings, framed in brownstone. Its proportions, color, and decoration are striking. The early interior has been most thoughtfully restored, with all later changes removed. The color treatment inside is excellent, and the furnishings are being carefully chosen. This is on its way to becoming one of the best house museums in the state.

¶ *Wyckoff*

VAN HORN–BRANFORD HOUSE
(1747–1760 and 1800)
> *Lafayette and Wyckoff Avenues; by request; donation to Bergen County Historical Society; Mr. and Mrs. Ray B. Lake.*

This is a small Dutch Colonial brown-fieldstone house of three parts; each part is of a different height and each built at a different period, but together they make a most harmonious and picturesque whole. The house belonged to a Loyalist, Barent van Hoorn, and was plundered in 1777 by the Whigs. It has been little altered, and its present owners, who are connoisseurs, have done much to preserve and enhance all its interesting features. As dealers in antiques (this is their home, not their shop), they have furnished it with some choice Queen Anne pieces, local slip ware, and other rare items.

¶ *Ringwood Manor Park (in Ringwood Valley, northern Passaic County)*

RINGWOOD MANOR (*c. 1780*)

> In park; daily 10 to 4 and Saturdays, Sundays, and holidays 10 to 5, May through October; parking 50 cents summer, 25 cents winter; state of New Jersey.

An outstanding example of how a cultivated and wealthy American family lived in the nineteenth century, the house, which has belonged to some of New Jersey's best-known families—the Erskines, Ryersons, Coopers, and Hewitts—was passed on to the state in 1936 by Erskine Hewitt, along with all of its furnishings. Of curious architecture, it seems to have been augmented and changed at will. The bays, gables, columns, and porte-cochere are all most suggestive of its Victorian era; however, a part of it is the early house, dating back at least to 1804, when it was advertised for sale in the New York *Herald* as "an elegant mansion with a 92 foot front." Of this, two rooms and a hall remain intact. A still earlier house may have burned down during the Revolution or may have been incorporated. It too was a mansion, for Washington, who stopped there frequently on his way from Norristown to West Point (it was then the home of Robert Erskine, official cartographer of the Continental Army) notes in his Journal, "Mrs. Erskine is a sensible and accomplished woman who lives in a style of affluence and fashion; everything indicates wealth, taste and splendor. . . ." And why not? From 1740 to 1931 iron of high quality was continuously mined on this twenty-thousand-acre tract, and the owners of Ringwood Manor directed the proceedings.

FROM TRENTON SOUTH

¶ *Burlington (Route 130 at Bristol Bridge)*

Burlington was once a flourishing river-port, and the Delaware was crowded with white sails; on its green banks stood the prim brick summer dwellings of Philadelphia Quakers. Today industry and superhighways are breathing down its neck, with the Bristol-Burlington Bridge looming over the town. Yet it manages to retain a lot of its eighteenth-century character. This lingering atmosphere can best be felt under the guidance of Mrs. Hugh Pugh, who requests one week's notice in advance.

HUGH PUGH HOUSE (*1725*)

> 130 West Broad Street; any time, on tour; tour 50 cents, proceeds to Historical Society; Mrs. Hugh Pugh (phone: Burlington 1491).

Distinctly worth a visit to acquaint you with the early brick-panel construction, typical of the small houses of the period. Unless you wish to drive your own car, Mrs. Pugh will take you on a walking tour which will include the two houses for the Historical Society (regularly open) and the houses listed below.

F. E. BELDIN HOUSE (*1797*)

> 312 Wood Street; any time, on tour; Mrs. F. E. Beldin.

Only the lower floor of this home may be seen.

GENERAL GRANT HOUSE (*1856*)

> 309 Wood Street; any time, on tour; Mrs. E. H. Slack.

Occupied by General Grant for a time during the Civil War; beautifully kept up, with some handsome family furniture.

CAPT. JAMES LAWRENCE HOUSE

(*rear c. 1767, front before 1800*)

> 459 High Street; daily 10 to 12 and 1 to 5 except Mondays, Sundays 2 to 5; state of New Jersey.

Birthplace of the naval hero of the War of 1812, whose historic words "Don't give up the ship" were spoken when he was fatally wounded in the battle between the U.S.S. *Chesapeake* and the H.M.S. *Shannon* in Boston Harbor. The house is joined to the

Cooper House, and they are similar in style—simple, sturdy, red-brick town houses of pre-Revolutionary character, with beautiful doorways and paneled shutters. When they were built, the town consisted of perhaps two hundred houses in all, and was on the way to becoming a summer resort for Philadelphians, who came up on Delaware River steamboats and built their summer houses on the green banks of the river. The house is well restored and furnished with antiques.

JAMES FENIMORE COOPER HOUSE
(*c. 1780*)
457 South High Street; Sundays 3 to 5, or by appointment; Burlington Historical Society.

This house, in which James Fenimore Cooper was born in 1789, was built by Samuel How about ten years earlier. The famous family subsequently moved to Cooperstown, New York, when the author-to-be was thirteen. The Burlington Historical Society has preserved the interior, in which old furniture, pictures, maps, and other Burlington relics make interesting exhibits.

THOMAS REVEL HOUSE (*1685*)
8 East Pearl Street; on request to C. H. McCray, 46 Riverbank Street; Colonial Burlington Society.

Often called the "Gingerbread House," this is probably the oldest in Burlington. It is a tiny red-brick structure, whose fame dates back to 1723, when a young man of seventeen by the name of Benjamin Franklin, who was walking from Boston to Philadelphia, missed his boat. The mistress of the house gave him hot gingerbread while he waited for the next one; this is the claim to immortality of both the owner and her house.

MC CRAY HOUSE (*c. 1850–1860*)
46 Riverbank Street; any time, on tour; Maj. and Mrs. Charles McCray.

A Victorian cottage with some nice paneling and some interesting French furniture.

There is still another Victorian cottage, the VAN RENSSELAER, designed by Strickland, at Talbot Street and the riverbank. It is a collector's item, though not open to visitors.

¶ *Rancocas (just west of turnpike 3 miles below Interchange 5)*

Rancocas is a charming and still unspoiled village containing an early Quaker meeting and schoolhouse. How long it can remain so in the midst of encroaching "progress" is a problem for its devoted inhabitants. Some of the owners of the old houses, other than the two listed below, will undoubtedly be glad to show them by appointment.

WILLIAM S. BAKER HOUSE
(*1767, addition 1820*)
By written appointment; Mr. and Mrs. William S. Baker.

One of the five small brick Quaker-style mansions along the banks of the Rancocas, with its original interior—its paneling, mantels, cupboards, and unique staircase—intact. It is furnished appropriately, which is to say, simply.

NORMAN S. WIGGIN HOUSE
(*c. 1760s*)
By written appointment; Mr. and Mrs. Norman S. Wiggin.

Also unpretentious and typical, its old woodwork and fireplaces are intact too. Mr. Wiggin may be able to help you to see some of the others.

¶ *Mt. Holly (3 miles east of Interchange 5)*

JOHN WOOLMAN MEMORIAL (*1771*)
99 Branch Street; daily 9 to 6, Sundays 1 to 6; maintained by a Friends organization.

Built on land once owned by the noted Quaker, John Woolman, one of the earliest opponents of slavery, it is a small red-brick building with adjoining gardens in which the present-day Quakers have tried to recreate the atmosphere of the place and period.

THE COURT HOUSE (1796) and the BURLINGTON COUNTY GAOL here were designed by Robert Mills; the latter was the first fireproof building in America and is not nearly so obsolete as you might think.

¶ Bordentown
(10 miles below Trenton)

An easygoing Quaker named Thomas Farnsworth established himself here on the banks of the Delaware in 1682. A little later Joseph Borden came by sailing vessel from Philadelphia and bought him out. Borden believed in progress and soon had his own stagecoach running between this place and New York, and boat service to Philadelphia as well. It was in no time a town taking his name. Even before the Revolution it was quite a famous place, with large schools whose students came from as far away as South America and the West Indies. It was also a summering place for many Revolutionary figures, among them Tom Paine and Francis Hopkinson. Such was its fame that Joseph Bonaparte, brother of Napoleon, and King of Spain and Naples, bought a large estate here in 1820, where he lived for twenty years or more. His French Colonial mansion stood in what is now Bonaparte Park; all that remains of the many buildings is the garden house.

Some of the old houses in the town are still standing. Should you want to know more about them, Mr. Orson H. Brown, 322 Prince Street, who has lived there more than 83 years, will be glad to give you directions. He must be notified in advance, and may on occasion conduct a small group personally.

The GILDER HOUSE was the home of the famous Gilder family and still breathes the atmosphere of the cultivated and remarkable people who lived here—poets, musicians, critics, explorers, and the celebrated editor, Richard Watson Gilder, of the old *Century* magazine.

The THOMAS PAINE HOUSE was used by him when he was carrying on his great work for the freedom of the Colonies.

The CLARA BARTON SCHOOLHOUSE, built in 1739, was used by Clara Barton, founder of the Red Cross, to establish the first public school in this country in 1844.

¶ Camden

WALT WHITMAN HOUSE (*1840*)
330 Mickle Street; daily 10 to 12 and 1 to 5 except Mondays, Sundays 2 to 5; 35 cents and 10 cents; state of New Jersey.

An unpretentious clapboard house joined to its taller brick neighbors, it sits flush with the pavement. The great poet lived in it from 1884 until his death in 1892. Many of his furnishings and mementos are here in place, as well as a valuable collection of original manuscripts.

POMONA HALL (*1726 and 1788*)
Northeast corner of Euclid Avenue and Park Boulevard; Mondays, Wednesdays, and Fridays 1:30 to 4, other days by appointment with E. H. Havens (curator); Camden County Historical Society Museum.

Built in two sections—the earlier by Joseph Cooper, Jr., and the later by his nephew Marmaduke—this impressive house of tapestry brick, with a double chimney at either end bearing the builders' initials, definitely represents one of the noteworthy pieces of New Jersey Colonial. Fortunately the staircase, fireplaces, partitions, and Colonial fittings are intact. The newer section (1788) typifies the post-Revolutionary changes in style. Its main function now is as a museum for the Camden County Historical Society, and it has on display exhibits of maps, Indian relics, and files of old newspapers, with only one room furnished in facsimile as this is written.

¶ Haddon Heights

GLOVER MANSION (*c. 1705*)
In park; Camden County Park Commission.

Much of its appearance was lost in remodeling. It was built by John Glover, who arrived in 1703 after being discharged from the British Navy. He sought and found his sweetheart Hannah Thorne, who had come to America earlier with her father, and brought her here as his bride. It is now an office of the Camden County Park Commission.

¶ *Haddonfield*

HADDONFIELD HISTORICAL SOCIETY (*1836*)

231 Kings Highway E.; daily Monday to Friday, 2 to 5; Haddonfield Historical Society.

This is a tall, narrow town dwelling much like those in Burlington and typical of the Jersey and Pennsylvania town houses of the well-to-do burghers of the period—plain and substantial as the Quakers who lived in them. It is well stocked with items of local interest, which include furniture, household decorations, and some of the belongings of Elizabeth Haddon, the town's first settler, sent here alone from England by her father when she was only twenty to look after a large property he had purchased in this area.

Old Indian King Tavern near Haddonfield.

INDIAN KING TAVERN (*1750*)

232 Kings Highway E.; daily 10 to 12 and 1 to 5 except Mondays, Sundays 2 to 5; 35 cents and 10 cents; state of New Jersey, Department of Conservation and Economic Development.

A landmark when Haddonfield was just another Jersey crossroads village during the Revolution. Among the distinguished figures who stopped over here were Gen-

eral Greene, Lord Cornwallis, Lafayette, "Mad Anthony" Wayne, Count Pulaski, etc. Innkeeper Creighton's niece, Dolly Payne, became President Madison's wife. Rescued and restored in 1903 by the state, the tavern is now maintained as an inn of its period. It houses a library of six thousand volumes, some Washington manuscripts, and earlier memorabilia.

¶ *Woodbury*

JUDGE JESSUP HOUSE or GLOUCESTER COUNTY HISTORICAL SOCIETY (*1750 or 1765*)

58 North Broad Street; Mondays 11 to 3, Wednesdays and Fridays 2 to 4, or by appointment with L. L. Lammert (phone: Woodbury 2–0211J); Gloucester County Historical Society.

Built by either John Tatem or Judge John Sparks, this is a typical early South Jersey house with Dutch Colonial features and Tudor touches. It has in all eighteen rooms, eleven of which are furnished, none in any one period, but with many interesting antiques. Records show that it was the boyhood home of the young naval hero, Captain Lawrence, born in Burlington. A mansard roof has been added to the house as well as a portico, though the building was better off without them.

¶ *Salem*

HOMELAND (*1729, wing 1784*)

By appointment; $1.50 to Salem County Historical Society; Dr. and Mrs. A. Ralston Green.

Built by a Whig colonel, Benjamin Holme, this is a perfect example of the red-brick manor house found only in this part of Jersey and in Delaware, usually with descending wings. They have fine style and proportions, and their personality is prim and English. Colonel Holme owned sixteen hundred acres and the ferry nearby, which was the terminus of the old King's Highway. Both the house and ferry were set afire by the British in March, 1778; fortunately the exterior of the house remained intact. It was the custom to carry the furniture to the waiting British ships before the houses were burned. A clock from this house, made by Wagstaff of London, was later recovered from British headquarters in New York. The house and

The dining room of Homeland is large enough to include a coffee-table grouping before the fireplace. The kitchen lies beyond.

grounds have been beautifully restored, and the charming interior has been treated with taste and skill. The kitchen and dining room are of particular interest, the kitchen containing modern equipment so artfully placed as to be practically invisible. The rare collection of molds here on the mantel shelf centers the attention on the vast hearth.

ALEXANDER GRANT HOUSE (*1721*)
81 and 83 Market Street; by appointment with Harry A. Crispin; Salem County Historical Society.

This is a typical South Jersey brick town house with a wing. It is not furnished as a home at the present time, but has large collections of furniture, glass, china, and apparel.

The kitchen at Homeland has become an extremely pleasant all-purpose room for dining, sitting, but primarily for cooking, filled with fascinating antiques.

The brickwork is a remarkable feature of the fine old Hancock house.

¶ *Hancocks Bridge (south of Salem)*

HANCOCK HOUSE (*1734*)

Daily 10 to 12 and 1 to 5 except Mondays, Sundays 2 to 5; 35 cents and 10 cents; state of New Jersey, Department of Conservation and Economic Development.

This Quaker house was the scene of a ferocious massacre of American patriots on March 21, 1778. A band of thirty men sleeping here was trapped by three hundred of the enemy and bayoneted. Still visible on the floor are the bloodstains. This was in reprisal for the food that was being sent to Washington's army at Valley Forge from this area, which is said to have prevented their starvation. As in a number of the houses in this area, the initials of the owner William and his wife Sara and the date are laid in the masonry which on one wall of this house forms a unique zigzag pattern with the use of only blue glazed bricks, while the front alternates red and blue. This use of bricks, an early brickmasons' fancy, can be seen as far west as the William Whitely House in Kentucky. The interior, furnished in antiques, has carved panels, moldings, and mantels, elaborate grillwork on a closet, and early Venetian blinds. In addition, there are such commonplaces of the day as bedbug traps, hoopskirt chairs, and tailors' gooses.

CEDAR PLANK HOUSE (*c. 1700*)

Behind Hancock House; daily.

This tiny one-story structure stands behind the Hancock House. It was built of cedar from the nearby swamps by the Swedes who settled here in 1643. The hand-hewn planks are dovetailed in Swedish fashion at the corners.

¶ *Greenwich*

RICHARD WOOD MANSION (*1797*)

Wednesdays and Sundays 2 to 5 April through December, other times by appointment; contribution; Mr. Theodore Wood.

This fine old house stands unchanged on a street laid out in 1684, and while it is not furnished as a house, it contains exhibits of local items and various private collections, changed from time to time. Mrs. Sara Sheppard Hancock, president of the Salem County Historical Society, lives a few miles distant in Bacon's Neck upon the land her ancestor Samuel Bacon bought from the Indians in 1682. Her own home is of interest, having been in her family since it was built.

THE ANCHORAGE *or* WHEATON HOMESTEAD (*1848*)

By request; Maj. Frank Ankenbrand.

Built by Providence and Ruth Foster Wheaton on the site of a library which stood here 1821–1838, it is a large frame house with a widow's walk and iron balustrades made by a local smith. The house has twenty-three rooms, twelve furnished with a variety of antiques and an unusual collection of paintings and prints, which include Morlands, Rowlandsons, and Knellers. One room contains a bedroom set identical to the one in the Lincoln Room in the White House. It was once the property of Charles Willson Peale's son, and the present owner purchased it from Peale's granddaughter. There are also some Lincoln and Peale items.

¶ *Somers Point*

SOMERS MANSION (*1720–1730*)

Shore Road and traffic circle at Somers Point; daily 10 to 12 and 1 to 5 except Mondays, Sundays 2 to 5; 25 cents; state of New Jersey, Department of Conservation and Economic Development.

John Somers, a Quaker born in England, purchased a three-thousand-acre tract from Thomas Budd in 1695; when he died in 1723, he left his "home lands" to his fourth child, Richard. He had been an important figure, operating a ferry from Great Egg Harbor to Cape May, and thence to East Jersey. Richard built the mansion of hand-made brick between 1720 and 1730. There are records of Quaker meetings held here in those days. The mansion remained in the family until 1937, when the heirs deeded it to the county historical society. It was renovated by WPA workmen, who removed the stucco and exposed the Flemish-bond brickwork; an original eight-foot fireplace in the great room was restored, disclosing a herringbone pattern in the back. The deck roof is particularly interesting, supported by hewn timbers which taper from a width of seven inches at the ridge to one or three at the heels, where they are pinned to the timbers supporting the steeper slope—undoubtedly an example of a shipwright's work. The mansion has been restored with great care to reveal as many as possible of its original features, including the paint.

Nothing could be more typical of the country furnishings and appearance of southeastern Pennsylvania than this children's dining room in Pottsgrove Manor, with one of the stone dwellings of the Furnace beyond. On the opposite page is Mt. Pleasant in Fairmount Park, considered by all and sundry to be one of the four or five greatest Georgian houses in the country.

PENNSYLVANIA

THE MANOR houses, such as ING-HAM MANOR near Lahaska and POTTSGROVE at Pottstown, are pure, un-adulterated Pennsylvania, not to be found anywhere else. And it is unmis-takably the same with the farmhouses that are so closely related to the manors. Then there are the celebrated country seats like MOUNT PLEASANT in Fair-mount Park and CLIVEDEN in German-town, which for all their striking indi-viduality also have a common character. All of these—the manor houses, the farmhouses, and the country seats—are boldly built and detailed, most of masonry. But there is more to it than

173

that; each one of them also has a quality of firmness and a generous scale, which helps to endow them with their robust regional character.

It is only when you come to the early town houses of downtown Philadelphia, such as the POWEL, SHIPPEN-WISTER, and MORRIS HOUSES, which are direct descendants of eighteenth-century London town houses and of the later, more delicate Georgian, that you feel these more sophisticated homes could have been built as easily almost anywhere else in the Colonies.

It goes without saying that the richest region for fine early houses is the old southeastern section, fanning out from Philadelphia across the adjacent counties and into the farmlands that sweep in a wide arc from the Delaware, through the Pennsylvania Dutch country, past York and Gettysburg to the Maryland border. The barns and houses are colorful to look upon, and the countryside is bountiful.

The best way to see some of the interiors is to attend the tours, which are numerous. Spring and fall are the best times of the year as far as visibility, brightness, color, and comfort are concerned, and it is during these two seasons that most of the visiting days in the various localities occur, all noted below in their proper places. The biggest is the Pennsylvania House and Garden Tour, taking place at the end of April and the first week in May and lasting three days; write for full information to the Penn-Sheraton Hotel, 39th and Chestnut Streets, Philadelphia. Also the guidance you get on these occasions is something to be grateful for, especially in the environs of Philadelphia, if you happen to be a stranger there.

IN & OUT OF PHILADELPHIA

While walking through the streets of present-day downtown Philadelphia, especially east and south of Independence Square, bear in mind that this was by far the largest of all our colonial cities. In 1775 its population was forty thousand, as compared with New York's twenty-five thousand and Boston's sixteen thousand. In fact, according to Carl Bridenbaugh in *Cities in Revolt,* "it was larger than any city in England except London itself and had taken its place not only with the largest provincial cities of the British Empire but with those of western Europe." The narrow lots in which the crowded city was laid out resulted early in a close-order formation of houses standing right up from the sidewalks, a characteristic that is not only historical but still current today on Philadelphia streets miles distant from downtown. It is a characteristic that gives great charm to Elfreth's Alley down below Independence Hall, where a Visiting Day is held in the spring by the Junior League of Philadelphia, 1715 Rittenhouse Street, to which you should write for dates; their tour also takes in other historic houses. It is a characteristic that gives both elegance and charm to several fine blocks on Clinton and Delancey Streets, which you will find by following Spruce Street a short way west after you have seen the POWEL, WHARTON, WISTER, and MORRIS HOUSES, in that order. With due respect to the houses, the noblest display of early American architecture downtown here (or anywhere in the country) is of course INDEPENDENCE HALL (1738–1741), a building which, with its entourage, contains many delightful details that are truly domestic in quality.

¶ The downtown houses

POWEL HOUSE (1765)

244 South 3d Street; daily 10 to 5; 25 cents; Philadelphia Society for the Preservation of Landmarks.

This is the only early house of high distinction in downtown Old Philadelphia which is regularly open to the public. Samuel Powel, who bought it shortly after it was built, was a cultivated gentleman, *bon vivant,* entertainer of celebrities, world traveler, and mayor of colonial Philadelphia. The house was beautifully suited to the social brilliance brought to it by the Powels and their friends, but for many years in its later life its handsomeness fell into such low esteem that it was on the point of disintegration. Its restoration came just in the nick of time, for dismantling had begun. Fortunately its marvelous drawing room got no farther away than the Philadelphia Museum of Art, where it can now be compared with the stunning recreation of the room in the house itself done by the late H. L. Duhring, Jr., architect of the restoration.

WHARTON HOUSE (c. 1795)

336 Spruce Street; open on written request to The Mutual Assurance Company, 240 South 4th Street.

Somewhat similar to but not quite in a class with the Powel House, this building with its beautiful brickwork is being used for business purposes, but with a keen appreciation of its interior beauty. Well worth seeing.

SHIPPEN-WISTER HOUSE (c. 1750)

4th and Locust Streets; open on written request to The Mutual Assurance Company, 240 South 4th Street.

A charming Georgian town house, larger and earlier than the Powel House, though again not quite its equal, it is, as is the Wharton House, owned and occupied for business purposes by the same appreciative and thoroughly "Old Philadelphia" firm.

ROBERT MORRIS HOUSE (1786)

225 South 8th Street; by appointment with N. W. Ayer & Son, Inc.

Perhaps the most impressive of these four fine Georgian houses is being used to good effect by the old Philadelphia advertising firm of N. W. Ayer as a house in which to

Downtown Philadelphia is given distinction by its notable early town houses, of which the Powel is a superb example.

entertain out-of-town guests. Throughout, the house is nicely maintained.

BETSY ROSS HOUSE (1700)

239 Arch Street; daily, 10 to 4:30; American Flag House and Betsy Ross Memorial Association.

The story goes that George Washington, Robert Morris (of the house above), and George Ross called at this very early unpretentious little town house to discuss the making of the first American flag with the seamstress who lived there. Both Betsy and her home have been famous forever since. The finely molded substantial cornices at roof eave and pent eave give the small-scale façade real Pennsylvania character. The rooms are all furnished for simple Philadelphia eighteenth-century living.

Nothing quite as remarkable in terms of the early German dwellings remains still standing in the Pennsylvania countryside as the house from which these rooms, now at the Philadelphia Museum of Art, were taken.

This house was at Millbach in Lebanon County, and the kitchen opposite, with its walk-in fireplace, and the stair hall, left, indicate the medieval quality of the first Pennsylvania "Dutch" homes.

EDGAR ALLAN POE HOUSE (*1800*)

530 North 7th Street; daily, 10 to 5; 50 cents; Richard Gimbel Foundation for Literary Research.

The poet lived for two years during the 1840s in this city dwelling typical of its date, meaning that, although plain, it has some personality. There are many possessions of Poe's here, and there is a fine research library for Poe students.

BARTRAM HOUSE (*1731*)

In Bartram Gardens, 54th Street and Eastwick Avenue, below Elmwood Avenue; daily, 8 to 4:30; no charge weekdays, Sundays and holidays 10 cents; city of Philadelphia.

Speaking of personality, this house is bursting with it, and most of it is John Bartram's, who built the place with his own hands of beautiful local stone laid up in ashlar courses. The tall Ionic columns were added, no doubt, when he remodeled it later in its century. One of the greatest of the early botanists, self-taught, his original touches—a recessed porch and carved-stone window casings—give the house its personality. The gardens are famous, of course, with rare and exotic plants, which his son-in-law continued to collect after

his death. This is in many ways one of the most rewarding old places to visit in the whole Philadelphia area.

WOODLANDS (*cemetery office*) (*c. 1770*)

Woodland Avenue and 39th Street; not open; Philadelphia Society for the Preservation of Landmarks.

This extraordinary "great house," of stone, was the community seat of the distinguished old Philadelphia family of Hamilton when the banks of the Schuylkill here were a lovely landscape of gardens and lawns. It is now surrounded by a vast city cemetery and occupied by the cemetery offices. There are immense porticoes front and back. Still quite a sight.

PHILADELPHIA MUSEUM OF ART

On hill overlooking river at entrance to Fairmount Park; daily 10:30 to 5.

1. Hall from the House of the Miller, Millbach, Pennsylvania.
2. Bedroom from the House of the Miller, Millbach, Pennsylvania.
3. Drawing room from the Powel House, Philadelphia, Pennsylvania.
4. Room from the Ezekiel Hersey Derby House, Salem, Massachusetts.

The rooms from the Millbach house are heavy, dark, and dour, with much medieval beauty and dignity. You won't see anything more pure in the whole Pennsylvania Dutch region, but there will be a lot out there which is more colorful and kindly. Here too is the original drawing room from the Powel House. And of extraordinary interest is the room from the great Ezekiel Derby House, in Salem, the one on which McIntire and Bulfinch collaborated, and which was torn down fifteen years after it was built. The room is mostly McIntire, furniture and all.

¶ The Fairmount Park houses

LETITIA STREET HOUSE

(1703–1715)

Daily 10 to 5 (closed holidays); admission by written (address bursar) or phone (Poplar 5-0500) request to Philadelphia Museum of Art; 25 cents and 10 cents; Fairmount Park Commission (custodians).

Not a country seat, obviously, but a little beauty of a brick town house brought out here in the 1880s from Letitia Street, in deep-downtown Old Philadelphia near Elfreth's Alley (noted above). Furnished in Queen Anne in accordance with its early date. The house is often called "Penn's Cottage," but it was never owned or occupied by William Penn.

SWEETBRIER MANSION *(1797)*

On right of park 300 yards along Landsdowne Drive; daily 10 to 5, except Sundays; 25 cents; Fairmount Park Commission (custodians).

A foursquare white-painted stone house with a lot of style, built by a man from Boston named Samuel Breck and now most handsomely maintained and furnished. Breck was a man with great social inclinations, and at Sweetbrier Mansion he lavishly entertained the *haut monde* of his day—royalty, nobility, and even Presidents. A perfect house for the purpose.

CEDAR GROVE MANSION

(1721 and later)

Beyond Sweetbrier Mansion on right fork; daily, 1 to 5 (closed holidays); 25 cents and 10 cents; Fairmount Park Commission (custodians).

As the date indicates, this fine sandstone house has developed in various stages; the end result is a sense of rambling informality. An unusually deep ground-level porch, brick-paved and roofed over, was an 1830 idea, and very becoming too. The house was moved here in 1927 from what is now the industrial section of Frankford, over by the Delaware. It contains the family furniture, and the old colonial kitchen is a favorite feature.

BELMONT MANSION (*a restaurant*)
(*before 1742, 1745, 1755, and 1760*)
Daily 5 to 8 except Mondays September through May, daily 5 to 9 June, July, and August, Sundays 1 to 8 year round; Fairmount Park Commission (custodians).

This distinguished old country mansion, built of stone, with early brick additions, has an interior that furnishes much pleasure along with the food. Outside the effect of the house suffers somewhat from an upper story added in the nineteenth century.

STRAWBERRY (*1798–1830*)
Near 33d and Dauphin Streets; daily, 11 to 5 (closed August); 25 cents and 10 cents; Fairmount Park Commission (custodians).

The older central section is oddly flanked by the two high later wings, one of them added, they say, to "entertain the City Troop." The ballroom, or music room, is a period chef-d'oeuvre done in richly colorful French Empire. The interior offers a complete change of pace from the other Fairmount Park houses. The original 1750 house here was called "Somerton" and was burnt by the British during the Revolution. The present central section is the second "Somerton," built in 1798 by William Lewis, a famous Philadelphia judge.

Joseph Hemphill was later responsible for the neoclassical wings and for quite a few other extravagant features, which contributed after his death to a foreclosure on the mortgage. It was the next owner, an energetic country woman, who made "Somerton" a going enterprise, with great fruit gardens and a dairy herd; she served refreshments on the side to the carriage trade from town, making a name for herself with her strawberries and cream. The house soon became known as "Strawberry Mansion," and "Strawberry" it still is, now delightfully restored.

WOODFORD (*1742–1756*)
Daily 1 to 5, except Mondays; Fairmount Park Commission (custodians).

This formal Georgian mansion, of tawny brick trimmed with white, is the personification of cultured elegance, true to type for early Philadelphia. It is one of the finest colonial houses in the country, and furnished to absolute perfection. "Woodford" had become a park guardhouse when it was restored under the direction of the Pennsylvania Museum and entrusted with the Naomi Wood Collection that helps to give the interior its present-day distinction.

MOUNT PLEASANT (*1762*)
Daily 1 to 5 (closed holidays); 25 cents and 10 cents; Fairmount Park Commission.

Another great magnificent Georgian mansion, richly done in stone, brick, and stucco, and complete with flanking dependencies, it is far and away the most

The music room of Strawberry in Fairmount Park is brilliant with the bright satins of its Empire furnishings.

"important" house in the park. As "Woodford" comes closest to perfection, "Mount
Pleasant" comes closest to grandeur. And
it is just as imposing inside as out. The
John Macpherson who built it in 1762 was
lavish with the money he made from
privateering, and expense was no object.
Seventeen years later it passed from Macpherson to Maj. Gen. Benedict Arnold, the
American commander at Philadelphia, who
bought it for his bride, the famous Philadelphia beauty Peggy Shippen. But before
the couple had a chance to occupy it, the
general was exposed as a traitor and fled
over to the British Army.

HATFIELD HOUSE (c. 1760–c. 1835)
*Daily except Thursdays, 10:30 to 5;
Fairmount Park Commission (custodians).*

This stalwart old country house of 1760,
which gained its impressively formal Greek
Revival portico in 1835, was brought here
in 1930 from what is now an industrial
section of the city, originally named "Nice-
town." A decidedly attractive addition to
the fine assembly of Fairmount Park
houses.

¶ The Germantown houses

STENTON (1728)
*In the small park at 18th and Cortland
Streets; city of Philadelphia, Society of
Colonial Dames (custodians).*

This was one of the first great houses you
would have come to approaching Germantown in colonial days, and one of the
finest. Standing now in its little six-acre
park surrounded by city, this noble old
mansion, of brick laid in Flemish bond,
once lorded it over a grand country estate.
The wide brick-paved entrance hall, like a
loggia, is a notable feature. James Logan,
who built it, accompanied William Penn
to America in 1699. Penn left him in
charge of the Province of Pennsylvania
during his long absence in England. He
was one of the greatest Philadelphians of
them all, and his house has the same
stature. Washington stopped here during
the Brandywine and Germantown battles.
The Colonial Dames maintain it, and a recent job of restoring original wall colors
and furnishings does them credit.

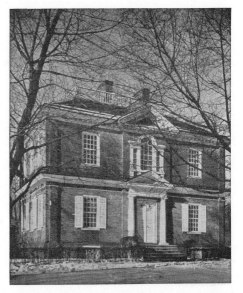

*Woodford is another of the great coterie of
Fairmount Park mansions.*

WAKEFIELD (1798)
*16th Street and Lindley Avenue; may be
seen by special arrangement; city of
Philadelphia, Fairmount Park and Colonial
Dames, Chapter VI (custodians).*

This large, attractive stone house, with a
lovely railed porch below the pediment,
looks down on a small public park, almost
as it must have appeared in its distant past.
It is used largely for meetings, and not all
of it is furnished.

HACKER HOUSE (1772)
*5214 Germantown Avenue; Tuesdays,
Thursdays, and Saturdays 1 to 5, except
Saturdays in August; Germantown
Historical Society.*

Typical of Germantown—meaning warm-
tinted, wide-jointed stonework, handsome
woodwork within, and reeking with history. It houses the library and museum of
the Historical Society.

GRUMBLETHORP (1744–1808)
*5267 Germantown Avenue; daily, 1 to 5;
Philadelphia Society for the Preservation
of Landmarks.*

Somewhat more manorial, this is the house
John Wister built. Wisters occupied it un-
til 1940, during which period it was called
the "Big House"; then they gave it to the
Landmark Society. It is the house in which
British General Agnew died of his wounds

The parlor of the Morris house, where the Washingtons lived when this was the Presidential residence.

The Morris house faces the site of the old market square in Germantown where Martha Washington did her marketing.

after the Battle of Germantown. The fine old house is now in gradual process of restoration and refurnishing.

MORRIS HOUSE (*1772*)
5442 Germantown Avenue; daily 9 to 5 except holidays; National Park Service.

This brownstone house on the square is famous as the place that Washington made his Presidential residence at the time when Philadelphia was the capital. In 1793 he

Upsala, another of the fine stone mansions that lined the old "Great Road."

brought his family here because of the yellow-fever epidemic in Philadelphia and the next summer rented it. His Cabinet met here often. A smallish house, it must have been bursting at the seams with guests, aides, etc. Washington comments on the fact that the cook might be seen from the dining room, where he was wont to receive. The house was well built but without any ostentation.

UPSALA (*1798*)
6430 Germantown Avenue, between Johnson and Cliveden Streets; Tuesday and Friday afternoons; 10 cents; Upsala Foundation, Frances A. Wister (President).

This beautiful house of ashlar-cut masonry is a lot simpler and less manorial than "Cliveden" across the street, but it stands as "Clivenden's" rival at this end of the "Great Road," for it has a graciousness and livability that the other lacks. When fully restored and furnished (a slow process for lack of funds), this is bound to be one of the Philadelphia "musts."

WYCK (before 1760), at 6206 Germantown Avenue, stands at right angles to the street behind its wall. It is one of the oldest and grandest but not open now. And farther out, opposite UPSALA, stands CLIVEDEN (1760), the most famous of them all in this area. Still belonging to a member of the Chew family, it is not open now, but at least you can get a good look at it from the street.

THE ADJACENT SUBURBAN COUNTIES

¶ *Delaware County: Upland; Essington; Chadd's Ford;*

Dilworthtown ¶ *Chester County: West Chester; Wayne;*

Bryn Mawr; Valley Forge; Pottstown ¶ *Montgomery County:*

Audubon; Whitemarsh; Hatboro

The number of houses listed for these three "Philadelphia counties" is no indication of how numerous the fine old houses are in this whole region. There are myriads of them, with a warm stone beauty all their own, making any rambling back-road drive rewarding. There are hardly any that are better than the houses listed here, but if you would like to see more, and particularly more private homes, you should send for the program of the annual house and garden tours managed by the Pennsylvania House and Garden Tour, Penn-Sheraton Hotel, 39th and Chestnut Streets, Philadelphia, which includes "Down the Brandywine." There are also local visiting days, which are mentioned below.

¶ Delaware County

Delaware County Day, usually in late May, shows as many as fifty historic buildings; the tickets are about two dollars and fifty cents, or four dollars including transportation. For dates, etc., write to Delaware County Day, 47 Long Lane, Upper Darby, Pennsylvania.

¶ Upland (*just out of Chester*)

CALEB PUSEY HOUSE (*1683*)
    Race Street; private.
This is not open ordinarily, but it does happen to be the oldest English-built house in Pennsylvania. Of brick-and-stone construction and of more than mere archeological interest.

¶ Essington (*down Broad Street, Philadelphia, onto 291*)

JOHN MORTON HOMESTEAD
    (*1654, 1698, and 1806*)
    Prospect Park; daily, 9 to 5; state of Pennsylvania.
If you have a taste for the truly primitive, these two log houses, with a later stone section in between, will be interesting. John Morton, a signer of the Declaration, was born here in 1724. The house is furnished in an appropriately primitive Dutch fashion and well cared for.

¶ Chadd's Ford (*322 over to Route 1*)

WASHINGTON'S HEADQUARTERS
    (*as of 1777*)
    Battlefield Park, on Brandywine River 15 miles from Wilmington on 202, 1½ miles south of intersection; weekdays 11 to 5 except Mondays, April through September, Fridays, Saturdays, Sundays, and holidays 11 to 5 October through March; state of Pennsylvania.

LAFAYETTE'S HEADQUARTERS GROUP (*as of 1777 with later additions*)
    Same.

HOWE'S HEADQUARTERS GROUP
    (*1754*)
    Same.
On the Brandywine Battlefield, where Howe's and Washington's armies met on September 11, 1777, these constitute three historically interesting and increasingly at-

tractive groups of houses and outbuildings. They are being furnished as of the Revolutionary period under the direction of Henry F. du Pont, of Winterthur, Delaware, one of the country's outstanding collectors of Americana.

¶ *Dilworthtown* (*on 202, 4 miles south of West Chester and about 1 mile from the Brandywine Battlefield*)

THE 1704 HOUSE (*1704*)

Old Westchester-Wilmington Pike ¼ mile from Dilworthtown; Tuesdays, Thursdays, and Saturdays 2 to 5 except holidays, also by appointment; 50 cents; Chester County Historical Society.

In the spring of 1648 Quaker William Brinton embarked with his wife and son William for Penn's colony, refugees of the religious struggle in England. Brinton in time prospered, acquiring more than a thousand acres of land. His son William married Jane Thatcher at the Birmingham Meeting, then held in the Brinton cabin. His father deeded the farm to him in 1697, and here he built a stone house for his wife and six children; the stone was taken from a nearby quarry. The walls were twenty-two inches thick, and the steep roof was pierced by dormers and pent eaves over the first-floor windows on the north and south sides of the house. In all there were

A recent remarkable restoration is the 1704 House near West Chester.

twenty-seven windows (an unusual number for the times) with leaded sash. Little of this early house remained when the society received it in 1947 from descendants of the builder, who had purchased it for preservation. The many descendants of the family have formed an association which has helped the Historical Society to finance the restoration. The restoration architect, Mr. Edwin G. Brumbaugh, made a careful study of the old house that existed under the modern wood and plaster after the removal of a large serpentine wing. It now stands much as it was originally—a medieval dwelling. The selection of furnishings is based on actual inventories taken after the death of the builder; only a very few of the original items have been located so far.

¶ *Chester County*

Chester County Day, the first Saturday in October every year, is the time to see the Chester County houses. Send for the illustrated program of nearly forty houses so that you can pick out the maximum of twelve houses which they advise you to attempt to see. This is truly a house-tour treat, beautifully organized. Address Chester County Day, Box 1, West Chester, Pennsylvania.

¶ *West Chester*

DAVID TOWNSEND HOUSE (*c. 1790–1830*)

225 North Matlack Street; Tuesdays, Thursdays, and Saturdays 2 to 5 (closed holidays), or by appointment (phone: 4755); 25 cents; Chester County Historical Society.

This tall town house was a small farmhouse in 1785; it had a three-story-front face lifting in 1830. It is well furnished with Hepplewhite and Sheraton pieces.

¶ *Wayne*

THE HOMESTEAD (*1789*)

Beech Tree Lane and Bellevue Avenue; open on request; Mrs. E. Dorothy Finley, Radnor Historical Society.

A tenant house put up on his Revolutionary farm by Squire John Pugh, this interesting

The best known and one of the most endearing of all of Washington's Revolutionary headquarters is this erstwhile ironmaster's residence at Valley Forge.

house has been for many years the home of the present owner's family.

❡ *Bryn Mawr*

IDLEWILD FARM (*1717*)
Follow Morris Avenue to Williamson Avenue; by appointment (phone: Lawrence 5-1234); Mr. and Mrs. Lawrence Saunders.

One of the very early Welsh stone farmhouses, beautifully kept and furnished. It is on a farm that has been in continuous operation since 1717, when the Welsh were beginning to filter into this part of Pennsylvania. There is a fascinatingly equipped early kitchen.

❡ *Valley Forge*

WASHINGTON'S HEADQUARTERS BUILDING (*1758*)
Daily; Valley Forge Park Commission.

This was built to be the ironmaster's residence for what was then the "Mount Joy Forge," but by the time John Potts bought it a few years later, the name had changed to "Valley Forge," which is the name that

has become immortalized by the man who occupied the house during the winter of 1777–1778 and the men who were encamped around it in the cold. It is a house so familiar in appearance that, paradoxically, few people really have a clear picture of it in their minds. To see it with your own eyes is to draw closer to that fateful winter. It is furnished mostly as it was at the time; much of the furniture belonged to the Potts family. Colonel Dewees' house and General Varnum's quarters are in the Park.

❡ *Pottstown*

POTTSGROVE (*1752*)
Route 422; daily 10 to 4, Sundays 1 to 4; state of Pennsylvania (owner), administered by State Historical and Museum Commission.

This, in a way, is "Valley Forge" five times as large—one of the great remaining manor houses of Pennsylvania. Built by the wealthy father of the John Potts who owned the Valley Forge house, it also served as Washington's headquarters—for

Pottsgrove is the embodiment of all that is most appealing among the stone country mansions of the state.

five days in September, 1777. This immense, handsome dwelling of mellow masonry is a thrilling house to visit; the colors inside and the furnishings couldn't be finer. It combines the best qualities of the early Pennsylvania manor and farmhouses.

¶ Montgomery County

¶ *Audubon (from Jeffersonville, on 422, take Egypt Road)*

MILL GROVE FARM (*1762*)
Pawling Road; daily, 10 to 5; Montgomery County Park Board.

This big stone house, with characteristically pented gables, was built by James Morgan, an iron man, who allowed the north wing to stand becomingly on a lower level. In the 1790s it was owned by Jean Audubon, the French father of the naturalist, and in 1804 it was occupied by the naturalist himself. It was at the Bakewell country place nearby, called "Fatland," that under tender circumstances John James met his future wife, Lucy.

FATLAND (*1845*)
Adjoining Mill Grove Farm; private (see above).

The house in which the Bakewells lived when Audubon was at Mill Grove Farm, of which no picture exists, was torn down in 1845, and on the same foundations was erected the remarkable Greek Revival mansion which today somehow manages to survive—an immense, bleak romantic edifice, with Ionic porticoes front and back, and one wing to match. It may or may not be preserved.

¶ *Whitemarsh*

HOPE LODGE (*1721*)
Route 309 on outskirts of town (house well marked); June 1 to November 1, Wednesday through Sunday, 12 to 5; no charge; Hope Lodge Foundation.

This is by all odds one of the finest Early Georgian houses in the country. Its fine five-bay brick façade bears some resemblance to "Wilton" in Richmond. A slightly recessed brick arch above the doorway is notable, and its interior woodwork is deeply molded, bold, and vigorous. The scale is lofty throughout. It was built by a wealthy, prominent Quaker named Morris for his English bride-to-be; but somehow the marriage never took place, and Morris lived and died here at Hope Lodge, a bachelor. An interesting house to see at any time, and when it is fully restored, it will be one of the prizes of Pennsylvania.

¶ *Hatboro*

KEITH HOUSE (*1722*)
Graeme Park, Keith Valley Road; by appointment; Mr. and Mrs. Welsh Strawbridge.

Built by Sir William Keith, this long, narrow, high stone house has a tall gambrel roof and two tall brick architectural chimneys rising from the central section of the roof. We agree with Wayne Andrews that "Keith's country home was an inspired creation of carpenters and masons (presumably Swedish) . . . an occasion when artisans were as eager as artists to stress the beauty of the materials with which they worked." While the exterior is unadorned, though with fine pattern and color in the wide white-jointed stonework, the interior is rich with paneling—in many rooms from floor to ceiling. The house is not at present maintained as a lived-in dwelling, but the passage of time has done wonders to the woodwork color.

Keith house is an edifice for connoisseurs. It is the work of Swedish artisans building proudly with the beautiful Pennsylvania fieldstone.

LANCASTER COUNTY

You are now in the country of the "plain people"; the villages, the countryside, and the people hereabouts are as picturesque as any in America. On market days in Lancaster the country people flock in, and it is something not to miss; they are Tuesdays, Fridays, and Saturdays (the five markets being open on different days). Out of town, try to get off the main roads once in a while. Lancaster farms are famous for their painted decorations as well as for their productivity.

You can get the current date (generally in mid-October) for Lancaster County Day by addressing the Lancaster County Art Association, Box 967, Lancaster, or else the Stevens House, Lancaster—a fine, old-fashioned hotel with a lot of style. Then, by writing the Women's Club of Ephrata, you can find out just when in May they'll be holding their Hospitality Day for Ephrata and northern Lancaster County. Not all the houses will be old, but don't let that stop you!

¶ *Lancaster*

WHEATLAND (*1828*)
> *Marietta Avenue; daily 9 to 5 April through October, weekdays 9 to 5 rest of year; The Buchanan Foundation.*

This handsome brick Federal mansion was purchased in 1848 for $6,750 by James Buchanan when he was Secretary of State in the Polk Cabinet—a bargain even then.

Wheatland, home of President Buchanan, in Lancaster, is now handsomely restored.

He lived here with a niece, who acted as hostess while he conducted the first "front-porch" campaign in our political history, becoming our first and only bachelor President. The house is furnished throughout in a style appropriate to its period, and contains many Buchanan-family pieces. The grounds, like the house, have been beautifully restored.

¶ *Ephrata (13 miles northeast of Lancaster on 222)*

EPHRATA CLOISTER (*1733–1749*)
Daily, sunrise to sunset; 50 cents; guides; state of Pennsylvania.

The cloisters comprise a set of buildings put up by the Seventh Day Baptists, a communal society founded by Conrad Beissel in 1732: the SAAL, the SISTERS' HOUSE, the CONRAD BEISSEL HOUSE, and others. A re-markably preserved, picturesque group of buildings, with a rich flavor of the Rhineland; not to be missed.

¶ *Reinholds (10 miles beyond Ephrata on 222; turn left on 897)*

MRS. HATTIE BRUNNER'S HOME AND ANTIQUE SHOP
On request to owner.

Mrs. Brunner's old Dutch house is a museum of wonderful Pennsylvania antiques. She has been a collector, connoisseur, and dealer for more than fifty years, and has made notable contributions to the Metropolitan Museum and others.

¶ *Manheim (10 miles northwest of Lancaster on 72)*

BARON STIEGEL MANSION (*c. 1762*)
Town square; by appointment (address: M. Luther Heisey, 237 North Lime Street, Lancaster); Lancaster County Historical Society.

Stiegel was no baron, but a glassmaker and iron founder of great fame who came here from Germany in 1750, laid out the town of Manheim, and built this remarkable house with a band platform on the roof. He owned the entire glassmaking town by 1770 but died penniless four years later. When, during the Revolution, Congress met at York, forty miles west, Robert Morris made this his residence; and Washington stayed here overnight on occasion.

BERKS COUNTY

The barns or the houses! Which are better here you will have to decide for yourself.

¶ *Baumstown (6 miles southeast of Reading on 422)*

DANIEL BOONE BIRTHPLACE (*c. 1735–1779*)
Birdsboro, R.D. 2; daily; 25 cents; state of Pennsylvania.

The wilderness scout of renown spent his youth in this beautiful example of an early Pennsylvania stone farmhouse. Small windows—for lack of glass and for protection—give it an ancient look. Now faithfully restored (by architect Brumbaugh), it contains early benches, tables, and other primitive furnishings. West of town is the house built by Lincoln's great-grandfather Mordecai, marked but private.

¶ *Birdsboro (a few miles beyond Baumstown)*

HOPEWELL VILLAGE (*c. 1740–1750*)
6 miles southeast of town in hills back on Schuylkill River; daily 8 to 4:45, Saturdays, Sundays, and holidays 9 to 6, May through October; National Park Service (superintendent in charge).

This represents one of the early manorial

ironmaking communities, built around a cold-blast charcoal-burning furnace. The community was medieval and self-sustaining, and stayed pretty much that way until the furnace was closed in 1883 after one hundred and thirteen years of activity. A fascinating, out-of-the-ordinary restoration, well worth seeing. (See Saugus, Massachusetts, for the ironworks restoration there.)

¶ *Douglassville* (*just beyond Birdsboro*)

MOUNS-JONES HOUSE or
OLD SWEDE'S HOUSE (*1716*)
> *Will be open when restored; R. H. Schurr.*

This fine stone house is the oldest in the region. It is being, or has just been, restored with the help of the Berks County Historical Society. The plan is to have it furnished with eighteenth-century pieces. It would be well worth finding out if it is ready.

¶ *Oley* (*5 miles northeast of Reading on 73*)

HENRY FISHER MANSION (*1801*)
> *By written or phone request (Yellow House 9–3276), preferably Saturday; Mr. and Mrs. Frank S. Fisher.*

Probably the finest example of a Georgian manor house in this section, it was three years a-building. A few family pieces are left. Each mantel is differently carved by master craftsman Gottlieb Drexel.

¶ *Womelsdorf* (*12 miles northwest of Reading on 422*)

CONRAD WEISER HOUSE (*1751*)
> *East of town in Conrad Weiser Memorial Park; Historical Society of Berks County, administered by Pennsylvania Historical and Museum Commission.*

This early stone house, typical of the region, was the home of the famous pioneer treatymaker and Indian interpreter.

BUCKS COUNTY

Bucks County is not only one of the biggest counties in Pennsylvania but in its venerable way one of the most beautiful. In covering the houses listed below you will pass through its finest towns and countrysides and see its early stone houses and barns at their best.

¶ *Tullytown* (*a few miles up from the Bristol bridge off Route 13 on the Delaware and near the Levittown development*)

PENNSBURY MANOR (*1683–1938*)
> *Well marked; daily, 10 to 4:30; state of Pennsylvania.*

When William Penn returned from England in 1736, he found his great country establishment "very near falling, the roof open as well as the windows, and the woodwork almost rotten." For two centuries after that it was left untouched; so the restoration which began in 1936, by the late R. Brognard Okie, had to be undertaken nearly from scratch. The manor is in fact a re-creation by this well-known architect, who was an authority on early Penn-

sylvania domestic architecture. The result is a grand success, comprising not only the manor house itself but many dependencies on the parklike estate by the bank of the wide Delaware. It is furnished appropriately.

¶ *Fallsington* (*near Washington Crossing*)

At this historic point ten miles up the Delaware from Trenton there are state parks on both sides of the river (see Washington Crossing, New Jersey) marking one of the more famous episodes of the Revolutionary War.

THOMPSON-NEELY HOUSE (*1701*)
> *East of Bowman's Hill section of Washington Crossing Park, at Clarksburg.*

The central part of this typical early brownstone house was built by John Pidcock, the first white settler in these parts. Here Washington had a meeting just before crossing the Delaware on Christmas night with his generals. The original part of this engaging house is furnished with pre-Revolutionary pieces, and more is being done.

The Thompson-Neely house in Washington Crossing Park is one of the handsome landmarks of this historic locality.

OLD FERRY INN (*1812*)

At the Crossing; daily April 15 to November 1, or upon special request during park hours; Washington Crossing Park Commission.

At the Pennsylvania terminus of McKonkey's Ferry, which played a vital part in the crossing, is an impressive brownstone of the period which was superimposed on the original ferryhouse by Mahlon Taylor. It was, of course, the scene of great activity that Christmas night when the Americans launched their desperate "Victory or Death" attempt, and also the scene of their triumph—the Hessian officers spending their first night of captivity here. The commission plans to make the Ferry Inn into a museum too.

TAYLOR MANSION

Across from the Old Ferry Inn.

This old stone beauty is now the Washington Crossing Park Administration Building.

¶ Newtown

One of the truly choice old towns of Pennsylvania, it is neither perfect nor spectacular but has plenty of mellow warmth and atmosphere. Charming old stone house rows and individual houses and inns line the main street. There is an Open House Day, generally in mid-May (address Open House Day Committee, Newtown). And let us suggest the drive from Newtown to Buckingham on 413 as one on which you will see any number of distinguished old stone country homes, delightful to look at as you pass. The town was Washington's headquarters before and after the Battle of Trenton.

LAVENDER HALL (*1742,*

older part prior to 1709)

Left on 532 just out of town; open as an eating place.

BIRD IN HAND (*1690*)

Near the Temperance House; Edward R. Barnsley.

Formerly a tavern, it is one of the oldest frame houses in the state.

FRIENDS' MEETINGHOUSE (*1817*)

The meeting held here was organized by Edward Hicks, the famous primitive painter.

¶ Solebury

A charming crossroads village with a fine Friends' meetinghouse, east of Buckingham via 202 and 263.

INGHAM MANOR (*an antique shop*)

(*pre-Revolutionary*)

Back on 202 between Aquetong and New Hope about 1 mile from New Hope.

One of the most likable and unspoiled tailored stone houses in the county, the massive exterior walls, the paneled living room, and the huge fireplaces reflecting the finest features of the local architecture.

LEHIGH & NORTHAMPTON COUNTIES

¶ *Allentown*

TROUT HALL (*museum and library*)
(*1770*)

Allen Park, 414 Walnut Street; Wednesday and Saturday afternoons; city of Allentown, headquarters of Lehigh County Historical Society.

The impressive stone exterior of this two-and-a-half-story country place shows how well the early settlers here managed to set themselves up. This was the house of the son of the William Allen who laid out the town, and was named from a nearby stream in which trout abounded. Allen ignored the "Dutch" architecture of the neighborhood and built a Georgian Colonial mansion. It once housed Muhlenburg College.

¶ *Egypt*

TROXELL-STECKEL HOUSE (*1756*)

Daily (caretakers' house nearby); Lehigh County Historical Society.

This is the real thing, a big early fieldstone farmhouse, with pent eaves, a heavy-beamed kitchen with an enormous walk-in fireplace, and fine early-farmhouse furniture. There is a wonderful cast-iron German stove of 1758 inscribed "Verachte das Alter ni" ("Never despise old age"), an appropriate motto for most of the entries in this book.

¶ *Catasauqua*

GEORGE TAYLOR HOUSE (*1757*)

Lehigh County Historical Society.

This fine old stone house, now in process of restoration, was the home of the signer

of the Declaration of Independence after whom it is named.

¶ *Bethlehem*

There is a group of old stone buildings in the vicinity of the Moravian church which housed one of the many early communal religious sects. While all are being used, it is possible that some of them may be seen on request. They are well worth seeing from the street at any rate, and be sure to pay a visit to the Moravian burying ground above the church, where the famous Easter Dawn Service is held each year.

¶ *Easton*

MIXSELL HOUSE (*1833*)

Southwest corner 4th and Ferry Streets; Saturdays 2 to 5, or by appointment; Northampton County Historical and Genealogical Society.

The Mixsell House was occupied by the family until 1928, when it was willed to the Historical Society, which exhibits here county historical items, Indian artifacts, pottery, books, old deeds, and furniture.

GEORGE TAYLOR HOUSE (*1757*)

4th and Ferry Streets; national holidays, or by appointment; D.A.R.

The George Taylor House was built by William Parsons, founder of Easton, and then became the town house of the signer of the Declaration after whom it is named. Some of the original furniture is here, along with other pieces of the period.

CENTRAL & NORTHERN PENNSYLVANIA

¶ *Harrisburg*

JOHN HARRIS MANSION (*1766*)

219 South Front Street; daily 2 to 5, except Sundays; headquarters of Historical Society of Dauphin County.

This fine stone mansion was built here on the banks of the Susquehanna by the

founder of Harrisburg, and is the oldest building in the city. Now a most rewarding historical museum, it was from its front porch that John Harris in 1775 watched the final review of the Harris Ferry company of Thompson's Rifle Battalion when this body of Pennsylvanians marched off to join Washington at Cambridge, among them Harris's namesake son, who was later killed at Quebec. From the same spot a year later Harris called the people of Harris Ferry together and read to them the Declaration of Independence, two days after it was signed in Philadelphia.

¶ *Sunbury*

HUNTER MANSION (*1852*) *and*
FORT AUGUSTA (*scale model*)

> *Open daily; Pennsylvania Historical and Museum Commission.*

Fort Augusta was Pennsylvania's stronghold in the Upper Susquehanna Valley from the days of the French and Indian War to the close of the Revolution. It was an extraordinary wilderness construction, containing considerable living accommodations within the fortifications. Residing in the fort during the Revolution was Col. Samuel Hunter, County Lieutenant of Northumberland, who occupied the commander's quarters while the fort disintegrated. Finally this last log building burned, and Capt. Samuel Hunter, the colonel's grandson, built the present Hunter Mansion, now a museum containing many fascinating relics of Fort Augusta and early Sunbury. Not the least interesting feature is the large-scale model of the fort which has been built on the lawn in front of the mansion.

¶ *Boalsburg*

BOAL MANSION (*1789–1798*)

> *Estate near Route 322; being restored, partially open daily May to November; 60 cents and 25 cents; Pierre L. Boals.*

It is probably best to begin by quoting a historical note furnished by Mr. Boals.

"The first of the Boals family came to this country before the Revolutionary War. Its ancestors had lived in Ireland after one of the captains of the Spanish Armada was shipwrecked on the coast of that country and married and settled there. Always an adventurous family the Boals served in nearly every war and became allied in a later generation with a French family of equally romantic history. Through the present owner's mother, Mathilde de Lagarde Boal, the family has inherited the

family chapel, complete with all its antique furnishings, works of art and religious accessories, of Christopher Columbus's descendants in Spain. . . . The house, the chapel, and the museum contain many heirlooms which are rich in historical association, from chain mail of Crusading days to Simon Bolivar's pistol. . . . The house is especially rich in fine china and crystal and objets d'art. The museum at present contains examples of both early Pennsylvania furniture and elegant European pieces."

Not only does the estate here, now on display, live up to the promise implicit in this description, but there is a further inducement to visit the vicinity if you can arrange to be on hand for the annual Old Boalsburg Day, generally held in May or June and sponsored by the community's P.T.A. In addition to ten or more old houses, taverns, and schools in Boalsburg itself, the tour takes in old buildings of interest in the nearby villages of Oak Hall, Linden Hall, and Shingletown. Here is an opportunity to get a rounded picture of the past and present of one of the most appealing countrysides in Pennsylvania. (Observe the enthusiasm taken here in the local history.) Write to Dr. D. W. Russell, Boalsburg, for dates and further information.

¶ *Altoona*

ELIAS BAKER MANSION (*1844*)

> *Baker Boulevard, near 36th Street; Saturdays and Sundays, 1:30 to 4:30, June to October; Museum of Blair County Historical Society.*

Baker was an ironmaster, and he built a house in keeping with the importance of his status—limestone walls, all interior trim of black walnut, Italian-marble columns in the drawing room, carved furniture, inlaid piano, and so on. Renovated in 1951, and a good job.

¶ *Northumberland*

DR. JOSEPH PRIESTLEY HOUSE AND MUSEUM (*1797*)

> *Open by arrangement with Pennsylvania State University.*

On a dramatic eminence where the Susquehanna divides into its east and west branches, there is a house of considerable size, built in 1797 by Dr. Joseph Priestley, the celebrated English chemist who discovered oxygen and other gases. The house is of clapboard, with many interesting details and some of the doctor's furniture. It is preserved as a memorial, and the small adjacent brick laboratory is a museum. The view is magnificent.

WESTERN PENNSYLVANIA

¶ *Farmington (near the southern border of western Pennsylvania 15 miles southeast of Uniontown on Route 40)*

MOUNT WASHINGTON TAVERN (*1816*)
On site of Fort Necessity; daily, 8:30 to 5; National Park Service.

The tavern is a big beautiful brick house with great double-chimney gable ends, one of the more impressive of the early-nineteenth-century stagecoach inns that lined the famous old National Road leading from the Atlantic to the West. And don't miss the old tollgate house a few miles farther east with its cut-stone octagonal tower. The tavern, of course, contains many relics of the battle as well as the furniture of its early inn days.

¶ *Ambridge (about 15 miles northwest of Pittsburgh on Route 88)*

OLD ECONOMY (*1824–1826*)
In the town; daily; 50 cents; state of Pennsylvania.

Here is not only the relic of an interesting experiment in communal living and industry but a fascinating museum of the domestic manufactures of the early nineteenth century. The Harmonist Movement began in Wurttemberg, then a kingdom in southern Germany, whence the adherents of lay preacher George Rapp followed their leader to this country in 1803. They made their first settlement at what is now Harmony, twenty miles north of Ambridge, where there are some interesting remains. Ten years later they sold their Harmony holdings most advantageously and moved to the banks of the Wabash in Indiana, where they founded New Harmony (see Indiana). This successful settlement they also sold again ten years later, and again to good advantage, this time to the English social theorist Robert Owen, and moved back to Ambridge here. The thirty-five-room "great house," built by the Harmonists with their own handmade brick, was originally two separate homes for Father Rapp and his chief lieutenant, Frederick Reichert Rapp; it was made one house in 1832 by a connecting wing. Decline followed the adoption of celibacy in the colony and the death of Father Rapp. The society was finally dissolved in 1905. But in its halcyon days everything the Harmonists did, from weaving to wagon-making, could hardly have been done with more skill and enterprise. This is evident here at Ambridge.

¶ *New Geneva (a few miles north of Point Marion, on the West Virginia border, on Route 166)*

FRIENDSHIP HILL (*1789–1823*)
Daily, May to November; 75 cents and 50 cents; Mr. and Mrs. Sherwood C. Martin.

Albert Gallatin, who came as a young man to this country from Geneva, Switzerland, and later became Jefferson's Secretary of the Treasury, built the brick first section of "Friendship Hill" just before his marriage. Then, thirty-four years later he added the stone mansion to the earlier house, making of it today, in its ivy-covered beauty, a pleasant memento of this colorful and famous figure of our republic's early years.

¶ *Scenery Hill (on Route 40 between Brownsville and Washington near both "Friendship Hill" and Fort Necessity)*

CENTURY INN (*1794*)
Daily; Dr. G. F. Harrington.

This is said to be the oldest tavern on the entire length of the National Pike. Built as an inn by Stephen Hill, founder of the village, it has been operated continuously as a tavern ever since. It is a cut-stone structure, typical of the region, and if it has not been preserved exactly as it was originally, we must bear in mind that concessions have to be made now and then to the changing necessities and tastes of the patrons.

¶ *Pittsburgh*

CROGHAN HOUSE, *now* PICNIC HOUSE (*1830s*)
Daily; state of Pennsylvania.

The main feature of this great Classical Revival mansion is the remarkable quality of its interiors, ornamented with Corinthian details of a very high order, if a little heavy in places. But it was meant to be a house in which to entertain, and the name it now enjoys fits it to perfection.

¶ *Russell (8 miles north of Warren on Route 62 near New York State)*

THE LOCUSTS (*1835*)
Just out of town; by appointment, June 1 to October 30; Mrs. W. A. Walker.

This historic old Warren County house was built in 1835 by Guy Irvin, who was one of the largest lumber operators in western Pennsylvania at the time. On his many raft trips down the Allegheny, Ohio, and Mississippi Rivers, which carried him into the Deep South, he found the houses he passed to his liking and decided to make his own home a composite of those which he liked the best. And though he made a

Unfortunately not many of the fine western Pennsylvania early houses can be opened on occasion to the public. The Locusts, near Warren, is luckily an exception.

remarkably good job of the house, to tell the truth it turned out to be more than anything else a rather choice example of western Pennsylvania Georgian. The brick was made on the place, the lumber came from Mr. Irvin's own forests, and the stone from nearby quarries. The restoration and furnishings are well done.

¶ *Washington (at junction of Routes 19 and 40, southwest of Pittsburgh)*

LE MOYNE HOUSE (*1812*)
49 East Maiden Street; daily, 1 to 5; Washington County Historical Society.

This cut-stone domicile, with its rather severely classical details, stands flush to the sidewalk and has a dignified if slightly dour appearance from the street. A smaller door to the left of the somewhat monumental entrance led at one time into what was the office and pharmacy of Dr. Francis J. Le Moyne, who built the house and later made of it a station of the Underground Railway. He was a leading abolitionist and at one time an unsuccessful candidate for the Vice-presidency.

¶ *West Overton (near Scottdale on Route 119 about 30 miles southeast of Pittsburgh)*

OVERHOLT HOUSE (*1838*)
Just out of village; Saturdays and Sundays 2 to 5, other times by appointment; Westmoreland-Fayette County branch of Western Pennsylvania Historical Society, Richard T. Darsie (Secretary).

This charming old brick hillside house, with its high white porch, was built by Abram Overholt, maternal grandfather of Henry Clay Frick, who was born in a cottage on the place and became one of the greatest steel magnates and art collectors of his day. The rooms are furnished with more than usual interest, and a Federal room, a Mennonite room, and a historical room with wallsize murals of the French and Indian War are especially notable.

Ohio is famous for its broad, flat-arched, fanlighted doorways, many of them much more ornamented than this one that belongs to the Mower house in the very good town of Granville. And within the tall, two-story portico of the President's house at Marietta, on the opposite page, is another doorway of similar form and proportions.

OHIO

*I*F YOU had been planning to try your fortunes in the wilderness that was then Ohio in the late eighteenth century, and had been making your way from Tidewater Virginia, Maryland, or the Carolinas, you would have struck for the Ohio River; there at some point you would most likely have loaded your worldly goods on a barge or flatboat and floated down the river toward your destination. But if you had been coming from the New England states, you would in all probability have trekked along the southern shore of Lake Erie on horseback, if you were lucky enough to own a horse, your family jolting along behind in a Conestoga wagon. After

1798 there was yet another route— Zane's Trace, which connected Wheeling, West Virginia, with Maysville (then Limestone), Kentucky—a vital road for those determined to settle in the central portion of the state. In fact, later it was to be known as the "National Road," and today it stretches across the continent from Atlantic City to San Francisco under the designation "Route 40."

Naturally the influence of the New Englanders is plain to be seen in the early building in the northern part of the state, still known as the "Western Reserve," and many of the place names too are of Yankee origin. In the southern part occasional stately Georgian houses

195

and even a few columned mansions of the plantation type have survived. But it was to accommodate the great influx that came surging over Zane's Trace, swelling to still greater proportions after it became a highway, that the characteristic Ohio building—the inn—sprang up; in fact, it seems that almost every house in the state today has been an inn at some time during its career. Of the old houses that have survived the blights of commerce and fire, there are actually more inns than private dwellings. But the inns were, after all, built exactly like any large-family house of the period; and thus, even when there are few other old places in a neighborhood, the inn tells us quite as much about domestic building as would a private dwelling.

In recent years, Ohioans, increasingly conscious of their architectural heritage,

have been restoring not only the early homes but many of the inns as well. Together they are a reminder of one of the most fascinating episodes in America's development.

¶ *Northeastern Ohio*

¶ *Kinsman*

ALLEN HOUSE (*1820–1830*)
Open as a tearoom; Miss Alice Logan.

Built by Dr. Peter Allen and inherited by his grandson Dr. Peter Dudley Allen, this can be truthfully described as one of the most delightfully unusual exteriors in Ohio. Richly but lightly ornamented, the exquisite carvings on window frames, doorway, and entablature are something to behold. The four full-height fluted pilasters with Ionic capitals are echoed by the short pilasters which stand on either side of the door, whose entablature is a little master-

Another familiar feature so typical of early Ohio houses is the pilastered front. The Matthews house at Painesville is a particularly fine example, with good Greek Revival details.

piece of sunbursts and delicately carved moldings. It is a mansion in miniature, and its interior detail is equally fine in quality.

¶ *Unionville (between Painesville and Ashtabula)*

SHANDY HALL (*1815, enlarged 1825*)

Near Cleveland on Route 84, 1 mile east of Unionville Tavern; daily 10 to 5 except Mondays, May 1 to November 1; 50 cents and 15 cents; Western Reserve Historical Society.

A pioneer homestead of weather-beaten clapboard, of whose rambling seventeen rooms the banquet hall is the chef-d'oeuvre. It has a flat, barrel-vaulted ceiling, and between it and the low dado is a magnificent French wallpaper that made this room the wonder of the frontier countryside.

¶ *Painesville*

MATTHEWS HOUSE (*1829*)

497 Mentor Avenue; campus of Lake Erie College; by appointment to limited groups; Mrs. Dean C. Matthews.

This house is one of a small group in the town built by the Western Reserve's architect-builder Jonathan Goldsmith, who came here from Connecticut in 1811 and died here thirty-seven years later. His work also survives in Mentor, Willoughby, and Cleveland. The Matthews House was moved to the campus of Lake Erie College and restored. It is a choice Greek Revival house whose owner has furnished it appropriately with antiques, some of them here originally. The stairway with its carving and delicate spindles is a good example of Goldsmith's fine detailing, as is the ornate exterior of the doorway with its drape carvings.

LUTZ'S TAVERN (*1822*)

792 Mentor Avenue (Route 20); open all the time; Park and Gerald A. Lutz (proprietors).

Originally Rider's and Randall's Tavern, it was first a stopping place on the Indian trail between Buffalo and Cleveland. Its "Mt. Vernon" front was added shortly after the inn was first built. Its six square piers are built around rough-hewn posts; a small door has been cut in one of them so that the guest may examine the construc-

tion. The inn has been well restored fairly recently and is furnished with antiques.

¶ *Cleveland*

DUNHAM TAVERN MUSEUM (*1842*)

6709 Euclid Avenue; daily 12:30 to 4:30 except Mondays; contribution; Society of Collectors.

An important stopping place on what was the old Buffalo-Cleveland-Detroit stage road, it was built by Rufus and Jane Pratt Dunham, immigrants from Massachusetts. A tavern until 1857, it was a country home from then until 1930. Meanwhile, Cleveland had swallowed up almost everything of this nature, and the Society of Collectors there did a great service to the community in preserving this fascinating old landmark. There are appropriate period furnishings as well as special exhibits.

¶ *Hudson*

SEYMOUR HOUSE (*1841*)

15 Prospect Street; by written or phone request; Mr. and Mrs. C. K. Reynolds, Jr.

Nathan Perkins Seymour came to Western Reserve Academy in 1834 from Yale, of which his grandson was later President. Nathan brought his bride, joined the faculty here, and built this finely proportioned brick house. Its construction was in the competent hands of the Connecticut carpenters, the Porters, who had come here to build the college buildings. It is said that, in spite of their excellent reputation, young Dr. Seymour watched every brick being laid; since he was a classical perfectionist, he wanted his home to be perfect. The present owners mean to keep it that way too and have left some of the rooms completely unchanged. The furniture is antique, with occasional contemporary pieces.

The PRESIDENT'S HOUSE and the BLISS or SLAUGHTER HOUSE on the campus of Western Reserve Academy are occupied by members of the faculty, and while no particular attempt has been made to furnish them in keeping, they are houses with much period charm whose interior woodwork has been left intact. Requests may be made to the residents, Mr. and Mrs. E. Mark Worthen, and Mr. and Mrs. Richard MacFarlane, respectively.

OLD STAGE COACH INN or **SINGLETARY HOUSE** (*an antique shop*) (*1828*)
> *Near Hudson at Streetsboro; Mr. and Mrs. Carlton Close.*

Considered a showplace throughout the area, like so many others of an early vintage in this state, it was built as an inn. It is a handsome white clapboard dwelling with possibly one of the most interesting doorways in Ohio.

❡ *Zoar* (*near New Philadelphia*)

This historical village was established in 1817 by a group of three hundred Separatists from Wurttemberg, led by Joseph Baumeler. Although the Zoarites came for religious freedom, they were not a severe sect, and their houses reflected German comfort and color. They were roofed with red tile, and both interior and exterior were brightly painted, several colors sometimes being used in one room. Painted decorations may be seen on the furniture, much after the manner of the Pennsylvania Dutch. The town was surrounded by apple orchards and a magnificent community garden, much of which is still maintained. Love of flowers and music seems to have predominated in this industrious community, which soon became self-sustaining. Its beer has become legendary.

WILLIAM AND LILLIAN BIMELER HOUSE, NUMBER ONE HOUSE, JOSEPH BAUMELER'S HOUSE (*all prior to Civil War*)
> *Daily 9 to 5 except Mondays, April 1 to October 30; state of Ohio.*

These homes were built simply, with the exception of Baumeler's house, which was originally intended as a home for the aged and certainly reflects the success of the colony. Of red brick, and two and a half stories high. it is an ornate mansion in the Late Georgian Colonial style, pillared, porticoed, and iron-railed. The Bimeler House, a plain two-story brick, is more typical. Both houses have indigenous collections of Zoar products of all kinds, including interesting pottery, weaving, and musical instruments. A few rooms are furnished.

❡ *New Philadelphia*

SCHOENBRUNN MEMORIAL STATE PARK
> (*Thirteen log cabins, church, and school*) *daily; state of Ohio.*

Three Moravian missionaries from Pennsylvania led a band of Christian Indians to the banks of the Tuscarawus River, where they founded the first village in what is now Ohio. Here all the Christian Indians were killed and scalped by whites—one of the uglier episodes in our frontier history. The village is an expert and edifying reconstruction.

❡ *Central Ohio*

❡ *Mt. Vernon*

CURTIS-DEVIN HOUSE (*1834*)
> *208 North Main Street; by written request; Fletcher M. Devin, 208 North Main Street.*

This house was altered in 1850 according to the prevalent Greek Revival fashion, at which time the balconies to the front, the huge scrolled acroteria surmounting the gable, and the balustrade at the eaves were doubtless added. The marble mantels were probably done by two English stonecutters in Gambier who came here to work on Kenyon College. The staircase is particularly noteworthy, with its simple, delicate spindles and its finely carved stringers. The narrow paneling which forms the wall beneath is repeated in the deep dado broken by a niche midway up the stairs. The whole thing is executed with real taste and skill.

❡ *Granville*

AVERY-DOWNER HOUSE (*1842*)
> *221 East Broadway; on request; Denison University.*

Now a sorority house, this is a remarkably

pure example of Greek Revival, built by Benjamin Morgan for Alfred Avery. The central two-story portion has four fluted Ionic columns supporting a deep unornamented pediment. The one-story wings repeat the central design. The effect of the place is chaste and charming.

MOWER HOUSE (*1824*)
233 East Broadway; open with advance notice; Mr. and Mrs. A. H. Heisey.

This was the residence of Granville's leading citizen back in the second quarter of the nineteenth century. Later it was used for many years as a local bank, but it is now again a very gracious and attractive home, beautifully furnished in periods preceding the date of the house itself.

¶ *Newark*

DAVIDSON HOUSE (*c. 1815*)
In Moundbuilders Park; Wednesday and Sunday afternoons; Licking County Historical Society.

A white clapboard house moved here from downtown Newark in 1948 and now set in a green park with its own walks and brick-walled gardens, this is a delightful and unusual piece of architecture with strong Federal feeling. The delicacy of the detailing on the doorway is extraordinary, and the recessed bay under the side gable, with its flat-arch form and its gallery, is a striking feature. In fact, it is considered one

of the finest doorways in the Middle West. It is furnished in period, many of the articles having been made in Newark or nearby, and there is an interesting collection of Ohio primitive painting.

¶ *Zanesville*

HEADLEY INN (*now a restaurant*) (*1802–1865*)
Between Zanesville and Springfield on Route 40; daily 9 to 5 except Mondays, June 1 to October 1; Mrs. Harry Ackerman and Mrs. E. B. Howard.

One of the most famous of all the famous early inns of Ohio, it was originally a drover tavern. Mrs. Uzdal Headley was known the whole length of the old National Road for her cooking. Built of huge blocks of dressed sandstone two to three feet long, a foot high, and eighteen inches wide, it is a kind of Ohio landmark, whose owners have preserved much of the early atmosphere. Big open fireplaces in the dining rooms still glow cheerfully in cold weather. In one of the beamed rooms the old sassafras tables and benches are still in use. See the upstairs rooms and the narrow, enclosed stairway that leads to them, with its rare grapevine pattern painted in polychrome on the riser baseboards—the work of Amos Edgerley, who married Uzdal's sister. A fascinating old inn, and the fare deserves its fame.

This early example of split-level planning is the Headley Inn outside Zanesville on Route 40— one of the most popular stopping places along the old National Road to the West from pioneer days to the present.

HILLSIDE (*1834*)

461 Luck Avenue; May 15 through July, by appointment only; Mr. and Mrs. Clarence Graham.

This impressive house with its classical portico crowns a hilly section of the city which was nicknamed "Natchez" by the river boatmen because it reminded them of the famous Mississippi town on its hill. There is a notable pair of mantels in the immense living room.

ROBBINS HOUSE

115 Jefferson Street; by written request; Mrs. R. M. Taylor.

Occupied for sixty years by the owner's parents but not lived in now. The unusual cornerstones and quoins draw the attention of many passers-by. Other houses to note are the GUTHRIE HOUSE (1842), a stunning brick house with a classical portico supported by four fluted columns; the BUCKINGHAM HOUSE and the MATTHEWS HOUSE, with their very good Ohio doorways.

UNITY FARM (*1834*)

McConnelsville, 15 miles south of Zanesville; April and May, by appointment; Mr. and Mrs. E. C. Jones.

Unity Farm was built as a stagecoach inn on the banks of the Muskingum when the mail route ran between Zanesville and Marietta. It is a long white building of simple distinction which has been thoughtfully restored by its owners. It has some of the original stenciled walls, as well as firebacks of museum quality.

¶ Chillicothe

ADENA (*1806–1807*)

April 1 to October 30, Daily 9 to 5 except Mondays, balance of year, daily 1 to 5; state of Ohio.

"Adena" was known first as Mt. Prospect. Thomas Worthington, one of the first two United States senators from Ohio, made the acquaintance of Benjamin Latrobe in 1805, when the famous Baltimore architect was at work on the south wing of the Capitol. He commissioned Latrobe to design this twenty-room mansion for his fifteen-thousand-acre estate. It remained in the family until 1903. Worthington, who came from Virginia, was Governor of Ohio from 1814 to 1818. He was buried in a Duncan Phyfe casket; the governor desired good cabinetry at all times. "Adena" has been beautifully restored. The chastity of the interior is enlivened by the wonderful color treatment of walls and ceilings. Six of the rooms have handmade wallpapers and authentic draperies in which the materials are at least a hundred and fifty years old. The family has returned many of the original pieces of furniture, and the collection now includes an outstanding set of Duncan Phyfe and other pieces of Sheraton and Hepplewhite used

The hand of a truly talented architect is apparent in the north front of Adena near Chillicothe—one of the best country houses Benjamin Latrobe ever designed.

Adena is now strikingly furnished with heirloom pieces that have been returned to the house; one of the handsomest early houses in Ohio.

by the governor. The masons were the two Morris brothers from Virginia; the iron, carpets, and brasswork came from Philadelphia; the window glass from Albert Gallatin in Gallatin, Pennsylvania; and the wallpapers from Baltimore. Local carpenters made many of the chairs, bedsteads, bureaus, wardrobes, tables, sofas, and clockcases, using mahogany and local cherry. This is a house that illustrates its own story to perfection.

¶ *London*

RED BRICK TAVERN (*1837*)
Halfway between Columbus and Springfield on Route 40; open March to January; Mrs. Nell Brasket (phone: London 401).

A handsome red-brick tavern with double end chimneys and spanking white trim, this old inn is one of the best-looking in the state. It can boast of having served six Presidents, beginning with John Quincy Adams and ending with Warren Gamaliel Harding. Harrison and Van Buren met here in a "smoke-filled room," and the famous slogan "Tippecanoe and Tyler too" is said to have been hatched here.

¶ *Lakeview*

MANARY BLOCKHOUSE MUSEUM (*1812*)
On Route 69, at northern end of town; May to September; 25 cents.

A log house built by Captain James Manary during the War of 1812, it served as a refuge for pioneers following the Hull Trail. In 1823 James McPherson bought it, plugged its rifle ports, and made it into his home. It now contains more than 1,000 relics of the period 1800–1825, rare cotton prints of the 1770s, and willow and hickory chairs.

¶ *Northwestern Ohio*

¶ *Norwalk*

STURGIS-KENNAN-FULSTOW HOUSE (*1834*)
99 West Main Street; by written appointment during summer months; Col. and Mrs. Philip H. Fulstow.

One of the finest homes here, and Greek Revival, of course. The pediment, supported by four octagonal columns, is decorated with an oval sunburst. Said to have been designed by William Gale Meade, who also built the Vredenburgh House that is owned by Mrs. Fulstow's brother. Contemporary furnishings.

Other good examples are the VREDENBURGH-GARDINER HOUSE (1832), 133 West Main Street; the WOOSTER-BOALT HOUSE (c. 1830s), 114 West Main Street; the KIMBALL-WOOSTER-MARTIN HOUSE (c. 1830s), 54 Main Street, a real Greek Revival beauty; and the OLD BAKER HOUSE (1830), 207 East Main Street.

¶ *Waterville (southeast of Toledo on 24)*

THE COLUMBIAN HOUSE (*1837, wing 1828*)

Ethel N. Arnold, 405 West Sandusky Street, Finley, Ohio.

Built as an inn by John Pray, one of the earliest settlers in the Maumee Valley, it was a stagecoach stop between Detroit and Dayton, and the social center of the community. An old lady told the owner that she could remember riding horseback over forty miles as a girl, her party gown in the saddle bag, to attend the balls given here. It is a fine-looking three-story building, well proportioned, with three doorways flush with the pavement. It has all its original woodwork: six-panel black walnut doors, dados in almost every room, and carved moldings in the ballroom on the third floor. Reopened as an inn some years ago, its owner hopes to open again soon.

¶ *Milan (a few miles north of Norwalk)*

In the 1840s, thanks to the canal that linked it with the Great Lakes, Milan was one of the leading grain ports of the world—for ten prosperous years. Then came the railroads!

MITCHELL-TURNER HOUSE (*1828*)

128 Center Street; not open now; Mr. Jay Fenn.

This is a charming Greek Revival house with a most handsomely wrought Ionic portico, as ornamental and appealing as an old-fashioned valentine. A lovely sight from the sidewalk. May be seen at some later time.

GALPIN HOUSE, MILAN HISTORICAL SOCIETY (*1840s*)

10 Edison Drive; May 1 to October 1; daily 1 to 5 except Mondays; Milan Public Library and Milan Historical Society.

A three-story red-brick house of substance and distinction, with the white trim and white shutters typical of the better Ohio town houses of the period, it was owned by Dr. Loman Galpin, who delivered a neighbor's baby christened Thomas Alva Edison. The parlor and kitchen are furnished in the period, and there is an Indian room. The remaining rooms are used for collections and exhibits but are due to be furnished.

EDISON BIRTHPLACE (*1841*)

11 Edison Drive; April 1 to December 1 Tuesday through Saturday 9 to 5, Sundays 1 to 5, January 1 to April 1 Thursday through Saturday 9 to 5 and by appointment (closed December); 50 cents and 25 cents; Mrs. Madeleine Edison Sloane.

This charmingly simple little brick house was designed and built by Samuel Edison, father of Thomas, when the town was a flourishing grain port. The family lived here until 1853, when they moved to Port Huron, Michigan. The house is appropriately and very pleasantly furnished, and contains many of the great inventor's personal possessions. Very engaging.

¶ *In & out of Lebanon*

GLENDOWER (*1836*)

Route 42; daily 9 to 5 except Mondays; 25 cents and 10 cents; state of Ohio, Ohio State Architectural and Historical Society, Mrs. William Mason Phillips (curator).

This is the chef-d'oeuvre of the Lebanon area. Greek Revival was going great guns when Amos Bennett, carpenter and joiner, built "Glendower" for J. Milton Williams, an outstanding lawyer and public figure of his day. Its recessed panels and entrance columns, its window grille in the attic, and the frieze on its low flanking wings are typical manifestations of the fashion which produced this truly distinguished brick mansion. It has been beautifully restored and furnished with original pieces from Warren County homes.

THE GOLDEN LAMB (*an inn*) (*1815*)

Mr. and Mrs. Robert H. Jones (proprietors).

This is a landmark—the oldest hostelry in the state, licensed December 23, 1803. It is known that in 1807 a two-story log inn existed on the spot, for, when the first copy of *The Western Star* came out in that year, advertisers located their shops in relation to Mr. Seamon's tavern. Ichabod Corwin built the present commodious brick building. "Charles Dickens, Esq. and Lady" registered here in 1842. Ten Presidents and many other celebrities have also been guests; some have had rooms named for them.

LEWIS HOUSE (*1846*)

144 East Mulberry Street; by written or phone request (Lebanon 3–2306); Mrs. Hazel Brookes, Lebanon.

The house has been occupied by the present owner's family since it was built, and, except for the 1900 porch, nothing has been added. The present owner's thrice-married mother was her thrice-married father's last wife; she was alive until 1945. Thus the house was occupied continuously by one husband and his wives for ninety-nine years—probably a record. Aunts and uncles moved in from time to time and in passing left their things in the house. "Therefore," says Mrs. Brookes, "it is a conglomeration and we are sentimental about some of the most insignificant items." The double parlors are impressive, and the walnut railing of the three-story open-well staircase has an unusually free form and newel post, spokes, and rail of rare finesse. There are fireplaces in almost every room; in the parlors the mantels have rare tile facings. Twin Venetian-glass chandeliers are reflected in pier glasses reaching to the ceiling. The original cornices and draperies, the excellent furniture and old family portraits all create in this fine period piece an atmosphere of well-to-do Midwestern family life in the mid-nineteenth century.

BRYNFRYD (*1840s*)

Cincinnati Avenue; by written or phone request; Mr. and Mrs. Wallace S. Howell.

A most impressive foursquare Greek Revival mansion in its own little park. With two-story columns across the front and a balustraded deck on the flat hip roof, it is engagingly romantic, yet eminently livable. A nostalgic touch is the old coach house on the grounds with its iron window grilles.

THE GOTHIC (*1840s*)

Cincinnati Avenue; by written or phone request; Mr. and Mrs. J. Alfred Jackson.

The ornamental bargeboards, sharp rooflines, balconies, and narrow Gothic windows provide the romantic flavor that gave this house its name. Victorian can be winning when it wants to be. The detail is equally attractive inside, with finely designed Gothic arches in the halls, spacious rooms, and antique furniture, some of it much earlier than the house.

BRANSBY FARM (*1855*)

Route 48, 5 miles north of Lebanon; on written request; Mrs. William Mason Phillips.

This well-proportioned white frame colonial is as sound today as when it was built a hundred years ago by John Plunkett, a native of Virginia. Among the rare items here is a pressed-glass punch bowl, one of a pair that belonged to Henry Clay; the other is in his home "Ashland" in Kentucky.

Stately and stylish, Glendower is one of the outstanding country mansions in the neighborhood of Lebanon.

ASHLEY (*1850*)

> *Maple Street, Harveysburg, northeast of Lebanon; on request; Mr. and Mrs. J. E. Welsh, Box 81.*

Colloquial Greek Revival, with a tall central section with foursquare columns and pediment, and low flanking wings, this was an active station on the Underground Railway. Furnished entirely with fine antiques.

OAK HILL (*1838*)

> *9 miles south on 48 at Morrow; open on request; 50 cents toward public library and upkeep of extensive grounds; Mr. and Mrs. Richard S. Whitacre.*

The house might be called "Ohio antebellum," exemplifying as it does the days of the 1840s and 1850s. The present owners' great-grandfather, who built it, was General Superintendent of the Little Miami Railroad (now the Pennsylvania), which ran nearby, and was the son-in-law of Cincinnati's pioneer cabinetmaker and clockmaker, accounting for much of the furnishings. The original draperies in the drawing room are of East Indian sailcloth, more than a century old, and painted in exquisitely faded colors. The crystal chandeliers are still lit with candles. Servants' quarters and carriage houses are also on the lovely grounds.

FERNEYCROFT (*1842*)

> *Lebanon; by written request, 1 to 5; voluntary donation accepted; Mrs. Georgette Glosser Stubbs, R.F.D. 3.*

As Mrs. Stubbs remarks, "The outstanding fact is that 'Ferneycroft' has been owned and occupied by the family for five generations. Visitors enjoy the evidence of how 'living the hard way' was accomplished a century ago."

¶ Up the Ohio from Cincinnati

¶ Cincinnati

SINTON-TAFT HOUSE (*a museum*) (*1820*)

> *4th and Pike Streets, near center of town; weekdays 1 to 5, Sundays and holidays 2 to 5; Cincinnati Institute of Fine Arts.*

This is in many ways the most unusual Classical Revival house west of the Eastern seaboard states. Said to have been designed by Benjamin Latrobe, it is quite Adamesque in its delicacy and adornments. Full of Federal-period style and dazzling white, its impressive entrance portico is approached by a graceful flight of steps. Steps and porch are guarded by ornamental iron railings. It contains much excellent furniture, creating a homelike but palatial setting for its fine collections, including Rembrandts, Turners, Goyas, and Corots.

KEMPER LOG CABIN (*1804*)

> *Zoological Garden, 3400 Vine Street; daily 10 to 5 May to October, rest of year Sundays, weather permitting; 10 cents and 5 cents; Colonial Dames.*

Really a two-story log dwelling, reputed the oldest within the Miami Purchase, it is furnished with primitive pieces of the pioneer variety.

¶ *Pt. Pleasant* (*on the Ohio southeast of Cincinnati*)

GRANT HOUSE MUSEUM (*before 1822*)

> *Grant Memorial State Park, junction of Routes 52 and 232; daily 9 to 5 April 1 to October 30, rest of year 1 to 5; state of Ohio.*

The house in which the President was born is tiny and unpretentious. It contains many personal belongings, including his cradle, his Bible, the trunk he took to West Point, and his favorite cigar case.

¶ *Ripley* (*on the Ohio northeast of Cincinnati*)

JOHN RANKIN HOUSE (*date unknown*)

> *Daily 9 to 5 except Mondays, April 1 to October 30, rest of year 1 to 5; state of Ohio.*

The state honors the Reverend John Rankin, a great abolitionist, by making his small brick house into a memorial for him. It was a station on the Underground Railway and because of its high location could cast a light which might be seen for miles across the Ohio River. Local legend claims that Eliza of *Uncle Tom's Cabin* crossed on the floating ice near here and was one of the many slaves to be succored at this house. After the war Ripley became a haven for freed Negroes, who also made, across the river, settlements named "Pomposity" and "Africa."

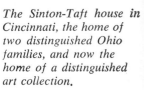

The Sinton-Taft house in Cincinnati, the home of two distinguished Ohio families, and now the home of a distinguished art collection.

¶ *Marietta*

Named in gratitude for Marie Antoinette, the Queen of our Revolutionary allies, this town at the junction of the Ohio and the Muskingum is the site of Marietta College and was one of the most important pioneer outposts during the western migrations after the Revolution. It is the oldest surviving Ohio settlement.

RUFUS PUTNAM HOUSE
(*before 1788*)
In the Campus Martius State Memorial Museum; daily, 9 to 5; state of Ohio.

Putnam is the man who led an important early group of settlers to this section where an elaborate scheme of dwellings in the form of a hollow square, which they called the "Campus Martius," served as a fortification. His house was one of the four substantial corner houses and is the only structure of the development still standing. It is now in the Campus Martius Museum. The framework is mortised and braced at the corners with dovetailed diagonal pieces held in place by wooden pins. The house is furnished in keeping with the style of its period. In it are some of Putnam's possessions, many others being in the museum itself, along with a host of relics from this extraordinary pioneer project. In the rear of the museum is the little 1788 land office of the Ohio Company, a fascinating restoration by the Colonial Dames.

THE PRESIDENT'S HOME (*1818*)
301 5th Street; on request to President's office; Marietta College, W. Bay Irvine (President).

Built by Henry P. Wilcox, who came here from Alabama in the early part of the century, this house is a small Southern Colonial mansion, even to the high-terraced approach with its double flight of steps, whose wrought-iron railings are supposed to be the midcentury work of a professor at the college here. The inside stairway, which terminates in a dome, or shell, is sculptured of wood. In 1825, a year after the house was finished, the builder departed, leaving a few debts to be settled. The property went to the Mills family, in which it remained for more than a hundred years, after which the college acquired it.

¶ *Gallipolis (junction of 7 and 23, on Ohio River)*

OUR HOUSE (*1819*)
434 First Avenue; daily except Monday 9 to 5, rest of year 1 to 5; state of Ohio.

Of Late Georgian colonial design, this two-story brick house with its end chimneys and two arched and paneled doorways was built as a hostelry by Henry Cushing, whose hospitable "Come up to our house" created the name. Much of the interior is original; the carving on the mantels is unusually refined for a tavern in the wilderness, as are the arched doors with their graceful fanlights. Beautifully made also is the circular stairway of walnut and cherry. The original lighting fixtures are in place, as well as the taproom chairs, tables, and settees, and the bed in which slept Louis Philippe, later to become King of France. Lafayette stopped here in 1825, and Jenny Lind in 1851. The third floor has possessions of the ill-fated early French refugees, who arrived in these parts in 1790, five hundred strong. Mostly small tradesmen from cities, they were unable to cope with the wilderness and were practically wiped out by disease, starvation, and Indians.

One of the best hunting grounds for good early houses in Indiana is down along the Ohio River, and one of the best towns along the river is Madison, where stand both Shrewsbury House and the Lanier home, two of Indiana's best, both the work of the remarkable early carpenter architect, Francis Costigan. The staircase in Shrewsbury House, above, is one of his tours de force; the Lanier home opposite one of his most monumental mansions.

INDIANA

HOOSIER is the name given to a state which has its own strong individuality, yet seems more typically American than almost any other. Pioneer traffic east and west flowed unceasingly through it, and earlier still it flowed north and south as well, for the French fur trappers and traders who first settled around Vincennes came north from New Orleans and south from Quebec. At that time they did not go farther west because the prairie lay beyond. Thus it was here that the English, German, and Scotch-Irish pioneers met up with the French; consequently a melting pot for our dominant ancestral strains came into being. Yankee shrewdness and toughness of fiber were to combine with the politesse of gentlemen adventurers from Virginia and the Carolinas to produce a kind of special type: a sturdy and substantial individual who was knowing rather than shrewd, and friendly rather than polite—a man in essence democratic. All this does not explain how he came by the name Hoosier but it does throw some light on the particular meaning the name has taken on—a name which next to Yankee seems to be a kind of joking symbol for "real American."

From this confluence of different peoples you might expect to find several styles of home building, and indeed you will. For once the necessary log-cabin stage was in the past; the early houses and buildings that are found in the state represent a wide range of influences. On the whole, Hoosiers do not seem to have amassed the great fortunes encountered in many other sections of the country during the days of cheap land and cheaper labor. Nor, for the most part, were they a folk given to ostentation. Mansions of the Lanier variety in Madison occurred infrequently. But of comfortable town houses on the modest scale there were numbers, and we can see some of them today in the Ohio River towns such as Madison and Vevay, neat, stylish, well-built, denoting a pleasant way of life.

¶ *Bruceville*

BRUCE HOUSE (*1811*)
Open any time; Mrs. Ruth McClure Ashby.
This is the house in which Lincoln slept one night when he came here to address a political meeting for Henry Clay. Lincoln's host had twenty-five children, who bedded down on the unfinished second floor, since then removed. The famous guest's bedroom on the first floor is still intact with the bed he slept in; so are the wide plank floors, deep window sills, heavy hinges on the doors—everything as it was, very simple and utilitarian.

¶ *Corydon (25 miles west of Louisville on Route 62)*

The site of Corydon, on a steep hillside, was originally owned by Gen. William Henry Harrison. After the Northwest Territory had been divided, the seat of the government was moved here from Vincennes and in 1816 it became, for a time, the state capital, which accounts for some of its fine little buildings.

STATE TREASURY (*1817*)
Mulberry Street; by phone appointment; Mr. and Mrs. William B. Doolittle.
Occupied until recently by the Doolittles, descendants of Amzi Brewster, the original householder. The Doolittles are glad to show this most interesting early example even though the interior is not presently in exhibition form.

See also the old STATE CAPITOL between Beaver and Walnut.

HENDRICKS-PORTER-GRIFFIN HOUSE (*1817*)
Walnut Street; upon written request; Miss Olive Griffin.
William Hendricks, third Governor of the

state (1822–1825), lived here. In 1841 Judge William A. Porter purchased it, and his granddaughter now occupies it. A small brick house with a two-room wing of limestone two feet thick, the house has its original woodwork, and has been little changed since the days when it was the governor's residence.

MANSION OF COL. THOMAS LLOYD POSEY (*1818*)
Oak Street at west end of Cherry; weekdays, 9 to 4; Hoosier Elm Chapter of D.A.R.
The Colonel Posey in question was the son of the famous territorial governor Thomas Posey, and was known as a great church worker. He never married, but as part of his good works he reared fourteen orphan children. He was the state Adjutant General. The brick house is furnished with local material dating from the early part of the century—pioneer relics for the most part.

¶ *Crawfordsville (Home of Wabash College, 45 miles northwest of Indianapolis on Route 34)*

HENRY S. LANE PLACE
(*1836, remodeled in 1845*)
212 South Water Street; weekdays, except Mondays; 10 cents; city of Crawfordsville (headquarters of Montgomery County Historical Society).
The builder was the first chairman of the Republican Party, a Governor of the state, and a United States Senator; he was a potent factor in the nomination of Lincoln as well. The house, a handsome fourteen-room brick mansion, sits in a little park which is beautifully landscaped. The detail of the interior has considerable style. There is a large and interesting collection of furniture of the 1845-to-1865 vintage, a doll room, and a pioneer room, among others. The rooms are well arranged and the whole place well kept up.

¶ *Greenfield (20 miles east of Indianapolis on Route 40)*

RILEY HOMESTEAD (*1849*)
304 West Main Street (Route 40); April 15 to November 1, daily; 25 cents and 10 cents; city of Greenfield.
Birthplace of the poet, this is a simple but

The unpretentious Posey house is one of the many attractions of the old river town of Corydon.

spacious and comfortable ten-room frame house situated in the heart of the farm land. With large fireplaces and walnut woodwork, it is furnished as it was when Riley was a boy. It contains his pictures, letters, and manuscripts.

¶ *Hanover (5 miles west of Madison near the Ohio River)*

BIRD HAVEN (*1858*)

> *In summer and early fall; to visitors not staying here, 25 cents; Miss Jane Rogers, Box 153.*

Now a guest house, this is Victorian Gothic at its most charming, with steep roof, gables, and lacy scroll trimming. Its furniture is heirloom, some much earlier than the house.

¶ *Indianapolis*

BENJAMIN HARRISON HOME (*1874*)

> *1230 North Delaware Street; daily 10 to 4 May 15 to October 15, daily 1 to 4 October to May (closed two weeks in March and during Christmas holidays); 30 cents and 10 cents; Arthur Jordan Foundation.*

Built by the most illustrious son of Indiana, the twenty-third President of the United States, descended from the long line of Har-

risons who have served the country with such distinction, this house offers a beautiful demonstration of the differences in architecture and decoration between the pioneer days when William Henry Harrison built his home near Vincennes (see "Grouseland") and the plush period of Benjamin Harrison, when Indians and buffaloes were a thing of the legendary past and life in these parts was established and prosperous. Here you have the fashionable house of its period—a two-story brick Regency with bay windows and ornate stone trim; its draperies, mirrors, carpets, and ornaments, stiff gilt and carved furniture evoke the gaslight era.

JAMES WHITCOMB RILEY HOME (*1872*)

> *528 Lockerbie Street; 10 to 4 daily except Mondays, open Sundays; 25 cents; James Whitcomb Riley Association.*

Riley, the pride of Indiana, whose poetry is now part of our cherished regional literature, lived in later life in this tall, stately Victorian house with its high-arched, stone-trimmed windows and doors. Definitely the dwelling of a successful man, it is furnished exactly as it was when the poet lived here, the atmosphere unique and personal.

The Riley home in Indianapolis has much to offer admirers of the Hoosier poet as well as the nostalgic eccentricities of Victorian.

¶ Madison

(on Ohio River halfway between Cincinnati and Louisville)

When the Ohio River was a main artery of commerce, Madison, located almost midway between Cincinnati and Louisville, was the most prosperous town in the state. Two remarkable houses survive this era, and a number of others of considerable interest line the streets near the river. Francis Costigan, who learned his trade as a carpenter's apprentice in Baltimore, is responsible for the two mentioned. Much of the elaborate carving in the Costigan houses was his own handiwork. Both are distinguished not only for their opulence but for the bold skill and ingenuity of their execution. They were built only thirty years after Madison was hacked out of the wilderness.

JAMES F. D. LANIER HOME *(1844)*

1st Street between Elm and Vine Streets; daily; 25 cents and 10 cents; Indiana Department of Conservation.

Sitting on its eminence facing the broad, brown Ohio, the south portico is impressive in every way. Richly carved are the capitals of the four great columns, which support a deep two-story portico whose ceiling is stunningly ornamented with three enormous squares centered in medallions. Engaged columns of the Tuscan order flank the ends of the front entrance and

The famous Lanier home is furnished completely in character.

the windows. The noble scale of this façade is further accented by the graceful iron grille, which repeats the octagonal pattern used in the windows of the frieze and used again in the glass cupola to which the spiral staircase in the hall ascends. Lanier, a North Carolinian by birth, and a financier and patriot who is said to have financed Indiana's part in the Civil War, built the place, and it remained in his family until it was given to the state by his granddaughter in 1925. She was then over eighty. She helped to furnish it as it had looked when her family lived there. The substantial carved furniture of the period of her childhood suits the massive scale of the house. It was a completely successful re-creation, for, in spite of its great size, this house has a wonderfully homelike quality. The emphasis is on the solid, comfortable impression of good living.

SHREWSBURY HOUSE *(1849)*

Southwest corner 1st and Poplar Streets; during January and February advisable to make appointment; 25 cents for house only; Mr. and Mrs. John T. Windle (antique dealers).

In many ways just as much a masterpiece as the Lanier Home and actually built before it, the two-story brick mansion cost about fifty thousand dollars (a tidy sum in those days), which indicates that the Shrewsburys were, to say the least, prosperous. Shrewsbury, as a member of the state supreme court, was one of Madison's outstanding citizens then. Set close to other houses, it has large side galleries and a very fine Regency doorway framing a twelve-foot door; this sets the scale for what follows. As you enter the hall, therefore, the grace and lightness of the staircase is astonishing. Freestanding, it spirals upward like a climbing vine, and is considered something of a structural marvel. There are twelve large rooms in the house and thirteen fireplaces. The ceiling height is impressive. The division between the twin drawing rooms, with their black-marble mantels, is made by double pairs of Corinthian columns, and the heavy framing of the windows reflects the Empire forms and figurations which were a result of Napoleon's Egyptian Campaign. All the woodwork is of temple proportions, yet it is paradoxically domestic in feeling. The first coats of white paint on these walls have never been covered and still look perfectly fresh. Here too are the original Louis Philippe crystal chandeliers. Architecturally the house is unaltered; indeed, this would be a job terrible to contemplate in these times. It is still in excellent condition. The Windles, who house their antique collections here, have been fortunate in acquiring the four Shrewsbury portraits, which hang in the drawing room.

OLD SULLIVAN HOME (*1816*)
1st and Poplar Streets; open by request; Mrs. Louise K. Gibb.

The first two-story brick house in Madison, this neat Federal-style home was built by Judge Jeremiah Sullivan, who named Indianapolis. Floors, woodwork, and carved mantels are all original. Care has been given to conforming to the period in the furnishing.

¶ *Mitchell (between Bedford and French Lick on Route 37)*

SPRING MILL VILLAGE
(*restored houses of early-nineteenth-century Indiana*)
Route 60, Spring Mill State Park; state of Indiana.

The following buildings were moved here from various places and restored in order to give an authentic picture of a typical village as it might have developed between 1815 and 1830: the APOTHECARY SHOP (c. 1830), the DISTILLERY (1825), the GRANNY WHITE HOUSE (1824), the GRISTMILL (1814), the HAT FACTORY (1816), the MILL OFFICE (1818), the MONTGOMERY TAVERN (1816), the MUNSON RESIDENCE (c. 1830), the POST OFFICE AND GENERAL STORE (c. 1830), the SAWMILL (1825), and the SPRINGHOUSE (1840).

¶ *New Albany (across Ohio River from Louisville, Kentucky)*

SCRIBNER HOUSE (*1814*)
East Main Street; open on application to caretaker, daily 9 to 5; Piankeshaw Chapter, D.A.R.

This is a simple frame house, restored and furnished with pieces of the pioneer period

The great double parlors of Shrewsbury House are big-scale Greek Revival.

given by friends, and with a few Scribner family pieces brought from New York (probably by covered wagon). A typical pioneer home of the time.

¶ *New Harmony (in southwest corner of state on Illinois line, on Route 460)*

OLD FAUNTLEROY HOUSE (*1816*)
West Street, on Route 460; weekdays 1 to 5, Sundays 2 to 5, summer 9 to 12; 35 cents; New Harmony Memorial Commission.

This is an historic community and the birthplace of two of the most widely known utopian experiments ever tried in this country. The first was under the leadership of George Rapp (see Ambridge, Pennsylvania) from Germany, and the second under Robert Owen, a Scotch reformer, who, in association with William McClure and other early scientists, helped to bring their idealistic brand of culture and education to the Middle West. There are a number of houses here built by the Rappites, of which one of the first is the Fauntleroy House, a spacious dwelling later the home of Owen's sons David Dale and Robert Dale, which derived its name from Robert Fauntleroy. Incidentally, it housed the first women's club in this country, the Minerva, founded by a granddaughter of Robert Owen.

The RAPP-MC CLURE HOUSE, the OWEN HOUSE, and the SCHNEE HOUSE, all built around this time or a little later, are all of interest, but privately owned at present. However, the New Harmony Community is a big restoration project of the Indiana Department of Conservation, and eventually there will be much to visit here.

¶ *Rockport (32 miles east of Evansville on Ohio River)*

THE LINCOLN PIONEER VILLAGE
(*a replica*) (*1816–1830*)
7 to 5 daily; 50 cents and 25 cents; city of Rockport, Park Department.

This is a memorial to Lincoln and to his fourteen boyhood years spent in this neighborhood. The Lincoln home was seventeen miles north of Rockport, and he often walked from it to John Pitcher's law office here to borrow or return books. The Village, a replica of the way the village looked at that time, was originally built as a WPA project under the direction of the sculptor, George Honig. Gentryville, a mile and a half from the Lincoln cabin, was where Lincoln spent much of his time. The well-to-do Gentry family were his great friends, and among the jobs that he was hired by James Gentry to do was taking a flatboat with cargo down the Mississippi to New Orleans—at a salary of eight dollars a month.

Of particular interest are JOHN PITCHER'S LAW OFFICE, where Lincoln spent his spare time reading, and the JONES STORE, where Lincoln clerked. Note the courting tube lovers used in the crowded one-room

log cabins; with the family all sitting around they could whisper into it. The AARON AND SARAH GRIGSBY HOME, where Abe's sister Sarah came as a bride, contains a bridal bed made of boughs. The GENTRY MANSION has been furnished by the Gentry family with pioneer pieces. The LINCOLN HOMESTEAD and a dozen other replicas complete this evocative museum of Lincolniana.

¶ *Terre Haute*

PRESTON HOUSE (*1820–1823*)
1339 Poplar Street; by appointment, between May and September; Miss Natalie Preston Smith.

Built of stone in the Georgian Colonial style, the mansion's furnishings were brought from Baltimore in 1835. The house, on its shaded grounds which were once the very edge of the prairie, is now a landmark in the city.

¶ *Vevay (20 miles above Madison on the Ohio River)*

Vevay, settled by a group of Swiss in 1801 and upriver about fifteen miles from Madison, has somehow managed to escape the "blight of progress" and remains a town of many charming old houses. It was early known for the wine produced in its vineyards. Edward Eggleston, a native son whose novel *The Hoosier Schoolmaster* is a classic of early days in Indiana, lived here. Vevay had its architect too—a builder-carpenter named George A. Kyle, who inserted silver plates with his name inscribed thereon in the newel posts of several of the houses he built—a very handy device for remembering himself to posterity. The houses are for the most part rural brick, versions of Georgian, neat and serviceable. The MOREROD HOUSES, the DUMONT HOUSE, the HENRY HOUSE, the FERRY HOUSE, as well as a number of others, form an interesting group with a certain homogeneity, thanks to Mr.

Kyle. They were built between 1810 and 1820, or thereabouts. The SWISS INN has been open for business since 1823. The homeowners are hospitable to interested visitors.

¶ *Vincennes (on the Wabash halfway between Terre Haute and Evansville on Route 41)*

This town, the oldest in Indiana, was the capital of the Old Northwest. It was first a thriving French trading post on the Wabash where hunters and trappers, arriving with their "bag" after days or weeks spent in the green depths of the forests, were blinded by the sunlight and overcome with the joy of seeing sparkling white houses and other men. Then it became the seat of the government for an area greater than the original thirteen states—so great, indeed, that no one quite knew its boundaries at that time.

WILLIAM HENRY HARRISON MANSION *or* GROUSELAND

(1803–1804)

3 West Scott Street; 9:30 to 5 weekdays, 1 to 5 Sundays; 30 cents and 15 cents; Francis Vigo Chapter, D.A.R.

Called "Grouseland" by its master and known also as "The White House of the West," it was the home of the dramatic and adventurous son of the illustrious Harrison family of Virginia, whose seat was "Berkeley," on the James. Chosen to govern the vast territories, he held a kind of dictatorial sway over lands which at one time included the whole Louisiana Purchase, west of the Mississippi to Wyoming and Oklahoma, so distant from the center of government that his power was virtually autonomous. The house, with twenty-six rooms and thirteen fireplaces, is built largely of black walnut and tulipwood. To the left of the hallway as you enter is what was formerly the council chamber, a bowended room in which many treaties were

The William Henry Harrison mansion in Vincennes is one of the most impressive presidential homes west of the Alleghenies.

concluded with the Indians, and which the great Indian Chief Tecumseh refused at one time to enter. An unsolved mystery are the two false windows in the front.

At 505 Main Street is the BONNER-ALLEN MANSION (1824). Like a large number of impressive early homes throughout the country, this excellent brick colonial house has become a funeral home. On the whole, it is perhaps a happier fate for a fine old house to be, so to speak, "embalmed" in this fashion, with its outward aspect preserved, than to be hopelessly disfigured or destroyed. This one has been called one of the most perfect examples of Colonial architecture west of the Alleghenies. A friend of Lincoln's, Cyrus A. Allen, purchased it from David Bonner, the Virginian who built it. Lincoln once passed the night in it. He was also often entertained at the old JUDGE ELLIS MANSION (1830), at 11 North 2d Street.

The Greek Revival fashion in the thirties and forties wended its way with Eastern pioneers as far west as Wisconsin, leaving its mark in the so-called Southern Peninsula of Michigan with classical gems of charm and naïveté, of which the Wilson-Wahr house in Ann Arbor is one of the excellent few that remain in anything approaching mint condition. On the opposite page, a relic of the rich early fur-trading days in a picturesque part of the Northern Peninsula is the beguiling old Beaumont house on Mackinac Island.

MICHIGAN

¶ In & out of Detroit: Dearborn; Toward Farmington
¶ The Greek and Gothic Revival houses of the Southern
Peninsula: Ypsilanti; Ann Arbor; Adrian; Marshall; Grand
Rapids; Niles ¶ The outpost houses of the Northern Peninsula:
Mackinac Island; Sault Ste. Marie·

*A*S INDICATED by the headings above, the houses now to be found in the Northern Peninsula either represent military installations, both British and American, or are relics of the fur trade and trapping which flourished there. Those in the Southern Peninsula towns designated above represent the influx of settlers from the Eastern states, and the fervor with which Eastern fashions in home building were utilized. It is unfortunate that so few examples of residential Greek Revival architecture have been preserved here in their original quality and condition, for few states have dealt with this thoroughly American style in such a charming way

and with the naïveté that is so essential to it.

What happened architecturally in the settlement made by Antoine de la Mothe Cadillac at the *place du détroit* ("place of the strait") between its founding in 1701 and 1760, when the British took over from the French, or even what happened up to 1796, when the United States took over, is anybody's guess. But we do know that, during the nineteenth century, easy going and well-to-do Detroit was famous for its comfortably housed, home-owning population. Someone who has carefully examined old photographs made in the neighborhood of the original 1850 NEWBERRY HOUSE long before its

1876 transformation has described the pictures for us.

"They show a peaceful, tree-lined Jefferson Avenue with large homes, well-kept lawns, a dirt road and what seems to be a board sidewalk. At its edge, in regular rhythm, ran horse-blocks, hitching posts, and, at the top of their poles— gas street lamps. Among the trees down toward the river, could be seen pleasant streets and comfortable frame houses."

And then [as historians are fond of repeating] came Ford!

The automobile industry transformed Detroit as few cities other than Pompeii have ever been transformed in so short a time. The transformation left us with but one "early" house to list for the city: the Newberry House, as remodeled in 1876. But it must be said that in return for what the industry took away, Ford gave us GREENFIELD VILLAGE. The Village is Henry Ford's own very personal statement of American homes, schools, factories, and products. But his remarkable conception has done one thing: it has given to Michigan a collection of Americana that is scarcely equaled in scope and variety anywhere else.

¶ In & out of Detroit

¶ Detroit

NEWBERRY HOUSE (1860–1876)
1363 East Jefferson Avenue; open by request; Louisa St. Clair Chapter D.A.R.

The 1850 mansion that was handed down to John S. Newberry and his bride can now be examined in the wonderfully flamboyant form it took on in 1876. In that year Newberry, a man of wealth who had made railway cars for the Union Army in the Civil War, engaged a Detroit architect, Gordon W. Lloyd, to enlarge the original house. Lloyd was an Englishman, and was said "to favor, in design, the French influence." He faced the house with two sets of bay windows rising from the sidewalk to the roof, which he crowned with a cupola from which an excellent view could be had of pleasure boats and barges going by under sail on the river. He ended up with thirty rooms, "not counting closets, storerooms, lavatories, and toilets." A Louis XV flavor dominated the drawing room. Birch, maple, rosewood, and mahogany were effectively employed in the mantels and cabinetry of the reception room and in the dining salon, where the walls and ceiling were entirely paneled in birch. Now the house is rapidly being restored to its former exuberant appearance, with furnishings being returned and restorations made where required, and it will soon take its rightful place as an exemplar of the period somewhere between the Campbell House in St. Louis and the Victoria Mansion in Portland, Maine.

DETROIT INSTITUTE OF ARTS
Tuesday through Friday 1 to 10, Saturdays and Sundays 9 to 6, in summer 9 to 6 except Mondays (closed holidays).

Incorporated in this interesting four-room exhibit are some of the amazing rooms from Whitby Hall moved here from Philadelphia, where Col. James Coultas built his home at what is now 58th Street and Florence Avenue. He named it "Whitby Hall" after his ancestral home in Yorkshire, England. In addition there is a bedroom from "Vauxhall Gardens," a seventeenth-century stone house which stood in Salem, New Jersey, and another bedroom from Spring Garden Mansion, built in 1760, in New Castle, Delaware.

¶ Dearborn

GREENFIELD VILLAGE
9 to 4 weekdays, 9 to 4:30 weekends and holidays; nominal fee. (It is suggested that you ask for the guidebook Greenfield Village, *which describes the whole area and the buildings, and offers a good map with the buildings located.)*

Greenfield Village is unique in America. It covers over two hundred acres and takes in over ninety buildings. Many old buildings of Michigan and the country at large have been bodily transported to it. The Village was planned by Ford to show the development of American customs, institutions, and early industry. He said of it that "by looking at things people used and that show the way they lived, a better and truer impression can be gained than could be had in a month of reading . . ." Maybe so; at any rate, it is an easy and entertaining way to learn. The streets of the Village are lined with mills, shops, schools, stores, and homes; some of the shops are "in business." There are planing mills, sawmills, cider mills, carding mills, silk mills—just about every kind of mill that existed in the old days (some of them running too). There is a weaving shed, a blacksmith's shop, a tintype studio, a toll house, a post office, a Sandwich glass plant, a pottery, a boiler shop, a carriage shop, and a brickworks, and there are other buildings too numerous to mention. In addition there are the actual (not facsimile) homes of Ford's heroes and friends: Luther Burbank's (homeplace), Stephen Foster's, George Matthew Adams's, McGuffey's (of primer fame), Noah Webster's, and, most important in this group, Edison's. The Edison complex includes his Menlo Park laboratory, office, and library, as well as several other buildings in which he made his experiments and discoveries—and even the boardinghouse where some of his workmen stayed; all these are structures of the '70s and '80s. The Edison Illuminating Company plant where Ford himself worked in the '90s, a very sizable factory, is part of this group. Nor has Ford forgotten to commemorate his friend George Washington Carver in a log cabin such as the great Negro agronomist was born in. An attempt has also been made to trace the development of domestic architecture in America as well as to preserve the homes of those whom Ford thought worthy of such notice. The development starts with a group from the Cotswolds in England—cottage, barn, forge, and dovecote—and is followed by the PLYMPTON HOUSE from Massachusetts, one of the oldest in America. Next comes the SUSQUEHANNA HOUSE (1652) from southern Maryland, with its wide veranda and dormers, and then the SECRETARY HOUSE from Exeter, New Hampshire, typical of early-eighteenth-century New England. Another group is all Michigan architecture and shows the development there from the log house to the fine Greek Revival mansion lifted bodily from Ann Arbor. Ford's own birthplace (1863)

stands where it did originally near 58 Bagley Street, with barns, sheds, and picket fences arranged as they were in his boyhood, as are the pictures and furniture inside. The emphasis, it is evident, is on historical and social interest, but there is also an architectural and esthetic appeal. A number of the Michigan buildings are used in the public-school system of Dearborn now and may not be visited inside for that reason. However, there are plenty of houses which are furnished in their period, just as the shops and barns are; for Ford was as tireless a collector of Americana as he was a creator of it—in his own fabulous way.

¶ *Toward Farmington*

BOTSFORD INN (*1836*)
> *Route 16, 16 miles from Detroit; open all year, lunch and dinner; same management as Dearborn Inn.*

One of the oldest landmarks in the state, this inn was serving the public when Detroit was a dusty village. It was built as a home for Orrin Weston before Michigan became a state, and stood on the Grand River Road, soon to become a much-traveled highway for stagecoaches and covered wagons. With the advance of the motor age the inn fell into disuse, but Henry Ford—whose nostalgic pleasure it was to preserve the evidences of the horse-and-buggy age in which he grew up—acquired it in 1924 and had it completely rehabilitated. Today a spacious, old-fashioned place with double porches, sitting well back from the humming highway, it maintains its tradition of hospitality and good cooking. The taproom and the huge old cooking hearth are much as they were when the inn was frequented by trappers and traders.

¶ *The Greek & Gothic Revival houses of the Southern Peninsula*

¶ *Ypsilanti*

BALLARD HOUSE (*1830–1842*)
> *218 North Washington Street; by appointment; The Ladies Literary Club.*

Built by Arden Ballard at the height of the Classical Revival, this house is fronted by four great Roman Doric columns, an order that is repeated in smaller scale at the doorway. The house is an entertaining example of the fashion that made its mark on this part of Michigan and one of the rare examples that have remained relatively unscathed. It is furnished with a feeling for its place in the past.

¶ *Ann Arbor*

WILSON-WAHR HOUSE (*c. 1840*,)
126 North Division Street; by written request; Mrs. James A. Sallade.

Considered the finest example of Greek Revival in the state by many authorities, this house has chaste and classical details and elegant proportions, and is furnished with the taste it deserves.

There are other good houses of the period to be seen here, where once the Greek Revival flourished; and at Dexter, nearby, there is one that was the finest of all—the JUDGE DEXTER MANSION—though now there is only just enough left of its former glory to stir the pulse.

¶ *Adrian*

GOVERNOR CROSWELL HOUSE (*c. 1840*)
228 North Broad Street; upon request; Lucy Walcott Barnum Chapter, D.A.R.

Home of an early Michigan governor who served two terms from 1876 to 1880, this is an attractive, smallish red-brick house, Greek Revival in character, with an odd and interesting set-back one-story wing ex-

actly duplicating the main portion. The furnishings are early-nineteenth-century.

¶ *Marshall*

Marshall is a town where the Greek Revival flourished early. Of its several fine examples of the style, there are two adjoining houses which are outstanding: STONE HALL (1837), the home of Mr. Louis E. Brooks; and the JABEZ FITCH HOUSE (1839), owned by Mr. Harold C. Brooks. At this point we can only call attention to the houses. Both have impressive Ionic porticoes with magnificent columns two stories in height; both have their entrances on the side, through a small one-story portico; and each sits in its own little park. They have been preserved by connoisseurs well known for their fine collections.

¶ *Grand Rapids*

GRAND RAPIDS ART GALLERY (*1840*)
230 Fulton Street E.; daily 10 to 5, Sundays 2 to 5 (closed Mondays and holidays); Grand Rapids Art Association.

This is one of the outstanding Greek Revival houses in Michigan, built by Abram Pike and occupied as a family residence until 1922. The fine fluted columns, repeated in miniature in the one-story match-

The fine Greek Revival house built by Abram Pike in 1840 now houses the Grand Rapids Art Gallery.

Remarkable for the fact that it is not only still standing but well cared for, the Sanford house in Grand Rapids exemplifies a style of architecture that was once to be found in great abundance all through the Southern Peninsula of Michigan; now a rarity.

ing wings, were brought from the abandoned Ottawa House at Port Sheldon. The interior has been completely changed, and is used for exhibits of painting and sculpture.

SANFORD HOUSE (*1847*)
540 Cherry Street S.E.; open by written request; Mr. H. P. Dix.

This very good example of the Greek Revival indicates the fervor with which this fashion was applied in what were then such out-of-the-way places. The scale of the Doric portico is almost monumental.

¶ Niles

In Niles the Greek Revival jostles the Gothic Revival, and for picturesque interest the latter wins out. When that romantic style comes into its own, as it is bound to with the passage of time, some of the best examples of it will be discovered in the Middle West. Many of us remember them or their like in the towns where we were born. They symbolized a type of comfortable family life that just managed to straddle the gap between the age of the ice pond and that of the Frigidaire.

While the owners of a number of Gothic houses have offered to allow visits by advance appointment, a stroll along Grant Street might be pleasure enough. Look at the CASPER GROTHWOHL HOUSE (c. 1850), at "552," a brick house, crisp with white trim. The porch, with its daintily railed second-story gallery, un-

If present plans materialize, the old fort and the buildings of the early fur-trading post on Mackinac Island will soon combine to form a vivid reminder of an era that was filled with many colorful characters and occasions.

covered, is like a starched lace petticoat standing out around this solid mansion; the brackets of the wide roof overhang, make a kind of ruching. Then there is the COTTAGE OF DR. JOHN W. STRAYER, at "553," a small gem of board-and-batten construction, steeply gabled; and the RALPH KING HOME, at "1218," a stately dark-brick mansion in a parklike setting, which presents a façade that is almost ecclesiastical. At 519 BOND STREET, shorn now of some of its Victorian lacework, is a house to include in this collection of Gothic heirlooms if only because it was the birthplace of Ring Lardner.

For further local information here, inquire of Mrs. Gertrude MacAhan, curator of the Fort St. Joseph Museum. An authority on the Niles homes, she lives at 991 South 3d Street in a tiny well-preserved log cabin of the 1830s.

¶ The outpost houses of the Northern Peninsula

¶ Mackinac Island

Proposals were made by the state historian in 1956 for developing the historical features of this fascinating old resort island (pronounced *Mackinaw*). Already certain restorations have been started, as will be noted.

THE STUART HOUSE *or* AGENT'S HOUSE *or* JOHN JACOB ASTOR HOUSE (*1822*)

June 1 to September 15; 25 cents; city of Mackinac Island.

This long, large Colonial building, with its double-stairway approach, served, like most agents' houses in fur-trading days, as both office and home. It is now furnished and fitted out as nearly as possible the way it was when Robert Stuart and the great Henry R. Schoolcraft were the factors here, and the American Fur Company an Astor monopoly. The warehouse buildings of the company, restored also, serve now as a community house, while the log Biddle House, oldest on the island, is in process of restoration. The home that belonged to William Backhouse Astor (1817) is now used to accommodate employees of the hotel.

THE BEAUMONT HOUSE (*1820*)

Daily 10 to 4, during summer; city of Mackinac Island.

This attractive old-stone-house restoration was the retail store of the American Fur Company and the house in which Dr. William Beaumont first treated the gunshot case that enabled him, because the wound refused to heal, to do historic research on the activities of the stomach.

¶ Sault Ste. Marie

THE JOHN JOHNSTON HOUSE (*1815–1827*)

Daily, 10 to 4; city of Sault Ste. Marie.

The builder of this recently restored house of the trading-post period was an Irish aristocrat who married an Indian princess. The legends she passed on via her son-in-law, Henry Rowe Schoolcraft, found their way to Longfellow, a cousin of Schoolcraft's, who wove them into *Hiawatha*.

ELMWOOD *or* THE INDIAN AGENCY HOUSE (*1827*)

Daily, 10 to 4; headquarters of Chippewa County Historical Society.

Considerably changed since it was built as a large agency house, it is interesting for having been the home into which Henry Schoolcraft moved with his bride, the daughter of John Johnston and the Indian princess. The skillful restoration has made the house interesting also as a piece of true pioneer Colonial.

This is the front parlor of the house in which the Abraham Lincolns lived for seventeen years just before the momentous move to Washington from Springfield. Many of the furnishings belonged to the family; the rest are from friends and neighbors of the President. The Gothic stove is a piece to cherish. On the opposite page is the Gen. John E. Smith house in Galena.

ILLINOIS

ACCUSTOMED as we are to thinking of Illinois as having been settled mainly by pioneers of the early 1800s, it is easy to forget that the French were masters here more than a hundred years before, and that the oldest permanent settlement the whole length of the Mississippi Valley is Cahokia, which was established by the French in 1698 and was soon to become a great trading center and the most populous place on the river. The long French occupation accounts for the fact that the few buildings left from the early 1700s might easily have been built in Louisiana.

The next period of settlement, when young America began to stream across the continent, was a long barren time as far as building was concerned, for pioneers had to think in terms of shelter, pure and simple, and conditions were not conducive to furbelows. Few of the early crude structures have stood the test of time, but you will see that in New Salem a careful re-creation has been made of the log-cabin village where Lincoln lived as a young man.

At about the time Lincoln moved from a log cabin into a frame house, the Greek Revival was beginning to sweep the country in epidemic proportions. As a fashion, it constitutes the flower of what remains of Illinois architecture of the pre-Civil War period, and while only a few examples of these homes are presently in a state of preservation to be listed in this book, more are bound to be restored. The State Historical Society has plans of large scope and can be expected to add houses to the following list from time to time. Since this movement is rapidly gaining headway in Illinois, it is suggested that you write to Illinois State Historical Library, Springfield, Illinois, for current information in addition to that concerning the houses listed here.

¶ *Bement*

BRYANT COTTAGE (*1856*)
9 to 5 daily, except Thanksgiving, Christmas and New Year's; state of Illinois.

A small house of historical interest, for it was here that Lincoln and Douglas, friends of the owner, hatched the great debates and decided when and where they should be held. The owner was Francis E. Bryant, a cousin of William Cullen Bryant.

¶ *Bishop Hill*

BISHOP HILL (*1848–1860*)
On Route 82, 18 miles from Kewanee

Near Bishop Hill at an intersection with Route 34 the state has placed a marker which reads, "At Bishop Hill two miles north of here, Eric Jansen and Jonas Olson founded a colony of religious dissenters in 1846. Organized on communistic lines the colony at one time had 1,100 members and property worth a million dollars." The venture ended with internal dissension and the murder of Jansen. In spite of this, thirteen of the sturdy buildings erected by these pioneers are still standing. The largest one was a four-story structure which had ninety-six rooms, but this burned down in the 1920s. South of the four-acre government-owned park, which makes this such a pretty spot today, stand three large brick houses, neatly faced with cement trim, with a style all their own. One was a hotel and the other two were communal apartment houses, which is pretty much what they all remain today. Many of their occupants are descendants of the settlers who, since the break-up of the colony in 1862, have owned their apartments cooperatively. This may be the earliest example of cooperative apartment dwellings in the country. In town there are the old bakery, the brewery, the cheese factory, and the Steeple Building, which, to give you an idea of its size, houses several stores, a garage, the phone exchange, and the post office. The Old

Colony Church (1848), owned by the state, is a frame structure, one of the few, for most of the first buildings were made of a soft adobe brick until a local clay was found suitable for firing. These were industrious people, for their record shows that once they had got under way with their brick making, they were turning out five million a month. No wonder the colonists sometimes worked eighteen hours a day, women included; and no wonder the colony broke up in dissension. To get a brilliant picture of how these people lived and worked, look at the exceptional collection in the church of primitive paintings, by Olaf Kraus, which depict the life in homely detail. Talbot Hamlin was greatly impressed by these buildings. He speaks of their excellent proportions in spite of crude detailing and says that "Their efforts have that true impressiveness which good proportions and adequate size always produce . . . they show the architectural amenity and formal grandeur for which the colony was striving." If this may somewhat exaggerate their qualities, it is none the less true that they constitute an unusual group of buildings, perhaps unique in this section of the country.

¶ *Cahokia (on Route 3, 4 miles south of East St. Louis)*

JEAN BAPTISTE SAUCIER HOUSE (*1737*)
Daily, 9 to 5, except Mondays; state of Illinois.

Since this is the oldest private dwelling in the Middle West, it has great interest for those who are concerned with antiquity as such. With the distinctively French stamp that the early fur traders and *coureurs de bois* left on this section of the Mississippi, it is built like some of the houses in Ste. Genevieve and certain other early ones in lower Louisiana. The walls are vertical logs, plaster-filled. Its bonnet roof projects out on all four sides, making a wide covered terrace surrounded by supporting posts. This seemingly primitive structure, built by the French military engineer, who built Fort de Chartres, has unexpected niceties inside, for the walls were plaster on split lath, and the windows had glass

Note the vertical log construction—à la française—of the Jean Baptiste Saucier house in Cahokia.

panes when oiled paper was customary out here. The floors are of sassafras puncheons on walnut beams. The house went to the St. Louis World Fair in 1904, then stood until 1939 in Jackson Park, Chicago. It is now back home to stay.

¶ Cairo

If the houses of the 1860s and the 1870s in Cairo continue to be occupied—and there is no reason why they should not, for they were built to last—Cairo will some day be a museum town, exhibiting that flavorsome period to perfection. Cairo was "a steamboat metropolis," situated where the Ohio and Mississippi meet; as such it was wealthy, and its surviving homes of the era tell the story well.

MAGNOLIA MANOR (*1869–1872*)
2900 Washington Avenue; daily 9 to 5, Sundays 2 to 4; 50 cents; Cairo Historical Society.

The Charles A. Galigher House is a perfect example of this ornate style as well as the solidity of building, for the walls are of double brick with a ten-inch air space between. The exterior with its heavy eaves, heavy cupola, double arched lintels, and New Orleans ironwork railings on porch and upper balcony, is also decorated in double courses of white trim at three separate levels. The effect is amazing. The drawing room, where President and Mrs.

Grant received hundreds of guests when they visited the Galighers for two days, is perfect for its period: fluted columns, paneled arches, a great bay window, and quite remarkable cornice with plaster carving of grapes and leaves, of a high order. The Cairo Historical Society is furnishing it with great care to perpetuate its gaslight-era atmosphere.

RENDELMAN HOME (*1865*)
2723 Washington Avenue; open by arrangement; Mrs. Adelaide Rendelman Grieve.

Built somewhat earlier than "Magnolia Manor" by a river captain, this is a three-story mansard-roofed mansion of brick and stone, the stone painted white. It stands in a three-acre park of its own in the midst of the city, with caretaker's house and stables. The entrance door contains panels and fanlight of prismatic glass. A winding staircase with heavy mahogany posts and a balustrade rises to a glass-enclosed "pilot house." Tall doors and window frames are of carved yellow poplar. The parlor and library have a plaster cornice of oak-leaf-and-acorn pattern that looks as though it may have been done by the skillful workmen who executed the cornice in "Magnolia Manor." This pattern is repeated in the border of a large rug whose central medallion depicts the Statue of Liberty. Blue-and-gold stained glass is in the big bay window.

Other houses to note in passing are those of Mrs. Oscar Herbert (1879),

2606 Washington Street; Miss Effie L. Neff, 2009 Walnut Street; Miss Margaret Rust, 703 Walnut; Mrs. George McClung, 603 Walnut; and Miss Sarah Alice Reed (1861), 419 20th Street.

¶ *Cantrall*

GEORGE POWER HOME AND LAW OFFICE (*1850*)

At Power Farms, 10 miles north of Springfield; by written request; Mrs. June Power Reilly.

Also known as "Fancy Creek Farmhouse," this pleasant brick country house with wide veranda, set in its ancient grove of maples, is now being occupied by the fourth generation of the family of Judge George Power, who settled in Sangamon County in 1821 and also eight years later built the little white frame courthouse now standing on the grounds. The first seat of justice in the county, it is claimed to be the one in which Abraham Lincoln tried his first case, a suit involving the killing of a dog. The last case that Lincoln filed before he became President was before the judge's son William, who then presided over the county court. George Power, like many another pioneer, came from Kentucky and began life here in a log cabin. It was not until almost thirty years later that he was able to realize his dream of a spacious dwelling built of brick like those he remembered from his Kentucky boyhood. In the meantime both the prairies and the Indians had been tamed. Little has been changed in this homestead. Its heirlooms and the mementos of its famous visitors have been cherished by the family. We could not offer you a better example of the way of life of a worthy pioneer family who gained their local importance the hard way.

¶ *Carmi*

GEN. JOHN M. ROBINSON HOUSE (*1816*)

110 South Main Cross Street; by appointment only; Miss Mary Jane Stewart.

One of the oldest houses in the state, it has been called a "living museum" by John Drury, historian of Illinois houses. Miss Stewart's grandfather bought the house in 1835 from John Craw, one of the earliest settlers in White County. It was built as a log house and served as courthouse for several years in its earliest days. General Robinson added wings to the log house and no doubt covered it with clapboard at the same time. A portico, a hooded doorway in the wing, and a white fence set this low dwelling quite apart from its surroundings, for Carmi was a busy town even then, during the oil boom. General Robinson spent eleven years in Washington as Senator from Illinois and much of the furniture in the house today was purchased while he was in the East. The general's father-in-law was James Ratcliff, a tavernkeeper here, one of whose distinguished guests was Abraham Lincoln who was campaigning for Harrison at the time. Lincoln was connected with the family more closely than this, however, for General Robinson's brother-in-law Edwin B. Webb was said to have been a rival of Lincoln's for the hand of Mary Todd and was incidentally the last Whig candidate for governor of Illinois. There are so many interesting heirlooms in this house that space does not permit cataloguing them. But in a rosewood secretary you can see original letters of Lincoln, William Henry Harrison, and Henry Clay, and an autographed copy of a speech of John Quincy Adams to John M. Robinson.

¶ *Carrollton (on Route 67, 32 miles north of Alton)*

BLACK HOMESTEAD (*1823*)

202 East Walnut Street, 2 miles west on Route 208 and then south ⅝ mile; 9 to 11 and 2 to 4, daily, or by appointment; Robert T. Black.

The land here was registered in 1821 by the owner's grandmother, and the deed, signed by President Monroe, hangs on the wall today. It is the oldest brick house in Illinois north of East St. Louis, and, when it was built, it stood conspicuously fine among the little group of log cabins that formed the hamlet, surrounded by open prairie. It was built facing east, but years later a new road was surveyed in back of it, and so it ended facing west. Later a frame addition with a deep overhang was added across the front, making it look much like a Southern plantation house with its two-story columns and balustraded second-story gallery. The rooms are large and there are fifteen of them, with many fireplaces. This is a comfortable family home with some furniture and relics of the wars still here.

¶ *Cedarville (5 miles north of Freeport on Route 20)*

JANE ADDAMS HOMESTEAD (1849)
On request by letter or phone; fee nominal; Henry J. Haldeman, Box 3, Girard, Kansas.

Jane Addams of Hull House was born here. Built of brick, the family house is pleasantly rural in appearance, with a recently added porch. The interior has several fireplaces and fine woodwork and floors. The furniture is of interest because much of it was there when Miss Addams was a child in this village. In back of the house is a bank barn (1848) put together with wooden pegs; next door, a brick building once the Addams's general store. Inside of this last is a buggy in which Jane drove to hear the Lincoln-Douglas Debates.

¶ Galena

Like many another booming river town, Galena's prosperity disappeared with the advent of railways, leaving a number of notable pre-Civil War mansions whose style is sometimes linked with the name of Gen. U. S. Grant, who was in fact for some years a resident of Galena, as will be noted. A yearly "open house" is held here in September under the auspices of the First Presbyterian Church. About eight homes are shown, most of which are open to you through the *Guide* year around. Write to Mrs. Walter Ehrler or the church for further information on the tour.

ELIHU WASHBURN HOUSE (1830s)
908 3d Street; on written request, small groups only, May and early June; Mrs. Frank T. Sheean.

The most imposing and handsome Greek Revival house in town, it was purchased by Mrs. Sheean's family from the Washburns seventy-five years ago. Elihu Washburn was General Grant's Minister to France. In 1861 Grant drilled Galena's first company of volunteers on the lawn, captained by Augustus Chetlain, who became a famous general in the war. At one time the Indians occupied this lawn once a year when they came to trade and receive government rations.

CHALATAIN ACRES (1836)
Route 20, 2 miles west of town; by written appointment, June, July, and August; 50 cents for the First Presbyterian Church; Mr. and Mrs. W. Clifford Stauss.

The original log cabin put up in 1826 by Louis Chetlain, a Swiss settler, is still part of the structure of this house. Ten years later he enlarged it to its present size. It is the oldest farmhouse standing in northern Illinois. It passed out of the Chetlain family only when the present owners bought it in 1943. They restored it without any important change. It is a long, white clapboard house with a deep pillared porch and an open gallery above. The three dormers are reminiscent of early clapboard houses in Virginia. Perhaps the porch was added later. The name of the house, by the way, is not misspelled here but appeared this way in the deed by mistake, and the owners left it so. The furniture is in keeping, much of it heirloom.

GEN. JOHN E. SMITH HOUSE (1845)
807 Bench Street; write or phone (350) for appointment, except in winter; Mr. and Mrs. Louis I. Nack.

A one-story-and-basement house built of red brick on a stone foundation, this is a good example of Middle Western Greek Revival. It has nice proportions and some charming detail, which includes a very pleasant portico supported by fluted Ionic columns. John Smith was a Galena jeweler who later became a staff officer for General Grant. The house is furnished with many old Galena items and several from the Duncan Hines home in Kentucky.

MINER'S COTTAGE (1838)
901 4th Street; open on request; Miss Katherine Delihant.

This is a double stone cottage which once belonged to miners working at nearby Muddy Hollow. Each side has three rooms and two fireplaces which have been unchanged. The original floors and windows are also there. Some of the furniture is old Galena, pine and maple, and all is in keeping with its simplicity.

MELVILLE HOUSE (*before 1840*)
1009 3d Street; on written request; Mr. and Mrs. Walter Ehrler.

This was originally a double house occupied by Maj. Thomas Melville and his married daughter. Major Melville was Herman Melville's favorite uncle, and the author of *Moby Dick* spent the summer of 1840 in this house. Remodeled fifty years ago into a single dwelling, both halls were thrown together at the time which gave the house a new spaciousness. Three of the main rooms are furnished with antiques, largely early Galena Victorian and Empire. There is a collection of glassware.

NORRIS HOUSE (*1853*)
3 miles west on Route 20, then south 1 mile on Norris Lane; on written request; Miss Katherine and Mr. Ralph Norris.

A rosy-brick home with wide eaves supported by brackets and tall double windows, the whole house is typical Galena of the period when it was built. The furniture has been used by the Norris family for three generations and there are many local articles, among them such kitchen equipment as dasher churns, wooden molds, and a fine old cookstove. This is the real thing.

THE ROCK HOUSE (*antique shop*) (*c. 1830*)
Virginia Fitzgerald.

An interesting stone house with stone window lintels and corner quoins, used as a shop. Can be seen any time.

The bracketed overhang of the roof gives considerable character to the General Grant house in Galena.

GENERAL GRANT HOUSE (*1857*)
Bouthilier Street; daily 9 to 5 except holidays; State of Illinois.

Grant came here some years before the Civil War and clerked in his brothers' leather store for six hundred dollars a year. The store is still at 120 Main Street, as is the plain little house where he lived with his wife and four children until the war. As a graduate of West Point, Grant volunteered at once and was commissioned a Colonel. When he returned to Galena, world-famous, the people here purchased the Alexander Jackson House by a subscription of sixteen thousand dollars, furniture and all, and presented it to the hero. The Grants intended to live there permanently, but three years later they were settled in the White House. The house today is much as it was when they lived in it. Most of their furniture has been retrieved and its personal interest is further enhanced by the fact that it represents so well the manner in which a prosperous and important family lived in the Middle West at that period. The exterior of the brick house, with its corner porch and unusually deep overhanging eaves, is pleasantly unpretentious.

¶ *Kankakee*

DR. A. L. SMALL HOME (*1855*)
Eighth Avenue and Water Street; Saturday and Sunday afternoons 2 to 5, and by appointment; Kankakee Park District.

Dr. Small not only carried on his country practice from this trim two-story limestone house of the prairie, but, being a horticulturist of note as well, surrounded his house with many acres of nursery and arboretum. The house is therefore far from being the sole attraction. One of the doctor's six children born in the house became the late Governor Len Small of Illinois, of whom there are many mementos here. The parlor, dining room, and office are as the doctor left them when he died.

¶ *Kaskaskia*

PIERRE MENARD HOME (*1802*)
50 miles southeast of St. Louis; daily; state of Illinois.

Kaskaskia was the first capital of Illinois,

and Pierre Menard, its first Lieutenant Governor, built this lovely Louisiana-like house after he was appointed Judge by Gov. William Henry Harrison. It is a spacious raised cottage with a long, sweeping roof projecting out over a gallery with delicate columns. The windows (with original hand-pressed French panes) which open onto the gallery are unusually large. The delightful old house contains a few of the Menard belongings, among them old Pierre's flute and flageolet, his barber chair, his embroidered vest, and his mahogany chest. In one room is an elegantly carved mantel, said to be a French import. The stone kitchen is interesting, with its enormous fireplace and its water basin carved out of a huge piece of rock. The Randolph County Historical Society is about to furnish it.

¶ Marengo

ANSON ROGERS' HOUSE (1846)

East Grant Highway (Route 20); open as a dress shop called "Coach and Four" with "Coach House" in rear (modern) operating as restaurant; Delmar and Marjorie Stevens.

This fine Greek Revival house has fortunately suffered few changes, except for the building in its rear. The house is of wood on a stone foundation, with six impressive supporting columns. Most of the original woodwork, the fireplace, and the mantels remain as they were. The house is furnished with antiques throughout.

The ORSON P. ROGERS HOUSE (c. 1846) stands nearby and is built similarly. It is used by tenant farmers at present.

¶Nauvoo

MANSION HOUSE (1841)

Open daily.

The pilaster decorations across the front of this house give it a kind of Greek Revival elegance. It is one of the few homes in this country on record which was built according to divine revelation. Often referred to as the "Joseph Smith House," it is now a Mormon shrine. At nearby Carthage is the old jail in which Smith was murdered, now something of a shrine as well.

The houses in Nauvoo "have a quality

The Pierre Menard home near Kaskaskia is one of the Mississippi River houses that show the influence of the early French cottage architecture brought up from Louisiana.

almost Dutch" in Talbot Hamlin's opinion. The BRIGHAM YOUNG HOUSE (1840), with its stepped gables and its interesting general composition, he finds "especially Continental in flavor."

¶ New Salem

NEW SALEM STATE PARK

(a completely restored village of the 1830s)

Daily, 9 to 5, except Christmas, New Year's Day, and Thanksgiving Day; staff of Park Guides, Department of Conservation, Division of Parks and Memorials of Illinois.

This is a reconstruction of the town in which Lincoln spent six of his formative years. Arriving by flatboat in 1831, he remained here to take an active part in the life of the village as postmaster, store clerk, and surveyor. Thirteen log cabins, plus the Rutledge Tavern, a school and church, and ten shops and stores have been reproduced and fitted out appropriately. The furnishings include many articles used by New Salem citizens of the time, such as wheat cradles, flax shuttles, and dough and cornmeal chests. Doctors' offices and cobblers' shops contain early implements; stores, bolts of old calico and other staples of the period. Vegetable gardens, flowers, and trees have been planted to re-create accurately the village scene as it was. At the homes of the two doctors, herbs used for medicinal purposes are grown in the gar-

One of the most interesting houses at New Salem State Park is the Onstot Cooper Shop of early log construction, in which Lincoln studied his law books by the light of the open fire.

dens, just as they were by wilderness medicos. There is only one original building—the Onstot Cooper Shop, built 1835, the shop in which Lincoln studied Blackstone, Shakespeare, and Burns by the light of Cooper's burning wood shavings. The whole village, in its humble simplicity, constitutes a moving memorial to one of the world's great men. There are overnight accommodations at the Wagon Wheel Inn and in several nearby towns.

¶ *Ottawa*

VALLEY VIEW (1842)
> *2011 Canton Road, North Bluff; by phone or written request; Mrs. Philip S. McDougall.*

Abraham Lincoln visited here frequently. His host, a wealthy Kentucky aristocrat, Judge T. Lyle Dickey, was a political foe, though reputedly a great friend. He served as an officer in the Mexican and Civil Wars and was an Illinois supreme court justice. In spite of various enlargements, the house retains quite a bit of original character. The furniture is mostly English.

JOHN HOSSACK HOUSE (1854)
> *210 West Prospect Avenue; by written request to Mr. Philip H. Godfrey.*

A grand old house of the plantation type, its deep double galleries with their well-proportioned square columns in widely spaced rows of six give it an impressive and yet comfortable appearance. The hip roof is crowned with a small railed-in plat-

form which is little more than a decoration but may well have served John Hossack as a lookout—for this house was a well-known stop on the Underground Railway.

¶ *Quincy*

GOV. JOHN WOOD HOME (1835)
> *425 South 12th Street; weekdays 10 to 12, Mondays and Wednesdays 2 to 5; Historical Society of Quincy and Adams County, Mrs. Edna Williams (curator).*

John Wood, one of the early Governors of Illinois, came here from Cayuga County, New York, where the Greek Revival was going strong. This accounts for the style of the house that he built here in Quincy after he had made his fortune. In it are the governor's Civil War pistols and the sword and medicine book his surgeon father carried in the Revolution. Among the fine furnishings is a chandelier of French drop crystals which once glistened in the great salon of a Mississippi River steamer.

¶ *Springfield*

ABRAHAM LINCOLN'S HOME (1839)
> *8th and Jackson Streets; daily, 9 to 5, except Thanksgiving Day, Christmas, and New Year's.*

This is the only house that Lincoln ever actually owned. Sold to him ready-built by the Reverend Charles Dresser, who had married the Lincolns in 1842, it cost only fifteen hundred dollars in cash, with a mortgage of nine hundred dollars. After two years of married life spent for the most part in boardinghouses, the Lincolns settled here with their little boy, Robert Todd. When built in 1839, the house was a one-story-and-a-half cottage. It was later enlarged. Some historians say Mrs. Lincoln had the second story raised during one of her husband's absences. The house is constructed of native hardwoods: framework and floor are of oak, lathes and weatherboarding of hand-split hickory, and door and window frames of black walnut. The Lincolns lived here for seventeen years, except for the year he was sent to Congress, when it was rented to Cornelius Ludlum for ninety dollars. Three of Lincoln's sons were born here; one died here. When the Lincolns went to Washington in 1861, they sold their house furnishings to their tenant, who subsequently took them to Chicago and lost them there in the fire. Some Lincoln pieces may be seen now on the first floor, but for the most part the house has been furnished from the homes of friends and relatives who lived in the town during Lincoln's time.

BENJAMIN S. EDWARDS HOME
(1833)
700 North 4th Street; daily, 2 to 5; Springfield Art Association.

When the early part of this house was built by Dr. Thomas Houghan, there was not another house in sight. Benjamin S. Edwards, who was to become the third Governor of the state, had the simple farm-

This is the Lincoln home in Springfield, of which the front parlor is shown on page 222, now preserved as one of the most personal of Lincoln memorials, a gift to the state from the President's son.

house transformed into a most romantic and imposing Italianate villa, remodeled in the 1850s. Its flat hip roof and wide overhanging eaves, its Corinthian-columned veranda, and the ornamental cupola are all the height of a fashion that was veering away from the Greek Revival. Lincoln once spoke to a crowd from an upper window. At that time the house was the center of the town's social and political activity, and the 1850 atmosphere has now been beautifully restored in the furnishings which are those of a wealthy and prominent citizen of the period and place. The wing which houses the Springfield Art Association, a separate building, conforms to the style of the house.

This is the house that Judge George Power built thirty years after starting life in Illinois in a log cabin. Elsewhere on the grounds is the tiny court house in which Lincoln is said to have tried his first case.

When the Tallman house was built at Janesville before the Civil War, it represented the utmost in Middle Western magnificence, and it is regarded today as the state's most ambitious Victorian mansion, and is so restored and preserved. On the opposite page, by contrast of transplanted Colonial, is the old Indian Agency house at Portage.

WISCONSIN

¶ Southwestern Wisconsin: Prairie du Chien; Cassville; Mineral Point ¶ Southern Wisconsin: Portage; Cooksville; Milton; Janesville; Beloit ¶ Southeastern Wisconsin: Watertown; Wauwatosa; Milwaukee ¶ Northeastern Wisconsin: Sheboygan; Greenbush; Neenah; Kaukauna; Green Bay

HAT the early houses of Wisconsin, at least the ones listed here below for visiting, lack in numbers is more than made up for in variety and surprise. The range is wide indeed between the 1776 Tank Cottage of wattle and daub, at Green Bay, and the elegant Italianate Tallman Mansion of the 1850s, at Janesville—and in between the two a lot of Wisconsin history was made. And at Green Bay, who would expect to encounter from the outpost period there as chaste an example of Greek Revival as the Cotton House? Towns like Cooksville are numerous in New England, but what about these New England houses clustering around their village green out here in Wisconsin? And where else in the country will you come across a group of Cornish stone cottages, built long ago by immigrant miners from Cornwall? The answer is: nowhere but here in Wisconsin.

¶ Southwestern Wisconsin

¶ *Prairie du Chien (where Route 18 crosses the Mississippi by toll bridge to Marquette, Iowa)*

VILLA LOUIS *or* **HERCULES L. DOUSMAN HOUSE** *(1843)*

> *Take Villa Louis Road at toll bridge; daily 9 to 5, May 1 to October 31; 50 cents and 10 cents; State Historical Society.*

The history of this amazing mansion is closely connected with the early career of the whole territory, for the builder of the house served as confidential agent for the John Jacob Astor interests. Dousman delivered hundreds of thousands of dollars in goods to the Indians and white trappers, and in return received millions of dollars in pelts. His intuitive understanding of the Indians and his reputation with them for honesty gave him enormous influence. When in 1844 he married a great beauty, Jane Fisher Rolette, he was already a millionaire; and what he built on an Indian mound above the river for his bride was a two-story brick house on Georgian lines, large and luxurious. His wife named it "Le Château Brillante," for when she arrived here after their honeymoon, five hundred candles were burning for her on the glassed-in front porch. This porch of the early house has been preserved, but little else. The Georgian lines disappeared under the Victorian remodeling undertaken by Madame Dousman in 1872, four years after her husband's death, when the outside walls were clad in yellow Milwaukee brick and a third-floor ballroom was added. The heirs of the family lived in the house until 1934 and assisted in its restoration as a Victorian period piece when it was taken over by the State Historical Society. Many of the heirlooms were brought back to the house by the family, and today it represents a perfect picture of ornate comfort, just as if a wealthy and hospitable family of that era lived there.

BRISBOIS HOUSE (*1808*)

> On river front; daily, 9 to 5; 30 cents and 10 cents; John Cornelius and Mrs. Louise Root.

In 1781, following the trail of Marquette and Joliet, Michael Brisbois, a young Canadian baker, came down the Mississippi to what was then an Indian village called Prairie of the Dog, named for the chief of the Fox Indians, who lived there. Since "Prairie" later became one of the great fur marts, Brisbois was destined to prosper. In 1808 he built his plain but ample cut-stone dwelling on an Indian mound on the river front; and the house stands today much as it did when it was built—one of Wisconsin's oldest landmarks. The last descendant of Michael died here in 1935, leaving most of the original family furnishings still in the house. Strong and simple, and heated by four fireplaces,

it furnishes an excellent picture of how life was lived by a prosperous trader in those early times. This story it tells better than the Dousman House nearby, for though Brisbois was well known, his career was not exceptional. Apparently he continued to bake bread; he also farmed and traded furs like everyone else. Of peculiar interest is the fact that his asparagus beds are still producing. The Indians told him of the new plant that had been brought over from England and was growing at Lake Pepin, and he sent his son there to get plants.

¶ *Cassville (about 30 miles south of Prairie du Chien via 133)*

STONEFIELD-NELSON DEWEY HOMESTEAD (*c. 1850*)

> In Nelson Dewey Memorial Park; open 9 to 5 daily, May 1 to October 31; Wisconsin Conservation Department.

The first Governor of the state (1848–1852), Nelson Dewey, was born in Lebanon, Connecticut, came to Cassville in 1836, and prospered. After his governorship he bought the entire village of Cassville and decided to develop on this two-thousand-acre tract a kind of plantation, self-sustaining, with all its dependencies. Something went wrong, however, and Dewey died a poor man in 1889. His wine cellar, smokehouse, barn, and servants' quarters, built of stone in a kind of sharp French Gothic style, are still standing, maintained as a crafts museum. The residence, a brick mansion that was swept by fire in 1873 and reconstructed, is furnished with many of Governor Dewey's possessions.

¶ *Mineral Point*

TRELAWNY, PENDARVIS HOUSE, POLPERO, *and* NEWLYN (*c. 1835*)

> Open daily; Robert Neel and Edgar Hellum.

These four houses in this astonishing village, where Cornish tin miners came in the 1830s after hearing of the Wisconsin lead mines, are built of local buff sandstone and are much like the ones the miners left behind in their native Cornwall—face or smooth stone used in front and around the windows and doors, the rest rough. The walls are eighteen inches thick and the fireplaces niched at the corners. In winter wood stoves were also used for heating. The stubby chimneys are red brick and the roofs of split-pine shingles. The first three houses have been furnished with interesting and authentic old pieces, effectively arranged to create a "lived-in" look; "Newlyn" is a guest house. The re-creation of a workmen's community is as unusual as it is interesting. You can eat a Cornish dinner if you stop for a while, or take your tea with saffron cake, plum preserves, and scalded cream.

¶ *Southern Wisconsin*

¶ *Portage*

AGENCY HOUSE *or* KINZIE'S HOUSE (*1832*)

> *At Fort Winnebago; daily, 9 to 5:30;*
> *35 cents and 15 cents; Colonial Dames.*

In 1830 when John Kinzie brought his New England bride here close by Fort Winnebago, their furniture had to be taken over the rapids of the Fox River, and much of it arrived water-soaked. Kinzie had been sent out by the government to take charge of the Winnebago Indian Agency here at the portage, where the Indians in large numbers were already government charges. Very neat and New England-looking, the house, although of frame, had brick fill for insulation. Jefferson Davis made some of the furniture for the house while he was a prisoner at the fort, one talent of his which is little known. Mrs. Kinzie tried to make it a place of hospitality for both Indians and voyageurs; her piano was the marvel of the settlement. Later in life she wrote an account called *Waú Bun*, now published by the Colonial Dames there.

SURGEON'S QUARTERS (*1826*)

> *Fort Winnebago, across canal from Indian Agency; daily 10 to 5 and Sunday and holiday afternoons Memorial Day to Labor Day, during May by appointment; 35 cents and 15 cents; D.A.R.*

The house is built of hand-hewn logs, the adze marks plain to be seen. The shape was evidently meant to be defensive, with two ells shielding the door. Support for

original floors are tamarack logs. The quarters are furnished with appropriate austerity.

¶ *Cooksville (25 miles southeast of Madison on 38)*

A COLLECTION OF EARLY HOUSES (*1848–1856*)

The town stands on a piece of land transferred to Daniel Webster by the United States government in 1837. Webster sold it in 1848 to Dr. John Porter of Massachusetts, who had it plotted out like a New England village, arranged around a green. Several of the homes around the green which date from that period are still occupied today, and although some of them are built in the Gothic Revival mode, then coming into fashion, the whole effect is oddly New England, with prim gardens and old shade trees. The people of the town, conscious of their unusual heritage, staged their first "open house" in 1949 under the auspices of the Rock County Historical Society. For further information it might be best to write to Mr. Miles T. Armstrong, who operates the Cooksville Store and owns one of the houses himself. There are about five houses in all, dating from 1848 through 1856, and they are well cared for. Mr. and Mrs. Armstrong are willing to be of help to anyone wishing to visit some of them, since the tour is not held regularly. Typical houses here are the MORGAN HOUSE (1848), Classical Revival; the ROBERTSON HOUSE (1850), modified American Gothic (owned by the Armstrongs); the DUNCAN HOUSE (1848), Classical Revival; and the HOXIE HOUSE (1852), American Gothic.

¶ *Milton*

MILTON HOUSE *and* GOODRICH LOG CABIN (*1844*)

> *Daily, 10 to 5; 50 cents and 10 cents; Milton Historical Society.*

The house is an early inn of unusual concrete construction, with a unique hexagonal three-story lobby. The inn and cabin were connected by an underground tunnel and together were an important station for escaping slaves. They are being restored and furnished appropriately by the local historical society.

¶ Janesville

LINCOLN-TALLMAN HOUSE
(1855–1858)
440 North Jackson Street; daily 9:30 to 5 and Sundays and holidays 1 to 5, May to November; 40 cents and 10 cents; city of Janesville.

In 1859 Abraham Lincoln spent a weekend here in the thirty-three-room mansion of William Morrison Tallman, which had been completed two years before. Built at a cost exceeding forty-two thousand dollars (paid in gold) and designed in the style of an ornate Italian villa, it was Wisconsin's showplace at the time. Lincoln addressed the Republican Club Saturday night, attended church with the Tallmans Sunday, and left for Springfield the next day where three weeks later he announced his candidacy. Could he have suspected that his wealthy host had built his mansion with

Octagonal houses keep cropping up all over the country—not many so notable as this famous one at Watertown.

special features to aid escaping slaves, and that the house was already one of the most important stations on the Underground Railway? At that time Lincoln did not advocate the violation of the Fugitive Slave Act. His friend Tallman, an ardent abolitionist, was the first person to present to Congress a petition for freeing the Negro; a man of both courage and vision, he had been twice mobbed for his speeches against slavery. Coming from Rome, New York, to Janesville, a frontier village, he had grown wealthy on Western land. He owned one tract alone of 1,700,000 acres in Texas. His house reflects his wealth—three floors, sixty feet in height to the top of its cupola. Built of Milwaukee pressed brick, with arched double windows and elaborate Italianate carving, and both baroque and rococo in style, its heavy mass is architecture at its most exuberant. A heating plant as well as fireplaces, running water in four bedrooms provided by drainage from the roof, gaslights and speaking tubes, and dumb-waiters for the servants were luxuries never before heard of on the frontier at this period. Two carved walnut doors open from the drawing room into a conservatory whose windows are topped with crescents of colored glass. The oriel window on the second floor in the east hall, with its bright panes, served as a signal for fugitive slaves who were coming up from the Rock River. Slaves stayed in the basement, where there were beds and food for them, unless there was a search, when they were hidden in the attic by way of secret staircases or spirited out and sent on their way again. The carriage house, which now serves as a museum for the Rock County Historical Society, is similar in style to the house. The house has been restored to its original Civil War appearance.

¶ Beloit

RASEY HOUSE (1848)
517 Prospect Street; daily 9 to 5, Sundays 1 to 5; 25 cents; D.A.R.

Built of cobblestones picked up in Turtle Creek by the college students at nearby Beloit in 1848, the house was sold right after it was erected in order to raise funds to roof and put windows into the first building on the Beloit campus.

The Kilbournetown house in Milwaukee marks one of the western reaches of the Greek Revival.

¶ Southeastern Wisconsin

¶ Watertown

OCTAGON HOUSE (c. 1854)

> *Daily 1 to 5, Sundays and holidays 10 to 5; 40 cents, 30 cents, and 15 cents; Watertown Historical Society.*

The invention and originality displayed in the design of this house make it one of the best octagonal houses in the country. Of cream-colored Milwaukee brick, it is crowned with four chimneys. It has eight rooms to a floor—fifty-seven altogether with halls and closets. The owner John Richards, a lawyer from Hinsdale, Massachusetts, came to Watertown when it was a village and stayed to see it boom. The staircase is spectacular, rising to the fourth story in a tightly curled spiral; the climb is made easy by the well-dimensioned treads and risers. The third floor was designed to shelter some of Mr. Richards' mill hands. Sixty-three doors have been counted in the house. The narrow balconies running the whole way around the house had to be removed for safety, but the society plans to restore them. The furniture, of the gaslight era, is all virtually intact, with the original wallpapers and carpets.

¶ Wauwatosa

LOWELL DAMON HOUSE
(1844–1845)

> *2017 Wauwatosa Avenue, Sundays, 2 to 5; Milwaukee County Historical Society.*

As typical a piece of Colonial architecture as can be found in the entire state. The man who built it was a cabinetmaker who also made buggies that lasted a lifetime. His house reflects his rare abilities. It contains various collections of antiquarian interest.

¶ Milwaukee

KILBOURNETOWN HOUSE (1844)

> *In Estabrook Park; 2 to 5 Sundays only; Milwaukee County Historical Society, Colonial Dames (custodians).*

Here is another unexpected Greek Revival temple from the pioneer period. Built by Benjamin Church, an early architect and builder, long before Milwaukee existed, it is a small house with great style featuring four fluted Ionic columns. The low wings, each with its own door and window, outlined in a chaste molding decoration, complete a picture of fine proportions and perfect restraint. As usual, the Colonial Dames have done well by its furnishings.

¶ Northeastern Wisconsin

¶ Sheboygan

TAYLOR HOUSE (c. 1848)

*½ mile west of city on Route 23;
Sheboygan County Historical Society.*

This is a picturesque foursquare Italianate residence with an immense cupola, a strange edifice to have been built as a farmhouse in the country. Judge Taylor was a notable of the neighborhood; his house, a prominent local landmark, is furnished as a museum, whose aim is to preserve the history of the county.

¶ Greenbush

WADE HOUSE (1850–1851)

Route 23, in state park, 6 miles west of Plymouth; daily 9 to 5, May 1 to October 31; 50 cents and 10 cents; Kohler Foundation, Inc.

Located now in a state park, this place was originally Stage Coach Inn on the plank road from Fond du Lac to Sheboygan and was built by Sylvanus Wade, who brought his family here in 1844 when it was still Indian country. It is a typical spacious country tavern, with heavy square pillars and a roofed second-story gallery. It has been furnished with great attention to the details of the period and very well done indeed, even to the proper carpets, china, and stoves.

BUTTERNUT HOUSE

*(same period as Wade House)
In state park near Wade House.*

West of the Wade House, Sylvanus helped his son-in-law Charles Robinson to build this charming Greek Revival abode. That Robinson was a carpenter is very evident. It is a story-and-a-half house with a cupola and a recessed porch which divides the front and carries around the corner, odd and very stylish in appearance. The severe cupola crowns a flat-hipped roof neatly. Altogether, this is quite a model of unsophisticated originality in adapting Greek Revival to personal needs and desires. It is furnished as a family would have done at the time it was built. Other buildings are being restored, and the entire site is being returned to its original landscaping, planted with butternut trees, sugar maples, wild crab apples, and the high-bush cranberries which grew there. This was the project of the late Mrs. Herbert V. Kohler, and much of it was carried out by her.

¶ Neenah

DOTY GRAND LOGGERY (c. 1845)

5th and Lincoln Streets in Doty Park; daily 9 to 12 and 1:30 to 5, Saturdays, Sundays, and holidays, 1:30 to 5; city of Neenah.

This was the home of James Duane Doty, territorial Governor of Wisconsin from 1845 to 1861.

¶ Kaukauna

GRIGNON HOUSE (1838–1839)

On banks of Fox River, just off 41; open all the time; 25 cents; Kaukauna Historical Society; William Wolf (curator).

Known as "The Mansion in the Woods," it was built here on the banks of the Fox River by Charles A. Grignon, son of the pioneer fur trader, Augustin. He brought his workmen as well as most of his materials from Buffalo, New York, and the house is reminiscent of the simple and sometimes somber Greek Revival houses that are scattered all over that section of New York State. With its balustraded open gallery at the second-floor level and its portico, it is M. Grignon's adaptation of the new fashion in building in the East. The solid-cherry stair rail and the handsome carved newel post and banisters in the house were brought from New York City, the final stage by canoe up the river. It was Charles's great-grandfather Charles de Langlade who was regarded as the founder of the first permanent settlement in Wisconsin, and it was he who married the sister of the Ottawa chieftain. The Charles who built the house could sit on the long balcony of his white clapboard mansion in the woods and watch the camping grounds of the Indians, who paddled up and down the Fox River below him. He lived, alas, to see the advance of industry and with it the withdrawal of his ancestors from the river. The house is three stories with twelve rooms that now, largely through the efforts of its curator, have been restored even as to much of the original Grignon furniture. During restoration the original log cabins were found under the edge of the bluff where Charles was born.

¶ Green Bay

TANK COTTAGE (1776)

Union Park; daily 10 to 5, Sundays and holidays 2 to 5; 50 cents and 10 cents; city of Green Bay.

This farmlike home of wattle and daub is the oldest in the state. The various owners could give a complete picture of the way the state was settled and how it grew. While the Great Lakes region was still under British control, a French fur trader named Joseph Roi built himself a cabin here with a huge fireplace, which may still be seen. Roi, who could neither read nor write, represents those intrepid French explorers and traders who first braved the wilderness which was then the Mississippi Valley. Why he built of wattle and daub is unknown, for it was a method seldom used in these crude cabins, nor was it in general use in France. However, the method (stuffing the inner and outer walls with twigs and leaves held together with mud clay) is interesting architecturally because it was so rare in our own early buildings. It was Nils Otto Tank, a missionary from Norway, who made a house of the cottage, clapboarding and plastering it and adding the two sloping, shedlike wings which give it its interesting lines. In the Tank Cottage, whose mistress, Madame Tank, was a wealthy and aristocratic Hollander, her Dutch heirlooms may still be seen, as well as her paintings and silver.

The Tank cottage at Green Bay is not only by far the oldest house still standing in the state but one of the most ingratiating early farmhouses to be found anywhere, its furnishings as fascinating as its story.

FORT HOWARD SURGEON'S QUARTERS (*c. 1817*)

Kellog and North Chestnut Streets; Tuesday to Saturday 10 to 5 and Sundays and holidays 2 to 5, May 1 to November 1; 50 cents and 10 cents; city of Green Bay.

This building and the hospital near it were once a part of the old fort but were moved here for preservation. It was the home of Dr. William Beaumont, whose discoveries, made at the fort on Mackinac Island, Michigan, (see page 221) were continued here. The house contains Beaumont's possessions, furniture, china, pictures, and library.

COTTON HOUSE (*1840s*)

2632 South Webster Avenue, Allouez; daily 10 to 5 except Mondays, Sundays 2 to 5; donation; Brown County Historical Society.

As an example of pure Greek Revival on a modest scale, its wide siding painted white, the house is interesting if rare in these parts. It was built by Capt. John Winslow Cotton, whose early home was in this very hamlet.

The Cotton house at Green Bay has an unusual recessed Greek Revival portico formed by its advancing wings.

INDEX

PHOTOGRAPH CREDITS

MASSACHUSETTS Page 3, Wayside Inn: Samuels; page 5, Harrison Gray Otis House: Society for the Preservation of New England Antiquities; page 5, Paul Revere House: Samuel Chamberlain; page 7, Henry W. Longfellow House: Frank O. Branzetti; page 8, Royall House: Samuel Chamberlain; pages 9, 10, Gore Place: Ezra Stoller, Ladies' Home Journal; page 11, Lyman House: Dwight O'Hara; page 16, Strawberry Hill: Zaharis; page 17, Lee House: Ezra Stoller, LHJ; page 20, House of Seven Gables: Haskell; page 21, Derby House: National Park Service; pages 23, 24, Parson Capen House and Fairbanks House: Samuel Chamberlain; page 25, Jabez Wilder House: Arthur C. Haskell; page 28, Adams Mansion: Ralph H. Anderson; pages 29, 32, 33, 35–38, Harlow House, Sturbridge Country Store, Narragansett Historical Building, Parson Ashley House, Frary House, Hall Tavern, Old Manse and Storrowton: all by Samuel Chamberlain; pages 40, 41, Shaker Farm: Ezra Stoller, LHJ; page 42, Thomas Cooke House: Samuel Chamberlain; pages 44, 45, Dell House and Nantucket: Ezra Stoller, LHJ.

NEW HAMPSHIRE Page 49, The Warner: Samuel Chamberlain; page 50, Gov. John Langdon House: Kingsbury Studio; page 51, Richard Jackson House: Samuel Chamberlain; pages 52, 54, Franklin Pierce House and Fort Acres: Eric M. Sanford; page 55, Ocean-Born-Mary House: L. M. A. Roy; pages 58, 59, Orford: Samuel Chamberlain.

MAINE Pages 60, 71, Ruggles House: Ezra Stoller, LHJ; pages 61, 62, 64–66, Hamilton House, Lady Pepperrell House, Sarah Orne Jewett House, and Holmes House: all by Douglas Armsden; page 67, Tate House: Ezra Stoller, LHJ; page 71, Field House: Douglas Armsden.

VERMONT Pages 73, 80, Dutton House, Shelburne: Ezra Stoller, LHJ.

RHODE ISLAND Page 88, Eleazer Arnold House: Laurence E. Tilley; page 89, Hunter House: Ezra Stoller, LHJ; page 92, John Brown House: Rhode Island Historical Society; page 93, Carrington House: Ezra Stoller, LHJ; page 94, Nathaniel Greene Home: L. E. Wagner; page 96, Barnum House: Laurence E. Tilley; pages 97, 98, Hunter House and Vernon House: Preservation Society of Newport County.

CONNECTICUT Pages 100, 102, Bonnet Hill Farm: Ezra Stoller, LHJ; page 101, Glebe House: Connecticut Development Commission; pages 106, 108, Denison House and Stonecrop: Ezra Stoller, LHJ; page 111, Buttolph-Williams House: Meyers Studio, Inc.; pages 112, 114, 118, Webb House, Royce House, and Nathan Hale Homestead: all by courtesy of Connecticut Development Commission.

NEW YORK Pages 120, 126, Rock Hall: Ezra Stoller, LHJ; pages 120, 149, Campbell-Whittlesey House: Society for the Preservation of Landmarks in Western New York; page 123, Dyckman House: E. P. McFarland; page 130, Home, Sweet Home: Ezra Stoller, LHJ; page 133, Philipse Castle: Laurence D. Thornton; page 139, House of History: Ezra Stoller, LHJ; page 142, Hasbrouck House: Cortlandt V. D. Hubbard; page 145, Constable Hall: Fynmore Photos; pages 146, 147, Fenimore House and Farmers' Museum: New York State Historical Association; page 150, Eastman Birthplace: George Eastman House, Inc.

NEW JERSEY Pages 154, 169, Homeland: Ezra Stoller, LHJ; pages 155, 156, Zabriskie–von Steuben House and McKonkey Ferry House: Department of Conservation and Economic Development; page 161, Boxwood Hall: M. W. Barish; page 161, Mead Hall: Peter A. Juley & Son; page 162, Ford Mansion: Ralph H. Anderson; page 164, Dey Mansion: Nathaniel Ewen; pages 168, 170, Indian King Tavern and Hancock House: Department of Conservation and Economic Development.

PENNSYLVANIA Pages 172, 184, Pottsgrove: Ezra Stoller, LHJ; page 175, Powel House: Cortlandt V. D. Hubbard; pages 176, 177, Rooms from Millbach: Philadelphia Museum of Art; page 180, Morris House: Ezra Stoller, LHJ; page 180, Upsala: Cortlandt V. D. Hubbard; page 182, 1704 House: Theodore B. Hetzel; page 186, Wheatland: Frederic S. Klein.

OHIO   Page 194, Mower House: Columbus Dispatch Photo; page 195, President's House: Marietta College; page 196, Matthews House: Hunter Studio; page 199, Headley Inn: Ohio Power Company; page 203, Glendower: Harold Rueppel; page 205, Sinton-Taft House: Taft Museum.

INDIANA   Page 209, Posey House: Wallace Studio; page 211, Shrewsbury House: Metzger & Metzger; page 213, Harrison Mansion: Read Studio.

MICHIGAN   Pages 215, 220, Mackinac Island: Emerson Dufina; Sanford House: Bernie Photographs.

ILLINOIS   Pages 212, 225, 228, 230, 231, Lincoln Home, Saucier House, Grant House, Menard House, Onstot Cooper Shop: all by courtesy of Illinois Division of Parks.

WISCONSIN   Page 237, Kilbournetown House: Milwaukee Journal; pages 239, 240, Tank Cottage and Cotton House: R. S. Sivesind, State Historical Society.

ABOUT THE AUTHORS

It would not be unnatural if the readers of the *Guides* were to wonder what kind of a house the Pratts live in. It is an old house but not very old, having been built by Jonas Calf in 1845. It stands in the rolling country of Bucks County, Pennsylvania, where all the old houses are built of the native fieldstone. In this case the walls are a monolith, two feet thick, plastered on both sides, and prone to sweat indoors in hot humid weather. In the moldings throughout there is a certain delicacy, bespeaking a natural sense of nicety in the farmer-builder. There is no elegance, to be sure, but there is feeling. The house was probably built in two sections—simultaneously, the Pratts suspect—and the second section was to accommodate a married son. As functional for its time and place as any modern design, it is still prized for its excellent utilitarian qualities and the peacefulness of its appearance. To compare it for distinction with most of the houses listed in the *Guides* would be presumptuous. But anyone who has an interest in simple farm dwellings, simply adapted, is welcome to visit it by written appointment in April and May when everything about the house looks its best.

Dorothy Pratt was born in Rochester in the midst of a city and countryside redolent with Greek Revival mansions and cobblestone houses. Richard Pratt was born near Harrisburg, between the Pennsylvania Dutch counties of Lebanon, Lancaster, and Berks, and the Scotch-Irish county of Cumberland, in a region where the great masonry barns are masterpieces of American building. He has been architectural and garden editor of the *Ladies' Home Journal* for the past twenty years. Since 1944, one of his magazine projects has been the well-known Regional Series of Early American Homes on which he and his wife have worked as a team, finding and photographing the houses and writing about them. This fine color series resulted in *A Treasury of Early American Homes* in 1950 and *A Second Treasury of Early American Homes* in 1955, on which the Pratts collaborated.

A GUIDE TO EARLY AMERICAN HOMES

South

A Guide to

EARLY

AMERICAN

HOMES

South

A GUIDE TO EARLY AMERICAN HOMES—SOUTH

Copyright © 1956 by Dorothy and Richard Pratt. All rights in this book are reserved. It may not be used for dramatic, motion-, or talking-picture purposes without written authorization from the holder of these rights. Nor may the book or parts thereof be reproduced in any manner whatsoever without permission in writing, except in the case of brief quotations embodied in critical articles and reviews.

Library of Congress Catalog Card Number: 56-10868

This edition published by Bonanza Books,
a division of Crown Publishers,
by arrangement with the copyright owners.
Printed in the United States of America

(EE)

PREFACE

The South as we see it here in terms of the early houses takes in all the states below the line drawn in the 1760s by the two British astronomers, Mason and Dixon. Where that line ends we have let the Ohio River take over. And across the Mississippi we have brought in the historically Southern states of Missouri and Arkansas. We were strongly tempted to take in Texas too, even though she is more rightly labeled Southwest than South; but at some point we had to draw a line of our own.

It is hardly necessary to introduce the South as a place where stately and romantic early homes abound. Too many people have heard by now of the glamorous charms of Natchez, New Orleans, and Charleston; of Williamsburg's patrician splendors, the matchless country mansions of Virginia, and Maryland's aristocratic tidewater manors. These are of course all covered in the *Guide*; but they are only a beginning. There are still many other major localities and collections. There are still any number of out-of-the-way towns and hidden-away houses.

For the South is vast; the early settlements where good houses were clustered were few and far between; the palatial plantations were widely separated as a rule, leading their lives apart and enriching their own solitudes. Except in the centers of trade and government, houses of consequence were built off in the country, to reign over their own private agricultural communities. The roads that led to many of them are not now the roads you ordinarily travel, a fact which makes them hard to find without some help and guidance, and this we hope our book will be able to provide.

As to what constitutes earliness, we have seldom included any houses later than the Civil War. As to where earliness begins, there are claims but no documentary evidence to convince us that houses still stand in the South which were built before 1650; the same being true, for that matter, of the North, where claims and claimants are much more numerous. If here and there you find earlier dates than 1650, we have put them down because we were not prepared or zealously inclined to dispute the claims. But as a rule we have let any convincing and commonly accepted date stand as a useful approximation of the house's age. To us the important thing was that the house still should stand to tell the story of its place and time and people.

There are two categories of houses in the *Guides*. There are the houses that are open to the public and maintained for that purpose, and there are the houses that are private homes and maintained for *that* purpose. We believe you will find here—for the first time anywhere—virtually every open early house of any merit in the South. We *know* that you will find here, for the first time anywhere, the several hundred private homes whose owners, through the *Guide*, have generously agreed to let their homes be visited under conditions set down in each case. The authors are as pleased to have helped make possible this unprecedented privilege as they are grateful to all the various owners involved for granting it. Readers will readily appreciate that to abuse this

v

privilege will be to run the risk of ending it for others.

Restoration towns, villages, and communities are described as we come to them, though with the notable exception of Colonial Williamsburg and the very promising restoration of Old Salem at Winston-Salem, North Carolina, there is nothing like the number of these in the South as in the North.

In the South, on the other hand, the organized house-and-garden tours have become major annual events of national importance; and you will find these described under the locality where each originates. In terms of scope and attendance, the following take precedence: the Maryland House and Garden Pilgrimage, Virginia Garden Week (both state-wide), the Natchez Pilgrimage, Charleston's Historic House Tour, the New Orleans Fiesta, and the Tennessee Antiquities Pilgrimage.

¶ Things to remember

Automobile road maps are accurate, up to date, and free. We believe that with the *Guide* and a good road map you can find every house listed herein, except some of the *private houses*. For these, which are often isolated, get explicit directions from the owners when making appointments by letter or phone.

For further local guidance, we suggest that the town or county historical societies, the chambers of commerce, the public libraries, the post office, and even sometimes the gas station or the police, will prove helpful—more or less in the order given.

It goes without saying that days, hours, and entrance fees are subject to change. Advance inquiries sometimes save disappointments. When two fees are given, the first is for adults, the second for children. If no fee is mentioned, no fee is required. Voluntary contributions are suggested in many cases but not obligatory.

¶ To those who helped

Mention of all the individuals who have given helpful information, and all the books which have been consulted, would fill a volume in themselves. We have tried the patience of countless homeowners, of house custodians and curators, of endless officers of state and local historical societies, of development commissions, of landmark and antiquarian societies, of pilgrimage and house-tour people, of chambers of commerce, women's clubs, librarians, town clerks, of the Colonial Dames and the D.A.R.—and we thank them all for the time they have taken in our behalf during the more than three years we have been working intensively on the books. For expert assistance on the manuscripts, we wish to give sincere thanks in particular to Miss Lorinda Ballard and Mrs. Anthony Salisbury—bless their hearts!

To the LADIES' HOME JOURNAL *and its editors, Bruce and Beatrice Blackmar Gould, and to the parent organization, the Curtis Publishing Company, a special note of appreciation for putting picture material at our disposal, along with indispensable facilities and advantages of many kinds, without which it would have been impossible to produce these Guides.*

CONTENTS

A GUIDE TO EARLY AMERICAN HOMES

South

With all its Palladian and classical qualities, Monticello is one of the most fascinating and personal of early American houses: Jefferson's architectural autobiography, in a way. The portico of the Myers house in Norfolk is across the page.

VIRGINIA

THERE is such an array of vintage architecture in Virginia, and most of it of such exciting merit and historical eminence, that the state might well be called in this respect the showplace of the nation. Williamsburg, with its remarkable restorations and reconstructions, comes immediately to mind; every year more than six hundred thousand people from all over the world come to this stunning exhibition town. Yet twice as many come to see Mt. Vernon; and while it is off the beaten track compared with Williamsburg and Mt. Vernon, two hundred thousand visitors annually find their way to Monticello, Thomas Jefferson's Palladian dream house, on its hill outside Charlottesville. Stratford and Gunston Hall, two of the greatest, are still standing, along with many other lovely and distinguished great houses such as "Kenmore," "Wilton," and "Woodlawn," all open to visitors at practically any time.

In addition, there are such private homes of importance as "Shirley," "Berkeley," and "Carter's Grove" along the lower James; "Tuckahoe" just outside Richmond; "Federal Hill" in Fredericksburg; "Oak Hill" and "Oatlands" in the Leesburg country; and "Edgemont" and "Estouteville" in the Charlottesville area. Most of these are open by appointment through the intercession of this *Guide.*

Then, of course, during the last week in April the famous Virginia fixture called "Historic Garden Week" takes place, providing, in addition to most of the homes mentioned above, the only opportunity thus far to visit such houses of outstanding importance and beauty as "Westover," "Brandon," "York Hall," "Toddsbury," "Morven," and many others.

All in all, there is more to be seen than can be covered in a single session. Perhaps the most rewarding method would be to do it piecemeal at various times. To make possible a program along these lines we have divided the state into sections, each one with a center, so to

3

speak, of special interest in which it should also be pleasant to stay.

And so, on to the Colony and Commonwealth of Virginia!

¶ In & out of Alexandria

As you walk around old Alexandria, keep an eye open for the BENJAMIN DULANEY HOUSE, 601 Duke Street, and the HOLLAND HOUSE, 415 Wolfe Street; they are usually open, along with quite a few others, during Alexandria's spring and fall tours, noted below. And don't miss the cobbled part of Prince Street with its prim and colorful colonial and federal airs. It was cobbled by Hessian soldiers. Also see GADSBY'S TAVERN, never a home but the next thing to it,

with its stunning doorways and a ballroom so beautiful that the original woodwork is now in the American Wing of the Metropolitan Museum, which returned the door as a gift in 1949. Try to see the GILPIN HOUSE, a private restoration with a gift shop on the ground floor —and while you're wandering around through this section, the old Stable-Leadbetter APOTHECARY SHOP, patronized by Washington and Lee, with its remarkable collection of pharmaceutical glass.

In addition to Historic Garden Week in April, throughout which Alexandria houses are open, there is a spring tour which precedes it and a fall tour on a Saturday in October, both local projects. Check on dates ahead of time. William

M. Kabler, Alexandria Historic Foundation, Alexandria National Bank Building, will furnish further information and maps and answer inquiries about seeing private homes by special arrangement.

Look inside the Arlington monumentality for Lee personality.

ARLINGTON HOUSE, now the LEE MANSION MEMORIAL (1802–1820)

> *At the Virginia end of the Arlington Memorial Bridge; daily, October through March 9 to 4:30, April through September 9 to 6; small admission charge; National Park Service.*

The monumental Doric portico of this house is almost the first thing you see if you enter Virginia, and then Alexandria, from the nation's capital. It is the Temple of Theseus, no less, translated from the Grecian into the Classic Revival that marked the architectural mood of America in the early 1800s. It was really a Custis house, built by the foster son of George Washington; but when Lt. Robert E. Lee, freshly out of West Point in 1831, married here the only child of the Custis family, it became his name with which the place was destined to be associated. It is a house of rather massive formality whose family living quarters and service rooms yet provide a personal and intimate flavor.

Left: Prince Street in Alexandria is a practically perfect museum street.

Right: The most frequently pictured and visited of early American houses, Mt. Vernon is bursting with history and beauty.

CARLYLE HOUSE (1752)

> *Entered through Wager Building, 121 North Fairfax Street; daily, 10 to 6; 30 cents and 20 cents; Lloyd Diehl Schaeffer.*

In Alexandria itself the section to see lies within the eight blocks between Franklin and Queen Streets and the six between Washington Street and the Potomac. The one open house there is the "Carlyle"; this is Alexandria's great Palladian mansion, though it must now be approached through another building. Its blue room is a beauty, and the house itself is a fertile ground for historians. It was here, for instance, that the colonial governors met in 1775 to draw up their stand on the "taxation without representation" policy that led to the Revolution. It has been subsequently called the "birthplace of the Constitution."

GADSBY'S TAVERN (1752–1790)

> *Cameron and North Royal Streets; daily, 30 cents; Gadsby's Tavern Board, Inc. (Mentioned above.)*

FRIENDSHIP FIRE ENGINE HOUSE (organized 1774)

> *107 South Alfred Street; daily, 9 to 5.*

A collection of early fire-fighting equipment and a small engine, donated by Washington.

MT. VERNON (1743)

> *Mt. Vernon Highway 7 miles south; daily, 9 to 5; 50 cents; Mt. Vernon Ladies Association*

The big show hereabouts is the three plantation houses south of Washington. Mt. Vernon would be the big show anywhere, not only for its significance as a symbol and shrine but for its tangible appearance

as a familiar and fine plantation house that belonged to the greatest of all Virginia gentlemen farmers, still as carefully cherished as when George and Martha Washington lived here. Now seen by over a million people a year, the plantation was originally an inheritance, much of its 8,073 acres indifferent in quality. Washington was deeply concerned with its improvement and development. Even during one of the most crucial periods of the new republic he found the time to write constantly to his manager; one of the letters runs to 2,500 words! No detail was too minor for his attention; when a new barn was to be built, he knew how many bricks it would take. Far ahead of his time he evolved the idea of a six-year crop rotation to improve the land; it is known that in his spare moments he wrote memos to himself about it. While a poor businessman, he was undoubtedly one of the best farmers of his day. Only at the close of his ardent life was Washington able to settle down here permanently. Even then there was little enough of privacy; he complained at one time that he and Martha had not been able to eat a meal alone in fifteen years! Friends, relatives, and even total strangers often dropped in at Mt. Vernon to pay homage. In one year alone the consumption of pork at Washington's table amounted to 1,600 pounds!

Woodlawn is filled with Federal stateliness and personal charm.

WOODLAWN PLANTATION
(1802–1805)
5 miles beyond Mt. Vernon; daily except Mondays, winter 10 to 4:30, summer 10 to 5 (closed Thanksgiving, Christmas, and New Year's); 50 cents; National Trust for Historic Preservation.

Closely associated with Mt. Vernon is this splendid Late Georgian mansion nearby that has only recently been restored with genuine éclat. It is the former home of Nelly Custis Lewis, granddaughter of Martha Washington, foster daughter of George Washington, and the wife of Maj. Lawrence Lewis, Washington's nephew. Lafayette, Henry Clay, Zachary Taylor, Millard Fillmore, and Andrew Jackson stayed here. Exquisitely furnished with English and American antiques of before 1839, some of which belonged to the Lewises and the Washingtons; the children's rooms are especially enchanting. The whole house is a vivid re-creation of elegant living not to be missed. We would like to suggest to the annual million visitors to Mount Vernon that they see Woodlawn too.

GUNSTON HALL (1758)
5 miles beyond Woodlawn; daily, 9:30 to 5; 50 cents; maintained by Board of Regents of Gunston Hall, National Society of the Colonial Dames of America; owned by Commonwealth of Virginia.

Somewhat farther down along the river, Gunston completes this practically perfect trio of Potomac plantations. It was the home of George Mason, one of the most civilized and courageous of colonial gentlemen. The house is the result of a collaboration between this author of the Virginia Bill of Rights and his greatly gifted woodcarver, William Buckland, who was brought for him from England and who later did the Hammond-Harwood House in Annapolis, another masterpiece. Gunston is a Georgian mansion with certain exterior cottage characteristics, such as the one-story eaves, and demioctagonal porch. Within, what wonders of woodcarving are to be seen in its Palladian room, and in the Chinese Chippendale room adjoining! This is one of the hardest houses to leave that we know of. With the painstaking research of experts the Colonial Dames have

Gunston Hall gives the impression of being less large than it is, especially now that it is dwarfed by the greatly grown boxwood hedges of George Mason's garden.

The superb interior details are evidence of William Buckland's woodcarving genius. His famous Chinese Chippendale room has no counterpart in the country.

The Palladian room is the supreme example of colonial carving to be found anywhere in America, and its restoration a triumph of skill and taste.

restored the house to its former luster. The authenticity of the red silk damask hung on the walls of the Palladian room, for example, was deduced from a shred discovered just beneath a molding. The furniture is being selected with equal care.

¶ In & out of Leesburg

The trip from the Alexandria neighborhood to Leesburg and nearby Middleburg takes you through the beautiful fox-hunting farmland surrounding these two towns. In each town there is an unusually good (and good-looking) early inn. There are no museum houses, but there are four private homes of great beauty and distinction, whose owners have kindly consented, through the *Guide,* to show by appointment; so it is a place for which to plan ahead.

As for the two inns, both the LAUREL BRIGADE in Leesburg and the RED FOX TAVERN in Middleburg are much older than the houses here described. Rather late in life the former took on the name of a gallant local Civil War unit. It has a ballroom built especially for Lafayette's Leesburg visit. Red Fox Tavern was built by a man named Noble Beveridge; thus it is only natural that drinks there should be dispensed from the Beveridge Bar.

The bridal chamber has a carved four-poster of museum quality, and the whole inn is beautifully done. The food in both inns could hardly be better.

BELMONT (1800)
Route 7, 5 miles east of Leesburg; by appointment; George C. Clarke.

Five miles before you get to Leesburg, Belmont is the tremendous mansion you see set back a half mile from Route 7. It was built by Ludwell Lee, son of Richard Henry Lee, nephew of "Light Horse" Harry, and host here to President and Dolly Madison after the British burned the White House. Keep in mind the fact that it is considerably larger today than when it was built. The two marble drawing-room mantels were gifts from Lafayette after he had been a guest here on his triumphal tour.

OAK HILL (started 1821)
Route 15, 2 miles north of Gilbert's Corner; by appointment; voluntary contribution to Loudoun County Hospital; Mr. and Mrs. Thomas N. de Laschmutt, Aldie P.O.

Two of the fine marble mantels at "Oak Hill" are also from a grateful guest—Lafayette again. The house, a little later than Belmont, more Classic and less Georgian. Coming north on Route 15 you get a good view of this splendidly porticoed yellow mansion built by James Monroe from Thomas Jefferson's plans. Boldly colorful inside and handsomely furnished, it has a complete bedroom of Madison furniture from Montpelier, a Madison mansion of renown down near Orange. "Oak Hill" stands above a famous terraced garden of aboretum quality. Very choice.

OATLANDS (1800)
Route 15, 6 miles south of Leesburg; by appointment; Mrs. William Corcoran Eustis.

"Oatlands" four miles north, is likewise distinguished, but in a very different way. Fronted by a two-story Corinthian portico and surmounted by a balustraded attic, it combines, as often happens in happy instances like this, both beauty and impressiveness. Built by George Carter, a grandson of "King" Carter, it remained a Carter home for almost a hundred years. There

Oak Hill from its famous gardens.

are balancing stairways at either end of the house, an octagonal drawing room, and fine carving. The old terraced boxwood gardens are very special, as is the celebrated grove of oaks.

CHESTNUT HILL (1796–1812)
Route 15, 12 miles north of Leesburg near Point of Rocks on the Potomac; by appointment; Mr. and Mrs. C. Coleman Gore.

This is the last and most northerly place of interest in the Leesburg vicinity, a beauty of a stone country mansion in a locality where mansions of brick predominate; you can tell you are nearing the Valley of Virginia, where stone comes into its own. The portico here again is a tall one, and there are unusually tall corner mantels in the four principal first-floor rooms.

¶ In & out of Charlottesville

In the city itself the great sight is, of course, what Jefferson did at the University of Virginia, whose architecture has a nearly domestic grace and scale. And indeed some of it is used as living facilities —namely, the pavilions occupied by University professors, and open during Historic Virginia Garden Week. It was Jefferson's genius as a designer to create with romantic devotion to the Palladian principles. This occasionally gave his work a somewhat cool and academic look, but it just as often produced effects of incomparable charm—and nowhere more so than here at the University. On Carr's Hill the PRESIDENT'S HOUSE is open only during Historic Garden Week, as are the JAMES MONROE HOUSE and the JAMES MONROE LAW OFFICE on Monroe Hill.

MICHIE TAVERN (1753)
1 mile south of 53; daily; 50 cents; Vestal Thomas Milton.

On the way to Monticello don't miss this, one of the most famous of colonial inns. The clapboard-covered hillside house with veranda was built by Patrick Henry's father. Jefferson gave parties in its ballroom; Lafayette dined here with Monroe;

and goodness knows how many other great figures were guests at the place. Interestingly furnished.

MONTICELLO (1772–1803)
Route 53, 3 miles out; daily, 9 to 5; 90 cents; Thomas Jefferson Memorial Fund.

This famous house attracts you as much for its livable homelike scale as for its patrician beauty. "Architecture is my delight," Jefferson wrote, "and putting up and pulling down one of my favorite amusements." This applies here; for thirty-one years after he had put up the original house, he did pull a great deal of it down, and then erected it again in its present form, which was more pleasing to him in both plan and appearance. And one of his great delights was to design the various fascinating devices and furnishings which make the Monticello interior as personal as it is impressive.

Redlands is one of the finest old family homes in this part of Virginia.

ASH LAWN (1799)
2 miles beyond Monticello; daily; 75 cents; Mr. and Mrs. Jay Winston Johns.

Nearby Jefferson designed this quiet and retiring residence for his dear friend James Monroe. Through a garden arch Monticello is framed in the distance. The house is furnished with warmth and affection, and the boxwood is of rare size and beauty.

REDLANDS (1798–1808)
Near Carter's Bridge; by appointment only; Robert Hill Carter, P.O. Box 1638, Richmond.

Because the homemade bricks could not be produced on the premises in a hurry, nor the lumber and lime, it took nearly ten years for Redlands to get built. It is a Virginia Georgian house of gentle restraint and fine proportions, designed, as far as can be learned, with at least no active help from Jefferson. An elliptical drawing room greets you as you enter, and tall windows, delicate cornices, and Adam mantels make the whole downstairs a rare delight. It has been a Carter estate since 1730.

ESTOUTEVILLE (*1830*)
Near Keene, 15 miles south of Charlottesville via 20; by appointment; Mr. and Mrs. J. Prescott Carter.

This is an immense country mansion with an imposing classic portico. It was designed by a young protégé of Jefferson's from Philadelphia, James Dinsmore, and the master's influence is unmistakable. The woodcarving within, said to have been done by Hessians who settled here after the Revolution, is of a high order. All in all, a house well worth seeing, including its Blue Ridge Mountain view.

With porticoes on every side, Edgemont is replete with Jeffersonian charm.

EDGEMONT (*1796*)
Route 712, about 10 miles from Keene near North Garden; by appointment; Mr. and Mrs. William Scott Sneed.

Built from a Jefferson design derived from Palladio's Villa Rotonda, this version is in white-painted wood, raised above a full basement, with porticos on all four sides, and with a pair of detached matching dependencies reached by underground passages. It makes a picture that will charm all lovers of Palladian grace.

¶ Southside Virginia

The great old houses begin to thin out in this scenic countryside. Only two of any interest at all can at this time be listed as open.

MILLER-CLAYTOR HOUSE (*1791*)
Riverside Park, Lynchburg; by appointment; Mrs. Langhorne Taylor (custodian).

This is a very pleasant house to visit. It is said that in its garden Jefferson demonstrated to an awe-struck gathering the edibility of the tomato.

MC LEAN HOUSE (*date unknown*)
Appomattox Courthouse; daily, 8:30 to 5; April to November; National Park Service.

Many people, us included, find *all* old houses of interest, even when, as here, the attractions are largely historical. For this is where, on April 9, 1865, Grant and Lee signed the Articles of Surrender.

¶ In & out of Richmond

WICKHAM-VALENTINE HOUSE (*1812*)
1015 East Clay Street; weekdays 10 to 5, Sundays 2:30 to 5:30; Valentine Museum.

While Richmond was, of course, a pre-Revolutionary city, the traditional flavor is now very much that of the nineteenth century, making this house seem truly typical of the city in that respect. Indeed, the history of its construction is a vivid picture of the life and history of the city itself. Built originally in the Federal style, it may well have been designed by Robert Mills. But in 1853, when the house was sold to a John P. Ballard after Mrs. Wickham's death, the Adamesque interiors were changed to fashionable Victorian. If Victorian is your dish, here it is at its most lush and delicious. The garden has its own character too.

POE SHRINE (*1680s*)
1916 East Main Street; March through November, Tuesday through Saturday 10 to 5, Sundays and Mondays 2:30 to 5:30; 50 cents and 25 cents; Poe Foundation, Inc.

This is the oldest house in the city, low, narrow, stone-walled, and with diminutive windows and dormers. Although it has no

No photograph of Wilton, inside or out, can convey the full delight and distinction which this great old Queen Anne mansion brings to the eye of the visitor. The paneling is supreme.

known actual associations with Edgar Allan Poe, he did live and work nearby, and the house is now filled with priceless mementos of the poet, including manuscripts—the largest Poe collection anywhere. There is a lot to see, for in addition there are the memorial building, the garden, and the teahouse.

JOHN MARSHALL HOUSE (*c. 1790*)
Ninth and Marshall Streets; Monday to Friday, 10 to 5; 25 cents; city of Richmond, A.P.V.A. (custodian).

This house of immense character was the home of our most celebrated dissenter, the first and greatest Chief Justice of the Supreme Court. It is probably the best Richmond town house of its time still standing. Each of the two street-entrance doorways opens directly into one or the other of the two principal downstairs rooms. It is fortunately unchanged, with many of the original furnishings from the Marshall family.

WILTON (*1750*)
Wilton Road, via Cary Street Road; weekdays 10 to 5, Sundays 3 to 5; The Colonial Dames of America in the State of Virginia.

This is, of course, one of the finest Queen Anne mansions in Virginia, and one of the choicest house museums in the country. It now stands in the outer residential district of the city as though it has always been there, though it was really brought here

from several miles down the James River. It is a tour de force of restoration, furnished with the dignity and richness it merits. An outstanding feature is its floor-to-ceiling paneling. Since it was the home of the Randolphs of Virginia, it goes without saying that all the famous figures of its day were lavishly received here.

VIRGINIA HOUSE (*reconstruction*)
Off Cary Street Road in Windsor Farms district; Tuesday through Friday 10 to 4, Saturdays and Sundays 2 to 5; 65 cents and 35 cents; Virginia Historical Society.

This place was built of materials from the ancient priory (1125) at Warwick in England, and further contains a copy of Sulgrave Manor, in part, as well as another English ancestral home of the Washington family.

TUCKAHOE (*1700–1710*)
River Road 6½ miles west of city; by appointment; $1.50; Mr. and Mrs. N. Addison Baker.

Here we have a very early Virginia great house, with much magnificent walnut paneling and carving. Few large houses still stand today with so much of their original structure intact, even to the windows and weatherboarding. It is not, happily, furnished in museum fashion. A street of slave quarters and other plantation houses, and a schoolhouse nearby where Jefferson was a pupil at an early age, make a visit to Tuckahoe all the more worthwhile.

¶ In & out of Fredericksburg

It will help you to get the full flavor of
Fredericksburg if, in addition to visiting
the four fine houses in the town itself
listed here and described below, you will
stroll through the old streets to the LAW
OFFICE OF JAMES MONROE, now containing the furniture the Monroes purchased
in Paris for the White House, and on to
the RISING SUN TAVERN and HUGH MER-
CER'S APOTHECARY SHOP. By so doing
you will pretty well cover the colonial
parts of the present city, one of the most
historic in the state, and will come face
to face with many fascinating (and some
fearsome) aspects of your country's past.

FEDERAL HILL (*mid-eighteenth
century*)
> *Hanover Street; by appointment; October,
> November, and March through May;
> voluntary donation toward further
> restoration; Mr. and Mrs. Richard N.
> Lanier.*

This dignified dwelling seems to have been
built by order of Queen Anne as a state
residence for her high colonial officials, as
it was early occupied by the lieutenant governor of Virginia, Sir Alexander Spots-
wood, and his lady. It was already recorded
as an "old" house when purchased right
after the Revolution by Robert Brooke, a
founder of the Federalist Party, who gave
the house its name. A great white clapboard

mansion, outwardly styled with distinguished austerity and charmingly Queen
Anne within. The woodwork has great
elegance. An extremely interesting house
to look at and hear about; appropriately
furnished.

BROMPTON (*1730–1836*)
> *Adjacent to the campus of Mary
> Washington College; by appointment;
> residence of the college president.*

This mellow brick mansion adjoins the
campus of Mary Washington College and
crowns the hill that looked down on the
carnage of December, 1862, when 11,000
died in Burnside's vain attempt to drive the
Confederate forces from the heights around
the house. The early central section is now
dominated by a classic portico and wings,
added in 1836, which give the battle-
scarred house an attractive air of modest
impressiveness. This impression is true, too,
of its nicely restored interior, and in particular of the loggialike entrance hall.

KENMORE (*1752*)
> *Washington Street; daily, 9 to 6; 60 cents;
> Kenmore Association.*

This is the chef-d'oeuvre of the town, and,
like the town itself, overflows with history.
It is an impressively pleasant brick house
as you look at it from its gardens, but the
true excitement starts when you enter. The
intricate plaster ornamentation in the
drawing room is all you have ever heard
it to be; and other rooms are almost as
breath-taking. The whole beautifully de-

*Left: Brompton is a
pleasant, unexpected
private home to see
here.*

*Right: The Washington
Birthplace: a highly
recommended recon-
struction.*

tailed house is furnished to perfection, faithful to its period and to the people who first filled it with colonial eminence. The home of Washington's only sister, Betty, and her patriot husband, Col. Fielding Lewis, Martha and George were its most frequent house guests. The bed in Betty's room is the very one on which her brother threw himself after the battle of Yorktown and slept, too exhausted even to take his boots off.

MARY WASHINGTON HOUSE (*1772*)
Charles and Lewis Streets; daily, 9 to 6; 50 cents; A.P.V.A.

This is the charming white clapboard house that Washington built for his mother so that she might be near her daughter Betty at "Kenmore." It is an especially appealing homelike place. Mrs. Washington's personal belongings remain in the bedroom where George saw her for the last time as she lay dying.

MARMION (*very early eighteenth century*)
17 miles from Fredericksburg, Route 609, off Route 3 at Comorn; daily 9 to 5; 50 cents; Mr. and Mrs. R. Carter N. Grymes.

This is the first house to see after leaving Fredericksburg in the direction of the Northern Neck of Virginia, and one of the oldest great houses in America. It is also one of unusual interest, with beautiful paneling, though the original woodwork of the drawing room is now a prize exhibit in the American Wing of the Metropolitan Museum. Named after the Marmion side of the Scottish Fitzhugh family that built it, it was bought by George Washington Lewis. On its grounds are pecan trees that still bear which were planted from nuts brought here by Mr. Lewis's famous and well-traveled uncle, George.

CAMDEN (*1760–1857*)
Near Port Royal (get directions when making appointment); April 15 to June 15; voluntary contribution for restoration of St. Peter's Episcopal Church, Port Royal; Richard Turner Pratt.

This is an extremely interesting example of stylistic transformation, wherein a notable Queen Anne mansion was made over into Victorian. The drawing room, still intact, is fascinating.

GEORGE WASHINGTON BIRTHPLACE (*reconstruction*)
Pope's Creek, 38 miles from Fredericksburg, 2 miles off Route 3; daily, 8:30 to 5; National Park Service.

This is a skillful and sensitive reconstruction of a typical Virginia plantation mansion on the site of the house in which Washington was born, which was burned on Christmas Day in 1779, and of which no records remain. While only a tilt-top table in the dining room survives from the original house, the furnishings are all of the period of Washington's parents, and the mode of mid-eighteenth-century life is made remarkably vivid.

Stratford is another great Virginia mansion that all too often baffles the camera. What would seem to be its Van-brughian severity vanishes when you see it face to face, walk through its fabulous rooms, and taste the plantation luncheon.

STRATFORD HALL (*1725*)

42 miles from Fredericksburg; off Route 3; daily, 9 to 5; April 15 to October 1; 50 cents and 25 cents; Robert E. Lee Memorial Foundation.

One of the greatest of the great colonial country mansions in America, this is also one of the most English of early American houses, having been designed apparently after the manner of the English architect, Sir John Vanbrugh. Still very much in use, Stratford Hall offers a beautiful opportunity to recapture the life and atmosphere on a vast and wealthy plantation of early-eighteenth-century Virginia. The scale of the house is manorial, and the paneling and furnishings a sight to behold. It was built by Thomas Lee, a native Governor of the colony, and within its walls were born the five Revolutionary Lees and, in 1807, the great Robert E. Lee himself. Give yourself plenty of time to browse. An old-time plantation luncheon is served from April 15 to October 1.

EPPING FOREST (*late seventeenth century*)

Route 354, east from Route 3 at Litwalton; daily; 50 cents; James D. and Eoline Ball Jesse.

The present west wing and dependencies of "Epping Forest" were built in the 1680s or 1690s, making this for the most part a venerable house indeed. It is reverently occupied. Like the Mary Washington House in Fredericksburg, this is a white clapboard house of real quality, for it is where the first President's mother was born

—Mary Ball, known in her youth as the "Rose of Epping Forest." The house is filled with memories and heirlooms.

Other distinguished early houses at this end of the Neck for which permission might be granted to look at from the grounds are DITCHLEY (1752), near Kilmarnock; CLIFTON (mid-seventeenth century!), nearby; MONASKIN (1702), out of Litwalton, and VERVILLE (1690), on the Merry Point Ferry road. No harm in trying.

MANTUA (*c. 1785*)

Get directions when making appointment; Mr. and Mrs. Wayne Chatfield-Taylor.

This is one of the few very early Federal houses in this part of Virginia—with wings and portico added soon after the eighteenth century. The house is dramatically located on a hill, with a marvelous view northeast to the mouth of the Potomac.

¶ *In & out of Williamsburg*

Here, in the old colonial capital revived, restored, and re-created, there must be well over a hundred eighteenth-century houses on which to feast your eyes. The assortment of sizes adds enormously to the fascination of the show, for they range from the grandeur of the GOVERNOR'S PALACE to the almost doll-like scale of the little detached kitchen buildings, many of which now serve delightfully as homes. And all, of course, including the endless minor dependencies, domestic outbuildings, and fences which formed an integral part of the architectural picture in this colonial town, are now stunningly restored. Then, within a thirty-five-mile radius of the town, there is, as you will see, a superb assortment of plantation homes, country mansions, and smaller houses, including many of the finest in Virginia. Altogether it is probably as happy a hunting ground for houses as any spot you will find in what was colonial America.

WYTHE HOUSE (*1755*)
Palace Green; daily, 10 to 5; on combination ticket; Colonial Willamsburg, Inc.

A beautiful beginning, with its ancient pink brick and delicate dignity. Chaste without, charming within, it stands with its gardens and grounds as the complete and distinguished establishment of a complete and distinguished colonial gentleman. George Wythe was Jefferson's teacher and dearest friend, as well as the first Virginia signer of the Declaration of Independence. The house was built for him and his bride, Elizabeth, by his father-in-law Col. Richard Taliaferro, who also, no doubt, designed it. It is needless to mention with what taste and skill the interiors in Williamsburg are decorated and furnished, for here you come face to face with perfectionism. And one

of the remarkable things about Williamsburg perfectionism is how carefully it preserves the "lived-in" look.

BRUSH-EVERARD HOUSE (*1717*)
Across Green from Wythe House; daily, 10 to 5; on combination ticket; Colonial Williamsburg, Inc.

Across the Palace Green from the Wythe House, this place provides an excellent opportunity to compare a more modest early Virginia town residence of frame with a statelier one of brick; for this delightful white-and-ocher-painted dwelling, while smaller than the Wythe House, is just as much, in its way, a "complete gentleman's" establishment. The boldness of the color scheme inside is one of the striking contrasts.

GOVERNOR'S PALACE (*reconstruction*)
At head of Green; daily, 10 to 5; on combination ticket; Colonial Williamsburg, Inc.

A superlative reconstruction whose splendors speak for themselves. How those splendors, so beautifully recaptured here, must have burned up the colonial Virginia taxpayer when called upon to furnish the Crown with the means for such elegant comfort!

LUDWELL-PARADISE HOUSE (*c. 1717*)
Duke of Gloucester Street; daily, 10 to 5; on combination ticket; Colonial Williamsburg, Inc.

This stylish town house now contains a fabulous collection of American folk art, and is the only other domestic dwelling of

The wonderful old Wythe House may not be the most spectacular sight in Williamsburg, but it is close to being the most beautiful, and the most complete picture of how life was lived in the Virginia capital.

note regularly open in the restoration. But, as noted above, the number of beautiful old houses to be seen from the sidewalks of Williamsburg constitute an embarrassment of riches.

During Virginia Garden Week at the end of April, Williamsburg invites visitors to see eight of these private homes and gardens not regularly open to the public. Admission fee is either separate or with a combination ticket.

CARTER'S GROVE (*1751–1753*)

Route 60, 3 miles southeast of Williamsburg; at reasonable hours for limited time each spring; $1.50; Mrs. Archibald McCrea.

One of the greatest of the Virginia mansions, "Carter's Grove" is still a going plantation. The long, illustrious brick house rises with grace and dignity from the green pastureland and lawns that surround it and which then drop down in broad turf terraces to the James River. Carter Burwell was its talented first owner, and Richard Bayliss and David Minitree were the tal-

ented English craftsmen-builders Burwell brought over for the job. Various later changes to the roof and wings have luckily been all to the good.

The great entrance hall and the staircase are among the glories of domestic architecture in this country. The scale is very generous in all of the rooms, which spread out in both directions from the manorial central hall. As one walks through the hall toward the river side, a vista of rooms in both directions ends in a welcoming blaze from the fireplaces, casting their flickering glow on richly paneled walls. Furnished today with the great taste and largesse of its mistress, it manages, in spite of its grandeur, to reflect her gay and vivid personality.

EVELYNTON (*reconstruction*)

Just off Route 5 about 5 miles east of "Westover"; daily, at reasonable daylight hours; $1.10; Mrs. John Augustin Ruffin.

On the way to "Westover" is a reproduction of an eighteenth-century mansion, built of early brick. The skill with which "Evelynton" has been reconstructed in

modern times on the land that William Byrd III of "Westover" bestowed upon his wife Lucy Parke Byrd, gives it added interest; but the rarity and beauty of its heirloom furnishings are its special claim to your attention.

SHERWOOD FOREST (*original part 1780, additions 1840*)
Route 5 near Evelynton; daily, except Sundays; Mr. and Mrs. Alfred J. Tyler.

The home of John Tyler, tenth President of the United States. He purchased it in 1842 while he was still in the White House and doubled its size after retiring to it in 1845. It is still being lived in by Tylers—his grandson and wife. The clapboard, added to by the President for comfort rather than style, is on many levels and rambles on for a length of three hundred feet, said to be a record in this country. The house is only one room deep, and there are many staircases. The President remodeled the old part to conform to the taste of the day; consequently the mantels are of black marble, and the over-door cornices classical throughout. It was elaborately furnished, and many of the original Victorian pieces are still there, with appropriate additions. Wallpaper of the period from France is still on the parlor walls, and the ornate gilt window cornices and chandeliers remain. The house stands today virtually as it was in Tyler's time.

WESTOVER (*1730*)
Entrance lane a mile or so east of "Berkeley"; daily during daylight hours, grounds and gardens only; $1.00; Mrs. Bruce Crane Fisher.

If any one colonial house can be called the finest in the country, "Westover" is the one that has been called that the most fre-

quently. It can be seen within only during Garden Week, but to see it only from without is a tremendous experience.

BERKELEY (*1726*)
Just off Route 5 about 5 miles before Shirley; daily, 8 to 5; Mr. and Mrs. Malcolm Johnson.

This is probably the oldest three-story brick house in Virginia, and is full of Harrison-family history. It was built by Benjamin Harrison IV, three-time Governor of Virginia; owned next by Benjamin V., a Signer; and then by William Henry Harrison, ninth President, who was born here. The house today is at the height of its handsomeness—wonderfully colorful within and furnished in fine style, all thanks to the present owners, who deserve even more thanks for letting it be seen.

ROLFE HOUSE (*1652*)
Off Route 31 near Surry about 3 miles from Jamestown ferry; daily, 9 to 5; 50 cents; A.P.V.A.

If not the oldest brick house in Virginia, this is one of the most engaging from its era. It was built and lived in by a son of the John Rolfe who married Pocahontas in 1614. In 1928 it was purchased by John D. Rockefeller, Jr., in the nick of time before its destruction, then beautifully restored, and presented to the Association for the Preservation of Virginia Antiquities.

Left: Carter's Grove, one of the greatest of James River mansions.

Right: The Rolfe is one of the earliest fine restorations to be seen.

SHIRLEY (c. 1769)

Just off Route 5 about 30 miles from Williamsburg toward Richmond; daily, 9 to 5; $1.00; C. Hill Carter, Jr.

A wonderfully tall brick house, with a mansard roof dramatically dormered and two-story porticoes forming both principal façades. It has a character all its own, which is fitting, for it is another of the mansions of that individualistic Carter family of Virginia fame. The interior is of the same high order as the house itself, and some of the furniture, portraits, and silver have belonged there since the beginning. Careful restoration is in progress, including its eighteenth-century dependencies.

Lovely old Shirley on the James.

¶ Norfolk

MYERS HOUSE (1792)

325 East Freemason Street; Tuesdays, Fridays, and Sundays 2 to 5, Saturdays 12 to 5; 25 cents; city of Norfolk, direction of Museum of Arts and Sciences.

A fine brick example of the Georgian town house of a wealthy merchant. The house contains much of its original furniture, chosen to complement its exquisite woodwork. There are Adam mantels and portraits by Sully and Stuart.

ADAM THOROUGHGOOD HOUSE

(between 1636 and 1640)

Norfolk on Lynnhaven River; hours not set; fee probably 50 cents; Adam Thoroughgood House Foundation, H. C. Hoffheimer II, P.O. Box 420, Norfolk (President).

This ancient house, which originally depended on water transportation, is now approached through a pecan grove. It is believed to be the oldest brick house in the country and possibly the oldest dwelling in

the state. It has many other claims to distinction: for example, its medieval aspect— one-and-a-half stories of brick laid in Flemish bond, steep gable ends laid in English bond, and T-shaped chimneys. The slate roof, pierced by three small dormers, was probably added at a later date, when the heart-pine woodwork may also have been put in. Two of the rooms are beautifully paneled; high ceilings and an unusually wide, low door opening are also part of its charm. It is a fortunate old house for having been first restored under the direction of the late Charles Over Cornelius, Associate Curator of the Metropolitan Museum in 1923. The National Trust for Historic Preservations is now supervising its further restoration and furnishing, which ensures that it is being done by the best experts in the field.

MOORE HOUSE (c. 1750)

Near the battlefield at Yorktown; daily, March to December; small fee; National Park Service.

Near the battlefield at Yorktown, the Moore house is one of the most endearing hip-on-gambrel houses in the country, as well as being the house in which the Articles of Surrender, which brought the Revolution to an end, were drawn up. A good start has been made in furnishing it properly by several patriotic women's organizations.

And while in Yorktown, you can see from the street the NELSON HOUSE (1725–1740), a brick house of great character, as you can't help noticing. Nor should you miss seeing the LIGHTFOOT HOUSE (1725) and the WEST HOUSE (1706) on Main Street.

ELSING GREEN (c. 1719)

Near Lester Manor, about an hour from Williamsburg (get directions when making appointment); Edgar R. Lafferty, Jr.

This spreading plantation in the Pamunkey River country, readily reached from either Williamsburg or Richmond, has been in continuous operation since 1690. The immense house, a Georgian Colonial brick mass with flanking dependencies, is perfectly maintained. And among the eighteenth-century furniture in the mansion is the mahogany coltsfoot table on which Lord Cornwallis signed his surrender at Yorktown.

WINDSOR SHADES (c. 1745)
Near Sweet Hall, in the general vicinity of Elsing Green (get directions when making appointment); Mr. and Mrs. Donald W. Vought.

In contrast, "Windsor Shades" is a small gambrel-roofed clapboard house in a most picturesque river setting. Its four massive outside brick chimneys are among the largest in Tidewater Virginia, and beauties to boot; it is not surprising, therefore, that the fireplace in the basement dining room is also one of the largest in Virginia. Yet the place, a "river house," is rather small in scale. It is a rare home to see, inside as well as out.

Another house in the general vicinity which can sometimes be visited during Garden Week is CHELSEA (c. 1709). See it if you can.

¶ The Eastern Shore of Virginia

Not to be confused with the Eastern Shore of Maryland, though it is the lower part of the same peninsula, this is the oldest community of the Old Dominion next to Jamestown itself. It is true tidewater country, with the Atlantic on one shore and the Chesapeake on the other, neither body of water ever very distant from the other. The houses have a quality all their own: they are mostly brick, or brick and frame, or brick with later additions in frame. The main house, its wings, and its dependencies tend to string out in a straight, descending line— a style known locally as "Big House— Little House—Colonnade 'n' Kitchen." The ocean-highway ferry route runs right down the middle of the Shore, making it a simple matter to explore the best early houses here, now that so many of the owners have been kind enough, through the *Guide,* to give permission to visit by appointment. All names appear in local telephone directory, or letters may be mailed to the addresses given here.

VAUCLUSE (pre-1700 and later)
Near Bridgetown, off Route 618; by appointment; no charge for small party; Mr. and Mrs. Verne E. Minich.

Overlooking Hungar's Creek on the Chesapeake Bay side, this is one of the finest locations on the Eastern Shore. Like practically all its neighbors here, "Vaucluse" is interesting for the various additions that have been made through the years, showing the evolution of a regional type of architecture that is livable and easy going.

CORBIN HALL (1725–1787)
By appointment; Mr. and Mrs. Raymond C. Mackay, Horntown.

This great brick mansion, overlooking a wide sweep of Chincoteague Bay, was built by George Corbin on a 3,000-acre land grant. With fine original paneling throughout, including a full-paneled drawing room, and a charming staircase, this is surely one of the finest houses on the Eastern Shore. The water table has a beveled-brick top course, and there is a three-brick belt course at the second-floor level; the bricks above the lintels are rubbed. There are ogee modillions under the cornice, and below them a row of dentils, while a Palladian window enhances the elegance. A wooden annex has been carefully added in the style of the house. Woodwork and furniture are as handsome as the exterior.

WARWICK (1670 and later)
By appointment; Mr. and Mrs. Richard Hollerith, Quinby.

This is one of the oldest, a story-and-a-half house whose original portion is of brick, and one of the best houses here of its kind.

EYRE HALL (1755, enlarged 1804)
3 miles south of Eastville, mile west off Route 13; by appointment, March through November; Mr. and Mrs. Henry DuPont Baldwin.

The long, winding entrance road does not prepare you for the cozy white picket fence. The house, with its deeply set back wing, is as engaging as the fence which surrounds it, and in the rear is one of the finest box gardens in this section. Never out of the Eyre family, the house is little changed in any way and is a rare example of colonial good taste and homeliness. A wide cross hall, library, and formal parlor are beautifully paneled, and the furnishing is exquisite. Also to be enjoyed are two Sullys, one a copy of a Heselius, also there.

ARCADIA (*eighteenth century*)
> *By appointment; Mr. and Mrs. Robert H. Stockton, Modest Town.*

Attractive proof of the fact that the restoration of a small early house can be done with great success on less-than-spectacular terms. Here it is most interesting to see what the owners have done and how they have done it.

WHARTON (*c. 1800*)
> *By appointment; Mr. and Mrs. Charles R. Busch, P.O. Box 146, Mappsville.*

This is a beautiful restoration on a larger scale—a fine foursquare, hipped-roof, two-and-a-half-story brick mansion with a Federal flavor. It is something not seen elsewhere on the Shore, leading one to believe it may have been designed by an architect brought over from Philadelphia. The small widow's walk on the roof was probably used by John Wharton to watch his ships as they slipped through the inlet to Assawamen Creek at the foot of the hill. He is said to have done his share of smuggling, like many another marine merchant of the times.

SEVEN GABLES (*1786*)
> *Accomac, one block east of Route 13; on written request; Mr. and Mrs. E. Aylmer Ames, Jr.*

This rambling frame structure has been thoughtfully restored. It is furnished with antiques and has a fine boxwood garden. Decidedly interesting.

COKESBURY (*date unknown*)
> *Near Onancock; by written appointment; Mrs. W. S. Calcott.*

Exquisitely situated on Onancock Creek, this rambling white clapboard house is completely dominated by a huge cork-oak tree, said to be the only old one in the United States. It was the home of the three famous Poulson sisters of Civil War days. It is furnished with antiques for the most part and has undergone considerable restoration, not much of the old woodwork remaining.

¶ The Valley of Virginia

You can look upon the houses in the Valley of Virginia as an interlude, if you like; if so, by all means visit them at apple-blossom time. Many of the houses here are built of stone, and many of them probably by Swedish and German artisans working their way south and west in the mid-eighteenth century and later.

During Historic Virginia Garden Week in early May you may take advantage of the one-day tour of houses in the Valley. Beside those listed below, noteworthy stone houses for which to keep your eye open are ELMINGTON, LLEWELLYN, RIVERSIDE, NORWOOD, CARTER HALL, RED GATE, SARATOGA, and SPRING HILL. To visit the Washington houses you must go to West Virginia.

ABRAM'S DELIGHT or
HOLLINGSWORTH HOUSE (*1754*)
> *Route 50 just outside Winchester; usually open; no charge until restoration is completed; city of Winchester.*

This is the only museum house here in the valley. Fortunately it is a fine early stone example, and is now being restored.

The stone houses of the Valley of Virginia are a fascinating contrast to the brick houses of the rivers and the tidewater; and Abram's Delight, as an open house, is a choice introduction to the great private homes of stone hereabouts.

The Corinthian two-story portico of Annfield is easily one of the prettiest in the Valley, set off as it is by the random ashlar limestone walls, and the histories of many distinguished occupants.

LONG BRANCH (*early 1830s*)
> *3 miles from Millwood; by appointment; Mrs. Frank H. Masi (overseer), Millwood, or Boyce 107–J (phone).*

"Long Branch" is one of the great estates of the Valley. Designed by Benjamin Latrobe, the foremost architect of the Greek Revival, it is the only one of the three existing mansion houses executed by him that is not in public hands. It was built on a colossal scale for Robert Carter Burwell, great-grandson of "King" Carter. The interior woodwork, with its exquisite baroque ornamentation, was added in 1843 from the designs of Minard Lefever, who had a genius for this kind of detail. Its next owner, Maj. Hugh Nelson, brought back the scenic wallpapers for the bedrooms from Paris. The hanging staircase was praised by Washington Irving, who admired the place in his published notes.

ANNFIELD (*1790*)
> *South of Berryville on Route 340; by appointment, October through June, 10 to 1, weekdays 2 to 6; weekends, 10 to 1; Mrs. William B. Watkins, Berryville.*

One of the most attractive stone houses in the Valley, with its two-story pedimented porch and hip roof crowned by a balustrade. These delightful appendages were probably added in the early 1800s. Matthew Page built the place just before his marriage to Ann Randolph, who is said to have freed thirty-four of her slaves and colonized them in Liberia. And it was here in 1808 that Mary Custis, who married Robert E. Lee, was born.

FAIRFIELD (*c. 1770*)
> *North of Berryville on Route 340; by appointment; Mr. and Mrs. Ralph R. Richardson, Gaylord P.O.*

This is one of the great stone mansions of the region, with many features reminiscent of "Kenmore" in Fredericksburg. Certain authorities connect the house with John Ariss, the architect of "Kenmore," who, in fact, may have lived here. Washington surveyed the land in 1748, and the house was built by his cousin Warner Washington.

CLIFTON (*1830*)
> *West from Berryville 3½ miles, then left ¾ mile; on request; Mrs. Charles Edward Stuart, Gaylord P.O.*

This is another exception in the stone region of Virginia—a handsome painted-brick two-story house with four solid-pine columns, supporting its pedimented portico and framing a capacious doorway.

The Presidents' Cottage at Greenbriar has been occupied by fourteen U.S. Presidents and has served as the summer White House for three; now appropriately furnished and preserved as a shrine. The log house opposite is a rare example from an earlier period.

WEST VIRGINIA

Y THE time West Virginia had won her independence from the Old Dominion in 1863 and had been proclaimed a state by President Lincoln, all the houses noted here below had, of course, long since been built—some for more than a century. One outstanding great house, "Claymont," had been built, burned to the ground, and built again. So, while West Virginia is comparatively new in a political sense, she yet has her inheritance of early houses. And though the houses are perhaps not so numerous and so omnipresent as to divert attention from her marvelous scenery, they are nevertheless of extraordinary interest and variety both architecturally and historically.

The three areas indicated above—the county, the city, and the famous old health and holiday resort, each some distance from the others—contain without question the choicest items in the state as far as early houses are concerned.

¶ *The Washington Houses & Others of Jefferson County*

First and foremost as a collection are the houses of Jefferson County. This is the county that appears on the map to fit into the state at its eastern tip like the last piece of a picture puzzle, in a three-way involvement with Maryland and Virginia. Architecturally speaking, the houses here are related to those previously described in the nearby Valley of Virginia. They run from Georgian to Federal to Greek Revival in appearance, and are all quite free and easy as to style; consequently, they are a pleasure to look at.

But they are a pleasure to hear about as well, in part because of the Washington story that attaches to many of them in one way or another. For it was here that young George Washington first appeared on the scene as a sixteen-year-old member of a surveying party sent out by Lord Halifax in the spring of 1748. It was a case of falling in love with the land at first sight; and shortly after, as a young officer in the frontier campaigns, he had an opportunity to become further acquainted with it and confirm his feelings. So, when Virginia was granting land to her troops, Washington was instrumental in having 200,000 acres of this region divided among his men in 1768. He himself owned 30,000 acres in Jefferson County when he died. Two of his brothers built their stately homes here with the aid of his advice, and many of his descendants have built and lived here since. But the houses themselves tell the story.

Permission has been given by their owners to visit two of the finest of the houses, but it is possible to see all of them from the grounds and gardens, and many of them are open on a two-day tour conducted by the Shenandoah-Potomac Garden Council during the last part of April, when everything here is in bloom. Charles Town is the place to start; the chamber of commerce will be most cooperative with maps and directions, and may even be able to furnish guides and make special arrangements for seeing individual houses hereabouts. Local inquiries are also handled at the Washington Drug Store in Ranson (really the northern section of the city) and at the Jefferson Hotel.

Many of the streets are named after members of the Washington family—Samuel, Charles, Lawrence, Mildred, and George. Some town houses to note are the TIFFIN (1790) on West Liberty, first lived in by the Dr. Tiffin who became the first Governor of Ohio (two other early governors of Ohio were born in the county); the old SUNRISE TAVERN and SEMINARY nearby; and the cream-colored CRANE HOUSE (late 1700s) at East Washington and Samuel Streets that belonged to Washington's business agent, Bataille Muse.

HAPPY RETREAT (*1780*)
Blakeley Place; grounds only; Robert McCabe, Charles Town.

Later called "Mordington," this fine brick house was built by brother Charles Washington, who laid out the town as well. He wisely positioned his house to take advantage of its stunning view of the Blue Ridge. Only the two wings were built during his short life, during which they were connected by a colonnade; it was the next owner, Judge Douglas, who constructed the main house from Charles's plans. The place has genuine style. There is an octagonal powder (gunpowder) house in the yard which greatly resembles the one at Mount Vernon. A carved mantel was taken from a much earlier log house that preceded this elegant one, and fitted into the

Claymont is by far the most impressive of all the Washington houses in Jefferson County; one of the great West Virginia showplaces.

Blakeley stands across from Claymont, preserving the feeling of companionship these fine old family houses had for each other.

present west wing of "Happy Retreat." This is the wing in which there is a secret closet in the paneling—a hideaway from the Indians. One of the most frequent visitors to "Happy Retreat" was, of course, brother George.

CLAYMONT COURT (*1820*)

Get directions from chamber of commerce; grounds only; Mr. and Mrs. F. Edwin Mower, Charles Town.

Now called "Poca-Dot Farm," this largest and grandest of the Washington homes here was built by Bushrod, grandson of John Augustine, Washington's third brother. Destroyed by fire in 1838, it was immediately rebuilt in its own image. There is a main three-story brick section, and two great pavilionlike wings of eight rooms each; all are connected by high-walled gardens or courts in the grand manner, creating a façade 250 feet in length. The double galleries and long windows in the rear present a charming plantation aspect.

BLAKELEY (*1820*)

Visible from "Claymont"; grounds only; Mr. and Mrs. J. Glenn Brown, Charles Town.

John Augustine II, brother of Bushrod, built this elegant country seat at the same time that Bushrod was building "Claymont." More of a companion house than a counterpart of the more lordly "Claymont," "Blakeley" is of painted brick, with wide gable-end chimneys and a two-story portico crowned with a balustraded balcony across the whole façade. Here is a veritable mansion, with wings and dependencies, yet essentially homelike in feeling.

HAREWOOD (*1700*)

Route 51, 3 miles out; 50 cents; Dr. and Mrs. John Washington (see caretaker).

The first of the Washington houses and the one with the most architectural merit, it has been called the finest example of Georgian architecture executed in native limestone to be found anywhere in what was Virginia. They say G. W. himself did it; he speaks of it in his Journal as "Bro' Sam'l's Quarters." The paneling of the drawing room was brought from England. In front of the green porphyry mantel (from Lafayette, of course) Dolly Payne Todd and James Madison were married. Other house guests beside Lafayette himself included Louis Philippe, later King of France, and his two exiled brother princes. On the grounds are the unmarked graves of Samuel and of three of his five wives. The present owners are direct lineal descendants and have been carefully restoring the fine old house with pride in its great history.

LOCUST HILL (*1840*)

Not occupied as of 1956.

Built on the original Harewood Estate by Samuel's great-granddaughter Lucy Washington Packette, this was the last of the Washington houses to go up. It is a large brick house with raised porches, simply designed and with a tradition of overflowing hospitality. During the Civil War General Sheridan occupied "Locust Hill" as his headquarters. It was the scene of a battle with General Early's troops which left the house considerably scarred.

CEDAR LAWN (*1825*)

South of "Harewood"; on request; R. J. Funkhouser, Centerville, Maryland.

The last of the Washington houses on this side of town, "Cedar Lawn" is prim, four-square, and Federal in effect, and one of the most attractive of the group. This was the home of Samuel's eldest son, John Thornton Augustine Washington.

THE OLD WHITE HOUSE TAVERN, *now* WHITE HOUSE FARM
(*prior to 1740*)

Summit Point Road; by appointment; Edward L. Blake, Charles Town.

One of the most interesting of the limestone houses here, and one of the earliest in the county (for it was along the Big Bullskin that the best land lay), it is occupied now by a learned and enthusiastic historian of the locality. With its steep roof, tall dormers, and skillful masonry, this is a perfect example of the early country architecture hereabouts. It was built by a Dr. John McCormick, a native of Ireland.

Further along the stream is ROCK HALL, a small stone house of particular interest because it is known to be on the property which George Washington chose for his own. He only abandoned the idea of making this his "seat" when he inherited Mount Vernon.

PIEDMONT (*1736–1780*)

Route 51 just out of town; grounds only; Misses Louise and Daisy Briscoe.

Behind this stylish Late Georgian brick house is the wing of log-and-stone construction which formed the original dwelling, built by Robert Worthington, a Quaker, who obtained a grant of 3,000 acres here from the Crown. It was Dr. John Briscoe of Charles Town, ancestor of the present occupants, who built the main section in such a sophisticated manner, with its brick laid in Flemish bond, its central pedimented bay, and all its delicacies of cornice and trim. The early interior woodwork and the French wall-papers are as they were, and there are interesting portraits.

¶ *In & out of Middleway*

Where Route 51 crosses 48 is the town of Middleway, notable for its wealth of unspoiled ancient charm. East of town several miles out on Route 340 is RION HALL (1836), one of the most attractive Federal houses in the county. BEALLAIR (1830), off Route 340 on the Shepherdstown road, is another Washington house, built by Col. Lewis Washington, a descendant of Augustine. It has many rambling wings, and a main section remarkable for its Regency manner, as it were; but the house awaits the restoration it deserves. North of town you will find:

Prato Rio is most original in form and structure and its legendary "open planning" strikes a truly modern note.

PRATO RIO (*1780s*)
Near Leetown.

This home was built here by Gen. Charles Lee after he had been cashiered by Washington for advancing at Monmouth. It is one of the most architecturally interesting of the early limestone houses, with its widely separated pair of front doorways beautifully balanced under its long, low eaves. It is unusual also for the fact of having been built with no interior partitions; the general was content to mark off the rooms by drawing chalk lines on the floor, describing his house as being, therefore, "the most convenient and economical establishment in the world."

TRAVELERS' REST (*1773–1806*)
Near Kearneysville.

The home of another disappointed Revolutionary general, Horatio Gates, the hero of Saratoga, whose retreat at Camden, South Carolina, cost him his command. His house, like that of his friend Lee, is of stone, but of greater elegance and size.

Mention must be made of the towns of Leetown, Kearneysville, and Shepherdstown for the unusual interest and unspoiled quality of their old streets and houses. The last town was given serious consideration by Washington as the place at which to locate the national Capital. There is still a street here of steep-roofed log houses, as well as a number of other landmarks of considerable interest.

THE BOWER (*1763*)
Outside Leetown.

Of the plantation type, with a full-length, columned veranda. Here lived still another Revolutionary general, Adam Stephen, who was dismissed by Washington after the Battle of Brandywine. It was the wry jest of the three generals that one had been sacked for advancing, one for retreating, and one for having done neither.

¶ Two Northern Panhandle mansions

Wheeling is the principal city of this wedge of West Virginia thrust up between Pennsylvania and Ohio. It is here that the old National Road and the Ohio River, two historic routes of trade and travel, intersected.

SHEPHERD HALL, *now* **MONUMENT PLACE** (*1798*)
Elm Grove on Route 40, 1 mile beyond Municipal Park, house at State marker; daily; Osiris Temple, Masonic Order.

Only two families, the Shepherds and the Lorings, have owned this magnificent stone mansion. It was built by Colonel Moses Shepherd on the site of Fort Shepherd as a plantation home, and as such it had the usual dependencies. Three stories of cut stone, with tall chimneys, it is a Georgian manor house whose exquisite entrance bespeaks its owner's taste and wealth, and prepares you for the exceptional woodwork within. No expense was spared on the second-floor ballroom, with its Adam mantels at either end; the room is girdled above by one of the loveliest of carved cornices, and the sunbursts over the arched doorways are rare. Maj. Alonzo Loring, who purchased the place in 1865, continued its tradition of lordly living. His daughter was the last private owner. Such notables as Andrew Jackson, Henry Clay, James K. Polk, and the ubiquitous Lafayette were among its more celebrated visitors.

MANSION HOUSE (*1835*)
Route 88 from Route 40 (at Oglebay Park); weekdays 10 to 12 and 2 to 5, Sundays and holidays 2 to 7; 50 cents and 30 cents; Wheeling Park Commission and Oglebay Institute.

Dr. Hanson Chapline, who built this fine Greek Revival mansion, married the daughter of one of the first settlers in these parts, Elizabeth Sprigg, who inherited this vast acreage which is now Oglebay Park. Set among old trees and gardens, the house has a two-story portico with fluted Ionic columns which is almost deep enough to have been a drive-under for a coach-and-four. The doorway, with its paired columns on either side, repeats the pediment in miniature. The house contains rooms of several periods, beginning with a pioneer kitchen. Three rooms are devoted to the eighteenth century, and there is a parlor in Victorian style. The eighteenth-century dining room, with its Zuber wallpaper, is beautifully executed in all details. In one room is a fine collection of Wheeling glass dating from 1813.

¶ Bethany (6 miles from Wheeling)

ALEXANDER CAMPBELL MANSION (*c. 1810*)

Campus of Bethany College; daily; Bethany College.

Alexander Campbell, a canny young Scotch businessman, farmer, and preacher, built this unassuming hillside house for his bride Margaret Brown, whose father gave him the land so that he would not take his family to Ohio. Although there have been additions, it still looks little like a mansion. Here Campbell settled down to raise sheep and children—fourteen of the latter. From his preaching grew the Restoration Movement, an attempt at reversion to the early New Testament Church; the movement, which Campbell personally financed, is generally believed to be the most powerful to have taken root on American soil. Later additions to the house were made for a school to train young men for the ministry, which, in turn, developed into Bethany College. The little octagonal brick building in front is where Campbell composed his sermons. Many interesting antiques are within: a huge piano, one of the

first to cross the Alleghenies; the family spinning wheel; and several other Campbell items. The Dufour wallpaper in the guest parlor depicting the adventures of Telemachus is in good condition and is said to be the oldest wallpaper in West Virginia. Campbell was buried on the hillside overlooking his house in 1866, having had a fuller life than most men.

¶ White Sulphur Springs

This is one of the oldest spas in the country, the first water cure at the Springs having been made in 1778. By 1800 tidy cottages were superseding the log cabins that had sprung up around the miracle springs, and by 1830 the place was the favorite resort for the wealthiest families of the South and a rendezvous for statesmen and politicians. During its long history the Springs have played host to fourteen Presidents of the United States, and the President's Cottage, a summer White House for at least three Presidents, is now preserved as a kind of museum which can be visited at any time. It is a spacious white cottage with

Dr. Chapline's Mansion House in Wheeling's Oglebay Park is one of the outstanding Greek Revival houses in the state; delightful inside and out.

The fine old cottage rows at Greenbriar are among the most charming features of the famous resort.

a double tier of railed porches, sitting a half story off the sloping ground, and so inviting that it is easy to understand why President Tyler brought his Virginia bride here for their honeymoon. Inside there are interesting memorabilia of the various illustrious tenants of the house, and some of the bedrooms are furnished as they were.

This is by no means the only surviving reminder of the days when Lee arrived on horseback and when stagecoaches overflowing with crinolines, whose wearers might have spent several days on the road from New York, clattered dustily up to the main entrance. Although the grand old hotel has given place to a vast modern hostelry, many of the old cottages have been spared. It was the fashion to build them in rows, each cottage alike.

In Baltimore Row the first delightful cottage, done in the classical manner, is surrounded by a colonnade; it was designed by Benjamin Latrobe's son for his own use. Then a row of identical cottages sprang up next to it, one of which belonged to General Lee, who spent three postwar summers here pursuing his work of reconciliation even while he was being lionized socially—for Lee was the great hero of the spa, and endless were the balls in his honor. Built in the 1830s, these cottages still stand, outwardly much as they were. The Lee cottage may be visited.

Another charming and much earlier row, following the steep slope of the hillside, was known as "Paradise Row"; it was built about 1800 and set aside for honeymooners. The Georgia Row is even now undergoing restoration. The Alabama and Louisiana Rows are, like the others, attractively in use.

The Eastern Shore and southern Maryland are laced and lined with estuaries leading off the Chesapeake. In these tidewater regions the state stores its wealth of fine early houses; witness West St. Mary's Manor here and the Anchorage across the page.

MARYLAND

*W*HEN IT comes to eighteenth-century houses, Maryland, a relatively small state, is one of the richest in the country. No one can know how many there were to begin with, but we do have the word of an authority, Henry C. Forman, that, when he wrote his book in 1934, there still existed about five thousand of them. No one will ever see them all, but there is an opportunity to see quite a few of the finest every year during the Maryland house and garden tour, with all arrangements being made expertly for you; or, through this book, you are enabled to see a goodly number of them on your own. For many of them you will need to follow directions with care, for the dreamlike tidewater country in which most of them are located is a maze of bays and estuaries flatly fingering their way inland from the Chesapeake. These rivers and creeks were once the only travel arteries of the inhabitants, and, accordingly, they built their houses near the water, thus creating for themselves some of the loveliest settings in the world. If you were to visit them by boat, you would naturally see them from their handsomest angles. In this book, however, we will be content if we can get you there by road.

The fullest flavor of colonial days anywhere in this country is generally furnished to us now by the houses themselves. But occasionally from a contemporary writer of the time you can fill in the scene in a most colorful fashion. For instance, in the mid-1600s, when Maryland was being settled, John Aubrey, an extraordinary chronicler, was setting down in England hundreds of short biographical sketches of celebrated Britons, now collected as *Aubrey's Brief Lives*. Aubrey devotes a few lines to Cecil Calvert, Lord Baltimore, as "absolute lord and proprietary of Maryland and Avalon in America," then goes on to expatiate as follows: "Now if I would be rich, I could be a prince. I could goe into Maryland, which is one of the finest countries of the world; same climate with France; between Virginia and New England. I can have all the favour of my lord Baltemore I could wish. His brother is his lieutenant there; and a very good natured gentleman. Plenty of all things: ground there is 2000 miles westwards. I could be able I believe to carry a colony of rogues; another, of ingeniose artificers; and I doubt not one might make a shift to have five or six ingeniose companions, which is enough."

It was up the Great Bay of the Chesapeake that two boats, the *Ark* and the *Dove,* brought the first two hundred settlers to these shores in 1634. Wrote Father White of the landing, "The soil appears particularly fertile and strawberries, vines, sassafras, hickory nuts and walnuts we tread upon everywhere . . ." It was a bountiful country. Lord Baltimore, its proprietor, offered those settlers who paid their own way one hundred acres of ground apiece; but if they brought over five more adults, they were to receive 2,000 acres each. Thus, if the settler doubled or tripled his "catch," he became the owner of a vast tract. Later, the "lords" of these great "manors," as they were called, held an almost absolute authority over their domains. The riches, it soon became evident, were to be made in the growing of tobacco, and it is said that by 1667 it had virtually supplanted money as a means of barter.

The political and social unit throughout Maryland's development has been the county. Counties have conspicuously retained individuality and importance, accounting for a wide variety of building modes and a readily identified county character. This marked regional feeling may also explain the unique names given to many of them, for example, "Clean Drinking Manor," "His Lordship's Kindness," "Crooked Intention," and "Hockley in the Hole."

As wealth and families increased, Marylanders added on to their houses in a special way. Instead of the usual stepped-down wing addition, it became the fashion to step *up* the wing, so that you will find many houses today with two or three additions, each broader and higher than the one before. Another feature of the pre-Revolutionary period is the fact that many houses, even very grand ones like "Whitehall," are only one room deep, though, as "Whitehall," very long.

As the Georgian influence grew throughout the Eastern seaboard, the homes became more elegant and sophisticated, and by that same token, more like the mansions in the neighboring state of Virginia. Some of the outstanding examples of Georgian architecture in the American style are right here in Maryland, many of them in Anne Arundel County, where, at the time, Annapolis was fast becoming a city of rare beauty and importance. The later and lighter Federal had its day in Maryland too, of course, and there are some perfect examples of it; but, lovely as they are, it is the pre-Georgian buildings that re-create the distinctive flavor of the state.

¶ Maryland House & Garden Tour

The Maryland House and Garden Pilgrimage stands with the Virginia Historic Garden Week and the Natchez tours as the most extensive and the finest in the country. It is well established, having taken place seventeen times so far, and it is beautifully organized. The Pilgrimage takes ten days, usually the first part of May. During each day you may see different houses in different counties, all of them interesting and many of them surpassingly fine examples of our early architecture. The Federated Garden Clubs of Maryland and the Society for the Preservation of Maryland Antiquities run the Pilgrimage jointly; their headquarters are at the Sheraton-Belvedere in Baltimore. In 1954 over two hundred houses were included in the tour. Each house and garden is open one day only; in other words, there is an itinerary, allowing a day only to each county. The cost without transportation is three dollars and fifty cents a day, or, for single houses, one dollar. Upon application you will receive an official tour book which gives full information about all necessary arrangements and also lists each house with a brief description. If you want to see the interiors of some of the finest houses in America, in many of which gracious living has gone on continuously through the centuries, this is your chance. In 1953 there were eight thousand people from all over the United States who availed themselves of it. Many of the gardens are as notable as the houses; this is a wonderful way to spend a holiday, when the gardens are at their loveliest.

ANNAPOLIS & ANNE ARUNDEL COUNTY

Many of the mellow, meandering streets in early Annapolis are lined with pink-and-white colonial houses and superbly ornamented here and there with Georgian mansions of such masterpiece quality as to put the town in a class apart. In fact, there is so much here that is fine that, if by some miracle (in the form of one or two million dollars), Annapolis could run her wires underground, pull down her poles, and clear away some of the more expendable clutter, the town would emerge as something to view with unadulterated wonder and delight. Considered along with the county of Anne Arundel, the colonial houses of town and country hereabouts can well be said to have, as a collection, no equal in America.

The seven top houses in the town itself are the "Hammond-Harwood," the "Chase-Lloyd," the "Brice," the "John Ridout," the "Paca" (now part of Carvel Hall), the "Upton Scott," and the "Acton." Of these, the only one that is completely on view is the "Hammond-Harwood," and it happens to be, by a stroke of luck for all concerned, the best. Of the lovely and lofty "Chase-Lloyd," across the street, only a part of its main floor may be examined—but enough to appreciate its Palladian splendor. The "Brice," a famous brick beauty and a favorite of many, is private, and may be viewed only on special occasions, which will be noted; the same is true of the "Ridout." The Prince George Street façade is practically all that is left of the "Paca" (Carvel Hall), though there are a few interior features remaining which anyone may see. The "Upton Scott" is church property, and "Acton" is private. All can be clearly seen from the street.

Of the no-less charming minor houses of Annapolis there are many. Anyone who would like to see large and small to the best advantage will do well to get in touch, in advance if possible, with Historic Annapolis, Inc., at 64 State Circle. Through this organization it is possible once or twice a year to visit some of the fine private houses. The semiofficial society has both "directed" and "guided" tours of the town (the latter for groups). In summer it conducts a waterfront tour of the town by boat which makes the former appearance of the old colonial capital come to life. The tour takes you across the Severn to "Whitehall," the first great colonial country house in the classic style. The boat view of the shore simplifies for you the locating of the Anne Arundel county houses listed below; for in the county, as in the town, it is deceptively difficult to find your way about. Naturally the tour takes into consideration that one of the great sights of Annapolis is the Naval Academy. The society can furnish you with excellent maps and descriptive material, and the fees for its services are very moderate.

During the spring and fall tours some of the historic homes will take overnight guests, arrangements to be made only through Historic Annapolis, Inc.

HAMMOND-HARWOOD HOUSE
(*1770–1774*)

Maryland Avenue and King George Street; daily 10 to 5, Sundays 2 to 5, closed at 4 in winter; 50 cents; Hammond-Harwood House Association.

One of the great Georgian houses of America, this magnificent mansion was undoubtedly designed and built by William Buckland; certainly its brilliant woodcarving is by the celebrated craftsman who did Gunston Hall down below Alexandria. The woodwork of the doorway here makes it one of the most beautiful in the country, and Buckland's medallionlike decorations carved on the inside reveals of the dining rooms are high spots in the stunning interior of this admirable house. It has been wonderfully restored and furnished to perfection. It is said that Matthias Hammond agreed to make his house two stories high instead of three on the plea of Samuel Chase, his neighbor across the street, who didn't want to lose his view of the bay—but only on the condition that Chase pay for the two wings which Hammond would have to put on instead. The five-foot-thick foundations of the Hammond-Harwood House's central portion would seem to give at least a little substance to the story. Elise Lathrop, in her *Historic Houses of America,* for which she has gathered a fund of often fascinating gossip, tells us that Hammond intended this to be his honeymoon house, but that, while Buckland was still putting the finishing touches to it, Hammond's fiancée broke the engagement, declaring that Hammond cared more for his house than he did for her. As for the Harwood part of the name, Miss Lathrop has this to say of Judge William Harwood, who lived in the house at the time of the Civil War: Because he refused to take the oath of allegiance to the Federal government after the war, he was not permitted to ride on the trains, and thus would walk every week to and from his new office thirty miles away in Baltimore.

The Hammond-Harwood dining room: another Buckland masterpiece.

CHASE-LLOYD HOUSE

(*1769–1771*)

Opposite Hammond-Harwood house; daily (first floor only); voluntary contribution.

This tall, stately house rises a full story or more above the Hammond-Harwood House across the street. Probably one of the largest of early American mansions, it is comparable in size to the later Brown and Nightingale "great houses" in Providence. It was begun by the outspoken patriot Samuel Chase, long before he became a signer of the Declaration of Independence; and long before the house was finished he sold it, perhaps wisely, to one of the wealthiest landowners on the eastern shore—Edward Lloyd IV, whose account books mention William Buckland as one of the principals employed in its construction. An impressive staircase divides at the second-floor landing, which is brightened by a large Palladian window. A fine coffered Adam ceiling in the left parlor and unusually elaborate trim in the dining room are other notable features. The doors are embellished with silver hardware, and the paneled interior shutters decorated with carved medallions and rosettes much like those in the Hammond-Harwood House and the front parlor of the Paca House. All these details are certainly the work of Buckland. In 1802 the house was the scene of the wedding of Mary Taylor Lloyd and Francis Scott Key. The upper floors are now occupied in accord with the last owner's wish, by "destitute, aged and infirm ladies" —a noble endowment for a noble house.

CARROLL-DAVIS HOUSE (*1722*)

Campus of St. John's College, facing King George Street; to be open regularly; Historic Annapolis, Inc.

One of the oldest houses in the state, this venerable beauty has the typical heavy brick end walls and clapboard front and back The wide-paneled living room, corner cupboards, and graceful staircase are in excellent condition, as are the other early features. It was the birthplace of Charles Carroll, of Mt. Clare in Baltimore, one of Maryland's most famous sons. Moved here recently and now in process of restoration, it will soon be furnished in such a manner as to be able to take its place among the best houses in Annapolis.

CARVEL HALL (*1765*)

Prince George Street.

This was the home of William Paca, a signer of the Declaration and Governor of Maryland (1782–1785). It has been a hotel since 1899 and vastly built onto.

THE MARYLAND INN

(*between 1772 and 1780*)

Church Circle.

Recently restored and now operated as a hotel, this was originally the Hyde House, already a hostelry in 1795. A very fine job of adapting it to modern needs has been done, leaving the exterior and colonial lobby almost as they were.

Across from the Hammond-Harwood stands the stately Chase house.

One of the choice old Maryland mansions, Whitehall is famous for the earliness of its classical portico; first in the colonies.

¶ The houses in Anne Arundel County

(Request travel directions when making appointment.)

WHITEHALL (*1764–1765*)

Outskirts of Annapolis; on written or phoned request at owners' convenience; Mr. and Mrs. Charles Scarlett, Jr.

This is one of the great houses not merely of Maryland but of America. Its beautiful classic portico was the first of its kind ever to be placed on a Georgian country mansion in colonial times. The setting is magnificent, with the gardens leading in a long vista down to the shores of the Chesapeake. The famous portico has been attributed to William Buckland, and the superb interior carving was undoubtedly executed by the master, but there is nothing to prove that he was actually the architect. The story attached to the place is that Governor Sharp built it in the expectation of making Mary Ogle his bride, but that she married his secretary John Ridout instead. Much later Sharp sold the house to Mary's father, and so, when the governor went back to his native England, it became Mary's home anyway. George Washington is said to have "trod a measure" here to the accompaniment of Benjamin Franklin's musical glasses. Extensive restoration is going on as this is written, but it is expected that the house will be ready to see by the time the *Guide* is published.

IGLEHART (*prior to 1809*)

Outskirts of Annapolis; on written request; Mr. and Mrs. Howard Keith.

A double-galleried frame dwelling of interesting plan and appearance, with an unusual offset pent chimney at one end, it is now handsomely restored, and furnished in Empire. Juliana and Leonard Iglehart, who built the house at the time of their marriage, are buried nearby.

BELVOIR MANOR (*oldest part 1690*)

Crownsville; on written or phone request (South Shore 5012); Mrs. W. C. Rogers.

This fine old hilltop house is one of the ancients of the county. It has a seventeenth-century wing, a gambrel roof, beautiful brickwork, a cantilevered staircase, and a history of occupancy by a long line of old Maryland families.

PART OF PROVIDENCE (*1800*)

Crownsville; on written request at owners' convenience; Mr. and Mrs. Robert C. Adams.

An enchantingly simple farmhouse, rescued from decay by its devoted and skillful owners. The restoration has taken twenty years of patient work without aid—an inspiring and fascinating project.

RISING SUN TAVERN (*1658*)

Route 178 below crossroads near Gambrills; Thursday afternoons July through September; Anne Arundel Chapter of D.A.R.

Washington paused here many a time on his way to Annapolis, giving the road that runs by the door its name—the "General's Highway." A charming little clapboard affair, with two rooms now on view, this venerable inn was built by the Puritans, who were early but not too popular settlers here. The original heaven-and-hell hinges are still in the kitchen.

WHITEHALL FARMS (*c. 1760*)

Gambrills, 7 or 8 miles from Annapolis; after restoration by appointment only, exterior and gardens only at present; Mr. and Mrs. Stephen Duckett.

Not to be confused with "Whitehall" on the bay, this fine old white-painted brick house is famous for being the birthplace in 1795 of Johns Hopkins. The farm has been in continuous operation for two centuries or more.

BRIGHT SEAT (*1690 and 1790*)

Conways, near "Whitehall Farms"; on request; Mr. and Mrs. Benjamin King.

A very simply restored farmhouse which the owners fondly named "Promised Land" until they discovered that it already had a pretty fine name of its own. The living room was once the Old Bright Seat Tavern, reputed to be still another place where Washington was accustomed to stop for a thirst quencher on his way through the neighborhood. The rest was built one hundred years later, still before the 1800s.

TULIP HILL (*1776*)

Cumberstone, 15 miles south of Annapolis; on written or phone request allowing 1 week after confirmation (West River 4211); Mr. and Mrs. Lewis R. Andrews.

One of the most endearing of the great Georgian mansions in Maryland, "Tulip Hill" is set in a park of copper beeches, larches, and tulip poplars. Its proportions, color, and ornament approach perfection.

In back is a sweep of terraces, or "falls," as they are still called in Maryland, dropping down to the wide West River in the distance. The hallway with its double arch and the exquisite shell cupboard at the foot of the stairs filled with pieces of *blanc de chine* are breathtaking. The owners' distinguished Chinese collections complement the American and English antiques beautifully. Many were the celebrities who visited here. The house itself was built by Samuel Galloway, ship owner, race-horse owner, and often host here to George Washington.

LARKINS HUNDRED (*1704*)

Birdsville, Edgewater; by written or phone appointment; Mr. and Mrs. John C. Plews.

Once called "O'Hara's Castle," this place is only a short distance from "Tulip Hill," and is by contrast a modest early brick house, though nevertheless remarkably fine

Many is the time that Washington rode up to Tulip Hill to dine and dance in this delightful house.

on a smaller scale because of the excellence of its paneling and woodwork. Its "good-morning" stairway is beautifully executed, and its built-in cupboard a rare one.

ROEDOWN (*1669–1742*)
Davidsonville, near Annapolis; on written request; Mr. and Mrs. John Murray Begg.

The home of the Brogden family for generations, this lovely Georgian brick house on a hilltop is a typical country "town house" of its stately time. It has beautiful Dutch antiques and rare old paintings. Be prepared for great charm here.

HOLLY HILL (*1667–1720*)
Friendship; by appointment only; April through June and September through November; nominal fee for benefit of St. James Church.

Certainly one of the great treasures in a state of treasures! It is difficult to convey the charm of this early red-brick house whose most recent wing was added in 1720. It is a place that must be seen to be believed. Legend has it that pirates of the Chesapeake brought their loot here from the bay through an underground passage. One of the many fascinating features of this house are the original mural paintings on wood over the mantel, and one small, almost hidden painted panel high over the dining-room door. The furnishings combine in a pleasant fashion many American and French antiques of the early eighteenth century.

¶ Calvert County

Route 2, which runs down the middle of Anne Arundel, continues down the middle of Calvert County to Solomon's Island off the tip end of this long, narrow peninsula between the Chesapeake and the Patuxent.

The five houses listed here are private homes, to be seen by appointment, and directions to reach them should be obtained when the appointments are made. In addition to these, about five more may be seen on the Calvert County day of the Maryland Pilgrimage.

CEDAR HILL (*between 1660 and 1700*)
Barstow; by written appointment, April 15 to November 1; Col. and Mrs. Charles S. Hamilton.

This is a most unusual house. It is cruciform in plan like Bond Castle, most famous of Calvert County houses and long since destroyed. Its twelve fourteen-inch-thick walls are laid up in Flemish bond. This tall-chimneyed manor house was once the

seat of over a thousand acres. The estate was sold to Thomas Gantt in 1745, and continued in his family until 1780. Floors, woodwork, and windowpanes are all original. The vestibule has built-in seats with scroll supports. The house is furnished in eighteenth-century pieces, with a few even earlier.

THE CAGE (*part prior to 1700*)
St. Leonard, Preston-on-Patuxent; by written or phone appointment (Prince Frederick 261J), May to October; Mr. and Mrs. Benjamin Parran.

Built by William Parrot on the land granted him in 1649, this house, a story and a half, with two rooms to a floor, is one of the earliest types in Maryland. The brick is laid in Flemish bond, the glazed headers showing only on the river side. Many rooms have been added by the present owners in keeping with the early style. The new living room is paneled by hand in wild cherry, a native wood. The dining room in the old part is paneled in walnut from the premises, and is said to have taken two years to complete. The house is lived in all year by the owners, descendants of the builder, who frankly state that they do not try to keep it in museum condition.

HILL FARM (*c. 1670*)
By appointment only; Mr. and Mrs. Christian Wohlgemuth.

Here is perhaps as good an example as you will find anywhere in the state of a typical early farm, well but unpretentiously built, as you might expect it to have been by settlers in the middle of the seventeenth century. The post-and-beam frame, braced against wind pressure, is covered with random-width beaded white-pine siding, and has served sturdily for almost three hundred years. For durability this type of framing has never been improved upon. The steep roof, pierced by three small dormers, and the two brick end chimneys are all exactly right, and the almost medieval charm is enhanced by the low wing, a log cabin which was moved in and joined

Left: Holly Hill has to be seen face to face; pictures somehow fail to express the full charm, style, and distinction of this rare old home, beautifully lived in.

to the house later. It commands a view of the whole area, and the unearthing of an old telegraph instrument of the Civil War period indicates that it was a lookout or signal station at that time. A tiny post office, or store, built of ship's timbers has been moved from its former salient location and is now used as a guest house.

SPOUT FARM (*1700 and 1730*)
On written request at owners' convenience; Gen. and Mrs. H. Fuller.

The date of the original one-room log house built on land granted to Thomas Hatton here in 1636 has been lost in the mists of history, but the white clapboard section of the house, with its mammoth pair of chimneys connected by a two-story pent, was built in 1700, making this rambling and remarkable old place one of the most ancient dwellings in the countryside. The gardens are beautiful here, but no more so than the view from the high bluff which overlooks the wide waters where St. Leonard's Creek flows into the Patuxent. The "spout" for which the place was named, a gusher of crystal water, supplied sailors for the long voyages of another era when there was a landing place here for big vessels.

CHARLES GIFT (*1650*)
Lusby; by appointment, between April 1 and November 1; Capt. and Mrs. Don Smith.

Built by Richard Preston, this is said to have been the seat of the Puritan government of Maryland from 1653 to 1657. The Great Seal of Maryland was lost here and never again found. The house has the long, steep rooflines of the medieval manor, and its fine paneled living room, with a huge fireplace at either end, is beautifully proportioned. It is furnished in an informal, livable manner.

¶ St. Marys County

St. Marys is the southernmost county of southern Maryland and is penetrated by Routes 5 and 235, the former leading off 301 at Waldorf, 25 miles south of Washington. It was here, at St. Marys City, that the first capitol of the colony was erected, of which no trace remains.

❡ *Drayden*

WEST ST. MARY'S MANOR
(late seventeenth century)
On written request at owners' convenience; Col. and Mrs. Miodrag Blagojevich.

Sitting slightly above the confluence of the Potomac and St. Marys Rivers, this rare old home enjoys one of the choicest locations in Maryland. Seeing the small, medieval brick house set in an enchantment of land and water is an unforgettable experience. It was built on the first land grant in the Colony of Maryland, in 1634—an area of 4,000 acres. There are four sturdy chimneys with pents between and a very steep roof with brick gabled ends and tiny dormers. The restoration of the small rooms—two in American William and Mary and one in New England—is the work of perfectionists. Everything in the house is a collector's item.

❡ *California*

ST. RICHARD'S MANOR
(late seventeenth century)
On written or phone request; Mrs. Maynard Barnes, 1061 31st Street, Washington 7, D.C.

One of few remaining manor houses still standing with *no* structural changes, it was built on the earliest manorial grant of land on the Patuxent River (1640). It has fine patterned brickwork and a large corner fireplace, and has been perfectly restored.

❡ *Beachville (or St. Inigoes)*

CROSS MANOR (*1642*)
Route 5, 1 mile below town; May to September; $1.00; Mrs. Clyde Cruitt and Miss Dorothy Grayson.

This may easily be the oldest house in Maryland. It was built of brick by Thomas Cornwaleys on a land grant of 2,000 acres, and is noted for its box garden, some of the plants being thirty-five feet in circumference.

❡ *Hollywood*

SOTTERLEY (*1730*)
Mid-June to mid-September, daily 11 to 6, other times phone Mr. Charles Knott (Greenwood 5–6782); Mrs. M. S. Ingalls.

Built by James Bowles, whose widow married Governor Plater, this house was named after his ancestral English home. The front, which faces the Patuxent River, has a covered colonnade nearly one hundred feet long. The house follows no formal scheme, having been augmented gradually through the years. However, the interior contains some of the finest woodwork in Maryland—a Chinese Chippendale staircase, the rail carving similar to that of "Bohemia." The drawing room walls are paneled in pine, the window frames are of walnut, and the doors of solid mahogany. The carved recesses on either side of the drawing-room fireplace are perhaps the best examples of the shell pattern in the state, or anywhere else, for that matter.

West St. Mary's Manor is a museum piece of a very early small-scale house; one of the best-preserved private homes in Maryland.

¶ *Charlotte Hall*

OLD WHITE HOUSE (*1803*)

On grounds of Charlotte Hall School;
M. D. Burgee (principal).

TUDOR HALL (*1750*)

Beautifully restored, this building was once part of an old military school founded in 1774, and has been the continuous meeting place of one of the oldest literary societies in the country, The Washington-Stonewall Society. It is now used as a public library, the first floor of which can be seen any time.

¶ *Charles County*

¶ *Mt. Victoria*

WEST HATTON FARM (*c. 1790*)

By appointment; Mr. and Mrs. Foster M.
Reeder.

This most enchanting and unusual place was once called "Wicomico" because it is located on a point of land almost surrounded by that river. The Georgian house built by Maj. William Truman Stoddert has remained in his family to the present day. The current owner, his great-great-granddaughter, finding it in need of attention, restored and furnished it with taste and understanding. She has brought some of the original pieces back to it. A feature of the interior is an arched double door with an elaborate fanlight between the drawing and dining rooms.

¶ *Newburg*

MT. REPUBLIC (*1792*)

On written request; Mr. and Mrs. Robert
Kennedy Hanson.

This manorial house on the Potomac was built for the ages: the thirty-inch-thick brick walls, the massive stairway of walnut and pine, and the great, square rooms all attest an early owner of considerable substance. It is said that the gentleman kept a poker game going here for forty years; perhaps only a little less apocryphal is the story that he kept fifty *pairs* of foxhounds. There is an outstanding garden and naturalized hillside, and the interior contains many interesting features.

¶ *Port Tobacco*

HABRE DE VENTURE (*1742*)

On written or phoned request; Mr. and
Mrs. Peter Vischer.

This was the home of Thomas Stone, a signer of the Declaration. Three types of early construction are shown here: the all-brick, the all-frame, and the frame-with-brick-gable-ends. The house was built on the arc of a circle, in three connected but unbalanced parts. The drawing-room paneling is so fine that the Baltimore Museum has it, but it has been replaced by a replica. An unusual feature in this unusual house is the fireplace in the dining room, which tapers upward as it slopes back to the wall.

ROSE HILL (*c. 1734*)

2 miles from La Plata, adjoining "Habre de
Venture"; by appointment; Mr. and Mrs.
Herbert E. Ryerson.

This "great house" across the Potomac from Mount Vernon often welcomed President Washington, for it was the residence of his personal physician, Dr. Gustavus Richard Brown, Jr., the son of the builder. Incidentally, Dr. Brown, summoned from here, attended the great man on his deathbed and disapproved of the excessive bleeding to which he had already been subjected.

Of impressive proportions, "Rose Hill," with its stately entrance, its exterior chimneys, and brick end walls so typical of this part of Maryland, is one of the showplaces of the county. The balancing one-story brick wings with their low connecting aprons are harmoniously related to the main houses; one was the doctor's office and the other the kitchen. The "Greate" room with its paneled-pine dado is thirty feet square. The fireplace with its carved mantel is one before which Washington toasted his long-stockinged shanks on many a frigid day. The box garden is notable.

MT. EAGLE (*1796*)

Near Bryantown; on request; Mr. and Mrs.
Herbert E. Ryerson, "Rose Hill."

An excellent example of an early Maryland brick farmhouse in the Piedmont style. The thousand-acre tract on which it was built was a Lord Baltimore grant of 1640. The Ryersons planned its restoration so that the original woodwork, mantels, and

corner cupboards are all beautifully preserved, as are its many other interesting
features.

DENT'S PALACE (*1720–1775*)
Charlotte Hall; on written request;
Mr. and Mrs. Moultrie Hitt, R.F.D. 1,
Oliver's Shop Corner.

This is the traditional seat of the Dent
family. Once the proprietary manor of
Calverton, it is a twelve-room house architecturally typical of the section, the descending wings possibly built earlier than
the main portion. The wide center hall,
double drawing rooms, oriel windows, holy-
cross doors, and wide pine floors are intact, though some of the woodwork appears to be of later vintage. It is furnished
mostly with eighteenth-century pieces.

¶ Prince Georges County

¶ *Clinton*

HIS LORDSHIP'S KINDNESS
(*1735*)
Route 2, Clinton, 15 miles from
Washington; on written request; voluntary
contribution to Ursuline Academy;
Mr. and Mrs. John M. Walton,
P.O. Box 455.

Of red brick, with dark green shutters and
white trim, this dignified house is one of
the most stylish Georgian mansions in
Maryland, and that is saying a lot. Its
double hip roof, ample windows in triplicate over the entrance door, and low,
matching wings, the whole surrounded by
immense trees and with a proximate box
garden in the rear, are the last word in

good scale. This quiet dignity and balance
is evident within as well. The "His Lordship" in the name is none other than Lord
Baltimore. who fostered a romance by be-
stowing 27,000 acres on Henry Darnell.
This young man, while a student at Oxford,
fell in love with Ann Talbot, niece of the
Earl of Shrewsbury, who frowned on the
penniless young man's suit. After young
Darnell became land-rich, however, the
great lord relented even to the extent of
building this house for the young couple.
Much of the original woodwork is intact, as
are the floors and much of the handmade
hardware.

¶ *Mason Springs*

SMALLWOOD'S RETREAT
(*prior to 1775*)
Under reconstruction; Smallwood
Foundation, Mrs. F. J. Fletcher
(Secretary), La Plata.

This home of the famous revolutionary
hero, General Smallwood, was almost in
ruins. It is being reconstructed and will be
furnished in late 1955, after which the
house will be open to the public.

ARABY (*between 1685 and 1715*)
By appointment at owners' convenience;
Adm. and Mrs. Frank Jack Fletcher.

Once the home of Ann Eilbeck, wife of
George Mason, the builder of Gunston
Hall and author of the Virginia Bill of
Rights, this handsome early brick mansion,
with molded water table, was built with
skill and restored with taste. The woodwork is truly notable, and the sitting room
perhaps unique. There are fine open cupboards and original floors and hardware.

B A L T I M O R E   &   W E S T E R N   M A R Y L A N D

¶ *In & out of Baltimore*   ¶ *Carroll County*   ¶ *Frederick*
County   ¶ *Harford County*   ¶ *Washington County*

¶ *In & out of Baltimore*

The three great houses here are "Mount
Clare," in Carroll Park; "Homewood,"
on the Johns Hopkins campus on

Charles Street; and "Hampton," nine
miles north of the city near Towson.
Both "Mount Clare" and "Hampton,"
are on view and are described below. It
is some consolation that "Homewood"

may at least be enjoyed from the saucer-like entrance to the University grounds, and that it is sometimes opened for the Maryland Pilgrimage; for this early classical mansion, built in 1801 by Charles Carroll, a signer of the Declaration, for his son, is one of the most engaging old "great houses" in the country, with not a little nobility. The raised central section of pink brick, with its delicately scaled white-columned portico, is flanked by lower symmetrical brick wings. "Homewood" has inspired the styling of the Johns Hopkins University buildings that have been grouped about and beyond it, and for which it serves as administration offices.

BALTIMORE MUSEUM OF ART
Wyman Park, Charles and 31st Streets; Tuesdays, Wednesdays, and Saturdays, 11 to 6, Fridays and Sundays 2 to 6; city of Baltimore.

There are period rooms at the nearby Baltimore Museum of Art in Wyman Park, two of them from houses on the Eastern Shore and in southern Maryland both of which may be visited through the *Guide*—the Ringgold House in Chestertown, and "Habre de Venture" at Port Tobacco.

MARYLAND HISTORICAL SOCIETY
Monument Street and Park Avenue; daily.

There are more rooms at the Maryland Historical Society, as well as many priceless documents, manuscripts (including that of "The Star Spangled Banner"), portraits, and unique collections.

PEALE MUSEUM (*1814*)
225 North Holliday Street; Decoration Day to Labor Day daily 10 to 4:30 except Sundays, rest of year daily 11 to 5 except Mondays, Sundays 1:30 to 5:30.

While in the mood, you might visit the Peale Museum, erected in 1814 by Rembrandt Peale, son of Charles Willson Peale, and used as a repository for the paintings of this famous and fascinating family. Now devoted more to the Baltimore historical scene, it does contain one period Peale room of 1814.

MOUNT CLARE (*1754–1760*)
Carroll Park, Monroe Street and Washington Boulevard; daily 11 to 5, Sundays and Mondays 2 to 5; 25 cents all days but Mondays, Tuesdays, and Fridays; city of Baltimore.

This distinguished Georgian mansion is the oldest manor house within the city limits, a reminder of the days when many of them looked down across the Patapsco River. "Mount Clare," the home of Charles Carroll, was one of the finest, remaining in the family up to a late date. The manorial

Mount Clare has the double éclat of being a Carroll mansion restored and maintained by the Colonial Dames.

One of the most elegant of the Georgian mansions of Maryland, Hampton has the further personal interest of its fine old family furnishings.

paneling, the delicately carved mantels, and the arched cupboards, serve as a background for choice furniture, portraits, rugs, and drapes. As usual, the Colonial Dames, its custodians, have done themselves proud in its appointments.

FLAG HOUSE (*prior to 1814*)
844 East Pratt Street; daily, 10 to 5, except Sundays; city of Baltimore.

EDGAR ALLAN POE HOUSE
(*prior to 1830*)
203 North Amity Street; 30 cents; Edgar Allan Poe Society.

These two little, unpretentious, early nineteenth-century town houses are principally of historic interest. In the former Mary Pickersgill made the flag which flew over Fort McHenry and inspired Francis Scott Key to write "The Star Spangled Banner" on September 14, 1814. The latter was occupied by Poe in the 1830s during the period of his first literary success; it is furnished as of that era.

HAMPTON (*1783–1790*)
Dulany Valley Road 2 miles north of Towson; Tuesday through Saturday 11 to 5:30, Sundays 1 to 5:30; 50 cents and 25 cents; National Park Service and Society for Preservation of Maryland Antiquities.

This belongs among the ten houses of top importance in Maryland. Hardly any other has so strong an architectural personality as this vast country residence of stuccoed stone, with its two-story portico containing a Chinese Chippendale gallery. Its basic and rather academic Georgian design is embellished with roof urns and fanciful dormers, and crowned with a domed octagonal cupola. Built by Capt. Charles Ridgely, it remained for a hundred and fifty years in the Ridgely family until it was turned over in trust to the Federal government, with its family furnishings intact. The old terraced gardens are a famous feature. But it is a sight to see in its entirety, so spare it plenty of time.

¶ Carroll County

Westminster

SHRIVER HOMESTEAD (1797)

On written request June 1 to September 1, other times Saturdays and Sundays only; Mr. Frederick Shriver Klein and brothers.

At Union Mills on Pipe Creek, where Meade had planned to stop Lee's army in 1863, is one of the oldest homes still occupied by the original family in this section. It is a great, rambling farmstead of twenty-four rooms, which grew out of the original four. Intimately involved in the history of the neighborhood, it has been an inn, a general store, a post office, and always a home. It was visited by Roger Taney, Audubon, Washington Irving, and other notables who passed this way. The family furniture of the nineteenth century is still intact, and the house is being occupied as it was then.

OLD SHERMAN HOUSE, or HISTORICAL HOUSE (1807)

206 East Main Street; daily, 2 to 5; voluntary fee; Historical Society of Carroll County.

Built by Jacob Sherman, a retired tavern keeper, this is a pleasant brick town house with three dormers. The rooms are of the Colonial, Federal, and Victorian periods. Although a museum, it is appointed informally so as to look like an inviting home.

¶ Frederick County

STEPHEN STEINER HOUSE (c. 1807)

368 West Patrick Street; daily 10 to 5, May 1 to October 31; voluntary fee; Historical Society of Frederick County.

A handsome house whose arched doorway, with its leaded fanlight in a pattern of miniature pineapples and flowers, should be especially noted. (The pineapple emblem represents hospitality, and can be found in many Maryland houses.) The place features fine antiques of the locality, china, and silverware.

ROGER BROOKE TANEY HOUSE (1799)

123 South Bent Street (Route 40); daily 10 to 12 and 1 to 5 May 1 to October 31; voluntary fee; Historical Society of Frederick County.

Taney came here in 1801 with Francis Scott Key and married Key's sister Anne; they lived in this interesting two-story brick town house. First Attorney General of the state, Taney was later appointed Chief Justice of the Supreme Court to fill the vacancy left by John Marshall. Here is the table on which he wrote his famous Dred Scott Decision, which aroused much resentment among liberals of the day. The house is furnished with many other things that belonged to him and to his friend Key.

BARBARA FRITCHIE HOUSE AND MUSEUM (1780)

154 West Patrick Street; daily, 8 to 9; 25 cents; Barbara Fritchie Home, Inc.

A story-and-a-half brick building with a steep-pitched gable roof and two dormers, it is furnished with Fritchie's family relics and mementos of many famous visitors to the house. There isn't any flag, though!

The Historical Society suggests that "a remarkable group of Federal buildings which surround Court House Square" is called to your attention.

¶ Harford County

OAKINGTON (1810)

Havre de Grace on Chesapeake Bay West; by written appointment only; Mr. and Mrs. Millard Tydings.

On a beautiful old property with a magnificent view of Chesapeake Bay, this house has been much changed. Wings were added by Stanford White, one of which was torn down in 1908 and replaced by another of stone. There are Adam ceilings, teakwood floors laid by Tiffany (early 1900s), and family antiques and portraits.

¶ Washington County

JONATHAN HAGER HOUSE or HAGER'S FANCY (between 1739 and 1745)

By appointment; Mrs. Frank W. Mish, Falling Waters, West Virginia; Washington County Historical Society.

A recent and very handsome restoration of a primitive type of house with certain Jacobean details. The exterior is cut fieldstone; heavy timbers were used in the construction, and mud and rye straw in the plaster. Two free-flowing springs are under the house. Artifacts of the eighteenth century were unearthed during restoration.

EASTERN SHORE

¶ *Kent County (In & out of Chestertown)* ¶ *Queen Annes County (In & out of Queenstown)* ¶ *Talbot County (Out of Easton)*

¶ Kent County

In & out of Chestertown

This is a fine old college town filled with atmosphere. The view of the Water Street houses from the bridge is a real period picture.

RIVER HOUSE (*1753*)

> *107 Water Street; by appointment;*
> *Miss Marion Weeks.*

A handsome brick town house with very fine mantels and paneling, it was owned by a wealthy Barbados merchant, William Timbull, whose ships plied between the West Indies, Philadelphia, and the Eastern Shore. It is full of interest. Do not miss a remarkable Chinese Chippendale mantel on the third floor.

RINGGOLD HOUSE

(*1735 and 1750*)

> *Water Street; by appointment only;*
> *President and Mrs. Daniel Z. Gibson,*
> *Washington College.*

One of the features of this house is the manorial paneled entrance hall with its antler-type staircase. The right-hand drawing room is a reproduction, the original being in the Baltimore Museum of Art; the left-hand room has the original paneling, said to have been brought from England. The mantel in the right drawing room shows the *Ark* and the *Dove,* the ships of Lord Baltimore, at the landing for the settlement of Maryland. The house is gradually being furnished appropriately.

BACCHUS HOUSE (*c. 1780*)

> *201 Water Street; any time;*
> *Mr. James L. Bacchus.*

Standing above the Chester River, with terraces descending to the water, this is a fine town house with an unusual staircase. It contains an excellent collection of antique furniture, mostly of the eighteenth century, most of which is for sale.

PROVIDENCE PLANTATION (*1781*)

> *Near Chestertown; by appointment, May 1*
> *to September 30 Wednesdays and*
> *Thursdays 10 to 4; Mr. and Mrs. Bartus*
> *Trew.*

One of the most entertaining small houses in the state, the second or third to stand on the land that has been in the family since 1668. It was a Lord Baltimore grant. The initials of the builders and the date are in the brick of the east wall. All paneling, sheathing, and woodwork are in their original state. Some of the original furniture

and china is still around. In the nearby family burying ground are the graves of all the owners down to 1912; Alexander Hamilton's brother is one of them.

THE REWARD (early eighteenth century)
On Langford Bay, Pomona; on written request; Mr. and Mrs. Edward A. Hurd.

On Langford Bay with five miles of waterfront, this is an interesting and unusual house with the long, sloping roof of earliest colonial days. It has its original stairway and original paneling throughout.

¶ Queen Annes County

In & out of Queenstown

BOWLINGLY (1733)
Queenstown; by written appointment; Mr. and Mrs. W. Randolph Burgess.

You will have noted by now that brick has always been the favored building material in Maryland, and that the men who did the early work were craftsmen par excellence. "Bowlingly" happens to be one of the finest examples, and is distinctively colored. Its glazed Flemish bond describes two diamond patterns in each gable end, with the date in kingsize figures. One reason why the delightful divided staircase seems small in scale is that it supplants a single staircase in the same space. The furniture is all eighteenth-century English and European—no American!

WYE PLANTATION (1747)
Carmichael; garden only, by appointment; Mrs. Arthur A. Houghton, Jr., 718 Fifth Avenue, New York 19, New York.

The terraced gardens here are considered to be among the finest in the country. The historic home of Gov. William Paca, a signer of the Declaration, who lies buried nearby, this grand old manor may not yet be fully restored. But meanwhile the magnificent garden may, fortunately, be seen. The extraordinarily long house, rather Flemish in appearance, was built by Col. Edward Tilghman.

Left: There is no rarer privilege made available through the Guide *than to visit Providence Plantation, of which two views are given here.*

PRATT MANSION
(early part 1710, restored 1770)
Route 304, Ruthsburg, 6 miles east of Centerville; on phoned request (Centerville 122W1); $1.00, benefit of St. Luke's Church (1728); Mr. and Mrs. John Robert Grove.

The brick walls of this great Georgian house are thirty inches thick. All the original woodwork is intact, with graceful arches in the hall, and fine wainscoting and paneling in many rooms. Above the front door are thirteen stars carved in stone by direction of Henry Pratt, the 1770 builder, a true colonial patriot. The primitive section, with its brick kitchen, eight-foot fireplace, and hewn beams, makes an interesting contrast. It is fittingly furnished throughout with fine American antiques.

¶ Talbot County

Out of Easton

THE ANCHORAGE (1720)
By appointment; Mr. Milton Campbell.

This long-drawn Georgian mansion with its impressive later portico is an imposing sight from across the Miles River. During the 1760s it was occupied by the Rev. John Gordon, who operated a race track behind his church nearby for the pleasure of his congregation after services. It is furnished in keeping with its age but not as a show house; its owner says, "We aim to keep it a home."

MYRTLE GROVE (1730–1777)
By written appointment only; Mr. and Mrs. Robert Goldsborough Henry.

Since the day Robert Goldsborough built the clapboard section, which is now the wing, the house has always been in the hands of his descendants. The whole place has the air of having been cherished carefully and long. The library has exceptionally fine raised paneling. The drawing room contains an Adam frieze and original cornices with decorations of American eagles over the windows. The steps of the magnificent hanging staircase are solid blocks of wood. There are family portraits by Peale and Heselius. This is a home in which character and quality have always predominated, and its owners are as distinguished as their dwelling.

Aspendale, deceptively plain outside, is a perfect example of the Delaware brick house so like its south Jersey neighbors. Opposite is the drawing room of Aspendale, which sets the tone for the rest of the house, of excellence and restraint.

DELAWARE

¶ *Dover* ¶ *Laurel* ¶ *Lewes* ¶ *Milford* ¶ *New Castle*
¶ *Odessa* ¶ *Rehoboth Beach* ¶ *In & out of Smyrna*
¶ *Around Wilmington*

ELAWARE was the first of the thirteen original states to declare its independence, and the last to remain Federalist. Its name was given by Captain Argall of Virginia, the next person after Henry Hudson to sail into the Delaware Bay. He named it after the Governor of his own state, Lord De La Warr. In 1621 the first settlement, a Dutch whaling colony, was made near what is now Lewes, but Indians massacred all twenty-eight men. About twenty years later, Peter Minuit, representing the Swedish Crown, landed at the mouth of the Christiana River, later to become the site of Wilmington. Nothing in the way of houses is left from the early Swedish and Dutch settlers, and though the Swedes were a strong influence here for more than a hundred years no traces of their influence in architecture may be found now except the Old Swedes Church (1698) in Wilmington.

The three lower counties on the Delaware, those which were first settled, contain a sizable number of pre-Revolutionary houses, most of them of the simple cottage type, many reflecting the influence of the later English incursion and much resembling the humble early shingle cottages on Long Island. However, by the mid-seventeenth century, many were built more pretentiously and solidly of native stone or brick. George Fletcher Bennett mentions that five-inch-thick oak planks were used in some

49

buildings. You will find small brick houses with overpowering chimneys in Yorklyn and Newport; clapboard and shingle in Lewes; and stone in Marshalltown. The "great houses," which were beginning to show themselves at this time, as wealth began to flow into the state, can still be seen in New Castle, Dover, and Odessa.

There are four "days" in Delaware. A Day in Old New Castle is held the third Saturday in May each year, when a choice collection of private homes is open from 11 to 5. A fee of $3.50 goes to the restoration of Immanuel Church. Old Dover Day, under the auspices of Friends of Old Dover, is held the first Saturday and Sunday in May, and the fee of $3.00 not only takes you into a fine assortment of early houses, but enables you to take tea with the Governor and see folk dances on the Green. Odessa Day is held the second Saturday in October, but it would be well to confirm this with the Community Center Association there. Wilmington Garden Day, which includes a half-dozen homes, is the first Saturday in May, sponsored by the Wilmington Garden Club at Shipley and 8th Streets, Wilmington.

¶ Dover

Although we are unable to state that any of the fine early private homes of Dover may be seen except on Old Dover Day, the charm of the old capital can be enjoyed to great advantage by a stroll around the Green in the center of town.

JOHN DICKINSON HOUSE (1740)

Kitts Hummock Road 5 miles southeast of Dover just off 113; 10 to 5 Tuesday through Saturday, 1 to 5 Sundays; Delaware State Museum.

Originally called "Kingston-upon-Hull," this very substantially built brick mansion is named after the son of its builder, one of the state's most brilliant and illustrious early citizens, called "The Penman of the Revolution" and author of the famous *Letters of a Pennsylvania Farmer* (written when Delaware was the three lowest counties of that state). After the house was swept by fire in 1804, Dickinson determined to substitute a simpler scheme of things for its former elaborate pre-Georgian interiors. The present restoration has followed this as closely as possible, using the original materials and furnishing it with eighteenth-century pieces, many of Philadelphia origin. Before the Revolution Dickinson felt that more could be accomplished by conciliation and refused to sign the Declaration of Independence. But all

History makes the Dickinson house outstanding. Another typical brick, one of the state's most important restorations.

was forgiven because of his courageous conduct in the war, and he became President of Delaware before the title of "governor" was given to that office. His portrait hangs in the State House.

¶ Laurel

GOVERNOR MITCHELL HOUSE or COLLINS HOUSE (1764)
Delaware Avenue.

This old town on Route 13 seven miles above the Maryland border was laid out on a tract called "Bachelor's Delight" and was an important shipping center in the early days. It is an up-and-coming community now, and the house that was the home of Governor Nathaniel Mitchell (1805–1808) is one of the few surviving originals.

¶ Lewes

Called the "saltiest town in Delaware" and pronounced *Lewis,* it is about forty miles down from Dover off 14 at the mouth of Delaware Bay.

DAVID HALL HOUSE
(late eighteenth century)
107 Kings' Highway; on written or phoned (Lewes 2441) request; Mr. and Mrs. John M. Vessels.

Like most of the early houses hereabouts, the Hall House is simple, cypress-shingled, and painted. There are the customary Christian-cross doors, and each of the six rooms has its paneled wall with fireplace and overmantel, nicely molded cornices, chair rails, and baseboards. The entrance hall is the most elaborate; the living room, the next; then the dining room; and so on. There is a Cape Cod quality here, with a special Delaware flavor.

CAESAR RODNEY HOUSE
(early eighteenth century)
Pilot Road; any time; Mr. Daniel H. C. Littleton.

If you are passing this way, you might want to make a "pious pilgrimage" to the house in which Caesar Rodney, great Delaware patriot and fourth President of the state, spent his childhood. From here he made his famous eighty-mile ride to Philadelphia

to cast his vote for the resolution for independence, which enabled Delaware on July 2d to be one of the twelve colonies to vote for the Declaration of Independence. It is considered the most important historical event in the history of the state. The house is long and low, with large dormers, and once stood on a nine-hundred-acre tract inherited by Caesar from his father, William. Of interest now chiefly for historic reasons.

¶ Milford (between Dove· and Lewes on 113)

MORDINGTON (1777)
By phone appointment (Frederica 5–5293); Leslie I. March.

A handsome early brick house in the Georgian style, with a beautiful millpond setting and a fine collection of antiques, it is said to be haunted by a pretty slave girl who was unjustly punished and jumped from a window to her death.

¶ New Castle

The oldest town along the Delaware, only six miles south of Wilmington and girdled by superhighways and jet-plane bases, New Castle sits peacefully on the bank of the river looking and behaving much as it did in the late eighteenth and early nineteenth centuries. Most of its fine houses have survived and are being lived in, typified by the particularly lovely Late Georgian READ HOUSE, on The Strand near Harmony Street.

Here is a Williamsburg that needed no rebuilding and little visible restoration. When Peter Stuyvesant, Dutch Governor from New Amsterdam, anchored in the harbor in 1651, the farmers who lived on the nearby plantations were Swedes and Finns. Later in the Dutch period, the Public Square was laid out under Peter's direction. One of the loveliest early buildings in the country, THE OLD COURT HOUSE, a twenty-foot section of which was said to be standing when William Penn landed here in 1682, still

Immanuel Church is one of many lovely sights in New Castle.

when George Washington kissed the Governor's daughter at her wedding, and also, it was said, all the other pretty girls there "as was his wont." On either side of the central hall, the two rooms are furnished with authentic and very fine pieces of the early period of the house, whose great kitchen hearth dates from 1706 or earlier.

OLD DUTCH HOUSE (*prior to 1704*)
Between Harmony and Delaware Streets; April 1 to December 1, 11 to 4; 25 cents; New Castle Historical Society.

Considered to be the oldest in the state, the style, unmistakably Dutch, places it sometime before 1704. Restored in 1938, it is small, with one of the lowest, widest eaves we have ever seen, a huge central chimney, a solitary dormer, and solid shutters. It is completely furnished with very early Dutch pieces and constitutes an unusually perfect example of life at the end of the seventeenth century in colonial America. A particularly fine example.

IMMANUEL PARISH HOUSE (*1801*)
Harmony Street and The Strand; on request; New Castle Historical Society.

This Late Georgian house was designed as a hotel and stands three and a half stories high, with a deck on the roof which has made it a landmark for the river boats for a century and a half. It has double entrance doors. The interior has been preserved with less success than others in the town; the Historical Society agrees that only one carved mantel is to be recommended.

VAN LEUVENEIGH HOUSE (*1732*)
2 The Strand West; on written request; Mrs. J. Danforth Bush.

This distinguished town house wears a veil of smooth plaster over brick. What sets it off is the cornice, whose rectangular modillions, sufficiently emphatic, along with the odd and interesting gambrel roof, help create its character. The fine paneling of the interior and an unusual irregular chimney breast and fireplace are features of a house that is furnished in keeping with its quality.

KINSEY JOHN HOUSE (*1789–90*)
East 3d Street facing the Green; by appointment unless a guest; Mrs. Lewis Booker.

Now a guest house, this is one of the love-

dominates the Green, whose ancient Immanuel Church, with its graveyard full of illustrious names, and the Old Academy and Arsenal form an unspoiled scene out of the past. All public buildings may be visited.

Through the courtesy and cooperation of Historic New Castle, Inc., special arrangements may be made to visit some of the private residences not listed below as regularly open. Write or phone to this nonprofit organization which encourages preservation, and allow a little time if you wish to see particular houses.

AMSTEL HOUSE (*c. 1730, wing c. 1700*)
4th and Delaware Streets; weekdays except Wednesdays and holidays, Sundays by appointment; 50 cents; New Castle Historical Society.

The first Governor of Delaware, Nicholas Van Dyke, lived here in this broad house built of locally made brick laid in Flemish bond, with a belt course and water table to lighten its sturdy design. The music room has been exquisitely restored by Mrs. Coleman du Pont, a great-great-granddaughter of the Governor, who has returned the room to its appearance on that gala day liest Georgian houses in a town of treasures, with some exceptionally fine interior detail to recommend it, along with its attractive accommodations. Take note of the staircase designed by Lampton Surrette.

RESIDENCE OF MR. AND MRS. SAMUEL H. CAROTHERS (*c. 1830*)
> *170 East 3d Street; by request;*
> *Mrs. S. H. Carothers, The Nonesuch Shop,*
> *Old Town Hall (phone: 3120).*

The only one of the few old clapboard houses in the town so far restored. There are two rooms upstairs and two down. The detail is simplicity itself, and the owners have restored it with taste and furnished it charmingly with heirlooms.

GUNNING BEDFORD HOUSE (*1730*)
> *6 The Strand; on request; Mr. and Mrs.*
> *Elmer E. Bailey.*

This stunning town house was built by John Van Gezel, grandson of one of New Castle's Dutch founders. It was one time residence of the Governor whose name has been given to it, and of another Governor as well, Caleb P. Bennett. It has exceptional staircases, fine fireplaces and floors. The present owners, who have recently restored this ancient beauty, have done so with the respect it merited.

Note: There is a KINSEY JOHN, JR., HOUSE at the northeast corner of Delaware and 4th, built in 1823. John succeeded his father as Chancellor of the state; his house represents Federal elegance.

¶ Odessa

Twenty-two miles south of Wilmington, this was once a busy port and market place called "Cantwell's Bridge." In 1825 six large granaries stood on the banks of its creek, shipping forty thousand bushels of grain annually to coastal cities. Because of this it was given the name of the famous grain port in Russia. The several distinguished homes that have survived the town's early prosperity are an indication of its early culture as well.

Odessa Day, in the middle of May, is likely to be a yearly occurrence. At this time, ten to fifteen houses are on view, including the great William Corbit House. The tour is sponsored by the Community Center Association.

CORBIT HOUSE (*1782*)
> *Main and 2d Streets; on written request*
> *only at owner's convenience and on special*
> *occasions; H. Rodney Sharp, Wilmington.*

There are few houses that touch this for Georgian perfection, both inside and out. A brick house, once called "Castle William," it was built according to plans drawn up by the English firm of Robert

Brick again gives the Kinsey John House its trimness, but note the elegance of doorway and windows lacking in the country cousins.

May and Company, who also designed the David Wilson Mansion next door. The Quaker Corbit family from Philadelphia prospered here for more than a century and a half. Until 1938 the family still occupied the house and it was therefore little changed. Mr. Sharp, a connoisseur and antiquarian, who purchased it at that time, removed certain unflattering additions such as added porches and bays, but otherwise he found its elegance intact. His fine color sense and the beautiful furniture and portraits have made it a house of museum quality. In fact many museums might envy its perfection. On the second floor is a reception room of really noble proportions, with walls paneled to the carved cornices. Fluted pilasters rise at either side of the mantel to a ceiling height of almost twelve feet. Chippendale carving of the chair rail and rope carving on the baseboard give the room great richness, although the ornamentation is restrained. Doorways have broken pediments, as do a number of the overmantels in the house. Although the house is large and its character solid, the detail is light throughout. The outside doorways have delicate fanlights, the doors being protected by lightly louvered shutters of unusual design, while the Chippendale railing near the roof peak seems to give it a triumphant crown.

EARLY BRICK HOUSE
(eighteenth century)
May; Mr. and Mrs. J. C. Calloway.

The brick portion of this home is believed to be the original manse of OLD DRAWYERS CHURCH, which is another May masterpiece begun in 1773. The frame addition of the house is well done. Its owner says it is loveliest in May, when the locust trees are in flower.

THOMAS HOUSE (*c. 1740*)
On request two weeks in advance;
Mr. and Mrs. Robert C. Heller.

The original part is built of hand-hewn logs, hand-split shingles and lath; the partitions are of plank. In the later section is some excellent paneling.

CYRUS POLK HOUSE (*c. 1852*)
On request; Mr. and Mrs. Gantt William Muller, Jr.

Of a later period than most of the houses

here, it is nevertheless very lovely and its Chinese antiques, dating from the Han Dynasty, together with other Chinese articles representing various periods, make this an exceptionally interesting house to visit.

DAVID WILSON MANSION (*1769*)
Tuesdays 12:30 to 4:30 and 7 to 9,
Saturdays 9 to 12 and 1:30 to 4:30;
Mary Corbit Warner Museum and Library.

The exterior is similar to the Corbit House. Robert May of London also designed it and the paneling here is second to none in the state. The Mary Corbit Warner Museum and Library was once the first free library in the state. The living room and two bedrooms remain furnished with Mrs. Warner's own things.

FAIRVIEW (*1773*)
On written request when owners are in residence; Mr. and Mrs. George F. Kelly.

Another fine example of the work of Robert May and Company, it was built for Maj. James Moore, one of the charter members of the Society of the Cincinnati. The Moore family were still living here until 1928. It is now beautifully restored by its new owners, Mr. and Mrs. George F. Kelly.

COLONIAL BRICK (*1772*)
Mr. and Mrs. William A. Deibert, (residents).

COLONIAL FRAME AND LOG HOUSE (*c. 1740*)
Mr. and Mrs. Jesse A. Loven, (residents).

LORE HOUSE (*original log end 1740*)
Mr. and Mrs. James Shallcross, (residents).

These three houses have all been restored by Mr. Rodney Sharp and are owned by him. Permission to see them must first be obtained from him and will also be subject to the residents' convenience.

¶ *Rehoboth Beach (An ocean resort town several miles below Lewes)*

HOMESTEAD (*1742*)
Henlopen Acres; on written request; Mr. W. S. Corkran.

Beautifully restored and maintained, this cypress-shingled house has had recent addi-

Aspendale's dining room in the low clapboard wing is the only primitive room in the house and may have been the first building here.

tions so carefully made that you cannot tell them from the original. Built by Peter Marsh, the framing is of hand-hewn walnut. It contains interesting primitive paneling, original doors and floors. The gardens have long been considered a show place.

¶ In & out of Smyrna
(halfway between Odessa and Dover on 13)

ASPENDALE (1771)
Route 300, 7 miles southeast of Smyrna and less than a mile beyond Kenton; May 1 to December 31 on written request; Donald V. L. Downs, Attention The Farmer, "Aspendale," Downs Chapel, Kenton.

The distinguished exterior of this charming old brick house hardly prepares you for the chaste and elegant perfection of its interior. It is definitely Delaware. The house has always been in the owner's family. Mr. Downs' work on it should be termed preservation instead of restoration, for he has altered nothing in the basic features. The paneling throughout the house is subtle and delicate, rather than rich and luxuriant; its beauty lying in the way it is composed, detailed, and put together. The woodwork is still covered with its first and only original coat of paint, the beautiful colors in the various rooms having been brought back by nothing more than soap and water. The house is furnished with chastity and taste; the whole thing a personal and intimate performance on the part of the owner. A "must" for connoisseurs.

BELMONT HALL (1773, rear lower wing 1686)
Route 13 on left as you leave town south; on written request; Mrs. Cummins E. Speakman.

One of the historic mansions of the state, this colorful large house occupies a little park of its own and has sheltered the Speakman family for generations. In a radical departure, the roof presents its wide

Belmont Hall, an impressive brick manor with a fine setting.

low gable end to the front, with a balustraded captain's walk flanked by fine chimneys. It is most impressive as to height, as to its nice doorway, and as to its windows with their stylish Delaware keystone lintels. The state legislature met here when the British burned the State House in Dover in 1777, and two Windsor chairs used at the time are still in the breakfast room. There is also a splendid accumulation of Empire and Victorian furniture.

¶ Around Wilmington

ELEUTHERIAN MILLS (*1802*)

> *Bucks Road; on written request, spring or fall only; Mrs. Francis B. Crowinshield.*

Éleuthère Irénée du Pont built this handsome house the year after he had established the now fabulous du Pont industrial empire in Delaware. The house that then looked down over the infant mills is now owned by the woman who has been one of the prime movers in the preservation and enhancement of great early American houses. One of her masterpieces was the refurbishing of the PINGREE HOUSE in Salem, Massachusetts. It is a privilege to see one of the houses in which she lives.

CLAYTON HOUSE *or* BUENA VISTA (*1846*)

> *State Road; on written request; Mr. and Mrs. C. Douglas Buck.*

The year after he built this impressive man-

sion, John M. Clayton, who was a United States Senator and a Secretary of State, named it in honor of Zachary Taylor's famous victory in Mexico. Prominent in politics, Mr. C. was notable at home among his friends as a concocter of diamond-back terrapin delicacies.

LATIMER HOUSE (*1800*)

> *102 Middleboro Row, Richardson Park; on request; Mr. and Mrs. James L. Banning, WY 4–9798.*

The Banning and Latimer families have always lived here and been active in Delaware affairs. The fine brick house is an excellent example of country Georgian, handsomely furnished.

HENRY FRANCIS DU PONT WINTERTHUR MUSEUM (*1817*)

> *Winterthur Lodge off 52 (Pennsylvania Avenue) a few miles out of Wilmington; by written application for tickets of admission; $2.00; daily except Sundays, Mondays, New Year's Day, Washington's Birthday, Memorial Day, Independence Day, Thanksgiving, and Christmas; The Winterthur Corporation.*

This extraordinary museum contains one of the largest and certainly the richest and finest collections of Early American rooms, furniture, and decorative arts ever brought together, the result of thirty years of searching, assembling, and arranging on the part

The stair hall of Montmorenci is one of the glories of Winterthur Museum.

Winterthur Museum has been endlessly enlarged to hold the finest rooms and collections of Americana in the country.

of Henry Francis du Pont. He and his family made their home here among his growing collections from 1926, when he inherited the house, until 1951 when the museum was deeded to the Winterthur Corporation and formally opened to the public. The original building itself began as the home of Mr. du Pont's great aunt Evelina Gabrielle du Pont de Nemours Biedermann and her husband. James Antoine Bidermann had come from Switzerland in 1814 with letters of introduction from Lafayette, married this daughter of Éleuthère Irénée du Pont de Nemours in 1816, and built this house a year later, naming it after his mother's birthplace in Switzerland. It was a large, foursquare, flat-roofed house whose original size has no longer any significance, so many enlargements having been made to hold the harvest after yearly harvest of Mr. du Pont's remarkable collecting. The place in fact is overwhelming, but the arranging has been done with such orderliness and truly dramatic skill that the interest never flags.

"The visitor enters one room after another, replete with rare and beautiful objects," wrote the late Joseph Downs, Winterthur's first curator, "and feels the richness of life at its best in successive periods of our early history." Here you will find authentic rooms stunningly displayed like the parlor and porch from the 1764 Stamper-Blackwell house in Philadelphia, long gone—the gayest and most opulent of Quaker City houses. The parlor and stairhall of 1744 "Readbourne" are here; the great country house itself still standing in elegant style on the Chester River near Centerville, Maryland. And while the notable North Carolina mansion called "Montmorenci," near Warrenton, is slowly disintegrating, its gracious hallway, with one of the finest of free-standing staircases, is permanently preserved here as one of the glories of the museum. But these are the merest sampling. Get a good rest the night before, wear your comfortable shoes, and save some time to see the gardens. Mr. du Pont is a horticulturist par excellence, as well as a collector.

Dumbarton House is a fitting headquarters for the National Society of Colonial Dames. The oval music room is as graceful as the harp through which you see it, a foretaste of its many other delights. The house opposite needs no introduction for you will recognize it as the home of American Presidents.

DISTRICT OF COLUMBIA

¶ *City of Washington* ¶ *The Georgetown Tour*

*B*ACK IN 1790, when the District of Columbia was created, this ten-mile-square tract of land mortised between the states of Maryland and Virginia contained two of our most charming colonial cities, Georgetown and Alexandria. The latter, charming as ever, has long since reverted to Virginia, where you will find her today—across the river out past the great Lee Mansion that greets you on the Arlington shore. Fortunately, too, you will also find Georgetown today, charming as ever, still very much herself as to personality and appearance, though otherwise part and parcel of the city of Washington.

Except for Georgetown, the great governmental city as we know it today began from scratch in 1790. The vicissitudes of politics and real estate speculation were stumbling blocks whose bad effects have not been altogether overcome. Even so, the city has achieved in official architecture and arrangement a kind of

classical countenance and monumental character in keeping with the nineteenth-century conception of what a nation's Capital should look like. Washington is really an inspiring spectacle, at its best both beautiful and thrilling.

Residentially, however, the city has always been rather catch-as-catch-can. Several early houses of considerable distinction are listed and described below; but one of the very finest and earliest, far from being a native home, was recently brought here from Massachusetts, as will be noted. And only one of the really good early houses here—"Dumbarton"—is open to the public as its primary function, though this one is a beauty. The rest may be viewed from without at will, but, with a few exceptions, may be visited only on certain occasions or by special arrangement, as noted below.

It will explain a lot to consider the appearance of Washington proper in the early days. Georgetown, a neat and trim entity in itself, was the "court end" of the District, whereas by comparison the new Capital City was a countrified place, its few and far apart important houses reached only by muddy roads. As late as 1851 Lady Stuart Wortley commented, "It could be a beautiful place, if it were built." It was bogged down in mire when the weather was wet, as Charles Dickens told the world testily, and after dark you could hardly see your hand in front of your face. It continued for some time to be a town of occasional mansions. It is interesting to note that the same William Thornton who designed without particular charm the notable Octagon House in the new city designed with great charm indeed the even more notable Tudor Place House in Georgetown. It is as though the official atmosphere of Washington proper had a somewhat stultifying effect on this first architect of the Capitol, whereas the effect of Georgetown on this talented man had altogether delightful results. And it is likely that the two sections of the city will have a similarly contrasting effect on the lover of early houses today.

¶ City of Washington

THE WHITE HOUSE (1792–1800)

On the axis of Pennsylvania Avenue, facing Lafayette Square; mornings, 10 to 12, except Sundays and Mondays; United States government.

In terms of public importance this house looms larger than any other described in the *Guide*. And in terms of actuality, it is by all odds the biggest. In the living quarters alone there are now fifty-four rooms and sixteen baths—one hundred and thirty-two rooms and twenty baths altogether! And the White House has housed quite a few occupants, first and last—thirty-three Presidents of the United States as of 1956 (all but George Washington himself, who passed on the plans and lived to see it practically completed). Even when the John Adamses moved in, in November, 1800, however, the East Room was far from finished, a fact which didn't floor Mrs. A.; she simply used the room in bad weather to dry the family wash. The plans that Washington approved were prepared by an Irish-born architect named James Hoban, who modeled the main façade after a mansion he'd designed in Dublin for the Duke of Leinster. Hoban also handled the reconstruction of the house after it was burned by the British in 1814, and in 1824 and 1829 put on the south and north porticoes. It was after the fire that the badly discolored sandstone walls were painted white, coining its present name; up to then it had been called the "President's House," or even the "President's Palace." It is now known officially as the "Executive Mansion." The White House has undergone many alterations, restorations, and "improvements" over the years in conformity with fashion, necessity, and Presidential desires. Gaslight was installed in 1848, and five years later hot-water heating. During the administration of President Truman, on the recommendation of a special commission, the White House underwent a complete and thorough renovation, its first since the 1814 fire. This took nearly four years, from 1948 to 1952, the Trumans living meanwhile in Blair House, across the way. It was an extraordinary feat of engineering which made it possible for the old sandstone walls to remain with the old familiar features of Hoban's neoclassical façades intact, while the famous interiors were being restored with historical accuracy, so that in the main it is today still very much the White House of most Americans' memories: East Room, Blue Room, Red and Green Rooms, Lincoln's Victorian bedroom, and all reconstructed to last for the foreseeable future.

BLAIR HOUSE (1810)

1651 Pennsylvania Avenue; on written request; Division of Protocol, Department of State, Washington.

Known as the "Guest House of the Nation," it is now used for visiting notables. It was built by the first Surgeon General of the Army, Dr. Joseph Lovell. As advertised in the *Globe* in 1836 after his death, it was "a spacious two-story brick building with a well of excellent water in the yard." During three generations of Blair ownership it received a third and fourth story and a Georgian portico and classical cornice, so that today it is large and imposing enough to play its important part in the affairs of the Capital. The Blair family was instrumental in the election of Lincoln, and Montgomery Blair served as Lincoln's Postmaster General. Much history was made in the house: here Robert E. Lee came to his fateful decision to cast his lot with the Confederacy, and here Admiral Farragut was given his command for the attack on New Orleans. Sometimes the events were not so portentous, as General Sherman's wedding here in 1850, at which President Taylor and his whole Cabinet were present. The innumerable historical events have left in their wake many mementos and treasures which are still here as a part of the furnishings.

DECATUR HOUSE (*1819*)

Lafayette Square; soon to be opened regularly; United States government, National Trust for Historical Preservation, 712 Jackson Place N.W. (beneficiary).

It can be seen at present only in the yearly tour of notable Washington houses. Built from designs of Benjamin Latrobe, it was commissioned by Com. Stephen Decatur, hero of the Barbary Wars, with the prize money from his famous exploits. Only fourteen months after its completion Decatur was killed in a duel with Commodore Barron. Mrs. Decatur, retiring to a house in Georgetown, refused to set foot ever again in Washington proper. The house then passed into the hands of many famous people: Secretaries of State, ministers of foreign powers, and finally the late Truxton Beale, our Minister to Persia and Greece. It was his widow who generously made it a part of the public domain. The gracefully ornate interior of this rather plain brick house is to be left virtually furnished as it is and always has been. So very few of the old Washington houses have survived the growth of the city that it is a most fortunate thing for the public that Mrs. Beale had so arranged it that this house is bound to outlive many contemporary structures. With Dumbarton House it now continues to show Americans

how their forebears lived when the Capital City was in the making.

HOUSE WHERE LINCOLN DIED, or PETERSON HOUSE (*1849*)

516 10th Street; weekdays 9 to 5:30, Sundays and holidays 12:30 to 5:30; United States government, National Park Service.

A plain house occupied by modest people, it stands across from Ford's Theater, which is now a Lincoln museum, and is outwardly as it was the night of April 14, 1865, when Lincoln was shot. As the Peterson House was the one nearest to the theater, Lincoln was carried there to a small first-floor bedroom, where he died at 7:22 A.M. the next morning. A meeting of Lincoln's Cabinet was held in the rear parlor of the house during the night. It is furnished now as it might have been the night of the tragedy.

THE OLD STONE HOUSE or WASHINGTON'S HEADQUARTERS (*1766*)

3051 M Street; United States government, National Park Service.

Saved from demolition recently as the result of special legislation, it is one of the few "ancients" here that have been little changed. It is thought to have been Suter's Tavern, where Washington and L'Enfant planned the Capital. Pennsylvania Dutch in style and probably in derivation, it has many interesting features, which, brought to the attention of the experts, saved its life. It is a story-and-a-half stone house with a full-story basement where the ground slopes off. The stonework, the roof pitch, and certain other details indicate its Pennsylvania ancestry. A heavy outside chimney and two dormers complete its primitive impression.

THE OCTAGON HOUSE (*1798–1800*)

1741 New York Avenue N.W.; Tuesdays to Saturdays, 10:30 to 4:30, except legal holidays; 30 cents; American Institute of Architects (headquarters).

Finished the same year as the White House, this *hexagonal* house was designed by William Thornton, first architect of the Capitol. It was built for a wealthy Virginia sportsman, Col. John Tayloe, at the instigation of his good friend, President Washington. Tayloe, who was owner of another splendid home—MT. AIRY in Vir-

The formal mass of the Octagon House must have been an impressive sight when Washington was only a village with muddy lanes.

ginia—built what was then considered the finest house by far in the new Capital. Today it is still high on the list of choice examples of architecture of the early republic period, and filled with memories of famous people and events. It was here that President Madison and Dolly stayed for more than a year after the British had burned the White House in 1814. Here in the circular room on the second floor which served Madison as a study, on the day before Christmas of that same year, was signed the Treaty of Ghent, which ended the War of 1812; the round table on which it was signed is still there. The drawing and dining rooms have been restored with formal dignity. The rest of the house is used for exhibitions of art and as offices for the American Institute of Architects.

THE ARTS CLUB (*1802–1805*)
2017 I Street N.W.

It was built by Gideon Granger, then Postmaster General, on a tract known as "The Widow's Mite." The fanlighted doorway of Mr. Granger's nearly palatial brick mansion, its stone-capped windows, and other refinements are still intact. The original staircase with its elaborate bas-relief gar-

lands shows how well Mr. Granger did for himself. The old house, so well preserved now by the Arts Club, is famous for having been James Monroe's residence while he was Secretary of War and State. Later it became Washington's most fashionable boarding house, with a clientele largely made up of foreign diplomats. The interior may be seen on the tour. There is a steward in residence, and students of architecture may apply to the President of the club, Mr. Lorenzo S. Winslow, for admission.

THE PARISH HOUSE OF ST. JOHN'S CHURCH (*1836*)
H Street adjacent to Lafayette Square.

It was at one time a center of Washington social life. In 1842 it was leased by Lord Ashburton, British Minister to the United States, who is said to have outdone any of his predecessors in the lavishness of the entertainments that he offered. Then Great Britain purchased the house for use as the British Legation until 1852. Now, as the parish house of a church, it is rounding out its days in a more restrained manner. Known as the "Church of the Presidents," St. John's, built in 1815, was designed by Latrobe, and is one of his little masterpieces. Students of architecture may address the resident minister by letter for permission to see the parish house.

THE LINDENS (1754)
2401 Kalorama Road N.W.; on written request to qualified students; Mrs. George Maurice Morris.

Although many would agree that "The Lindens" is one of the most striking and beautiful houses in Washington, it is not a native here. It was built as a country house at Danvers, Massachusetts, and its early New England origin sticks out all over it, even though it stands on a street of the Capital as if it had been there forever. Yet it was as recently as 1928 that it was moved down from Danvers in marked pieces. Its putty-colored wooden walls are carpentered to imitate ashlar masonry.

"The Lindens'" balustraded gambrel, the tall chimneys that give it extra height, the pilasters, and the doorways, can all be studied from the street. The interior has a museum perfection, and if you can convince the gifted antiquarian who owns it that you will benefit from seeing it, you will look upon a masterpiece of re-creation. To quote the owner, "Not even the design for a curtain valance is later than the year the house was built." The outstanding feature of the interior is the stairway, which is considered by many the finest in America. It certainly ranks near the top, and its beauty is further enhanced by the exciting pattern of the hand-blocked French wallpaper The furniture throughout is Queen Anne and Chippendale, museum pieces for the most part. There are four immense paneled bedrooms on the second floor, and in one of them is a unique set of matching English crewelwork drapes and bed furnishings from the reign of Charles II.

The Lindens, complete with fencing, marched to Washington from Massachusetts without losing a trace of its New England distinction.

The brilliant crewel-work drapes and bedspread are undoubtedly the most complete set in the country. The highboys, too, are unique.

DUMBARTON HOUSE (*1799–1805*)

2715 Q Street N.W.; daily, 10 to 5, except Sundays and holidays; National Society of Colonial Dames.

This beautiful brick house of the Federal period, whose graceful garden front with its two semicircular bays rivals its more formal street front, and whose Adam interiors are furnished to perfection, has, like "The Lindens," been moved from its original site. But whereas The Lindens was brought nearly 500 miles from beyond Boston, the Dumbarton House was taken apart and rebuilt less than that many feet from where it stood before. It had been obstructing travel on Q Street and was in danger of being demolished when it was acquired by the Colonial Dames for their national headquarters and shifted to its present nearby location. The mantels are exquisite, particularly the famous one in the dining room; and the elliptical music room, looking out on the gardens, with its white-and-gold paper and its antique Rus-sian chandelier of sapphire crystal, is the last word in elegance.

¶ The Georgetown Tour

Duncan Emrich has rhapsodized about Georgetown as "a carriage lamp, a door knocker, brick sidewalks and ivy . . . the great estates of EVERMAY and TUDOR PLACE and the little houses, eight, nine and ten feet wide . . . the yellow, red and pink doors fronting the cobblestones along the Canal." The doors of the red-brick houses swing open only once a year to the public—on the annual Georgetown Tour, lasting two days, usually early in April and including fifteen or more houses each year. Write to the Georgetown Tour Committee, St. John's Church, 3240 O Street N.W., for information. Otherwise, walk down

Q, P, and O Streets, Dumbarton Avenue, N and M Street, and you will have met with many of the choicest. See the row houses on N Street, paying special attention to NUMBERS 3255 and 3263, built about 1803 for Col. James Smith. There is much to admire in these prim, reticent houses, usually of brick and three stories high. They are often beautifully dormered, with recessed stone panels over the windows for decoration and arched or fanlighted doorways.

Lovely TUDOR PLACE, on Q Street, is one of the exceptions. It sits in a little park of its own, but you can catch glimpses of it through the trees. This yellow-stuccoed house, designed by Dr. Thornton, is pure classicism; its semi-circular south portico is modeled after the Temple of Athene. Originally the home of Martha Parke Custis, who was the granddaughter of Martha Washington and who married Thomas Peter, the house still belongs to the Peter family.

Another house of great distinction, known as "THE BODISCO HOUSE" or the "RUSSIAN LEGATION," is at 3322 O Street. The severity of its three-story brick façade is relieved by an entrance of great style. A classic portico and massive eight-panel doors are approached by a gently curving double sweep of stairs almost as wide as the house itself. It is owned now by the Francis C. de Wolfs.

THE DECATUR HOUSE here in Georgetown, to which the widow of Com. Stephen Decatur retired after his death in a duel, is at 2812 N Street—a charming and typical eighteenth-century Georgetown house with a lovely doorway. Its garden affords a sweeping view of the Potomac. The present owner, Mrs. Franklin Mott Gunther, has restored it with taste.

The house of former Secretary of State and Mrs. Dean Acheson, at 2805 P Street, is late Federal (1840) and presents to the street a "musket-barrel" fence in which a former owner made use of some surplus Mexican War guns.

THE YELLOW HOUSE (prior to 1733), at 1430 33d Street, of painted brick, is the oldest in Georgetown.

The rear of Dumbarton House with its curving bays is a favorite view for visitors.

The Colonial Dames take pride in the Cornwallis House on which they have long lavished attention—most recently on the restoration of an old-fashioned garden in the rear and the choice little dependencies. Opposite page shows a very different kind of architecture, the Old Salem Community Store, part of one of the most interesting restorations in the country.

North Carolina

*Y*OU will look in vain for North Carolina's very earliest houses, as you will for the most part in other colonial regions. What happened to the several settlements established by **Sir Walter Raleigh** in 1585 *et seq.* on Roanoke Island nobody knows for sure; but anybody who gets excitement from unspoiled sea and duneland can drive down Route 158 from Kitty Hawk (where the Wright brothers made history of another sort) and at least observe the tragic site of this earliest of all our colonial settlements. Not only Raleigh but Hakluyt himself had a hand in this one, and so did Sir Francis Drake and Sir Richard Grenville. It was also on Roanoke that the first colonial child —Virginia Dare—was born. But that's about all we know. And we know even less about the North Carolina houses

built by planters from Barbados in 1664 on the Cape Fear River, down below what is now Wilmington.

And what happened to the houses built at New Bern by colonizers from Switzerland in 1711—another ill-fated settlement? In the lovely town of New Bern today there are later and naturally more elegant early houses to be seen. But there is nothing at all of what might have been our only instance of Swiss Colonial.

Not only the very earliest houses have vanished; later casualties have also been great, particularly among the large frame plantation houses of the Piedmont, so heavily hit by long periods of depression and neglect. Great houses like "Prospect Hill" are going fast, and "Montmorenci" is practically gone, though its finest rooms are gloriously preserved at the Winterthur Museum.

It is some consolation that "Tryon's Palace," at New Bern, destroyed by fire in 1791, which has been called "the finest early house of North Carolina, if not of the American colonies," is now being reconstructed. This will indeed be something to see! Built to serve as both the residence of the colonial governors and the headquarters of the Carolina government, this truly palatial creation was one of those exceedingly rare examples of a colonial building for whose design and assembly an architect (in this case John Hawks) was actually brought over from England. By some miracle his plans were preserved.

Very likely because of its decidedly difficult seacoast, North Carolina is the only one of the American colonies which was not settled by seafarers from abroad; which accounts for the diverse style you will find in colonial houses throughout the state. Leicester B. Holland calls them "Colonial Colonial." They were built by settlers coming down overland from Virginia, Maryland, and Pennsylvania, and by colonial carpenters from Connecticut and Massachusetts who would land at New Bern and Edenton from little trading vessels that made triangular voyages between New England, the British West Indies, and here.

There are Tidewater houses with Ba-hamian verandas that have features common in houses up the Connecticut River and along the shores of Massachusetts Bay. There are Piedmont houses with Williamsburg characteristics and treatment typical of South Jersey and Delaware, while the Moravian settlement of Winston-Salem is almost pure Pennsylvania Colonial. Even so, most of the houses have a "North Carolina look" as well, and a very distinctive look you will find it to be on further acquaintance.

To facilitate this acquaintance, we have arranged the order of the localities here so as to cover the more fruitful regions of the state. As you spot the areas on your road map, you will find that they fit into an orderly progression for both the Tidewater and the Piedmont houses—a progression which can readily be revised to suit the direction you are taking.

People who plan to take a thoughtful and appreciative look at early North Carolina houses will be grateful, we believe, for our suggestion that they first go to the nearest good public library and consult *The Early Architecture of North Carolina,* by the late Thomas T. Waterman, with fabulous photographs by Frances Benjamin Johnston. Few colonial states have been documented in such a scholarly fashion and so beautifully.

THE TIDEWATER HOUSES

¶ *In & out of Edenton*

At the first architecturally outstanding Tidewater town on the way down the coast, be sure to see ST. PAUL'S CHURCH (1736) and the CHOWAN COUNTY COURT HOUSE (1767), said to have had the largest paneled room in the colonies. And while HAYES PLANTATION (1789–1801), a private home on the outskirts of town, is not open, it is only fair to acknowledge its presence, for it is one of the truly distinguished Tidewater mansions of North Carolina.

Contact Mr. and Mrs. Leland G. Plant to learn which Edenton houses may be visited. Note that of the fifteen houses listed, twelve are private homes, open by appointment (through the *Guide*). There is also Edenton's biennial

The Cupola House merits a long look, for you will see nothing else quite like it in the South.

spring tour, usually in April (but check the date with the Edenton Women's Club, with headquarters in the Barker House).

CUPOLA HOUSE (*c. 1712*)
South Broad Street; daily, 10 to 12 and 3 to 5; 25 cents; Cupola House Association.

This has been called one of the most striking essays in the Jacobean style in America. What extraordinary character it has, with its corbelled overhangs and massive brick chimneys, crowned with its splendid cupola! To see the original paneling of the lower floor, you will have to go to the Brooklyn Museum in New York.

JAMES IREDELL HOUSE (*1759*)
East Church Street; State of North Carolina.

The Iredell House is furnished with English pieces, as it must have been by its original owner, Justice Iredell, appointed by Washington. Visitors are conducted by guides supplied by the D.A.R.

PAXTON HOUSE (*c. 1790*)
West King Street; 50 cents; Dr. and Mrs. Frank Wood.

Built by Samuel Butler, it is being restored.

ELLISON HOUSE (*date unknown*)
106 West King Street; Mrs. Fred P. Wood.

EDMUND HATCH HOUSE (*1744*)
East King Street; 50 cents; Mr. and Mrs. J. W. Davis.

LITTLEJOHN HOUSE (*1769*)
218 West Eden Street; 50 cents; Mr. and Mrs. T. C. Bynum, Sr.

The Ellison House, built by Robert Lemax and confiscated during the Revolution, is furnished with American and English antiques, as are the Hatch House and the Littlejohn House, which has lovely paneling.

PENELOPE BARKER HOUSE (*1782*)
Edenton Women's Club, Business and Professional Women's Club, and Junior Chamber of Commerce; Mr. and Mrs. Leland G. Plant.

Here we have the reconstruction of a fine place built by Thomas Barker, London Agent for the colony before the Revolution. His wife Penelope presided over the Edenton Tea Party of October 25, 1744, the first known occasion when ladies took part in colonial politics. The house has been moved to the waterfront. It will be a community center, and visitors must be accompanied by a member.

ALBANIA (*date unknown*)
West Queen Street; 50 cents;
Mrs. M. G. Brown.

Furnished with American and English antiques, it belonged to Dr. Edward Warren, Confederate Surgeon General of the state, a gentleman who usually added to his name the title of "Bey," once conferred on him by the Khedive of Egypt.

BOOTH HOUSE (*c. 1756*)
108 North Granville Street; by appointment; 50 cents; Edenton Tea Party Chapter, D.A.R.

The Booth house, with its four dormers, is faintly reminiscent of the Moore house at the battlefield of Yorktown. The wainscoted living room, with its paneled mantel, is of heart pine. There is an unusual Chippendale stairway, and the authentic period furniture has been well chosen.

PEMBROKE HALL (*1841*)
121 West King Street; 50 cents;
Col. and Mrs. William B. Rosevear.

This place was built by the same Josiah Collins who built "Somerset," down the coast. His great-granddaughter has recently restored the house and furnished it with many of the pieces he brought with him from England.

SYCAMORE (*prior to 1775*)
Albemarle Sound; Mr. Grayson H. Harding.

This typical plantation dwelling of the early period was in the Norcom family for over two hundred years and still retains its original floors, paneling, and mantels.

GREENFIELD (*c. 1752*)
Albemarle Sound; Mrs. George Collins Wood.

Also on the sound, and also typical of the Albemarle pre-Revolutionary plantation houses, "Greenfield" is famous for genera-

One of the oldest and most attractive is Booth house in a town that has more than its share.

tions of hospitality and for its fine double galleries.

MULBERRY HILL (*1784*)
5 miles out on Albemarle Sound;
Mr. and Mrs. Thomas B. Wood.

Nearby is this distinguished four-story brick house, unusual in this section and somewhat like the Smallwood-Ward House in New Bern. The west gable contains a window with a five-foot radius, made from a single piece of wood. The delicate detail is lovely.

CLEMENT HALL (*c. 1758*)
Route 32, 1 mile from town;
Mr. and Mrs. W. P. Bond.

This out-of-town plantation was originally owned back in 1744 by the rector of St. Paul's, whose wife and daughter both attended the Edenton Tea Party.

BANDON (*c. 1790*)
Route 32, 15 miles up the Chowan River;
Mr. and Mrs. John G. Fletcher.

Still further out of town on the Chowan River is one of the prize homes of this locale. Three of its dependencies still stand, one of which was a boys' school dating back to 1754. The house itself, built by a Senator Johnson during Jefferson's administration, is lovely both inside and out—a work of connoisseurs.

SOMERSET (*1830*)
Pettigrew State Park, Routes 172 and 64 via Creswell; daily, 8 to 5; state of North Carolina.

Now in process of restoration, "Somerset" once looked out on its private race track, where tournaments were held. It is the kind of house that recalls the days when Southern knighthood was in flower.

¶ New Bern

This is the town that was settled in 1711 by an expedition of Swiss Palatines under the leadership of Baron de Graffenried, though nothing but the name remains of that ill-fated attempt at colonization. The oldest houses now standing were built more than a half century after all landmarks of the departed Swiss had disappeared. Where the streets of early houses remain reasonably undisturbed,

Greenfield is typical of the plantation houses that commanded vast lands on lovely Albemarle Sound when the area was beginning to be settled.

The plantation owner of Mulberry Hill must have liked the town houses he visited in New Bern and ordered his to be built like them.

they have great charm and character.

Contact Mrs. Bess Hyman Guion, 311 Johnson Street, for all New Bern houses; when it comes to old homes in New Bern, she is the "last word." She is the person to see for information on the two-day tour, held usually the first week in April. Tickets include guides if you wish. Of the private homes listed below, only five will be open simultaneously— Monday through Friday, 10 to 12 and 2 to 5.

The fee of 50 cents each is for the benefit of the New Bern Historical Society.

TAYLOR-WARD HOUSE
(*prior to 1800*)
228 Craven Street; Mr. and Mrs. William F. Ward.

The Taylor-Ward House has a tall, trim brick town-house exterior and a stylish interior that is uncommonly warm and friendly. It has an elaborately carved master bedroom which was formerly an upstairs drawing room, as in the Charleston mansions, as well as beautiful furniture and mellow coloring.

LIVELY-VAIL-MOULTON HOUSE
(*1776*)
519 East Front Street; Mrs. Celia Lively.

One of the four fine houses along Front Street, known as "Louisiana House" because of its double galleries which were introduced here, as elsewhere, by English planters and American artisans who had sojourned in Barbados.

SMALLWOOD-WARD HOUSE (*1810*)
534 East Front Street; Mr. and Mrs. David L. Ward.

Thought by many to be the best of the New Bern Late Georgian brick houses, its handsome interiors are furnished with respect and affection.

JARVIS-HAND HOUSE (*1810*)
East Front at Johnson Street.

Exquisitely carved woodwork and spacious proportions.

FULSHIRE-IVES HOUSE (*1775*)
211 Johnson Street; Mr. and Mrs. G. Allen Ives.

With its dog trot and old kitchen at the rear, it is furnished with antiques, including lighting fixtures dating back to 1860 and still in use.

HOLLISTER-SWAN HOUSE (*1840*)
George and Broad Streets; Mr. and Mrs. Hugh Swan.

Owned and occupied by the same family for five generations, it is furnished with family pieces.

BRYAN-ASHFORD HOUSE (*1802*)
605 Pollock Street; Dr. and Mrs. Charles H. Ashford.

This home has rare rosewood folding doors and Sheffield silver knobs, as well as some

The Smallwood-Ward house represents the tall brick New Bern style at its peak.

The arched recesses in the dining room of the Smallwood-Ward contain identical tables, mirrors, and candelabra. Note the cornice and rope molding below the chair rail.

fine pieces of early furniture. The adjoining doctor's office (formerly a law office) was a common feature here in New Bern.

TRYON'S PALACE (*1767–1770*)
George Street.

Now being reconstructed, it will be described in subsequent editions of the *Guide.*

¶ In & out of Wilmington

Considering how numerous and noble the great early plantation and town houses were hereabouts, it is a pity that so few still stand. You can tell from the Greek Revival BELLAMY MANSION (1859) at Fifth and Market Streets, and from the Federal-style DUDLEY MANSION (1830–1835) at Front and Nun Streets, what a lot of early Wilmington was like.

CORNWALLIS HOUSE (*1771*)
224 Market Street; Tuesday through Friday, 10 to 1; 50 cents and 25 cents; North Carolina Society of Colonial Dames.

This fine white weather-boarded mansion, with superimposed colonnaded porches, a Palladian doorway, and elegant interiors beautifully restored and furnished, was where the British commander made his residence prior to the Battle of Yorktown. With its garden and dependencies now all refurbished, this is one of the most fascinating houses in the state.

The drawing room in the Cornwallis House has a sumptuous severity which is emphasized in the furnishings.

ORTON PLANTATION (*1725–1840*)
> *4 miles west on Route 17, then 14 miles on Cape Fear River Road; house on occasion, gardens any time; January through April $1.50, May through December $1.00.*

The road following the river out of town, along which the Barbadians tried their best to colonize in the 1660s, was once lined with fine plantation houses; now Orton alone is left. It has rather outgrown its original form, though the present mansion is an impressive remodeling made in the Greek Revival period. The house is open only on occasion, but it may be seen at any time from the azalea gardens, which are one of the famous sights of the South.

THE PIEDMONT HOUSES

Whereas the houses of the Tidewater sections show clear signs of having been influenced by the work of New England craftsmen, or even actually built by New England carpenters brought in by the sailing-ship trade, the architecture in the foothill section of the great expanse of the Piedmont derived its form and fashion, as indicated above, from builders who came by land from Virginia, Maryland, Pennsylvania, and other regions in the North.

❡ *Between Halifax & Warrenton*

Aficionados will find this forty-odd-mile stretch of country rewarding for its numerous minor (and some not so minor) early houses with Virginia mannerisms— some of stylistic distinction, some of romantic regional charm, and some hardly more than empty shells of bygone beauty. There is no largesse here of well-preserved elegance and fine furnishing, but there is plenty of the past. Many of these souvenirs are rapidly disappearing, however, so hurry!

CONSTITUTION HOUSE
(*prior to 1776*)
> *Halifax; on request to custodian in house opposite; 25 cents to D.A.R.*

This small clapboard building with its fine doorways and the outside brick chimneys characteristic of this area was the place where, on April 12, 1776, the famous Halifax Resolves—the first official action of any colonial legislature for national independence—were drawn up.

PROSPECT HILL (*1825–1827*)
> *Near Airlie 20 miles out via Routes 461 and 48.*

It may already be too late to see more than the imposing exterior of "Prospect Hill," one of the "giants" of North Carolina: as we wrote this, the woodwork was being removed and taken "up North."

While in the Airlie neighborhood, inquire about the WILLIAMS-MACON HOUSE (1825) and the graceful THORNE HOUSE of the same period.

MOSBY HALL (*1774*)
> *Route 158 near Littleton 10 miles up Route 48 from Airlie; on request; voluntary contribution for restoration; William Thomas Skinner II, Linden Hall.*

Originally called "Little Manor," it "shows some ravages of time and vandalism," as the owner acknowledges, but there is a wealth of interior woodwork, plasterwork, and marble, detailed with great delicacy. It is unfurnished. But Mr. Skinner, a descendant of the builder, who lives in nearby Linden Hall (1840–1844), which was part of the same colonial grant, tells us that Linden Hall is furnished with such heirlooms as have survived fires and wars.

Also nearby is the OLD ORDINARY, restored by the Colonial Dames. It has entertained many distinguished personalities, including Lafayette, Horace Greeley, and Aaron Burr—and you will no doubt find it entertaining yourself.

In the neighborhood of Warrenton, about ten miles west on Route 158, you can see clearly how choice this area must have been, for among the many "ghosts" there are some houses still being kept up and occupied: for example, ELGIN and the COLEMAN-WHITE-JONES, both of the 1830s. It is too late now in this area to demand the spectacular, though it did exist, as you can see in the Johnston-Waterman book and by observing the "MONTMORENCI" (1825) interiors, some of which are now in the Winterthur Museum in Delaware.

❡ Raleigh

JOEL LANE HOUSE (*1760*)
728 West Hargett Street; any time; Wake Society of Colonial Dames.

A pleasant early gambrel type styled very much in the Virginia manner, this was the home of a famous pre-Revolutionary family of pioneer settlers. It was the best for a

hundred miles around when erected. It was here that Raleigh was chosen to be the permanent capital, Lane donating the whole site of the present city.

ANDREW JOHNSON HOUSE (*c. 1802*)
Pullen Park; daily, 2 to 5; donation; city of Raleigh.

This humble dwelling, in which the President was born, is tiny, with only one window downstairs in the front and one dormer in the gambrel roof. Johnson's father was hostler and janitor at the inn; his mother, known as "Polly the Weaver," did all the weaving at the inn. Johnson himself started as a tailor. The house is furnished simply as its first humble occupants must have furnished it.

HAYWOOD HALL (*1793*)
211 New Bern Avenue; Mr. and Mrs. Walter Stearns.

Built by the great-grandfather of the present owner in the year following the establishment of Raleigh as the capital, this handsome white clapboard house has unusual delicacy of carving and paneling, and a

Haywood Hall, always lived in by the same family, is destined to become one of the most engaging house museums in the country.

wealth of heirloom furnishings. The two-story porch with its slender fluted columns is as graceful and appealing as they come. Its owners have willed it complete to the North Carolina Society of Colonial Dames as a house museum, a future for which it is admirably fitted.

¶ Out of Durham

DUKE HOMESTEAD (*1851*)

> *Route 501, 3 miles north; Sundays 2:30 to 5, April 1 to October 1; other times call Durham 9011, extension 328; Duke University.*

This tiny house stands on the tobacco farm on which the modern tobacco industry was born. After Appomattox, J. B. Duke walked one hundred and thirty-seven miles back to his Piedmont home with a working capital of two blind army mules and fifty cents—the foundation of a fantastic fortune. The six-room pine-board house is furnished just as it must have been then.

FAIRNTOSH PLANTATION (*1799–1804*)

> *12 miles north off Route 501; on written request; Mr. and Mrs. John W. La Bouisse, Bahama R.F.D. 1.*

In contrast, this mansion still has much of its original furniture. Built by Judge Duncan Cameron, it was at one time the manor of a 30,000-acre plantation. The house appears today exactly as it was when built, of heart pine cut on the place. The family chapel, school house, slave cabins, office, and other dependencies are still standing, as is the great-grandfather's house (1740), nearby on the estate.

¶ In & out of Hillsborough

Mrs. T. E. Lloyd, Margaret Lane, Hillsborough (phone 4395), has compiled for the *Guide* this list of homes from which at least three will be shown to visitors upon request, and more if desired; one has a very fine garden. Address her or the Garden Club for information on the tour. Hillsborough had an "open house" in 1953 to celebrate its two hundredth anniversary.

There are many old houses in Hillsborough that are famous locally and full of interest, though few lay claim to magnificence. For the most part frame, these homes have a simplicity and character that is typical of much North Carolina building before 1800. AYR MOUNT, a stately brick affair, is an exception here, but MOORFIELDS, with its rare Chinese Chippendale staircase, is otherwise an unpretentious house. Both can be seen only on the annual tour. The latter was the birthplace of Thomas Hart Benton, the painter. A program sponsored by the Julian S. Carr Chapter of the United Daughters of the Confederacy is under way for reconstructing the BENNETT HOUSE here, where Generals Johnston and Sherman met to agree on surrender terms. Only its foundations and the great chimney remain.

LLOYD HOME (*1754*)

> *50 cents; Mr. and Mrs. T. E. Lloyd.*

The pre-Revolutionary Lloyd House is the one remaining wing of the summer home of colonial Governor Tryon, who journeyed here to escape the heat of the New Bern summers.

NASH-HOOPER HOUSE (*1772*)

> *50 cents; Mr. and Mrs. H. H. Brown.*

Home of the Revolutionary hero for whom Nashville, Tennessee, was named, and later the residence of William Hooper, a signer of the Declaration, it contains some fine furniture.

NASH-MOORE HOME (*1790*)

> *50 cents; Dr. and Mrs. H. W. Moore.*

SANS SOUCI (*prior to 1800*)

> *Mr. and Mrs. Samuel Latta, Jr.*

Somewhat more elaborate is the carefully restored Moore Home, while "Sans Souci," on its hilltop is a delightful small-scale manor house, reminiscent of early Virginia. With its steep roof, dormers, and chimneys, it has some very neat interior detail as well.

COLONIAL INN (*1781*)

Comfortably restored recently and open to guests.

J. L. CONNERS HOME (*prior to 1830*)
50 cents; Mr. and Mrs. J. L. Conners.
Once a tavern and stagecoach stop, it has random-width pine paneling in every room.

¶ *Winston-Salem*

The interest here is mainly in "Old Salem," the ancient Moravian part of the present city, established in 1753 by a band of Moravian brethren from Bethlehem, Pennsylvania. The architecture bears a marked resemblance to the Moravian buildings in that and other Pennsylvania towns, though stylistically it is more English than German. A restoration project of some magnitude is now under way. Of the planned community of sixty houses which stood here in the late 1700s, forty remain, most of them still in use. Ten or twelve public buildings still stand too. The whole section is a unique survival of an early American communal venture. Architectural direction for the restoration comes from the same Boston office that designed and directed the Williamsburg restorations. Even at this stage there is much to see. A regular tour can be arranged any time through Miss Jane Carter, Old Salem,

Inc., HEADQUARTERS HOUSE, 614 South Main Street. At Easter there is always a three-day tour which includes the lovely Moravian Dawn Service.

LICK BONER BLOCK HOUSE AND BOYS' SCHOOL (*1787*)
512 South Liberty Street.
These are now complete, the former a very fine log house with two rooms furnished, the latter a museum.

JOHN VOGLER HOUSE (*1819*)
Open to public.
A fine restoration of a typical brownstone dwelling, this home is furnished with the articles and furniture made here at the time. These houses have a special simple style, having been built by good craftsmen who obviously wanted to make them handsome as well as sturdy. The German influence is strong.

ADAM SPACH HOUSE (*1754*)
Open to public.
This fortresslike home, built of uncut stone laid without mortar, is a gem.

THE FOURTH HOUSE (*1768*)
Not open at present; Colonial Dames.
The oldest in Salem, this was the first house restored (1940). It received its name from being the fourth to be built in the community. It is occupied at present by tenants and will be open in due course.

The Lick Boner block house with its gun ports shows that the Moravians had to think first of protection when they arrived here.

BELO HOUSE (*1849*)
455 South Main Street; not open.

Not open now either, but well worth looking at from the street. Quite a magnificent affair of the Classical Revival, with Corinthian porticoes and much remarkable ironwork from the old Belo Foundry, it is in another key entirely.

¶ In & out of Charlotte

This region covers considerable territory and merits careful advance planning, correspondence where necessary, and a good road map. There is a tour in Huntersville in May sponsored by the Alexandriana Chapter of the D.A.R., and Charlotte conducts a garden tour in October. Write to the chamber of commerce.

ROSEDALE (*c. 1780*)
3427 North Tryon Avenue; not open at present but may be later; Mrs. Craighead Davidson.

HEZEKIAH ALEXANDER HOUSE (*1774*)
On grounds of Methodist Home, 6 miles out on Shamrock Road; Sunday afternoon; 25 cents; Mrs. Benjamin Wyche; Five Chapters of Charlotte Daughters of American Revolution.

It is called the "Rock House"—and you can see why. This fine solid stone dwelling was the home of a signer of the Mecklenburg Declaration of Independence (1755), and has been well restored and furnished.

POTTS HOUSE (*1811*)
Cornelius, 5 miles from Huntersville; on request; $1.50; Mr. and Mrs. Clifton Eugene Smith.

Built of hand-hewn logs pegged together and clapboarded, this enchanting little house is preserved in its original state and with most of its original furnishings, made expressly for Robert Potts, its first owner, whose descendants are still here.

CEDAR GROVE (*1831*)
3 miles west of Huntersville and 15 miles north of Charlotte; phone request (Charlotte exchange); Mr. and Mrs. R. T. Banks.

To the north of Charlotte, this unusual brick house with stepped-gable shoulders has much carved-walnut woodwork by Jacob Stirewalt, an architect of local fame, and a three-flight "unsupported" spiral staircase. The hall is forty feet long. The wine cellar and rock stables are still intact. It is gradually being restored, and is well worth it.

ZEB VANCE HOUSE (*c. 1840*)
501 West Sharpe Street, Statesville, 44 miles north of Charlotte by Route 21; Wednesday or on request to caretaker; voluntary fee; United Daughters of Confederacy.

The home of the Civil War Governor of that name, it is furnished in keeping with his position and period.

MILL HILL (*1821*)
Concord, 12 miles out, 24 miles north on Alternate Route 29; spring and summer by appointment; $1.00; Mr. and Mrs. Jacob Stirewalt, IV, R.D. No. 2.

Jacob Stirewalt, an early North Carolina architect and cabinetmaker of talent and ingenuity, designed and built this house for himself. The lines are traditional, but he gave it, out of pure romantic impulse, a charming full-length Doric porch. He also made most of the furniture, as well as a violin, a piano, and a wooden organ—all still in the house.

FOR PITY'S SAKE (*1850*)
Off Route 29, 5 miles above Kannapolis, and 35 miles north of Charlotte (ask directions when making appointment); on request; $1.00 for benefit of Elizabethan Herb Garden at Manteo, Roanoke Island; Mr. and Mrs. Charles H. Cannon.

Another Stirewalt house, this one built by Jacob's son Jacob, Jr. The owner is president of the North Carolina Society for the Preservation of Antiquities and is now growing an herb garden for the blind; so both house and garden are of special interest.

KISTLER-JONAS HOUSE (*1826*)
Lincolnton; by appointment; Mr. and Mrs. C. R. Jonas.

The brickwork in this fine four-story town house is most unusual. The cornice is four bricks thick, alternately convex and concave. The outer brick walls are twenty-four inches thick. The wooden construction of the interior is of heart pine, still in perfect condition, and the woodwork is beautifully ornamented. Interesting metal shields serving as covers for the drainpipes bear the date 1826.

OLD STONE HOUSE *or* MICHAEL BRAUN HOUSE (*1766*)

6 miles east off Route 29 at Salisbury, 43 miles above Charlotte, and 1½ miles northeast of granite quarry; daily; contribution; the Brown family (see caretaker next door).

This fine early-Pennsylvania-style stone house has a lot of solid-walnut woodwork. "It is not really prepared for public enjoyment," says the owner, but it may be ready by the time you read this.

INGLESIDE (*1817*)

Alexis on Route 1, 17 miles east of Lincolnton, 32 miles above Charlotte; by appointment; Mr. and Mrs. David Clark, Lincolnton.

A brick mansion of considerable distinction, with a heroic portico, said to have been designed by Benjamin Latrobe. It has some very fine plasterwork inside. It is not furnished at present, but is in otherwise perfect condition.

VESUVIUS FARM (*1792*)

Lincolnton; on request at owners' convenience; Mr. and Mrs. B. C. Lineberger, Sr.

The birthplace of Gov. William Graham, who was also Secretary of the Navy under Filmore and a senator as well, was built by his father the general, who established one of the earliest iron furnaces in the area in 1790. The house has been restored and is somewhat changed. It is not furnished with antiques.

¶ *Other houses here & there*

CREEKSIDE (*c. 1835*)

Morgantown; anytime at owners' convenience; 50 cents; Mr. and Mrs. Harry Ariail Boggs.

This fine brick Classical Revival house, which Waterman calls "the most monumental in the Piedmont," is the showplace of its period and region. Built here toward the western part of the state by Col. Thomas George Walton, whose granddaughter occupies it now with her family,

it is beautifully furnished with pieces purchased in Philadelphia and Charleston. Many of the originals were destroyed during the Civil War but have now been painstakingly replaced with replicas. This place cannot fail to be the high spot in a trip covering this area.

CLOVER HALL, *formerly* CLOVER HILL (*1841*)

Route 5 near Lenoir, Caldwell County; on request by phone (Plaza 4-5461); Mr. and Mrs. Palmer D. Kountze (Mr. Glenn Collis, caretaker).

This fine old brick manor house in Happy Valley was up for sale at the time of writing, so it would be well to inquire of the caretaker. Or maybe you will be the one who buys it. If you do, let us know if it may be looked at by readers of the *Guide*.

HOUSE IN THE HORSESHOE (*1760*)

Route 15–501 near Carthage on eastern edge of Uharie National Forest; state of North Carolina and Society for Prevention of Cruelty to Animals.

This place has a dramatic Revolutionary history and is interesting architecturally. An important restoration is now under way.

SHAW HOUSE (*prior to 1862*)

Southern Pines; Southern Pines Garden Club and Moore County Historical Association.

WOODFIELD'S INN (*1850*)

Flat Rock; June 1 to October 1.

NU-WRAY INN (*1833*)

Burnsville near Mt. Mitchell; any time.

In the scenic western part of the state, both of these inns attempt with considerable success to preserve an authentic early atmosphere. Woodfield's Inn, a Victorian building, is virtually unchanged outside. The Nu-Wray Inn serves all meals except Sunday supper.

BILTMORE HOUSE (*1895*)

Biltmore, near Asheville; Biltmore estate.

The Vanderbilt version of "Chambord" and "Blois," designed by the famous Beaux Arts architect, Richard M. Hunt, who also did "The Breakers" in Newport and many others. There is everything here that money can buy.

This entrance gate is one of many that contribute to the charms of Charleston. On the facing page is Rose Hill, an Up Country plantation house which became the home of the Confederate Governor Gist. Its broad fanlighted doors open onto iron-railed galleries in a portico of more than usual elegance.

South Carolina

HEN English King Charles II gave Sir John Colleton, a Barbados planter, carte blanche to form a colony on this low-lying coast—whose boundaries then appear to have been as ill-defined as the landscape of the moon —his Carolinian name had already been attached to the territory in honor of the French King Charles IX. But the first band of Huguenot refugees had been murdered by the Spanish, who had earlier renounced the area as unprofitable.

Of Colleton's West Indian planters who settled on the Cape Fear River no trace remains. Of the Spanish influence only an occasional house of tabby shows any sign. But later waves of immigration from both England and Barbados and later settlements of Huguenots began to establish a wealthy and distinctive society. Of course, Charles-Town was its center, attracting trade because of its location and attracting successful planters from their malarial rice plantations to spend the summers in the healthy Atlantic breezes. From the beginning it was destined to be a brilliant center of society for the leisured and pleasure-loving.

"State, magnificence and ostentation, the natural attendance of riches, are conspicuous among this people: the number and subjection of their slaves tend this way," said Josiah Quincy, a Bostonian who visited the Brewton Mansion in 1773. He speaks too of their chief occupation as "cards, dice, the bottle and horses." But Josiah was a Puritan, of course.

In such a society of wealth and leisure, little wonder that the houses designed for hospitality, elegance, and spaciousness should constitute, as a group, the finest perhaps in the whole country. Of the opulent rice and indigo plantations built in the early days there are relatively few survivals. While there is, possibly, a typical Low Country plantation style of building, as at MARSHLANDS on the Cooper, at SEABROOK on Edisto Island, HARRIETTA near Hampden, and PALMETTO HALL, near Frogmore—tall, porticoed houses, whose high living floors defy dampness, still far more Georgian in character than West Indian—the sparse survivals are by no means all alike. For instance, MULBERRY on the Cooper, early and great, is a Jacobean brick house, square, with a pavilion at each corner, with roofs and cupolas like fanciful Chinese pagodas. Another deviation is medieval MEDWAY. DRAYTON HALL, on the banks of the Ashley, a few miles out of the present Charleston limits, is an equally magnificent, if less charming, brick dwelling, Georgian in feeling. Its flankers and gardens are only a memory, but its princely interior is intact and its manorial entrance hall is still fit for royalty. Of MIDDLETON PLACE only a restored wing of the original Jacobean mansion remains, but the great gardens open to the public illustrate well the inspired extravagance of these early American gentlemen. They sent to England, of course, for their landscape artists whose fluid work has survived better than the buildings which it was originally supposed to enhance.

This same variety of styles noted above may also be found in Charleston, whose builders were merchants as well as planters. Here the double house of William Gibbes, three stories of graceful whiteness, vies in distinction with the formidable brick pile of the MILES BREWTON HOUSE, with its truly splendid two-story portico. The somewhat later Federal mansions of the town show the same disparity of tastes, even though their interior ornament may stick to the Adam predilections of the day. For instance, compare the exterior of the MANINGAULT MANSION to the dignified and very formal brick dwelling of Nathaniel Russell, both of which may now be seen in their entirety at any time.

If there is a Charleston style, it must be a long narrow house with its gable end looking rather blankly at the street, with tiers of piazzas facing the side lawns which generally catch the prevailing breeze. These are three-storied, high-ceilinged houses, generous in proportions. But there are many other styles of building to be found in town and just as many more throughout the state. Perhaps the variety reflects the independent nature of the Low Countrymen, who established the right to have their say before the first boatload of them landed from England in 1669. The historian Samuel Stoney says that "upon its arrival, it was to hold a disputed election, even before it had come ashore." This set the tone for a people whose pride of place was to become paramount, whose sense of private rights has remained passionate, and who, therefore, have often been "a law unto themselves." These qualities have made for much freedom of choice in architecture, much of it bearing the stamp of splendor and intransigence. It makes for something worth looking at.

The history of the Up Country people, so opposite in most respects from their neighbors of the Low, has produced, as you might expect, fewer homes of architectural interest. The emphasis is on comfort, rather than elegance, for the most part. For a long time, the Up Country was a kind of stepchild of the state, not even possessing equal political rights. The descendants of the Scotch-Irish and Germans who settled inland were small farm holders, a poor people who had to be industrious and thrifty to "get along." Not until the introduction of the cotton gin did the cities of this section begin to develop and such towns as

Columbia, now the capitol, Cheraw, Winnsboro, etc., begin to thrive. Thus, since wealth came slow and hard, the domestic architecture, as elsewhere, reflects this condition.

The South Carolina House and Garden Tour, with headquarters at the Fort Sumter Hotel in Charleston, has the Beaufort, Cheraw, and Winnsboro Tours under its aegis. All have local headquarters, noted in place.

THE LOW COUNTRY

¶ In & out of Charleston

Charleston is one of the least spoiled cities in America. Age has only added to its transcendent charms. Many of its winding streets remain much as they were in the past and the houses, too, are little changed. The annual tour lasts a month, usually taking place around the middle of March, but it is timed to coincide with the blooming season when the world-famous gardens of Magnolia, Middleton, and Cypress are gorgeous with color. The tours are arranged to leave afternoons free to enjoy the gardens, the countryside, or the town itself. They are scheduled for leisurely pleasure, to be taken at your own pace, the program changing each week to include different houses. All arrangements and information will be supplied by the Historic Charleston Foundation, the sponsor. There is nothing quite like Charleston and for lovers of old houses and beautiful furniture the tour is "a must." The five houses regularly open plus those you will see on the tour will give you a well-rounded picture of the pomp and affluence that was Charleston.

On one of your forays into the country, get directions from the Foundation to find Goose Creek Chapel, a small baroque chapel tucked away in the

woods, a rare experience in a very different key.

MILES BREWTON HOUSE (*1769*)
> *27 King Street; daily except Sundays, Good Friday, and Christmas, 10 to 1 and 3 to 5; $1.00; Miss Susan Pringle Frost.*

One of the great Georgian houses of America, it is willed to the city by its owner, who personally shows the house with its many family heirlooms and mementos. The upstairs drawing room has recently been restored. Hanging from the painted center panel of the carved ceiling is one of the finest crystal chandeliers in the country, and there is a portrait of Miles Brewton by Sir Joshua Reynolds.

The magnificence of the Miles Brewton house façade hardly needs pointing out.

NATHANIEL RUSSELL HOUSE (1807)

51 Meeting Street; any time; variable fee; Historic Charleston Foundation.

One of the outstanding examples in the country of Adam design and decoration, it served magnificently as a private home until 1955, when it began to serve equally magnificently as a museum house and headquarters of the Charleston Historic Foundation. The tall brick house has been immaculately preserved, and in it you will find mantels and paneling of incredible delicacy, and, as time goes on, there will be more and more furnishings to match. An extraordinary staircase that appears to sweep up in a free-floating curve to the hall above is a chef-d'oeuvre of the joiners' art.

MANINGAULT HOUSE (c. 1800)

350 Meeting Street; daily, 10 to 2; 50 cents; Charleston Museum.

This museum house is an Adam town mansion of considerable acclaim, built in the

prosperous post-Revolutionary era. The wide two-story piazzas follow the curves of the brick house walls in a way that is flamboyantly Maningault. There is an enormous ballroom on the third floor, and a lot of the carved woodwork throughout the house is first rate, but the fine place is sadly in need of a face lifting that only money can buy.

HEYWARD-WASHINGTON HOUSE (1770)

87 Church Street; daily, 10 to 2; 50 cents; Charleston Museum of Art.

This earlier and more austere house, which the period perfectionists here have been restoring with the utmost skill and care under the direction of Mr. Milby Burton, curator of the museum, can now be seen in all its original colors. It is furnished much as it must have been the day President Washington received a delegation of Charleston ladies in the downstairs drawing room in front of the stylish mantelpiece paneling. Washington's host, Thomas Heyward, was a signer of the Declaration, and this finely proportioned brick house he built is one of the older beauties of the town.

SWORD GATE HOUSE (1776)

32 Legare Street; daily, 10 to 1 and 3 to 5; $1.00; Mr. and Mrs. Henry T. Gand.

The wrought-iron gateway to the grounds here is a Charleston showpiece (others to note are at 23 Legare Street, 83 Pitt Street, and at 14 Green Street). And don't by any means overlook the house itself. The ornate ballroom, all gold and white, is worth a long look.

ASHLEY HALL (1816)

172 Rutledge Street; daily, hall and parlor only.

A superb Regency villa whose parlors, hallway, and spectacular spiral staircase can be seen. The beautifully bizarre portico with its recessed porch is one of the most splendid sights of the city. The interior furnishings are appropriate, and the delightful little park in which this villa-

The formality and stateliness of certain English town houses is called to mind by the Nathaniel Russell house.

The woodwork throughout the Russell house is considered among the finest examples of Adam in the country. The furniture shown here belonged to the former owner.

turned-school stands is tropically exotic.

Other outstanding private homes (usually all open on tour), as described by Samuel Stoney, are:

THOMAS ROSE'S HOUSE (c. 1735)
59 Church Street.

"His unsymmetrical floor plan is almost unaltered. His large, dignified panels, robust cornices, and other simple Early Georgian decorations are nearly as he left them. A delicate little Adam mantel was evidently placed in the drawing room as a "modernization" at the beginning of the nineteenth century, but this adds a touch that is rather charming.

"Though most of the things in it might fit well in a museum, it is still happily a home. Thus you will find furnishings from a number of countries, ages, and styles, all combining to enhance its beauty.

"A magnificent Tabriz animal carpet dating from the late fifteenth or early sixteenth century now gives the drawing room a golden glow. This is emphasized by window hangings carefully suited to the period of the house. These, together with its superb furnishings and pictures, make this one of the most distinguished rooms in Charleston. It is owned by Mr. and Mrs. Henry P. Staats."

CAPERS-HUGER SMITH (c. 1745)
69 Church Street.

"When this old house was still a shell-torn wreck from the bombardment of the Civil War, it was purchased by Mrs. William Mason Smith. Her children and grandchildren have lived here ever since and most evidently cherished it. It was, and is still, one of Charleston's earliest and handsomest examples of the large double house.

"The Smiths' old and beautiful furniture fills these rooms amply and delightfully with a fine history of the family's good taste. Miss Alice R. Huger Smith, the noted watercolorist, lives here now."

BRANFORD-HORRY (c. 1751)
59 Meeting Street.

"Built so strongly and beautifully that in an architectural survey it was classified as 'of national importance,' this house contains some of the most impressive woodwork in Charleston. The cypress paneling and the carved tulip and mahogany in the upstairs drawing room, freed of paint and rubbed down to the finest finish, are some of the architectural delights in a city where they are manifold. It has been beautifully restored and furnished with many local and some English pieces by the owners, Mr. and Mrs. Percy Kammerer."

GEORGE EVELEIGH'S HOUSE
(c. 1738)
39 Church Street.

"George Eveleigh was a wealthy Charlestonian whose agents bartered British goods to the Indians of the Southeast for the thousands of deerskins that were then shipped to Europe.

"The rooms are splendidly paneled with wide cypress boards brought in from the Low Country swamps. Here also Adam mantels have replaced the originals. As in most old Charleston houses, the drawing room is on the second floor. Here it gives a deceptively spacious effect by taking up the entire front of a comparatively small house.

"For many years this house has been the home of Miss Mary O. Marshall. Much of her furniture was made in Charleston, and most of it has served many generations of her kindred."

COL. JOHN STUART'S (1772)
106 Tradd Street.

"This house, with its dignified facing of shiplap weatherboarding that still carries one of the old insurance plaques under a third-story window, as well as some of the most imaginatively carved decoration in the city, represents the peak of Georgian design in this part of the world.

"About a score of years ago the woodwork from the two principal rooms was sold to the Kansas City Museum of Fine Arts. Shortly after this the celebrated architect, John Mead Howells, made this his winter home and restored most exactly the fine paneling and beautiful carving. Mr. Howells added the garden wall and redesigned the Victorian west wing so as to be more in keeping with the body of the house. It is now the residence of Mr. and Mrs. John D. Wing."

WILLIAM GIBBES (c. 1772)
64 South Battery.

"This splendid mansion, built at the height of Charleston's Georgian period, was ex-tensively redecorated again in the midst of her craze for Adam decor. The result is both extraordinarily distinguished and pleasing. The present owner's fine furniture, in addition to this, makes it one of the handsomest houses in the city.

"The house was started soon after 1772 by William Gibbes. The Ashley River then came up to the opposite side of the street. Gibbes had a long wharf running out to its channel on which he conducted his business. The wharf had another most agreeable function: in hot weather a place of 'genteel entertainment' used to be set up at its far end, where Charlestonians might partake of both the cooling air and some light refreshment.

"In the 1930s Mrs. Washington A. Roebling, widow of the builder of the Brooklyn Bridge, bought the house and made extensive restorations and alterations. For her collection of Oriental art and ceramics the southeast room on the principal floor was remodeled in the mode of Chinese Chippendale."

It is now the home of Mrs. Roebling's grandson Mr. John Ashby Farrow, and his wife, who allow it to be open during the whole month of the tours.

Other homes of almost equal interest which are often on the tour are: COL. WILLIAM RHETT'S HOUSE (1712), 54 Hasell Street; COL. OTHNIEL BEALE'S HOUSE (1740), 101 East Bay Street; THOMAS LEGARE'S HOUSE (c. 1760), 90 Church Street; and MRS. WILLIAM HAYWARD'S HOUSE (c. 1789), 31 Legare Street.

¶ Beaufort

An ancient seacoast town (dating from 1521), its sea breezes are laden with an aroma of the past, there is nothing else quite like it in the country, and five of its old private homes may be seen by appointment through the generous co-operation of their owners with the *Guide*. In addition to the listings below, what is now the LAFAYETTE BUILDING, or VERDIER HOUSE, an early 1795 Adamesque mansion of the Low Country plantation-house style, is in process of restoration, but the halls and ballroom (perhaps more by now) are exceptional, and may be seen any time. The Beaufort Museum has it in charge. Write to them or the Garden Club for information about the open house day in the West Low Country in the spring.

TABBY MANSE (*1768*)
1211 Bay Street; by appointment;
Misses Clara and Alma Greenwood.

This was the first house in Beaufort to be built along the Bluff, the summer location chosen by the rice planters for its sea breezes. It is one of the few tabby houses left in this section (tabby being a composition of crushed oyster shells). The house shows English influence, quite typical of the early Low Country plantations. Three of the rooms have their original paneled walls and hand-carved mantels. It is simply and artistically furnished.

SECESSION HOUSE (*1850s*)
1113 Craven Street; by appointment;
Mr. and Mrs. Claude McLeod.

They say the first draft of the Ordinance of Secession was drawn up here. Edmund Rhett, who built this house, was the brother of the United States Senator Rhett who was called the "Father of Secession." It was used as officers' quarters during the occupation by the Union Army. Architecturally it is an imposing town mansion with double porches and graceful iron stairs at either end. It is being (or has been) carefully restored and furnished by its new owners.

JOHNSON-DANNER HOUSE (*1850*)
411 Craven Street; by written or phone
(411) appointment, March, first floor and
garden only; Mr. and Mrs. Howard
Danner.

It was called "The Castle," meaning it appears, "The Castle of Indolence," a reference to its earlier and less energetic inmates. The massive house, showing a North Italian influence, but built by local artisans, has an interesting floor plan, a complete grid of solid brick walls on a cribwork of palmetto logs. The furniture is American antique and some contemporary. The interesting garden overlooking the sea was laid out by the first Mrs. Johnson and has been restored by the Danners. With the exception of the azaleas and camellias, the trees and shrubs were those planted in the 1850s, although they have been covered with salt water in many a storm.

Beaufort is an unspoiled town that attracts artists. Places like the Secession House create the dreamy atmosphere.

Another survival of plantation days is the McLeod house, presently the home of the mayor.

MC LEOD HOUSE (*c. 1813*)

> *Bay and Wilmington Streets, overlooking bay; by appointment, first floor only; Mayor and Mrs. Angus D. Fordham.*

A handsome town house built by a wealthy planter, John Joyner Smith, whose plantation was at Old Fort. There is no access to the front yard from the street (probably never has been) and this oddity is accompanied by a still greater one—namely a false doorway on the front of the house. Anything can happen in Beaufort! The plaster cornices and center medallions in the high-ceilinged rooms are ornate and beautiful.

PALMETTO HALL (*1790*)

> *Frogmore; by written appointment; Mr. and Mrs. W. H. Graham.*

Typical of the tall-built Low Country plantation houses, of which so few are left. The delicately carved mantels seem to be characteristic of the fine craftsmanship found in these earlier homes. Furnished throughout with antiques. Don't miss it.

¶ *Georgetown*

In the Low Country near Charleston, Georgetown is the heart of an old plantation country. No houses can be seen here except during the three-day tour in the latter part of March. The Woman's Auxiliary of Prince George Winyah Church sponsors it annually and will furnish information. It is not a guided trip, but maps and histories are furnished and you can go at your own pace. You will find the people hospitable.

It covers a day in the Santee River region, another in the Black and Pee Dee River country and Waccamaw; three dollars a day or eight for the three. In all there are about twenty houses shown, mostly typical plantation houses and some being lived in very much as they must have been a hundred years ago. Included are BROOK GREEN, BELLE ISLE GARDENS, and some churches.

The low marshy country, full of little lakes and reflecting ponds, grew rich on rice at one time. Now it has a singularly remote feeling; some of the places tucked away in the moss-hung trees are as if lost in a dream. Their names are evocative— CHICORA WOOD, RICE HOPE, BLACK RIVER HOUSE. Any of these tours provide an interesting contrast to the polished and urbane Charleston houses which you will naturally see if you are that near at this season. This was a comfortable country society where very large fortunes were not the rule. The tours offer a good picture of what life was like here when the plantations were all being cultivated.

But it may not last much longer, so see it before the machine age plows it under.

¶ McClellanville

This is somewhat more than halfway from Charleston to Georgetown (where the plantation tours are held in the spring) just off of coastal highway 17. "Belle Isle Gardens" are between here and Georgetown, and halfway between Georgetown and Myrtle Beach are "Brook Green Gardens." Both are worth a visit.

HAMPTON PLANTATION (1735)
Near McClellanville; any time; $1.00; Archibald Rutledge.

One of the most photogenic plantation houses in South Carolina, its portico cries out for the camera. The ballroom needs work, but what a room! And what a worthy cause toward which to make a contribution. Don't overlook the contribution box. Washington, who appeared to pick only the best, stayed here, and there is a Washington oak in the yard. The owner is poet laureate of South Carolina.

¶ Eutawville

Once prosperous indigo and then cotton and plantation country, many of the plantations hereabouts have been inundated by the waters of man-made Lake Marion.

THE ROCKS (1803)
6 miles east of Nelson Ferry Road, near Route 6; on request; Mr. and Mrs. J. Rutledge Connor.

This has been called the finest of the early plantations in this part of the state and is now one of the best maintained. Built for the most part of hand-hewn cypress, the woodwork within resembles that of the Nightingale House in Providence, though less ornate. The mantels may have come from New England. The house, which in 1942 was moved a mile from its former location because of the new lake, is of two-story, hip-roof design, with a portico supported by attenuated Tuscan columns.

UP COUNTRY

¶ In & out of Columbia

Almost exactly in the geographical center of the state and approached by highways from all directions, the capital city of South Carolina, an Up Country town, is close to the fall line of the Sand Hills and separates Up Country from Low. Many of Columbia's best early houses were burned when Sherman set fire to the city in 1865. There must have been considerable Charlestonian charm before that, for some of it has survived. Then, too, Robert Mills lived here through the 1820s, and one gets the feeling that this distinguished early American architect has left his mark here and there.

GOVERNOR'S MANSION (1855)
"800" block of Richland Street; usually daily, 11 to 12; state of South Carolina.

The "Mansion," which has been used by South Carolina governors since 1868, was originally the officers' quarters of the Arsenal Academy, all of which except this one building was burned by Union troops. The whole group may have been designed by Robert Mills. The austerity of the house is relieved by some gracious old ironwork. The interior architecture has a classic simplicity and several fine crystal chandeliers are noteworthy.

CRAWFORD-CLARKSON HOUSE (1842)
On request; contribution; Harriet J Clarkson.

The slender, square, metal-framed columns that line the iron steps leading up to the first-story portico are a surprising feature of this house, for they are faced with glass, forming tall hollow lanterns, which once used candles but are now fitted for electricity. The yellow frame house, with its flat copper roof, is raised above the ground by its brick basement. Within there are hand-stenciled wallpapers, much heirloom furniture, and atmosphere galore.

MIRACLE HILL (*c. 1815*)

1332 Pickens Street; any time; Mrs. Edwin G. Seibels.

The fact that it was built by a German botanist and entomologist, whose wife taught school in the little house next door, may account for many of its unusual qualities. The gardens are especially luxuriant, and early spring is definitely the time to see the house, as well as Columbia itself, at its best.

BOYHOOD HOME OF WOODROW WILSON (*1871–1874*)

Weekdays 9 to 5, Saturdays 9 to 12; state of South Carolina.

Built by Wilson's father, Dr. Joseph Ruggles Wilson, who was President of the Presbyterian Theological Seminary, it is a simple frame house with no pretensions, but very well maintained and furnished comfortably in its period, which is now beginning to benefit from the enrichment of time. The bed in which Wilson was born is here, also a desk and chair which he used while Governor of New Jersey.

What used to be the old Chicora College nearby was formerly the HALL-HAMPTON-PRESTON MANSION, attributed to Robert Mills, as was the Greek Revival DEBRUHL-MARSHALL HOUSE at 1401 Laurel. And another of the same vintage is the BOYLSTON HOUSE at 829 Richland. Strolling past these three places will pretty much round out your picture of Columbia's picturesque past.

¶ *Edgefield (on Routes 23 and 25 about 60 miles southwest of Columbia)*

OAKLEY PARK, RED SHIRT SHRINE (*c. 1835*)

Eastern edge of town between highways to Columbia and Augusta; Tuesdays and Fridays 9:30 to 11:30 and 3:30 to 5:30; voluntary fee; Edgefield Chapter, United Daughters of Confederacy.

Built by Daniel Byrd of Virginia, it was later the home of Gen. Martin W. Gary, who led a movement called "The Red Shirts" which sought to free the state of carpet-baggers and misrule in 1876. Recently the home of his nephew, John Gary Evans, a former Governor of South Carolina, it is still an impressive mansion, furnished in period, and serving now as a shrine to honor The Red Shirts.

¶ Winnsboro

On Route 218 twenty-three miles north of Columbia, containing a wonderful Robert Mills courthouse with double curving staircase embracing the portico. Write to the Garden Club about the tour in April.

WYNN DEE *or* THE OLD BRATTON PLACE (*1795*)

On request; Mr. and Mrs. Joe Cathcart.

A typical Up Country house of the early prosperous times, with many unusual details in its generally Adamesque decor. The chimney pieces are particularly fine. The old kitchen still stands in the yard, and in the cellar is the old cooling well "where many a morsel of food was kept." The builder was Richard Winn, a settler from Virginia, for whom Winnsboro was named.

HUNSTANTON, *formerly* SWEET BRIAR (*prior to 1820*)

Route 218, 2 miles south; on request at any reasonable time; Mr. and Mrs. C. E. Strange.

Houses raised off the ground on a high basement story used to be called "mosquito cottages," though "Hunstanton," with eighteen rooms, is hardly a cottage. The wide-spread portico across the front is approached from either side by flights of broad curving staircases of whitewashed brick. It is an impressive white house, handsomely furnished.

¶ Cheraw

Cheraw was settled by Philadelphians around 1820 (and many street names still attest the fact). Write to the Cheraw Garden Club about the tour here, usually in April.

LAFAYETTE HOUSE (1823)

235 Third Street; March, April, May, and on request, downstairs only; Mrs. Margaret A. Malloy (owner), Mr. and Mrs. Manning W. Malloy (occupants).

When Lafayette visited here in 1825, this is where they held the ball and reception, and you can see why. The balustraded residence, with its splendid white fence, was the largest in town. Built by Col. William Eberle, it was sold to Dr. Archibald Malloy in 1835 and is still in the family. The house has an odd plan—entrance halls on all four sides cross in the middle, and all the rooms open into the halls, but none into each other. The dining room, living room, formal parlor, and downstairs bedroom are all furnished in traditional pieces.

EDWIN MALLOY HOUSE (1825)

321 Third Street; on request at owners' convenience; variable fee; Mr. and Mrs. Edwin Malloy.

This house was built by Maj. M. H. Lazarus of Charleston. In 1940 the Malloys had it moved back from the street and it now sits in the midst of its lovely gardens with the original paths, walls, and slave quarters. It is furnished largely with antiques.

OLD MALLOY HOUSE (late 1700s)

219 Kershaw Street.

Oldest house in town, it may be seen outside only. Woodrow Wilson's father was often a guest here.

CHEROKEE INN (1833)

232 Market Street; any time on request; Henry Carter Harrall.

This sturdy brick house was designed by a Philadelphia architect and it is not hard to see its affinity to the houses of that period in the Quaker City. It was built for a banker and his family, the bank being housed there as well as the family. The present owner found a large supply of individually signed bank notes, mostly fivers, which he has been passing out liberally

Hunstanton is an unusual house to find in the Up Country. It is a sturdy "raised cottage" whose curving flights at each end of the porch are unexpected.

A handsome brick house now privately owned, Cherokee Inn, before it became a hostelry, housed a bank as well as the banker and family.

ever since. The building was still used in the early 1900s for banking purposes, but it was bought by the mother of the present owner and restored. The first and second floors are entirely furnished in antiques.

ENFIELD (*c. 1820*)
McIver Street facing Cedar Avenue; by appointment; Mr. and Mrs. John D. Nock.

General Erasmus Powe, who fought in the War of 1812, built it and planted the avenue of cedars still standing. Beautifully restored, the house has much lovely old furniture.

¶ In & out of Union
(about 70 miles northwest of Columbia)

WHITE COLUMNS, *or* THOMAS C. DUNCAN HOME (*1854*)
Keenan Avenue (Route 176); by appointment; Mrs. D. M. Eaves and Miss Fannie Duncan, P.O. Box 245.

This is a mansion-type house with a tremendous portico supported by Corinthian columns, in back of which are lesser columns supporting a deep porch which runs around three sides of the house, with a balustraded balcony above. It was owned by the great-grandfather of the present occupants and contains many heirlooms and family portraits, of which the most remarkable is a rosewood piano with mother-of-pearl keys and a keyboard inlaid with scenes and flowers. The frescoed ceiling is unusual. The owners call it "a house of hospitality and a happy home."

J. A. SAWYER'S HOME (*1812*)
By appointment; 50 cents; Mrs. Foster Bentley.

It was the residence of Judge William H. Wallace, speaker of the famous "Wallace House" during the Reconstruction and a Brigadier General in the Confederate Army. Jefferson Davis stayed here en route to Abbeville. The house was built by a German count in exile, of eight-inch-square bricks, each inside partition wall thirteen inches thick. The front door was imported from Italy.

ROSE HILL, *or* GOVERNOR GIST MANSION (*1828*)

Gist Bridge Road, 8 miles southeast toward Sedalia; daily, 9 to 5; 50 cents; Clyde F. Franks, Laurens (caretaker on premises).

William H. Gist was the Confederate Governor of South Carolina, the first state to secede. His house is an unusually graceful example of Greek Revival influence on Up Country plantation architecture. It has an attractively light two-story pedimented porch, with fanlighted doorways and tall wide windows. The workmanship on the woodwork of the mantels, moldings, and paneling shows an expert hand. The house is furnished throughout in pieces of its period.

¶ Clemson

This attractive college town is at the junction of Routes 76 and 123, forty miles southwest of Greenville.

FORT HILL, *or* JOHN C. CALHOUN HOUSE (*1803, enlarged 1825*)

Weekdays 10 to 12 and 2 to 5, and Sunday afternoon; voluntary fee; Clemson College.

Home of the famous statesman, whose son-in-law, Thomas Green Clemson, founded and endowed Clemson College, by whom the house is now maintained as a shrine to Calhoun. The large white clapboard house has great Up Country architectural charm, two-story porticoes at both the front and side and big columns of stuccoed brick. It is beautifully maintained and furnished in the fine domestic Empire, Duncan Phyfe, and early Victorian pieces handed down from the Calhouns and the Clemsons. While her husband was in Washington, Mrs. Calhoun did the designing and, with Andrew, the head slave carpenter, much of the actual building. Calhoun's letters indicate that he was fearful of the cost and cautioned his wife to await his return before proceeding, but like many a wife, she paid no heed.

Enfield is one of the many excellent old places that help to give Cheraw its character and which are still being much appreciated by their owners.

*The drawing room in the Thomas house is exactly as its last owner left it—
for the pleasure of the public. Its feminine décor, which suits the architecture
so well, is to remain unchanged. Opposite, in the Greek Revival town of
Athens, stands the splendidly pillared Du Bose house.*

GEORGIA

¶ Athens ¶ Augusta ¶ Covington ¶ Crawfordville ¶ Forsyth
¶ Indian Springs ¶ La Grange ¶ Macon ¶ Madison
¶ Marshallville ¶ Middleton ¶ Milledgeville ¶ Rome ¶ Millen
¶ Rosswell ¶ Savannah ¶ Out of Savannah ¶ Spring Place
¶ Thomasville ¶ Toccoa ¶ Washington ¶ Out of Waynesboro

*B*ACK in the second quarter of the nineteenth century when the Greek Revival became more of a national style than the United States ever had, nowhere was it adopted with a more princely flourish than in the state of Georgia. The style came close to perfection as a way of expressing the prosperity and hospitality of the great plantation owners in the country and wealthy merchants in the towns. With its lofty ceilings, spacious rooms, open planning, and cooling colonnades, it also suited the climate.

Luckily a lot of these mansions remain, many of the finest of them splendidly preserved and maintained. And, happily, now a grand assortment can be listed here for you to learn about and visit as described below.

Naturally, not all the houses here are Greek Revival. Savannah, which has the feeling of an imaginary city somewhere in the south of France, has notable examples of town houses reminiscent of the Regency style. And elsewhere you will come across houses done in the Late Georgian manner with dignity and restraint, some of them surprisingly ancient.

Athens is a classical college town of enchanting purity and distinction. Milledgeville and Washington are collector's items in the true sense of that overworked term. But everywhere the *Guide* leads you, there will be something as different and delightful as the novelist Thackeray found Macon to be in the 1850s.

If you go to Georgia in early spring, you will walk between banks of azaleas; camellias will not quite have passed their peak of perfection, and the soft air will be saturated with the scent of tea olive and banana shrub. That is the time to see her white columns at their glamorous best.

That is the time, too, when there is a succession of house and garden tours throughout the state. To acquaint yourself with each year's changing plans, write to Mrs. Mercer Poole, 899 West Wesley Road, Atlanta, spark plug for the Garden Club of Georgia and president of the Atlanta Garden Center. She has consented to help readers of the *Guide* get the last word on places to visit on these special occasions; likely localities being Athens, Atlanta, Augusta, Covington, Marietta, Madison, Macon, Milledgeville, Savannah, Statesboro, and Saint Simon Island. Some of them are listed below. When in doubt, check with her or the Georgia Chamber of Commerce which cosponsors the tours.

¶ Athens
(66 miles east of Atlanta and 100 miles west of Augusta on Route 78)

Athens is an unbelievable town—unbelievable in the sense that so many beautiful buildings have survived, not only unscathed by time but enriched by it. The town came into being in 1801 at the site of America's first chartered state university, where the first classes were conducted out of doors under the curious eyes of the red men. What a picture it must have made, the peaceful Cherokees in their paint and feathers, peering at the young students in the dappled shade cast by the first growth of trees. The University has prospered, and now many of the

stately columned private homes of the early period are being used for educational purposes; many others have become fraternity and sorority houses, and some remain as private houses. Most of them are still there, and, through the help of Mrs. Carlisle Cobb, we have been fortunate in listing a large number for you, both private and semiprivate. There is much for you to see at your leisure.

THE PRESIDENT'S HOUSE (*1854*)
570 Prince Avenue; by appointment; University System of Georgia, Dr. and Mrs. Aderholt (residents).

This is the second and finest residence of Benjamin Harvey Hill, United States Senator and brilliant orator, who moved to Athens in 1869 from "Bellevue" in La Grange (listed later) because his home constituency had turned against him after the war when he urged the acceptance of the inevitable. To him goes much of the credit for influencing President Hayes to withdraw the Federals from Georgia. This great house, with its peristyle of sixteen tall Corinthian columns, is now the residence of the presidents of the University of Georgia. Fiske Kimball called it "the most superb of all." Probably no other house in Georgia has more elaborate plasterwork on ceilings and cornices, and there are magnificent crystal chandeliers and gilt mirrors of the period. It is now furnished in eighteenth-century English and some Empire. Dr. and Mrs. Aderholt have graciously said that it may be visited upon request when they are able to show it. Otherwise it may always be seen outside in its lovely garden settings, its portico extending the length of the front and sides, with a Doric colonnade in the rear.

MAGNOLIA HALL, UPSON HOUSE (*1840*)
1022 Prince Avenue; not open at present; Mr. and Mrs. Bradbury Foss (residents), Mrs. Stephen Upson (owner).

Perhaps next in interest, this monumental house is occupied by descendants of the Upson and Lumpkin families. The furniture has always been handed down by grandfathers, including some exceptional Queen Anne and Chippendale chairs. Grandfather

The Presidents of the University of Georgia are privileged to live in one of the loveliest mansions in the South.

Stephen Upson was a savant, one of the youngest men ever to graduate from Yale, and he finished at the University of Paris. Mrs. Bradbury Foss, who lives here with her husband, remembers that her grandfather spoke Latin and Greek fluently as well as several other languages. (Athens seems to have lived up to its name in those early days, for its sons were more interested in culture and learning than making cotton fortunes.) The parquet floors of quarter-sawed oak are of a different design in each room, edged with inlaid mahogany patterns. Much of the door hardware, door knobs and keyholes, is silver, and there are magnificent early portraits of the fam-ily. Please write the authors of the *Guide* to find when this house can be visited.

MELL HOUSE (*1848*)
> *897 South Milledge Avenue; by appointment; Mrs. John Mell.*

Built by the Lumpkin family, this house is Victorian, superimposed on the Greek Revival. The columns, though greatly attenuated, extend all the way across the front. They are connected with an iron-work rail and other Victorian ornament.

More of this exquisite ironwork can be seen on the OLD HONNICUT HOUSE (1865), 325 North Milledge Avenue. Look for a most unusual porch roof there. The house is not open at present.

The Mell house is earlier than it looks, for the unusually delicate Victorian trimmings were added later. It is one of the several Lumpkin homes, the family which was largely responsible for Athens' educational prestige.

FERDINAND PHINIZY HOME (*1857*)
250 South Milledge Avenue; not open at present.

A delectable dwelling resembling something you might see in the French Quarter at New Orleans. Both of its porches, first and second story, are delicately decorated in iron dentelle. Please write the authors of the *Guide* to find when this house may be visited.

BRUMBY HOUSE (*1818*)
343 East Hancock Avenue; by appointment; Misses Anne and Mary Brumby.

Built by New England workmen for Alonzo Church, President of the University from 1829 to 1859, since 1831 it has been occupied by the Brumby family, and the direct descendants are living here now. A house filled with lovely old furniture, silver, and some rare Waterford glass, and a particularly remarkable Sheraton sideboard. This should be a rare treat and a chance to learn much about the early Athenians.

E. K. LUMPKIN HOUSE (*1848*)
973 Prince Avenue; any time; Young Harris Memorial Methodist Church.

Now used for educational purposes, it was in this parlor that the first Garden Club in the world held its meetings. It is festooned with iron grillwork, reminiscent of some of Savannah's finest.

HENRY GRADY HOUSE (*1845*)
634 Prince Avenue; by appointment; Miss Lois Lumpkin.

A stunning Doric-columned temple at the end of a solid street of columns, this was the boyhood home of one of the most beloved figures of the South, one who helped more than any other man of his time to heal the wounds of the War. As managing editor of *The Atlanta Constitution,* Grady made the paper one of the best known in the country. He was a constructive and brilliant writer and orator. The thirteen Doric columns represent the thirteen colonies and are symbolically linked together by iron grillwork.

The buildings on the University grounds are a remarkable group and should not be missed. The original college, now the administration building, dates back to 1801. DEMOSTHENES HALL, 1824, is the home of the oldest college literary society in North America. The WILSON LUMPKIN HOUSE, built of two-by-three-foot stone blocks brought from Scotland to Savannah and then dragged here by oxsled, is now the library of the College of Agriculture. Other old houses on the campus, added as the University enlarged, are the BISHOP COTTAGE and the LUSTRAT, STRAHAN, LUCAS, and REED HOUSES. These and many others on the campus are worth seeing, along with the churches and fraternity houses off campus. Please take your time and walk all around town. The interiors of almost any of the fraternity or sorority houses may be seen on request, but we particularly recommend the following.

DEARING HOUSE (*1856*)
150 South Milledge Avenue; by appointment; Kappa Alpha Theta Sorority House.

A stunning red brick with Doric columns. Beautifully maintained and handsomely furnished in period.

HAMILTON HOUSE (*1858*)
338 South Milledge Avenue; by appointment; Alpha Delta Pi Sorority House.

Of French Colonial design with eleven elegantly carved mantels; beautifully maintained and handsomely furnished in period.

JAMES CAMAK HOUSE (*1830*)
Faces Meigs Street; on request; The Masons.

When it was built, the old James Camak house stood within the borders of the Cherokee nation, just outside the town. An impressive brick house with iron trimmings and a beautifully carved interior, it is now a Masonic Lodge.

CRANE HOUSE (*1842*)
247 Pulaski Street; on request; Sigma Alpha Epsilon Fraternity House.

The Garden Clubs of America consider it "one of the three most perfect examples of southern architecture."

Henry Grady's house was a Greek temple, but the lacelike iron railing joining the thirteen symbolic columns changed Grecian purity to Southern grace.

In late April, Athens generally holds a tour in which about fifteen houses and many lovely gardens are opened for a day. For the latest information write to the Garden Club Council.

¶ Augusta
(as you enter Georgia from South Carolina on Routes 1, 25, and 28)

MEADOW GARDEN (c. 1800)
13th Street; Saturday 2 to 6, Sunday 3:30 to 6; 25 cents; D.A.R.

A simple house of plantation style, it was the home of one of Georgia's great men, George Walton, a signer of the Declaration, also Governor of Alabama in 1789. It contains early furniture, portraits, a rocking chair in which Washington sat when he visited, and a colorful quilt made by Mrs. Walton.

THE WHITE HOUSE (1750)
1822 Broad Street; Saturdays 10:30 to 6, Sundays 12:30 to 6 (may close for restoration); state of Georgia.

Built as an inn, it was later a trading post and then British headquarters during the Revolution, when thirteen patriots were hanged here over the stairwell. The Historical Society considers it their number one historical house in the state and, therefore, restoration has been slow and care-ful. Moldings and trim are Early Georgian and were evidently made by a country carpenter who used the wooden molding plane of the day. The mantels are copies of Georgian prototypes, but the front doorway may have been done at a later date for it is very finely detailed. The spiral staircase is also evidence of experienced builders.

THE OLD GOVERNMENT HOUSE (1801 and 1821)
423 Telfair Street; will be opened to public; Augusta Junior League, Mrs. Thomas Richards (President), 2815 Lombardy Court.

Known to the people of Augusta as the "Dr. Eugene Murphy Home," it was designed by Maningault of Charleston fame. It is said to contain "the finest drawing room in the state." The detail is characteristic of Maningault, elaborate and elegant: massive gilt mirrors and gilt cornices are intact, as it is to be hoped are the gaslight chandeliers, the wonderful velvet drapes, the Victorian carpets, and many other features of this Augusta landmark. The ironwork outside and the gardens are notable.

KILPATRICK HOUSE (1751)
1314 Comfort Road; on request; Dr. Andrew Jones Kilpatrick.

Built as an inn, it has solid brick foundations, said to have been brought over from

England. Lafayette spoke to the Augustans from the balcony in 1825. The downtown location of this home became so noisy that the Kilpatricks had it moved piece by piece to its present commanding location in 1929 at a cost of forty thousand dollars rather than give it up. The furniture is Victorian.

WARE'S FOLLY, *now* GERTRUDE HERBERT INSTITUTE OF ART
(1818)
506 Telfair Street; by appointment, Tuesday through Friday 10 to 5, Sundays 4 to 6; city of Augusta.

Now an art museum, it was built as a home by Maningault at a cost of one hundred and forty thousand dollars, quite a sum for 1818. You can see how it got its name. Only one room is furnished now, but it is certainly worth a look for its sheer magnificence.

APPLEBY HOUSE (*c. 1830*)
John's Road and Walton Way; city of Augusta.

Now being restored, the house is sold to the city and will be a branch library. It was one of the best in town, alas. It will be worthwhile just to look at the woodwork.

THE MANSE (*1840s*)
419 7th Street; W. C. Peeples.

Now an apartment house, this is the boyhood home of Woodrow Wilson, a simple, dignified Late Georgian brick dwelling. It is under consideration by the state for designation as a national shrine.

The tour takes place in late March or early April. Write Mrs. Henry Perkins, 1118 Milledge Road.

¶ *Covington*
(*35 miles southeast of Atlanta on Route 12*)

WHITEHALL (*c. 1850*)
506 Monticello Street; by written or phone appointment; Mr. and Mrs. N. S. Turner.

An impressive town house built by Judge John Harris, whose plantation to the east of town was used as a camp site by General Sherman. Three stories high, it has tall Corinthian columns, connected by a handmade balustrade which is repeated in the

Whitehall represents high, wide, and handsome Southern hospitable living.

hanging balcony of the second floor. It is beautifully kept up and furnished by the second generation of Turners to live in it. With hand-painted wallpaper and Baccarat chandeliers, it is worthwhile.

OLD PRESIDENT'S HOME (*1838*)

John Wesley Street, on campus of Emory University, Oxford, 1 mile north of Covington; on request by phone or letter; Dean Virgil Y. C. Eady.

Built by Igatius Few, the first President of Emory University. The second President added the two flanking rooms which connect with the porch but not directly with the rest of the house. One was used for a study and the other for students. The main part of the house sits snugly back between the wings and looks very private with its pretty porch and big shade trees. Six bishops have lived in it—Chandler, Dickey, Pierce, Haygood, Key, and Ainsworth—all of whom boarded here first as students. Bishop Key purchased the house so that his daughter-in-law might use it for boarders, but it was said that she was such a "flirt" that the plan proved unfeasible.

For the Covington tour in mid-April, write Mrs. N. S. Turner, as above, or The Green Thumb Garden Club.

¶ Crawfordville (about 10 miles southwest of Washington)

LIBERTY HALL, *or* ALEXANDER H. STEPHENS HOME

(*1834, remodeled 1872*)

Daily, 9 to 5; state of Georgia, Department of Parks.

Alexander Stephens was Vice-president of the Confederacy and United States Senator. During the Civil War his house became an inn. The house and grounds are now part of a state park. Much of the original furniture is still there; carpets and wallpapers are copies of the period. Stephens, who, by the way, never weighed more than a hundred pounds had "a whim of iron." He did things to suit himself; he kept bachelor's hall and the room at the head of the stairs was called "the tramps' room"—anyone could sleep there who wanted to. His friends lived with him here for long periods

of time and everybody did as he pleased. Hence, the name of the house.

¶ Forsyth (24 miles northwest of Macon)

NEWTON HOUSE (*c. 1810*)

By written appointment, April to October; 50 cents; Mr. and Mrs. Howell Newton.

Moved from across the river by wagon in 1830, it could easily be mistaken for a New England house with its clean simplicity and hip roof. You will find many American antiques here—a beautiful eight-panel Coromandel screen, a fine collection of small eighteenth- and nineteenth-century oils, and some American primitives. The oils include works by Innes, Church, Shattuck, Wight, etc. In the rear, there is a very formal garden where much out-of-door entertaining takes place.

¶ Indian Springs (20 miles north of Forsyth)

GREAT INDIAN CHIEF GENERAL MC INTOSH HOUSE, *now* VARNER HOME (*1821*)

Route 23, 50 miles south of Atlanta; daily, 9 to 6; 50 cents and 25 cents; J. H. Elliott.

An extraordinary dwelling of thirty-five furnished rooms, the owner calls it the forerunner of the motel. All windows on the ground floor open onto the porch. The original owner of this huge house (eighteen columns on the front) was said to have had nine wives, so no doubt he needed the space. The house was built by Indians for him, their Great Chief; he himself is said to have carved the mantels and doors. The bricks used in the construction were carried on foot over two hundred miles from the coast. The interior walls are made of vertical hand-hewn boards. There are nine fireplaces. It is furnished throughout with pieces dating from 1750 to 1840 and its collection of Indian relics is said to be the finest in the South. It contains thirty oil paintings of Chiefs who visited the house, together with the desk at which fifty Chiefs gathered to sign the treaty ceding all their lands from Georgia to the Mississippi (which negotiation in the end cost McIntosh his life at the hands of the Indians he had thus betrayed).

¶ *La Grange*
(71 miles southwest of Atlanta)

BELLEVUE (*1853*)

204 Ben Hill Street; weekdays, 9 to 5; contribution; La Grange Woman's Club, Mrs. R. S. O'Neal (President).

This is the other Ben Hill House, the one he lived in before he moved to Athens in 1869. It is a two-story frame house with tall Ionic columns and a massive carved cornice. Hill was arrested here by the Federals and taken at ten minutes' notice.

FERRELL GARDENS (*prior to 1855*)

1200 Vernon Road; on request; Mr. and Mrs. Fuller E. Callaway, Jr.

Unusual and extensive formal gardens, started in 1841 by Sarah Coleman Ferrell with the help of an Italian gardener and slave labor. There are trees and shrubs from all over the world and unique box arrangements, much of them growing for a hundred years or more.

The tour takes place here the second week in May. About fourteen homes are shown but not all old ones. Write to The Garden Club for particulars.

¶ *Macon*
(almost directly in center of state)

SKELTON-NAPIER-SMALL HOUSE (*c. 1850*)

156 Rogers Avenue; at reasonable hours; R. B. Small, Jr.

The house, which is a studio of decoration, may be seen downstairs. It is an outstanding example of Greek Revival, even in this region where there are many good ones.

SIDNEY LANIER COTTAGE
(*prior to 1842*)

213 High Street; usually open.

Essentially unchanged in structure, this is one of the earliest houses in town. It was, of course, the home of the South's most

Bellevue, the first Ben Hill house, shows once more that the Senator of Reconstruction fame knew how to pick his dwellings.

The Ralph Small house is notably pure in its style.

popular poet whose name it bears, although he did not build it. Private parties are catered.

THE COLUMNS (*c. 1850, remodeled 1895*)
315 College Avenue.

A remodeling job (superimposed on Greek Revival), done in 1895 to the tune of one hundred thousand dollars. Dinner is served by reservation, and it makes a place that is fun to eat in. The food is said to be in keeping with the house.

A few interesting houses have survived what a native calls "the wolf of progress." They are worth looking at outside.

The COWLES-BOND HOUSE, the work of Alexander Elam, is at Cowles Hill and Bond Street and sits back on lovely grounds. The house, begun in 1836, took four years to build and is one of the most interesting Greek Revival mansions in the state. The proportions of the columns are excellent and the balustrades girdling the roof in an inner and outer encirclement add to its loveliness. This same talented architect, Elam, built the THADDEUS GOODE-HOLT HOUSE (1840),

Georgia at Orange Street, with its graceful double steps, and very likely designed the lovely COWLES COTTAGE (1829) at Walnut between 2d and 3d Streets, also perfect on the small scale. Lastly you might like to see the outside of the JOHNSON HAY HOME, 934 Georgia Avenue, a twenty-four-room Italianate palazzo, built more than a hundred years ago at a cost of two hundred and fifty thousand dollars. It took seven years to build. The honeymoon couple who built it saw its counterpart in Italy and brought back the plans.

A tour is held in Macon the early part of April and some of these houses can be seen. The Macon tour usually includes a number of contemporary houses as well. Consult the chamber of commerce about it.

¶ Madison
(28 miles south of Athens)

Many of the ante-bellum homes here have been in the same families for gen-

Boxwood, with its Late Victorian porch, is throughout a period piece.

erations. Miss Kitty Newton, who lives in "Boxwood," one of the loveliest, has done us the great favor to say that she will try to make arrangements for interested visitors to see some of the homes listed here—at the owners' convenience, of course. If she is away, the chamber of commerce, in the city hall, has agreed to help you in her place. Miss Newton is also chairman of a tour sponsored by La Flora Garden Club during the latter part of April (not every year).

BOXWOOD (*c. 1851*)
510 South 2d Street; on request; (phone 119); Miss Kitty Newton.

Two large gardens, where peacocks fan their tails in the green aisles of boxwood, give their names to Miss Newton's place. The house has elaborate and extremely elegant period parlors, whose every feature—carpets, draperies, chandeliers—is the unspoiled original furnishing of the days when Victorian could be regal. The house is a magnificent period piece, something to behold.

MC HENRY HOME (*c. 1820*)
610 1st Street; Mrs. J. G. McHenry.

This is another beauty; earlier yet, furnished for the most part in the same vintage. Six generations have occupied this house, and the exquisite velvet scroll carpet in the drawing room was purchased by the

first. Much of the furniture here has stood just where it is now for more than a hundred years. Ask to see the hoop-skirt closet under the stairs. It had to be roomy.

BONAR HALL (*1832*)
Mrs. W. T. Bacon and Miss T. Newton.

A Georgian manor house of handmade brick; adjacent to it is its orangery, now a tea house.

Then there is HONEYMOON, still earlier, and the C. R. MASON HOUSE, recently restored. Drive out of town a mile to THE OAKS, a plantation of two thousand acres, land as it used to be parceled. Here you will see more peacocks on the lovely grounds and handsome antiques. In Madison you can almost feel that you are back in the Old South.

¶ *Marshallville (30 miles southwest of Macon)*

WADE HOME (*1840*)
By appointment; Mr. and Mrs. John Wade.

A simple, lovely Southern Colonial manse with six two-story columns in front, whose owners, Mr. and Mrs. John Wade, are principally interested in their fine garden, as it seems are most people in Marshallville, widely known for its great yearly camellia show. Their garden is loveliest in January and February when the camellias are in full bloom and many other flowers as well. They are *always* pleased to show it and will show the house when convenient.

¶ *Middleton (40 miles east of Athens on Route 72)*

ROSE HILL (*1810*)
At reasonable times, preferably spring and summer; Mrs. John Wade Johnson, Sr.

The traditional home of the Heard family is a white frame house with a narrow two-story central porch. It was built during or shortly after the Revolution by the widow of the famous Revolutionary Governor of Georgia, Stephen Heard. The original building is now the central part; wings were added later. The grounds, with their spacious flower gardens and avenues of oaks and cedars, are noted throughout this part of the state. The stairway in this house was used in the filming of *The Birth of a Nation* but was subsequently removed along with the wainscoting.

¶ *Milledgeville*
(36 miles northwest of Macon)

It is a town of many homes erected by master builders. Writing of it, Talbot Hamlin said "nowhere did the Greek Revival produce a more perfect blending of the dignified and the gracious, the impressive and the domestic than in the lovely homes of the '30s and '40s in up-state Georgia." It is of a piece with the graciousness of this architecture that the people who live in it are equally gracious in their willingness to show their homes to strangers, and, except for the annual tour which takes place the first week in April, no charge is made to see any of them.

To appreciate the town and its lovely homes, more than a few hours is essential, so leave your things at the Sanford House, only recently become an inn.

SANFORD HOUSE (*1820*)
Opposite Courthouse; on request; Miss Fannie White.

Now an inn, it had always been lived in by the Sanford family and never much remodeled. The mantels, woodwork, and wainscoting are intact—the work of master builder, John Marlon. The food is said to be fine, and it might be well to reserve in advance.

The Sanford-Powell-Binion house is likely to be your first stop. The hospitality behind these stately columns is not hard to imagine.

The old Executive Mansion now regally serves the Presidents of Georgia State for a home.

EXECUTIVE MANSION (1838)

Clark Street; on request; Board of Regents, University System of Georgia; Dr. Henry King Stafford, President, Georgia State College for Women (resident).

Formerly serving as the home of eight successive governors of Georgia, this is one of the finest and best preserved Greek Revival houses in the state. About sixty feet square, it has a central rotunda lighted by a skylight at the top of the dome. The plaster-coffered dome has gold decorations on the ornamental moldings. All the main rooms in the first story have plaster cornices and ceiling medallions four feet in diameter. All downstairs windows are paneled beneath. There are black marble mantels in the salon; white in the parlor and four bedrooms. There is an immense ballroom and the basement kitchen, with its massive fireplace, has now been restored. It is filled with many other interesting features.

ELIZABETH JONES HOUSE (1820)

Corner Liberty and Greene Streets; on request.

Miss Jones is librarian at the College and the authority on the old homes of Milledgeville. Perhaps better than anyone else here, she is qualified to answer your questions. Her house is an adaptation of Greek Revival, furnished in perfect taste with rare Charleston and New Orleans pieces, mostly of the eighteenth century. The house was built by Charles J. Paine. If she can spare the time, she will gladly share some of the lore of the town with you.

PETER J. WILLIAMS HOUSE (1818)

Corner Washington and Liberty Streets; on request.

Built by the grandfather of the present owner, the house contains, besides its lovely furniture, a notable collection of paintings which include Rembrandt, Corot, and Kneller. The boxwood and gardens here are very fine indeed.

JOHN W. GORDON HOUSE (1820)

Greene Street; on request; Mrs. Mary Cline.

This was a governor's mansion in 1838. It has beautiful mantels and fine old furniture, glass, and silver.

METHODIST PARSONAGE

(early nineteenth century)
Columbia and McIntosh Streets; on request; Mr. and Mrs. Frank Bell.

A one-story-and-basement Greek Revival house with a very pretty clapboard exterior.

THE CEDARS (c. 1825)

At Columbia between McIntosh and Hancock Streets; on request; Mrs. J. I. Garrard.

A Greek Revival mansion, having extensive and lovely old gardens.

LOCKERLY (date unknown)

Irwinton Road, Midway.

Built by Judge Daniel Tucker, it also has its gardens. Within are fine antiques, silver, china, and portraits.

SAMUEL ROCKWELL HOUSE (1834)

Allen Memorial Drive, Midway; on request; O. M. Ennis family.

Governor Johnson's home for some time. You cannot miss it, for the wonderful iron fence cost almost as much as the house. It has beautiful carved woodwork and a circular staircase. Joseph Lane was its architect.

The tour, held usually the early part of April, is not likely to show any more houses than we have mentioned here. There is a modest fee, of course, and information about it can be had from either the United Daughters of the Confederacy or the Rotary Club.

¶ *Rome (70 miles northwest of Atlanta)*

OAK HILL (*1860*)
> *On grounds of Martha Berry School; by appointment; Mrs. Inez Henry, Administration Building.*

Former home of Martha Berry, wealthy planter's daughter, who started this remarkable school for young Georgians unable to afford to pay for their education and which has achieved a countrywide reputation.

Rome has a tour from time to time, sponsored by the Garden Study Club in late April. Headquarters are at Hotel General Forrest.

¶ *Millen (50 miles south of Augusta on Route 25)*

BIRDSVILLE PLANTATION
> (*rear 1770, front 1847*)
> *By appointment; $1.00; Mrs. Ben Franklin, Sr.*

Behind its Greek Revival portico the early part of "Birdsville" is one of the two oldest houses still standing in the state, except for the Savannah plantations. It has been occupied by eight generations in succession. You can be sure it has seen its share of history, and that it is filled and furnished with many souvenirs of the past.

¶ *Rosswell (18 miles north of Atlanta)*

MIMOSA HALL (*1840*)
> *By appointment at owners' convenience; $1.00 for Rosswell Women's Club; Mr. and Mrs. Granger Hansell.*

This is an elegant house of brick, plastered over. The interior is spacious and rather simple. The furniture is eighteenth-century English and French, some American, and there is one Victorian "Gone with the Wind" bedroom. In the hall are unusual murals.

A glimpse of a Greek Revival street in Rosswell.

BARRINGTON HALL (*1837–1842*)

Daily except Sunday; 50 cents; Misses Evelyn and Katherine Simpson.

Built by Barrington King, the co-founder of Rosswell, it is now the home of his great-granddaughters. It contains many heirlooms, much original furniture. The exterior with its fluted columns is handsome indeed, with a beautiful gate and fine boxwood.

HOLLY HILL (*1842–1847*)

By appointment to those seriously interested in early architecture only; Mr. and Mrs. Robert L. Sommerville.

The builder, Robert A. Lewis, was a relative of Barrington King. The house is the type called "Low Country," but there are three floors instead of the usual two. Both front and back have identical columned galleries. It is a vast place with three halls, all the same size, and all rooms eighteen feet square. Because of its size, restoration is to be gradual.

¶ Savannah

You can stroll along Savannah's semi-tropical streets and get the feel of a foreign city. Laid out in a series of open squares, the houses with their iron grill railings and balconies, their graceful flights of steps, form architectural girdles for the little green parks, gaudy with azaleas in the spring. There are many colorful exteriors, and in the early part of March when the flowers are blooming, the tour will permit you to visit about a dozen of the best. For information write to The Women's Auxiliary of Christ Church or the De Soto Hotel, where the tours generally start. The second day of the tour takes you out of town to some plantations. However, the four fine "open houses" here, the products of a talented

One side of a typical Savannah square, the houses tall and comfortable, each with its steep stoop and plenty of iron dentelle like the fence in the foreground.

The sophisticated portico of the Owens-Thomas house faces another leafy square. Even the fence is carefully designed to enhance the stylishness of the house.

young English architect, William Jay, give you the complete picture of the heyday of this charming city.

OWENS-THOMAS HOUSE (*1816*)
Tuesday through Saturday 10 to 5, Monday 12 to 5, Sundays 3 to 6; $1.00; Telfair Academy.

Recently opened as a museum, it was left to the Academy intact by its last owner, Miss Margaret Thomas. This was young Jay's masterpiece, a house of remarkable charm and grace, which rather resembles some of the English Regency houses in Bath and elsewhere. Furnished with a feminine taste, which suits it admirably, it is an excellent example of William Jay at his most inventive, and of a time and place that appreciated his gifts. The "lived-in" look, so difficult to create in a museum house, is here to stay.

JULIETTE GORDON LOW BIRTHPLACE (*1819–1821*)
Bull Street and Oglethorpe Square; Girl Scouts of America.

Credited to William Jay, and it may very well be his design, the house was built after he left Savannah. Mrs. Low, founder of

the Girl Scouts (who are honoring her in this restoration) and a farseeing feminist at a time and place when this was unusual in women, was born and grew up here. The parlor floor is to have the Low family furniture of the '60s—and as far as possible the rest will be in keeping. Also the nursery and Mrs. Low's bedroom will have the original furniture that belonged there. The top floor will be used for visitors and the basement for meetings.

LOW HOUSE (*1848*)
329 Abercorn Street; Monday through Friday for visitors accompanied by professional guide; Georgia Society of Colonial Dames.

One of the Regency beauties of Savannah, as you might expect when you know that the Colonial Dames of Georgia chose it for their headquarters. Juliette Gordon Low lived here during her marriage and old age. Within, the house is a skillful re-creation of the taste of the period and place, where culture and the amenities, rather than wealth, set the key—although wealth was not lacking. Wrought-iron balconies and a jalousied piazza face on the back garden; the carriage house was made into Scout headquarters by Mrs. Low, which it continues to be until the day when the birthplace house is finished.

TELFAIR ACADEMY OF THE ARTS AND SCIENCES (*1818*)

Tuesday through Saturday, 10 to 5, Monday 12 to 5, Sundays 3 to 6; Telfair Academy.

William Jay again, but altered a good deal for the Academy, which was founded in 1875 by Mary Telfair as a gift to the city. The Telfairs have played an important part in the history of the state, beginning with Edward, the early Governor and hero of the Revolution. Most of the furniture here has belonged to the family and includes Colonial, Regency, and Victorian, a setting for the museum collection of early American portraits, engravings, and statuary. It is altogether fascinating and full of character.

¶ *Out of Savannah*

By arrangement with the *Guide,* two of the oldest plantations in Georgia may be visited.

WILD HERON PLANTATION (*1756*)

From midtown Route 17 south 12 miles to sign, 3 miles left on Grove Point Road; March, 10 to 5 except Sunday; other times for large groups only by appointment two weeks in advance; contribution for Garden Club of Savannah; Mr. and Mrs. Shelby Myrick.

Built by Francis Harris for a country house on a grant from George II, it is said to be the oldest house in Georgia and has never been greatly changed. It affords an unusual opportunity to see how these very early plantation homes were constructed. Mrs. Myrick, one of the leading spirits in the preservation of Georgia's architectural heritage, has kept this place, in so far as modern living permits, representative of a simple early rice plantation, the crop mainly grown in this area. At the southeast corner, Mrs. Myrick can show you a palm tree which was planted in 1780 by Elizabeth, bride of Harris. Some of the descendants of the slaves who were on the land still live in the neighborhood. Their spirituals, not recorded, are unique to the locality. In line with the tradition of the place, tea or coffee is served to all guests.

WORMSLOE

On Isle of Hope; garden only; on request by phone or letter; Mrs. Craig Barrow.

"One of the loveliest gardens in the world" is the description usually given of "Wormsloe," Georgia's oldest plantation. In the course of time, most of this garden has become naturalized, for much of it has been growing on for a century or two. Consisting of eight hundred acres, the original grant was presented to Noble Jones in 1756 by King George II, some time after he had leased it from the colony. Little of it except the avenues, walks, and gardens has ever been cultivated so it remains a kind of pristine paradise for birds and wild things. For more than two hundred years, nature with the helping hand of man has added to the beauty of this place, which has been continuously owned by the same family. The house, which has been greatly changed in the course of time, still rests on its tabby foundations built by Noble Jones. It may be seen from the garden, of course.

¶ *Spring Place (just off Route 76, near Chatsworth)*

CHIEF JOSEPH VANN HOUSE (*1804–1809*)

Open during restoration; 25 cents and 50 cents; Georgia Historical Commission.

Vann was a half-breed Cherokee Indian who operated an inn and ferry near Gainesville and owned thousands of acres of rich valley lands and hundreds of slaves as well. It is said that he was run out of Georgia in 1865. He moved to Tennessee where he operated a steamship line and was killed in a boiler explosion while racing another steamer. The house is a late, striking brick structure stunningly restored by Henry C. Forman. Moravian diaries provided data on what it had been. It will house early Georgia and Cherokee exhibits and some furniture. An unsupported stairway and free-hanging balcony are outstanding interior features. On a marker in front of the house, it is stated that "John Howard Payne, author of Home, Sweet Home, suspected as a spy of the Cherokee Indians was imprisoned here in 1835, but released."

¶ *Thomasville*

GREENWOOD (*1845*)

> *By appointment; Mr. and Mrs. John Hay Whitney, E. V. Komarek (superintendent).*

"Greenwood" is one of the great estates of Georgia, both the huge Greek Revival mansion and its lovely grounds can match any for their beauty. The house is an outstanding classical example, the work of John Wind, an English architect. The sunken garden here was designed by Stanford White, while more recently other parts of the extensive grounds have undergone restoration by Umberto Innocenti, of Italian repute.

¶ *Toccoa (60 miles north of Athens)*

JARRETT MANOR (*1787*)

> *Route 123, 8 miles north of Toccoa; usually open; Jarrett Manor Foundation.*

Its former mistress, Mrs. White, was still alert in her late eighties, a remarkable personality, and the first woman in the state to avail herself of suffrage. Until recently she showed the house and told about its long history of which she has been an important part. She has given the house to the Georgia Historical Society. Called "Traveler's Rest," it was built by Jesse Walton, brother of Georgia's signer of the Declaration, George Walton. It was a famous inn visited by many notables. Probably the only pioneer house in Georgia still standing with its original furniture, it is one of three houses in the state that the Department of the Interior recommended for preservation. The old tavern is one hundred feet across the front and contains twenty-one rooms, many of them paneled in walnut and chestnut. At one end is an elevated room in which silkworms were raised, and down the hill are quarters for slaves which Joseph Walton brought from Africa in his own ship.

¶ *Washington*

> *(41 miles east of Athens, 60 west of Augusta, on Route 78)*

In this town of enormous charm with narrow, shady streets, the citizens have

The Gabe Toombs home, raised high off the ground with its plain Greek Revival portico, is the prototype for Washington homes.

steadfastly held out against industrial incursions. The precedent seems to have been established by Gen. Robert Toombs, who purchased the TOOMBS HOUSE, still on the avenue named for him, and remodeled it elegantly back in 1837. After the Civil War, the townspeople wanted to build a hotel but General Toombs repudiated the idea heartily: "If a respectable man comes to town, he can stay at my house; if he isn't respectable we don't want him here anyway," said he. To this day his opinion prevails for there is still no hotel. "Washington is one of the last dreaming places of the south," says Mrs. H. C. Standart, its historian, who may be thanked for arranging with four of the owners to allow their homes to be visited. There are over fifty buildings of historic interest in the town, she will tell you, and she has described all of them and located them in a six-page guide with map which the chamber of commerce is glad to furnish on request. If given due notice they will probably help you to see other homes of particular interest to you with the help of Mrs. Standart.

In addition to the historic homes, there are eight historic trees. To save one of these trees, the citizens of Washington turned down an offer of three hundred thousand dollars in state highway funds a few years back. In Washington you might discover a new aspect of conservation—one that has been going on quietly over a century.

HOLLY COURT
(older part 1825)
301 South Alexander Avenue; by appointment; $1.00; Mr. and Mrs. R. R. Johnson.

Although the oldest part was built in 1825, the rest of the house was moved from

The Tupper-Barnett house is one of the prizes in this "last dreaming" town of many tall columns and spacious galleries.

seven miles away and joined to it in 1851. In this home Mrs. Jefferson Davis awaited the arrival of her husband who was fleeing before the Northern troops after the fall of the Confederacy. It has deep windows, high mantels, and a fine stairway; many lovely pine and mahogany ante-bellum family pieces, large mirrors, tester beds. The grounds are very lovely here, too.

TUPPER-BARNETT HOUSE
(*older part early 1800s*)
W. Robert Toombs Avenue and Allison Street; by appointment; Mr. and Mrs. Marion Barnett.

In 1850 the peristyle of eighteen columns was added here. It was the home of Dr. Henry Allen Tupper, Baptist minister (grandfather of the wife of Gen. George Marshall), so much loved by his congregation that they were called Tupperites and accused of loving the Lord *next* to Dr. Tupper. It has handsome ante-bellum furnishing with especially magnificent pier mirrors and Oriental rugs, figurines, vases, and fine engravings.

THE CEDARS (*older portion 1790s*)
Sims Street; any time by appointment; $1.00; Mrs. T. J. Barksdale.

The furnishings are fabulous. There are twenty-eight rooms in the house, built by a Frenchman, Anthony Poulain, whose son was personal physician to Lafayette. There are four parlors each opening into the other, making a room ninety feet long. The dining room holds three dining tables, three sideboards, china cabinets galore and is still not crowded. If size and scale interests you, here it is.

CAMPBELL-LINDSAY HOUSE
(*early 1800s*)
212 East Liberty Street; $1.00; Mr. and Mrs. W. C. Lindsay.

This was originally the home of Duncan Campbell who introduced college education for women to the state of Georgia. The house is an exceptional example of Greek Revival, the columns added in 1860. Encircling the house are a balustraded Doric portico and balcony. There are a pair of fanlighted front doors. The mantels are richly carved. It is furnished in the massive mahogany of the '60s and '70s.

¶ Out of Waynesboro

BELLEVUE (*1768*)
12 miles from Waynesboro; by appointment; Peter Wilkins Carswell III.

The oldest Up Country plantation in the state, "Bellevue" has been continuously occupied and added on to by the Carswell family since it was built. The "courting parlor" was an addition of 1850. This is the real thing.

The Fatio house here on the right helps to give St. Augustine's Aviles Street a soft and pleasing effect of Spanish provincial, while across the page, The Grove, in Tallahassee, besides being historically picturesque, is a good example of Floridian Greek Revival.

FLORIDA

Although St. Augustine is the oldest city in North America, founded in 1565 on the Saint's own day by Pedro Menéndez de Avilés, quite near where Ponce de Leon made his landing a half century before, and though other settlements were made from time to time by the French and the Spanish in their see-saw occupations of the territory—very little remains to tell the story; and outside of the town itself, nothing remains prior to the 1800s. It is true that the Spanish rule lasted at one period for almost a hundred years and that it left its imprint on the manner of building in the little city, even though so few of the actual constructions remain. The English too had their hand in it—they held it during the Revolution and made it a safe and out-of-the-way refuge for rich Tories from the

North. It was claimed by France again in 1795 and it came to us through the Louisiana Purchase. Never more than thinly settled until the twentieth century, it was not organized as a territory until 1822 and during all this time and later Indian troubles persisted.

The Tallahassee area had been visited by De Soto as early as 1539, but the town was not founded until 1824. Key West had its early explorers, being almost a part of the Bahamas, but its prosperity awaited the nineteenth century too.

In this century the state has flourished mightily because of its salubrious climate. In the twenties it had another fling at Spanish architecture, or perhaps more properly Spanish-Floridian. But it will be left to a later chronicler of houses to classify this indigenous manifestation of twentieth-century wealth and taste.

¶ St. Augustine

A few narrow winding streets running into the central square, the Plaza de la Constitucion, are all that remain of the old city that was built on the narrow peninsula between the Matanzas and the San Sebastian Rivers. Aviles Street (now an art colony) and Treasury and St. Francis Streets keep some of their Spanish manners. The houses sit flush to the street, their ground floors of coquina (a durable shell rock) lengthening out into walls that protect tropical gardens from curious eyes; their windows grilled; and their decorative little balconies, hanging over the street, making fine sunny spots from which to gossip with a neighbor, or flirt with a friend below. According to Spanish custom, the Plaza was the business center. At the east end, the OLD SLAVE MARKET (1824) is still standing, built where a general market existed as early as 1598. This is authenticated as is the 1690 date of the OLD TREASURY at St. George and Treasury Streets; and at the northwest corner of St. George stands old CITY HALL, dated 1821. At 14 St. George Street, what is said to be the oldest wooden schoolhouse in the United States is open daily for a fee. It was built of hand-hewn red cedar some time before the Revolution. The OLD CURIOSITY SHOP (1803–1813) was once a house, as was the PUBLIC LIBRARY (1785) at 5 Aviles Street. Its pleasant patio with its fountain is a good place to take a pause in the sun, but there are other gardens to which you will have access, as well. The great sight, of course, is the Fort on Matanzas Bay, which has seen such a lot of history that it was declared a national monument and is now called by its original name, Castillio de San Marcos, more familiar to most of us

as Fort Marion. The Historical Society has a letter by a Spanish governor referring to its completion in 1690. At the same time he spoke of the necessity of rebuilding certain official houses with stone because "they were built of wood and in bad condition." It was at that time, no doubt, that ground floors were built of the native coquina which insulated them from heat and cold and made them sturdy survivors for us to enjoy. On Anastasia Island nearby, there are coquina quarries that have been working since 1600. All of the places mentioned above are open to visitors, as well as those which follow.

HOUSE ON ST. FRANCIS STREET
(*late sixteenth century*)
14–22 St. Francis Street; daily, 9 to 5:30; 50 cents; St. Augustine Historical Society.
When the Society can prove their house's date, the other contestants for "oldest house" will have to concede the honor. At the time that the English, under Sir Francis Drake, burned the town in 1586, a map was drawn by one of his men showing a cluster of houses right here, and an earlier Englishman reported seeing a house here with the date 1571 on it. So the claim is far from fanciful, even though it is not proved. The first floor of the house is coquina; the second story, wood. The floor inside is tapia, a shell and lime mixture two feet in thickness. In its long history, many families have lived in it. When in 1764, during the British occupation, the Spanish moved in a body to Cuba, it was commandeered by Maj. John Peavett, a wealthy Britisher, who added fireplaces to the house which previously had been heated only by charcoal braziers. He may have added the steep roofs as well. There is a detached Spanish kitchen.

FATIO HOUSE (*1806*)
22 Aviles Street; Fridays 2 to 4 during winter season, or on request; National Society of Colonial Dames in Florida.
The main body of the house, built by a Spaniard named Andreas Ximinies, is of coquina mined on nearby Anastasia Island and plastered outside to keep out moisture.

The Llambias house on St. Francis Street in St. Augustine has recently been expertly restored and invitingly furnished.

It is one of the few remaining here that was built by a Spaniard. The slave kitchen in the rear, built before 1750, contains the only example of a stone baking oven left in the town. The house takes its name from Miss Louisa Fatio who bought it in 1855 and in whose family it stayed until the Colonial Dames took it over. It has many interesting features—a long inner gallery, the old cedar doors, unusual moldings, recessed windows with the old glass panes. Rooms are furnished in different periods. In the Spanish room is a beautiful hand-painted prayer desk made of Jacaranda wood in 1784 and a carved ebony chest of 1803, which came from an old house down the street.

LLAMBIAS HOUSE (*prior to 1763*)
31 St. Francis Street; to be open regularly; city of St. Augustine, administered by St. Augustine Historical Society.
The restoration here has just been completed and the house today represents the period 1765–1830. It commemorates the group of colonists and their descendants who came to Florida in the mid-eighteenth century. Its construction is of coquina like the others, but its roofline differs as does its balcony which extends the full length of the front of the house. The roof, without dormers, is vaguely reminiscent of certain dwellings of this period in Mississippi, also largely influenced by the Spanish

occupation. The double porches in the rear with jalousies were used as outdoor sitting rooms. The furnishings are from the period 1800–1840.

CASA DE CANNONOSA (*1740*)
18 St. Francis Street; daily, 9 to 6.
Formerly a residence, it now houses a museum collection.

¶ Tallahassee

Tallahassee was founded in 1824 by an arrangement with the Indians. As the capital and the center of a rich cotton-growing region, it naturally became the most prosperous place in the state before the Civil War. Here the planters made a gay life for themselves and built some stately mansions for show and entertainment. Of these a few remain; outstanding are "The Grove," family seat of the present Governor's lady, and "Goodwood."

THE GROVE (*1836*)
Across from the Governor's Mansion; to be open on request; Governor and Mrs. LeRoy Collins.
"The Grove" is of particular interest because it happens to be the childhood home of the present Governor's wife and has been occupied by her family continuously

since it was built by her great-grandfather, Richard Keith Call, the territorial Governor of the state in 1836. He was a lieutenant on the staff of President Andrew Jackson, who helped him to elope with the first Mary Call, a native of Nashville. They were married at "The Hermitage" there. "The Grove" is said to represent Richard Call's desire to make a home for his Mary as beautiful as those she was accustomed to in Tennessee. The construction took years; all walls, both inside and out, and the massive columns were made of bricks burned on the place. The room walls extend from the ground three stories to the roof. Interesting features of the façade are the brackets over the main entrance which were to hold an iron balcony imported from England. The balcony was lost in a shipwreck, but the brackets remain. The stairway is particularly fine and somewhat resembles that of "The Hermitage," but there the similarity between the houses ends. During the Reconstruction the family was forced to sell much of its fine furniture. However, a few of the early pieces and some silver and glassware remain. Governor Collins and his wife are giving its original beauty back to "The Grove."

GOODWOOD (*1839*)
Miccosukee Road near Tallahassee; by appointment; Mrs. Thomas Hood.

Built by Bryan Croom in 1839, "Goodwood" was four years in the building.

Croom sent to New York for his bricks, doors, and windows; he and his master carpenter, with the help of his slaves, did the work. He lived only four years to enjoy it, for he and his family were drowned on a trip to New York. The great house, built square on simple lines, has unusually pleasing proportions; the detail is so restrained that you hardly realize its size. The delicate columns support an open gallery; both porches are gracefully railed. There is an octagonal cupola like that of Mount Vernon. In point of fact, the house is immense, for the central hall is one hundred feet long. Heavy mahogany doors swing on silver hinges and are capped by fanlights. The ceilings of drawing room and library were frescoed by a French artist and the paint is still remarkably fresh. Through the wide French windows of the drawing room, a delicate tracery of iron balcony is visible. Magnificent gilt mirrors and window cornices add their richness to the Victorian decor. This house has a reputation for lavish hospitality. At one time it had its own private race track.

BOWEN HOUSE (*1830*)
325 North Calhoun Street; by appointment; Mrs. N. M. Bowen.

This is one of the first prefabricated houses in the country. The lumber, New England white pine, was framed in New York State and shipped to St. Marks via New Orleans, then hauled here overland. The pieces

Look for great interior style of the Victorian variety when you visit Goodwood in Tallahassee, even though its exterior in a Late Colonial style may not indicate the charmingly romantic rooms within.

were numbered so that it would be easy for the builder to figure out how to put them together. The whole house was mortised and held together with long wooden pegs. There are two large identical rooms upstairs and down. Handsome cornices, marble mantels, and fine chandeliers were part of the original and are still there today. Gas was actually installed here before the Civil War.

¶ Torreya State Park

GREGORY MANSION (*1833*)
Neil's Bluff, 13 miles northeast of Bristol; Florida State Park Service.

A heavily columned mansion, plainly but handsomely designed for the climate, it was the center of social life in West Florida during the middle of the last century. It was dismantled, floated across the Apalachicola River on barges and reconstructed where it stands in this 1,138-acre park. It has been, or is about to be, furnished in antiques of its period.

¶ Ellenton

GAMBLE MANSION (*1843–1850*)
On the Manatee River; daily except Mondays, Christmas, and New Year 9:30 to 4:30; 25 cents; State Board of Parks and Memorials.

After the Seminole War in 1842, the Manatee country was opened to settlement. Major Gamble held thirty-five hundred acres here, and from his plantation in Tallahassee he brought one hundred and fifty slaves to build his house and create his gardens. The mansion is impressive—built of brick made of lime, sand, and shells, and plastered with a mixture of tabby, the walls are two feet thick. Eighteen massive columns support the roof of the two-story structure, which is ninety-three feet long by fifty feet in depth. In the rear is the kitchen, separated by a breezeway. In 1858 the mansion was sold for $190,000, a tidy sum for a house today and a fortune then. Looted during the Civil War, it was not otherwise harmed. In May, 1865, two men drove up and asked for lodging here; one, a "Mr. Howard," was Judah P. Benjamin, Secretary of State of the late Confederacy. But the house proved unsafe for him; he moved on and after several narrow escapes

reached Cuba. His later career as Queen's Counsel in England is well known. His own memorial you will find in Louisiana, where he lived.

¶ Key West

Key West, too, had its early fling. The furthest west of the string of keys stretching toward Cuba and, by that token, almost a Bahamian city, the influence of the Bahama plantation architecture is clearly seen here. It had its great days in the 1820s and 1830s, the result of sponges and cigars, an export trade largely to Europe which was, in point of fact, easier to reach than New York. The salvage of the cargoes of ships which foundered on the treacherous reefs beyond the harbor was the foundation of many a Key West fortune, for in the laws of salvage the race was to the fleetest. A number of the Bahama houses of the middle 1850s are still comfortably and solidly standing, spacious, easygoing houses that were meant for spacious, easy living. Many of them now have rooms that may be rented by visitors during the season, large airy rooms that suit the climate. The distinctive features of these places are their girdles and festoons of porches with every variety of wooden railing, some of them made a long time ago by hand. Cypress, the native wood growing profusely in the swamps, and mahogany are used for building.

WATLINGTON
322 Duval Street; at regular hours; small fee.

The only "open house" in Key West and the oldest as well. None can tell you its date. Built of cypress and mahogany, it is steep-roofed; a tall double dormer in the center is a later addition not too becoming to it. It sits on a high stone foundation which slopes with the street, and its railed porch or balcony almost hangs over the sidewalk. It is not "kept up," but it is interesting and suits the prevailing mood of Key West, which is easygoing, like the houses.

The Gorgas house on the University of Alabama campus at Tuscaloosa is set apart not only as the home of one of the South's most famous families but as an unusually gracious example of Southern residential architecture. Note the dignified double porch, the sweeping stairways, the sunlight and shadow. Done by the same architect, William Nichols, the President's Mansion across the page, a companion on the campus, is striking in its white and classic splendor.

ALABAMA

¶ *Mobile* ¶ *Montgomery* ¶ *Boligee* ¶ *Selma*
¶ *Greensboro* ¶ *Lowndesboro* ¶ *Tuscaloosa* ¶ *Birmingham*
¶ *Talladega* ¶ *Jacksonville* ¶ *Huntsville* ¶ *Florence*

*D*URING the thirty prosperous years before the Civil War, Alabama's plantations became the principalities of their owners, so to speak. In many cases the great plantation houses took on a palatial splendor, a reflection of the great fortunes being harvested along with the cotton crops.

In the northern part of the state the earlier Georgian treatment introduced by the settlers from Virginia and the Carolinas was superseded by the Greek Revival fashion that conveyed so well the new plantation opulence. Even many of the smaller houses reflect this affluence in one way or another with their own touches of classical grandeur.

In the southern part of the state Mobile, one of the earlier settlements, set its own style as will be seen. While visiting there in 1770, John Bartram, the great Philadelphia botanist, wrote about the French colonial houses in the city. They were apparently built in the same manner as the raised cottages of Louisiana, and for the same reasons—the dampness and prevalence of malarial fevers. But even as far north as Tuscaloosa and Talladega the raised-cottage influence is evident, here endowed with such stateliness that you may not at once recognize its ancestry. Time has taken its toll, of course, but there are still many distinguished survivors.

The arrangement of towns here is one that works its way north from Mobile; it can be followed just as easily in reverse.

¶ *Mobile*

In Mobile there are just enough old places to give enchantment to the town, especially in March, when the azaleas make it a miracle of color. To get the feeling of the old town, walk down Government Street. There is still much "iron-lace" to be seen here, as well as on Conti, Jackson, and North Conception streets; through the delicate iron gateways you can occasionally glimpse quiet patios, all very much in the style of the French Quarter.

The Bellingrath house itself was opened to the public just as we went to press. The fabulous furnishings and priceless collections here, along with the famous gardens, make this one of the outstanding sights in the South.

A good time to take in Mobile and its environs is during the Azalea Trail festivities in early March (for annual dates address P.O. Box 172, Mobile, or the Battle House Hotel). The event lasts a week or more and draws crowds from far and wide, so reserve accommodations well in advance.

KIRKBRIDE HOUSE (1820–1850)

104 Theater Street; daily; Historic Mobile Preservation Society, city of Mobile.

Now the headquarters of the Historic Mobile Preservation Society, it has some homelike rooms furnished from its 1850 period. But of more ancient note, it contains part of old Fort Conde (1717), built by the Sieurs de Bienville and d'Iberville when this region was all part of French Louisiana. It is a good place to obtain local lore which will make for better browsing through this town where the old French and Spanish influences are still pervasive.

GEORGIA COTTAGE (1840)

2564 Spring Hill Avenue; on written request (also during Azalea Trail festival, which lasts several days); small fee; Mrs. E. A. Sledge.

One of the choicest of the old homes, built by Col. John Murrell for his daughter. A tree-lined avenue, bordered in March by brilliant azaleas, leads into a twenty-acre estate. This Greek Revival house has lovely mantels and other fine architectural details. There are many historical pieces among the antique furnishings, such as the marble-top table which belonged to Jefferson Davis. It was inhabited by Augusta Evans, famous Mobile author.

DR. G. G. OSWALT HOME (1870)

964 Government Street; on written request; small fee; Dr. G. G. Oswalt.

Its pleasing façade belongs to the grand period of Mobile's history too. In addition to more recent architectural features, it is famous, even in Mobile, for its large collection of exceptionally interesting antiques.

PALMETTO HALL (early)

55 South McGregor Avenue, Springhill; on request; Mrs. Maisie M. McKeon.

A Southern mansion of the raised-cottage type in a setting of live oak, magnolias, and azaleas. The six fluted columns at second-story height supporting a Greek Revival pediment, and laced together with a lovely balustrade, look as though they may have been added later. The old French influence is strong here. The flight of stairs leading up to the veranda is interesting: beginning as a double flight, the arms turn at a sharp angle where they join. The owner is in process of a leisurely restoration.

¶ Montgomery

A short stroll along Court and Perry between Adams and High Streets will give you the old-time flavor here.

FIRST WHITE HOUSE OF THE CONFEDERACY (1852)

Across from the capitol; daily, 9 to 4:30, except Christmas; state of Alabama.

Moved from its original neighborhood, the First White House is where Jefferson Davis was inaugurated in February, 1861. A simple but substantial town house of the time, lovingly restored, it contains many pieces of the Davis family furniture, as well as other personal possessions of interest.

TEAGUE HOUSE (1848)

Chamber of Commerce; any time.

The chamber has done as handsome a job as you could wish on a distinguished example of Greek Revival by Berry Owens. It is the state headquarters now, but no radical changes have been made, the first

Montgomery's famous Teague house is now her beautiful Chamber of Commerce headquarters.

floor has been furnished in suitable Empire and Victorian for the enjoyment of the public. The iron furniture on the porches and lawn was made at the Jannery Foundry, operated here since before the Civil War. This is proof of the view that old buildings can be useful as well as ornamental.

¶ *Boligee*

ROSEMOUNT (*1830*)

Route 43 between Eutaw and Livingston, from Forkland (on U.S. 43), left on dirt road 10½ miles; daily, 8 to 6; 50 cents; Mrs. Edward de Vesci.

A beautiful blend of Southern charm and grandeur, with columns and cupola, all of period perfection. The Empire furniture traveled from France to Mobile up the Tombigbee River, and then by oxcart to the top of this star-shaped hill.

¶ *Selma*

KENEN PLACE (*1826*)

50 miles west of Montgomery, Summerfield Road; by appointment only; Dr. James Kenen.

A fine example of a house well lived in since ante-bellum days, with a lovely garden. You will hear how Wilson's Raiders burned part of the parlor in 1865. Ask here what else to see in Selma.

¶ *Greensboro*

MAGNOLIA GROVE (*1835–1838*)

At head of Main Street; daily; contribution; state of Alabama (Miss Margaret Hobson, hostess).

The home of Adm. Richard Pearson Hobson, Spanish War hero, whose memory is kept green here by his sister, the resident. Built of handmade brick, with a portico of six great Doric columns, it sits in a grove of giant magnolias. Frescoes and elaborate plasterwork decorate the hallway and several rooms. Family furniture, portraits, and silver are all as they were during Hobson's lifetime.

Rosemount's crown is a kingsized cupola of noble proportions.

¶ *Lowndesboro*

THE COLONNADE (*1852*)

> *20 miles west of Montgomery, on U.S. 80;*
> *by written or phone request; Mrs. R. B.*
> *Hagood.*

Good old Greek Revival inside and out, with elaborate plasterwork friezes and ceiling rosettes. Furnished for comfort, with some antiques.

¶ *Tuscaloosa*

At the fall line of the Black Warrior River, this town has a style all its own. How any of it has survived, however, is hard to understand, for, according to Davy Crockett, it was "wiped from the face of the earth" when, during the Indian revolt against the whites of 1813, Crockett's commanding officer captured and burned it. Later, in 1865, the University of Alabama buildings were burned, and much other damage done by Northern troops. In spite of all this, the houses here date from the period when Tuscaloosa was the state capital (1825–1846).

GOVERNOR'S MANSION (*1834–1835*)

> *Now the Faculty Club, on campus; on*
> *request; University of Alabama.*

The third of the three buildings on the campus that survived the burning, this mansion housed the governor when Tuscaloosa was the state capital. The mansion, including its very elegant interior features, has not been disturbed.

WHIGHAM HOUSE (*1824*)

> *1217 Greensboro Avenue; March and*
> *April; $1.00; Mrs. J. H. Whigham.*

Furnished in excellent taste, with exquisite iron grillwork.

GORGAS HOUSE (*1829*)

> *Also on campus; Monday to Friday, 10 to*
> *12 and 2 to 5; University of Alabama*
> *(Mrs. Bertha L. Miller in charge).*

With a façade of even greater elegance and grace, this is part of the original University group designed by William Nichols. Fully furnished as it was when the home of the Confederate general, Josiah Gorgas,

one-time president of the University, and of his son Gen. William C. Gorgas of yellow-fever fame.

PRESIDENT'S MANSION (*1841*)

> *On the University campus; on written*
> *request; University of Alabama (residence*
> *of Dr. Oliver Carmichael, President).*

An unusually harmonious and stately house, with an exquisite iron railing and double-wing stairs leading up to the story-high first floor. The original interior is still intact, furnished with serviceable antiques from near and far.

Not open, but well worth looking at, are the DEARING-SWAIM HOUSE (1835–1837), 21st Street and Fourteenth Avenue, with its sixteen Ionic columns—one of the finest of Alabama's domestic temples; the old STAGECOACH INN (1827); and CHEROKEE (ante-bellum), an extraordinary Italianate villa crowned by an observation tower.

¶ *Birmingham*

MUDD-MUNGER HOUSE (*c. 1842*)

> *331 Cotton Avenue, S.W.; daily, 9 to 5,*
> *except Sunday 2 to 5; 50 cents and 25*
> *cents; city of Birmingham (Arlington*
> *Historic Association in charge).*

This impressive mansion with its gardens was here thirty years before the city itself, which explains its country-seat appearance. Ballroom with Waterford crystal chandelier; Sheraton, Hepplewhite, and Empire galore, as well as some beautiful china collections.

¶ *Talladega*

This is a town decidedly worth seeing if you are anywhere in the vicinity. Sometimes a house tour is conducted in October, about which the Talladega Pilgrimage Club can inform you. There is real Southern charm here.

SALTER PLACE (*date unknown*)

> *East Street; April; by appointment only;*
> *no charge; Dr. and Mrs. C. L. Salter.*

Surely one of the loveliest Greek Revival structures in the state—a mansion so carefully proportioned that its scale is minimized. The detail is classical, except for the ornate iron rails which lead up the wing steps and lace the porch. Please observe the "julep pavilion," which was formerly just a step from either the dining room or kitchen, and is now joined to the house by a breezeway. Large collections of glass.

MC ALPINE PLACE (*prior to 1830*)
> *505 East Street S.; April, preferably by written request; $1.00; Mrs. T. R. Williams.*

A large, unusual arcaded porch, with a balustraded Palladian dormer above. The house and its lush setting remind you of the New Orleans Garden District. Furnished with family heirlooms.

ELLIOTT HOUSE (*c. 1845*)
> *511 East Street; April, by appointment; $1.00; Mr. and Mrs. Julian Elliott.*

A gracious Southern mansion with four great fluted columns supporting a balconied portico; sumptuously furnished with antiques throughout.

THORNHILL (*1834*)
> *R.F.D. 2; daily in summer, on request; no charge; Mrs. Scears Lee.*

An attractive and impressive early plantation home built by a Scotsman, James Hardie, who had a mile-long race track, now gone. Mrs. Lee describes it as furnished in Victorian collected by "a family in moderate circumstances."

IDLEWILD (*1829*)
> *Near town; by request in advance (please give ample notice); Mr. and Mrs. Turner Jones (telephone number 4153).*

A tall, impressive brick mansion built by Gen. William B. McClellan. You can tell it by its two-column, two-story portico. "Betsy" Hamilton, well-known dialect writer, lived here.

MT. IDA (*1830*)
> *10 miles south, near Winterboro, 1½ miles off Route 241 at historical marker; April, at other times only by appointment; $1.00 and 50 cents; Mr. and Mrs. Raleigh B. Kent, Talladega 6782.*

This seat of fifteen hundred acres of grazing land is a tall, square dwelling of such imposing mien that it rates a historical marker. The original house was converted by its builder, Walker Reynolds, into this mansion before the Civil War. Furniture is Victorian and earlier.

The square-columned Mudd-Munger house in Birmingham is now the Arlington Shrine.

¶ *Jacksonville*

THE MAGNOLIAS (*1850*)
> *603 North Pelham Road; on written request; $1.00; Mrs. C. W. Daugette.*

The Magnolias is inhabited by the daughter of the famous Confederate general, John H. Forney, a hero of Vicksburg. The house is redolent of its region and period, and, with its association and memorabilia, is well worth visiting for any student of the Civil War era.

¶ *Huntsville*

Called "City of Governors" because six of them have lived here, Huntsville has, for a town hard hit by the Civil War, a remarkably unscathed number of its oldest homes, handsomely kept. Tours of twenty or more of them are generally conducted in May (for exact dates inquire of the Huntsville branch of the American Association of University Women). However, the owners of the home listed below have graciously consented to let them be seen at almost any time on request. They are open daily and at no charge if no dates or conditions are stated below.

BASSETT-YOUNG HOUSE
(between 1819 and 1823)
600 Franklin Street; Miss Sophye L. Young.

The spirit is Georgian, the stair hall spacious, the ceilings high, the rooms enormous, and the furnishings heirlooms of four preceding generations, of which Miss Young is the fifth to live here.

CABANISS HOUSE *(1832)*
602 Randolph Street; on request two weeks in advance; Miss Ellen D. Roberts.

Most of the furniture remains just where it was placed by "Ma" Virginia Shepherd Cabaniss, who lived here for sixty-four years and whose hospitable spirit, which still pervades the house, is a Huntsville legend.

WATKINS HOUSE *(1850s)*
603 Adams Avenue; by appointment; any fee to charity; Mr. and Mrs. Milton K. Cummings.

This home has a two-story Corinthian portico and three spiral staircases, one of them ascending to the cupola. Built by James Bell, a Negro slave carpenter from Charlottesville, Virginia, who devoted three years to the task. All interior woodwork is walnut, and the Carrara mantels are elaborately carved. There is also a complete

Belter suite by the New York cabinet-maker who carved rosewood as though he were spinning sugar lace.

WEEDEN HOUSE *(1819 and 1832)*
Gates and Green Streets; on request by letter or phone; Mrs. Ben Lee Bibb.

A good example of the Georgian Colonial in Alabama. Jeffersonian in feeling, its double walnut doors are crowned by a fanlight of high quality. Windows are large. The interior has carved mantels and baseboards and family furniture of the eighteenth and nineteenth centuries. It was the lifetime home of Miss Howard Weeden, poet and painter (1847–1905), whose grandniece lives here now.

EWING-THORNTON HOUSE, *or* CEDARHURST *(1825)*
2000 Whitesburg Drive on Route 38, 2 miles out; April and October; Mr. and Mrs. J. D. Thornton.

An exceptionally fine example of a wealthy planter's home, it sits among giant trees and commands a sweeping view. The rooms are tremendous, and furnished with old family pieces. Don't miss it.

THE TOWERS *(c. 1820)*
558 Franklin Street; by appointment; $1.00; Mrs. B. A. Stockton, Jefferson 6–3623.

Birthplace of Gen. John Hunt Morgan, the rebel raider, whose family moved to Kentucky in 1830. The Neal family (1850–1949) remodeled the old fourteen-room

One of the most eye-catching features of Mapleton in Florence is the delicacy of its carved mantels and doorways.

brick house into a twenty-four-room town house and brought in an English gardener, much of whose fine landscaping remains today. Most of the furniture is at least one hundred years old and belonged to the Neal family; the present owner, Mrs. B. A. Stockton, bought it intact.

ERSKINE-HENDRICK HOUSE
(c. 1818)
527 Franklin Street; year round except December, January or July, by appointment only; Mrs. Ada V. Hendrick.

Has the early, indigenous look. Some of the furniture was brought by oxcart from Nashville.

POPE-PATTON-WATTS HOUSE
(c. 1815)
100 Echols Street; May and October, on written request; Mr. and Mrs. James F. Watts.

A mansion with a magnificent setting and furnished in Queen Anne, Chippendale, and Sheraton (rare enough in these parts where Victorian predominates).

GEN. JOE WHEELER HOUSE
(1818, west wing 1860s)
47 miles west of Huntsville on Route 20; those interested should inquire of University of Alabama in Tuscaloosa to whom it has been willed.

Both historically and visually interesting, this was the family home of the colorful "Fighting Joe" Wheeler, lieutenant general in the Confederate Army, major general in charge of volunteers in the Spanish-American War, lawyer, planter, author, and member of Congress.

¶ Florence

FORKS OF CYPRESS (1818)
Route 4; on request; small fee for large party; Rufus B. Dowdy.

Famous for its peristyle of twenty-four Ionic columns, its restoration and furnishing in period authenticity is a hobby of the owner's, who lives elsewhere; but a

The portico of Rogers Hall, with its paired Ionic columns, is one of the fine sights of Florence.

caretaker or nearby relatives will show on request. "No charge unless traffic becomes too heavy," says the owner.

MAPLETON (1820)
420 South Pine Street; any time by appointment.

This is a place of rare beauty. Double front doors with a fine fanlight; double parlors with exquisite McIntire-like carving; authentic furniture of the period.

WAKEFIELD (1825)
450 North Court Street; at all times; Mr. J. Hurd Walker.

Built by James Sawyer for his bride Parthenia McVey, daughter of the early Georgia Governor Wakefield, it is now kept open by the present owner in memory of his wife, whose hospitable spirit still pervades the lovely house.

ROGERS HALL, *formerly* COURTVIEW (1855)
Used as social hall for State Teachers College; daily.

At one time the showplace of the town. Although the exterior is intact, its use for group activities has made appropriate furnishing difficult.

The fine old homes of Mississippi are of many moods, styles, and states of preservation, but predominantly of the Greek and Gothic revivals and for the most part remarkably well preserved, notably at Natchez. Imagine the classic Corinthian splendor of Windsor Plantation in its prime, as it stood proudly above the river at Port Gibson—now a spectacular ruin. Consider the Gothic charm of Cedarhurst at Holly Springs, across the page.

MISSISSIPPI

*T*HE RIVER from which it takes its name has given this state much of its character. The great "Father of Waters," which flows the length of the state to the sea, has deposited the wealth of the soil of half a continent right in the lap of Mississippi, as well as furnishing the means for transporting the yield from this soil. Caprice is another of its aspects: often it has turned enemy, flooding the farms and towns. And finally, it has produced its own climate, moist and warm, strongly affecting the whole tempo of life and thought in large sections of the state.

That the French, Spanish, and English all early recognized the territory as a prize accounts for the fact that these three influences are all visible in the architecture of the state. In many of the buildings of Natchez, whose justly fam-

ous houses have made its name familiar throughout the country, can be traced the influence of the Spanish dons who, though they ruled there only briefly, left a strong impression. The French, of course, have left their imprint both here and in Louisiana with the raised cottage, the dominant style in both states. Raised a story or a half story to avoid the damp and the floods in the lowlands, their construction is reminiscent of the provincial French farmhouse. But a humid climate soon made the addition of long, wide porches and galleries, on which the family might spread out and cool off, a standard feature. Thus a special style came into being, distinguished by a casual spaciousness and simplicity. Cypress, being plentiful, was used most frequently, and it stood the climate well; it is for this reason that so many of these homes still

129

exist in spite of neglect. Owners who had more slaves were more likely to use handmade brick; it was considered more elegant.

The English, especially the wealthy Tories who were refugees during and after the Revolution, brought their money, their aristocratic manners, and their Georgian architectural preference with them, making certain adaptations to the climate and the easy way of life. The Georgian style speaks here with a Southern accent in spite of itself.

¶ Holly Springs

This town is located just south of the Tennessee border 40 miles from Memphis on Route 78. Five houses may be seen, at 50 cents each, through an arrangement with the *Guide*. Requests must be cleared through the Holly Springs Garden Club, the proceeds going to its restoration fund.

The Chickasaw Indians gave Holly Springs its lovely name because they stopped here, where their trail crossed a high ridge on the way from the Mississippi to their tribal headquarters, to drink at a crystal spring in a glade of

The Magnolias is one of Holly Springs' choice collection of early homes.

holly trees. In 1832 they ceded the land to the United States, and the glade on the ridge soon took on the aspects of a boom town in what might well have been called the "cotton rush." It was rapidly populated by fortune seekers from Tidewater Virginia and their slaves—the richness of the soil and the high, healthy location of the place caused a mushroom growth of greater than usual speed. Fortunes were made so rapidly that the settlers were building themselves mansions almost before they had passed through the log-cabin stage, and, as you will see, they well remembered their Tidewater homes when they built. But the period of prosperity was brief, for the fortunes of the Civil War brought the town within the pincers of Grant's and Sherman's converging attack on Vicksburg, and it was raided some sixty-one times in all. Later, in 1878, half of its population was wiped out by yellow fever. Also, the first waves of planters had ruthlessly exploited the land, and by this time erosion was taking its toll of the soil. Fortunately for us, however, the houses of its early grandeur have survived all the disasters; and age, which with a little help treats stone, brick, and wood so kindly, has only added to their quality.

THE MAGNOLIAS (*1850s*)
Mrs. Everett Sladen, President of Garden Club.
The elaborate ironwork of the porch throws its delicate shadows over the broad Tudor arch of the entrance like a lace mantilla. The house was built as a wedding present, and really looks like one. Inside are spacious double parlors, a spiral staircase, and fine antiques which include Dresden china and beautiful silver.

CEDARHURST (*1857*)
Mr. and Mrs. Fred Belk.
Another Gothic house, but delightfully ornate, of red brick with white trim. It looks like an outsized valentine. Built by

Miss Sherwood Bonner, gifted writer of Southern-dialect stories and secretary to Henry Wadsworth Longfellow, it contains Venetian glass and plush period furniture.

FEATHERSTON PLACE (*1834*)
Mr. and Mrs. George M. Buchanan.

A raised and rather classical cottage, with deep portico porches whose corners are supported by triple columns. The basement here is used as a dining room, kitchen, and cool summer living room. The Chippendale parlor furniture is said to be by Savery of Philadelphia.

GREY GABLES (*1830*)
Headquarters of Garden Club.

Behind its valentine porch and Victorian gables are the simple, old, familiar forms of Eastern Colonial. It is the first restoration of the Garden Club, and its pride. The design of the richly carved woodwork is repeated on the ceilings in plaster, and Bohemian stained glass decorates the transoms above the doors. There is a fine spiral staircase, and the furnishings throughout are well chosen.

WALTER PLACE (*1855*)
On request, through Garden Club (not regularly included); Mrs. Oscar Johnson.

This is the showplace of Holly Springs—an extraordinary large-scale brick house, with an imposing Corinthian portico flanked by octagonal Gothic corner towers. Of the four tower rooms, one is a study and three are bathrooms. It was built at the height of the wealth and largesse of this area, and includes spacious rooms, graceful staircases, and much ornamentation. General and Mrs. Grant stayed here during the Vicksburg campaign.

MONTROSE (*1858*)
On request, through Garden Club (not regularly included); Mrs. Jackson Johnson.

Another impressive brick mansion of the same period whose Corinthian columns support a fanlighted pediment and whose window heads are of ornamental ironwork from a local foundry that flourished here when ironlace was the fashion. The interior is equally ornate, with molded cornices, ceiling medallions, and other elaborations of the place and period. Fine furniture here as well.

Maxland's tall-columned façade is made even more impressive by the ancient cedars that line its broad brick approach.

Fant Place is another of Holly Springs' show pieces: the two-story columns, the towering evergreen magnolias, the ornamental ironwork, and naturally the noble scale of the rooms within.

THE MIMOSAS (1838)

Mrs. L. D. Tucker and Mrs. Heath Loftin.
The first two-story house in Holly Springs, it was built by Roger Barton, one of the four men who planned the town. Its "Mount Vernon" front and Colonial look place it in the period just before the rage for Greek Revival and Gothic. It is filled with family heirlooms.

MAXLAND, FANT PLACE, BOX HILL, STRICKLAND PLACE (1821), and many others may be seen on the annual tour sponsored by the Holly Springs Garden Club, which usually takes place the last week in April. The entire town has a very special appeal.

¶ Pontotoc

The county seat, where the Federal land office was located after the Chickasaw Indians had ceded their northern territories and the rich delta land was attracting many settlers from the east, was known as a center of cultured and independent-minded people in the early days. The county seems to have had its own mores, and something of this individualism still clings.

LOCHINVAR (1836)

On request; J. B. Fontaine.
Standing on the highest hill in the county, this great, white, porticoed monument to the storied past is another emblem of the vast fortunes that are gone. It was the home of Robert Gordon, a young Scotsman, who fell in love with the country, struck it rich, and founded the city of Aberdeen. The house was built the hard way—every timber cut by hand of heart pine. Eight of its fifteen rooms are twenty-two feet square. There are two wide halls and, beneath them, three cellars. A free-standing staircase ascends in graceful curves three stories to the observatory. Its present owner has restored the mansion in so far as means allow.

Other houses of interest here are the TURNER THOMASON, 705 South Congress Street; the JACK FONTAINE, 1210 South Congress Street; the FRANK A. CLARK, a half mile northeast on 6 on the site of the old land office; and the SPENCER HOUSE, a mile out, the best example of a pioneer home in this section.

¶ Aberdeen

Once the center of a highly prosperous cotton-growing region on the Tombigbee River, with steamboats carrying the rich cargo to Mobile, it is now removed from the main stream of progress, and so retains, along with many of its homes, the unhurried pace of the Old South. The wide streets are lined with shade trees and white columns. Eight of the ancestral homes, all of whose owners have graciously consented to allow visitors "on request," are listed here.

THE MAGNOLIAS (1849)

Dr. and Mrs. J. M. Acker.
Considered one of the finest of the antebellum homes in Aberdeen, it was owned for many years by Capt. T. B. Sykes, the Confederate hero. In the same family for five generations, it is filled with a museum collection of heirlooms.

GEN. REUBEN DAVIS HOUSE (1852)

Mrs. Chester Brummett.
Diagonally across the way from "The Magnolias" is this pillared mansion of a noted soldier and lawyer whose niece Mrs. Edmonia H. Nichols lived here until recently. The house is impressively simple with its seven fluted columns and deep, shady porch. Its owner will show the lower floor.

LAURI MUNDI (1845)

March and April; Mrs. Mary Therrell Paine and Mrs. T. A. Claiborne.
Once the home of Methodist Bishop Paine, and still owned by a direct descendant. The family has been in possession since the days of the Indians, the original deed having been signed by the Chickasaw chieftain,

Lotty James. The beautiful grounds and magnificent trees enhance this delicately columned mansion.

MAGNOLIA HILL (*1849*)
Dr. and Mrs. N. S. Dickson.

Not far away is "Magnolia Hill," furnished in the period and with a most attractive garden as well.

HOLLIDAY HAVEN (*1850*)
Mr. and Mrs. Julian Evans.

Owned by the fifth generation of the family that built it—you may be greeted by the fifth "Marian" to live in this splendid old colonial house built by Col. John Holliday. The art treasures and heirlooms have been zealously preserved by the present generation.

TEN ACRES (*1850*)
Mrs. John B. McFarland.

Stands on the original ten-acre block bought by this family when the town was laid out in 1838. Interesting antiques here.

MC FARLAND HOME (*1852*)
Mrs. Ben H. McFarland.

Belonged to Judge J. Baxter McFarland. Its present occupant, Mrs. Ben H. McFarland, the widow of the judge's son, is justly proud of the fine library of 3,000 books, many of them first editions, which belonged to the judge.

GREENLEAVES (*c. 1865*)
Mrs. Guy Hartwell Watkins.

An "Old Betsy" cannon from Reconstruction days guards the entrance and the formal gardens. This place has the somewhat later appearance of the Classical Revival.

THE OAKS (*1842*)
Mrs. John Whyte Donelson.

The oldest house in town, built of logs and covered with plank sheathing. You may find others like it if you look or consult Miss Lucille Peacock, the librarian, who knows all about them and has helped us to make the special presentation here.

¶ Starkville

The first settlers here were wealthy landowners from Virginia and the Carolinas who grew still wealthier on the rich, black Prairie soil. The wide, tree-lined streets of this once-prosperous town give ample if faded evidence of the opulence which prevailed here. Here and nearby can be seen a few houses with the Georgian lines which their owners brought with them from the seaboard states.

OUTLAW HOUSE (*1835*)

The two-story Outlaw House has a distinctly Georgian appearance. Its slender columns are characteristic of the neighborhood, where the lightness of the frame structures needed no stronger support.

RICE HOUSE (*1842*)

Of the same vintage as the Outlaw House, with a two-story portico, slender columns, and hipped roof.

MONTGOMERY HOUSE (*1839*)

Attractively proportioned, it was built by an Englishman, and is known as an "imported house" because he chose to reproduce his eighteenth-century English manor in the twilight of this grove of cedars.

DR. JAMES GILLESPIE HOUSE (*1850*)

A Prairie (meaning, of course, the so-called "Black Prairie" of Mississippi, once its richest soil) adaptation of Greek Revival.

It may be possible to visit all these houses and perhaps others of equal interest by getting in touch with Mr. John K. Betterworth at State College, who will be able to advise you further and furnish directions.

¶ Columbus

The chamber of commerce will arrange for you to see four of the lovely homes for a fee of one dollar per house at any time of the year. These will be chosen to suit the convenience of the owners from a group of about eight or ten which are in the annual three-day tour. The tour

The graceful double staircase of the Thomas house is a delightful feature of this little classic gem.

takes place the last week in March, when more than a dozen homes may be seen for five dollars.

Columbus is the first place mentioned in any existing record of Mississippi, for De Soto crossed the Tombigbee River here in 1540. Today it is within easy driving distance from Birmingham, Mobile, Memphis, Jackson, and Greenville. There are about forty old houses in all here, many of them essentially unchanged, dating from the 1830s to the 1860s and covering every architectural style that existed in this section of the South.

W. PRATT THOMAS HOME (*1833*)

Of the raised-cottage type but with unique features. Its central part, the proportions of which are delightful, is approached by an unusual banistered double flight of steps and crowned by a balustrade. The wings, only slightly recessed, rest on a solid-brick foundation. The exterior is so interesting that you should not miss it, even if the interior is not on view when you are there. The brick walls which surround the grounds were built after the Civil War of bricks

from the old Confederate arsenal. The furniture here is heirloom.

FAIRLEIGH MANOR (*1838*)

Of painted brick with an oval light in the pediment, it reflects the growing Federal influence of the period in its fine proportions and air of restrained dignity. Mrs. Leigh is a descendant of one of the early owners, and her grandchildren make the eighth generation of the family to live here.

RIVERVIEW (*1844*)

A baronial mansion whose cupola house alone, with its three long, colored windows on each side, would constitute today a penthouse dwelling for a small family. The house has six chimneys, and the homemade bricks used in its construction weigh eleven and a half pounds each. The window headings, the capitals of the pillars, and the porch floors are of marble. The rich decorations in plaster on the ceiling and cornice are among the finest examples of plasterwork in the state.

THE CEDARS (*1830*)

A good example, by contrast, of the chaste charm of the earlier dwellings, this was the second house built here and had the first cooking stove in town. It was constructed as a two-story log house; additions were made in the 1830s. Much of the original atmosphere is retained.

FRANKLIN SQUARE (*early 1840s*)

This impressive red-brick town house has pillared porticos front and side, fine furniture, silver, and glass, and portraits of five generations of the family.

HOMEWOOD (*1836*)

A combination of the classic and romantic to which much of the ornamentation was obviously added later. Crystal chandeliers, handsome furniture, silver, and glass.

SNOWDOWN (*1840s*)

Jefferson Davis was serenaded here while standing in his nightshirt on the balcony. Its octagonal hall and other features are the result of a visit to Monticello by its builder, Gov. James Whitfield.

¶ *Scooba*

GILES PLANTATION (*c. 1830*)

4½ miles east by Routes 16, 17, and 45; on request only; Mr. and Mrs. Shepherd Spencer Neville.

Built by the owners' great-grandfather, Jacob Giles, this is an H-shaped building with three porticoes and hand-hewn columns on the front. Each of its ten rooms opens onto a porch. It has some fine plastered ceilings. The cornices in the drawing rooms have an unusually chaste and lovely ornamentation, and the furniture and mirrors throughout are the original pieces. The owners feel that much work needs to be done on the house, and they expect to do it gradually.

¶ *Grenada*

S. F. WILLIAMSON HOUSE (*1850*)

201 Margin Street; on request; Mrs. Sam I. Williamson.

In 1829 Mr. Williamson arrived here from Virginia with his slaves by oxcart. Using the broadax, mortising the joints, and fastening them with wooden pins, he and the slaves built this house of the virgin timber in the area. The stone columns were shipped from France via New Orleans and the Mississippi, Yazoo, and Yalobusha Rivers; for in those days, when a man needed something for his house, he couldn't get it from Sears, Roebuck. The place is furnished with antiques.

There are others listed at one time or another as open by appointment; courteous request will undoubtedly enable you to visit now some of the following: the IDA CAMPBELL HOME (oldest house in town); CUFF'S HILL; the ESTELL ROLLIN HOME (1830s), 422 Doak Street; the JOHN NASON HOME, 410 College Street; and the GOLLIDAY LAKE HOME, 605 Margin Street.

¶ *Indianola*

There are some lovely old places here. The owners are usually willing to show them to interested people on request, the mayor assures us.

DUNLEITH (*1847*)

10 miles from Indianola plus ½ mile on gravel road; by appointment; W. R. French.

A rambling stucco house with red-tile roof, once valued at a million dollars and still considered one of the finest of the Delta plantations.

¶ *Jackson*

EXECUTIVE MANSION (*1834–1841*)

On capitol grounds; on request by phone or letter to the hostess at the Mansion; state of Mississippi.

The front entrance is a replica of the east entrance of the White House in Washington—a semicircular portico supported by four Corinthian columns. William Nichols was the architect, and he saw that the interiors received the elaborate formality considered fitting. The red-brick exterior is now painted white, adding to the impressive effect of the whole.

¶ *Vicksburg*

Few cities have suffered such a variety of violence—war, floods, and hurricanes. In order to appreciate her old homes, it would be well to brush up on her history.

DUFF GREEN HOUSE (*1840s*)

Southwest corner Locust and First East Street; now used by Salvation Army.

A four-story brick mansion once noted for its hospitality and its magnificent balls, the exterior is still exquisite, with galleries, cornices, and railings of the finest ironwork creating a series of six frames, top and bottom, for the great doors and long French windows which open onto the galleries.

PODESTA-KLEIN (*c. 1838*)

2200 Oak Street; daily to visitors accompanied by official guide; 50 cents; Dr. A. J. Podesta.

Standing but a few hundred yards from the Mississippi, this is an imposing brick mansion with Ionic portico and wings. It has a ballroom, banquet hall, and reception hall on the first floor, not uncommon in the type of Southern home where the entertaining was on the grand scale. The second floor generally became the family living quarters. That part of the house which is now open to the public contains some rare antiques. The family occupies other portions. One of the walls still holds a cannon ball which tore into it during the siege of Vicksburg.

ALEXANDER MC NUTT HOUSE
(1828)
East and Monroe Streets.

Built by an early governor of the state, this house, of the New England Colonial type, is anomalous here with its simple, almost severe lines. Although recently sold, it may still be seen on request as in the past.

And note these in passing: the MARSHALL-BRYAN (1835), 1128 Grove Street; the THREE OLD HOUSES on Crawford Street; and the COOK-ALLEIN HOME (1826), 1104 Harrison Street.

¶ *McGarry's Forks*

SPRINGFIELD PLANTATION *(1791)*
2 miles from McGarry's Forks in Jefferson County; 25 cents; R. G. Allen.

This two-story "planter-style" home recalls vividly the Spanish occupation, for the woodwork and mantels, of unusual interest, were carved by Spanish workmen. Andrew Jackson and Rachel Donelson were married here soon after it was completed in 1791.

RICHLAND *(1840s)*
½ mile from McGarry's Forks; 25 cents; R. G. Allen, Springfield Plantation, Jefferson County.

The granddaughter of Col. Thomas Green, who built Springfield, inherited the plantation, and her husband built Richland. Located in a grove of cedars and surrounded by shade trees, crape myrtles, and camellias, it is a wide, well-proportioned mansion with square columns and broad galleries.

¶ *Port Gibson*

SERENITY *(1817)*
702 Church Street; on request; Mayor Frank C. Englesing.

This one-story frame dwelling still de-

serves the name. According to its owner, descendant of the builder and mayor of the town, it represents the average town house of a comfortable planter prior to the Civil War. It happens also to have been the birthplace of Constance Cary, who made the first Confederate flags out of silk dresses, and whose father had been raised in the Jefferson household. The house is low, spreading, comfortable-looking, and surrounded by century-old lawns and gardens. The furniture is mainly of about 1850, with some earlier family pieces and two portraits by Healey. Here is a tradition of culture without ostentation.

GAGE HOUSE *(1851)*
602 Church Street; June and at other times when owner is at home; Mrs. Robert Douglas Gage.

Another typical house of the midcentury, with the slender columns in double tiers characteristic of this section of the state. When Grant came through the town, he said it was too pretty to destroy; however, he is reputed to have taken fifty of the old people here to Vicksburg as hostages, and Mrs. Gage, the owner, says that her grandfather, James Alexander Gage, was one of them. The house still contains many of the pieces that he placed there originally.

THE RUINS OF WINDSOR *(1861)*
About 10 miles out of town; inquire.

Twenty-two massive fluted Corinthian columns are all that remain of the glory that was Greek Revival here. Laced together at the level of what was the second-story gallery by an ornamental iron railing, these romantic columns must eventually give way to the vines that are already rampant. When the house was built in 1861, it was considered the final word in the "grand manner," standing five stories and cupola high and furnished in keeping. Mark Twain and other steamboat pilots on the Mississippi charted their course here by its tower. In 1890 it was gutted by fire; only the columns remain to tell its story.

¶ *Natchez*

For our readers, Natchez is one of the most fascinating towns in America, a perfect mirror to the past. In Natchez, once the territorial capital, flourished a society of graceful culture based on a fabulous prosperity founded on cheap land, cotton, and slaves. The town's many mansions are one of its by-products. The successive French, English, and Spanish rules, which in turn gave way to the surge of American immigration from the East, all left traces of their influence on the homes. Everything conspired here to create an architecture of opulence, where limitless personal service was available, where hands were so many that the need for machines was not even considered.

Of the homes of the French who came here first under Bienville back in 1716, and who fought it out with the Chickasaw Indians, there is no trace, though their influence can be identified in places of later date. The British were here for only a little more than ten years, and then they ceded the territory to the Spanish in 1797. Under the dons Natchez began to prosper. Although their occupation lasted scarcely a lustrum, they, more than any other influence, gave the town its flavor. Their houses had a Castilian somberness, the severe exteriors showing the Mediterranean orientation, the ornate interiors intended for stately, luxurious living. Their fastidious love of style left its imprint on the whole social fabric.

After 1800 the territory was organized by the United States and the Mississippi opened to navigation. As the river traffic reached fantastic proportions, Natchez was on its way to becoming one of the richest ports in the South. Next came the opening of the Natchez Trace, the land road which helped to carry the growing wealth of the area to the North and East—molasses, pelts, grains, and tobacco, and, a little later, the cotton, and ever more cotton, that was to make everybody rich. Adventurers flocked in as well as wealthy planters from Virginia and the Carolinas and other parts of the East who wanted to become still wealthier, and did.

Eventually Natchez became a center of a sophisticated, pleasure-loving society, where manners were as important as wealth and where both were present to a high degree. In many ways this society was unique in America, and it produced something quite distinctive in the way of architecture. That so many of the

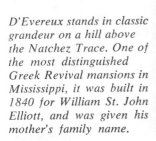

D'Evereux stands in classic grandeur on a hill above the Natchez Trace. One of the most distinguished Greek Revival mansions in Mississippi, it was built in 1840 for William St. John Elliott, and was given his mother's family name.

houses built at the peak of that spacious and affluent period have survived and have been preserved, many even furnished as they then were, is indeed one of the more commendable miracles of our industrial era. Benign have been the fortunes of progress that left Natchez a backwater to be rediscovered by lovers of antiquity.

The Natchez Tour, which lasts from February 27 through March 31, takes in all the houses listed and described below, and the following others as well: HAWTHORNE (1814), GLOUCESTER (prior to 1803), MONMOUTH (1818), D'EVEREUX (1840), and CHEROKEE (1794), one of the oldest.

General information about the tour may be received, and inquiries about room reservations for accommodations in ante-bellum houses on the Tour or in other private residences may be answered, by writing to the Natchez Pilgrimage, Natchez, Mississippi. For hotel accommodations write direct to the Eola, the Natchez, or the Belmont Motor Hotel. There are two tours daily; a ticket for all thirty houses is $20.00, for five houses $4.00, for ten houses $8.00, and so on. Make reservations well in advance—the tour season is popular.

ARLINGTON (*1816*)
Daily, 9 to 5; $1.20; Mrs. Hubert Barnum.
Sure to be one of the high points of your trip. A square, red-bricked mansion with tall white columns, its fanlighted doors and pediment give it lightness in spite of its great size. In spring the delicate effect is enhanced by towering shell-pink azaleas. The architect, James Hampton White of New Jersey, built it during the days when Indians still inhabited the region. Part of the great interest of this place lies in the fact that some of the original furniture is preserved, along with priceless portraits by

One of the great beauties of the Natchez neighborhood, Arlington has a quality that could almost be called Charlestonian; and as lovely and chaste as it looks from without, so rich and rare are its interiors.

Sully, Vernet, and Audubon, a notable glass collection, and a century-old library of eight thousand rare volumes purchased in London.

DUNLEITH (*1848*)
Daily, 9 to 5; 60 cents; Mr. and Mrs. Leslie Carpenter.

With its many tall white columns gleaming through the trees, its tall chimneys and its dormers, its deep galleries laced round with iron railings, and its various brick dependencies, Dunleith has been the home of the Carpenter family for five generations. It has all the look of a gracious country dwelling designed for spacious living and is perhaps the best example of the manner in which the wealthy planter adopted the classic to suit his easy, casual, and luxurious way of living.

CONNELLY'S TAVERN (*1795*)
Ellicott's Hill; daily, 9 to 5; 60 cents; Natchez Garden Club.

Built during the Spanish rule, it is deemed by many the architectural gem of Natchez.

There is probably no better example of Spanish provincial architecture in the South. Its immensely long double galleries, broken nine times by slender posts, the typical outside staircase, and the deep brick foundation and brick-walled terraces give it extraordinary distinction. No wonder the Natchez Garden Club made it their project to restore it. Here, in defiance of the Spanish, Andrew Ellicott raised the American flag for the first time in the lower Mississippi Valley. Here also Aaron Burr is supposed to have met with Blennerhasset to prepare their treason defense in 1807.

ELGIN PLANTATION
(prior to 1812)
Daily, 9 to 5; 50 cents; Mrs. S. R. Beane and family.

A typical plantation house of the early period, it was built by Sir William Dunbar and named for his birthplace in Scotland. The oldest part was occupied in 1780; its blue poplar floors and blown-glass panes establish its antiquity. The main part, how-

Almost surrounded by its two-story colonnaded porches, Dunleith is one of the most palatial plantation houses in the South, a true embodiment of the wealthy, aristocratic, slave-holding society of its time and place.

Green Leaves is incomparable among the Natchez mansions for the lovely detailing of its woodwork, the delicacy of its ornamental iron, and the colorfulness of its interiors—its twin parlors in particular.

ever, was built in 1840 for Annis, Sir William's granddaughter. The front galleries are ninety feet long, not unusual for Natchez. The present owner's grandmother made the trip to Philadelphia as a bride in 1848 to purchase most of the furniture. Many of the lovely pieces she chose are still here, including a four-poster once slept in by Jefferson Davis.

THE ELMS (*1782*)
Daily, 9 to 5; 60 cents; Mr. and Mrs. Joseph P. Kellogg.

There is little doubt as to the Spanish origin of this fascinating house, one of the earliest in Natchez and thought to have been built by the Spanish governor, Don Pedro Piernas. Almost primitive in its simplicity, it is unlike most of the other plantations, with low ceilings, narrow window facings, paved courts, and other features that bespeak the Spanish influence. It is surrounded by a beautiful garden containing a summer house which once caged a pet eagle, and a brick arch which may have been part of a Spanish mission here.

GREEN LEAVES
(*prior to 1812*)
Daily, 9 to 5; $1.00, with guide 75 cents; the Beltzhoover family.

That this place was built prior to the War of 1812 is almost certain, although it was remodeled in 1840 by the present owners' great-grandfather. It is a raised brick-and-

frame house with a narrow portico, almost lost in the green light of the giant shade trees that surround it. Inside, the fourteen rooms seem to epitomize all that was most charming in the town life of the era; nothing has been changed in the identical twin parlors, except for certain details in their priceless accessories. Carved rosewood, bronze chandeliers, magnificence in gilt, it is all here—with Watteau fans and china painted by Audubon, to boot.

HOLLY HEDGES (*1795; altered to Greek Revival in 1832; restored in 1949*)
Daily, 9 to 5; $1.20 (including tax); Earl Hart Miller.

Built by Gov. de Lemos Gayosa, sometimes known as plain John Scott, many changes have been made in this house from time to time by its various owners to conform with the vogue. Now, with the help of a gifted New Orleans architect, Richard Koch, it has been restored once more to its original simple elegance as a town house of the eighteenth century, and today it is one of the showplaces of a showplace town. The owners, decorators of distinction, have lavished their special talents on its interior and created a house of museum quality. There are several superb scenic wallpapers here, and the eighteenth-century furniture and portraits are of a high order. An interesting patio and garden may be seen as well.

HOPE FARM (*1774–1789*)

Daily, 9 to 5; $1.00; Mr. and Mrs. Balfour Miller.

Hope Farm is really two separate houses joined by galleries. The older and larger portion is said to have been built during the brief English occupancy, and the front and smaller part by Carlos de Grandpré, a French adventurer who was governor during the Spanish regime. It is built in the early manner, the detail chaste and the lines almost severe in their simplicity. The owner, who is the long-time president of the Pilgrimage Garden Club, has furnished it with taste and skill as you might expect. The furnishings show many influences, from the Early Federal of the dining room, to the Victorian of the cool inside parlor, to the Early American of the bedrooms.

KING'S TAVERN

Not open.

The oldest house in Natchez, standing on what was once the Natchez Trace, it was the stagecoach stop. It is built of timbers taken from a flatboat, portions of which were used frequently in the earliest buildings on the river.

LANSDOWNE (*1853*)

Daily, 9 to 5; 75 cents, 60 cents with guide; Mr. and Mrs. George W. Marshall and Mrs. James H. Ward.

A house whose excellent proportions may mislead you as to its scale. However, you have only to look at the six tall chimneys and the massive hallway with its lofty ceiling some eighty or ninety feet long to see that it was built in the grand style. The wealth of this family, which at one time possessed more than a thousand slaves, almost created a style of its own. One of the drawing rooms contains a marble mantel of Sèvres carved in calla lilies. Don't miss this one (or any of the others, for that matter).

LINDEN (*prior to 1790*)

Admission only with guide, 75 cents; Mr. and Mrs. Frank Fauntleroy.

Linden is one of the most interesting houses, architecturally speaking, in the area. The old central portion, dating be-

Linden betrays its early date by its colonial lines that becoming additions cannot conceal. A feature of its immense dining room is a punkah, or breeze fan, hung from the ceiling and swung by a servant.

fore 1790, is two stories in height with a deep portico, while the long, one-story wing extensions added in 1825 create a gallery ninety-eight feet long, balustraded all the way across on the second-story level. With its ten slender, hand-hewn columns and its low steps running the full length of the veranda, the total effect is remarkably light and fresh. The fanlighted door with its beautiful sidelights has been photographed as much as any doorway in the South, and deserves its fame. From time to time additions have been made to the house, but none has spoiled its lovely façade. There is much heirloom furniture here.

LONGWOOD
(under construction during Civil War)
Daily, 9 to 5; 75 cents; Dr. Haller Nutt.

Under construction during the Civil War but never completed, it is a weird, five-story structure dominated by a great fat cupola. Only the first floor was finished, and the house is not lived in. A curiosity.

MISTLETOE (*1867*)
Mr. and Mrs. S. H. Lambdin.

Built as a honeymoon house, it is a charming small-plantation-type cottage with a canted roof forming the porch shade and a pretty doorway. The interior comes as a surprise, for this is a "mansion in minia-

ture." The woodwork and mantels, carefully restored, are fine, simple, and early. Hepplewhite and Hitchcock pieces, good family portraits, and lovely drapes and rugs make this house a small gem, a contrast in scale to the many mansions.

MONTEIGNE (*1855*)
Daily, 9 to 5; only on special occasions during off-season months; $1.00; Kendall family.

One of the showplaces of Natchez, it is comparatively new—in fact but ten years built when Union soldiers were stabling their horses in its drawing rooms. It not only survived the vandalism but is today one of the most perfectly preserved and appointed of all of these cherished homes. Its rosy-pink plaster set off by white columns and trim, its lush gardens and ancient trees, make the first look at this well-proportioned mansion an experience. In point of fact, Monteigne marks the close of Natchez's golden age, just as Hope Farm and Gloucester mark its beginning. The interior is in keeping with the elegant perfection of the approach: a vast entrance hall with a black-and-white marble floor, scenic French wallpaper, and a staircase whose balustrade is harplike in its delicacy as a mere introduction to a series of rooms whose furniture and appointments may be called uniformly splendid.

OAKLAND (*1835*)

Daily, 9 to 5; 60 cents; Alan Ward Graning.

A son-in-law of Don Estevan Minor, governor under the Spanish regime, built this simple raised-brick cottage whose spacious rooms, with their sixteen-foot ceilings, are still furnished as they were in 1830 with relics from "Concord," one-time mansion of the Spanish governors. An interesting collection of Sèvres, Spode, and majolica may be seen here.

ROUTHLAND (*prior to 1779*)

Mrs. Charles Everett Ratcliff, Sr.

Mournfully beautiful, moss-hung trees form the setting for this ancient plantation tucked away in dense woods between the bayous. The exterior simplicity of the great rambling house with its pleasantly canted roofline and dormers does not suggest the elegance of its interior, which has been beautifully restored by its present owner. Among its many fine features are the triple arch which separates parlor and drawing room, the black-and-pink marble mantels, the door panels outlined in gold leaf, and the fine furniture, china, and family portraits.

ROSALIE (*1820*)

Daily, 9 to 5; $1.00; D.A.R.

The D.A.R. is rightly proud of its restoration of "Rosalie," a massive brick Georgian mansion whose stunning white columns are almost hidden by mountains of shubbery. The hill behind this house was the site of Fort Rosalie, where the terrible massacre of the white garrison by Natchez Indians took place in 1729, and which passed through Spanish, French, and English hands during its historic career. "Rosalie" was the headquarters of General Gresham of the Union Army, and Grant, too, stopped here. It is furnished in keeping with its importance.

STANTON HALL (*1852–1857*)

Daily, 9 to 5:30; $1.00; Garden Club headquarters.

Since it is the headquarters of the Pilgrimage Garden Club, and since you may consequently stay the night there in one of its enormous bedrooms, it will probably be the house that you will see first. You could not start with a better one; it is considered the most palatial house in the town, and some think it the most beautiful as well. Built in the flush times, the owner chartered a whole ship to bring from Europe materials and furnishings for his home—not to mention further importations during the five years of its construction. The lacy iron grillwork on the side and rear galleries came from Italy, as did the carved white

If you think Stanton Hall, opposite, is grand from without, wait till you see it inside!

Down in Pass Christian, along the Gulf Coast, the house (right) known as the Dixie White House (because Woodrow Wilson spent a winter there), is well worth seeing for its own attractive sake.

Carrara mantels; the solid-silver hinges and doorknobs came from England, and from France the massive gilt mirrors and the bronze chandeliers. In keeping with the scale of the house, the double drawing rooms may be combined into a ballroom seventy-two feet long and with twenty-two-foot ceilings. Frederick Stanton, an Irish cotton broker and the first Natchez millionaire, built it.

MT. LOCUST (*1780–1784*)

Just north of town on new Natchez Trace Parkway; being restored as an information center.

One of the oldest and most historic homes in the area, it served as an inn on the trace.

¶ *Woodville*

HAMPTON HALL (*1832*)

Highway 61; by appointment only; no charge; Mr. and Mrs. Maxwell Bramlette.

Formerly known as "Ararat" because it stands on a hilltop out of danger of high water, this handsome plantation is almost buried under the great oaks and sweet-olive trees as old as the house. There are also lovely boxwood and magnolias here. The place is beautifully furnished with nineteenth-century originals and reproductions.

GENERAL POSEY HOME (*1842*)

Church Street; by appointment only; no charge; Mr. Richard A. J. Sessions.

A cottage-type house whose exterior has been much remodeled, the interior still has its original carved woodwork and marble mantels, and is furnished in keeping. The owner is proud to show his rare china and equally rare camellias.

ROSEMONT PLANTATION

(*early 1800s*)

Near Woodville, 1 mile east of Route 24; daily; small fee; Mrs. Henry Johnson.

A Jefferson Davis shrine, it is the home where he spent his boyhood. Davis's father bought the place in 1810 when he moved here from Kentucky. Here lived and died his mother and two sisters; they are buried in the plantation graveyard.

MAJOR FELTUS HOME (*c. 1820*)

By appointment only; no charge; Dr. C. E. Catchings.

A very early house, the parlor still has the Louis XV set of the family who built it.

¶ *Waveland*

(*near Bay St. Louis*)

PIRATE'S HOUSE (*1802*)

By appointment; Garfield J. Ladner.

A fine example of the early-Louisiana-planter type of raised cottage, with brick ground floor, outside stairway leading to the first floor, and well-spaced dormers. There are sixteen square white columns supporting the gallery which runs the length of two sides of the house; these are laced together with delicate ironwork much like that seen in the New Orleans French Quarter. Legend has it that the builder was the chief of the Gulf Coast pirates; hence its name.

¶ *Pass Christian*

East Beach Boulevard is worth a stroll if you are passing through, for there are at least two old houses there of considerable interest: The DIXIE WHITE HOUSE (Number 767), so called because President Wilson used it for a winter White House in 1913, and a very early French type of dwelling at Number 551 generally accepted as the oldest in "Pass." The "White House" is a raised cottage in the grand style, an immense, low white mansion whose double curving flight of steps leading to the columned veranda gives it panache. Its owner Miss Gertrude Todt lives in New Orleans. When in residence she may allow you to visit; otherwise, consult the chamber of commerce, for they are willing to be helpful. The oldest house is a long, plain structure which is owned by the Mrs. Donald Rafferty Estate in town, and would be of interest mainly to antiquarians.

OSSIAN HALL (*1830*)
>*Daily, 9 to 5; Col. and Mrs. Hubert De Ben.*

A typical Greek Revival mansion with verandas and fluted columns. It has fourteen rooms furnished in French Empire and Louis XIV, the heirlooms of Mrs. De Ben, who features hospitality. By making an appointment in advance, you will be served a delectable tea with Swiss cookies and cheese ribbons made nearby from old French recipes handed down in her family. Twenty acres of gardens here.

¶ *Biloxi*

BEAUVOIR (*1852–1854*)
>*Terminal of Route 90, midway between Biloxi and Gulfport; daily, 9 to 5; $1.00; state of Mississippi.*

The home of Jefferson Davis, President of the Confederacy, is now a state shrine filled with memorabilia of his life and times. It also happens to be a delightful example of a raised cottage, vast in size and well proportioned, with the West Indian influence strongly marked. Its ground floor was used for servants' quarters when the balanced end pavilions were detached from the main portion. The sturdy, square, paneled columns and the fine dentil detail over doors and windows as well as cornices give the house a finish that would mark it as the home of people of wealth and taste even if the ownership were unknown. Most of the rooms are exactly as they were when the Davis family lived here; many pieces have been returned by the descendants. To give you an idea of the scale of the house, the family carriage and boat are both on display in the hallway.

THE OLD BRICK HOUSE
>(*1790–1800*)
>*410 East Bay View Street; daily, 2 to 5; contribution; city of Biloxi.*

A one-story cottage of brick with later wings and rambling additions, typical of Spanish Colonial architecture in the Deep South. The Biloxi Garden Center is restoring it and will make a home museum of it when it is properly furnished.

A spring pilgrimage is held in this area annually about mid-March which takes in Biloxi, Gulfport, Long Beach, Bay St. Louis, and Pass Christian, all resorts. The tour lasts a week, each day being devoted to a leisurely visit to one of these areas taking in new as well as old mansions and some very fine gardens. Write for information to the Mississippi Gulf Coast Council of Garden Clubs at Biloxi or to Mr. Anthony Ragusin, president of the chamber of commerce.

¶ *Pascagoula*

LONGFELLOW HOUSE (*1830*)
>*The Ingalls Ship Building Corporation.*

This was an old house in which Longfellow never lived; there is no knowing how it came by its name. In any event, it is today a very up-to-date inn with five modern three-room guest houses on the grounds and a view of the Gulf beyond. It should be a pleasant place to spend some time.

Beauvoir is one of those elusive houses that for some reason look larger and lovelier in real life than in pictures. Historically famous as the home of Jefferson Davis.

Greenwood, above St. Francisville in the Audubon country, epitomizes the look of luxuriance which is so much a part of the Louisiana legend in fact as well as fancy. Nowhere else in this country were great houses built with such bravado and romance almost as a matter of course. Houmas, across the page, is another case in point.

LOUISIANA

WHEN the French explorer La Salle claimed the entire tributary system of the Mississippi in 1684 for France, the vast territory was named after his king, Louis XIV. Louisiana proved to be an unremunerative colony, and in 1762 Louis XV gave it to his cousin Charles III of Spain, whereupon the French settlers revolted and were able to keep their independence for a period of ten months, making them the first colony in America to throw off European rule.

The territory was undeveloped up to the nineteenth century, except for the land along the banks of the Mississippi, the Red, and the bayous in the south.

Thus it is in these regions that the oldest houses in the state may be found, of a distinctive style known as "raised-cottage." Although France and Spain, and later the West Indies, furnished the method of building, it was the climate and the materials at hand which actually so modified the method as to create a recognizable mode. Thanks to its practical advantages for periodical damp conditions, the raised-cottage style spread beyond the area to Mississippi and even to Missouri and Alabama. Because of the annual flooding of the Mississippi and its tributaries, the houses had to be raised above the ground six or eight feet on stone or brick piers. An-

147

other necessity in this hot climate was shade; this was ensured by extending the roof in a sloping overhang from the upper floor over a wide porch (called "galerie") supported by slender columns. The porch in turn shaded the ground floor, which in early days was used for cooking and sometimes dining space and for offices. The ground floor was later built a full story high. The porches furnished additional living space as well as shade and often became the focal center of the house for the traditionally large Creole families, the children sleeping there in the hottest weather.

Cypress, so plentifully supplied by nature, was the ideal wood for withstanding the dampness, and durable as well. It weathered beautifully. Before good bricks were made that could "take" the climate, a construction called "briquette entre poteaux" (bricks between posts) was popular; the wall space between the cypress posts and the struts was filled with brick and mortar and then sealed against the dampness with a smooth coat of plaster. A still earlier filler called "bousillage" was made from nearby clay and the druidic moss with which the trees were lavishly hung. Later, as slave labor became plentiful and as better clays were found, it became possible to make bricks which would keep out the damp, and they soon took the place of wood in many homes.

By 1830, when Louisiana began to boom, the Greek Revival craze was sweeping the country, and wealthy Louisianians adopted the style with striking results. Its naturally big scale suited their needs and desires, and furthermore it adapted itself nicely to the climate. Not only did the great columns look well in their settings of immense trees and mysterious mosses, but they furnished the definition and support for the wide galleries and linked exquisite iron railings or handmade balustrades. These mansions managed to look less like Greek temples, as they were inclined to in the North, and more like the lavish family headquarters for a vast plantation which they usually were. They came to be identified by the label "the Southern plantation house," and although not as individual in style as the raised cottage, they were destined to have a wide effect on Southern domestic building and more than occasionally on Northern architecture as well.

IN & OUT OF NEW ORLEANS

You can see what Mark Twain meant when he called this city a Paris in America; although the comparison isn't exact the flavor of the old Creole Quarter is decidedly French provincial. The streets have names like Iberville, Toulouse, Bienville, Bourbon, Dumaine, and Chartres; and as you walk along under galleries of ironlace, you may hear snatches of Creole French. You can look through dark passageways into patios filled with sunlight and palms. For a flavor of another sort, you encounter in one block of Moss Street on the Bayou St. John (no distance at all from the Vieux Carré) a few remaining country-like plantation houses. They are now in the city, of course; but their water setting provides a shifting mirror from moss-hung trees and dwellings. From the Old Quarter out along St. Charles Avenue in what is called the "Garden District," where the air is scented with sweet-olive blossoms in spring and the houses give off their own special aroma of ante-bellum splendor in settings of almost tropical lushness, you find still another flavor that could be called "crinoline." Altogether, it is a unique and romantic potpourri—French, Spanish, English, and American—that makes up New Orleans (with the accent on the "Or").

The old houses here are picturesque and spectacular beyond compare, and they are so abundant as to be an embarrassment of riches. But hardly any are maintained as museums open to the public, nor are many "open on request." To visit any but a very few of the fine old New Orleans houses you have to take the tours.

Of these, the most varied and comprehensive take place during the first two weeks after Easter under the auspices of the New Orleans Spring Fiesta Association, and if you plan to visit here at any time, by all means send ahead for their splendidly prepared program (address: Upper Pontalba Building, 546 St. Peter Street). And, by the way, in the Lower Pontalba Building there is a newly restored suite of rooms to see.

In addition to the tours that cover some of the most fascinating houses in the Old Quarter and the Garden District, there are two tours that take you out into the country. One of these is conducted in St. Tammany Parish, on the other side of Lake Pontchartrain, covering a collection of early Louisiana country houses in settings that, at this season of the year, are a blaze of beauty. Another goes across the Mississippi River to visit some of the outstanding plantation houses along the Bayou Lafourche. There are also candlelight tours of the Old Quarter patios and "crinoline" tours of the courtyards, all very atmospheric.

During the month of February there are semiweekly tours run by the Louise S. McGehee School in the Garden District that take you into a choice assortment of the mansions in this area, but write ahead to the school (2343 Prytania Street) for fresh information. And in March there is a locally sponsored tour of the best Bayou Lafourche houses; for the date each year write the Fiesta Association. Included in the tour until recently was "Glenwood," home of Mrs. Edward P. Munson.*

So much for tours on special occasions. If you are on your own as far as time and inclination are concerned, you will find listed below all the early houses that can be visited, and certain others that should be looked at even if only in passing.

It has been the practice of the *Guide* to avoid strict itineraries like the plague, but here in the Old Quarter and Garden District we shall weaken to the extent of setting down our selection of houses in such an order as to suggest a kind of getting-acquainted stroll.

¶ *The Old Quarter (Vieux Carré)*

This ancient Creole section of the city is bounded pretty completely by Canal Street, Rampart Street, Esplanade Avenue, and the Mississippi River. The listing below might be called "On and off Royal Street," but to give it a real New Orleans beginning and ending, let's let it start at 209 Bourbon Street with an early lunch at Galatoire's, which is New Orleans cuisine at its finest. After lunch *turn left, cross Bourbon at the Old Absinthe House, and walk down Bienville to Royal; turn left again.*

301 ROYAL; the SHOP OF PRUDENT MALLARD, one of the two great New Orleans furniture makers back in the 1830s.

339 ROYAL (1800); never a house,

* The regrettable news that Glenwood, described on page 158, is no longer open to visitors, was received too late for its notation to be removed. The authors owe much to Mrs. Munson's expert local knowledge.

but notice the ironwork of the balcony railings.

401 ROYAL (1821); never a house either, but designed by Benjamin Latrobe for La Banque de l'Etat de la Louisiane.

417 ROYAL (1801); the PATIO ROYALE, one of the great romantic and historic residences of the Quarter, now a restaurant with a delightful courtyard. *Turn left on St. Louis.*

713 ST. LOUIS (date unknown); ANTOINE'S. The best date here is for dinner.

820 ST. LOUIS (c. 1820); the GRIMA HOUSE. Another beautiful courtyard; food served. *Back to Royal.*

520 ROYAL (1816); built by a wine importer named Seignouret who became, with Mallard down the street, one of the two great local furniture makers. You can see his "S" in the guard screen of the third-floor balcony.

529 ROYAL (1792); the OLD MIRO HOUSE, one of the oldest. *Turn left on Toulouse.*

723 TOULOUSE (c. 1800); CASA FLINARD. Named after its first owner, Gerome Flinard, a Spanish grandee, it is one of the best of the few that survive from this era, and is typically Spanish provincial in feeling. Hand-hewn cypress timbers in floors and ceilings, delicately hand-wrought hinges and latches, carved walnut staircase, beautiful mantels, and fine furnishings make it a sight to see if you hit it at the right time. The present owner, Mrs. Alvin Hovey-King, operates a *parfumerie* on the ground floor, and the patio is lovely.

THE "600" BLOCK, ROYAL; this is one of the best blocks on the street. As most of the houses speak for themselves, it is needless to elucidate. *Turn left on St. Peter.*

619 ST. PETER (reproduction); this is an exact copy of the early-nineteenth-century house that was found to be tumbling down because of termites. It is now used as a meeting place for the Daughters of 1812. Open daily, 10 to 5, except Sunday; no charge; owned by the Louisiana State Museum.

628 ST. PETER (Spanish period); this is the home of the Countess von Einsiedel, and is open on written request winter and spring. The house, one of the choicest and oldest in the Vieux Carré, was erected under the Spanish regime by Jean Batista Mercier, son of a distinguished French family of writers and physicians. Mercier left it to his widow Dame Marie Gracieuse Fontenelle, who left it in 1824 to her daughter Justina, the last of the Mercier line to own it. It is of plastered brick and presents one of the most agreeable façades in the Quarter. Furnished in keeping with its period and location, it yet represents the interesting taste of its owner. The salle centre between the very high-ceilinged upper and lower floors is one of the two known examples in New Orleans. The original ceiling beams are exposed in the provincial manner. *Return to Royal.*

700 ROYAL (1830s); LABRANCHE HOUSE. Some of the best ironwork in town. *Turn left on Dumaine.*

632 DUMAINE (c. 1780s); MADAME JOHN'S LEGACY (she inherited it from "M'sieu' John," according to a story in George W. Cable's *Old Creole Days*; hence the name). This raised cottage has the off-the-ground gallery, colonnettes, and rooflines typical of Louisiana Colonial. Two rooms are furnished in that period; the rest are used for exhibits. Open daily, 10 to 5, except Sunday; owned by the Louisiana State Museum. *Return to Royal.*

915 ROYAL; the cornstalk fence here is of an unusual pattern; there is more of it at Prytania and Fourth Streets, in the Garden District.

1132 ROYAL (mid-nineteenth century); you can tell this was an architect's home; it belonged to James Gallier, Jr., who, with his father, James, Sr., did many a splendid house in and out of town in his day.

1140 ROYAL (1832); MADAME LA-LAURIE'S HOUSE. A kind of French Empire house with a fantastic history, much of it lurid. Although sometimes known as the "Haunted House," it is now a social-welfare center. *Turn left on Governor Nichols Street*; after passing the Spanish Stables on the left and the "Arts and Crafts" pottery establishment on the right, *turn right on Bourbon, left on Barracks to Dauphine, and right to Esplanade.*

908 ESPLANADE (1830s); FABACHER HOUSE. Once the home of Celeste Destrahan, daughter-in-law of Bernard de Mandelville de Marigny. The *haut monde* lived along this broad avenue when it was known as the "Promenade Publique."

704 ESPLANADE (1856); JOHN GAUCHE HOUSE. The shutters on this proud foursquare brick house are generally closed, as though there were little life within.

But this is one of the most fabulously furnished "grand-manner" interiors in the South, as can be seen in the *First Treasury. Take Royal to Barracks and turn left to Chartres.*

1113 CHARTRES (1826); the BEAURE-GARD HOUSE. This beautiful private home is open on request to special groups. It is owned by the Beauregard House Association, Inc. Basically the familiar Louisiana raised cottage, but here very much the dignified town house, and as fine as anything in the Quarter. The furnishing is elegant and formal, ranging from a three-hundred-year-old carved set from Peru to Empire pieces owned by General Beauregard. Aubusson carpets and valuable paintings add to its *ton.* The house was designed by the Spanish architect, Correjoles. Beside Beauregard, it has been the home of the "greatest chess player of all time," Charles Morphy. Not the least of its distinguished occupants is the present lessee, the popular novelist, Frances Parkinson Keyes.

Turn left down Ursulines Street to the old French Market for a cup of *café au lait* and a cruller—a true New Orleans period to your tour.

While most of the houses of the Quarter are attractively caged, as it were, in lacy ironwork, the portico of the Beauregard house is clean-cut and classical.

This columned and railed veranda fronts a typical Garden District mansion.

¶ The Garden District

This dreamy section developed as a kind of *faubourg américain* where wealthy "American" families, as opposed to Creoles, began to build their palatial homes in the 1830s. It runs from Jackson to Louisiana Avenues between St. Charles Avenue and Magazine Street. The listings here suggest a kind of introductory stroll.

1450 4TH, at the corner of Prytania (1859); the old SHORT HOME, with iron-work on three sides, and the cornstalk fence you saw on Royal Street in the Vieux Carré.

1448 4TH; the old O'DONNELL HOME.

1213 3D (1850s); the old HERO HOME, still another example of the work of James Gallier, Jr.

1331 3D (1838); the old MUSSON HOME, now OGDEN, also called the "Iron Lacework House." The fence and the garçonnière (boys' quarters) in the rear are original.

1415 3D (1840s); the JORDAN HOUSE; another of the younger Gallier's palatial conceptions. This one is furnished spectacularly by its very knowledgeable owners.

1427 2D (1830s); the old D'ARCY HOME, now MEHURIN. This great galleried edifice has been beautifully restored by the distinguished New Orleans architect, Richard Koch.

1134 1ST (1848); the STRACHAN HOME, sometimes called the "Jefferson Davis" because it was here that the President of the Confederacy died while visiting his daughter. It is as choice within as

without, as you will see if you are taking a tour or if you will look in the *First Treasury*.

1239 1ST (1840); the WISDOM HOUSE, one of the most attractive in the District.

2340 PRYTANIA (1830); the WEST-FELDT HOUSE, also known as "Toby's Corner" because the original part, in which the living room is now contained, was built by a Thomas Toby from Philadelphia and used as an overseer's cottage. Its age and its expertly constructed additions give it a very special charm.

OLD HURST HOUSE (*1830*)
> *3 Garden Lane, in the Métairie District; by special appointment November 1 to April 1, 2 to 4:30, except Saturdays, Sundays, holidays, and from December 20 through January 5; Mr. and Mrs. Lawrence M. Williams, Galvez 3949 (evenings), Raymond 6052 (daytime).*

This is a stunning example of a fine Mississippi plantation house, raised off the ground and with pillared porches on three sides and a long sloping roof with dormers. It was brought here from the riverbank five miles away and restored in this perfect setting under the direction of Richard Koch. The interior woodwork is unusually fine, with carved acanthus leaves on doors and window frames. Handsomely furnished.

¶ Down the river

There are four houses of considerable interest undergoing restoration which would make worthwhile a drive down the east bank fifty miles to the ferry at Pointe a la Hache, across, and back up the west bank. The Four Oaks and the Judge René Beauregard house are at Chalmette, eight miles down the east bank, where the Battle of New Orleans was fought. Magnolia is on the west bank where the ferry crosses and where the orange belt begins; and on the way back you will come upon Bellechasse, just below Gretna and about six miles before you reach the Huey P. Long Bridge.

FOUR OAKS (*date unknown*)
> *8 miles below city near the Chalmette Slip; open certain days; American Sugar Refinery, Chalmette.*

The pillared galleries of the former home of the Cerias family may be seen beyond the buildings of the sugar refinery, which is considering restoration. Phone the office for further information.

The Old Hurst house at the left is a good example of an important Louisiana raised-cottage plantation from Greek Revival times.

An extraordinary Coromandel screen dominates the drawing room of the Hurst house.

JUDGE RENÉ BEAUREGARD HOUSE
(1840)

In Chalmette adjacent to battlefield; being restored by Louisiana; will be open to the public.

This old mansion facing the river embodies the Greek Revival style for which the elder Gallier was renowned. There are wide ground-and-upper-floor galleries in both front and rear, and the low-pitched, dormer-windowed roof is supported by eight massive columns. This place should be well worth seeing when fully restored.

MAGNOLIA PLANTATION HOUSE
(1795)

35⅗ miles from bridge on Route 31; on request; Joseph Vaccaro, Jr., 17 Breeze Park, New Orleans.

A great plantation house, the walls, of plastered brick, are thirty inches thick, and all the lumber hand-hewn. There are ten rooms, each measuring twenty-two by twenty-eight feet, with fine wood carving throughout done by slaves. This was the home of Reconstruction Governor Henry Clay Warmoth, famed for his lavish hospitality. It sits now in the midst of a great orange grove.

BELLECHASSE (*prior to 1844*)

Below Gretna on west bank, 6.3 miles from bridge on Route 31; by request (caretaker on duty part of time); Judah P. Benjamin Association, New Orleans.

This white-painted, three-story plantation house contains twenty rooms and has sixteen-foot hallways. Upper and lower galleries supported by square cypress columns surround the house. It was purchased by Judah P. Benjamin in 1844 and remodeled. Famous as a showplace of wealth and splendor, it fell on bad times after the war. Benjamin, who was Secretary of State and War for the Confederacy, fled to England and there became Queen's Counsel; he had a great career and lived there the rest of his days. House is under restoration as a Civil War museum.

THE MISSISSIPPI RIVER PLANTATIONS

The order followed here, as you will see from any good road map, is up the "east" bank of the river from New Orleans, the last listing on that side being "The Cottage," eight miles below Baton Rouge. You can take the River Road the whole way and see them all, or else cut in from the Baton Rouge highway and see only certain ones. You can then cross the river by the Darrow-Donaldsonville ferry, see "Mulberry Grove" and the ruins of "Belle Grove" just above Donaldsonville, and then drive down to "Oak Alley." If you've had enough, you can ferry across just below "Oak Alley" to Lutcher, which is close by the Baton Rouge highway; or you can continue on down the "west" bank. If there is a chance of seeing "Evergreen," by all means continue. The other two high spots in a tour of the river plantations are "Houmas" and "Oak Alley," in case you want to shorten your drive by skipping some of the others.

It might be pointed out here that the Bayou Lafourche houses can be easily tied in with the above, as they lie between Donaldsonville and Thibodaux.

¶ East Bank

DESTREHAN (*c. 1790*)

In Destrehan; Clarence J. Elisier, Pan-American Southern Corporation.

In process of restoration and being furnished in period, this place should be opened to the public, at almost any time now. Jean Lafitte, the pirate, was a frequent visitor here, it is claimed.

ORMOND, built in the 1780s, is half a mile above Destrehan. It is not open, but, handsomely restored, is a beautiful sight from the road. It is illustrated in *First Treasury.*

VOISIN PLACE (*c. 1785*)

1 mile beyond Reserve; any time, preferably spring or summer; 50 cents; Miss Lydia Voisin.

A typical raised cottage which has never changed hands, nor has the house itself changed, except to grow older. The furniture is also original. Miss Lydia Voisin, whose accent is still French, owns a dueling set which has been in her family more than two hundred years. The house is made of spliced, mortised, and interlocked timbers, with mud and moss as a filler. This is the real thing.

TEZCUCO PLANTATION (*1855–1861*)

River Road near Burnside, just below "Houmas"; on request by letter or phone (Donaldsonville 8662); Dr. and Mrs. Robert Hollingsworth Botts.

The owners of this delightful plantation are a gifted young couple and most hospitable. It was a home belonging to the Bringiers, early French settlers here, and was built by Benjamin F. Trudeau. The house is furnished with many interesting pieces by the famous New Orleans cabinetmakers, Mallard, Seignouret, and Seibrecht. This furniture, massive in scale and usually

of mahogany or rosewood, is distinctive in character; it might be called "Deep South Empire."

HOUMAS (*prior to 1800, and 1840*)

River Road near Burnside; on request by appointment; Dr. George Bernard Crozat, Maison Blanche Building, New Orleans.

One of the most beautiful and dreamlike plantations of the Deep South, set back a little from the river in a grove of massive live oaks. Fortunately it has fallen into the hands of Dr. Crozat, whose *expertise* has re-created not only a house but a whole manner of living. Under his guidance, patience, and enthusiasm, and with some of the work done with his own hands, the house and its gardens and dependencies are already as lovely as ever—a perfect example of the casual dignity, the polite informality and largess of such great houses when they were lived in by wealthy French

An interior entrance courtyard separates the main house of Houmas Plantation from the wing in which is to be found this delightful informal dining room of Spanish provincial.

planters. The furniture that Dr. Crozat has collected is for the most part the work of the New Orleans cabinetmakers, of great interest because of its local character; many pieces are signed by the makers.

THE HERMITAGE (1812)

In Darrow; special written permission given from time to time; Dr. C. Walter Mattingley, 1800 Canal Street, New Orleans 16.

Under restoration, it is not furnished. Visitors may come within twenty-five feet of the house at any time without permission.

BELLE HELENE, *formerly* ASHLAND (1841)

In Geismar 9 miles above Darrow; any time on request by phone (Donaldsonville 7029) or letter (Hohen Solms); Mrs. Helene Reuss Hayward.

Under restoration and not furnished as yet.

THE COTTAGE (1824)

Route 63, 8 miles south of Baton Rouge; daily; 50 cents; James J. Bailey.

A Greek Revival mansion with twelve Doric columns enclosing a brick-paved gallery. Lafayette, Zachary Taylor, Henry Clay, and others stayed here. It was on the flour-spread lawn of "The Cottage" that victims of the blazing *Princess* were brought on the midnight of June 20, 1870; their steamboat had caught fire while they were watching the *Robert E. Lee* and the *Natchez* steam past in the famous race up the Mississippi.

¶ West Bank

ST. LOUIS PLANTATION (1858)

Near Plaquemine about 10 miles below the Baton Rouge Bridge on Highway 168; on written request; Mr. Andrew P. Gay.

Capt. Joseph Erwin stopped here on his way down the river from Tennessee in 1807 to establish his plantation, and built such an elaborate mansion that it was known as "The Castle." Swept away by the Mississippi flood of 1850, it was replaced by the present spacious and charming house. Surrounded by wide galleries supported below by six fluted columns, the hipped roof, crowned by a very low square belvedere, is, in turn, supported by Corinthian columns. The plan consists of a central hall and four rooms, each twenty by twenty with a sixteen-foot ceiling, on both upper and lower floors. There is a kitchen wing at the rear. The interior woodwork is of a most graceful design, and on the ceilings there are elaborate medallions. St. Louis is not so monumental as some of the other old Louisiana houses, but it has a delicate elegance. In conjunction with the house is a lovely formal garden which was laid out by a French landscape gardener at the time the house was built.

TALLY HO (c. 1850)

Near Bayou Goula, a short distance on Route 168 above the ruins of "Belle Grove" and below St. Louis Plantation; by written appointment; Mr. D. Dennis Murrell, 1584 Jefferson Avenue, New Orleans.

The brick piers of this raised plantation house are of unusual height, allowing for the full-length French windows at ground level. Six square wooden columns support the roof. The walls of both stories of this solid structure are of brick fifteen inches thick covered with clapboard. The house is traversed by double galleries. It has been closed for some time but is now slated for restoration.

MULBERRY GROVE PLANTATION (1836)

In Hohen Solms on Route 30 between Donaldsonville and White Castle; spring; 50 cents; Mrs. C. C. Clifton, Sr.

A typical sugar-plantation home some of whose land is still planted in that crop today, this is a fine example of the spacious way in which the wealthy planters lived. The lower part is of brick, the upper frame. All of the original woodwork has been preserved. A special feature of the house is a hidden circular staircase. This was the ancestral home of the Dr. Edward Duffel from Virginia, who married Anne Marie Antoinette Desirée Landry, whose father was an expelee from Nova Scotia. With its heavy, square painted brick columns below and its shaded double galleries across the front, typical of many of the other large plantation houses of the period, its very simplicity and size give it a kind of grandeur. It has been furnished with antiques and reproductions.

Oak Alley is a plantation house that refuses to be dwarfed even by the immensity of its great avenue of live oaks.

RUINS OF BELLE GROVE (1857)
Just above "Mulberry Grove."

A gloomy but fascinating sight, wonderful to photograph. This was one of the masterpieces of the younger Gallier.

OAK ALLEY (1836)
Vacherie, 2 miles north on Route 30; daily, 9 to 5; $1.22; Mrs. Andrew Stewart.

The first owner, Jacques Telesphore Roman, was the brother of Gov. André Roman. Originally called "Bon Sejour," it is a Greek Revival mansion, seventy feet square and girdled by twenty-eight massive Doric columns. The brick, covered with plaster, is painted pale pink, the shutters and railings greenish blue. The house is first seen down a monumental avenue of stately live oaks which form a vault overhead. At the rear stand two garçonnières, replicas of the main house, one of which is now used as a guest house and the other as the manager's home. The owner graciously allows you to picnic in the beautiful garden if you have brought lunch along. Do, by all means; you are far away here from anything that Duncan Hines would recommend.

EVERGREEN (1830s)
18 miles below Vacherie; on written request only; Miss Matilda Gray, 704 Esplanade Avenue, New Orleans.

Now being extensively and expertly remodeled, when complete it will undoubtedly be one of the finest restorations on the river. Its owner has the resources and taste with which to re-create its atmosphere brilliantly.

THE COTTAGE (1830s)
River Road near Hahnville; any time on request; Richard L. Keller.

A typical raised-cottage plantation house, furnished now in a simple, unpretentious present-day fashion.

Back from either bank of the river are raised cottages, of which The Cottage is an excellent example.

¶ *Bayou Lafourche*

ARMELISE (*1804*)

Paincourtville, 1 mile north on Route 29; by appointment; Mr. and Mrs. Frank A. Vought, Armelise Planting Company.

The oldest house on Bayou Lafourche, it was built by Henri Landry, who came here from Nova Scotia to escape religious persecution. The site, on a Spanish land grant of 1797, was chosen for its setting of mighty oaks, many of them still standing. It is one of the few estates on the river that remains in the possession of the descendants of the original owners, nor has it ever been mortgaged. The Landrys arrived here on horseback and lived on a houseboat on the bayou while their home was being built. Henri was a victim of the tidal wave that swept away Last Island in the Gulf in 1856. The present occupants of "Armelise" restored it in 1946 and made a point of altering the original structure as little as possible. It is not an elaborate house but a typical one, constructed of handmade brick chinked together with mud-and-moss filling; hand-hewn timbers were also used. It is presently furnished for simple country living with a few family pieces.

GLENWOOD PLANTATION HOUSE (*1840*)

Napoleonville, 1 mile north on Route 29; Mr. and Mrs. Edward P. Munson.

Dr. Ebenezer Eaton Kittredge built the original old plantation house as a wedding gift to his daughter Marie Louise, and the family has continuously occupied the house ever since. Enlargements were made in 1885 to accommodate a big family. Today it is a spacious guest house of twenty rooms, with fifteen-foot ceilings. The downstairs hall, eighty feet long, is broken by a triple arch. The furniture is for the most part priceless family heirlooms, including a rosewood Seignouret bedroom suite and a hand-carved mahogany banquet table, on which visitors dined who were fortunate enough to enjoy the charming hospitality here. The owners are authorities on life on the river, including its old houses.

MADEWOOD (*1840–1848*)

Napoleonville, 2 miles south on Route 77; by appointment only; $1.00; Madewood, Incorporated.

A great white two-story house of stucco-covered brick, a very fine example of Greek Revival. Six fluted Ionic columns rise from the terrace to support the well-proportioned pediment. At either end two wings repeat the details in miniature. The interior is elaborate but as yet only partially restored; ceilings are twenty feet high, and walls eighteen inches thick. Built entirely by slave labor, it took four years to finish. The plantation, a private wildlife preserve, covers three thousand acres.

WHITE PLANTATION (*c. 1790*)

Route 29, 5 miles north of Thibodaux; 25 cents; Chief Justice White Memorial Association, state of Louisiana.

A good example of the earliest type of construction, it was built by Chief Justice

Madewood is a plantation house in the pure Greek Revival tradition.

Edward Douglas White, a member of the Supreme Court for twenty-seven years. It is a raised cottage built of hand-hewn cypress, its wooden portions put together with pegs. Tall brick pillars elevate the house. The family was among the first settlers in this section, and the father served as Governor. It is being restored and furnished by the state as a memorial to the former Chief Justice.

ACADIA PLANTATION (*1828–1830, addition in 1889*)

Route 29, 1 mile east of Thibodaux; on request by letter or phone (Thibodaux 3427); Mr. and Mrs. Richard C. Plater, Sr. and Jr.

The land was owned originally by Acadian refugees, and after 1820 by Philip Barton Key, nephew of Francis Scott Key, whose mother was a Plater. The heroic knife fighter, Jim Bowie, and his brother Resin built the first three houses here in the 1830s, as well as the first steam-driven sugar house. In 1879 the new owners combined the three houses and added several rooms to form

an odd cruciform plan. The mansion is now divided between the senior and junior Platers, and is full of fine family heirlooms and portraits. The lawns are planted with semitropical trees and shrubs. The plantation is still a sugar-cane farm.

MAGNOLIA (*1858*)

Route 82, 7 miles southwest from Thibodaux; daily, 9 to 6; $1.00; Mrs. Bessie Schaffer.

Stands amid the great flowering monarchs for which it was named. Of brick and frame construction, with hand-wrought iron railings, it was built by Thomas Ellis. It served as a hospital during the Civil War. "Magnolia" contains eighteen kingsize rooms and a twenty-two-foot entrance hall with an arched ceiling and elaborate plaster detail. The mahogany staircase was imported from France. Look at the rosewood parlor suite, gold-leaf mirrors, portraits, and fine Sèvres and Dresden, heirlooms of the Schaffer family, who have lived here since 1874.

BAYOU TECHE

¶ *Franklin*

OAK LAWN MANOR (*1816*)

From 167–90 turn right on Irish Bend Road (gravel); daily during daytime; $1.20 (grounds only, 25 cents); Mrs. C. A. Barbour.

This is one of the showplaces of the Teche country. The massive Greek Revival mansion is approached through a magnificent grove of oaks a mile and a half long and bordered by a double row of cedars, an approach unique in America. It is strikingly lit up at night. The mansion was built by Alexander Porter, noted jurist and close friend of Henry Clay, as the manor for his huge sugar plantation. Constructed of brick and stone, with an impressive façade of six tall Doric columns, broad fanlighted doorways, and wrought-iron balconies, it suffered a near-disastrous fire in this century, but was restored by Capt. Clyde Barbour in 1927. The furniture is both European and American, the latter of the type used hereabouts when the house was built.

¶ *Baldwin*

OLD FUSILIER PLANTATION (*c. 1800*)

It exemplifies perfectly the style and sturdiness of the early building mode—a French Colonial farmhouse, much modified by the necessities of the hot, moist climate.

¶ *Jeanerette*

ALBANIA (*1842*)

On request to Mr. Stephen C. Munson, Delgado-Albania Plantation Commissioner for city of New Orleans, when in residence.

Of great historic interest because the ground on which it stands was part of a double grant from the Spanish Crown to Carlos Grevenberg for services rendered, of which the present 2,200 acres is only a fraction. The plantation has grown sugar cane for over 125 years. The house is of tremendous proportions; its simple balustrade repeats itself on the second floor across the length of the house, the slender posts rising the full two stories in height. The first-floor gallery sits close to the ground. The house is furnished with antiques inherited from several old Louisiana families.

¶ New Iberia

THE SHADOWS (*1830*)
> *Route 167–90 near town; by appointment; $1.25; Weeks Hall.*

One of the most fabled ancestral homes of Louisiana, it was built by David Weeks, and is now occupied by his descendant Weeks Hall. It is a hauntingly beautiful house of rosy brick, with eight columns rising two stories from the level of its lovely garden to support a roof with three dormers. The second-story balustrade is perfection in its fine simplicity. The furnishings are as chaste as the elegant detail of the woodwork. This home was long famed for its hospitality. When the invading army made their headquarters here during the Civil War, its mistress withdrew to the upper story of the house, never leaving her room again until she was taken to be buried soon after in the garden she herself had planted.

STEAMBOAT HOUSE (*1870s*)
> *On request (phone: 2–9612); Mr. and Mrs. James P. Cross.*

This place was originally bedizened with the fancywork that frosted the river steamboats of the period. The present owners removed the trimmings and made of the house a most impressive white-columned

The Shadows is one of the most evocative old houses in the bayou country.

manor, given unusual character by great curving bays, repeated in galleries and roof balustrade. These bays form two circular guest rooms on the second floor. An unusual reconstruction.

¶ St. Martinville

ACADIAN HOUSE MUSEUM (*eighteenth century*)
> *Longfellow-Evangeline Memorial Park, 1 mile from town; daily; state of Louisiana.*

This is the Acadian house which is supposed to have sheltered the "Gabriel" of the poem *Evangeline*. The spot is very near where the Acadians landed when they first arrived here. The old house is a raised cottage of the type one sees so frequently throughout the state, except that it lacks the usual dormers in the steep-sloping roof, attesting to its age. It is surrounded by moss-hung oaks and highland cypresses. The kitchen is detached as was the custom. The house was built by the widow of the Chevalier de la Houssaye, but the actual date seems to be lost. It has been furnished for the most part with primitive pieces from the neighborhood, as simple as the house itself; furniture, clothing, and implements of the early settlers are also on display. A good example of pure French Colonial.

In St. Martinville you will also find the Acadian Craft Shop of André Olivier, a descendant of the Acadians, who is the "official" historian of the area and can tell you more delightful stories about it than anyone around. He will be able to help you to see whatever you wish, for this is truly his country. He will probably suggest that you look at the handsome POST OFFICE, once a private home of the '80s; the OLD CASTILLO HOTEL on Main Street, typical of the exotic architecture of the early Spanish and French; and the OLD GOVERNMENT HOUSE (now a school), where the first commandant of the fort resided. At the corner of Main and Market is the HENRY FOURNET HOUSE, of red brick, built in the 1830s; its pyramidal roof has three

Now the Acadian Museum, this is the charming old cottage in which Louis Arcenaux may have lived. He was the Gabriel in Longfellow's Evangeline.

gables. And further along the banks of the Teche you can see Mrs. Emile Martin's CREOLE MANSION. A mile and a half out of town is the grand old ST. JOHN PLANTATION MANSION.

¶ Lafayette

LAFAYETTE MUSEUM (*prior to 1845*)
1122 Lafayette Street; 50 cents; Lafayette Museum Association.

The Lafayette Museum, recently restored, is a two-story frame house with cupola and balustraded galleries, owned by the first Governor Mouton. In the rear is a separate kitchen built of brick, with moss and clay filling—a traditional type of construction known in this area as "bousillage." The house is devoted to various exhibits, with two or three of the rooms being furnished in the early local style. During March and April the museum plans bus tours of the surrounding area taking in plantations, houses, and gardens; consult Mrs. Frederick J. Nehrboss, President.

¶ Opelousas

GOVERNOR MOUTON HOUSE (*1848*)
Sterling Avenue; on written request; George A. Voitiers.

The oldest city in the state and the center of government for the southwest part of Louisiana during the Spanish rule, Opelousas retains much of its ancient charm. The Governor Mouton House was the seat of government during Opelousas' second period as capital. It has a modestly impressive Greek Revival façade. Its owner has informed us that little of the interior is original.

The DIETLIN and BOAGNI houses on Main Street, and the ESTORGE and GARLAND are all distinctive and interesting old places. The DIETLIN and HEBRARD homes are open at times upon special request, the former having an especially agreeable façade of a Georgian character; their small iron balconies remind you that you are in the Deep South.

RINGROSE PLANTATION
(1810–1830)
Prudhomme Road near Catholic convent; exterior only at present; Leo Austin Fontenot, Jr.

The plantation home of the Fontenot and Prudhomme families at present may be seen from the outside only. A typical bayou dwelling, the ground floor is of soft-pink brick, as are the round columns, and the upper floor and gallery of wood. The interior is plastered throughout and has open-beamed ceilings. The beauty of this house is that it has never been "restored" and has indeed had few alterations of any sort since it was built. The original barns and flanking pigeonniers are all there. To recapture the feeling of a real Teche plantation of long ago, you could not do better than to visit here.

¶ *Washington (6 miles north of Opelousas on Route 5)*

WARTELLE HOUSE (1828)
Grand Prairie Road; on written request; Miss Aline and Miss Maude Wartelle.

Built by their grandfather Pierre G. Wartelle, a captain under Napoleon.

MAGNOLIA RIDGE MANSION
(completed 1831)
Bayou Coutableau; on written or phone request; Mrs. Valéry Mayer.

Formerly known as the "Prescott House," this massive brick structure was the great social center of the area in the days before the Civil War, when the bayou was a shipping point of some importance. During the war the house was used at various times as a headquarters by both armies. It is furnished with antiques of its period.

THE FELICIANA PARISHES
(The Audubon Country)

¶ *In & out of St. Francisville*

Known as the "Audubon country," for the artist-naturalist who lived briefly and painted some of his finest bird pictures here, this region, roughly halfway between New Orleans and Natchez, has a number of delightful old homes, many of them in the hands of the same hospitable families for generations. A moderate fee is asked to see some of these places, which are more or less continuously "open" when their owners are in residence. Mrs. Josie Leake Stirling, who owns the Woodhill Crafts Shop in West Feliciana Parish a few miles from St. Francisville on Route 61, is the authority on this neighborhood and its people. It might be well to contact her first for advice and information, which she gives most generously to those who desire it.

A good pamphlet to direct you through this area, called "Louisiana's Plantation Homes in the Audubon Country," is issued by the Tourist Bureau, Department of Commerce and Industry, Baton Rouge, Louisiana.

VIRGINIA
(1839, enlarged 1852)
Royal and Felicity Streets; daily; 75 cents; Miss Oriana Pillet.

The Pillets, driven out of France during the Revolution, fled to San Domingo and thence to America. This stately town mansion has a small rear wing, so old that its date is unknown. The so-called "cottage part" was built by Thomas Jacobs, while Judge Brewer added the imposing two-story section in 1852. Although all was built by slave labor, fashions had changed in the interim, and the two sections of the house are quite different. It is furnished completely with heirlooms, plumed mahogany sofas, a Duncan Phyfe table, Queen Anne chairs, a table dated 1770 and brought over by English ancestors, and century-old painted window shades of lavender linen.

ROSEDOWN (1830)
¼ mile northeast on 35.

When this was written, it could only be seen from the outside because its surviving occupant, Miss Bowman, was too old to be disturbed. *So Red the Rose,* written by Stark Young, is about "Rosedown" and its inhabitants—once a beautiful example of gracious living but now in a state of decline.

THE OAKS
Just north on 61–65; during blooming season; 25 cents.

A Late Victorian house, this has one of the finest gardens in the parish and contains antiques handed down in the owner's family.

WAVERLEY (*1821*)
3 miles north on 61–65; on written request; Mrs. George M. Lester, St. Francisville.

Georgian Colonial "Waverley," charmingly restored, is of particular interest because it was here that Audubon taught young ladies their music lessons.

AFTON VILLA (*1820s*)
4 miles north on 61–65; Daily; $1.00; Mr. and Mrs. Wallace Percy.

A forty-room villa modeled by D. Barrow after one near Tours, France. It is of stucco-covered cypress, buff with dark red trim. Its towers, Moorish galleries, and stained-glass cathedral windows give it a highly romantic aspect. The interior is ornate, with plaster friezes, marbleized woodwork, and Dresden doorknobs, and is furnished in keeping. In the beautiful terraced gardens roses and azaleas bloom in profusion.

THE COTTAGE (*1795–1859*)
6 miles north on Route 61–65; unless a guest, $1.00; Mr. and Mrs. J. E. Brown.

This rambling cottage-type plantation house, now a guest house, is a delightful place to stay. Built in the shape of an L, it still has its original school, slave quarters, and offices—one of the few plantations in which most of the outbuildings are intact. The house, built in the Spanish tradition, is 147 feet long, with spacious galleries. All the pillars are hand-wrought, as is the woodwork. Most of the furniture, including many early Louisiana pieces, is original. The French damask draperies, Brussels carpet, and gold-leaf wallpaper in the parlor date back to its days of affluence. If you stay overnight, you will sleep in a huge old four-poster, and your room will have a fireplace with an original hand-carved mantel.

OAKLEY PLANTATION, AUDUBON MUSEUM (*1799–1810*)
Audubon Memorial State Park, off Route 61–65 a few miles south of the town; daily; state of Louisiana.

Begun while Louisiana was under the Spanish rule, this plantation house shows a curious mixture in mantels and exterior details of the Adam influence combined with West Indian informality. Its great interest lies in the fact that Audubon came here to live in 1832, hired by Mrs. James Pirrie to tutor her daughter Eliza. He was

Oakley Plantation is where Audubon brought his wife and children in 1832. Though he himself stayed here only a few months, he did some of his most important paintings in the vicinity.

Parlange on False River is one of the finest of the raised-cottage plantations.

paid sixty dollars a month, and had his afternoons free to paint. Since Audubon had been in straits, he was glad to come to Feliciana Parish, which abounded in wildlife. It marked a turning point in his career, for, although he stayed only a few months, he painted thirty-two of the birds in the large folio. His young assistant, Joseph Mason, who was allowed to come with him, painted the backgrounds. Mrs. Audubon, who acted as governess, remained here for seven years with her children. The plantation has been called the "Shuttered House" because its jalousies entirely enclose the upper gallery and extend four feet down over the second floor. It is gradually being furnished in keeping.

PARLANGE (*1740*)
Route 93 on north bank of False River and west bank of Mississippi River; daily; $1.00; Mr. and Mrs. Walter C. Parlange.

One of the oldest and most charming houses in the state, it is on the other side of the Mississippi, and is reached by ferry from St. Francisville. It is a one-and-a-half-story raised cottage of cypress construction set on a brick basement, encircled by galleries and with a steep-pitched roof and dormers. The drive is flanked by octagonal pigeonniers. The original builder, Charles Parlange, is the ancestor of the present owners, who are the seventh generation of the family to live here. The imported French furniture, purchased before the

Civil War, is all intact. This is, in truth, an ancestral home.

GREENWOOD (*1830*)
10 miles north on 124; unless a guest, $1.00; Frank Percy.

One of the finest examples of Classic Colonial in Louisiana, surrounded by twenty-eight massive columns and with a belvedere on the roof. It took seven hundred slaves to build this mansion. The owner accommodates night guests by reservation.

HIGHLAND (*1799*)
10 miles northwest; daily, preferably 2 to 5; Mr. and Mrs. D. I. Norwood.

This house was constructed of the virgin cypress timbered to make room for the dwelling itself, and of blue poplar as well. It was built by William Barrow, who came here with his family from North Carolina in a covered wagon; Mrs. Norwood, the present occupant, is his great-granddaughter. The land was then under Spanish dominion, and Barrow was one of the leaders who, in 1810, helped to overthrow the Spanish rule. The settlers proclaimed the country "The Republic of West Florida," with St. Francisville as the capital. President Madison then took over "The Republic," to the relief and joy of the populace. The floors of this remarkable house are of unpainted one-and-a-half-inch cypress, scrubbed beautifully white. The wainscoting in the hall and parlor is hand-carved, as are the doors and frames. A Palladian window upstairs is an unusually elegant ornament for the location and period. Cypress logs had to be shipped by boat to Cincinnati for the shutters to be made there. The house, on a commanding elevation, sits in a large grove of magnificent live oaks planted by Mr. Barrow's son. Mr. Norwood delights in showing the house, and you will delight in seeing it.

¶ In & out of Clinton & Jackson

Clinton is almost a Greek Revival town, with its rows of white columns on Court House Square and "Lawyer's Row." Through the courtesy of some of the home owners, six homes are listed here. Others of interest in the town are the MARSTON HOUSE (1840s), now a community center; the WILLIAM BENNETT HOUSE (1825) and the STINE HOUSE (1806), both on Baton Rouge Street; and the CHASE HOUSE (1830) on St. Helena Street.

ASPHODEL (*1821, wings 1833*)
>   *Route 74, 3 miles from Route 61 out of Jackson; by appointment only; $1.50; Mr. and Mrs. John H. Fetzer.*

This house, of the raised-cottage type, is built of patterned brick unusual in the Deep South, giving the front wall, seen through impressive Doric shafts, a very rich texture. There are six columns on the main building and two on each wing. It was built by Benjamin Kendrick. The furniture is Victorian, Empire, and Early American.

THE SHADES (*1803*)
>   *Route 314, 1½ miles west of Wilson; on request; Miss Eva Scott.*

A lovely old garden with brick walks and boxwood borders surrounds this early brick house built by Alexander Scott, whose descendant Miss Eva still lives here.

HICKORY HILL (*1810*)
>   *2 miles beyond "The Shades"; by request; Mrs. Mabel Richardson, Box 84, Jackson.*

Built by David McCants in what was then Spanish West Florida. He owned three hundred slaves, and they built this tall, narrow house of red brick baked on the scene. Only the central portion of the original house, with its four tall columns, still stands. It has been called a monument to the two sisters who risked their lives during the Civil War after the surrender of Baton Rouge to make trips there to get food and clothing for the hard-pressed guerrillas in the countryside. One of these sisters was Blanche McCants Freeman, who died in 1939 at the age of 91. Her daughter and grandchildren live here now.

BONNIE BURN (*1850*)
>   *On outskirts of Clinton; on request; Mr. Richard H. Kilbourne, District Attorney General.*

A Southern plantation house surrounded by moss-covered trees, with long French windows both upstairs and down, graceful square columns, and delicate balconies. It was purchased by the owners' great-grandfather from the Courtney family, its original owners. The furniture is mostly Victorian.

KERNAN GROVE (*1836*)
>   *On outskirts of Clinton; on request; Mr. and Mrs. Benjamin W. Dart, Sr.*

A farm cottage whose owners are much interested in antiquity. They will furnish information about the annual "open house."

RICHLAND PLANTATION (*1820–1824*)
>   *Norwood, near Clinton; by appointment; Mr. and Mrs. C. B. Dudley.*

Another of the fine early plantation homes whose brick was made and whose timber cut on the spot. The brick is plastered over and painted white, as are the four heavy Doric columns which rise through a two-story portico and gallery. An exterior feature is the massive double chimney gable ends. The house is furnished with Early American pieces, as well as some modern for greater comfort.

¶ In & out of Natchitoches

Natchitoches in the Cane River country, which was once called "La Côte Joyeuse" ("Joyous Coast"), is the oldest town in the Louisiana Purchase, having been established in 1714. It has an annual tour of about ten homes, all built by the French who settled here. Many of the older houses have galleries and fences of cast-iron filigree. The houses are not maintained as showplaces nor, for the most part, furnished with an emphasis on antiquity; however, they are most interesting to visit. Since the owners are hospitable, visits can be arranged by advance request to Mrs. Nita Sutton, President of the Garden Club, or to the chamber of commerce.

By all means see MELROSE, down the Cane River. Mr. Mignon, the custodian of "Melrose" and the able historian of this area, may be able to help you to see other plantations in the vicinity.

LAUVE HOUSE (*1806*)
202 Washington Street.
A raised-cottage type with square wooden columns and two full-length windows on each side of the entrance.

JOSEPH TAUZIN HOUSE (*early*)
436 Jefferson Street; Leopold Levy.
Originally built as an office, but before the Civil War an upper floor was added with an ornamental iron railing.

HOUSE OF BRIDES (*c. 1775*)
706 Second Street.
So called because it was a dowry house.

OLD LEMÉE HOUSE (*c. 1830*)
308 Jefferson Street; on request; the Women's Club.
The original house built in 1792 was burned in 1830 but immediately replaced by a copy of the original. It was purchased by Aléxis Lemée (pronounced Le-*may*) in 1849 for $2,300. It is a plain house, with blackwood mantels, simple moldings, and wide cypress-plank floors, and is furnished with antiques.

OLD NEVILLE PRUDHOMME HOUSE (*c. 1850*)
530 Jefferson Street.
Owned by the grandson of the founder of La Côte Joyeuse (his name you will often hear in this neighborhood), who built himself a great three-story house with spacious galleries.

WILLIAMS HOME (*1776*)
East Natchitoches.
The oldest residence in northwest Louisiana. The hewn-cypress rafters and sills were floated down Red River from Tauzin Island, and the walls built of an adobe mixed with deer hair—for the owner was a tanner of deer hides.

ANDRÉ CHAMARD HOUSE (*1735*)
104 Amulet Street.
Built by a gentleman of that name descended from the royal Bourbons and knighted by Louis XIV, the house, although many times remodeled, is still in the same family.

¶ Out in the Cane River country

Of these plantations François Mignon has this to say: "None of them were designed to awe the public but rather conceived as ample plantation residences. Perhaps it is for that reason—the feeling of authentic home places—that they appeal so strongly to the pilgrims passing this way."

MELROSE (*1835, stone buildings 1750*)
Route 20, 15 miles south of Natchitoches on Cane River; daily; François Mignon, custodian.
The famous home of Cammie G. Henry, patron of the arts, is unique in that it contains two of the original colonial buildings dating back to 1750. The central section of "Melrose" itself is a typical spacious plantation mansion. Its octagonal flankers are unusual, however; apart from this, its most striking architectural features are its nine-foot mantel and the fact that its outside staircase is the only staircase of the whole house.

YUCCA HOUSE *and* **AFRICAN HOUSE** (*1750*)
On grounds of "Melrose."
Even more interesting are the "Yucca House" of mud and cypress and the "African House" of brick and cypress, part of the original group dating back to 1750. The land was a Spanish Crown grant to a freed slave, Marie Therese, who built these

When you get to Melrose you are truly in the Cane River country.

houses with the image of her native Congo architecture in mind. These are definitely the only old buildings of African architecture that exist on this continent, and they are among the thirteen "unique buildings in the South" classed by the Federal government. On the wall in the "Yucca House" is an extraordinary collection of portraits in oil of famous Afro-Americans, and also of some of the former owners of "Melrose."

ALPHONSE PRUDHOMME HOME, *or* OAKLAND PLANTATION (*1818–1821*)

Route 20, 7 miles below city on Cane River; daily; 50 cents; Mrs. J. Alphonse Prudhomme.

Eight generations of the family have lived here where the first Prudhommes settled on this rich cotton land. The owners still have the tools used to plant the first cotton crop in the state. There is a portrait of the first Prudhomme, Emmanuel, holding cotton in his hand, and the medical instruments used by the first Dr. Prudhomme are

also here—along with much fascinating heirloom furniture. Built of hand-hewn cypress, with mud-and-moss walls ("bousillage") in which deer's hair is used as a binder, the house has eleven rooms. The fanlight between the living and dining rooms is most unusual.

NARCISSE PRUDHOMME HOUSE, *or* BEAUFORT PLANTATION (*c. 1840*)

Near Oakland; by appointment only; Mr. and Mrs. C. Vernon Cloutier.

Built in the same period before the war on the site of St. Charles Fort. Mr. Cloutier, a descendant of the Prudhommes, has recently restored the house, and it, too, contains much family furniture. It is the last word in interior elegance and grace.

Other plantations in the vicinity to ask about are METOYER, former residence of Lyle Saxton, OAK LAWN, CASHMERE, and BEAUFORT PLANTATIONS.

Tennessee, first and last, had a lot to do with Andrew Jackson, and Jackson had a lot to do with Tennessee. This is his bedroom in the Hermitage, his library beyond in the room with the flag. And on the opposite page is the columned portico across the front. On page 178 is a picture of the parlor.

TENNESSEE

TENNESSEE, like Gaul, is divided into three parts. The eastern part, which was settled first by the intrepid men who dared to intrude upon the Indians' happy hunting grounds, is a mountainous region, heavily forested, which for the most part was divided up into small holdings. Knoxville is today its center. The western part, between the two great rivers, the Mississippi and the Tennessee, remained Indian domain until 1818. Then it was settled rapidly, with Memphis becoming the bustling focus of the cotton boom, which grew so fast that the settlers had little time for cultural pursuits for the next thirty years. The middle section was settled by the same pioneers who had come into Kentucky only a few years before. Now, braving the Cumberland Plateau, men like Daniel Boone, Davy Crockett, and John Sevier were the first to see the fertile paradise which was to produce the vast land fortunes of Tennessee, with Nashborough (Nashville) as its center.

It is in this middle section, four years after the founding of Nashville, that the first so-called "great house" was built—"Rock Castle," near Gallatin. Then came "Spencer's Choice" and "Cragfont." The names, along with such others as "Roll Stones" and "Rock Jolly," listed here, give you an idea of the prevailing building material. However, limestone soon gave way to brick when slave labor became plentiful, for it is only to be expected that the settlers, largely from North Carolina and Virginia, should have favored the Georgian to which they were accustomed. In spite of the fact that most of the houses have Greek Revival façades, a more careful inspection will show you that Georgian continued to be favored for a long time after it had been replaced by the Federal style back East. The Greek façade was an appliqué used mostly for ornament, as in Kentucky, until William Strickland moved to Nashville in 1844 and left his own stamp on the architecture of these parts. The genius of Strickland, America's first indigenous architect of real importance, was, it appears, in perfect sympathy with these people and their needs and tastes. His architecture is big in scale and scope, and it has a forceful and yet simple character, although he could turn out an Italianate villa or a church with impressive Egyptian detail when he had a mind to. And he often had.

Perhaps nowhere else in early America does the feeling that the early home builders were actually vying with one another to see who could build the finest house hit you so strongly as in this region; and this competition, whether conscious or not on their part, seems to have been to the benefit of the houses. Such a concentration of interest on building bigger and better was bound to produce something rather extraordinary, especially in a situation where labor was plentiful and cheap. The great Polk and Pillow Mansions, "Belle Meade," "The Hermitage," "Riverwood," the Chears Place, "Rattle and Snap" and "Fairfax" (all listed here), centering, for the most part, around Columbia, were the result. They set a style for Tennessee which has both force and individuality, even

though the detail may sometimes be lacking in finesse.

Beside the "great houses" you will not fail to notice the high percentage of abodes which were inns or taverns at one time, or, for that matter, still are. In the index of the Tennessee book of the American Guide Series you can count no less than twenty-nine still standing. The role of Tennessee in the settlement of the West and the restless comings and goings that marked its history almost from the beginning meant that many of the early buildings had to serve as hostelries as well as family homes. In every border state even the finest families at times accommodated strangers who could press on no further.

¶ Between Bristol & Knoxville

¶ *Blountville* (*9 miles southwest of Bristol on 11W*)

OLD DEERY INN (*1785*)
April, May, and June; admittance upon request; Mr. and Mrs. Joseph Anderson Caldwell.

William Deery, a wealthy Irish merchant, built the tavern which offered entertainment to travelers in these parts for more than a hundred and fifty years. Sitting flush with the street, this is a long, low building which still looks as though it has the welcome sign on the door. In its day it greeted such notables as the two Andrews, Jackson and Johnson, Lafayette, and Louis Philippe, who seems to have been everywhere in this country. Naturally the famous Polk family of Tennessee stopped here frequently too. Everything in the house is handmade, down to the nails and the hardware; the mantels and woodwork are hand-carved. The owners love its tradition and preserve it, although they want it understood that they do not treat the place as a museum or an inn, but live in it as a home. They have furnished it in keeping, and there are interesting things from the locality.

¶ *Kingsport (12 miles beyond Blountville on 11W)*

NETHERLANDS INN (*1811*)
2144 Lee Highway; Mr. Bruce and Miss Mary Nelms.

Not in good repair but unchanged.

ALLANDALE (*1830*)
Open to lovers of architecture; Mr. and Mrs. Harvey Brooks.

This house is a reconstruction of the Dickinson-Atkin House which was located in Knoxville at 518 West Main Avenue and which was in turn originally a copy of the poet Emily Dickinson's home, built by her relative, Perez Dickinson. It is a two-story stuccoed house, to which the Brookses added colonnades when they rebuilt it.

RIDGEFIELD FARMS (*1850*)
By appointment; Mr. and Mrs. C. P. Edwards, Jr.

This place is Early Victorian and beautifully furnished. Built by Martin Roller of brick made on the premises, it overlooks the island where the first treaty with the Indians in this region was signed. Thoroughbreds are raised here.

¶ *Rogersville (on 11W, 30 miles southwest of Kingsport)*

AMIS HOUSE (*1782*)
Old Stage Coach Road 2 miles out; on request; Miss Anne Amis.

Built like a fortress because, in the very early days of its building, the Indians were a constant menace, this stone house was erected by Capt. Thomas Amis. Miss Anne is the sixth generation to live in it. Among its distinctive features is the fact that each room has a separate staircase leading to the upper floor, as well as its own fireplace.

While you are in Rogersville, look at the old ROGERSVILLE INN (1782) at 108 Rogers Street, now converted into a two-family house, though some of it is still intact. Visit, too the MASONIC TEMPLE (1846), a very fine specimen of Greek Revival. If you have time, there are two other inns to see nearby, neither of them in the best of condition or furnished.

The ANDREW JACKSON INN (1856), two miles west of town, has plasterwork by Allison (also connected with "The Hermitage") and a good circular staircase. The owner is Mrs. G. C. Lyons in Surgoinsville. The NETHERLANDS INN, at 2144 Lee Highway, remains virtually unchanged.

¶ *Greeneville*
(about 30 miles south of Rogersville via 66 and 11E)

SEVIER-SUSONG HOUSE (*c. 1790*)
202 South Main Street; by appointment; Mrs. Edith O'Keefe Susong and Mrs. Quincy Marshall O'Keefe.

This began as a two-story log house, now the central part of the present long clapboard structure close to the street. The dining room has the original hand-hewn horizontal panels of pine. Attractively simple, it is furnished in Early American, and there is an immense Aubusson in the living room. It was built by Valentine Sevier, nephew of John Sevier, perhaps the most famous of the Tennessee pioneers, who became the first Governor when the state was still named "Franklin."

The Sevier-Cowles house (see next page) is trimly built of bricks made on the place; finely carved woodwork within.

SEVIER-COWLES HOUSE (*1810–1815*)

214 North Main Street; by appointment; Dr. and Mrs. R. S. Cowles.

This impressively tall, trim, four-chimney brick house, also known as "Sevier Place," is the one that Valentine Sevier built when his fortune began to be sizable. Special features are its beautiful entrance porch, its carved interior woodwork, its Cross-and-Bible doors, and its Haymaker hardware.

BOXWOOD MANOR (*1855*)

By appointment; Mr. and Mrs. S. J. Milligan.

A fine foursquare brick house with a flat hip roof and robust chimneys. Its Early Victorian trim is not in the least unbecoming, and inside its great high ceilings, large windows, and winding walnut staircase give it considerable distinction. It is said to have been designed by an architect from Ogdensburg, New York.

ANDREW JOHNSON HOUSE (*1851*)

Main Street; by arrangement at tailor shop of President Johnson at Depot and College Streets; National Park Service.

Andrew Johnson bought this simple brick house in 1851, before it was even complete, and lived in it until his death in 1875. His descendants continued to live here until 1941, when it was purchased by the government. Johnson's trade was tailoring, and the shop which he once owned and worked in is nearby; in it he employed young men to read to him as he worked, so that he might remedy his lack of education. Southerner and slaveholder, he none the less stood firmly by the Union. Johnson was the only President ever to be impeached, though the impeachment did not succeed, and also the only President ever to return to Washington as a Senator afterwards. In many ways his post–Civil War job was one of the hardest and most thankless in our history. His shop and house are a monument, fittingly modest and unpretentious. The furnishings used by the family have been preserved as they were in 1941, when the government purchased the house from his descendants.

¶ *White Pine (at junction of 25E and 66)*

FAIRFAX (*1832*)

Open to students and lovers of architecture on request; Mr. and Mrs. Thomas H. Berry.

Perhaps the most unusual house in the state, almost pure Georgian despite its date. It was built by Maj. Isaac Franklin, close kinsman of Benjamin Franklin. Descendants of the family say that a New Orleans architect probably designed it, since the family spent much time there; some experts, on the other hand, attribute it to Benjamin Latrobe. The similarity of the stairway and woodwork to that in "Long Branch" in Millwood, Virginia, gives support to this last theory. The woodwork is elaborate and includes a spiraling rosewood staircase which ended at a cupola, no longer there. The house needed extensive restoration. It is being furnished for the most part with antiques. Already almost completed, it is bound to be spectacular.

Fairfax, with its effectively pilastered walls, begins to give you some idea of the grandeur that was Tennessee.

Earlier and simpler, the Blount mansion is more reminiscent of the Colonial of the Seaboard states.

¶ Between Knoxville & Chattanooga

¶ Knoxville

BLOUNT MANSION (1792)

> *200 West Hill Avenue; Monday to Friday 9:30 to 5, Saturdays and Sundays by appointment; silver contribution; Blount Mansion Association.*

Gov. William Blount, "Governor of all territories south of the Ohio River" (quite a stretch of country!), built the first frame house west of the Alleghenies. Here, too, was born the state of Tennessee on June 1, 1796. An unostentatious Georgian mansion, fittingly furnished, this two-story house has balanced one-story wings. Hand-carved mantels, chair rails, and wide-paneled doors, along with an old-fashioned garden tended by the Garden Club, make this a rewarding place to visit.

OLD STRONG HOUSE

> *(late eighteenth century)*
> *120 West Cumberland Avenue; any time; Volunteers of America.*

This house was built by **Dr. Joseph C. Strong**, who was surgeon on the U.S.S. *Trumbull* during the Revolution. Coming south, he copied the Massachusetts home of his father Caleb Strong, Governor of and Senator from that state. The brick house contains distinguished carved mantels and cornices, as well as a free-standing

staircase built by craftsmen brought from New England—the same ones who had ornamented the Caleb Strong Home there. Although a very fine house, it is in need of restoration and is not furnished in keeping.

LONGUEVAL (1823)

> *2728 Kingston Pike southwest of city; Mrs. Alfred Sanford, Sr.*

On a sweeping curve of the Tennessee River, it was first called "Crescent Bend." This two-story brick house sits on its "long view" among huge old oaks. Its gardens slope in terraces down to the river. It was the plantation home of Drury P. Armstrong, banker and planter. Inside is a stairway branching two ways from a balcony landing. The spacious rooms are beautifully paneled, and furnished in antiques of the period.

RAMSEY HOUSE, or SWAN POND (1797)

> *Thorn Grove Pike near Marbledale, via Riverside Drive and Boyd's Bridge, 8 miles east of city; by appointment; Association for Preservation of Tennessee Antiquities, Mrs. W. N. Garrett (phone 2–0460) or Mrs. T. H. Berry (phone 6–1812).*

In the words of the builder's son, Dr. J. G. M. Ramsey, author of the famous *Annals of Tennessee*, "It was a large stone structure, with a deep basement and an attic, besides two tall stories. Its corners, its arches, the top of the chimneys, and one row of building rock midway between the ground and the top of the square, were built of pure blue limestone, while the walls throughout were built of red granite. Its style was Gothic, long narrow windows, cornices richly carved in wood but painted to resemble stone, massive, elaborately finished and ornamented." At the census of 1800 it was the most costly and most admired building in Tennessee. The miracle is that everything in this house has been left unchanged, even to the first stone steps and the window shutters with their hand-wrought hinges in place. It was the first house in Tennessee to have plastered walls, and the original paint, enhanced by time, is still on them. The house is being furnished in keeping; restoration was well under way when this was written. If your taste runs in this direction, you will never see anything to touch it.

CHISHOLM'S TAVERN (1792)
217 Front Street; to be restored.

Capt. John Chisholm built this tavern during the first year of the city's history. It was constructed of logs on a fieldstone

foundation three feet thick. The hand-hewn weatherboards were added later and pegged together. Two huge pent chimneys at the gable ends assured cheer and hot food. Tradition has it that the ubiquitous Louis Philippe was attacked by vicious insects (which shall be nameless) while stopping here, greased himself with hog lard to no avail and finally rushed forth and jumped screaming into the nearby river. Double front doors flanked by fluted pilasters open into the main hall. Heart pine was used in the woodwork throughout, and there are solid-pine doors, beautifully paneled. Many a huge joint must have turned on the spit of the huge fireplace in the "great room." Typical of the better hostelries of the day, this tavern, when restored, will be another of the "must" places in Knoxville.

SPEEDWELL (prior to 1861)
Old Peter Blow Farm; on written request; Dr. Frank T. Rogers, 608 West Main Avenue.

This was the family home in Tazewell of Dr. Rogers's mother and was moved here to the city piece by piece, along with

At the time of the 1800 census Swan Pond was deemed the most admired and the most costly of Tennessee houses. The walls throughout are of red granite, while the corners, arches, and chimney trim are of pure blue limestone.

most of its original furniture. A beguiling brick house with four large end chimneys and a large-scale classic portico, it commands a grand view of the Great Smokies.

¶ *Loudon* (*31 miles from Knoxville*)

BUTLER PLACE (*prior to 1861*)
Kingston Pike, 3 miles out on River Road; by written appointment; Mr. and Mrs. J. W. Butler.

The builder of this charming colonial brick house reminiscent of Virginia was Albert Lenoir; thus it is sometimes called the "Old Lenoir Place." It is said to be one of the oldest houses in the county.

¶ *Concord*

STATESVIEW (*1809*)
By appointment; Dr. and Mrs. Lucien Bailey.

It was built by Charles McClung, who laid out the streets of Knoxville and who also wrote the first constitution of the state. The place was rebuilt after a fire which destroyed most of it in 1823; only a lower wing survived. The distinction of this simple brick house is in its excellent proportions and in the quality of its workmanship. Moldings, mantels, etc., are stylish in a plain way. It is furnished with antiques.

¶ *Madisonville*

JUDGE STICKLEY HOUSE (*1846*)
Route 129–411, from Knoxville to Chattanooga; daily; 50 cents.

Built by an English architect, Blanchard, who brought his craftsmen from Pennsylvania, the outside walls of this big house with two-story pedimented veranda are five bricks thick. Inside there are carved mantels, paneled doors, and a three-story spiral staircase.

¶ *Tellico Plains* (*between Madisonville and Etowah*)

MANSION HOUSE (*c. 1847*)
Cherokee National Forest, Route 3, on Tellico River; May 1 to November 1 daily 10 to 5, remainder of year Saturdays and Sundays 12 to 5; 50 cents and 25 cents; Mrs. Sarah Key Patten and Z. Carter Patten.

In a picturesque wilderness setting in the heart of the Cherokee Indian country, with the Tellico River running swiftly in front

Statesview presents a distinguished and inviting silhouette above the hill where it stands near Concord.

of its door, is Mansion House, built around a log cabin erected by John Sevier, the great pioneer and first Governor. The owners are converting the land into a natural garden and bird preserve. The house, which overlooks the old trail of the early Carolina explorers and Indian traders, was the pride of the area, having four spacious rooms on each floor and a fine stairway. The ever-present Louis Philippe, according to his diary, was feted by a Cherokee chieftain nearby; the hospitality included a bed with two squaws. The house now makes an excellent background for the owners' unusual collection of antiques. There are modern cottages for tourists on the grounds, also furnished with antiques.

¶ *Chattanooga*

HENDERSON HOUSE, *or* **GENERAL GRANT'S HEADQUARTERS**
(*prior to 1840*)
110 East First Street; donation; Cotton Ball Association.

Jane Henderson, widow of a census taker killed probably by the Cherokees, built this place, the first frame house in Chattanooga. It served as an inn at one time, and later as the headquarters of General Grant. Many notables of that era stopped in this modest hostelry, since in those days there were no others nearby. The house is being furnished with antiques and is used as a museum of local history.

THE CRAVENS HOUSE
(*mid-nineteenth century*)
Side of Lookout Mountain overlooking city; United States government, J. Eugene Lewis (restoration chairman), Bonny Oaks Drive.

A frame house owned by Robert Cravens, a pioneer in iron manufacturing. It stands on a spectacular spot—Chickamauga Park. The house has been leased to the Association for the Preservation of Tennessee Antiquities by the government. There is much local interest in its restoration, though little seems to be left of the original buildings.

¶ North & south of Nashville

¶ Nashville

RIVERWOOD (*1798*)
Porter Road, 4 miles from downtown; on request; Mrs. Lucius E. Burch.

A magnificent mansion and a seat of Southern hospitality for a century and a half, it stands at the end of a half mile of driveway amid gentle hills and meadows. Built at the turn of the century by Alexander James Porter, who had fled Ireland and started a successful linen business here, it was then located deep in the forest and called "Tammany Wood" after his home near Londonderry. In 1858 the last Porter to own the house made extensive additions,

which included the impressive pillared portico on the end. Since William Strickland was in Nashville at the time designing the capitol, and since the Egyptian fad that influenced him strongly is found here in the window and door frames and in the lotus-blossom theme of the capitals on the exterior columns, it is more than likely that he was responsible for it. The boldness of scale bears out this theory. On the right side of the hall there are three parlors opening by double doors into one another, each with its massive Egyptian-style framing and its black marble fireplace. The vista looks like a long reflection in a mirror and gives the impression of a place able to swallow up crowds of guests; there are, in fact, records of the great dinners given for Gen. and Mrs. Andrew Jackson here. The fine furniture, drapes, and rugs are in keeping with the manorial house. Mrs. Burch's family, the next to own it, have lived here more than a hundred years.

BELLE MEADE (*1853*)
Leake Avenue, 6 miles on Route 70; by appointment; Association for Preservation of Tennessee Antiquities (phone 2-0460 or 6-1812).

This home started with two log cabins built in 1798 by John Harding when he came here from Virginia. They still stand near the great mansion erected by his son, who

Here again you get the grandeur that was Tennessee in the great hallway of Belle Meade, the pride of Nashville.

was born in one of the cabins and who built this house after his first attempt in 1830 had burned down. But by 1850 he had made this one of the most prosperous farms of the state and one of the largest. He was said to have disbursed over five million dollars for the Confederate cause. His mansion, certainly built by Strickland, has a two-story white marble portico with square stone pillars extending across the front. Later, when "Belle Meade" passed to Harding's daughter and her husband, it became one of the most famous horse-breeding farms in America. The Ohio newspaper, the Cincinnati *Enquirer,* was named after one of the great stallions, and when he died here the paper sent three hundred people to cover the dedication of his monument on Leake Avenue.

TRAVELER'S REST (*1793*)
Radnor Yards, 7 miles toward Alabama line; to be opened after restoration and furnished by Colonial Dames of America in Tennessee.

At the end of a half-mile driveway, this two-story house of wood and brick with long windows is the impressive place built by Judge John Overton, before Tennessee attained statehood. The first house was built for his bride, Mary White, whose father founded Knoxville. As a restoration, it promises to be second only to "The Hermitage" in importance. It grew from a log cabin, enlarged and beautified through the years, as Overton became one of the wealthiest and most important men in the state and Jackson's closest friend and adviser. The Colonial Dames plan to keep it "a simple, dignified dwelling" and will undoubtedly furnish it with their usual good taste, using Overton material whenever they can find it. Overton, a horticulturist of sorts, imported gardeners from all over the world to enhance his grounds. These, it is hoped, will be part of the restoration.

BELMONT, *now* WARD-BELMONT ACADEMY (*1850*)
Sixteenth Avenue and Belcourt Street; any time.

Now part of Ward-Belmont Academy, the main building of the group is "Belmont," which was originally built as a home on the grand scale for Col. J. A. S. Acklen.

No expense was spared here. Almost certainly designed by William Strickland during his ten-year residence in Nashville (1844–1854), it is a lavish production and well preserved. The wrought-iron balconies and window guards are of a delicacy unmatched in this country; they were imported from Italy. Other academy buildings have been added facing the garden in the rear, but the façade is unspoiled, as are the vast entrance hall and drawing room, separated from each other only by an open row of fluted Corinthian columns. The ornamentation of cornices, ceiling rosettes, etc., is highly elaborated, and the antler stairway is a masterpiece of skillful craftsmanship. Its builders were evidently striving to make it the finest house in Tennessee. Some think they succeeded.

MAXWELL HOUSE (*1859*)
Corner of 4th Avenue N. and Church Street.

A four-story brick hotel designed by Francis W. Strickland, son of the master, for Judge John Overton of "Traveler's Rest," who is said to have purchased the land on which it stood for fifteen dollars, at an auction, thinking at the time that he was bidding on a cow. The hotel was so oversized for the town that it was also known as "Overton's Folly." It was named Maxwell House for his wife, and the well-known brand of coffee was named after the hotel.

¶ *Donelson*
(northeast outskirts of Nashville)

THE HERMITAGE (*1834*)
Route 70, 12 miles below Nashville; daily, 8 to 6; 50 cents; Ladies Hermitage Association.

This was the house of President Andrew Jackson, furnished as when he lived there, the grounds and gardens also maintained to perfection as he laid them out with the aid of Ralph E. W. Earl, an artist who married Mrs. Jackson's niece. Jackson acquired the plantation early in 1805 and lived here first in log cabins, some of which are on the grounds now. He could not afford a better home until 1812, and the simple two-story brick house erected then was almost burned to the ground in 1834. Rebuilt under the direction of Joseph Rieff, a dis-

The double parlors of the Hermitage evoke the lovable virtues and vices of the Victorian era.

tinguished architect of the period, the finest of furnishings were ordered from Philadelphia. They were sailed to New Orleans, and thence by steamboat to Nashville, where the wharf burned and the furniture with it. Rachel Jackson never lived to see her fine new home finished. The detail here is somewhat less ornate than in most mansions of the period and has considerable dignity, along with the unmistakable flavor of an outstanding personality.

TULIP GROVE (*1832*)
Near "The Hermitage"; daily, 10 to 6; $1.00; Mrs. Charles Buntin (owner).

Approached through a curving driveway lined with tulip trees, in a tree-shaded park as lovely as anything in England, it was the home of Andrew Jackson Donelson, who had been the President's political secretary and whose wife had been Jackson's official White House hostess. Jackson, himself, hired Joseph Rieff to design it. While it was being built, the nearby "Hermitage" caught fire. It is in many ways the equal of "The Hermitage," a spacious square brick mansion with an ell. The recessed façade has a splendid Doric frieze. Interior detail is ornate and massive. The walls of the hall were marbleized, then a new fashion in America, by the ever useful Mr. Earl, and the eight panels of the hall doors as well as the eight panels in the door-reveals are painted to simulate a dark grained wood, an art much practiced in Pennsyl-

vania at the time. In any event, the effect is quite a tour de force. You can see why the building and decoration of this house absorbed the whole attention of the Jackson-Donelsons at the time.

BELAIR (*1838*)
Route 70; by appointment; Harry H. Chitwood.

Begun by Joseph Harding for his daughter, Elizabeth, it was not completed until 1838 when a new owner, William Nichol, purchased it and added the flanking wings, winding stair, rosewood doors with their silver knobs, and, no doubt, many of its other elegancies. It resembles many Virginia houses of the early part of the century and the deep entablature and rather heavy double porches appear to be almost a Greek Revival afterthought. The garden is similar to that of "The Hermitage."

¶ Gallatin

TROUSDALE PLACE (*1815*)
First Saturday in each month, other times by appointment; Clark Chapter, United Daughters of the Confederacy, Mrs. Henry S. McKoin, Sr. (Secretary).

It was the home of two early governors. This is an unusual brick building with interesting detail—semicircular brick crowns over the windows with ornamented frames as well. The neatly balustraded balcony is supported by delicate columns. It was first the home of Gov. William Campbell and then of Gov. William Trousdale, known as "The War Horse of Tennessee" because he served in the Creek, Seminole, and Mexican Wars. His son's wife willed it to the United Daughters of the Confederacy, who use it as a chapter house, meeting place, library, and historical museum. Closed in 1955 for extensive repairs, it may be open now.

ROSEMONT (*1847*)
On request; 50 cents; Mrs. Lewis Guild.

Built by Judge Joe Conn Guild, author of *Old Times in Tennessee*, the house is a fine brick structure with the windows framed in white and a Greek Revival porch and balcony. It has double basements in which valuable racing colts, as well as the silver, were hidden during the Civil War. It is now occupied by his daughter and her son.

If you are a devotee, two other very interesting stone houses in the Gallatin area are SPENCER'S CHOICE (1798) and CRAIGFONT (1802); both badly run down at this writing, but the latter, though neglected, is noteworthy.

¶ *Madison*

GLEN ECHO (*1794*)

> *Route 31 (Gallatin Road) 6 miles from Nashville; on written request; $1.00; Misses Fanny and Alice Walton, Box 432.*

One of the oldest houses in the vicinity, this colonial brick was built on the site of an Indian mound. The first log cabin on this ground was burned down by the Indians. Although it was built by a pioneer teacher and educator, Thomas Craighead, who had a school nearby which became the nucleus of Peabody College, the Walton family has lived in it since 1870. The dreamy old house, which resembles its name, has most of the original Walton furniture.

¶ *Castalian Springs*

CASTALIAN SPRINGS TAVERN, now WYNNEWOOD FARM (*1829*)

> *May 15 to September 15, by appointment at owner's convenience; Mr. and Mrs. George W. Wynne.*

Wynnewood Farm was a pioneer inn of more than average interest. Built entirely of logs, it is a long structure of eighteen rooms, and still unsheathed. It was considered a tour de force, the joining of these heavy logs being a feat accomplished here by only four men. One of them was Col. Alfred Wynne, who subsequently purchased it. The interior has features of considerable refinement, carved mantels and woodwork. Here you can see the breezeway (sometimes called the "dog trot") which was typical of the very early log cabins, and which grew to be a characteristic of Tennessee houses, later being used to connect kitchens, servants' quarters, and other outbuildings. Colonel Wynne planted a hickory tree the day of Andrew Jackson's death in his memory and you can still stand in its shade on the lawn. His descendants are living here today, farming and still enjoying the place.

¶ *Portland (31 miles north of Nashville via 31W)*

ROCK JOLLY (*c. 1830*)

> *Rock House Road 3 to 4 miles from state line; on written or phone (Cross Plains 2041) request; Mrs. George J. Gale.*

By all means phone for directions. On the way you will see the old stone bridges whose construction is so similar to that of "Rock Jolly." Be sure to find out how it got such a wonderful name, too. Good Early American furniture here.

Rock Jolly is an out-of-the-ordinary old house in an out-of-the-way place.

Wyatt Hall's proportions are of interest: eight rooms long, one room wide.

WINGATE (*1821*)

> *Route 31W near Portland, and the Kentucky-Tennessee state line; on written or phone request; Mr. and Mrs. Allison Buntin.*

"Wingate" is one of the few Tennessee homes remaining in the family of the original builder. John Buntin built it and brought his wife, Adelia Allison, here from North Carolina. The two names are combined in the present owners. A classical Georgian house of handmade brick, none of it has been changed. The unusually lovely interior woodwork was made to Bun-

tin's order in Philadelphia and hauled to this remote spot by long stages of travel. A feature not to be missed here is the enormous old kitchen with its original brick flooring, massive overhead beams, and "cooking" fireplaces at either end. The Buntins appreciated the good life, even though they were far from a city.

¶ *Franklin*

WYATT HALL (*1797–1800*)

> *By appointment; Mr. and Mrs. William Hubert Wyatt.*

Built of handmade brick laid in Flemish bond, it is six rooms long and only one room wide. Each room has its own fireplace. It is furnished with taste in American and Southern antiques. That the house was in the heart of the Battle of Franklin was attested by unexploded cannonballs.

CARTER HOUSE (*1830*)

> *Route 31, 8 blocks south of the square; daily; 50 cents and 25 cents; state of Tennessee, managed by Carter House Association, Mrs. Thomas P. Henderson (President).*

When Fountain Branch Carter came here from Virginia, he built a little house that is reminiscent of Williamsburg except that it has stepped gable ends. Coupled Doric

Homes of Presidents have a personality interest apart from the interest of their architecture, which gives the Samuel Polk home a double attraction, for there is much here to see and admire.

columns frame the door with fanlight and sidelights. The two large front windows are capped with emphatic lintels. It's very neat and stylish. Rare features inside are a drum-ceiling attic and doors with Cross-and-Bible panel pattern. All materials are of poplar, ash, and cedar, hewn from the virgin timber. It is being furnished in the mid-nineteenth-century period of its construction. The office, gin house, kitchen, and smoke house are part of this restoration. Carter's son fell mortally wounded during the Battle of Franklin, not two hundred yards from home, and was taken to his mother's room to die. Many of the wounded were cared for by the Carter family and it is said that stains on the floor were made by their blood. At any rate the bullet marks in the ell are plain to be seen.

¶ *Spring Hill*

CHEAIRS PLACE, *now* HOUSTON HALL FARM (*1855*)
By appointment; Mr. P. D. Houston; 326 Union Street, Nashville, or Houston Hall Farm.

Now the heart of a stock farm, it is considered one of the showplaces of Tennessee. Built by Strickland of red brick for Maj. Nathaniel Francis Cheairs, the handsome columns with their lotus capitals are unmistakably the work of "the master," as is the emphatic cornice and the palatial solidity of the place. It has two-story recessed entrances on three sides. This house is historically famous for the fact that the five generals who were killed in the Battle of Franklin breakfasted here before they went forth to battle and to their death. Furnished to suit its importance, it stands in a park of great old trees.

¶ *Columbia*
(44 miles south of Nashville on 31)

SAMUEL POLK HOME (*1816*)
301 West 7th Street; daily 9 to 12 and 1 to 5, Sunday 1 to 5; James K. Polk Memorial Association.

Of whitewashed brick, with French windows and balconies, it is now a memorial to the eleventh President, who was born here. It is a spacious town house, with little ornament and much style. Young Polk left here to go to the University of North Carolina; his wedding took place here; and he opened a law office nearby. It is furnished in authentic period pieces, many of which belonged to his White House period and others to Polk Place in Nashville, including mirrors, portraits, glassware, and silver and the rosewood and crimson brocade furniture in the parlor. The house next door, almost an exact duplicate, was built by Samuel Polk for his daughter. It is privately owned and not open.

RATTLE AND SNAP (*1845*)
Mt. Pleasant Road, 5 miles from Columbia; on written request; Mr. and Mrs. Oliver M. Babcock, Jr.

At the end of a quarter-mile drive sits the greatest of the Polk houses, a noble edifice which climaxes the other Polk and Pillow mansions of the vicinity. Its noble façade of ten Corinthian columns and its exquisite interior, whose cornices and ceiling medallions are as delicate as any you will find anywhere, bespeak the skill of craftsmen who had been brought here from other parts of the country, for there is nothing else quite like it in Tennessee. The columns are believed to have been made in Cincinnati and transported by river boat and ox team. The architect is unknown but it is considered most unlikely that it was Strickland. Built by George Knox Polk, cousin of the President, it acquired its odd name, it is said, because he won the land in a dice game with the governor of North Carolina. Be that as it may, the unique name is hardly descriptive of this greatest of Tennessee mansions. The present owners are doing a very careful work of restoration on it; nothing inside had been altered, fortunately, and you will see it, therefore, much as it was originally. The furnishings are both handsome and appropriate.

If you are an *aficionado,* you may wish while in the neighborhood to make an effort to see the PILLOW-HALLIDAY HOUSE (c. 1845) and the PILLOW-BETHEL HOUSE (1845), both said to have considerable interest and to be in good condition. At this writing they are under lease, and arrangements to visit would be better made in person.

¶ *Pulaski* (*31 miles south of Columbia*)

CLIFTON PLACE (*1847*)

7 miles from Pulaski and 1 mile from Wales Station; on written request; Mr. and Mrs. John Kilpatrick.

Of brick laid in Flemish bond, it was built by a Virginian named Tyree Rodes, who is said to have employed an English architect and an English landscape gardener named Barret to plan the boxwood garden. The whole delightful place is being carefully restored.

¶ *Mt. Pleasant*

MANOR HALL FARM (*1849*)

By appointment; $1.00; Mrs. John S. Frierson.

Manor Hall Farm was built by Martin Luther Stockard, in spite of his name a gay blade, who built a race track in front of his house and who took his bride to London to buy furnishings for their stately new home. By good fortune some of these things are still here. The drawing rooms and halls are about sixty feet long, with fourteen-foot ceilings. Two marble mantels come from Italy, and the crystal chandeliers, cornices, and velvet carpets were brought from England, as were the fine gilt mirrors. The staircase is remarkable. The smokehouse and servants' quarters are still standing. The house is in need of repair but is still of considerable interest.

¶ *Smyrna*

SAM DAVIS HOME (*1810–1847*)

Near Smyrna; off Route 41, 20 miles from Nashville; daily 8 to 6, Sunday 1 to 6:30; 50 cents.

This was the farm home of the boy hero of the Confederacy, whose story is much like Nathan Hale's. Young Davis, who was offered a pardon on the gallows if he would tell the name of his informer, said "If I had a thousand lives to live I would lose them all before I would betray a friend or the confidence of my informer." (A lesson for our times.)

The house, a simple but substantial one, was built of red cedar logs, now clap-boarded. It follows the style of the period, the original floors and hardware still intact. Kitchen, smokehouse, and overseers' cabin are separate buildings, all original. The old-fashioned garden tended by the Nashville Garden Club has a long season of bloom. At the rear of the garden, young Sam Davis found his last resting place.

¶ *Murfreesboro*

ELMWOOD (*1842*)

Route 41 toward Nashville; by appointment at owner's convenience; Mrs. Thomas Epps Hord, Jr.

Built by Thomas Hord, this house has always been lived in by the same family and has a wealth of original furniture. The owners speak of it as "truly a home that is lived in." During the Civil War it was occupied by Federal troops for two years and was used for the wounded during the Battle of Murfreesboro.

CASTLEWOOD (*1845*)

Route 231, 2 miles north on Lebanon Road; on request; Mrs. James M. Haynes.

A fanciful house, built by David Spence whose imagination was early stirred by his father's descriptions of English castles. Built of brick, it now, alas, is stuccoed over. In spite of medieval turrets at each end (now used as clothes closets), Spence built a second story whose grilled balcony and French windows are as Southern as they can be. The furniture here is for the most part heirloom. The house was also used for the wounded during the nearby battle.

While here, take a look at MARYMONT (1859), not open, but has some worthwhile exterior details.

¶ *Memphis*

HUNT PHELAN HOUSE (*1835*)

533 Beale Street; on request; Mr. Stephen Rice Phelan.

It is a pure example of Greek Revival, reminiscent of the classic quality found in some of the Greek houses in New England, of brick construction with a monumental Ionic portico. Its present owner has performed a public service in rescuing the great house which had come near to the verge of ruin. In 1861 it was occupied by Leonidas Polk, Confederate general during the organizing of "The Provisional Army of Tennessee," but it was soon after seized by Federals and used by General Grant as his headquarters in 1862. In Memphis, it stands with the old ROBERTSON TOPP HOUSE at 537 Beale Street, as a unique survival of the short era of building which Memphis enjoyed during the ten or fifteen years before the Civil War.

NEELY HOUSE (*1849*)

652 Adams Street; October 1 to May 15, by written or phone appointment; Mrs. B. L. Mallory.

A Memphis landmark, it was originally a two-story house of the French type; a third story and cupola was added in 1890 somewhat changing its character. At this time the marble mantels were removed and other changes made which were not for the better. Its style might perhaps be described as kind of Memphis Victorian, which merely means that the French influence is strong as well as the exuberance of Southern life in the cotton belt. It was built by James Kirkland and contains twenty-eight rooms. The parlors are wonderful with lush Victorian furniture, elaborate cornices, and plaster work on the ceiling, crystal chandeliers, red silk damask, and Oriental screens.

RAMSAY HOUSE (*1864*)

487 Goodwyn Street; on request in advance; 50 cents; Mr. and Mrs. John Woolfolk Ramsay.

Handmade brick with an interesting two-story portico, in the Regency manner, it is a spacious house whose entrance hall is uninterrupted by a staircase. Each room has its own fireplace. The original crystal sconces are still on the walls, as are many family portraits. The drawing room is furnished in Victorian carved rosewood, while the dining room is Jacobean.

¶ *The Pilgrimage*

The Tennessee Statewide Tour, still an infant of three or four years, is nevertheless very well organized, as its tour booklet demonstrates. It takes place the last week in April and the first week in May, covering the eastern section in one week and the west and central in the other. The territory is extensive and well over fifty homes have been included in the past, but it may all be seen if you put on your boots and spurs.

Full information and programs are available which describe each house at the Tennessee Pilgrimage State Headquarters, The Hermitage Hotel, Nashville 3, Tennessee.

The three areas fan out from Knoxville, Nashville, and Memphis roughly, although there are a number of places like Kingsport and Blountville at some distance from any focal point. If your time is limited, you would do best to stick to the Nashville and Columbia areas for it is here that the houses are thickest, and here that the great Polk and Pillow mansions, which usually open their doors for the tour, are located. What with the grandeur that was and is Tennessee and the increasing interest in preservation, this tour should soon take its place with the big three or four.

Stony Lonesome is well named. It is located in what might be called lonesome country, in the region of Versailles. The house is of Kentucky stone, the floors and indoor trim of native ash and walnut, and it is filled with Kentucky furniture, for which the state enjoys a special fame. It is the earliest Kentucky house listed in the Guide. *On the opposite page we have Kentucky at its more grandiloquent, the Yeiser-Kinnard-Chestnut house at Danville—yet in this case too, Kentucky through and through.*

KENTUCKY

*T*HE limestone that lies under most of central Kentucky has been the rock on which good fortunes have been founded. Limestone has caused the twelve thousand square miles of Bluegrass country to produce unsurpassed horses and cattle, as well as tobacco and other crops; it is responsible for the sweet water in Kentucky's flowing springs that has made Kentucky whisky famous all over the world; and it also was used (limestone, that is) to lay up the walls of her earliest permanent homes.

The central location of the state in relation to the tides of migration and commerce brought the home builders from the Eastern-seaboard states, and they in turn brought their own home-building ideas. A few of the permanent dwellings which began to appear in the latter part of the eighteenth century, when planters from Virginia and the Carolinas followed the pioneers, are still being cherished. They are houses that show the Georgian influence of their predecessors but whose character was much modified by local materials and workmanship. This is particularly true of the stone houses, whose flinty pale-gray limestone still looks newish after a hundred and fifty years and whose interiors attest the great variety of virgin wood from which the builders could choose.

Later, as you will see, when wealth accumulated, the houses took on the more florid aspects of plantation living

185

and entertaining. This sometimes consisted simply of the addition of porticoes and pillars; somehow the Greek Revival failed to hit Kentucky with quite the same impact as it did some of the other states to the south, and the columns one sees, while impressive, seem to have been the product more of a desire for stateliness than of a passion to be in style.

As in every other state, in spite of a common fount of inspiration, the houses took on their own regional character, conditioned by the climate, materials, and economy. Beside the early stone houses there was a typical one-story brick house with flankers which comes close to being a genuine regional style. Although these are often referred to as "farmhouses," they were beautifully built, with charming proportions and rooflines, and are veritable little manors. Occasionally they astonish with their finely wrought detail. Some of the best examples are MALVERN HILL, near Lexington, THE GRANGE, near Paris, RIDGEWAY, near Louisville, and BURFORD HILL, near Harrodsburg. In spite of their elegant manner, they possess in common an indefinable quality that can only be called "homelike." Stephen Foster felt it and wrote his immortal song to express the feeling.

If you were to spot on your road map the towns mentioned in the heading to this introduction, you would see that they form a little cluster in the northeast center of the state. There is a good reason why the best early houses of Kentucky should all be found in this comparatively small area, for this is the region of the bluegrass. At any rate, it will not only simplify your sightseeing to have everything within rather easy reach, but the beauty of the countryside will greatly enhance your pleasure.

❡ *The Kentucky House Tours*

"Open house" in Kentucky has been taking place for sixteen years as an established custom which occurs in the middle of May. Needless to say, the gardens are then at their late-spring best and the air is fresh and balmy. The garden clubs of Kentucky sponsor the event; write to Mrs. H. Alvin Stiltz, Chairman, Newtown Road, R.R. 6, Lexington, or to the feature editor of the Louisville *Courier Journal,* for information. The thirty-or-more houses shown, running in date from the late eighteenth century to the mid-twentieth, make it possible to see the entire history of home building in the state. The tours are unhurried, the houses in Lexington, Louisville, and Frankfort remaining open for three days; the fee is fifty cents a house. The houses are for the most part out of the towns, but roads are well marked for the tour and maps plentifully supplied. Proceeds are used for the maintenance of the garden at LIBERTY HALL in Frankfort and for the planting of the garden at ASHLAND, home of Henry Clay (both listed herein). Here is a good chance to see many of these homes at their best.

❡ *Louisville*

FARMINGTON (*1810*)
3031 Bardstown Road (street number to be changed); by phone appointment, March, April, May, September, and October; Mr. and Mrs. Porter Smith.

Lincoln visited here in 1841, suffering from an unhappy love affair. It was built by John Speed, whose two sons were among Lincoln's most intimate friends. It is a one-and-a-half-story brick house with a central pedimented portico of slender Doric columns and a doorway with oval fanlight and sidelights. Because of the two octagonal rooms separated by a hall and flanked with massive square rooms, an arrangement recalling one of Jefferson's designs, the house

It is clear that Farmington was built under the influence of Jefferson's classical enthusiasm.

has been ascribed to him; but so have others. However, the house is handsome and spacious, and its present owners are furnishing it in keeping.

¶ In & Out of Lexington

Bluegrass country surrounds the town of Lexington. Within a radius of some thirty miles of this verdure there are as many as four hundred houses a hundred years old or older. Not many of them are unchanged, but a goodly number still retain some of the original construction. To see a section which is virtually unspoiled in Lexington proper, walk to the quadrangle known as "The Gratz Park Scene," where the CAPT. JOHN STARK HOUSE (1812) faces the BENJAMIN GRATZ HOUSE (1819), with its delightful doorway. Here also the DR. FREDERICK RIDGELEY HOUSE (1794), considered by some to be the finest example of colonial architecture in the "West," faces the house once occupied by Gideon Shryock—the young man who left his mark on the Greek Revival mansions of the whole area.

But outside the town there is some-

thing more important than houses: on lush pastures whose turf has never been disturbed, the finest horses in the world are bred. In the center of town there is a monument to Man O' War; here he was buried in state, and the funeral of few public figures has attracted more attention in Kentucky. But even way back in the early 1800s Patrick Henry was so fretted about the proper burying ground for his own horse, "Henry Clay" by name, that he prevailed upon his close friend, Dr. James Moore, President of Transylvania, who lived near town in lovely "Malvern Hill," to grant the steed a plot in his garden, where he rests today.

In 1797, when Clay came riding into Kentucky from Virginia on the back of this very same horse, he found a thriving city—at the time the largest and wealthiest west of the Alleghenies. Yet it had been only a scant twenty years since a little group of rugged (and probably ragged) frontiersmen had named the wilderness spot after they got the news of the Battle of Lexington. This little band of pioneers had stumbled onto one of the richest areas in the country, whose potentialities the westward-moving floods of emigrants were not slow to develop. Those who stayed prospered greatly; the homes hereabouts illustrate their success story.

HUNT-MORGAN HOUSE (*1814*)
201 North Mill Street; daily, 10 to 4:30, except Monday; 50 cents and 25 cents; The Foundation for the Preservation of Historic Lexington and Fayette County.

The great brick town house of John Wesley Hunt, the first millionaire in the West; later the home of his grandson, Gen. John Hunt Morgan, C.S.A., called the "Thunderbolt of the Confederacy"; and finally the home of Thomas Hunt Morgan, distinguished Nobel prize winner in genetics. It is both historically and architecturally the "first" house in Lexington. The outstanding feature of the big brick place is the gable end with its broad, fanlighted doorway facing Gratz Park, the leaded glass in fan and lunettes exquisitely designed and repeated in the Palladian window above. The building has an unusually good plan in terms of convenience and livability: an office with a private entrance on 2d Street; a service court screened from the street by a seven-foot wall, which runs down to the stable and the coach house; and a two-story pavilion for servants' quarters. Some changes were made in the house during its many years in the same family which were not for the better, but presumably an able restoration will take care of them. It bids fair to be the big attraction here (after the racing season is over).

WINDWARD, *formerly* ROSE HILL (*1813*)
Parkers Mill Road 8 miles west of town, opposite entrance to Lane Allen Road; on request; Laurie J. Blakely.

The land on which this solid-brick house stands once belonged to the pioneer Simon Kenton. The thick walls, the original white-ash floors, and the walnut woodwork are again as good as new. The simple plan of a central hall and two ample rooms both upstairs and down creates a symmetrical simplicity for the chaste façade with its

delicate proportions. The Blakelys rehabilitated what was considered a total wreck and have made a lovely home of it. They have an interesting interior furnished principally in pine and cherry—the emphasis being on color.

BRYAN STATION FARM (*1795*)
Route 956, 5 miles northeast of Lexington, and 3 miles below New Circle Road; daily, May through October, by phone appointment (Lexington 2–6621); $1.00 and 50 cents; Mr. and Mrs. W. C. H. Wood, Jr.

The defense of Bryan Station, besieged in 1782 by a band of Indians, halted the invasion of Kentucky by their British allies. The house, now of white-painted brick and a story and a half high, sits on a rise where presumably the fort from which the place was defended stood. The house, built by Joseph Hale Rogers, began as one story. The beams, joists, and sills were taken from the blockhouses of the old fort, mortised, and pegged together. In 1800 it received additions at front and center; the paneling and carving must have been done at the later date. The woodwork, of cherry and poplar, is beautifully reeded and carved—by skilled slaves, of course. The floors are of ash and the hardware imported from England. The house has been maintained in good condition and has been in the hands of the Wood family since 1879. It is furnished with some antiques, and the owners plan to take further pains to furnish it authentically.

ASHLAND (*c. 1810, rebuilt 1857*)
Route 25, 1 mile east of Lexington; daily, 9:30 to 4:30, except Monday; 50 cents and 25 cents.

The early house, the home of Henry Clay, was built in 1810 after the designs of Benjamin Latrobe; but in 1811 an earthquake unsettled its foundations, and it was later taken down. Rebuilt in 1857 from Latrobe's plans with the original materials, the details were none the less much changed. It is set in a grove of trees planted by the great orator himself. The thick pine grove near the house is where he liked to stroll while composing his speeches. Behind the house is Mrs. Clay's garden, designed by the famous French landscapist,

L'Enfant. Clay lived in this house until his death in 1852. He was Speaker of the House, Senator, and finally Secretary of State, but he failed to achieve the Presidency. Inside you can see the campaign banner for his 1844 race. His chairs, desk, chess table, family portraits, and clothing are all here, and the place still has a "lived-in" look.

WHITE HALL (*1834*)

> *312 North Limestone Street; on written or phone request; $1.00 to Polio Fund; Dr. and Mrs. James C. Carrick.*

This was once the home of Chief Justice Thomas A. Marshall, descendant of John Marshall. Its columns were designed by Gideon Shryock. It was sold by Justice Marshall in 1857 to Mayor Claudius Johnson, husband of Rose Vertner, the famous Bluegrass poet, who also lived here. The drawing and dining rooms are furnished in the "grand style," and there is a charming mid-Victorian parlor.

PARKER HOUSE, or STONY POINT FARM (*1784*)

> *Parkers Mill Road, 8 miles west of Lexington; on written request; Mr. and Mrs. William B. Gess.*

A very early house for Kentucky, this is a simple white-plaster structure, built by Revolutionary War General John Parker. The farm itself is called "Stony Point" as a reminder of his victory at Stony Point, New York. The interior, with some appealing early features, is also plain, and furnished largely with antiques.

WINTON (*1823*)

> *Newtown Road, 6½ miles north of city; daily, 1 to 5, April through October; $1.00; Mr. and Mrs. Howard Evans, R.F.D. 6.*

Maj. Samuel Meredith III, nephew of Patrick Henry, named his Kentucky home "Winton" after his father's house in Virginia, though it was, to begin with, only a crude three-room log cabin. His second dwelling was five rooms in all, the two sections built of squared logs and connected by a dog trot; these are still on the property. The third house, a four-room brick affair, built in 1806, has been torn down. His final house, the one now standing, was built in his more affluent days of brick laid

in Flemish bond on a stone foundation. The house was enlarged in 1865 by a granddaughter of Major Meredith and her husband Dr. Robert Peter, but they left a large part of the old place unchanged. The original white-ash floors are here, as are the window and door frames, baseboards, and chair rails. The Christian doors are of natural walnut, but they have been painted over and then finished to imitate the grain. All partitions are of brick, and the hardware is English import. The present owner is the sixth generation of the family. Since farming, except on a large scale, is no longer profitable, and since she loves the house and its associations, she and her husband have decided recently to open it to the public. What they will tell you of its history will give you a memorable picture of a typical Kentucky pioneer family, whose descendants have treasured their traditions. The furniture in the house has been little changed in the last hundred years; some of it was brought by Major Meredith from Virginia, and many other pieces were made especially for various owners of the house.

The owners of Winton find that part of the pleasure they get from their home and its history is in sharing its interest with others.

¶ Paris

(17 miles northeast of Lexington on Highway 68)

HARKAWAY (1787–1789)

Ruddles Mill Pike north of Paris; on written or phone request; Mr. and Mrs. Edward F. Spears.

Another very old house for Kentucky, built by a miller, Laban Shipp, who sold it to Abraham Spears, the great-grandfather of the present owner. It is built of stone in three wings, resembling somewhat a Pennsylvania farmhouse. Although it has been restored, no changes were made; the original ash floors, put down with handmade nails, are still there, and most of the fine woodwork is the original. The house and lovely grounds have much character. It is not easy to find, so make careful inquiries.

DUNCAN TAVERN (1788)

Public Square; daily and Sunday afternoon; 70 cents; D.A.R.

This is an uncommonly fine-looking old structure, dominating the square. It was built by Maj. Joseph Duncan before the town existed and four years before Kentucky became a state. It was a meeting place for the first settlers in the wilderness, Daniel Boone, Simon Kenton, James Smith, and many other well-known frontier characters. It has been well restored and furnished appropriately. Descendants of several of these famous visitors have dedicated and furnished various rooms, a practice which has ensured much good furniture but a diversity of tastes. The effect, while hardly that of an inn, nevertheless enables the visitor to see a lot of interesting furniture. It contains the John Fox library.

GREENTREE, *formerly* FAIRLAWN (1834)

The Georgetown area, 7 miles from Lexington; by appointment; Mrs. Charles S. Payson (owner), Mr. Clarkson Beard (manager), Box 1110, Lexington.

As early as 1830 this was a great horse-breeding farm, and it still is. The great house is on the formal side, of brick, with white columns and a pilastered façade. No expense was spared in its construction, and this fact is reflected in the spacious interiors, in which a graceful walnut stair-case corkscrews from the vast entrance hall to the attic. This is one of the best of the large Bluegrass farm mansions; it is a pleasure and a privilege to visit it.

THE GRANGE (c. 1816)

Maysville Pike (inquire location); on request at owners' convenience; Mr. Ben Harbeson.

We would like to let the owner tell the story of the house he loves: "My house was built by Edward Stone, who came here from Virginia about 1800. He built the kitchen about 1805, and lived in the bedroom above it while he was constructing the balance of the house. In those days the cellars were dug, the limestone foundations laid, and this was allowed to settle two or three years before any brick was laid atop it. The main house was completed in 1816 and was entirely separate from the kitchen. Stone was one of the large slave traders in this section. He bought outlaw slaves, kept them in total darkness in a dungeon under the main hall of the house until he broke their spirit, marched them in a chain gang to Maysville where they were loaded onto flatboats to New Orleans and sold there at market. On one such trip the slaves mutinied, killed Stone and his companion and were tried and hanged at Stephensport."

"The Grange" is one of the typically regional houses referred to in the introduction. The chaste portico with its twelve-sided columns shades a broad, fanlighted doorway. The two arched dormers have leaded panes which repeat the fan theme. But the end pavilions are unique, for in the slightly curved walls are set Palladian windows of great elegance, with fluted frames which appear to cover most of the wall space. The scale of the whole building is a delight.

¶ Carlisle *(14 miles northeast of Paris)*

FOREST RETREAT (1817)

Route 68, 2 miles from town; any time; house $1.00 for benefit of Nicholas County Hospital, garden free; Dr. and Mrs. Eslie Asbury.

An interesting group of buildings, for not only may the restored Federal house, built in the wilderness by Gov. Thomas Metcalfe, be seen here, but also the cabin of

Daniel Boone (1788–1794), the only place he occupied in Kentucky. The Half Way Tavern and post barn, which was the overnight stagecoach stop between Maysville and Lexington, is here as well. At that time Route 68 was Zane's Trace, or Limestone Trail, which was originally beaten by the herds of buffalo traveling to Blue Lick Springs. These buffalo trails were the only roads through the wilderness when the pioneers made their way west. The house, named by Henry Clay, is one and a half stories, of painted brick, with a unique cornice. It has fine woodwork, and is furnished carefully with American antiques, some pieces used by Governor Metcalfe, who is buried in the rear of the garden. Its present owner breeds thoroughbreds; Determine, 1954 Kentucky Derby winner, was bred here, along with many other famous ones.

¶ Frankfort

Christopher Gist's journal tells of his being here in this region in 1751, probably as the first white man. More than twenty years later the governor of Virginia sent a survey party to explore the land. On December 5, 1792, the town which had sprung up became the capital of the state and has remained so. The old capitol, at St. Clair Street and Broadway, was rebuilt in 1827 after two destructive fires by Gideon Shryock in the Greek Revival mode. It is a good example of the use of the native white limestone, and cost the state ninety-five thousand dollars; it is open weekdays.

LIBERTY HALL (*1796*)
218 Wilkinson Street; daily, 9 to 5; 50 cents; Liberty Hall Association.

Home of John Brown, first U. S. Senator from Kentucky, this house remained in the hands of his heirs until 1937, when it was taken over by the state. A letter from Thomas Jefferson to Brown, one of his law students, substantiates the theory that Jefferson gave him some help on the plans for this house, although it does not resemble Jefferson's work. The furnishings are the former possessions of the family; among them are a Gilbert Stuart portrait and some piano music belonging to Margarette, Brown's wife. The house has a lived-in, personal feeling. Monroe, Lafayette, William Henry Harrison, Jackson, Taylor, and even "Teddy" Roosevelt were guests of this illustrious family. Of Late Georgian Colonial style, the house has quiet dignity. Above the entrance is a fine Palladian window. The interior has large fireplaces and carved mantels. At one time the necessary ballroom occupied half of the second floor.

THE OLD HOUSE (*c. 1840*)
218 West Campbell Street; by appointment; 50 cents; Mrs. Eleanor Hume Offutt (phone: 4-2149).

This home of an authority on early Kentucky furniture is filled with notable pieces —a collector's holiday. There are fine examples of the cabinetmaker's and silversmith's art, and interesting Kentucky paintings, an expert's collection of over forty years. The house is a simple farmhouse type, flush with the sidewalk, with its garden in the rear. Woodwork from earlier houses has been incorporated in some of the rooms; notable is a pair of concave doors from the Hannah Mansion, described in *The Kentuckians*.

GOVERNOR'S MANSION (*1798*)
Open to public after restoration; state of Kentucky.

Originally known as "The Palace," it was first occupied by the second Governor of Kentucky, James Garrard. Isaac Shelby, the first Governor, lived here during his second and later term. For a total of one hundred and thirteen years all the governors of the commonwealth lived in this stately but unostentatious house, including two who worked as laborers on its construction—Gov. Robert Letcher, a brickmason, and Gov. Thomas Metcalf, a stonemason, known as "Old Stone Hammer." The large brick house with its delightful doorway, its delicate modillioned cornice, and its twenty-four-paned windows is decidedly reminiscent of the chaste quality of some of the brick houses in Williamsburg and no doubt Governor Garrard knew the Virginia capital very well, as did some of the other

The Orlando Brown house in Frankfort is one of the most recent of the distinguished early Kentucky homes to be restored and opened to the public.

governor-builders who worked on its construction. When completed, it will be one of the gems of the state, and especially interesting in comparison with the new Governor's Mansion across the river.

ORLANDO BROWN HOUSE (*1835*)

Wapping and Wilkinson Streets; to be restored, furnished as a museum, and opened to public; Colonial Dames of America in the State of Kentucky; write Mrs. E. D. Taylor, 220 South Highland Street, Winchester.

For several reasons this is bound to be an important restoration. Gideon Shryock, called the "pioneer Greek Revival architect of the Middle West," designed it, and it is "one of the few departures of this architect from strict Hellenism." Shryock, among many other buildings, designed the state capitol and Morrison College at Transylvania. In drawing up the plans for this large, homelike brick house, he followed a pattern already set in Kentucky, for he felt that the Greek temples which were springing up all over were ill advised for comfortable living. Kentuckians seemed to feel this too, and preferred to cling to

Georgian domesticity while making a bow to the prevailing fashion with porticoes and columns which did not interfere with interior comfort. You cannot find a better example of the typical popular brick town house of that era in Kentucky than this one, pleasant in its proportions and well built without ostentation. You can be assured that the Dames will restore it as it should be and that the furniture will be as genuinely Kentucky as the house.

¶ *Versailles (halfway between Frankfort and Lexington)*

STONY LONESOME (*1784*)

Grier's Creek Road, Versailles; by appointment; $1.00; Mr. and Mrs. Edward Clay O'Rear II.

Built by Joel Dupuy before Kentucky achieved statehood, this is a superb example of the type of stone house that came after the log cabin. It is constructed of almost white Kentucky River marble quarried from the nearby cliffs, and is laid in even ashlar. Although the house is simple to the point of severity without, its interior is spacious, and the detail borders on the elegant. The trim throughout is black walnut and the floors ash, all cut nearby, of course. The thickness of the walls and the Indian bars on the doors were a needed protection in the wilderness. Much of the furniture in the house is of early Kentucky make; in the dining room the console is of Kentucky wild cherry inlaid with holly. The owner is collecting early children's pieces. You will discover that the house is well named.

WELCOME HALL (*1790 or before*)
Clifton Road; by appointment; Mr. and Mrs. W. Henry Graddy, Sr., Clifton Road, Versailles.

Since this lovely old stone house has been in the Graddy family through seven generations, the house has lived up to its name. Built by a pioneer, John Long, the brick wings were added, one before 1813, one in 1822. The original woodwork and even the colors have been lovingly preserved by the family. It is beautifully furnished, mostly with heirlooms—eighteenth-century Virginia and Maryland, Queen Anne, and Chippendale. For those especially interested in early Kentucky architecture and furniture, here is another opportunity to enjoy a true old Kentucky home. It was advertised for sale in *The Western World* in 1806 as "an elegant stone residence [giving dimensions], having an established orchard, mill and distillery," the customary appurtenances of any big Kentucky establishment in the early days.

¶ In & out of Harrodsburg
(*24 miles southwest of Lexington on Route 68*)

Harrodsburg, the oldest white settlement in Kentucky, is in itself a kind of museum, showing all of the styles in architecture that have flourished since it was laid out in 1774 by James Harrod and Daniel Boone. Here you can still see Harrod's Fort, the friendly stockade that furnished the pioneers with protection and help, where George Rogers Clark wrote his famous journal, laying his plans for the conquest of the territories which were to become Ohio, Indiana, and Illinois. You can see the cave where Boone spent the winter of 1769–1770, and within five miles of it the old stone house the McAfee brothers built in 1790.

In addition to the houses listed there are any number of other interesting and romantic homes in and near town. Of the

Welcome Hall, near Versailles, is another of the fine old stone houses of the locality.

Diamond Point gives further Greek Revival interest in Harrodsburg.

Georgian type, beside those listed here, is BURFORD HILL, on the right of the Louisville Pike as you leave town, a small house whose fanlighted doorway and Palladian side windows are unusually elegant. With the town's growth came the handsome Greek Revival mansions. Be sure to take in College Street where the pillars, Doric and Ionic, stand in ranks. Stop and look at the RIKER HOUSES: both DORICAM and RYKON are exceptionally interesting. So are FOREST PILLARS, the home of Mrs. Ensminger;

FAIR OAKS, home of Dr. and Mrs. C. B. Van Arsdall, Jr.; and DOSSETT PLACE.

If you are staying long enough to see them all—and you could not find a pleasanter place to spend time—the chamber of commerce will be glad to give you some help; ask for Mr. Gabhart there, whose own house, CLAY HILL, is one of the best. The people of Harrodsburg respond to genuine interest with sincere hospitality.

DIAMOND POINT (*1840*)
> *On phone request; portion only; Miss Clara E. Chapelle.*

Although the interior has been divided, this is still one of the loveliest Greek Revival houses in the state. Professor Newcomb remarks on "its extreme originality." The deep two-storied portico, set between square end piers, shelters an elaborately carved doorway and a narrow balcony, at second-story level, traced in a delicate diamond pattern. It is impossible to describe it adequately, so be sure to see it; Miss Chapelle will show you the part in which she is living.

CLAY HILL (*1812*)
> *Near inn; on request; Mr. and Mrs. Willard Gabhart.*

A handsome two-story brick structure with one-story wings, originally somewhat resembling "Federal Hill." The splendid

Clay Hill has been meticulously restored and is lived in with full appreciation of its many splendors. This is one of Harrodsburg's best.

pediment and pillars were successfully added later. The remarkable interior wood-carving over doorways and mantels here has been most carefully treated by the owners, who are restoring and furnishing the house gradually. It is well worth the effort. In the rear is a columned loggia which, according to Professor Newcomb, the authority on Kentucky architecture, is unique, to his knowledge, except where it is repeated almost exactly at nearby SHAWNEE SPRINGS.

MANSION MUSEUM (*1800, front 1830*)
At gate of Pioneer Memorial State Park; daily, 8 to 4:15 except Christmas and New Year's; 35 cents; state of Kentucky.

The interior of this handsome brick post-colonial building has been little changed, although it is used largely for museum collections. The fine woodwork is intact in this house built by Maj. James Taylor, which has certainly justified its name. One room has interesting Lincoln collections, another has memorabilia of George Rogers Clark, and there is also a collection of Shaker furniture and other objects.

LINCOLN MARRIAGE TEMPLE, THE DOCTOR'S SHOP, DENTIST'S OFFICE, *and* FIRST SCHOOL, *in park*

Step inside the gates of the park here and you will see a variety of log cabins, including the one in which Lincoln's mother and father were married. These will give you a good idea of how the first settlers lived. South of the main entrance is the Doctor's Shop, a one-story brick building containing early medical books and instruments.

ASPEN HALL (*1840*)
Near Beaumont Inn; at reasonable hours; contribution to James B. Huggin Memorial Hospital, unless a guest; Mr. and Mrs. J. T. Cotton.

An imposing Greek Revival house with massive Ionic columns, one of the loveliest exteriors in town, it was built by Dr. James Shannon, President of Bacon College and Minister of the Christian Church. Later it was occupied by Dr. Bowman, who founded the University of Kentucky. Its parlors are furnished in livable Victorian, and the door and window frames carry the massive Egyptian detail frequently used by William

Strickland, Latrobe, and others. It is now a guest house, and rooms here for the night are delightful; but see it anyway, even if you are not staying over.

BEAUMONT INN (*1840*)
Danville Street; open as an inn.

A six-columned mansion which was once exclusive Daugher's College. There are three vast parlors furnished in Victorian ease with crackling open fires in winter. The food and the old-time service cannot be bettered in the South. The overnight accommodations are probably spacious too.

SHAWNEE SPRINGS (*1791*)
Curry Road; on request; Mr. and Mrs. Louis G. Bonta, Harrodsburg.

The owners have a letter from Col. George Thompson to his grandsons stating that work was started on this house in 1791. A distinguished Georgian structure of fourteen rooms with a huge attic and a basement under the entire house which was once used as slave quarters, it is now occupied by tenant farmers. It is essentially unchanged, though the pediment and

In addition to its other noteworthy qualities, Beaumont Inn enjoys a culinary reputation par excellence.

Ionic columns are, of course, a later addition—perhaps the work of the same architect who gave "Clay Hill" its splendid Italianate colonnade in the rear, for this house has the same features. The interior is quite remarkable, architecturally; the two halls in the main part of the house are divided by high carved arches, and the staircase is carved as well. The floors are of ash and poplar, and the woodwork of cherry, walnut, and poplar. All the original hardware is intact. A family burying ground, each headstone giving the life story of the individual, is nearby.

¶ *Shakertown (or Pleasant Hill, 7 miles north of Harrodsburg on Route 68)*

SHAKERTOWN INN (*1817–1839*)

What is now the inn was originally one of the dwellings of the Shaker colony which sprang up here in 1806. Built with the usual Shaker care, skill, and simplicity, this severe three-story brick building, with its two entrance doors, contains a rather unusual feature for a Shaker construction, namely a self-supporting twin spiral staircase of remarkable delicacy. The inn is furnished with antiques but as yet not many Shaker items. However, the owner proposes to restore and furnish each of the other four or five Shaker buildings appropriately. We hope he does, for when it is

finished it should be a rare place to visit. Incidentally, the food here is said to be in the best Shaker tradition—plentiful and good.

SHAKERTOWN GUEST HOUSE (*1817–1839*)
Daily, 10 to 10; Mr. Renfrew (manager), B. K. Marshall (owner).

The Guest House nearby, a neat and charming brick building with a fine fanlighted doorway, looks more like Kentucky than Shaker architecture.

¶ *McAfee (1 mile from Salvisa)*

MC AFEE HOME (*1790*)
On request; Mr. W. C. Knight, Harrodsburg.

Anyone in Salvisa will tell you how to find it, for it is a landmark here. The McAfee brothers—there were four—share the honors with James Harrod, Daniel Boone, Simon Kenton, and others for the opening up of this part of America. They met Harrod on their way down the Ohio and joined forces with him in the spring of 1773. In 1779 they came back again with their families, built a fortified hamlet, and resisted the Indians; by 1790 they were established in the new country. James, the eldest, built this two-story gable-roofed house, said to have been modeled after his home in Ireland, out of the native stone. The

Early additions to the Dr. McDowell house in Danville were done with forthrightness and originality. With the restored garden, they help to make the rear of the house its most interesting exterior aspect.

walls, thirty inches thick, show that men of the time were still thinking first of protection. The woodwork is hand-carved, and some of the strap hinges are the originals.

Only a few miles away in Salvisa still stands the SAMUEL MC AFEE HOUSE, a clapboarded log structure which, though built probably about the same time, shows that the brothers had different ideas. The deep portico on this house was added much later, of course.

¶ Danville

DR. EPHRAIM MC DOWELL HOME
(1790–1802)
> *Daily 10 to 5, Sunday 2 to 5; 50 cents and 15 cents; Kentucky State Medical Association.*

This simple yet stately house stands in its pretty garden on a street which has long since been given over to small stores and gas stations. It is a state shrine dedicated to the doctor who performed the first ovariotomy here in 1809 upon a woman who had ridden over the rough terrain on horseback for three days to reach the place. Her life was at stake, but so was the great doctor's—for a mob of angry townsfolk stood in front of his house while he performed what may well be the first piece of abdominal surgery on record. If the woman had lost her life, so might the doctor have lost his. But she lived, and thus his name goes down to posterity. The house itself is a moving monument; its sturdy, well paneled rooms, simply but skillfully furnished with old Kentucky pieces, are exactly as you might imagine the surroundings of the dedicated physician. His small office in back of the house is intact, with the high desk that he used, the cabinet of instruments, the medicines, and all the primitive medical paraphernalia of the day. This little room, which played a unique role in the early history of surgery, is alone worth the admission. The whole house is a "must" if you are nearby.

OLD CROW INN, *or* BARBEE ADAMS HOUSE *(1784)*
> *Edge of town; lunch and Sunday dinner by appointment, will show on request; Miss Mary Adams, Box 196.*

This is a landmark of the neighborhood, far older than its Greek portico indicates. The house, completed by Col. Joshua Barbee, is a massive two-story gray-stone structure, of which the central portion is the original. The ends were built later; and finally, to keep up with the fashion, the heavy Doric portico, with its huge columns of stucco-covered brick, was added. The Adams and Barbee families have been the sole occupants. It is furnished for comfort, and the food is of the homemade variety.

The doctor's waiting room and office, which occupy the low brick wing in the foreground of the view on the opposite page, is preserved as a very personal memorial to the famous surgeon, in a house that has some handsomely furnished portions.

WAVELAND (*1800*)

Hustenville Pike near Danville; on phone request; Mr. and Mrs. J. D. Erskine.

The Erskines had lived peacefully in this brick farmhouse for thirty years until Adlai Stevenson became a nominee for the Presidency; then they began to have visitors by the score. The reason: Stevenson's great-great-grandfather Willis Green built the house after he had come here from Virginia as a surveyor. One of the visitors, who arrived unannounced one day, turned out to be Green's illustrious descendant, who was in Danville to receive an honorary degree at Center College. It was Green who named the place "Waveland" because of the contours of its surrounding fields. His marriage to Sarah Reed in 1783 was one of the first to take place in Kentucky, and by 1797 he was able to begin building her a fine mansion in the Virginia tradition. The great stands of black walnut and ash on the land furnished his woodwork and floors, while brick was made of the clay excavated for the basement. Skilled carpenters from Philadelphia were brought in to execute the detail, which is unusually fine here. The house has two floors, ten rooms, wide halls, and a spacious attic and basement. The present occupants have left it structurally unchanged. The paneling and carving in

some of the rooms is noteworthy, particularly in the back parlor—originally the front parlor when the house faced the Old Wilderness Road. It is furnished with a combination of antique and modern furniture.

NELSON-GUERRANT-CURRY HOUSE (*c. 1818*)

Lexington Pike, 2½ miles out; on written request; Mr. and Mrs. Robert K. Lewis.

Another one-story brick house of charming proportions and rooflines. Again, as in "The Grange," near Paris, you will find Palladian windows in the flankers; but here the wings stand forward, and the portico with its circular window is an unobtrusive break in the roofline, a mere capping for the lovely fanlighted doorway.

YEISER-KINNARD-CHESTNUT HOUSE (*1804*)

135 West Lexington Ave.; on written request; Mr. and Mrs. William P. Caldwell.

The original central section of this stunning mansion was built in 1804 by Philip Yeiser. The date of the remarkably carved architrave and the Ionic colonnade does not seem to be established, but they were probably added when Kinnard, a banker, purchased it. The balustrades which enclose the roofs of the flankers were added during

On the front of his house are William Whitley's initials; in the rear are his wife Esther's.

This stately brick structure on the edge of Bardstown is considered by many to be the state's most famous shrine—My Old Kentucky Home.

the occupancy of the Chestnut family. Far from spoiling its character, these successive embellishments seem to have added to its charm and stateliness. Doorways were widened during some of the later occupancies, but otherwise the original woodwork has been preserved. It is furnished mainly with antiques.

¶ *Crab Orchard*

WHITLEY HOUSE (1787–1794)

Route 150, 2½ miles from Crab Orchard and 8 miles from Stanford; daily, 35 cents and 10 cents; state of Kentucky, Division of State Parks.

Formerly called "Sportsman's Hill," this is considered the first brick house to have been built west of the Alleghenies. Col. William Whitley was a famous pioneer scout and Indian fighter. The old name of his house is significant; for here in the wilderness on the recently cleared grounds was built Kentucky's first race track, casting a long shadow on the future history of the state. The bricks, which were made on the premises, were laid in Flemish bond, with slightly darker bricks used to form diamond patterns on the gable ends. The initials "WW" on the front of the house and "EW" (for Whitley's wife Esther) on the back wall were set in lighter-colored bricks. The house has many unusual features evocative of the way of life of the frontier. First-floor windows were placed

high above the ground to prevent Indians from shooting effectively into the rooms. A third-floor ballroom, once used as a courtroom, contains a secret hiding place for women and children. Two layers of wood, with a heavy sheet of iron between, were used in the construction of each elaborately hand-carved outer door, which swung on leather hinges. A small dungeon was dug beneath the house for the secure imprisonment of captive Indians, for the home was used as a fort in addition to its function as a social and civic center in the community. Over the mantel in the parlor are thirteen panels, symbolizing the thirteen colonies. Careful research has gone into the furnishing in order to retain authenticity. To travelers facing the hardships and dangers of the wilderness, this must have been a haven of safety and comfort on the long trek.

¶ *Bardstown*

FEDERAL HILL or
MY OLD KENTUCKY HOME
(1795–1818)

1 mile east of Bardstown; daily, 60 cents and 20 cents; state of Kentucky.

This was and still is one of the showplaces of Kentucky, a town house of considerable size and style for its period and location. Since Civil War days the name "My Old Kentucky Home" has been attached to it, for it was about this house that Stephen Foster composed his immortal song. Stephen's cousin Judge John Rowan built the earliest part, and, of course, Stephen visited here. It was not until 1922 that the last of the family, Mrs. Madge Foster Rowan, sold it to be a state shrine. Its tremendous rooms are now furnished in Victorian and Empire, every colorful detail carefully carried out. It is much visited.

WICKLAND (*1813–1814*)

Route 62, outskirts of town; daily 9 to 5, April 1 to November 1, or by special appointment; 50 cents and 25 cents; Dr. Walter E. Wright (owner), Mrs. George Hagen (custodian) (phone: 3291).

Known as the "Home of Three Governors," this is probably the finest house in Kentucky. The three governors, not all of Kentucky, were all nevertheless descendants of Charles Anderson Wickliffe, a native Kentuckian of pioneer parents, who built it. Its informal composition adds up to an unusually pleasing exterior, beautifully proportioned and without ornament, the red brick mellowed by age. The interior is stately, with fine Adam carving on woodwork and mantel. Although the family is no longer in residence, much of the furniture has been left; the great gilt mirrors, the glass chandeliers, the Aubusson carpets, etc., are still in place. Be sure to see it while you are there. The caretaker lives nearby and is most obliging.

¶ *Hodgenville*

SINKING SPRINGS FARM AND MEMORIAL BUILDINGS

Abraham Lincoln National Historic Park; Route 61, 3 miles south of village; daily; National Park Service.

On a raw frontier farm on the edge of "The Barrens" was born the man whose studies carried him awkwardly, yet majestically,

Lincoln's close connection with the history of Kentucky from his birth through his boyhood has caused many early primitive buildings to be preserved as restorations or re-creations. This log house in the Lincoln Homestead State Park is one of the latter on the site where Lincoln's grandparents lived.

over a path that began in common Kentucky clay ai..! ended in immortality. His grandfather, Abraham, moved across the mountains between 1782 and 1784 and was killed by an Indian; his father, Thomas, bought this three-hundred-acre farm in December, 1808, for $200.00 cash. In this one-room log cabin, Lincoln was born in 1809. The Lincolns lived here only two and a half years since the place was lost to them through a defective title. The authenticity of the cabin is not entirely established. Furnished in primitive provincial.

¶ Cox's Creek

STARLINGS (*1790–1794*)
> *Route 68, 6 miles from Bardstown; May when owners are at home, other times on written or phone request; 50 cents; Mrs. Victor J. Dayton.*

A tall brick house, formerly the Old Star Tavern, which has been tastefully restored by the present owner and is now occupied by three generations. The house has some very fine mantels and a lovely hallway.

Treasures from all over the world collected by Mrs. Dayton, a noted concert pianist, furnish it—eighteenth-century English pieces, George III silver, Waterford glass, and a guest room done in Venetian and French style.

¶ Springfield

LINCOLN HOMESTEAD STATE PARK
(*log cabin reproductions*)
> *Just out of town; daily; state of Kentucky.*

Here may be found interesting replicas of early log construction, furnished with primitive pieces.

¶ Elizabethtown

BROWN-PUSEY COMMUNITY HOUSE
(*prior to 1825*)
> *128 North Main Street; daily 9:30 to 12, Sunday 1 to 5; Board of Trustees.*

A fine brick town mansion, well restored with some early furniture and used for community activities.

Just as the early English settlers along the Eastern Seaboard brought their building styles with them from England, so the settlers here in Missouri brought with them the styles to which they were accustomed in the Eastern states. Prairie Park, near Arrow Rock, is a possible exception that somehow proves the rule, for while it is said that the plans were procured from England, its Geek Revival style was all the rage in the East at the time. On the other hand, and on the opposite page, the much earlier Guibourd house at Ste. Genevieve is built in a style that was brought up the Mississippi by French fur traders when Missouri was part of Upper Louisiana, a province of Spain.

MISSOURI

HEN Missouri was ceded by the Spanish to the United States in 1804 it soon became, because of its central location where the two greatest rivers in America join, a vast kind of stopping-off place for wagon trains pressing westward toward the Pacific and for the traders plying up and down the "Father of Waters" and the Big Missouri. The pioneers were obliged to halt somewhere on their long trek before the final push across plains, to regroup, repair, and rest. Many of them were tempted to stay on in the fertile land watered by those two tremendous streams; but it was a restless society, composed of people from almost every section of the East, traders and adventurers seeking their fortunes, and it is not surprising that the regional imprint they left on their homebuilding here was reminiscent in a rough and ready way of the homes they had left behind them.

The scattered old houses of Missouri are mostly of 1840 vintage, reflecting varied sources of migration. Lexington is the center of a section where quite a number of houses of this period can be seen. The outpost and pioneer houses have their own personal flavor that brings history to life, and the old "sophisticated" houses, like "Prairie Park" and the "Campbell," give color and fascination to the past.

There is one survival of a very early rural settlement, where a number of the houses with great strength of character and individuality still stand. This is Ste. Genevieve, once a thriving fur trading center for the French, serving as the capital of the Upper Louisiana Territory throughout the French and Spanish occupations and even for a time after the

203

territory was granted to us. Eventually the town was superseded by nearby St. Louis; but some of the old families still live here in their ancestral homes.

¶ *Arrow Rock*
(*midway between St. Louis and Kansas City, about 40 miles from Lexington*)

ARROW ROCK TAVERN, SEMINARY, and GAOL (*1834*)
Arrow Rock State Park, off Route 41; daily, 8 to 6; 25 cents; Missouri Park System, Mary Low Pearson.

Only a short while before the town was built, the hostility of the Indians was so great that the fort here had to be abandoned for the greater safety of St. Louis, which was then a bustling center of trade on the upper Mississippi. Kansas City, now much nearer, did not exist. A plain brick building with no exterior ornament, the tavern was an important stopping point for travelers both east and west from St. Louis. The D.A.R. have done an outstanding job in restoring and furnishing it as a museum; the fact that they run it as an inn (on a nonprofit basis) has helped to make it a vital re-creation. It accommodates a hundred and twenty-five persons, and meals must be ordered ahead. All the rooms are papered in 1830 designs. The parlor, lobby, old dining or tap room, and five bedrooms are furnished in antiques. Seven of these rooms have their original fireplaces. The furniture and portraits are of local interest and include many articles owned by three of the early governors of the state. Most interesting, however, are the works of Kit Carson's comrade George C. Bingham, the pioneer artist, outstanding painter of early life in the state.

GEORGE CALEB BINGHAM HOUSE (*c. 1837*)
Part of reservation; Missouri Park System.

This small brick house nearby contains a few old pieces and is of interest chiefly because it is a reconstruction of the home of this gifted and humorous genre and portrait painter. In contrast to "Prairie Park," it shows how plain and primitive was the average house at the time.

PRAIRIE PARK (*1840*)
3 miles southwest; by special appointment; Dr. and Mrs. John R. Lawrence, Marshall.

One of the best examples of Greek Revival in the state, the fact that it was built almost contemporaneously with the Bingham House makes it especially interesting. Built from plans procured from England by William B. Sappington, son of the famous physician who introduced quinine to this malarial section of the country, it was obviously the home of a very prosperous man who had slaves and who could afford to have much of the material and even some of the workmen shipped in by river. Stone for the columns which form the two-story portico was brought by oxen from Cole County. Florentine marble was imported for the drawing-room mantels. These rooms still have the original paint on the marbleized baseboards and their original elaborate plaster cornices and ceiling medallions. Other features of the exterior are the refined detail of the cornice and lintels and the well-proportioned observatory and chimneys. The present owners have beautifully restored the house and furnished it in antiques throughout.

¶ *Defiance* (*20 miles southwest of St. Charles on Route 94*)

DANIEL BOONE HOUSE (*c. 1810*)
3 miles northwest of Defiance; on request; Col. Francis M. Curlee, 1001 Washington Avenue, St. Louis.

It should be called the "Nathan Boone House," for it belonged to Boone's son; but Daniel helped to build it and died here in 1820 at the age of eighty-six. He came here at the urgings of the Spanish, who were in possession at the time and who promised him vast lands as well as honors. When the United States took over, he lost most of the land, as he had already done in Kentucky, a result of faulty titles. In any event, here he stayed with his family on the thousand-arpent piece that was left to him. The house, built of blue limestone quarried nearby, was said to have taken seven years to build. It is not large, seven rooms in all, and resembles certain early limestone houses in Kentucky, which in turn seem to derive from similar types in Pennsylvania. It is solidly and simply built, but, within, all the woodwork is walnut and in each room is a fireplace carved with sunbursts which Boone himself is said to have executed when old age had slowed up his restless activities.

¶ *Hannibal*

MARK TWAIN BOYHOOD HOME
(*1844, a reproduction*)
> *206 Hill Street; daily, 9 to 5 May through September, 7 to 7 June through August; city of Hannibal.*

This is a reconstruction of the modest frame house built by Mark Twain's father, John Marshall Clemens, in which Samuel lived as a boy. It is furnished in keeping, with a number of the pieces that belonged to the family. A two-story museum adjoins which is also filled with memorabilia of Mark Twain and his family. The house has little of architectural interest; it was built a floor at a time because John Clemens could not afford to build it all at once. However, as the background for many of the experiences of Tom Sawyer and Huck Finn, and of the great man who gave them immortality, it has a special interest.

¶ *Hermann*

An unusual town, it was named for the hero of the Goth Wars when founded in 1836 by German-Americans from Philadelphia. Distressed by the threat that their children might lose the language and customs of the Fatherland, they decided to found a German "state" somewhere in the West where they could enjoy American advantages while preserving their own culture and customs.

They sent three scouts out west who found this beautiful valley, not unlike the Rhine Valley. By 1844, huge wineries had sprung up along the river, where the wild Ozark grapes were crossed with European stock. By 1856, Hermann was shipping one hundred thousand gallons of wine a year.

Their four-day "Maifest" is in celebration of the new wine and their own past. There are a few old houses rem-

iniscent of Pennsylvania Dutch of which they are very proud, among them the STREHLEY (1845) and GENTNER (1850) homes.

¶ *Jefferson City*

B. GRATZ BROWN HOUSE
(*1871–1873*)
> *109 Madison Street; Monday through Saturday, 1 to 4; 25 cents; Cole County Historical Society Museum.*

It was built by one of the state's greatest men, who was responsible for restoring peace between Southern and Northern sympathizers following the Civil War. The drawing room and bedroom are furnished in Late Victorian furniture from homes hereabouts and have a character all their own. What it lacks in elegance, it makes up for in color and dash.

¶ *Kansas City*

ALEXANDER MAJOR'S HOME MUSEUM (*1855*)
> *8145 State Line Road; Monday, Wednesday, Friday, Saturday, and Sunday, 2 to 5, and by appointment; 25 cents; Miss Louise P. Johnston.*

Miss Johnston, who lives here, is the great-granddaughter of the original owner, who operated the famous Pony Express to California, wagon trains to the south, and a stagecoach line to Colorado. The house, a pleasant-looking country manse of the Southern type, is being restored by the National Old Trails Road Association—a museum collection has to do with Miss Johnston's illustrious forebear. The HARRIS HOUSE (1854), at 4000 Baltimore Avenue, is one to note in passing.

ATKINS MUSEUM OF FINE ARTS
> *Rockhill Road and 45th Street; weekdays 9 to 5, except Monday and Sunday mornings and some evenings; George L. McKenna (registrar).*

1. Entrance hall from the Brockenbrough House (1743), Port Royal, Virginia.
2. Drawing room from "The Lindens" (1754), Danvers, Massachusetts, built for Robert "King" Hooper of Marblehead, Massachusetts; the house now in Washington, D.C.
3. Dining room (1795–1800) from Salem,

Massachusetts, attributed to Samuel McIntyre; magnificent scenic wall-paper.

4. Bedroom (1830) from a house built near Jacksonboro, South Carolina.
5. "Keeping room" (late seventeenth century) from Deerfield, New Hampshire.

These rooms comprise a very distinguished choice of Early American styles, and are beautifully and completely furnished. The museum includes the collection of the William Rockhill Nelson Gallery of Art.

¶ Lexington
(41 miles east of Kansas City)

Named for Lexington, Kentucky, the former home of many of its earliest settlers, it was plotted in 1822. Profits from hemp, cattle, and tobacco made this a very prosperous river town in the early part of the century and attracted a mixed population. It is one of the few towns in Missouri which has a number of old houses of the '30s and '40s still being lived in and which is proud enough of them to hold a yearly tour. The Lexington Garden Club sponsors it under the able guidance of Mrs. Harold Maib, 908 Highland Avenue, and shows about ten houses. Mrs. Maib estimates that here and in the vicinity there may be nearly a hundred more built between the '30s and '60s, of which the lines are likely to be Georgian, strongly influenced by the Kentucky background of many of their builders. The tour is held in September or October and the uncertainty of the date makes it particularly necessary to consult her in advance. Mrs. Maib or the chamber of commerce have agreed to furnish a walking tour to readers of the *Guide.* The following constitute a sampling of the town.

ANDERSON HOUSE (1853)
Battlefield Park, North 15th and Wood Streets; daily.

A massive three-story red-brick house with a one-story white portico, whose Corin-

thian columns seem to have been sawed off at some later period and set upon paneled bases which do not belong to them. The rear, however, is charming, with its double galleries running the length of the house and ell. There are eighteen rooms with a marble fireplace in each one; the woodwork, door frames, and graceful staircase are all of unpainted black walnut. The builder, a Col. William Oliver, spared no expense for his home, which was later to become a battle ground and hospital in the Civil War. The rooms, now being furnished by the D.A.R. and the United Daughters of the Confederacy, are gradually assuming their early elegance, with crystal chandeliers, fine draperies, and appropriate furniture. (The size of the house makes it a long-range job of restoration.) Some of the Anderson furniture has been returned here, among other things a Victorian bed of Brazilian rosewood with miniatures of the colonel and his lady inlaid in the headboard.

THE HOUSE BY THE SIDE OF THE ROAD (1870)
Weekdays 9 to 5, on request; 50 cents; Dr. and Mrs. A. W. Wright.

The Gothic aspect of this house, with its elaborate trim and fanciful second-floor balcony surmounted by a bracketed canopy, belies its late look, for much of the house is earlier. Back in the '50s a slave block was across the street. In a cabin, formerly behind the house, the slaves were quartered until "slave day." A cornice of lincrusta in the parlor, a carved leather dado in the hall, and a frieze between the double doors of the parlor are entertaining features which are bound to be prized for their evocation of the plush period. The furniture is in keeping.

STALLING HOME (1844)
1415 South Street; weekdays by written appointment; 50 cents; Mr. Robert F. Stalling.

This pleasant two-story brick house is early for these parts. Its one-story veranda was added later when the second owner, a son of William Waddell of Pony Express fame, enlarged the house to its present considerable size. The ell furnishes a protected galerie for outdoor sitting, like so many plantation houses further south. The man-

An unusually choice collection of period rooms is contained in the Nelson Gallery of Art in Kansas City, including the splendid hallway, above, from Port Royal, a famous Philadelphia mansion that has long since been dismantled and destroyed, and, below, the original drawing room of The Lindens, the great house that was moved from Danvers, Massachusetts, to Washington, D.C.

tels, heavy moldings, and staircase are Midwestern Victorian, as is the ornate furniture, so distinctive in character as to constitute its own style. The "gent's wig dresser," an artless and delightful piece of cabinetry, deserves your special attention. Note also the hanging lamps with colored-glass globes.

LINWOOD LAWN (1850)

2½ miles southeast of town; on written request during warmer months; 50 cents; Mr. and Mrs. Marshall Young (tenants), Mr. and Mrs. Edgar F. Cox (owners).

A large brick house of the 1850s whose heavy cornice, heavy corner quoins, downstairs bay, and triple upstairs windows appear to indicate later changes were made here. William Limerick, the banker who built it, spent eighty thousand dollars on it. His twenty-four marble fireplaces were imported from Italy, one to each room. There are marble-top lavatories, a built-in iron stove, speaking tubes, and, *mirabile dictu,* two furnaces and an air-conditioning system, four slaves having been employed in continuously stoking the furnaces. Lastly, the house has a spacious ballroom and a race track.

REMELEY-ARDINGER HOUSE (1839)

June and July; on written request; Mrs. Horace Ardinger.

Seems to be the oldest house in town. On either side of the entrance are two porches with rails and supports of beautiful iron grillwork that look as though they might have come up from New Orleans. A charming patio, created by Mrs. Ardinger, is in the rear. The interior is colorful and interesting with antiques, mostly Empire and Victorian, and china, silver, and glass.

¶ *Ripley (east of Kansas City between Independence and Lexington)*

FORT OSAGE (1808)

Route 24 and County Road 2E; daily; Native Sons of Kansas City.

The fort consists of officers' quarters, soldiers' quarters, Indian trading house, blockhouses, and other buildings and was the first to be built by the United States in the Louisiana Purchase. It is strategically located on the Missouri, twenty-five miles

east of the mouth of the Kansas River. Major Sibley was the government trading agent in charge. The immensely long trading house or factory, standing on tall stone piers, has been restored. Its steep sloping roof with dormers is much like the early houses in Ste. Genevieve, which in turn are reminiscent of the Louisiana plantation houses. The French Canadian farm influence is unmistakable. The factor's dwelling, with stone fireplaces, has been partially restored and some of it furnished in keeping. The blockhouses have their own hive-like architectural interest too.

¶ *St. Charles (30 miles west of St. Louis, Missouri, on Highway 40. First capital of Missouri)*

SIBLEY HALL (1857)

On campus of Lindenwood College.

This big three-story brick mansion with eight columns across the front and an imposing entrance was built and lived in by Maj. George C. and Mary Easton Sibley, who founded the college in 1827 and later gave it all of their possessions. It was lighted by rosin gas made on the place. Adjoining parlors remain as they were, furnished with many of the Sibleys' own things, such as a Mason and Hamlin organ which came by mule over the mountains from Virginia, and by water down the Ohio. Other interesting pieces as well.

¶ Ste. Genevieve

In the eighteenth century Ste. Genevieve was the principal settlement of Upper Louisiana, just as New Orleans was its focus in Lower Louisiana. Like Cahokia and Kaskaskia across the river in what is now Illinois, Ste. Genevieve was a conveniently located trading post for the French and Indians. Even after the vast territories west of the Mississippi were ceded to Spain in 1762, the French continued to be the chief explorers, traders, and settlers of the region. Their influence in the building of homes in Ste. Genevieve, where so many have fortunately

The Louis Bolduc house at Ste. Genevieve is the oldest important house still standing in this part of the country.

survived, is more marked than anything contributed by the later Spanish conquistadores. In many ways they resemble the raised cottages of lower Louisiana and Mississippi, which combine West Indian features with French provincial, although here it was the custom for the logs used in construction to be set upright, and the plastered houses were seldom raised more than a half story. Broad porches encircled by railings, end steps, and a simplicity of line and lack of decoration are their chief exterior characteristics. The interiors in some of them were more elaborate, for wherever there were numbers of slaves there was likely to be found some interior carving.

LOUIS BOLDUC HOUSE (*1785*)
123 South Main Street; under restoration by Colonial Dames; Mrs. Charles Galt, 4505 Pershing Avenue, St. Louis 5.

This is the largest and very likely the oldest of the surviving eighteenth-century Creole houses of Ste. Genevieve. The long, sweeping roof with its massive Norman trusses is as characteristic of the type as are the

galleries that surround the house on four sides. Ceilings are beamed, the walls plastered and whitewashed, and the stone chimneys and large fireplaces resemble French and English eighteenth-century types. The house will be furnished as it might have appeared in 1820, including some of the original furnishings; Creole pieces as well as locally made American pieces.

JEAN BAPTISTE VALLÉ HOUSE, *or* STATE HOUSE OF UPPER LOUISIANA (*1785*)
Northeast corner Main and Market Streets; Vion family.

During the Spanish rule lasting from 1762 to 1804, the French Vallés remained the commandants of this district. When Jean Baptiste Vallé was twenty-five, he built a house for his bride. According to a Spanish census in 1787, his household consisted of his wife, his two children, and thirty-seven slaves. Later when American control was established in 1804 and the vast territory came under the sole jurisdiction of Governor William Henry Harrison, Jean Baptiste was put in charge of the district and his house became, in effect, the state house for all of Upper Louisiana. Vallé lived on in his house while great changes occurred in this part of the country. Missouri became a state and the city of St. Louis, which had hardly existed when he was a young man, superseded Ste. Genevieve. In 1840 at the age of eighty he was remembered by a chronicler of the era "as an old gentleman of courteous manner who wore cocked hat, knee breeches and an old-fashioned coat with broad cuffs,—altogether a striking memorial of the ancient regime."

GREEN TREE TAVERN (1790)
244 Old St. Mary's Road; at reasonable hours; Mr. and Mrs. R. A. Grannerman.

It was built by François Janis, became an inn in 1810, and once again a private home in 1850. The house, all on one floor, is seventy-five feet long and built of upright logs, mud-chinked and plastered over inside and out. Originally the porch, typical of these Ste. Genevieve homes, ran all the way around the house. It is now

on three sides only. Doors, mantels, and chair rails are walnut; the outside shutters of black walnut are from New Orleans. Conveniences have been added for modern living but otherwise it is unchanged. It is furnished with antiques.

¶ St. Louis

EUGENE FIELD HOUSE (1845)
634 South Broadway; Tuesday through Sunday 10 to 5, except first Tuesday of each month; St. Louis Board of Education.

A tall three-story brick town house, an unpretentious but comfortable souvenir of a comfortable age, it was saved from demolition as one of a row of similar homes when the citizens of St. Louis demanded that it be preserved as a memorial to a well-loved personality. Most of his adult life was spent at Sabine Farm, his home in Chicago, and from there came the things that furnish this house. They are redolent of a cultivated individual and of the place and time in which he lived.

If you have an opportunity to visit the Campbell house in St. Louis, don't let a certain austerity in the exterior appearance dismay you. This is a period piece and a personality house par excellence.

CAMPBELL HOUSE MUSEUM (*1851*)

1508 Locust Street; Tuesday through Saturday 10:30 to 5, Sunday and Monday 1 to 5; 30 cents and 10 cents; Campbell House Foundation.

When Robert Campbell bought his three-story brick house from John H. Hall, who had built it but three years before, he was one of the richest men in this part of the country, a frontiersman who had gained his wealth the hard way. His Rocky Mountain Fur Company was the rival of the great Chouteau-Astor Company. Naturally his home was in the most fashionable section of town, and, being an open-handed Irishman, he entertained lavishly. His wife from North Carolina abetted his hospitality. They left two sons and several million dollars. By some freak of fate resulting in our good fortune, the two sons became recluses and for half a century few people ever saw anyone leave the house. In the 1930s they died, leaving the place exactly as it was when their parents had given some of the gayest parties of the 1860s—a perfect period piece furnished with the best that money could buy, everything in excellent condition. Brass and bronze chandeliers are still gas-lit; the magnificent gilt mirrors and cornices to match, the rosewood and the Brussels velvets, even the copper cook pots in the kitchen, all look as though the Campbell brothers had just stepped out, even though they never did.

TOWER GROVE (*1849*)

Missouri Botanical Gardens, 2315 Tower Grove Avenue; daily 1 to 4, except Christmas and New Year's; Missouri Botanical Gardens.

Both the town and country houses of Henry Shaw are on the grounds of this lovely park which was the setting for "Tower Grove," the country residence now open to the public. Mr. Shaw, English by birth, arrived in St. Louis in the early part of the nineteenth century with a small stock of cutlery. Twenty years later he retired with a quarter of a million dollars and spent the rest of his life cultivating his tastes, chief of which was his botanical garden. He traveled extensively in Europe and his travels influenced the building of his homes. "Tower Grove" is an impressive Regency villa for a gentleman of means, and its rather tall tower may have been his own fancy. The building has a kind of gloomy charm. The mantels, carved marble, the fine crystal chandeliers, Abusson carpets, and gilt mirrors were imported, of course, the furniture purchased in England for the most part. The house has been left as lived in by Shaw, a bachelor whose horticultural hobby developed into a life interest which resulted in these extensive botanical gardens now in the public domain. As part of his will, his town house was moved brick by brick to the gardens after his death and is now one end of the administration building. In it are two memorial rooms. His little museum and library, which he built as a necessary adjunct to his hobby, is said to be the oldest museum west of the Mississippi. However, William Clark opened his Indian Museum in St. Louis in 1818. In any event, it is a charming little building and may be seen when there is someone to show it.

CITY ART MUSEUM OF ST. LOUIS

Forest Park; daily 9 to 5, except Monday; Catherine Filsinger (Assistant Curator).

1. Living room (1750–1760) from 61 Tradd Street, Charleston, South Carolina.
2. Living room (c. 1785) from 201 South Lee Street, Alexandria, Virginia.
3. Dining room (c. 1790) from the Putnam–Hanson House (originally called "Frye's Tavern"), Salem, Massachusetts.
4. Bedroom (c. 1800–1810) from Newburyport, Massachusetts.
5. Parlor (1832) from Nicholas Burckhartt House, Howard County, Missouri.

Beautifully and fittingly furnished, these rooms comprise a distinguished selection.

By a stroke of luck and a lot of good management, a charming group of buildings has been preserved and restored in the heart of Little Rock which could well be a fragment of Williamsburg. What might appear in the picture here to be an unusually appealing pioneer home is the garden side of the old Territorial Capitol. On the opposite page is the nearby Old State House, designed by Gideon Shryock, one of the architect kings of the Greek Revival.

ARKANSAS

*T*HE TWO choice collections of early houses out here are in busy, balmy Little Rock, the capital, and in the charming, old-fashioned town of Fayetteville, in the Ozarks. In both places the flavor is predominantly antebellum, as it is in most of the early Arkansas towns, reminding you that Tennessee and Mississippi are next-door states and that Nashville and Natchez are not far distant. But in addition to the pre–Civil War houses dating from the 1840s to the 1860s, there is in Little Rock the attractive territorial capitol restoration of the 1820s and 1830s which is almost Virginian in its trim Georgian tone, and which is in fact a kind of frontier Williamsburg in miniature. Still earlier, and probably the oldest house still standing in the state, is the 1809 Wolf House near Norfolk in the Ozarks, a primitive gem of true pioneer character. So, while it is only natural that the early houses of a hundred years ago or more should be thinning out now that we have reached the southwestern limits of the *Guide,* there is still quite a bit to be seen.

¶ Little Rock

THE ARKANSAS TERRITORIAL CAPITOL RESTORATION (*1820s and 1830s*)

3d and Rock Streets; Tuesday through Saturday 10 to 5:30, Sundays and Mondays 1 to 5:30, closed holidays; 30 cents and 10 cents; state of Arkansas.

Surrounded now by the tall buildings of a modern city, this remarkable restoration of thirteen houses formed the heart of the early town as it clustered about the boat landing by the river. Though the old buildings had been augmented and altered in the course of time, by some miracle they had not been destroyed; and it was merely a matter (a prodigious one, of course) of returning them to their original condition. The most important of the houses, shops, and dependencies in the beautifully gardened group follow.

The GOVERNOR'S HOME AND CAPITOL (1820) is a simple, almost primitive structure, the largest of the group, built of oak logs covered with red heart-cypress siding, hand-beaded. Some remodeling in 1834 furnished it with certain refinements, such as the hand-carved mantel in the west room downstairs.

The NOLAND HOUSE (1830) is a little brick beauty that was the home of Lieutenant C. F. M. Noland, who carried the first state constitution of Arkansas to Washington on horseback. A columned terrace in the rear overlooks a garden whose boxwood border was grown from cuttings from the hedges at Mount Vernon. A pair of dependencies flank the intervening lawn.

The CONWAY HOUSE (1830) is a long one-story frame cottage, very trim and neat. The home of the fifth governor, a bachelor, it is now furnished with some of his belongings.

The WOODRUFF HOUSE (1824) is one of a little corner group which also contains the print shop of Woodruff's paper *The Arkansas Gazette,* the oldest newspaper west of the Mississippi, and a separate kitchen building, as was customary.

In contrast to the old capitol, the OLD STATE HOUSE, built by Gideon Shryock in the same part of town, indicates that the territory had already accumulated enough wealth to commission one of the leading architects of the day to build this magnificent and costly Greek Revival structure, which can hold its own with any public building of the period in the South.

TRAPNALL HALL (*1843*)
423 East Capitol Avenue; on request;
Junior League of Little Rock.

One of the most distinguished early dwellings in the city, this one-story brick house, with its white-columned veranda, has considerable Kentucky character, undoubtedly because of the fact that its builder came here from Harrodsburg, bringing with him the broad fanlighted doorway. This opens into a banquet hall which can be expanded to include the adjoining rooms. Part of the house is handsomely furnished; part is used for a social service project of the league.

The rear view of the Noland house shows part of the garden, the well, the lieutenant's office at the left, the kitchen at the right, all in the best Southern territorial tradition.

In the Territorial Restoration, this house at the left was the home of Lt. C. F. M. Noland, who delivered the state constitution to the nation's capital on horseback.

This is the front of the Territorial Capitol whose garden side is given on page 212.

A general view of the grounds of the Territorial Capitol Restoration gives the impression that as attractive as this group of buildings must have seemed to begin with, it has certainly never been more charming than it is today.

THE ALBERT PIKE HOUSE (*1840*)

411 East 7th Street; Tuesdays and Thursdays 2 to 5, or by phone request at any time; Mr. and Mrs. David D. Terry.

A fine example of Greek Revival in brick— even to its Ionic columns. It sits in its own pleasant park, in which it was built by one of the most distinguished citizens of the young state—scholar, lawyer, author, and explorer. It was the boyhood home of John Gould Fletcher, the Pulitzer prize poet.

THE OLD STAGE COACH INN *or* MC HENRY HOUSE (*1836*)

10 miles out of town on the Hot Springs highway; by written or phone appointment; Mrs. J. L. Murphy.

This is a handmade old brick house with great double chimneys that flank its ends like bastions. It has been carefully restored. It is said that all the interior woodwork was brought here from Kentucky. There are numerous tales connected with its history, most of them tragic; the saddest is that of a neighbor boy who, while spying for the Confederates, was captured by the Union soldiers who were quartered here and duly executed.

¶ *Pine Bluff*

The fact that this was a town of considerable wealth in the 1850s and 1860s is reflected in some of the larger houses here of that period. Though most of them may be seen on request, often the clearest impression of past splendor is obtained from the street; for within modernization has generally seemed to be more sensible than perpetuating the Victorian ideals in the furnishings and fittings. Some recommended residences are LA BOCAGE (1865), 1115 West 4th Street; the DEXTER HARDING HOUSE (1850), 1109 Texas Street; the PORTIS HOUSE (1844), 216 East 2d Street; the BELL-ROBINSON HOUSE (1852), 811 West Barraque Street; and the THOMPSON HOUSE (1860), 519 West Barraque Street. The last is quite a house—and Barraque is quite a street.

¶ *Magnolia*

This is oil country, and the only house listed here is 7 miles west of town— though the town itself, as a matter of fact, is famous for its magnolias.

FROG LEVEL, *or* FRAZIER PLANTATION (*1852*)

Get directions at Magnolia; notify in advance, as owner is not always at home; Mrs. W. A. G. Woodward.

The insistent bellowing of hundreds of great bullfrogs gave this fine ante-bellum mansion its name. The house, which has been handsomely preserved, derives much dignity from the two-story pedimented portico with its second-floor balcony. As it was one of the largest plantations in the locality, court sessions were held here in the early days; and from those early days and this locality have come most of its heirloom furnishings. The house is a delightful documentation of its place and period.

¶ *Fayetteville*

The largest city in the Arkansas Ozarks and the location of the University of Arkansas, it contains more early houses that have been continuously occupied than any other town in the state. Prof. William J. Lemke, of the School of Journalism at the University, will be found to be a most helpful authority on Fayetteville and Arkansas antiquities.

THE FUTRALL HOUSE (*1868*)

226 North College Avenue; by request; Mrs. J. C. Futrall.

Occupying the site of old Arkansas College, this is certainly one of the most delightful houses in town. Its deep double verandas, broken by a portico, sweep across the front of the ample dwelling. Built by E. I. "Ras" Stirman, said to have been the youngest colonel in the Confederate Army, the house is beautifully furnished with family heirlooms and interesting portraits—an excellent example of how a cultivated family lived here in Victorian times.

The fact that Fayetteville has always been a college town in the most scenic section of the state caused it to become well known for its fine homes well before the Civil War. Unfortunately, many of its best houses were destroyed during the war. The Futrall house, above, is one that rose from the ashes; the Tebbetts house below is a particularly good one that survived.

THE TEBBETTS HOUSE (*1850*)

118 East Dickson Street; by request in advance; Mr. and Mrs. P. R. Green.

This house, a Federal headquarters during the Civil War, still bears the scars of battle on its door panels. It is considered by Professor Lemke to be "the most beautiful and the most important ante-bellum house in Arkansas." It is a one-story Greek Revival, built in conformity with the residence of the college president, who lived across the street. Its present owners have restored it to perfect condition and furnished it with antiques.

THE YELL HOUSE (*1836*)

South College Avenue; by appointment; Mr. and Mrs. Bryan Walker.

Standing on a hill with a view in all four directions, this house, known formerly as "Waxhaws" after the Carolina home of its builder, offers much of interest. Its clapboard exterior, fine outside chimneys, and simple columned portico are reminiscent of early Carolina country houses. Among its remaining dependencies is Yell's little law office, with its stone fireplace, standing nearby.

Worth noting also is the WALKER-STONE HOUSE (1847) on West Center Street, once the showplace of the town, now an apartment house.

¶ Near Norfolk in Baxter County

THE MAJ. JACOB WOLF HOUSE *or* WOLF MEMORIAL (*1809*)

Open year round; donation; city of Norfolk.

This venerable house is as out of the ordinary as it is out of the way. It is a two-story log structure with more architectural style than is customarily encountered in a dwelling of such primitive and pioneer construction. The setting is dramatic, with a sweeping view of the north and south forks of the White River, which divided the territory from Indian country when the house was built. The two-story verandas on both faces of the house are supported by rustic posts carefully selected for their slender proportions, and the daubed and wattled logs of the house itself make most effective walls of horizontal lines in contrasting colors. The heavy stone end chimneys taper to brick above. Major Wolf came here as the Indian Agent, and the house was built for him by Negro slaves and Indians, who tongued and grooved the hand-hewn floor planks.

INDEX

PHOTOGRAPH CREDITS

VIRGINIA Page 5, Mount Vernon: Charles E. Peterson; page 7, Gunston Hall: Ezra Stoller, Ladies' Home Journal; page 13, George Washington Birthplace: National Park Service; page 14, Stratford: Charles E. Peterson; page 17, The Rolfe: Virginia State Chamber

WEST VIRGINIA Page 23, President's Cottage, The Greenbrier: Cummins Photo; page 28, Mansion House: Joseph E. Hoffmann; page 29, Cottage Rows, The Greenbrier: Cummins Photo

MARYLAND Page 37, Tulip Hill: Ezra Stoller, LHJ; page 40, West St. Mary's Manor: Mildred Capron; page 43, Mount Clare: The Hughes Company; page 44, Hampton: Ralph H. Anderson; page 46, Providence Plantation: Constance Stuart

DELAWARE Page 48, 55, Aspendale: Ezra Stoller, LHJ; page 50, Dickinson House: Delaware State Archives; page 56, Belmont Hall: Public Archives Commission

DISTRICT OF COLUMBIA Page 58, Dumbarton House: Ezra Stoller, LHJ; page 59, White House: Abbie Rowe; page 63, The Lindens: Cortlandt V. D. Hubbard; page 64, The Lindens: Ezra Stoller, LHJ; page 65, Dumbarton House: Woltz

NORTH CAROLINA Page 66, 73, The Cornwallis House: Knight Photo Company; page 67, Old Salem Community Store: Ed T. Simmons; page 69, Cupola House: North Carolina News Bureau; page 70, Booth House: Gus Martin; page 71, Mulberry Hill: Gus Martin; page 71, Greenfield: Gus Martin; page 77, Lick Boner House: Frank Jones

SOUTH CAROLINA Page 83, Miles Brewton House: Alma Crenshaw; page 88, McLeod House: Palmetto Studio; page 84, Russell House: Samuel Chamberlain; page 85, Russell House: Ezra Stoller, LHJ

GEORGIA Page 94, Thomas House: Ezra Stoller, LHJ; page 102, Bellevue: Lee A. Stietenroth; page 103, Ralph Small House: Ralph Jones; page 104, Boxwood: Christopher Early; page 107, Mimosa Hall: Macon Chamber of Commerce; page 108, Savannah: Ezra Stoller, LHJ

FLORIDA Page 114, Fatio House: J. Carver Harris; page 117, Llambias House: J. Carver Harris; page 118, Goodwood: Slade's Studio

ALABAMA Page 121, President's Mansion: John E. Thierman; page 123, Teague House: Laurens Pierce

MISSISSIPPI Page 134, Thomas House: The Gring Studio; page 139, Dunleith: Knabb Lane Studio; page 140, Green Leaves: F. M. Demarest; page 141, Linden: Knabb Lane Studio; page 142, Stanton Hall: Knabb Lane Studio; page 143, Dixie White House: Hinman; page 145, Beauvoir: Anthony V. Ragusin

LOUISIANA Page 147, 155, Houmas: Ezra Stoller, LHJ; page 167, Melrose: Lester Jones

TENNESSEE Page 168, 169, Hermitage: Ezra Stoller, LHJ; page 172, Fairfax: Bryon Hale; page 173, Blount Mansion: Thompsons Commercial Photographers; page 174, Swan Pond: Thompsons Commercial Photographers; page 176, Belle Meade: Ezra Stoller, LHJ; page 180, Samuel Polk House: Crescent Illustration Company; page 180, Wyatt Hall: Gerald Holly

KENTUCKY Page 184, Stony Lonesome: Ezra Stoller, LHJ; page 187, Farmington: John E. Thierman; page 189, Winton: John E. Thierman; page 196, 197, McDowell House: Ezra Stoller, LHJ; page 198, William Whitley House: John E. Thierman; page 200, Log building, Lincoln Homestead Park: Division of Publicity, Frankfort

MISSOURI Page 203, Guibourd House: Massie, Missouri Resources Division; page 207, Period rooms: The William Rockhill Nelson Gallery of Art; page 209, Bolduc House: Massie, Missouri Resources Devision; page 210, Campbell House: Massie, Missouri Resources Division

ARKANSAS Page 212, 216, Territorial Capitol: Phelps; page 214, 215, Noland House: Phelps; page 215, Territorial Capitol: Earl Saunders